GUIDES TO INFORMATION SOURCES

A series under the General Editorship of
Ia C. McIlwaine,
M.W. Hill and
Nancy J. Williamson

Other titles available include:

Information Sources for the Press and Broadcast Media
edited by Sarah Adair
Information Sources in Architecture and Construction (Second edition)
edited by Valerie J. Nurcombe
Information Sources in Art, Art History and Design
edited by Simon Ford
Information Sources in Cartography
edited by C.R. Perkins and R.B. Barry
Information Sources in Chemistry (Fourth edition)
edited by R.T. Bottle and J.F.B. Rowland
Information Sources in Development Studies
edited by Sheila Allcock
Information Sources in Engineering
edited by Ken Mildren and Peter Hicks
Information Sources in Environmental Protection
edited by Selwyn Eagle and Judith Deschamps
Information Sources in Finance and Banking
by Ray Lester
Information Sources in Grey Literature (Third edition)
C.P. Auger
Information Sources in Information Technology
edited by David Haynes
Information Sources in Law (Second edition)
edited by Jules Winterton and Elizabeth M. Moys
Information Sources in Metallic Materials
edited by M.N. Patten
Information Sources in Official Publications
edited by Valerie J. Nurcombe
Information Sources in Patents
edited by C.P. Auger
Information Sources in Physics (Third edition)
edited by Dennis F. Shaw
Information Sources in Polymers and Plastics
edited by R.T. Adkins
Information Sources in Sport and Leisure
edited by Michele Shoebridge
Information Sources in the Earth Sciences (Second edition)
edited by David N. Wood, Joan E. Hardy and Anthony P. Harvey
Information Sources in the Life Sciences (Fourth edition)
edited by H.V. Wyatt
Information Sources in Women's Studies and Feminism
edited by Hope A. Olson

GUIDES TO INFORMATION SOURCES

Information Sources in the
Social Sciences

Editors
David Fisher, Sandra P. Price and Terry Hanstock

K · G · Saur München 2002

Die Deutsche Bibliothek – CIP-Einheitsaufnahme

Information sources in the social sciences
/ ed. David Fisher.... – München : Saur, 2002
(Guides to information sources)
ISBN 3-598-24439-8

Printed on acid-free paper

Cover design by Pollett and Cole

Typesetting by Florence Production Ltd., Stoodleigh, Devon

Printed and Bound in Great Britain by Antony Rowe Ltd., Chippenham, Wiltshire

ISBN 3-598-24439-8

Contents

Series editors' foreword

The second half of the twentieth century has been characterized by the recognition that our style of life depends on acquiring and using information effectively. It has always been so, but only in the information society has the extent of the dependence been recognized and the development of technologies for handling information become a priority. Since the early 1990s the Internet and its adjunct the World Wide Web have transformed information retrieval. Online searching, which started in the late 60s and early 70s as a useful supplement for bibliographic retrieval, has become a means of finding directly current information of every conceivable kind. Networked computers enable us to track down, select, process and store more information more skilfully and transmit, via an intranet perhaps, more rapidly than we could have dreamt possible even 20 years ago. Yet the irony still exists that, while we are able to do all this and are assailed from all sides by great masses of information, ensuring that one has what one needs just when one wants it is frequently just as difficult as ever. Knowledge may, as Johnson said in the well known quotation, be of two kinds, but information, in contrast, is of many kinds and most of it is, for each individual, knowable only after much patient searching.

The aim of each Guide in this series is simple. It is to reduce the time which needs to be spent on that patient searching; to recommend the best starting point and sources most likely to yield the desired information. Like all subject and sector guides, the sources discussed have had to be selected, and the criteria for selection will be given by the individual editors and will differ from subject to subject. However, the overall objective is constant; that of providing a way into a subject to those new to the field or to identify major new or possibly unexplored sources to those already familiar with it.

The Internet now gives access to many new sources and to an overwhelming mass of information, some well organized and easy to interrogate, much incoherent and unorganized. Further, the great output of new information from the media, advertising, meetings and conferences, letters, internal reports, office memoranda, magazines, junk mail, electronic mail, fax, bulletin boards etc. inevitably tend to make one reluctant to add to the load on the mind and memory by consulting books and journals. Yet they, and the other traditional types of printed material, remain for many purposes the most reliable sources of information. Despite all the information that is instantly accessible via the new technologies one still has to look things up in databooks, monographs, journals, patent specifications, standards, reports both official and commercial, and on maps and in atlases. Permanent recording of facts, theories and opinions is still carried out primarily by publishing in printed form. Musicians still work from printed scores even though they are helped by sound recordings. Sailors still use printed charts and tide tables even though they have satellite directed position fixing devices and radar and sonar equipment.

However, thanks to computerized indexes, online and CD-ROM, searching the huge bulk of technical literature to draw up a list of references can be undertaken reasonably quickly. The result, all too often, can still be a formidably long list, of which a knowledge of the nature and structure of information sources in that field can be used to put it in order of likely value.

It is rarely necessary to consult everything that has been published on the topic of a search. When attempting to prove that an invention is genuinely novel, a complete search may seem necessary, but even then it is common to search only obvious sources and leave it to anyone wishing to oppose the grant of a patent to bear the cost of hunting for a prior disclosure in some obscure journal. Usually, much proves to be irrelevant to the particular aspect of our interest and whatever is relevant may be unsound. Some publications are sadly lacking in important detail and present broad generalizations flimsily bridged with arches of waffle. In any academic field there is a 'pecking order' of journals so that articles in one journal may be assumed to be of a higher or lower calibre than those in another. Those experienced in the field know these things. Research scientists soon learn, as it is part of their training, the degree of reliance they can place on information from co-workers elsewhere, on reports of research by new and (to them) unknown researchers on data compilations and on manufacturers of equipment. Information workers, particularly when working in a field other than their own, face very serious problems as they try to compile, probably from several sources a report on which a client may base important actions. Even the librarian, faced only with recommending two or three books or journal articles, meets the same problem though less acutely.

In the K. G. Saur Guides to Information Sources we aim to bring you the knowledge and experience of specialists in the field. Each author regularly uses the information sources and services described and any tricks of the trade that the author has learnt are passed on.

Nowadays, two major problems face those who are embarking upon research or who are in charge of collections of information of every kind. One is the increasingly specialized knowledge of the user and the concomitant ignorance of other potentially useful disciplines. The second problem is the trend towards cross-disciplinary studies. This has led to a great mixing of academic programmes – and a number of imprecisely defined fields of study. Courses are offered in Environmental Studies, Women's Studies, Communication Studies or Area Studies, and these are the forcing ground for research. The editors are only too aware of the difficulties raised by those requiring information from such hybrid subject fields and this approach, too, is being handled in the series alongside the traditional 'hard disciplines'.

Guides to the literature and other sources of information have a long and honoured history. Some of the old ones remain valuable for finding information still valid but not repeated in modern information sources. Where appropriate these are included in the updated Guides of this series along with the wealth of evaluated new sources which make new editions necessary.

Michael Hill
Ia McIlwaine
Nancy Williamson

Preface

The book is intended to provide an evaluative guide to key sources of information in the social sciences. It is not a comprehensive directory of resources, but rather an attempt to point the reader in the direction of the most useful materials, chosen by experienced subject specialists. It is hoped that the volume will be of use to researchers, library and information professionals and all those information seekers who require balanced, critical assessments of carefully selected resources.

In his introduction to the *International Encyclopedia of the Social Sciences* editor, David L. Sills, argues that there is no need to resolve controversies regarding the constituent members of a conceptual grouping called the *Social Sciences*. Rather, he suggests 'what is required is only that whoever uses the term "social sciences" make clear what he includes under this heading' (p.xxii). Following this principle, let us state clearly what can be found within the pages of this volume. After an introductory section on general social science information sources, we provide individual chapters on: anthropology, sociology, psychology, criminology, education, political science, economics, human services and human geography. Doubtless, many hours could (and may well!) be spent in heated debate about the pros and cons of such a selection, but we believe that all significant social science subject areas have been included.

Something needs to be said about the presentation of resources within the subject chapters. You will see that the primary classification is by material type – *annuals*, *bibliographies*, *dictionaries*, *directories*, *encyclopaedias*, *guides and handbooks*, *Websites*, *journals*, *abstracts, indexes and databases*, *official publications*, *statistics*, *research in progress*, and *organizations* – and then by subject divisions within material type. To aid navigation around the volume we have numbered the main divisions. Thus, in Chapter 1, *annuals* can be found at *1.2* and similarly in Chapter 2 they will be at *2.2*, in Chapter 3 at *3.2* and so on. The order of materials remains the same within each chapter, which we hope will assist the reader in locating the same type of information source across different subject chapters.

What about the terminology used? We believe that the meaning of the majority of the headings is self-evident, but several of them – *Websites*, *research in progress* and *abstracts, indexes and databases* – would probably benefit from further explanation. The heading *Websites* is used for major gateway sites which do not fall into any of the other categories of material type. However, you will see Web addresses throughout the sections, as we have asked the chapter authors to emphasize electronic materials.

The *research in progress* section is an attempt to offer advice on how to track down current debate and elusive, unpublished materials. This is one area where the Internet is playing a significant role in shrinking geographical space by digitally linking together people via ever expanding computer networks. In this section we have asked the authors to discuss some of the key electronic discussion and mailing groups in their subject areas. The heading – *abstracts, indexes and databases* – has been used to emphasize the changing nature of resources in this area. It is now common for a resource to be an indexing and abstracting service as well as a full-text database. It seems sensible to put all such resources together in one broad area.

In a work of this kind there will inevitably be some repetition of resources, as the authors have written their chapters to be largely, self-contained guides. However, cross-referencing has been used to reduce reiteration wherever possible. The distribution of resources across the headings is not always an easy matter as, for instance, an annual may also be a directory and so on. The final decision regarding the precise location of a resource has always been guided by the desire to produce a logical and easy-to-use text. The same principle has led us, where appropriate, to make a distinction between print and electronic sources by employing *(a) Print* and *(b) Electronic* headings. The reason for doing this is to make it straightforward for the reader to select their preferred format of information source.

We would like to thank all our authors for their contributions to this volume. Thanks are also due to Linda Hajdukiewicz, Elizabeth Green and Catherine Lain at Bowker-Saur and to Geraldine Turpie and Mary Warren at K. G. Saur. We would like to take this opportunity to gratefully acknowledge the assistance of our colleagues at The Nottingham Trent University. Finally, we would like to thank our respective partners for their support and encouragement.

DF, SP and TH

About the contributors

Krystyna Brown is a lecturer in Human Geography in the School for Geography and Environmental Management at the University of the West of England in Bristol. She is a specialist in the environmental applications of Geographical Information Systems GIS.

Rosemary Burton is a lecturer in Human Geography in the School for Geography and Environmental Management at the University of the West of England in Bristol. She researches ecological aspects of tourism.

Craig Conkie is an information consultant, combining a knowledge of information management and a political science background. He has a BA (Hons) in Political Science and Modern History and a Postgraduate Diploma in Information Analysis.

Heather Dawson has been Assistant Librarian, Information Services and Collection Development, at the British Library of Political and Economic Science since 1996, where she is subject liaison librarian for Social Anthropology. She is also SOSIG (Social Science Information Gateway) subject editor for Government and Politics and Secretary of the Aslib Social Science Information Group and Network (ASSIGN).

Helen Fallon is Deputy Librarian at the National University of Ireland, Maynooth. Previously, she was Sub-Librarian at Dublin City University. She is the author of *Women on the Web: A Study of Gender and the Internet*. She enjoys both academic and creative writing and has had work broadcast by Radio 4 and the World Service.

David Fisher is an Information Manager with the Library and Information Services at The Nottingham Trent University. Prior to this he was the Faculty Liaison Officer for the Social Sciences. He has a BA (Hons) in

Sociology and an MPhil in Criminology from the universities of Durham and Cambridge respectively. He is a regular contributor to the academic and professional literature and is the author of over 70 articles and reviews.

Terry Hanstock spent many years with Sheffield City Libraries. He now works for the Library and Information Services at The Nottingham Trent University and has special responsibility for the Law and Politics collections.

Roy Kirk has been Education Librarian at the University of Leicester since 1973. He is currently editor of the Carfax publication, *Technical Education and Training Abstracts*, and Business Manager of *Education Libraries Journal*, published by Librarians of Institutes and Schools of Education (LISE). He has held the offices of Secretary and Chair of LISE and similar posts with the Library Association Education Librarians Group.

Tamara Kuhn is a research associate and Director of Internet Development at the Sociometrics Corporation in Los Altos, California. She is currently serving as the Principal Investigator on the Multivariate Interactive Data Analysis System (MIDAS) project, an Internet based data analysis system. She has also worked on a number of federally funded projects related to web development, data archiving and research methodology. Prior to joining the Sociometrics Corporation, she received her masters degree in Sociology from Stanford University.

Eric L. Lang is a Senior Scientist with TRW Systems and Information Technology Group in Monterey, California, and President of the Prosocial Science Institute. Prior work has included positions as a Principal Research Scientist at the Sociometrics Corporation, as well as social science work at the American Institutes for Research and the Institute for Social Research. He has an MA and PhD in Social Psychology from the University of Michigan. He has served as the Principal Investigator on a number of federal grants and contracts related to social science methodology, health, data archiving, disability and the Internet.

Sandra Price is the Faculty Liaison Officer for Property and Construction at The Nottingham Trent University. Prior to this she was the Information Specialist for Economics, Surveying and Social Work. She has a BLS (Hons) and MPhil in Information and Library Science from Loughborough University.

Alison Sharman is a Chartered Librarian and works in a converged Learning Resources Centre, as a Learning Advisor for Management and Economics at the University of Lincoln. Prior to this she worked in the Business Library of the University of Hull, where she had special responsibility for the European Documentation Collection.

Richard Spalding is a lecturer in Human Geography in the School for Geography and Environmental Management at the University of the West of England in Bristol. He conducts research into sustainable food production systems.

Caedmon Staddon is a lecturer in Human Geography in the School for Geography and Environmental Management at the University of the West of England in Bristol. He is a specialist in the environmental aspects of post-communist transformations.

Alan Terry is a lecturer in Human Geography in the School for Geography and Environmental Management at the University of the West of England in Bristol. He studies local development issues in southern Africa.

Angela Upton has a BA (Hons) in English from the University of Sussex and a Diploma in Librarianship from the University of North London. She joined the Library and Information Service at the National Institute for Social Work in 1989 and is currently working on the Knowledge Floor of the eLSC (Electronic Library for Social Care).

Mark Watson is Director of Information at the National Institute for Social Work (NISW). He is currently working with the Department of Health in England, in setting up the Social Care Institute for Excellence. He also leads a team of staff engaged in a number of projects: developing a Scottish Executive funded social work reSearchWeb; working on the Department of Health funded electronic Library for Social Care; and managing the NISW Caredata database. Prior to joining NISW he worked for Essex Social Services Department.

1 General social science information sources

David Fisher, Sandra Price and Terry Hanstock

▶ 1.1 NATURE AND SCOPE OF THE SOCIAL SCIENCES

It is much easier to chart the rise of social science than to state, without equivocation, what it is. There is even debate over whether we should be talking about social science in the singular, or social sciences in the plural. Ralph Dahrendorf (1996, p.800) argues that: 'The singular implies a community of method and approach which is now claimed by few; thus the plural, social sciences, seems more appropriate'. Taking an opposite stance, Aiden Foster-Carter (1998) has put the case for an inclusive social science, rather than social sciences. David Sills (1968, p.xxi) reminds us of the fluidity of the subject area when he notes that 'the social sciences differ in their scope from one generation to another'. However, putting such conceptual quandaries to one side for the moment, there is general agreement that social science(s) as conventionally defined, is concerned with the study of human society and behaviour. In fact, in the USA, the phrase 'social and behavioural sciences' is often substituted for social science.

The history of the development of social science can be traced back to the Enlightenment of eighteenth century Europe, and was subsequently fashioned by the processes of industrialization and the rise of the nation-state. The social sciences grew out of moral philosophy which was transformed into positive philosophy. Positivism provided the scientific foundation for 'science social', a phrase popularized by the influential Auguste Comte, but coined by Charles Fourier.

As Dorothy Ross (1991, p.3) states: 'The social sciences began in America by importing and adapting models of political economy, political science, and sociology developed in Europe in the eighteenth and early nineteenth centuries. These were new ways of understanding the historical world, born out of a new kind of historical consciousness and shaped by the emerging contours of capitalist society'. The American Social Science

Association was founded in 1865, based on the British National Association for Promotion of Social Science. Much of the early progress of the newly cast social sciences was associated on the one hand with conducting ambitious fact-finding surveys – Charles Booth in Britain and the American Chicago School – and on the other, with the creation of theories based upon the principles of the natural sciences, two key figures being Emile Durkheim and Vilfredo Pareto.

Ralph Dahrendorf (1996, p.801) notes that the dominance of the scientific approach – although reincarnated at various points throughout the history of the social sciences – was first challenged by the German School of social theorists, and in particular by Max Weber whose notion of *Verstehen,* 'empathy and understanding', opened the door for the future development of the interpretive style of social science knowledge, which exploded in a variety of directions including the exotically named phenomenological and ethnomethodological paradigms.

The years following the Second World War witnessed the expansion of the social sciences across the world. International alliances and collaborative ventures gradually began to take off – the International Social Science Council was formed in 1952. But, as Kazancigil and Makinson (1999, p.11) note, 'an overwhelming proportion of the world social science output continues to be produced in North America and Europe'.

The social sciences are nothing if not diverse and are home to an ever shifting constituency of disciplines and perspectives. Kazancigil and Makinson (1999, p.14) make a timely observation regarding outstanding issues that need to be tackled: '... being at the same time critical and practical gives the social sciences a particular status ... The main challenge that the social sciences are to face in the next century is to bridge the dichotomy between the intellectual and professional cultures ... and transform it ... into a creative tension, as well as a factor of strength and further advancement'.

In this opening chapter our aim is to introduce you to key general social science resources and materials. Subsequent chapters will guide you to more specific sources of information used within particular social science disciplines.

▶ 1.2 ANNUALS

In this section we discuss a selection of broad-based reference works of use to the social scientist, together with a range of more narrowly focused social science materials. As is our aim throughout the book, emphasis is given to publications with an international perspective.

The Annual Register: a Record of World Events (Bethesda, MD: Keesing's Worldwide) has been published since 1758, employing Edmund

Burke as its first editor. It remains an authoratitive chronicle of events from every country in the world. In addition to its country-specific coverage it provides global perspectives on religion, the sciences, law, the arts and sport. International organizations, obituaries of eminent people and key documents are also included. Of related interest is *The Statesman's Yearbook: the Politics, Cultures and Economies of the World* (London: Macmillan), published annually since 1864. It is divided into two main parts: International Organizations; and Countries of the World A–Z. Like the *Annual Register*, it benefits from the inclusion of a comprehensive index. Taken together, these publications should satisfy most social scientists' needs for brief information about countries, people and newsworthy international events.

Those who require a little more detail and statistical surveys of key aspects of each country (e.g., industry, agriculture, finance, tourism and education) may wish to consult *The Europa World Year Book* (London: Europa Publications). Formerly *The Europa Year Book: a World Survey*, it was first published in 1926, adopting its annual two-volume format in 1960. Like the *Annual Register* and *Statesman's Yearbook,* it provides information on international organizations and country-specific reports. The introductory surveys of each country are of particular value covering among other topics: recent history, government, defence, economic affairs and social welfare. The publication also features what is termed a *Directory* for each country consisting of information about the constitution, government, judicial system, religion, the press, broadcasting, finance, trade and industry, transport and tourism, and including the names and addresses of important organizations.

Whitaker's Almanack (London: The Stationery Office) was first published in 1868 by Joseph Whitaker. It provides detailed coverage of the United Kingdom on such varied topics as: Parliament, religion, education, social welfare, transport, the environment, lotteries and gaming, taxation, the media and organizations. Data on the rest of the globe are far more sketchy, but the Almanack does offer information on the European Parliament, European Union, a brief A–Z compendium of facts (and maps) about the countries of the world and a profile of world events from the past year. The *Almanack* also includes a bibliography of annual reference books.

The *Yearbook of International Organizations* edited by the Union of International Associations (Munich: KG Saur Verlag) is published in four volumes: 1. *Organization Descriptions and Cross-References*; 2. *Geographic Volume: International Organization Participation: Country Directory of Secretariats and Membership*; 3. *Subject Volume: Global Action Networks: Classified Directory and Index*; 4. *Bibliographic Volume: International Organizations Bibliography and Resources*. It is also available in CD-ROM format. The *Yearbook* is an invaluable guide to nearly 30 000 organizations in 300 countries and territories. In addition to an alphabetical listing of organizations with detailed descriptions, the reader can locate organizations by topic/activity and find references to publications produced by organizations (including those featured in the *Encyclopedia of World Problems and Human Potential* – *see 1.6*). The CD-ROM version of the *Yearbook* usefully combines the information from the four volumes together with biographies from *Who's Who in International Organizations* (*see 1.5*). At the time of writing an online version of the *Yearbook* is being planned.

The well-established *Annual Reviews* (Palo Alto, CA: Annual Reviews, Inc) series in the social sciences is a useful resource for more narrowly focused academic information within specific disciplines. Six individual volumes are produced covering particular subject divisions within the field: anthropology; energy and the environment; political science; psychology; public health; and sociology. Literature reviews of major topics are provided, usually accompanied by comprehensive bibliographies. The individual subject chapters discuss the *Annual Reviews* of specific social science disciplines in more detail. The *Reviews* are also available in electronic format at: <arjournals.annualreviews.org/socialhome.dtl>. The Website provides access to the tables of contents and abstracts of the reviews free of charge, even if you do not subscribe to the full-text publications.

The annual reports of research and other national/international organizations in the social sciences can be valuable sources of information, examples of which are listed in the following subject chapters. The *Consortium of Social Science Associations* (*COSSA*) is an umbrella organization which makes its annual reports available on its Website at: <www.cossa.org/AnnualReports.htm>. *See 1.14.2* for further information about the organization.

The *International Social Survey Program* (*ISSP*) is an annual programme of crossnational collaboration between 31 nations including the four founders: Germany, the United States, Great Britain and Australia. The purpose of the collaboration is to supplement and coordinate national surveys in order to enhance the global social science knowledge-base. See <www.issp.org/biblio.htm> for an extensive bibliography of ISSP publications arranged by country of origin. *See 1.14.2* for further information about the association.

▶ 1.3 BIBLIOGRAPHIES

The individual subject chapters feature an extensive range of bibliographies covering specific topic areas within the social sciences. In this general chapter we restrict ourselves to major multidisciplinary works.

(a) Print

A London Bibliography of the Social Sciences (London: London School of Economics and Political Science, 1931–1960; London: Mansell Information/Publishing, 1970–1989). This classic bibliography, first compiled under the direction of B.M. Headicar and C. Fuller, arose out of a project to produce a subject catalogue for the Library of Political and Economic Science at the London School of Economics. Its first four volume edition covered over 600 000 items spanning 1650 to 1929. The following 60 years witnessed the publication of 24 supplements and 47 volumes. To a computer literate generation it may appear something of a cumbersome anachronism, but it remains a testament to one of the world's foremost social science libraries.

From 1990 onwards, materials that would have been covered by the *London Bibliography* can be traced via *The International Bibliography of the Social Sciences* (Andover, Hants: Taylor & Francis/Routledge). It is an annual publication (now published each December), a bibliography and, latterly, an electronic database (*see 1.10*). Thus its precise placement in a guide such as this is both problematic and arbitrary. The *Bibliography* has been produced since 1951, when it was created by the International Committee for Social Science Information and Documentation. For many years it was compiled at the Fondation Nationale des Science Politiques in Paris by Jean Meyriat and Jean Viet. Since 1989 it has been produced by the British Library of Political and Economic Science at the London School of Economics and Political Science. Published in four volumes – anthropology, economics, political science and sociology – it remains a key resource for all social science researchers. The four volumes cover some 24 000 titles (articles and monographs) spanning over 100 countries and include bilingual (French and English) subject indexes. Reprints of back issues dating from the first in 1951 are available from the publishers. The *Bibliography* is now available in a variety of electronic formats (*see 1.10*).

Those with an interest in the history of the development of social science journals may wish to consult *Social Sciences: an International Bibliography of Serial Literature, 1830–1985* by Jan Wepsiec (London: Mansell, 1992).

(b) Electronic

The *Bibliography of Social Science Information and Documentation* <www.stir.ac.uk/services/swp/docs/bibs/> is produced by the Helsinki School of Economics Library under the editorship of Kyllikki Ruokonen. It contains over 700 references in English, French, German, Russian, Spanish, Italian and Dutch, relating to information sources and information providers within the social science field. Although updated irregularly, it contains much useful information which will, hopefully, be added to in the future.

Bibliographic Records of UNESCO Documents, Publications and Library Collections (UNESBIB) <unesdoc.unesco.org/ulis/unesbib.html>. A large repository of over 52 000 documents produced by the United Nations Educational, Scientific, and Cultural Organization (UNESCO) since 1942. Subjects covered include: education, culture, social and human sciences and communication.

Social Science Bibliography of Northern Ireland 1945–1983 <cain.ulst.ac.uk/bibdbs/nissbib.htm>. This bibliography was compiled in 1983 by Bill Rolston and Mike Tomlinson. It remains an excellent resource for researchers interested in the history of Northern Ireland. The bibliography consists of some 6000 items across a wide variety of materials: books (and book chapters); government publications; journal articles; dissertations; pamphlets; unpublished conference papers; and mimeographed articles of limited circulation. The references were published between 1945 and 1983 and cover the period from 1921 to the early 1980s.

The Evolutionary Models in Social Science (EMSS) Web Bibliography <www.soc.surrey.ac.uk/~scs1ec/emssbib.html> is a work in progress by Edmund Chattoe, Associate Director of the Centre for Research on Simulation in the Social Sciences. In addition to the main bibliography, which attempts 'to cover all models making use of evolutionary analogies with social processes and focuses on recent models using computational techniques', the site includes many other useful bibliographies on, for example, systems theory, the literature of discontent, cognitive science and artificial intelligence, econometrics and forecasting, psychology and decision theory, organization theory and the philosophy and methodology of social science.

The Bibliography for Rhetoric, Composition, and Professional Communication <www.public.iastate.edu/~wsthune/research/bib1.html> is an extensive, searchable collection of over 7600 articles and books related to the topic of academic discourse. Its scope suggests it is likely to be of interest to practitioners and researchers from diverse disciplines across the social sciences.

▶ 1.4 DICTIONARIES

(a) Print

At the time of writing, an important new publication the *Dictionary of Social Sciences* (Oxford: Oxford University Press, 2001) is about to be published. Edited by Craig Calhoun – President of the Social Science Research Council in New York (*see 1.14.2*) – it will fill a significant gap in the market. For many years Duncan G. Mitchell's *A New Dictionary of the Social Sciences* (New York: Aldine, 1979) was a key text, but it is now showing its age. The *Dictionary of Critical Social Sciences* by T. R. Young and Bruce A. Arrigo (Boulder, CO: Westview Press, 1999) is of more current value as it describes and defines major social science concepts in progressive, radical, critical Marxist, feminist, left-liberal, postmodern and semiotic contexts.

In addition to the above text, social theory is well-served by *The Blackwell Dictionary of Twentieth-Century Social Thought* edited by William Outhwaite and Tom Bottomore (Oxford: Blackwell, 1994). Renowned authors cover all the main themes, concepts and schools of thought in considerable detail. The five-volume *Dictionary of Twentieth-Century Culture* edited by Catherine Savage Brosman (Farmington Hills, MI: Gale, 1994–1996) offers an alternative analysis of the twentieth century, focusing on cultural communication. Volume one looks at American culture after World War II; volume two concentrates on French culture; volume three features the Hispanic culture of South America; volume four continues with the Hispanic culture in Mexico, Central America and the Caribbean; and volume five concludes the series with African-American culture.

(b) Electronic

The *Online Dictionary of the Social Sciences* <datadump.icaap.org/cgi-bin/glossary/SocialDict/SocialDict> produced jointly by Athabasca University and The International Consortium for the Advancement of Academic Publication, has 1000 entries covering the disciplines of sociology, criminology, political science and women's studies, with an emphasis on Canadian materials.

▶ 1.5 DIRECTORIES

Those wishing to investigate the scope of directory publishing in the United Kingdom should consult, *Current British Directories*, 13th ed., (Beckenham, Kent: CBD Research Ltd., 2000). It features around 2500 directories, guides and yearbooks published across all subjects.

The *World Directory of Social Science Institutions* (Paris: UNESCO, 1990) contains details of over 2000 training institutions, professional societies and groups from 199 countries. The information is taken from the databank of the UNESCO Social and Human Sciences Documentation Centre. The *Directory of Social Research Organisations in the United Kingdom*, 2nd ed., edited by Martin Bulmer, Wendy Sykes and Jacqui Moorhouse (London: Mansell, 1998) has entries for 1000 social research organizations, covering: central and local government; quangos;

universities and other higher education research centres and units; independent research institutes; charities; market research companies; and management consultants. It also provides a number of essays, by respected academics and practitioners, on various aspects of social science research.

Of related interest is the *International Research Centers Directory*, 10th ed., (Farmington Hills, MI: Gale, 1998) which provides information on over 8000 government, university, non-profit and commercial organizations in around 125 countries. Offering a narrower North American focus, is another publication from Gale called, *Research Centers Directory*, 28th ed., (Farmington Hills, MI: Gale, 2001) which gives details (including Web and Email addresses) of over 13 000 non-profit research organizations in the United States. If information is required on British organizations, *Centres, Bureaux & Research Institutes*, 3rd ed., edited by Charlotte Edwards (Beckenham, Kent: CBD Research Ltd., 2000), will be of interest. It lists 2000 bodies across 750 different subject areas.

Directories of associations and learned societies may need to be consulted by social scientists. *The Encyclopedia of Associations: International Organizations*, 37th ed., (Farmington Hills, MI: Gale, 2001) provides detailed information on multinational and national membership organizations across the world, from Afghanistan to Zimbabwe. Geographic, executive (executive officers and other personnel) and keyword indexes facilitate ease-of-use. *Pan-European Associations*, 3rd ed., edited by Crispin A. Henderson (Beckenham, Kent: CBD Research Ltd., 1996) features over 2000 multinational organizations active in a wide range of areas. Excluding Great Britain and the Republic of Ireland, the *Directory of European Professional & Learned Societies*, 5th ed., edited by Susan Greenslade (Beckenham, Kent: CBD Research Ltd., 1995) provides details about over 4000 professional, academic, scientific and technical societies in every country of Europe. Useful features in both publications include translations of organizational names and an abbreviations index.

For British and Irish societies see the *Directory of British Associations and Associations in Ireland*, 15th ed., edited by S. P. A. Henderson and A. J. W. Henderson (Beckenham, Kent: CBD Research Ltd., 2000). It is also available in electronic format on CD-ROM. Of related interest is *The Aslib Directory of Information Sources in the UK*, 11th ed., edited by Keith Reynard (London: Aslib, 2000) which provides details of over 11 000 associations, societies, educational establishments, institutes, commissions, government bodies and other organizations. For libraries and documentation centres across the world see *The Selective Inventory of Social Science Information and Documentation Services*, 5th ed., prepared by the UNESCO Social and Human Sciences Documentation Centre (Paris: UNESCO Publishing, 1998). It is a country-by-country listing of major social science information services. Entries include: contact information; details of geographic and subject coverage; and titles of publications produced.

If you are investigating the people who populate organizations then you may wish to consult *Who's Who in International Organizations*, 3rd ed., edited by the Union of International Associations (Munich: KG Saur Verlag, 1999), which lists over 13 000 key personnel from around 12 000 organizations. The biographical information includes: career (current/previous positions and published works); personal details (family, education and leisure interests); and addresses. The indexes facilitate searching by organization, country and fields of activity (*See 1.2* for the *Yearbook of International Organizations*). For European information it is worth consulting *Who's Who in the European Union: Inter-institutional Directory 2001* (London: The Stationery Office, 2001). In addition to information on the organizational structure of EU bodies, it includes details of MEPs and the Members of the Economic and Social Committee.

► 1.6 ENCYCLOPAEDIAS

For assistance in gathering information on the scope, quality and range of encyclopaedias across all fields, see the two volumes of *Subject Encyclopedias: User Guide, Review Citations, and Keyword Index* compiled by Allan N. Mirwis (Phoenix, AZ: The Oryx Press, 1999). Of particular value is Mirwis' five-point scale, based on the findings of published reviews, used to give a quality rating for each encyclopaedia.

The two major social science encyclopaedias of the twentieth century are: R. A. Seligman and Alvin Johnson's 15-volume, *Encyclopaedia of the Social Sciences* (London and New York: Macmillan, 1930–35); and the *International Encyclopedia of the Social Sciences* edited by David L. Sills in 17 volumes (New York: The Macmillan Company & The Free Press, and London: Collier-Macmillan, 1968). The latter included a supplementary biographical volume published in 1979 and a dictionary of quotations in 1991. Both works offer the reader insightful overviews of the state of knowledge of their respective generations. However, their value is now largely historical, for as David Sills says in his introduction: 'Because an encyclopedia reflects a generation's contributions to and perspectives on knowledge, it must be revised, updated, or supplemented if it is to maintain its intellectual credibility' (p.xiii).

The Social Science Encyclopedia, 2nd ed., edited by Adam Kuper and Jessica Kuper (London and New York: Routledge, 1996) is testimony to the truth of Sills' statement, having first appeared in 1985 and recently published in a new edition to take account of the rapidly changing and fluid state of contemporary social science. It contains around 600 concise entries (which include references and suggestions for further reading), written by an international panel of contributors. The single volume spans all the major disciplines of the social sciences and ably covers new trends such as the development of environmental economics, cultural geography and psychological anthropology. The editors share the sentiments expressed earlier that a degree of conflict is healthy, because although they suggest that their work demonstrates the interconnectedness of the social sciences, this does not mean that diversity is dead, far from it: 'Through interchange, by a process of challenge and response, shared standards and concerns develop.' (p.viii). Hence, the reader will be exposed to the debates and controversies that make the social sciences so stimulating.

At the time of writing, a major new 26 volume work – *International Encyclopedia of the Social & Behavioral Sciences* – is being planned by Elsevier, to be available in both print and electronic formats. The editors-in-chief of the encyclopaedia are Neil J. Smelser and Paul B. Baltes. It is intended to include 4000 signed articles, 90 000 bibliographic references and 150 biographical entries, making it the largest social science reference work ever published. The online version will offer annual updates from 2003 onwards. Further information and sample entries can be found at: <www.iesbs.com>

The Encyclopedia of World Problems and Human Potential, 4th ed., edited by the Union of International Associations (Munich: KG Saur Verlag, 1994–5) comprises three volumes: 1. *World Problems*; 2. *Human Potential – Transformation and Values*; and 3. *Actions, Strategies and Solutions*. The publishers have also made the volumes available in a single CD-ROM format, which greatly enhances the speed with which the 3000+ pages of text can be searched. The publication's worldwide focus on social problems means that it is a resource which could be of value to a broad spectrum of social scientists.

The *Encyclopedia of Social History* edited by Peter N. Stearns (New York: Garland, 1994) is of potential interest to all social scientists. The alphabetically arranged entries provide brief, yet readable, overviews of key topics including: the family, industrialization, multiculturalism and nationalism. 'See also' references are given in addition to a name/subject index. The *Routledge Encyclopaedia of Philosophy* edited by Edward Craig (London: Routledge, 1998) is available in 10 print volumes or as a single CD-ROM, with augmented subject searching capabilities. International, multi-cultural and interdisciplinary in scope, it will be of assistance to social scientists seeking information on the philosophies of western and non-western cultures.

▶ 1.7 GUIDES AND HANDBOOKS

1.7.1 General

(a) Print

The *World Social Science Report 1999* (Paris: UNESCO Publishing/ Elsevier, 1999) edited by Ali Kazancigil and David Makinson, is one of a series of reports on specific subject fields from the United Nations Educational, Scientific and Cultural Organization (UNESCO). It provides a comprehensive review of the role of the social sciences on a global scale.

The *Reader's Guide to the Social Sciences* edited by Jonathan Michie (London: Fitzroy Dearborn, 2001) is an excellent guide to the literature for those new to the social sciences. Most of the main subject divisions are covered including: psychology, sociology, politics, economics and human geography. The A–Z format provides 1500 review essays across two volumes. Full bibliographic references for featured materials are included.

Walford's Guide to Reference Material. Vol. 2: Social and Historical Sciences, Philosophy and Religion, 8th ed., edited by Alan Day and Michael Walsh (London: Library Association, 2000), aims to be a selective and evaluative guide to the best sources of reference material in each subject area. It covers: journal articles, electronic resources, bibliographies, encyclopaedias, monographs and directories. Critical annotations and reviewers' comments are also included.

Social Science Reference Sources: a Practical Guide, 3rd ed., by Tze-Chung Li (Westport, CT: Greenwood, 2000), provides a useful update to the previous editions published in 1983 and 1990. It directs the reader around 1600 sources of information – dictionaries, directories, biographies, theses and statistics – within most of the major social science disciplines.

The Social Sciences: a Cross-Disciplinary Guide to Selected Sources edited by Nancy L. Herron (Englewood, CO: Libraries Unlimited, 1989) has been prepared by practising reference librarians and is aimed at both researchers and students. Coverage includes reference sources applicable across all disciplines: those relevant to social sciences and those defined as 'emerging' from the humanities or pure sciences into areas of the social sciences.

Sources of Information in the Social Sciences: a Guide to the Literature by William H. Webb, et al. (Chicago, IL: American Library Association, 1986) covers the literature of: history, geography, economics and business administration, sociology, anthropology, psychology, education, and political science. Its coverage and detail is impressive, but many of the resources referred to are now many decades old. Hence, its value is more historical than contemporary.

(b) Electronic

The *Resource Guide for the Social Sciences* <www.jisc.ac.uk/subject/socsci/> focuses on social science resources funded by the Joint Information Systems Committee (JISC) of the Higher and Further Education Funding Councils of the UK, and the Economic and Social Research Council (ESRC). Individual sections include bibliographic, reference and research information, and subject gateways.

1.7.2 Research and data analysis

Two books which will be of immense help to the novice researcher are: *A Handbook of Social Science Research*, 2nd ed., by Gary D. Bouma and G. B. J. Atkinson (Oxford: Oxford University Press, 1995); and the *Handbook for Research Students in the Social Sciences* edited by Chris Skinner and Graham Allan (London: Falmer Press, 1991). Both works discuss what it means to be a researcher in the social sciences, how to construct a research proposal and review a range of research methods.

The *Manual of Online Search Strategies: Volume III – Humanities and Social Sciences*, 3rd ed., edited by C. J. Armstrong and Andrew Large (Aldershot: Gower, 2001), offers researchers detailed advice on database selection, search service selection and search strategy compilation in the areas of social and behavioural sciences, humanities and education. Whilst there are reservations to be made about its currency – it focuses on the electronic environment of the early to mid-1990s rather than the twenty-first century – it will remain a useful introduction to electronic sources of information for a little while longer.

As in many other areas, the Internet is changing the nature of research in the social sciences. *Using the Web for Social Research* by Craig McKie (Toronto: McGraw-Hill Ryerson, 1997) is designed to help social science students and researchers make effective use of it. McKie provides details of Internet resources in the fields of psychology, sociology, anthropology, political science, economics and criminology, amongst others. It is a well-written guide and amply illustrated with screen dumps of apposite Webpages.

Social science researchers frequently have to make use of a number of statistical methods, tests and computer software applications. Fortunately, there are a growing number of publications offering guidance in this area. The *Handbook of Statistical Modeling for the Social and Behavioral Sciences* edited by G. Arminger, C. C. Clogg and M. E. Sobel (Dordrecht, The Netherlands: Kluwer Academic, 1994), introduces quantitative and statistical methods for a range of social science disciplines including: economics, education, political science, psychology and sociology. Alan Bryman and Duncan Cramer have established themselves as key interpreters of a social science data analysis software application known as SPSS. Their most recent works focus respectively on the quantitative and qualitative use of the package: *Quantitative Data Analysis with SPSS Release 10 for Windows* (London: Routledge, 2001); and *Qualitative Data Analysis with SPSS Release 10* (London: Routledge, 2001).

Locating tests, questionnaires and other measures can be difficult. Paula E. Lester and Lloyd K. Bishop have made the task considerably easier with the publication of the *Handbook of Tests and Measurements in Education and the Social Sciences*, 2nd ed., (Lanham, Md: Scarecrow Press, 2000). The authors have made a compilation of 120 important tests, questionnaires and inventories used in the social sciences.

1.7.3 Study and writing skills

Becoming conversant with the skills required for academic study, communication and writing can be a challenge for many students. There are several guides on the market designed to make the process as painless as possible. See, for example: *The Student's Writing Guide for the Arts and Social Sciences* by Gordon Taylor (Cambridge: Cambridge University Press, 1989); and *A Short Guide to Writing About Social Science*, 3rd ed., by Lee J. Cuba (London: Longman, 1996). For specific help with the use of references in academic work see the booklet, *Citing References* by David Fisher and Terry Hanstock (Oxford: Blackwell's Bookshops, 1998). Many of the reference examples are taken from the social science literature.

▶ 1.8 WEBSITES

In this section we discuss general social science gateways – quality rather than quantity is our aim! Subsequent chapters will detail key sites within specific social science disciplines.

ABYAN.net: Social Science <www.abyan.net/>. A well-organized commercial site covering links to information within many of the major disciplines within the social sciences, in addition to being a one-stop shop for access to the broad-based gateways. Recommended by the respected *Scout Report* (*see* its listing below and in *1.13*).

BUBL Link: Social Sciences <bubl.ac.uk/link/soc.html>. Extensive resources from the Bulletin Board for Libraries based at the University of Strathclyde, UK. The social science page provides an alphabetical listing of a very wide range of topics from Accountancy to World Travel and Tourism. Each quality Web resource is annotated and includes important information such as the author, resource type, location, subject coverage and date last checked.

Data on the Net <odwin.ucsd.edu/idata>. The Inter-university Consortium for Political and Social Research (ICPSR), based at the Institute for Social Research at the University of Michigan, provides access to a vast array of data archives and social science gateway sites.

Galaxy: Social Sciences <www.galaxy.com/galaxy/Social-Sciences.html>. Links to specific and general Web resources from Galaxy – a searchable directory first launched in 1994 and now part of the Fox/News Cor-poration. They employ qualified subject librarians to research, classify and organize information on the site. Social science disciplines covered include: anthropology, communication, education, geography, political science, psychology and sociology.

H-Net: Humanities & Social Sciences OnLine <www2.h-net.msu.edu>. Hosted by Michigan State University, H-Net provides networking and gateway resources for the social sciences. It describes itself as 'an international interdisciplinary organization of scholars and teachers dedicated to developing the enormous educational potential of the Internet and the World Wide Web'. In addition to providing links to quality Websites, *H-Net* also publishes peer-reviewed essays on a wide range of topics from radical religion in the time of Shakespeare to the history of the United Democratic Front in South Africa.

INFOMINE: Social Sciences and Humanities <infomine.ucr.edu/>. A searchable set of Web links from the libraries of the University of California. Currently over 900 resources are provided including full-text document archives and electronic journals, as well as online subject guides. Resources can be browsed by subject, keyword and title.

NISS Directory of Networked Resources: Social Sciences <www.niss.ac.uk/>. A quality gateway of classified hierarchical links from the UK-based National Information Services and Systems (NISS) organization. In addition to general social science gateways, the directory offers more narrowly focused resources for methodology, demography, politics, economics, government, social welfare, education and ethnology.

RDN Virtual Training Suite <www.vts.rdn.ac.uk>. Officially launched on Tuesday, 8th May 2001, the suite is 'a set of online tutorials designed to help students, lecturers and researchers improve their Internet information skills'. Currently, there are tutorials in: anthropology, economics, education, geography, politics, psychology, social policy, social research methods, social statistics, social work, sociology and women's studies. The Resource Discovery Network (RDN) is part of DNER (Distributed National Electronic Resource), a UK-based managed information environment 'designed to enable users to move seamlessly and easily between a variety of high quality information services'.

Research Resources for the Social Sciences <www.socsciresearch.com>. A useful page of links to a wide range of social science Websites. Based on the book *Using the Web for Social Research* by Craig McKie (Toronto and New York: McGraw-Hill Ryerson, 1997) – *see 1.7.2.*

Social Science Hub <www.sshub.com>. Maintained by Sharyn Clarkson, an anthropology graduate from Canberra, Australia, this site provides links to subject-specific resources as well as newsgroups, journals and universities. Not as comprehensive or authoritative as some of the more established sites discussed in this section, but this attractive and easy-to-navigate resource does put many of the more run-of-the-mill university Webpages to shame. A work in progress which is well worth a visit.

Social Sciences & Social Issues <www.clearinghouse.net>. Graded resources from the Argus Clearinghouse, a US organization founded by Louis Rosenfeld in 1993. Their mission is to provide 'a central access point for value-added topical guides which identify, describe, and evaluate Internet-based information resources'. The subcategories of the Social Sciences and Social Issues section include: anthropology, communities and urban planning, families, linguistics, political science, psychology, social issues and sociology.

Social Sciences Virtual Library <www.clas.ufl.edu/users/gthursby/socsci>. A major resource providing links to general and specific social science sites, edited by Dr Gene R. Thursby at the University of Florida. The homepage states that 'sites are inspected and evaluated for their adequacy as information sources before they are linked to from here'. In addition to covering standard disciplines such as anthropology, education, psychology and sociology, the site also strays into the arts and classics as well as what are termed 'systems' (Artificial and Natural). A useful feature is the highlighting of sites that are particularly recommended from amongst its extensive links.

SOSIG Social Science Information Gateway <www.sosig.ac.uk>. A key starting point for accessing Web-based social science information including: organizations, statistics, library catalogues and full-text documents. Since 1999, *SOSIG* has been known as a 'hub' and forms part of a cooperative network of information providers under the umbrella Resource Discovery Network or RDN. All the information on *SOSIG* has been checked for reliability and quality by librarians and academics. Despite being a UK-based service, its scope is international.

SRSOCSCI – The Scout Report for Social Sciences & Humanities <scout.cs.wisc.edu/report/socsci>. Very useful current awareness service providing information on new Websites selected by librarians and information specialists. The *Scout Report* has been published continuously since 1994 and is based in the Department of Computer Sciences at the University of Wisconsin-Madison. The biweekly *Social Sciences and Humanities* version can be accessed from the above Website, or you can take out a free subscription and receive it via Email. The resources are invariably interesting and are accompanied by detailed, evaluative descriptions. *See also 1.13 (b) Electronic.*

TRAMSS: Teaching Resources and Materials for Social Scientists <tramss.data-archive.ac.uk>. An innovative resource aimed at postgraduate students engaged in quantitative social science research. The site provides data samples and the tools needed to construct simple or complex analyses depending upon the individual's level of expertise.

Yahoo! Social Science <dir.yahoo.com/Social_Science>. This well-known directory offers numerous links to a broad selection of resources. It is perhaps let down by the fact that not all resources are described and those that are do not usually warrant more than a sentence. However, the pages are relatively easy to navigate and provide speedy access to a formidable selection of social science Websites, mailing lists/discussion groups and full-text electronic materials.

► 1.9 JOURNALS

The intention of this section is to offer a selection of key journals, with an emphasis on those titles which are international and multi-/inter-disciplinary in scope. Well-established journals are presented alongside notable newer titles. If a journal is available in electronic as well as print format, this is indicated. There is not a separate *Electronic* section as such, as most journals are available in both print and electronic formats. Web addresses are only given if they give free, full-text access to the journal.

If a comprehensive listing, rather than an evaluative selection, of journals is required it would be worth consulting the standard publication, *Ulrich's Periodicals Directory* (New Providence, NJ: RR Bowker) which lists around 164 000 serials from across the world. It is also available in CD-ROM format and on the Web at <www.ulrichsWeb.com>. In addition, the *World List of Social Science Periodicals* (Paris: UNESCO, 1991) could be consulted. It lists over 4400 journals arranged by title and country of publication. However, as it is some years since it was updated it is of declining utility. Those interested in historical bibliography may find Jan Wepsiec's book of interest (*see 1.3 (a) Print*). For statistical analyses of the most frequently cited journals see *Journal Citation Reports: Social Sciences Edition* (Philadelphia, PA: Institute for Scientific Information) which is produced annually on CD-ROM and on the Web <www.isinet.com/isi/products/citation/jcr>. It covers 1600 social science journals from anthropology to women's studies.

Cross-Cultural Research: the Journal of Comparative Social Science (ISSN 1069–3971) (Thousand Oaks, CA: Sage, 1966–). Quarterly. As its title suggests, this refereed journal is a useful source of comparative research in the social sciences. Available electronically.

Economy and Society (ISSN 0308–5147) (London: Routledge, 1972–). Quarterly. A well-established, interdisciplinary peer-reviewed social science journal, presenting radical and cutting-edge theoretical and political debate.

European Journal of Social Theory (ISSN 1368–4310) (London: Sage, 1998–). Quarterly. A newly established title offering a multidisciplinary and transnational approach to social theory. Includes a regular book review section. Available electronically.

History of the Human Sciences (ISSN 0952–6951) (London: Sage, 1988–). Quarterly. A refereed serial devoted to analysing the origins and theoretical underpinnings of the social sciences, with a particular focus on sociology, psychology, anthropology and linguistics. Available electronically.

Human Relations (ISSN 0018–7267) (New York: Kluwer Academic/Plenum Publishers, 1947–). Monthly. A refereed serial providing an interdisciplinary perspective for the analysis of human relations, and includes a regular book reviews section. Available electronically.

Information, Communication & Society (ISSN 1468–4462) (London: Routledge, 1998–). Quarterly. The journal identifies itself as 'devoted to the publication of high quality empirical research and theoretical works that include analysis of the emerging properties of the Information Age in a multi-disciplinary and transcultural perspective'. Available electronically.

International Social Science Journal (ISSN 0020–8701) (Oxford: Blackwell Publishers, 1949–). Quarterly. This refereed journal is published on behalf of the United Nations Educational, Scientific, and Cultural Organization (UNESCO) in English, Arabic, French, Spanish and Russian, offering a global perspective on the social sciences. Most issues are devoted to a particular topic which is covered in depth. Information is also given on forthcoming international conferences and new UNESCO publications. Available electronically.

International Social Science Review (ISSN 0278–2308) (Boone, NC: Appalachian State University, 1925–). Quarterly. Publishes qualitative and quantitative research across the social sciences.

Philosophy of the Social Sciences (ISSN 0048–3931) (Thousand Oaks, CA: Sage, 1971–). Quarterly. A useful journal for those interested in the philosophical foundations of the social sciences. Available electronically.

The Qualitative Report (ISSN 1052–0147) (Fort Lauderdale, FL: Nova Southeastern University, 1990–). <www.nova.edu/ssss/QR/index.html>. An *electronic*, peer-reviewed journal for the discussion of qualitative and critical enquiry.

Russian Social Science Review (ISSN 1061–1428) (Armonk, NY: M.E Sharpe, 1960–). Bimonthly. This refereed journal presents translations of key articles from major Russian-language social science journals. Available electronically.

Social Epistemology: a Journal of Knowledge, Culture and Policy (ISSN 0269–1728) (London: Taylor & Francis, 1987–). Quarterly. A multidisciplinary journal which engages in international debate on epistemological issues. Available electronically.

Social Forces (ISSN 0037–7732) (Chapel Hill, NC: The University of North Carolina Press, 1922–). Quarterly. A typical issue of this refereed journal ranged widely over such diverse topics as: contemporary forms of inequality; political economy in fifteenth-century Tuscany; nursing homes in Ontario; the effect of americanization on health; and African American church attendance. A good source of book reviews. Available electronically.

Social Research: an International Quarterly of the Social Sciences (ISSN 0037–783X) (New York: New School for Social Research, 1934–). Quarterly. A refereed serial which has regular themed issues. Past issues have included such diverse themes as: food, democracy and conversation.

Social Research Update (Guildford: Department of Sociology, University of Surrey, 1993–). Quarterly. <www.soc.surrey.ac.uk/sru/sru.html> Each issue of this electronic journal covers a particular research topic indicating the main directions of recent work and including a bibliography of sources.

Social Science Computer Review (ISSN 0894–4393) (Thousand Oaks, CA: Sage, 1982–). Quarterly. An excellent source of information on the application of IT within the social sciences and includes detailed software reviews. This refereed journal is available electronically.

Social Science History (ISSN 0145–5532) (Durham, NC: Duke University Press, 1976–). Quarterly. This refereed journal is the official journal of the US-based Social Science History Association and, as such, has a primary focus on American research, but European articles are also featured. Available electronically.

Social Science Information/Information sur les Sciences Sociales (ISSN 0539–0184) (London: Sage, 1954–). Quarterly. Written in English and French, this refereed journal is a good forum for global social science debate, particularly in the area of comparative and cross-cultural research. Available electronically.

Social Science Japan Journal (ISSN 1369–1465) (Oxford: Oxford University Press, 1998–). Semiannual. A good source of information on Japanese society from a comparative perspective.

The Social Science Journal (ISSN 0362–3319) (New York: Elsevier Science, 1963–). Quarterly. The official publication of the Western Social Science Association, but this refereed journal has a US-wide coverage and offers a good mix of theoretical and empirical articles on a broad spectrum of topics. Available electronically.

Social Science Quarterly (ISSN 0038–4941) (Austin, TX: University of Texas Press, 1920–). Quarterly. Published on behalf of the Southwestern Social Science Association, this journal ranges widely over all major social science topics from multidisciplinary, empirical and theoretical perspectives.

Social Science Research: a Quarterly Journal of Social Science Methodology and Quantitative Research (ISSN 0049–089X) (San Diego,

CA: Academic Press, 1972–). Quarterly. A research-based journal, specializing in the presentation of quantitative studies. Available electronically.

Social Theory and Practice: an International and Interdisciplinary Journal of Social Philosophy (ISSN 0037–802X) (Tallahassee, FL: Department of Philosophy, The Florida State University, 1970–). Three issues a year. A forum for the discussion of social, political, legal, economic, educational and moral philosophy.

Society: Social Science and Modern Society (ISSN 0147–2011) (Picataway, NJ: Transaction Publishers, 1963–). Bimonthly. This well-established, refereed journal acts as a forum for the discussion of social sciences and public policy. It can count many luminaries both within and beyond the social sciences amongst its contributors. Available electronically.

Theory and Society (ISSN 0304–3421) (Dordrecht, The Netherlands: Kluwer Academic, 1974–). Bimonthly. Founded by Alvin Gouldner, this is a key refereed journal for social theorists. Available electronically.

Theory, Culture & Society (ISSN 0263–2764) (London, Thousand Oaks and New Delhi: Sage, 1982–). Bimonthly. Refereed journal of social and cultural theory, published on behalf of the Faculty of Humanities, The Nottingham Trent University. The journal publishes articles by renowned scholars from around the globe. Available electronically.

Thesis Eleven (ISSN 0725–5136) (London, New York and New Delhi: Sage, 1980–). Quarterly. Refereed journal devoted to encouraging a multidisciplinary approach to social theory. It includes a regular book reviews section. Available electronically.

▶ 1.10 ABSTRACTS, INDEXES AND DATABASES

The following section details a number of important abstracting and indexing services within the social sciences field, together with broad-based multidisciplinary databases. Over the past few years, there has been a growth in databases that provide not only bibliographic information, but also link to full-text materials. It should be noted that a number of publishers such as Blackwells, Elsevier and Oxford University Press have table of contents access to the journals they publish and many publishers also offer full-text on a subscription basis. A number of other database providers have produced multidisciplinary databases that have supporting document delivery and alerting services.

Since the early 1950s, the *International Bibliography of the Social Sciences (IBSS)* <www.lse.ac.uk/IBSS/> (London: London School of Economics and Political Science) has been produced. It was originally compiled at the Fondation Nationale des Science Politiques in Paris and later, from 1989, at the London School of Economics and Political Science. The bibliography provides access to over two million records. Bibliographic details are also given for more than 2400 international social science journals and 7000 books each year. Over 30 per cent of the references are not written in the English language, although title translations are provided in English. From 1997, abstracts are also available for approximately five per cent of the journals. IBSS is available in print, CD-ROM and online. The electronic database includes over 1.5 million records and has been made available to all UK higher education institutions through Bath Information and Data Services (BIDS) at: <www.bids.ac.uk/ibss.html>. Bibliographic references and abstracts can be downloaded and results sent via Email. The BIDS IBSS service also links with the full-text ingentaJournals service. *See also 1.3 (a) Print.*

The *Social Sciences Index* (New York: HW Wilson) indexes more than 518 English-language journals. It has a broad coverage across social science disciplines including anthropology, area studies, criminology, economics, politics, geography, international relations, health and medical care, law, geography, policy studies, psychology, sociology, social work and urban studies. The bibliographic index is available in print, CD-ROM, magnetic tape and Web format from 1983 to date. See the following Websites for further information: <www.hwwilson.com/databases/socsci.cfm> and <www.silverplatter.com/>. HW Wilson also has a Web service called *WilsonWeb* that allows the user to access full-text and graphical information for a number of journals covered by the database. In addition, the database is also available as *Social Sciences PlusText* (Ann Arbor, MI: ProQuest Information and Learning), which provides full-text access to over 200 journal titles. For further information see: <www.umi.com>.

The *Applied Social Sciences Index and Abstracts (ASSIA)* <www.assianet.co.uk/> (East Grinstead: Bowker) gives access to over 168 000 bibliographic records for articles from over 600 key English-language social science journals that have been published worldwide. The service is available in print, CD-ROM and via the Web. The database has a very good UK and European journal coverage. It is particularly valuable for material relating to social issues, prison services, youth work, economics, politics, healthcare, employment, race relations and sociology.

The *Social Sciences Citation Index* <www.isinet.com/> (Philadelphia, PA: Institute for Scientific Information) is a multidisciplinary database that indexes more than 1725 journals, plus selective relevant articles from over an additional 3300 titles. The database is available to members of the UK Higher Education sector via the ISI *Web of Science* service hosted at Manchester Information and Associated Services (MIMAS) <wos.mimas.ac.uk/>. It covers material from 1973 to date and includes Email delivery of results. In addition, via the *ISI Links* service, selected full-text articles can be accessed. The Institute for Scientific Information (ISI) also produces the *Arts and Humanities* and *Science Citation Indexes*, which may be of use to social science researchers.

The *Index to Social Sciences and Humanities Proceedings* <www.isinet.com/> (Philadelphia, PA: Institute for Scientific Information), is a useful companion service to the *Social Science Citation* and the *Arts and Humanities Citation Indexes* discussed above. It offers multidisciplinary coverage of around 200 000 papers presented at over 2800 international social science and humanities conferences. It covers a wide spectrum of subject areas including: psychology, sociology, public health, economics, art, literature, philosophy and history. Source publications feature monographs, journals, series and preprints. The index is available in a variety of formats: print, CD-ROM, online and Web. It is also available via the ISI *Web of Science* service hosted at MIMAS <wos.mimas.ac.uk>, from 1990 to date.

Of related interest is the *Index of Conference Proceedings* (Boston Spa: The British Library). It lists the conference proceedings held in the British Library, which has a policy of collecting the proceedings of significant conferences from across the globe, regardless of subject or language. It currently stocks the proceedings of over 400 000 conferences. The index is published monthly and cumulated in an annual volume. Materials are listed in a single A–Z sequence of name and subject keywords derived from the catalogue record. *See also Zetoc* below.

British Humanities Index (BHI) <www.bhinet.co.uk/> (East Grinstead: Bowker) is a very useful UK-based service. It provides access to bibliographic records from over 400 academic journals, weekly magazines and newspapers. The database is multidisciplinary and it has particularly strong coverage of current affairs, economics, popular science, law, politics, urban environment, architecture, arts, literature, history, music and religion. It is available in print, CD-ROM and via the Web. The BHInet service is updated on a monthly basis.

Humanities Index (New York: HW Wilson) provides bibliographic records for articles published in approximately 500 English-language journals across the wide spectrum of the humanities subject field. The index is available in print, CD-ROM, hard disk and Web format from 1984 to present. See the following Websites for further information: <www.hwwilson.com/databases/> and <www.silverplatter.com/>.

Project Muse <muse.jhu.edu/> (Baltimore M.D: John Hopkins University Press) provides worldwide access to over 100 full-text scholarly journals within the subject fields of social sciences, arts, humanities and mathematics. It is an institutional subscription based service. Further information can be obtained from, Email: muse@muse.jhu.edu.

The *Periodicals Contents Index* (PCI) <pci.chadwyck.com/> (Cambridge: Proquest Information and Learning Company) contains information from the tables of contents of thousands of English and other language journals in the subject fields of arts, humanities and social sciences. The index has a worldwide coverage of 3536 journals. The index is available on CD-ROM and in Web format, PCI Web, and there is a full-text edition.

It includes the contents of journals from the latter part of the eighteenth century to the latter part of the twentieth century. The database is also available to UK higher educational institutions through EDINA (Edinburgh Data and Information Access) with a site subscription, <edina.ed.ac.uk/pci/>.

Studies on Women and Gender Abstracts <www.tandf.co.uk/swa> (Basingstoke: Carfax Publishing) was, until 2000, known as *Studies on Women Abstracts*. The service is published on a bimonthly basis and indexes both international journals and books. It focuses on education, employment, health, female sex and gender roles, women in the family and community, medicine, social policy, the social psychology of women, female culture, media treatment of women, biography, literary criticism and historical studies. Each issue contains both author and subject indexes. Cumulative author and subject indexes appear at the end of the year. The database is available in print and via the Web. The database version is available free to subscribers of the print version and covers material from 1995 to date.

The *PAIS International* database <www.pais.org/products/index.stm> (New York: OCLC PAIS) indexes current affairs, political, economic and social issues. The database includes references from over 3700 sources from 1972 to the present and is updated on a monthly basis. In January 2000, Public Affairs Information Service (PAIS) merged with OCLC to form the OCLC Public Affairs Information Service. Earlier publications produced by PAIS have included: *the Bulletin of the Public Affairs Information Service*; the *Foreign Language Index*; *PAIS International in Print* (a combination of both previous publications); *PAIS Decade* database; and *PAIS Select* (CD-ROM). Another useful resource for current affairs information is *Keesing's Record of World Events* (Cambridge: Keesing's Worldwide) that has been published since 1931 (Email: info.uk@keesings.com). *See also 7.2 (a) Print.*

European Access (Cambridge: Chadwyck-Healey) is published bimonthly and provides bibliographic references to recent publications from the EU and articles relating to EU issues that have appeared in a number of journals and newspapers. The publication is arranged in a classified sequence by subject and is available on a subscription basis. A further subject index appears at the back of each issue. It is available in print, or electronic form as *European Access Plus* <www.europeanaccess.co.uk/>. *European Access Plus* offers all the features of the printed version but it is more up-to-date (with weekly updates), and offers access to many full-text sources. Another useful database for locating references relating to EU publications is the *SCAD Database*, <europa.eu.int/scad/>. *See also 7.3.8 (b) Electronic.*

The *REGARD* <www.regard.ac.uk/> (London: ESRC) bibliographic database provides access to the Economic and Social Research Council (ESRC) research awards and all associated publications. It provides access to in-depth information on UK social science research. REGARD is managed by the Institute for Learning and Research Technology and the University Library at the University of Bristol. *See also 1.13 (b) Electronic.*

DARE <www.unesco.org/general/eng/infoserv/db/dare.html> (Paris: UNESCO) is a bibliographic database that contains 11 000 worldwide references to social science journals, social science research and training institutions, specialists, documentation and information services. It is provided by the Social and Human Sciences Documentation Centre of UNESCO's Information Services. Further information can be obtained by contacting Email: c.bauer@unesco.org. *See also 1.13 (b) Electronic.*

SIGLE – System for Information on Grey Literature in Europe is managed by an equally bizarre acronym: EAGLE, the European Association for Grey Literature Exploitation. The latter being a consortium of documentation centres and libraries in Europe, which work together to provide access to reports and other non-trade publications, including those produced by research organizations, universities, charities and pressure groups. The database of over 674 000 records from member countries is available with semi-annual updates on CD-ROM, hard disk and the Internet, from SilverPlatter Information <www.silverplatter.com> (Norwood, MA: SilverPlatter Information).

Dissertation Abstracts <wwwlib.umi.com/dissertations/> (Ann Arbor, MI: ProQuest Information and Learning) is the authoritative source for information about US doctoral dissertations and masters theses. The database includes 1.6 million titles, citations ranging from the first US dissertation in 1861 to the present date. The database includes 350-word abstracts for dissertations published after 1980. It includes citations for North American and some European universities. The CD-ROM version includes citations from 1861 with abstracts for material published after 1982 and is updated on a quarterly basis. (*See also 1.13 (a) Print* and *(b) Electronic*). The best source for theses accepted for higher degrees in Great Britain and Ireland is *Index to Theses* <www.theses.com/> (London: Expert Information Ltd). The Web version provides access from 1970, i.e. volume 21 of the print version, and the service includes abstracts for theses from 1988 onwards (*See also 1.13 (a) Print and (b) Electronic*).

The *Population Index* <popindex.princeton.edu/> (Princeton: Office of Population Research, Princeton University) provides abstracts of journal articles, books, working papers and dissertations, covering the subject fields of population studies, demography and related areas. The Web version contains references from 1986 to the present.

JSTOR <www.jstor.org/jstor/> (New York: JSTOR) is a subscription based service that provides tables of contents and full-text articles from journals in a variety of subject fields especially in the humanities and social sciences. JSTOR started out as a sponsored project by the Mellon Foundation in 1994 to provide electronic access to the backfiles of ten journals in two core fields – economics and history. JSTOR was established as an independent not-for-profit organization in August 1995.

UnCover <uncWeb.carl.org/uncover/unchome.html> (Denver, CO: UnCover) is a multidisciplinary database of current article information taken from more than 18 000 journals. UnCover contains bibliographic information for articles from 1988 onwards. The service also offers a document delivery service and a current awareness alerting service called *UnCover Reveal*, which provides journal tables of contents directly via Email. For further information Email: uncover@carl.org.

The British Library's new table of contents service is called *Zetoc (Z39.50-compliant access to the British Library's Electronic Table of Contents)* (London: British Library). The multidisciplinary database contains references from approximately 20 000 current journals and 16 000 conference proceedings published each year. The database covers the years from 1993 to the present date and is updated on a daily basis. It is made freely available to further and higher education institutions in the UK through MIMAS on behalf of the British Library, <zetoc.mimas.ac.uk/>. All of the articles and conference papers included in the database are available from the British Library's Document Supply Centre. There is also an alerting service called *Zetoc Alert*.

OCLC Online Computer Library Center, Inc., produces a number of database services. The *ArticleFirst,* <www.oclc.org> (Dublin, OH: OCLC) database provides an index of articles from approximately 12 500 journals covering the subjects of business, science, humanities, social science, medicine, technology and popular culture. The database includes material from 1990 to present. The *FirstSearch* (Dublin, OH: OCLC) service provides access to full-text, including full-image articles from over 3300 electronic journals.

In 1996, the *IDEAL– International Digital Electronic Access Library* <www.idealibrary.com> (London: Academic Press) was launched. It provides access to over 200 000 articles from over 250 journals published by Academic Press and Harcourt Health Sciences. Access to the service can be via a license that provides access within a consortium or institution to all the AP journals, or by an Institutional Publications License (IPL) allowing title-by-title selection for institutions. There is also a pay-per-view option for individuals outside a licensed institution. IDEAL also provides a contents page alerting service called *IDEALAlert*.

The *Lexis Nexis* <www.lexis-nexis.co.uk/> (Dayton, OH: Lexis Nexis Group) database services include a wide range of sources from newspapers, country reports, market research, government documents, legal journals and many more. There are over 29 000 source publications and more than 2.8 billion documents accessible through the service. The database is available online and via the Web through a number of different service options including a personal Alert service, Professional and Executive. The database provides full-text with a number of different delivery formats, Email, fax, print or download to disk. It is updated on a daily basis. The Nexis Lexis Group also provide a number of resources in both print and CD-ROM format.

▶ 1.11 OFFICIAL PUBLICATIONS

Our aim is to provide a brief introduction to a selection of key print and electronic resources. It is impossible in such a short section to discuss official publications from a large number of individual countries. Those readers who require such a detailed assessment might like to consult *Information Sources in Official Publications* edited by Valerie J. Nurcombe (London: Bowker-Saur, 1997). It is a comprehensive, evaluative guide to official publishing in most countries of the world. Each section provides guidance on further resources and gives details of major collections of official publications. Similarly, Gloria Westfall's *Guide to Official Publications of Foreign Countries*, 2nd ed., (Bethesda, MD: LexisNexis Academic & Library Solutions, 1997) is an authoritative list of major documents published by foreign governments, along with brief descriptions of content and a title index. In addition, The Law Library of Congress provides a useful starting off point for locating individual country Websites with its *Nations of the World* links at <lcWeb2.loc.gov/glin/x-nation.html>.

1.11.1 United Kingdom

(a) Print

Her Majesty's Stationery Office (HMSO) operates as part of the Cabinet Office, under the ministerial control of the Minister for the Cabinet Office. HMSO manages and regulates the use and licensing of all information produced by government which is protected by Crown copyright. In 1996 The Stationery Office acquired the trading and most of the publishing functions of HMSO. The key resources providing indexed access to official publications have traditionally been the annual, monthly, weekly and daily lists published by HMSO. These are now published by the Stationery Office and thus, have become, *The Stationery Office Annual Catalogue* (London: The Stationery Office), etc. The catalogues are divided into several segments: Parliamentary publications; classified section of non-Parliamentary publications; Northern Ireland publications and Scottish agency publications; and other agency publications which include British, European and international organizations for which the Stationery Office is an agent. *See also UKOP* under *(b) Electronic* below.

HMSO and latterly, The Stationery Office, have never claimed to publish *all* official publications. To keep track of the myriad materials which are not published by The Stationery Office, it is necessary to consult the prosaically titled, *Catalogue of British Official Publications Not Published By The Stationery Office* (Cambridge: Chadwyck-Healey). The catalogue is issued on an annual and bimonthly basis. It covers the publications of more than 500 organizations which are financed or controlled by the British Government. The main arrangement is by organization, supplemented by an alphabetical list of contributing organizations and a combined person/corporate author and subject index. *See also UKOP* under *(b) Electronic* below.

(b) Electronic

The majority of British official publications are now available from the online bookstore of *The Stationery Office* <www.clicktso.com>, although some material is still published by *Her Majesty's Stationery Office* <www.hmso.gov.uk/>. The clickTSO.com site provides a well-organized homepage that can be searched by keyword or browsed by material type. The full-text of the *TSO Daily List* is available on the clickTSO.com site.

UKOP – United Kingdom Official Publications <www.ukop.co.uk/> published by arrangement with Her Majesty's Stationery Office (HMSO), provides bibliographical details of all official publications published since 1980. It offers combined, searchable access to *The Stationery Office Catalogues* and Chadwyck-Healey's *Catalogue of Official Publications Not Published by The Stationery Office. UKOP* is updated daily which makes it the most up-to-date and comprehensive source of national, regional and local government publications in the UK. In addition, it has a growing archive of full-text documents – 12 000 are added each year.

BOPCAS – the British Official Publications Current Awareness Service <www.soton.ac.uk/~bopcas/> is a joint venture between Aslib and The University of Southampton, based on data drawn from the Ford Collection of British Official Publications in the Hartley Library at the University of Southampton. It provides detailed information on British Parliamentary and governmental publications.

For access to local government information visit the *UK Online Open Government Information Service* at: <www.open.gov.uk>. The Organization Index gives access to a comprehensive listing of the Websites of local, regional and national organizations, from Aberdeen City Council to the Wyre Forest District Council.

1.11.2 Europe

The Council of Europe Publishing based in Strasbourg, is the official publisher of the Council of Europe – the oldest and largest of all European institutions. Over 1500 publications in the official languages of English and French have been produced on a range of topics: human rights, law, health, society, environment, demography, education, culture and communications. Official documentation includes the *Official Reports of Debates* in the European Parliament. A complete catalogue of publications from the Council of Europe Publishing is available on the Web at: <book.coe.int>. There is also a gateway from this site to the full-text of European treaties: a trilingual (French, English and German) collection of *European Conventions and Agreements* concluded within the Council of Europe between 1949 and 1998.

The full-text of selected European documents can be located via *Eurotext* <eurotext.ulst.ac.uk>. This service, hosted by the University of Ulster, was established under the eLib Electronic Libraries Programme. It provides free access for all universities in the United Kingdom to treaties and a wide range of other European documentation from agriculture to tourism. At the time of writing, there is a message on the Website warning that the future of the service is currently under consideration.

Until recently, *EUDOR: European Union Documentation Delivery Service* <www.eudor.com> provided free access to European Union documentation. However, the content of the site has been transferred to *CELEX* (*see* below) and *EUR-LEX – The Portal to European Union Law* at: <eur-op.eu.int/portal/en/index.html>. The latter provides free, searchable, full-text access to the *Official Journal*, treaties, legislation, case law, Parliamentary questions, and related documentation.

CELEX <europa.eu.int/celex/htm/celex_en.htm> is a key source for European Union law. *CELEX* was established in 1970 and launched on the Web in 1997. It states that its multilingual, fully searchable full-text database of over 200 000 publications contains 'most acts published in the L and C series of the *Official Journal of the European Communities* within days of their publication.' It also contains the texts of some unpublished documentation – in all, a particularly valuable resource.

The *European Report* (Brussels: European Information Service) published 94 times a year is a good way of keeping up to date with what is happening in the European Union. It covers EU institutions, economic and financial news and monitors the relationship of the European Union with non-member countries.

1.11.3 United States

In the United States, the Government Printing Office is the main cataloguer of Federal Government documents. Its key publication is the *Monthly Catalog of United States Government Publications* (Washington, DC: GPO, 1895–), supplemented by semiannual and annual indexes – including author, title, subject and keyword entry points. Since 1994, the catalogue has been available as a CD-ROM. However, its most useful format is undoubtedly as an online database via the Web: <www.access.gpo.gov/>. It offers an excellent search facility including: keyword, title, depository item number and GPO stock number searches. The Web version also has two other main advantages over other media: it provides links to full-text documents where available and is updated on a daily basis. The downside is that coverage only starts from 1994 onwards, so the print catalogues and indexes must be consulted for earlier materials.

The easiest way to track down state and local government information is via a comprehensive Website called *State and Local Government on the Net* at: <www.piperinfo.come/state/index.ctm>. It provides A–Z links to US States from Alabama to Wyoming, together with multi-state information (e.g., the Multistate Tax Commission), federal resources (e.g., the Census Bureau) and national organizations (e.g., the National Association for County Community and Economic Development).

1.11.4 International

United Nations Publications <www.un.org/Pubs/sales.htm>. The Website of the UN publications section provides access to online catalogues of all official publications from the United Nations and other bodies within the UN system. It includes separate listings of journals and products available electronically. Of particular value is the list of key titles, which highlights the most useful sources and provides direct links to the publications on the Internet where available.

As UNESCO Publishing, the United Nations Educational, Scientific and Cultural Organization (UNESCO) <www.unesco.org> is a key publisher of international documents of interest to social scientists. It has a catalogue of over 10 000 titles translated into 80 languages. Its many series include: Communication, Development and Society; Culture and Development; Cultures of Peace; Democracy and Power; Environment and Development; Ethics; Family Plus; Human Rights in Perspective; Law in Cyberspace; Peace and Conflict Issues; Social Science Studies; The Philosopher's Library; The Researcher's Library; UNESCO World Reports; Women Plus; and Youth Plus. To view the current catalogue see <upo.unesco.org/books.asp>. To access the full-text of selected UNESCO documents including: Speeches of Directors-General since 1987; Executive Board since 1994; General Conference since 1993; and Resolutions and Decisions since 1946 see <unesdoc.unesco.org/ulis>.

▶ 1.12 STATISTICS

1.12.1 United Kingdom

(a) Print

The *Guide to Official Statistics* (London: The Stationery Office, 2000) provides a directory of statistical and data series from official organizations in the United Kingdom. The publication is produced by The Office for National Statistics (ONS) on an occasional basis. It provides a comprehensive, descriptive overview of UK official statistics produced in both paper and electronic format. Each chapter is devoted to a particular statistical theme such as population, health care, labour market, etc. There is a keyword index at the end of the guide. *See also (b) Electronic* (*StatBase*) below.

The *Annual Abstract of Statistics* (London: The Stationery Office) is a broad compendium of statistics compiled from a variety of official sources. At the end of each source publications are acknowledged and contact details provided. Subjects covered include demography, society, economy and industry. It is compiled from more than 100 source publications.

The *Monthly Digest of Statistics* produced by the ONS (London: The Stationery Office) provides the latest monthly data within 20 different themes. It provides the user with the latest statistics on a wide range of economic, business and social statistics within the UK. The publication also includes the 'Britain Update' which gives an overview of economic and social statistics. The publication was first published in 1946.

The *United Kingdom in Figures* leaflet, produced by the ONS (London: The Stationery Office) on an annual basis, is a useful resource for brief, core information relating to many aspects of life in the UK today, including the economy. The statistical data are taken from a number of Government Statistical Service publications and the leaflet contains time series for a variety of subjects. The publication is freely available from the ONS and via the Web, *see (b) Electronic* below. The *Key Data* (London: The Stationery Office) annual publication provides a selection of popular UK statistics in an easy-to-use format. The statistics are presented in textual, chart and graphical formats. A further compilation of up-to-date facts and figures concerning the United Kingdom structure and organization is provided by the annual publication, *Britain 2000: the Official Yearbook of the United Kingdom* (London: The Stationery Office, 2000). This was first published in the 1940s and formerly named *Britain: an Official Handbook*.

The *General Household Survey* (London: The Stationery Office) was first produced in 1971 with five core topics: education; employment; health; housing; and population and family information. The five core topics still remain and each year different special topics are also included. The survey is published by the ONS on an annual basis and the sample survey is carried out on approximately 9000 households.

Regional Trends (London: The Stationery Office) has been produced on an annual basis by the Central Statistical Office (CSO) and the ONS since 1965. It provides an extensive range of statistics for the 12 statistical regions within the UK. It also contains key data for the subregions of the UK and includes a chapter on European Union regional statistics. The publication provides: demographic, social, industrial and economic statistics.

The ONS produces *Region in Figures* (London: The Stationery Office) for a more in-depth coverage of regional statistics. This annual publication is similar in layout to *Regional Trends*, each of the nine Government Office Regions is covered in a separate volume. The chapters include: economy; labour market; population; transport and the environment; education and training; and living in the region. *See also (b) Electronic* below.

The first edition of *Social Trends* (London: The Stationery Office) was published in 1970. The publication provides an annual compilation of social and economic data from UK government departments and other bodies. It covers a wide variety of subjects, presenting a broad picture of British society. The subjects covered include: population; households; families; education; transport; and lifestyles. The *Social Trends Pocketbook* (London: The Stationery Office) was initially published in 1998 and provides a handy, compact mini-version specifically aimed at students. The Pocketbook contains 13 chapters relating to different social policy areas and includes tables and charts. *See also (b) Electronic* below.

(b) Electronic

The Web version of the UK Government Statistical Service's *Guide to Official Statistics* is available via the *StatBase* information service at the following Web address: <www.Statbase.gov.uk/GTOS2/dbguide.htm>. The freely available *StatBase* service provides a more extensive information service. The service has two main components: *StatSearch*, providing detailed information relating to sources of official statistics; and *StatStore*, containing a wide range of statistics covering social, economic and socio-economic affairs. In 2000, with the advent of the National Statistics organization, the Government Statistical Service and the Office of National Statistics Websites merged to form *National Statistics: the Official UK Statistics Site*: <www.statistics.gov.uk>. Data on this Website are divided into 13 themes.

The *United Kingdom in Figures* <www.statistics.gov.uk/stats/ukinfigs/ukinfig.htm> (London: The Stationery Office) leaflet produced by the Office of National Statistics is available via the Web. *See (a) Print* above, for further information.

A 30-year archive of *Regional Trends* (London: The Stationery Office) has been published in CD-ROM format covering the period 1965–1995. The database provides the facility to compare regional statistics over a 30-year period. It is available directly from the ONS. The 2000 edition of *Regional Trends* is also available in pdf format from the following Website: <www.statistics.gov.uk/nsbase/OnlineProducts/default.asp>. For further information relating to the content of *Regional Trends, see (a) Print* above.

The data for the *Region in Figures* (London: The Stationery Office) series are available on a CD-ROM database. Subscribers to the print version (nine volumes) receive a complimentary copy. Individual datasets for particular regions can also be purchased with individual volumes. The latest figures are also available via the Web from the following address: <www.statistics.gov.uk/nsbase/OnlineProducts/default.asp>. *See also (a) Print* above.

The *Facts about Britain 1945 to 1995* CD-ROM (London: The Stationery Office) contains the full-text from a selection of the *British Handbooks and Aspects of Britain* series. The CD-ROM is available from the ONS. It contains tables, maps, charts, diagrams and photographs that explore a wide range of topics.

A compilation of the first 25 years of *Social Trends* 1970–1995 (London: The Stationery Office) has been produced by the ONS on one CD-ROM. Both the latest issue of *Social Trends* and the *Social Trends Pocket Book* are also available in full-text via the following Website: <www.statistics.gov.uk/nsbase/OnlineProducts/default.asp>. *See (a) Print* above, for further information relating to the content of *Social Trends* or Email: social.trends@theso.co.uk.

The *UK Data Archive* <www.data-archive.ac.uk/home/> (Colchester: University of Essex) was established in 1967 by the University of Essex to support further analysis by the research community. It is now jointly funded by the University along with ESRC (Economic and Social Research Council) and JISC (Joint Information Systems Committee). Data are acquired from government, academic and commercial sources, there are over 4000 datasets. The Website includes an online catalogue for users to search, with some data available online. The archive provides data across the subject disciplines of the social sciences and humanities and it is accessible via the Internet, CD-ROM and other media. Major data holdings include the *General Household Survey* and the *ONS Databank*.

The *Manchester Information and Associated Services* <www.mimas.ac.uk> (Manchester: University of Manchester), or more widely known *MIMAS*, datasets service is a national service to UK universities, funded by ESRC, JISC and the University of Manchester. It provides access to key socio-economic data including cross-sectional surveys and longitudinal panel surveys funded by research councils and university research units. Time series data are available through: the ONS; the OECD (Organization for Economic Cooperation and Development) Main Economic Indicators; the UNIDO (United Nations Industrial Development

Organization); IMF (International Monetary Fund) databanks; and some free-of-charge world economic outlook data. MIMAS is accessible free-of-charge to members of UK higher or further education institutions, access to the datasets is via institutional registration.

The *r-cade – Resource Centre for Access to Data on Europe* <www-rcade.dur.ac.uk> (Durham: Durham University) was established in 1995. It is a collaborative project between the Centre for European Studies at the University of Durham and the Data Archive at the University of Essex. It provides free access to European and international datasets covering a wide variety of topics for academic institutions. The Centre is an official Eurostat datashop and disseminates data produced by UNESCO (United Nations Educational, Scientific, and Cultural Organization) ILO (International Labour Organisation) and UNIDO (United Nations Industrial Development Organization).

1.12.2 International

(a) Print

The Eurostat (Luxembourg: Office for Official Publications of the EC (OOPEC)) series includes statistics compiled from the various statistical offices of the European Union. It covers nine main themes, each one denoted by a different colour. The themes are: general statistics; economy and finance; population and social conditions; industry, trade and service; agriculture and fisheries; external trade; transport; environment and energy; and research and development. *See also (b) Electronic* below.

Statistical Abstract of the United States: the National Databook (Washington, DC: Hoover). This annual publication was first published in 1878. It is a compilation of social, political and economic statistics of the United States. It is also a useful guide to other statistical publications and sources. *See also (b) Electronic* below.

The United Nations (UN) publishes a wide range of international statistics from both developed and developing countries. The *UN Statistical Yearbook* (New York: United Nations) was initially published in 1948. It is a compendium of international statistics published annually on social and economic conditions at world, regional and national levels. The *Yearbook* provides basic data on economics, trade, socioeconomics, wages, education, culture, and science and technology. The *Demographic Yearbook* (New York: United Nations) provides demographic statistical data for over 200 countries.(*See also (b) Electronic* below).

The *UNESCO Statistical Yearbook* (Paris: UNESCO Publishing and Bernan Press) was first published in 1963 by the Division of Statistics. During 1999, a new UNESCO Institute for Statistics was created with responsibility for producing the *Yearbook*. It provides statistical data on education, science and technology, culture and communication. Selected tables from the 1999 *Yearbook* are available at the following Website: <unescostat.unesco.org/en/stats/stats0.htm>.

The World Fact Book (Washington, DC: Central Intelligence Agency) is a very useful resource, initially produced for the use of US Government officials. It contains many facts and statistical information for each country, including geographical data, population, transportation and statistics on the economy. *See also (b) Electronic* below.

(b) Electronic

The Organization for Economic Cooperation and Development (OECD) <www.oecd.org/std/> Website provides access to a range of statistics split into broad themes that are further subdivided by more detailed subjects. *See 8.12.11* for more specific information relating to OECD resources.

The Statistical Office of the European Community (EUROSTAT) <www.europa.eu.int/en/comm/eurostat/serven/home.htm> has a useful Website that includes statistical information for member countries, and press releases. Eurostat also has a supporting Email information service at: info.desk@eurostat.cec.be and a free alerting service. *See also (a) Print* above.

Uncle Sam's Reference Shelf <www.census.gov/statab/www> provides selected data from various statistical publications. It also gives access to a selection of data from the *Statistical Abstract of the United States*. A CD-ROM version of the *Statistical Abstract of the United States* is also available. *See (a) Print* above, for more information.

The *Council of European Social Science Data Archives* (CESSDA) <www.nsd.uib.no/cessda> promotes the acquisition, archiving and distribution of electronic data for European social science research and teaching. It cooperates with other international organizations and provides access to the catalogues of member organizations at: <dasun3.essex.ac.uk/Cessda/IDC>. The President is currently based at the Norwegian archive (NSD).

The United Nations (UN) <www.un.org/depts/unsd> produces a wide range of statistics. Information about statistical methods, sources, actual statistics and indicators can be accessed through the UN Website. The Website provides access to short statistical profiles of the 55 member countries: <www.unece.org/stats/trend/trend_h.htm>. For further information contact the UN at the following Email address: statistics@un.org. *See also (a) Print.*

The *World Factbook* <www.odci.gov/cia/publications/factbook/index.html> produced by the CIA is also available via the Web. It provides statistical reports on every country of the world. *See also (a) Print* above.

1.12.3 A selection of country-specific statistical and data archive Websites

ANU Social Science Data Archives (SSDA) (Australia) <ssda.anu.edu.au/>.

Arhiv Druzboslovnih Podatkov (ADP) Social Science Data Archive, Slovenia. <rcul.uni-lj.si/~fd_adp/index.htm>.

Archivio Dati e Programmi per le Scienze Sociali (ADPSS) (Italy) (Adpss – Sociodata Data Archive for Social Science) <www.sociologia.unimib.it/dipartimento/sociodata/eng.htm>.

Australian Bureau of Statistics <www.abs.go.au/>.

Banque de données socio-politiques (France) <solcidsp.upmf-grenoble.fr/>.

Belgian Archives for the Social Sciences (BASS) <bass.rspo.ucl.ac.be/bass/>.

Centraal Bureau voor de Statistiek <www.cbs.nl/> Official statistics from the Netherlands.

Central Archive for Empirical Social Science Research (Germany) <www.za.uni-koen.de/index-e.htm>.

The Centro de Investigaciones Sociológicas (CIS) (Centre for Sociological Research) Survey-based research relating to Spanish society. <www.cis.es/>.

Council of European Social Science Data Archives (CESSDA) <www.nsd.uib.no/cessda/>.

Dansk Data Arkiv (Danish Data Archive) <www.dda.dk/>.

Data and Statistical Services (USA) <www.princeton.edu/~data/index.html>.

Estonian Social Science Data Archive <psych.ut.ee/esta/essda.html>.

Federal Statistical Office Germany <Statistik-bund.de/e_home.htm>.

Fedstats <www.fedstats.gov/>. Provides a gateway to statistics from over 100 US Federal agencies.

Finnish Social Science Data Archive (FSD) <www.fsd.uta.fi/english/index.html>.

GESIS – German Social Science Infrastructure Services <www.social-science-gesis.de/en/index.htm>.

Harvard-MIT Data Center (USA) <hdc-www.harvard.edu/hdc/>.

Hong Kong Census and Statistics Department <www.info.gov.hk/censtatd/>.

Institut National de la Statistique et des Etudes Economiques <www.insee.fr/fr/home/home_page.asp> French statistical Website.

Instituto Nacional de Estadistica <www.ine.es/>. Official Spanish statistics.

Instituto Nacional de Estatistica <www.ine.pt/>. Portuguese official statistics.

Inter-University Consortium for Political and Social Research (ICPSR) <www.icpsr.umich.edu>.

Irish Central Statistics Office <www.cso.ie/>.
Irish Social Science Data Archive <www.ucd.ie/~issda/>.
Israel Social Sciences Data Center (ISDC) <isdc.huji.ac.il/>.
London Research Centre <www.london-research.gov.uk/ds/dshome.htm>.
Ministry of Statistics and Programme Implementation (India) <www.nic.in/stat/>.
National Statistics <www.statistics.gov.uk>. The official UK statistics Website.
NISRA <www.nisra.gov.uk>. Northern Ireland Statistics and Research Agency.
Norwegian Social Science Data Service (NSD) <www.nsd.uib.no/>
Scottish Executive <194.247.69.28/stats/default.htm>.
South African Government Statistical Site <www.statssa.gov.za/Logo.htm>.
Social Science Data Archives (USA) <sun3.lib.uci.edu/~dtsang/ssda.htm>.
Social Science Japan Data Archive <www.iss.u-tokyo.ac.jp/ssjda/>.
Social Sciences Data Collection (SSDC) (USA) <ssdc.ucsd.edu/>.
Sociological Data Archive (Czech Republic) <archiv.soc.cas.cz/enindex.phtml>.
Statistics Bureau and Statistics Center (Japan) <www.stat.go.jp/english/1.htm>.
Statistics Canada <www.statcan.ca:/start.html>.
Steinmetz – Dutch Social Science Data Archive <www.niwi.knaw.nl/us/navigate/rawdata.htm>.
Swedish Social Science Data Service (SSD) <www.ssd.gu.se/enghome.html>.
Swiss Information and Data Archive Service for the Social Sciences (SIDOS) <www.sidos.ch/new/index-e.html>.
TARKI Social Research Informatics Center (Hungary) <www.tarki.hu/index-e.html>.
Wiener Institut für sozialwissenschaftliche Dokumentation und Methodik (Austria) <www.wisdom.at/>.
UK Data Archive <www.data-archive.ac.uk/home/>.
USA Statistics in Brief <www.census.gov/statab/www/brief.html>. A supplement to the Statistical Abstract of the United States.

▶ 1.13 RESEARCH IN PROGRESS

Services and resources which will assist the reader in keeping up to date with ongoing and unpublished research are discussed. In addition, the reader is directed to *sections 1.5*; *1.9*; and *1.10* for additional directory, journal and database resources.

(a) Print

Current Research in Britain (CRIB) (London: Cartermill International, 1985–). Appearing every couple of years or so, this is a useful register of research being carried out in universities and other higher education institutions in the UK. Formerly a British Library publication, between 1995 and 1998 it was published by Cartermill. It is produced in four volumes: *Physical Sciences; Biological Sciences; Social Sciences;* and *The Humanities*. The main entries are organized A–Z by institution and detail the projects individual researchers are engaged in. Extensive subject and author indexes make the volumes easy to navigate. The work is now available in CD-ROM as well as print format. In 1999, *CRIB* was acquired by *Community of Science*, and at the time of writing its future is uncertain.

Theses are important sources of unpublished information for the researcher. They can be tracked down relatively easily via the following products:

Dissertation Abstracts (Ann Arbor, MI: Proquest Information and Learning) details theses from authors in over a 1000 North American graduate schools and European universities. *Index To Theses* (London: Expert Information Ltd, 1953–) abstracts theses across all disciplines accepted for higher degrees by the universities of Great Britain and Ireland. It has been published continuously from volume one in 1953, which covered the years 1950–51. For more information on both these services *see (b) Electronic* below and *1.10*.

(b) Electronic

Community of Science (COS) <www.cos.com/>. This is a searchable, international database of researchers from universities, government agencies and other R&D organizations. The database holds information on a number of social scientists which can be retrieved by both name and area of research.

Regard (Bristol: Institute for Learning and Research Technology, University of Bristol) <www.regard.ac.uk/> is a free service providing information on ESRC (Economic and Social Research Council) funded research. Its database can be searched in a variety of ways including: subject, person, institution and conference. *Regard* abstracts the research projects which have been awarded ESRC grants and links to any subsequent publications. *See also 1.10*.

DARE <www.unesco.org/general/eng/infoserv/db/dare.html> (Paris: UNESCO) is a bibliographic database that contains 11 000 worldwide references to social science journals, social science research and training institutions, specialists, documentation and information services. It is provided by the Social and Human Sciences Documentation Centre of UNESCO's Information Services. *See also 1.10*.

SRM Infobase <www.eur.nl/ub/srm/srmsearch.htm>. This useful database provided by the SRM-Documentation Centre at the Erasmus Univers-ity in The Netherlands, contains information on: researchers forums, meetings, projects, research and documentation centres and software for social science research. The database is searchable by information type, subject, or an alphabetical list of terms.

SRSOCSCI – The Scout Report for Social Sciences & Humanities <scout.cs.wisc.edu/report/socsci> (Email:listserv@HYPATIA.CS.WISC.EDU and in body of message put subscribe SRSOCSCI). Published every two weeks, the Scout Report provides useful updates on new social science Websites, selected by librarians and information specialists. The *Report* can either be viewed at the above Website, or Emailed to your mailbox. *See also 1.8.*

Social Science Research Network (SSRN) (Rochester, NY: Social Science Electronic Publishing) <www.ssrn.com>. They state on their Website that the SSRN 'is a worldwide collaborative of several hundred leading scholars that is devoted to the rapid worldwide dissemination of social science research'. They encourage networking by listing contact details for the authors of papers on the database. The SSRN's subscription service Emails research paper abstracts to subscribers. From their Website you can also search SSRN's database of abstracts of published and forthcoming working papers and journal articles, around half of which are available in full-text format which can be downloaded. The only negative side is that the resources are not as broad as the title of the network implies, as the main focus is on economic, financial, legal and Latin American materials. However, if you use the topic search facility on the database you will retrieve resources across a reasonable number of individual social science disciplines.

Dissertation Abstracts <www.umi.com/hp/Support/Dservices/products/da.htm.> This service includes citations from the first US dissertation in 1861, to those accepted last semester. From 1988 onwards the references include abstracts. It is available in a variety of electronic formats including the Web via ProQuest, which offers an easy-to-use, searchable interface. Its CD-ROM version is updated quarterly and consists of a current disc (1994–) and a four-disc archival set (1861–1993). *Dissertation Abstracts* is also available from the following commercial services: *Ovid Online*; *DataStar*; *DIALOG*; *EPIC and FirstSearch*; and *STN International*. (*See also 1.10). Index To Theses* <www.theses.com/> is the electronic version of the printed service mentioned above and consists of a searchable database, providing abstracts of UK theses from 1970 onwards. *See also 1.10.*

Mailing/Discussion Lists/E-Conferences are a good way of keeping in touch with members of the research and academic communities. Mailing/discussion lists, are electronic services which allow users to read and post messages on topics appropriate to the list in question. There are literally thousands of such lists, below are a few good starting points within the social sciences.

ABYAN.net: Social Sciences <www.abyan.net/>. The homepage of the social sciences section has a heading *Communities* which links to several useful discussion/mailing lists including those hosted by *Yahoo!* and *Meta-List*.

The Directory of Scholarly and Professional E-Conferences <www.n2h2.com/KOVACS>. A searchable index of discussion lists, newsgroups, mailing lists and interactive Web chat groups (e-conferences), edited by Diane K. Kovacs. An important feature of the index is its quality control: only those lists judged to be of scholarly or professional value are included.

JISCmail <www.jiscmail.ac.uk>. This organization runs electronic discussion lists for the UK higher education and research community. However, they are open to all academics regardless of their geographical location. There are lists covering all the major social science disciplines as well as broad-based groups like *SOCINFO* which is interested in discussing the use of new technologies within the social sciences.

SOS-DATA (Email: listproc@irss.unc.edu and in body of message put subscribe sos-data Firstname Lastname) is an American-based list which acts as a forum for the discussion of any topic related to social science data. Details of conferences and new data sources are often announced on the list.

H-Net Discussion Networks <www2.h-net.msu.edu/lists>. This site gives access to a significant number of social science related discussion lists from African–American Studies to Women's History.

See subsequent chapters for many more mailing/discussion lists relating to individual social science disciplines.

► 1.14 ORGANIZATIONS

The following section provides contact information for a selection of general social science based organizations. Throughout this book, further reference is made to more specialized organizations within specific social science disciplines. It should also be noted that many universities, particularly those with strong social science departments, have established important research centres and institutes within the field.

1.14.1 United Kingdom

Academic Librarians in the Social Sciences (ALISS)
Web: <www.blpes.lse.ac.uk/other_sites/aliss/>

ALISS is a group that provides a forum for information specialists and librarians working within higher education to discuss matters of interest, new developments and attendance at associated events.

Academy of Learned Societies for the Social Sciences (ALSISS)
4 Tintagel Crescent, London, SE22 8HT, UK
Tel: +44 (0)20 8693 0866
Fax: +44 (0)20 8693 0866
Email: andy.cawdell@the-academy.org.uk
Web: <www.alsiss.org.uk/>

The academy was formed in 1982 to provide support for individual learned societies. The Association of Learned Societies in the Social Sciences transferred its activities to the academy in July 2000. It provides a number of services including an information service, statistical resources, training, research and events.

Association of Commonwealth Universities
36 Gordon Square, London, WC1H OPF, UK
Tel: +44 (0)20 7387 8572
Fax: +44 (0)20 7387 2655
Email: info@acu.ac.uk
Web: <www.acu.ac.uk>

The Association of Commonwealth Universities is financed and governed by its membership throughout the Commonwealth. The Association promotes cooperation between Commonwealth Universities and publishes a number of publications including the *Commonwealth Universities Yearbook*.

Association of Research Centres in the Social Sciences
HUSAT Research Institute, Loughborough University, The Elms, Elms Grove, Loughborough, Leicestershire, LE11 1RG, UK
Tel: +44 (0)1509 611088
Fax: +44 (0)1509 611088
Email: d.hackett@lboro.ac.uk; husat-info@lboro.ac.uk

ARCISS was formed in 1997 from the merger of The Association of Social Research Organisations and the Directors of Research Centres in Social Sciences. The Association promotes, manages and disseminates the advancement of social science research.

Association for the Teaching of the Social Sciences (ATSS)
PO Box 61, Watford, Herts,WD2 2NH, UK
Tel: +44 (0)1704 877004
Web: <www.atss.org.uk>

The Association was formed in 1965 to develop and support the teaching of social sciences within schools and higher education.

Economic and Social Research Council (ESRC)
Polaris House, North Star Avenue, Swindon, Wiltshire, SN2 1UJ, UK
Tel: +44 (0)1793 413000
Fax: +44 (0)1793 413001
Web: <www.esrc.ac.uk>

The ESRC was established by Royal Charter in 1965. It is the main UK funding agency for research into social and economic issues. In particular, it supports high quality research and postgraduate training.

Fabian Society
11 Dartmouth Street, London, SW1H 9BN, UK
Tel: +44 (0)20 7227 4900
Fax: +44 (0)20 7976 7153
Email: info@fabian-society.org.uk
Web: <www.fabian-society.org.uk/>

The Fabian Society is affiliated to the Labour Party in the UK. The society was established in 1884 and undertakes research on a wide range of social and political fields. It also publishes a number of publications and arranges numerous events.

Joseph Rowntree Foundation
The Homestead, 40 Water End, York, North Yorkshire,YO30 6WP, UK
Tel: +44 (0)1904 629241
Fax: +44 (0)1904 620072
Email: info@jrf.org.uk
Web: <www.jrf.org.uk/>

Until 1990, The Joseph Rowntree Foundation was called the Joseph Rowntree Memorial Trust. It is the UK's largest independent social policy research and development charity. It supports a wide programme of research and development projects in housing, social care and social policy. It is particularly interested in research and development projects that contribute directly to better policies and practices.

The Leverhulme Trust
1 Pemberton Row, London, EC4A 3EX, UK
Tel: +44 (0)20 7822 6938
Fax: +44 (0)20 7822 5084
Web: <www.leverhulme.org.uk>

In 1925, the trust was established under the will of the first Lord Leverhulme. The trust provides grants to support further research within further and higher education and registered charities across a wide range of subject disciplines.

National Centre for Social Research (NCSR)
35 Northampton Square, London, EC1V OAX, UK
Tel: +44 (0)20 7250 1866
Fax: +44 (0)20 7250 1524
Email: info@natcen.ac.uk
Web: <www.natcen.ac.uk>

The NCSR founded in 1969, is an independent, non-profit social survey research institute that both initiates social research and undertakes government studies on a wide range of social policy subjects. It conducts social research amongst members of the public to provide information on a range of social policy issues in Britain. The NCSR has conducted the design and fieldwork for a number of important quantitative and qualitative UK surveys (e.g., the British Crime Survey) and it is a founding member of the International Social Survey Programme. (*See 1.14.2*)

The Nuffield Foundation
28 Bedford Square, London, WC1B 3EG, UK
Tel: +44 (0)20 7631 0566
Web: <www.nuffieldfoundation.org/>

Lord Nuffield established the foundation in 1943. The foundation provides research grants to support specific projects that aim to advance social well-being and it has several award schemes, including the Social Science Small Grants Scheme, that support academic research.

Social Market Foundation (SMF)
11 Tufton Street, London, SW1P 3QB, UK
Tel: +44 (0)20 7222 7060
Fax: +44 (0)20 7222 0310
Email: info@smf.co.uk
Web: <www.smf.co.uk>

The SMF commissions and publishes original papers on key topics in the social and economic fields. It provides a source of innovative economic and social policy ideas. The foundation is a registered charity and it is independent of any political party or group. The SMF maintains a network of links with sister organizations in the EU and US.

Social Research Association (SRA)
PO Box 6688, London, SE15 3WB, UK
Tel: +44 (0)20 8670 5640
Fax: +44 (0)20 7635 6014
Email: admin@the-sra.org.uk
Web: <www.the-sra.org.uk/index2.htm>

Founded in 1978, the Social Research Association is affiliated to ALSISS (the Academy of Learned Societies for the Social Sciences – see main entry above). It aims to advance the conduct, application and development of social research.

Society for Research into Higher Education (SHRE)
3 Devonshire Street, London, W1N 2BA, UK
Tel: +44 (0)20 7637 2766
Fax: +44 (0)20 7637 2781
Email: srheoffice@srhe.ac.uk
Web: <www.shre.ac.uk>

The Society for Research into Higher Education was established in 1964 and aims to promote excellence in learning and teaching and improve quality in higher education. It also provides a coordinating role for research into all forms of higher education.

The Tavistock Institute
30 Tabernacle Street, London, EC2A 4DD, UK
Tel: +44 (0)20 7417 0407
Fax: +44 (0)20 7417 0566
Email: central.admin@tavinstitute.org
Web: <www.tavinstitute.org>

The Tavistock Institute is an independent social science organization founded in 1946, providing many research services relating to the field of human relations.

1.14.2 International

The European Association for the Advancement of Social Sciences
ICCR – Interdisciplinary Centre for Comparative Research in the Social Sciences – International Schottenfeldgasse 69/1, 1070 Vienna, Austria
Tel: +43 1 5241 3931 00
Fax: +43 1 5241 3932 00
Email: office@iccr.co.at
Web: <www.iccr.co.at/ea/>

The European Association for the Advancement of Social Sciences was formed in 1990 to provide a European Social Sciences Network. The Association arranges a number of events, produces publications including the journal titled: *Innovation – the European Journal of Social Sciences*.

International Social Science Council (ISSC)
Web: <www.unesco.org/ngo/issc/>

The ISSC is a non-profit making organization based at the United Nations Educational, Scientific, and Cultural Organization (UNESCO) in Paris. Its members are from non-international non-governmental organizations. The Council's aim is to promote and facilitate the understanding of human society by encouraging social sciences across the world.

The International Social Survey Program (ISSP)
Secretariat: Tom W. Smith (Secretary General)
National Opinion Research Center (NORC), 1155 East 60th Street, Chicago, IL 60637, USA
Web: <www.issp.org/>

The ISSP is a self-funding association that brings together social science research projects, coordinates research goals and provides cross-national collaboration and perspectives to national studies. Each of the member research organizations funds all of its own costs as there are no central funds. The merging of the data into a cross-national data set is performed by the Zentralarchiv für Empirische Sozialforschung, University of Cologne, in collaboration with the Analisis Sociologicos, Economicos y Politicos in Spain. Since 1984, the ISSP has grown and currently has 31 member countries. A bibliography of ISSP publications is available via the ISSP Secretariat or via the Web – *see 1.2.*

Netherlands Institute for Scientific Information Services (NIWI)
PO Box 95110, 1090 HC, Amsterdam, The Netherlands
Tel: +31 20 462 8600
Fax: +31 20 665 8013
Email: info@niwi.knaw.nl
Web: <www.nsd.uib.no/cessda/europe.html>

The NIWI is an institute of the Royal Netherlands Academy of Arts and Sciences (KNAW). NIWI was formed in 1997, when six existing institutes merged together. The Institute aims to provide information in the fields of biomedicine, social sciences, history, and Dutch language and literature. NIWI also provides: information about research and researchers in the Netherlands across all scientific fields; data archives, publications; special collections; library; and a document delivery service. From January 2001, free access is available to databases available on the NIWI Website.

Social Behavioral and Economic Sciences
Suite 995, National Science Foundation, 4201 Wilson Boulevard, Arlington, Virginia 22230, USA
Tel: +1 703 292 5111
Web: <www.nsf.gov/sbe/ses/polisci/mcsbio.htm>

The Directorate for Social, Behavioral and Economic Sciences supports National Science Foundation research in relation to human behaviour, social interaction, economic systems and society. The NSF is an independent US government agency with responsibility for the promotion of science and engineering.

The Social Science Research Council (SSRC)
810 Seventh Avenue, New York, NY 10019,USA
Tel: +1 212 377 27001
Fax: +1 212 377 2727
Web: <www.ssrc.org/>

The SSRC is an independent, non-governmental, not-for-profit international organization that seeks to advance social science across the world, supporting research, education and scholarly exchange. Since 1923, the Council has helped to generate new ideas on key social issues. It has linked universities, foundations, social science disciplines, area studies associations, and government and non-governmental organizations in exploring new advances and developments, and testing theories and methods against both contemporary and historical problems.

Social Sciences and Humanities Research Council of Canada (SSHRC)
350 Albert Street, Box 1610, Ottawa, Ontario, K1P 6G4, Canada
Tel: +1 613 992 0691
Fax: +1 613 992 1787
Email: z-info@sshrc.ca
Web: <www.sshrc.ca/english/index.html>

The SSHRC is the Canadian federal funding agency for university based research and graduate training. It distributes funds to researchers and universities through a competitive grant programme. It is an independent body that reports to parliament through the Minister of Industry.

The United Nations (UN)
GA-57, New York, NY 10017, USA
Tel: +1 212 963 4475/ 963 9246
Fax: +1 212 963 0071
Email: inquiries@un.org
Web: <www.un.org/site_index/>
Or Palais des Nations, 14 avenue de la Paix, 1211 Geneva 10, Switzerland
Tel: +41(22) 917 4896/ 917 4538
Fax: +41 (22) 917 0032

The United Nations was established in 1945 by countries committed to preserving peace through international cooperation and security. The membership now totals 189 countries.

United Nations Educational Scientific and Cultural Organization (UNESCO)
Office of Public Information Documentation Centre,
7 Place de Fontenoy, 75352 Paris 07 SP, France
Tel: +33 1 45 68 16 81
Fax: +33 1 45 68 56 57
Email: opi.opdoc@unesco.org

UNESCO promotes collaboration with member nations through education, science, culture and communication.

▶ REFERENCES

Dahrendorf, R. (1996) 'Social Science', in *The Social Science Encyclopedia*, A. Kuper and J. Kuper (eds), pp. 800–2. London and Boston: Routledge and Kegan Paul.

Foster-Carter, A. (1998) 'Soapbox', in *Times Higher Educational Supplement*, 9 October, 16.

Kazancigil, A. and Makinson, D. (1999) *World Social Science Report 1999*. Paris: UNESCO/Elsevier.

Ross, D. (1991) *The Origins of American Social Science*. Cambridge and New York: Cambridge University Press.

Sills, D. L. (1968) (ed.) *International Encyclopedia of the Social Sciences*. London: Collier-Macmillan and New York: The Macmillan Company and The Free Press.

2 Anthropology

Heather Dawson

▶ 2.1 NATURE AND SCOPE OF ANTHROPOLOGY

A definition of what constitutes anthropology can be problematic. Among the general public there are often erroneous pre-conceptions that anthropology is only concerned with the study of primitive or 'exotic' cultures. Indeed several textbooks, such as *What is Social Anthropology?* by Jean La Fontaine (1985), have devoted themselves almost exclusively to refuting this claim. The history of the discipline has seen the expansion of anthropological study from a primary focus on foreign non-industrialized societies to a desire to apply its methods to modern urban societies. It has also seen the emergence of an increasing number of specialist subfields, such as medical anthropology and visual anthropology, which have drawn upon other aspects of the social sciences including economics, politics, sociology and psychology. Useful textbooks for tracing the history of the subject include: *The Rise of Anthropological Theory* by M. Harris (London: Routledge and Kegan Paul, 1976), a classic account of the development of the different schools of anthropological thought; and *Anthropologists and Anthropology*, 2nd ed., by Adam Kuper (London: Routledge and Kegan Paul, 1983), which focuses specifically on the history of the discipline in Britain, although it does give information on the influence of American and European work on the development of British theory.

A broad definition of anthropology is the study of all peoples and their ways of life, without limitation in space or time. Although individual practitioners differ, it is generally characterized by study based upon fieldwork methods of participant observation or close personal contact with the society being studied. Anthropology is traditionally divided into four fields of study:

1. *Physical Anthropology* – the analysis of the physical traits and genetics of human groups;

2. *Archaeology* – the study of ancient civilizations;
3. *Linguistics* – the study of language in the context of particular cultures; and
4. *Social Anthropology* – the examination of the social organization of particular societies.

Since the purpose of this text is to provide a guide to sources for the social sciences, this chapter will focus primarily upon social anthropology. Social anthropology has a close inter-relationship with sociology, which is also concerned with the analysis of social relationships and institutions. However, anthropology is usually distinguished by its humanist methods of fieldwork study. Within the discipline there are a number of distinctive subfields. There is no universal consensus on the number of these and, indeed, they are in a continual process of growth as the field develops. For a succinct discussion of this issue see Eric Wolf (1980) *They Divide and Subdivide and Call it Anthropology*. This chapter makes use of a number of subcategories recognized by the American Anthropological Association.

Applied Anthropology – this may be defined as the practical use of anthropology to solve specific problems in areas such as community development.

Economic Anthropology – focuses on systems of production, distribution and exchange in specific societies. It also considers the impact of global economic systems upon non-Western societies.

Medical Anthropology – this discipline examines social and cultural aspects of health care. It ranges from studies of traditional healers and medical systems, to studies of the social perceptions of disease. Reference is often made to epidemiological surveys.

Psychological Anthropology – this subfield is heavily influenced by cognitive psychology and linguistics. It seeks to examine how cultures are organized by underlying structures and rules.

Urban Anthropology – this subfield may be defined as the application of anthropological research methods to the study of urban communities. A primary focus is on the transformation from rural to urban life and the issues of adaptation and change, which this imposes for particular social groups.

Visual Anthropology – originally arose through the need for anthropologists to provide visual records of the societies which they studied. It now has a rich tradition of its own which is based upon the analysis of photographs, film and video and covers such issues as film techniques and the way in which other cultures are represented through them.

Reference will also be made to resources, which although not specifically designed for anthropologists, are of relevance for 'area studies' of particular regions of the world. However, one should note that due to the sheer quantity of material available, the coverage of these type of resources is necessarily more selective than elsewhere in the chapter.

▶ 2.2 ANNUALS

(a) Print

Annual Editions: Anthropology (Guilford, CT: McGraw-Hill, 1974–) is a compilation of articles previously published in academic journals. A useful source for highlighting important articles for students. All subfields of anthropology are covered. *See also AAA Guide* in *section 2.5.1.*

Voices (Arlington, VA: American Anthropological Association) is an official publication of the Association for Feminist Anthropology which is a section of the American Anthropological Association. It is published as an annual review of the year's activities in feminist anthropological theory and research. *See also 2.14.1* for further information on the society.

(b) Electronic

Annual Review of Anthropology (ISSN 0084–6570) (1972– , Palo Alto, CA: Annual Reviews). (Continues *Biennial Review of Anthropology 1959–71.*) The purpose of this publication is to provide a general overview of current anthropological research. Each issue contains approximately 15 review essays, which cover all subfields of the discipline. It is particularly strong at focusing attention on emerging areas of study and providing detailed bibliographies of further readings. Recent areas covered include: HIV transmission and human rights and the anthropology of cloth. Back issues of the title may be accessed electronically via the JSTOR service, which aims to create an archive of electronic journals. *See also 2.9.1 (b) Electronic.*

▶ 2.3 BIBLIOGRAPHIES

2.3.1 General

(a) Print

Annual Review of Anthropology (1972– , Palo Alto, CA: Annual Reviews. ISSN 0084–6570). *See 2.2 (b) Electronic.*

Anthropological Bibliographies: a Selected Guide edited by Margo L. Smith and Yvonne M. Damien (South Salem, NY: Redgrave Publishing Company, 1981). This has a listing of 3200 titles from the beginning of the twentieth century to the 1980s. It is broad in scope, encompassing texts from all the main subfields and in many languages. It lists both independently published monographs and journal articles, which may be difficult to trace elsewhere. Also included are filmographies of audio-visual materials and teaching aids. The main emphasis is on listing bibliographies relevant for area studies, although a subject index is also provided.

Anthropology Journals and Serials: an Analytical Guide by John T. Williams (New York: Greenwood Press, 1986) concentrates on English language sources, listing over 400 journals with anthropological content. Each entry includes publication details, intended audience and a summary of the subject area covered. Its age means that it is unable to provide guidance on titles published after 1985 or on electronic titles, but it is a useful starting point as the descriptions of content are detailed.

The *Bibliographic Guide to Anthropology and Archaeology* (Boston, MA: GK Hall, 1987–) is issued annually and based upon additions made to the holdings of the Tozzer Library, Harvard University (this was previously known as the Library of the Peabody Museum of Archaeology and Ethnology). It lists all monographs, series and fiche sets acquired by the library in the preceding year. It is international in scope, including strong coverage of foreign language materials. Journal articles are not listed. Entries are indexed by author and subject. Each entry offers bibliographic details and Library of Congress subject headings. Since 1997, it has also been made available electronically. *See (b) Electronic* below. The *History of Anthropology Bibliography* by Paul A. Erickson (Toronto: Canadian Scholars Press, 1997) is a useful unannotated source which lists several thousand books and journal articles relevant to the historical development of anthropology. Author, subject and geographical indexes are provided.

(b) Electronic

Anthropology Bibliography on Disc (New York: GK Hall, 1997–). This CD-ROM is issued annually. It offers access to a searchable database of monograph titles added to the Tozzer Library, Harvard University in the preceding year. Entries are taken from the library catalogue. Although annotations on content are not provided, each entry does have added Library of Congress subject headings which give an indication of the subject areas covered.

CSAC Anthropology Bibliography <lucy.ukc.ac.uk/cgi-bin/uncgi/search_bib2/Makhzan>. This project is maintained by the Centre for Social Anthropology and Computing, University of Kent at Canterbury. It is sometimes known as the Makhzan Social Anthropology Bibliography. Its aim is to cover social anthropology in its broadest sense. The project offers access to over 15 000 entries, including monographs and journal articles. Some brief annotations are also provided. Users should note that the site contains a warning that not all bibliographic details have been verified and as a result duplication of results may occur.

Hunter-Gatherer Bibliography <www.acs.ucalgary.ca/~helmer/hgbilio.html>. This extensive bibliography contains over 900 references to books and journal articles relating to the anthropology and archaeology of hunter-gatherer peoples worldwide. Most of the items have been published from the 1970s to date. It is compiled by Dr. J W. Helmer, an academic based at the University of Calgary. The list may be viewed online or downloaded in its entirety as a zip file.

2.3.2 Applied anthropology

Anthropology in Use: a Bibliographic Chronology of the Development of Applied Anthropology by John Van Willigen (Pleasantville, NY: Redgrave, 1980) is a bibliographic chronology of the development of applied anthropology prior to 1980. It includes over 300 annotated references to books, journal articles and technical reports. *Anthropological Fieldwork: an Annotated Bibliography* by Pierre Gavel and Robert B. Marks Ridinger (New York: Garland, 1988) offers over 700 references to books and journal articles relevant to all aspects of conducting anthropological fieldwork, including methodology and ethical issues. The entries are arranged by author, but there are also extensive subject and geographical area indexes.

Sociology, Anthropology and Development: an Annotated Bibliography of World Bank Publications 1975–1993 by Michael Cernea (Washington, DC: World Bank, 1994). The historical scope and coverage of grey literature offered by this bibliography make it of particular value to researchers. It includes annotated references to over 500 formal publications and 200 'informal' grey literature publications of the World Bank which are structured into six broad subject areas, including social science and development, social policy in sectoral analysis and social variables in environmental management. Indexes are also provided for titles, geographical region and author.

2.3.3 Area studies

(a) Print

Africa Bibliographies compiled by Daniel A. Britz and Hans E. Panofsky in *Anthropological Bibliographies: a Selected Guide,* pp. 4–54 (South Salem, NY: Redgrave, 1981) is a comprehensive listing of over 600 relevant sources published from 1968–1980. They include easily traceable books and journal articles, as well as listings of monographs and articles with significant attached bibliographies which would otherwise be more difficult to find. The listing is subdivided into 10 geographic regions of Africa. *East and Northeast Africa Bibliography* by Hector Blackhurst (Landham, MD: Scarecrow Press, 1996) is a detailed bibliography on eight nations: Djibouti, Eritrea, Ethiopia, Kenya, Somalia, Sudan, Tanzania and

Uganda providing over 3800 references to material published since 1960. Unfortunately, it is largely restricted to English language books. Periodical articles and government reports are also excluded. These restrictions necessarily place some limitations on its comprehensiveness and users will need to supplement it with access to other sources.

Southern Africa Bibliography by Reuben Musiker and Naomi Musiker (Landham, MD: Scarecrow Press, 1996) covers 10 nations: Angola, Botswana, Lesotho, Malawi, Mozambique, Namibia, South Africa, Swaziland, Zambia and Zimbabwe. It provides 4081 entries of material published since 1945, the majority of which are in the English language. As such, while it is detailed for the time period covered, it is not able to offer references to some classic titles published before this date and should be used in conjunction with other sources.

Americas Bibliographies compiled by Yvonne M. Damien is another excellent example which appears in *Anthropological Bibliographies: a Selected Guide,* pp.4–54 (South Salem, NY: Redgrave, 1981). It has approximately 400 examples of bibliographies on all aspects of Caribbean, Central, Latin and South American anthropological study. It includes journal articles and chapters within books, as well as monographs. *Asian Bibliography* compiled by Lucy B. Drews and Paul Hockings and published as a chapter in *Anthropological Bibliographies: a Selected Guide,* pp.4–54 (South Salem, NY: Redgrave, 1981) highlights over 500 important bibliographies relating to regions of Asia. The main organization is by geographical region. It provides an update to *World Bibliography of Oriental Bibliographies* by J. D. Pearson (Totowa, NJ: Rowman and Littlefield, 1975). *Oceania Bibliographies* compiled by Max L. Plaut and published as a chapter in *Anthropological Bibliographies: a Selected Guide,* (South Salem, NY: Redgrave, 1981) is a useful listing of over 500 references organized by geographical region. It includes books and journal articles (some with extensive bibliographies), published prior to 1980.

Cultural Anthropology of the Middle East: a Bibliography Volume 1: 1965–1987, by Ruud Strijp (Leiden: EJ Brill, 1992), *Volume 2: 1988–1992* (Leiden: EJ Brill, 1997). Together these volumes present a valuable reference tool for tracing ethnographies of the Middle East. Geographically, they cover the area from Mauritania in the West to Afghanistan in the East, and from Turkey in the North to the Arab Peninsula and Northern Sudan in the South. References are provided to studies published in English, French and German including bibliographies originally published as journal articles. Annotations are provided for the majority of titles.

(b) Electronic

Bibliography of Native North Americans (BNAA) (Norwood, MA: SilverPlatter) is available as either a CD-ROM or via the Internet. It is based on work collected for the Human Relations Area Files Project (HRAF) and the contents of the Ethnographic Bibliography of North America (EBNA), which was published in four paper editions between 1941 and 1990. The BNAA provides access to over 60 000 citations of books, book chapters, dissertations, government documents and journal articles concerning over 290 native tribes of North America and Mexico, published from the sixteenth Century to the present day. Updates are currently made twice annually. The database may be searched by region or subject area. For further information on subscription rates consult the HRAF Website at <www.yale.edu/hraf/>.

2.3.4 Economic anthropology

Social Science Bibliography on Property, Ownership and Possession, 1,580 Citations from Psychology, Anthropology, Sociology and Related Disciplines by Floyd W. Rudmin et al (Monticello, Il.: Vance Bibliographies, 1987). Although this book is essentially cross-disciplinary in nature, it contains many references of value to economic anthropology. These include ethnographies, monographs and journal articles on the social aspects of property and exchange. Unfortunately, annotations are not provided. *Economic Anthropology 1940–1972: an Annotated Bibliography* by H. T. Van der Pas (Oosterhout, Netherlands: Anthropological Publications, 1973) is a specialist historical resource which provides annotated references to over 500 largely English language books and articles written between 1940 and 1972.

2.3.5 Medical anthropology

The AIDS Bibliography: Studies in Anthropology and Related Fields by Ralph Bolton and Gail Orozco (Arlington, VA: American Anthropological Association Commission on AIDS Research and Education, 1994). This resource provides extensive references to over 1700 articles and books on the social and cultural aspects of AIDS. They include publications from scholars in sociology, history and psychology. Geographical and subject indexes are provided, although as the latter relies largely on keywords taken from titles it cannot be regarded as comprehensive. *Resources for Third World Health Planners* by Peter Singer and Elizabeth A. Titus (New York: Trado-Medic Books, 1980) includes references to over 1800 books and articles relevant to medical anthropology. Topics covered include: shamanism, traditional healing and social aspects of medicine and mental illness. Indexes are supplied for geographical area and cultural group, but there is no subject index. Medical Anthropology by Edward Wellin (*Choice* 26, November 1989, 441–52) is a useful introduction for undergraduate study, listing of over 100 core books on socio-cultural factors related to disease and illness.

2.3.6 Urban anthropology

Urban Anthropology in the 1990s: a Collection of Syllabi and an Extensive Bibliography edited by Irene Glasser and Lawrence B. Breitborde (Arlington, VA: American Anthropological Association, 1996). This guide was compiled by the Society for Urban Anthropology, a specialist subgroup of the American Anthropological Association. It is divided into two parts: the first provides information on the content of general, geographical and topically focused urban anthropology courses offered by American universities; the second part offers a detailed bibliography of books and journal articles relevant to the field.

2.3.7 Visual anthropology

(a) Print

Films for Anthropological Teaching, 8th ed., by Karl Heider and Carol Hermer (Washington, DC: American Anthropological Association, 1995) is a valuable resource for tracing relevant anthropological films. It lists over 1500 films and videos, indexed by topic and geographical area. Entries include annotations on running time, distributor, and warnings concerning any technical problems. Some examples also offer bibliographies of further readings and citations of reviews.

(b) Electronic

Documentary and Ethnographic Film: a Short Bibliography of Books and Articles in UC Berkeley Libraries <www.lib.berkeley.esdu/MRC/documentarybib.html>. This is a useful listing which relates to the collection of the University of California at Berkeley libraries which have particularly strong holdings in ethnographic film. It includes 250 items, the majority of which were produced after 1945. Although many are documentaries, a high proportion have ethnographic content. The list has one general section and an index for individual producers. Entries include full bibliographic details.

HADDON: Online Catalogue of Archival Ethnographic Film Footage <www.rsl.ox.ac.uk/isca/haddon/HADD home.html>. HADDON is an online catalogue of over 1500 films shot between 1895 and 1945 and stored in archives and museums worldwide. The project is coordinated by the Institute of Social and Cultural Anthropology at the University of

Oxford and supported by the Economic and Social Research Council. The content is primarily concerned with non-European societies. Information can be searched by region, film maker or subject keyword. Entries are detailed and generally include overviews of subject content, technical detail and information on where the materials can be accessed.

Royal Anthropological Institute Film Library Catalogue Volume I edited by James Woodburn (London: Film Committee, Royal Anthropological Institute in Association with the Scottish Council for Educational Technology, 1982) <rai.anthropology.org.uk/film/catalogue_1/catalogue_i.html>. *Royal Anthropological Institute Film Library Catalogue Volume II* edited by Margaret Wilson (London: Film Committee, Royal Anthropological Institute in Association with the Scottish Council for Educational Technology, 1990) <rai.anthropology.org.uk/film/catalogue_2/index.html>. These catalogues are alphabetical listings of holdings of the film and video library of the Royal Anthropological Institute. They are currently in the process of being made available electronically via the RAI Website. Although not completely up to date they are a useful starting point. The entries are arranged alphabetically and each gives details of subject content, the film makers and length of the film. For more up-to-date information consult the Film Library section of the RAI Website <rai.anthropology.org.uk/film/film_library.html> which gives information on holdings and current films for hire.

▶ 2.4 DICTIONARIES

(a) Print

The Dictionary of Anthropology by C. Winick (New York: Philosophical Library, 1956). This classic work covers the whole field of anthropology, including all the major concepts and terminology. The definitions are clearly worded and especially suitable for those new to the discipline. However, it should be noted that in an attempt to make the subject more accessible to the public, Winick tends to emphasize the consensus in anthropological theory. He does not discuss fully the divergence in viewpoints between different schools of thought. Also, as the dictionary was published in the 1950s, it does not offer coverage of more recent subfields such as aspects of medical anthropology and visual anthropology.

A Dictionary of Anthropology by C. Seymour-Smith (London: Macmillan, 1986) is an extremely useful source which places emphasis on theoretical discussion of the way in which concepts and issues are approached by the various schools within anthropology. Consideration is also given to an examination of the relationship between anthropology and other related disciplines such as sociology and linguistics. It contains over 1000 entries with 150 biographies. Each entry offers references for further reading.

The Dictionary of Anthropology edited by Thomas Barfield (Oxford: Blackwell, 1997) is a substantial and detailed reference work which should be standard reading for any undergraduate student. It provides access to over 3000 analytical articles on key concepts, technical terms and issues within social and cultural anthropology. Contributors include many famous anthropologists such as Jack Goody on succession rules and Laura Nader on legal anthropology. The volume also includes critical assessments of the work of leading anthropologists from the nineteenth and twentieth centuries such as Herbert Spencer, Henry Morgan and Ernest Gellner. Lists of further readings are provided.

The Dictionary of Concepts in Anthropology by Robert H. Winthrop (New York: Greeenwood, 1991). The main strength of this dictionary is its concise summaries of the main anthropological concepts. It covers 80 topics with lists of resources for further reading.

International Dictionary of Anthropologists edited by Christopher Winters and compiled by the Library Anthropology Resource Group (New York: Garland, 1991). This source provides essays on 752 people whom the authors regard as having made a significant contribution to anthropology. The key figures are covered, and while some of the essays are rather brief, they provide a basic coverage of the main points with bibliographies of further readings.

Women Anthropologists: a Biographical Dictionary edited by Ute Gas (New York: Greenwood, 1988). This dictionary contains 58 biographical essays on leading women anthropologists from the twentieth century. It includes geographical and subject indexes and offers citations to other sources.

(b) Electronic

Anthromorphemics <www.anth.ucsb.edu/glossary/index2.html>. This is an online glossary of a wide range of terms used in cultural anthropology, physical anthropology and archaeology. It is possible to browse the categories or search using Boolean operators. Definitions are succinct. The database is maintained by members of the Department of Anthropology, University of California at Santa Barbara.

▶ 2.5 DIRECTORIES

2.5.1 General

(a) Print

The *AAA Guide* (Arlington, VA: American Anthropological Association, 1962–) has been produced annually by the American Anthropological Association since 1962 and provides a wealth of detail about anthropological teaching and research. Its main emphasis is on North America, although there is some limited coverage of other parts of the world. It is currently subdivided into six sections: a directory of anthropology departments; a listing of departments by type (including academic, government, museum and research bodies); Email and address directories of AAA members; statistics on student enrolment and numbers of degrees awarded in anthropology; and an annual listing of PhD dissertations accepted in the past year. The latter is arranged by author and provides the title, university, and geographical area of coverage. Selected parts of the guide can be viewed online at the American Anthropological Association Website <www.aaanet.org/>. This site also provides information on many of the membership directories produced by its numerous special interest subject groups. A recent example is *The Association for Feminist Anthropology Membership Directory* which was published in 1996.

Biographical Directory of Anthropologists Born Before 1920 edited by Thomas L. Mann and compiled by the Library Anthropology Resource Group (New York: Garland, 1988) is a useful introductory guide to the founding fathers of the discipline. It provides brief biographical entries, with listings of all published works and citations to any published biographies of the figure.

International Directory of Anthropologists (Washington, DC: National Research Council, 1938); *International Directory of Anthropologists*, 2nd ed., (Washington DC: National Research Council, 1940); *International Directory of Anthropologists*, 3rd ed., (Washington DC: National Research Council, 1950); 'International Directory of Anthropologists', 4th ed., published in *Current Anthropology* (8, December 1967, pp.549–646); and *International Directory of Anthropologists*, 5th ed., (Washington DC: National Research Council, 1970). Considered collectively, these directories provide an impressive historical listing of practising anthropologists and academics from the 1920s to the 1970s. Information was compiled from membership lists of leading organizations worldwide. The preface to the fifth edition includes an overview of the development of anthropology during the twentieth century. Entries typically contain such information as: contact name and address, employment, education and areas of interest. The final edition also offers more detailed indexing by what it refers to as 'methodological speciality'. This pinpoints exponents of specific anthropological subfields such as medical anthropology and applied anthropology.

(b) Electronic

WEDA – World Wide Email Directory of Anthropologists <wings.buffalo.edu/academic/department/anthropology/weda/>. A searchable international directory of Email addresses of anthropologists, which is continuing to grow steadily. Anthropology is considered in its broadest sense, covering physical, social and cultural anthropology and related disciplines in the social sciences and humanities. Entries offer the name of the body/individual, contact address and research specialism. It is hosted at the University at Buffalo Website.

2.5.2 Applied anthropology

Directory of Professional Anthropologists Developed by the National Association for the Practice of Anthropology Society for Applied Anthropology (Arlington, VA: American Anthropological Association, 1996). The most recent edition of this reference source provides a listing of all current individual and institutional members of the National Association for the Practice of Anthropology. They include community workers, advisers and medical professionals. Details of the Society's events are also included. *See also 2.14.2* for further information.

2.5.3 Area studies

Society for the Anthropology of Europe Directory, 2nd ed., (Arlington, VA: American Anthropological Society) edited by Susan Parman et al. This directory was compiled by the Society for the Anthropology of Europe, a specialist subgroup of the American Anthropological Association. It provides a listing of researchers, mainly based in North America, who specialize in European anthropology. The directory is indexed by name, fieldwork region, geographic areas of interest and subject interest. *See also 2.14.3*.

2.5.4 Medical anthropology

Graduate Programs in Medical Anthropology, 1993–94 (Arlington, VA: American Anthropological Society). This directory was compiled by the Society for Medical Anthropology, a specialist subgroup of the American Anthropological Association. It provides details of courses of study relevant to Medical Anthropology in North America. Although the date of this work means that its information will become increasingly out of date if a new edition is not completed soon, it serves as a useful starting point for tracing graduate programmes and individuals working in the field, as it contains a directory of clinically applied anthropologists. *See also 2.14.4.*

► 2.6 ENCYCLOPAEDIAS

2.6.1 General

The *Companion Encyclopedia of Anthropology* edited by Tim Ingold (New York: Routledge, 1994) offers just under 40 long essays which encompass the breadth of the discipline, including culture and social life. All are well documented and include bibliographies of further reading. The *Encyclopedia of Anthropology* edited by David E. Hunter and Phillip Whitten (New York: Harper & Row, 1976) is most useful as an introduction for students new to the field, providing 1400 succinct dictionary type entries covering general theories and key anthropologists, but excluding detailed analysis of specific ethnic groups. Some entries offer guides to further reading.

The *Encyclopedia of Cultural Anthropology* edited by David Levinson and Melvin Ember (New York: Henry Holt, 1996) is an excellent introduction to the main methods, concepts and topics central to the study of social and cultural anthropology. Each article is signed and offers a brief but useful bibliography of further readings. An appendix to the four volume set contains a listing of significant anthropology journals. The *Encyclopedia of Social and Cultural Anthropology* edited by Alan Barnard and Jonathan Spencer (New York: Routledge, 1996) contains approximately 250 essays on the theory and history of anthropology and ethnographic fieldwork methods. The essays are succinct, but cover all the main points, including lists of further readings. Also provided, are over 200 biographical entries of leading anthropologists from the nineteenth and twentieth centuries, with lists of their key works and bibliographies of secondary commentary.

The Encyclopedia of the Social Sciences edited by E. Seligman (New York: Macmillan, 1930–35). Despite its age this remains an authoritative work. It contains one long article on the historical development of anthropology prior to 1930 and a number of smaller articles on particular concepts such as kinship. All offer extensive bibliographies. In *The International Encyclopedia of the Social Sciences* edited by D. Sills (New York: Macmillan and Free Press, 1968) there is one main section on social anthropology that is composed of six long essays that deal with the history and practice of the discipline. Biographies of researchers born before 1890 are also included.

2.6.2 Area studies

The *Encyclopedia of World Cultures* edited by David Levinson (Boston, MA: GK Hall, 1991–96) is a major 10 volume work sponsored by the Human Relations Area Files Project (HRAF). It provides information on the history, sociology, politics, economy, religion and social life of over 1500 individual twentieth century cultures worldwide. The majority of entries have been written by practising anthropologists and so provide authoritative accounts from the field. The CD-ROM version includes colour photographs and interactive maps. It can be searched by subject keyword using Boolean operators.

▶ 2.7 GUIDES AND HANDBOOKS

2.7.1 General

(a) Print

Anthropological Resources: a Guide to Archival, Library and Museum Collections compiled by the Library-Anthropology Resource Group (New York: Garland, 1999), provides a comprehensive guide to important North American and Canadian collections. Coverage of Britain, and Europe is more selective. It encompasses anthropology in the widest sense, including physical anthropology and linguistics. The primary focus is upon collections relating to non-industrial cultures. *Cultural Anthropology: a Guide to Reference and Information Sources* by Josephine Z. Kibbee (Eaglewood, CO: Libraries Unlimited, 1991) is an excellent source for guiding the user to the most relevant resources for research. It provides wide coverage of 12 main subfields of anthropology, including: physical, linguistic, cognitive and medical anthropology, and also information on related subject areas from the humanities, such as material culture and religion. A more selective coverage is provided of resources for seven broad geographical areas. Individual chapters document particular types of resource including journals, indexes and encyclopaedias. However, the age of the text means that coverage of electronic resources is sparse.

Funding for Anthropological Research by K. Cantrell (Phoenix, AZ: Oryx Press, 1986) is geared primarily towards the American market, listing over 700 sponsors of anthropological research. These include government and private institutions and bodies willing to provide grants for graduate students. *Introduction to Library Research in Anthropology*, 2nd ed., by John M. Weeks (Boulder, CO: Westview, 1998) is a good starting point for anthropology students. It has separate chapters on different types of resources including book reviews, theses, films, bibliographies and dictionaries. It also includes coverage of key Internet and electronic sources. Helpful, succinct annotations are provided.

2.7.2 Applied anthropology

(a) Print

Handbook of Methods in Cultural Anthropology edited by H. Russell Bernard (Walnut Creek, CA: AltaMira Press, 1998). A broad ranging introduction to anthropological research methods which is suitable for students. Areas covered include: ethics, methods of fieldwork research, data interpretation and applied anthropology.

(b) Electronic

Handbook on Ethical Issues in Anthropology edited by Joan Cassell and Sue-Ellen Jacobs. Special publication no.23 (Arlington, VA: American Anthropological Association, 1988). Available in paper or in full-text on the Internet at <www.ameranthassn.org/committees/ethics/toc.htm> this text provides useful information on the types of ethical dilemmas which anthropologists face in the field. It contains a history of the way in which these issues have been handled by committees of the American Anthropological Association and practical advice with case studies of solutions that have been found. Guidelines on how to teach fieldwork ethics to students are also included.

2.7.3 Area studies

Area Handbook Series (Washington, DC: Library of Congress, 1957–) prepared by the Country Studies Area Handbook Program at the Library of Congress. This series offers useful background information on the economy, politics, culture and social conditions of several hundred countries worldwide. The series is continuing and many of the volumes are periodically revised. Electronic versions of over 100 of the texts can be found at <lcWeb2.loc.gov/frd/cs/cshome.html.> *Atlas of World Cultures: a Geographical Guide to Ethnographic Literature* by David H. Price (Newbury Park, CA: Sage, 1989) provides maps of the geographical location of individual cultures and directs users to the main ethnographic works about them. Over 1000 books and journal articles are cited. Reference is made to the geographic classification used by the Human Relations Area Files. *Ethnic Groups Worldwide: a Ready Reference Handbook* by David Levinson (Phoenix, AZ: Orix Press, 1998) is a basic quick reference guide to cultures worldwide. It is arranged alphabetically by country and each entry offers a profile describing succinctly the ethnic composition and ethnic relations of each country.

European Anthropologies: a Guide to the Profession, volume 1: Ethnography, Ethnology, and Social/Cultural Anthropology edited by Susan Carol Rogers, Thomas M. Wilson and Gary W. McDonogh (Arlington, VA: American Anthropological Association, 1996). This 66-page guide was compiled by the Society for the Anthropology of Europe and offers a solid introduction to the anthropological study of Europe. It contains succinct country profiles of the main European nations and listings of selected reference works about them.

2.7.4 Medical anthropology

Medical Anthropology: Contemporary Theory and Method edited by Carolyn F. Sargent and Thomas M. Johnson (Westport, CT: Praeger, 1996) is an excellent guide to current research in the field. It covers the core theoretical issues including: methodology, health policy and interaction with biomedical practitioners. An extensive bibliography of further reading is offered.

▶ 2.8 WEBSITES

2.8.1 General

This section provides a guide to a selection of general Websites which are of value for anthropologists. Many of the leading anthropology organizations have detailed Websites and a listing of the major ones can be found in *section 2.14*.

Anthropology Resources on the Internet <home.worldnet.fr/clist/Anthro/index.html>. This site maintains a listing of Internet resources relevant to the study of archaeology, cultural anthropology and physical anthropology. Although it does not offer annotations it is up to date, containing over 1500 links. These are arranged by geographical area, specialist topic and resource type. The latter include: mailing list and Email directories, journals and organizational Websites.

Anthropology Web Sites <www.anth.ucsb.edu/links/pages/>. A listing of important sites for cultural anthropology, physical anthropology and archaeology, maintained by the Anthropology Department of the University of California at Santa Barbara. Access to the list is by the discipline, geographical area or resource type. The latter include electronic journals, online courses and syllabi and organizations. Annotations are not currently provided, but the site is updated frequently.

CSAC Ethnographics Gallery <lucy.ukc.ac.uk/>. This excellent Website is maintained by the Centre for Anthropology and Computing, University of Kent at Canterbury. It provides access to a wealth of full-text data and bibliographic databases, these include: *Anthropological Index Online* (*see* 2.10), *UK Anthropology Theses Listing* (*see* 2.10) and the *CSAC Social Anthropology Bibliography* (*see* 2.3). Also available on the site are a growing number of full-text articles and monographs. These include such classic texts as Paul Stirling's writings on a *Turkish Village* (1965), Phyllis Kaberry's *Women of the Grassfields* (Colonial Research Publication no. 14, 1952) and archival resources on the Mambilia. Other features include access to online fieldwork notes from University of Kent students and numerous links to other useful anthropology Websites.

Internet Anthropologist <www.vts.rdn.ac.uk/anthropologist/index.htm> is a self-guided Internet tutorial, which has been developed to cater for the needs of anthropology students, researchers and lecturers. It was launched in Spring 2001 and forms part of the RDN Virtual Training Suite, a publicly funded JISC initiative which offers free online training in Internet skills for the UK's higher and further education communities. The tutorial introduces users to key anthropology Internet sites and provides practical guidance on how they might use the Internet in their teaching and research. It also offers quizzes and interactive learning exercises that teach students how to search the Internet effectively and how to evaluate the quality of the resources they find.

SOSIG (Social Science Information Gateway) <www.sosig.ac.uk/>. This Internet subject gateway is funded by the Higher Education Funding Council for England (HEFCE) and compiled by a series of specialist subject editors who review the resources and provide helpful descriptions of their content. The anthropology section is currently maintained by the Centre for Social Anthropology and Computing, University of Kent and the University of Manchester Library. It includes specialist subsections for topics such as kinship, economics, medical and visual anthropology.

WWW Virtual Library Anthropology <vlib.anthrotech.com/>. This excellent resource, which is part of the WWW Virtual Library, is sponsored by Anthro-Tech. It covers all aspects of physical and social anthropology and includes several thousand links to directories, discussion forums, electronic journals and news services. There is a separate listing of featured sites, which highlights useful glossaries, news services and subject gateways, and provides a listing of recently added resources. All resources are rated and described by the editors. Users may register to receive regular notifications of updates and new additions via Email.

2.8.2 Applied anthropology

ANTHAP – The Applied Anthropology Computer Network <anthap.oakland.edu>. ATHAP is a Web guide to resources for applied anthropologists which is compiled by Oakland University. It includes links to useful Internet sites, ethical and research guidelines, discussion channels and lists of educational courses in applied anthropology.

Experience Rich Anthropology <www.era.anthropology.ac.uk/index.html> is a consortium of UK universities funded by HEFCE and led by CSAC (Centre for Social Anthropology and Computing) based at the University of Kent (*see also 2.8.1*). It aims to provide electronic teaching materials that will help students explore the relationship between field data and subsequent disseminated analysis in monographs and journals. This site reports on the project's development as it happens and contains links to a number of sample teaching materials, data sets and working papers.

Fieldwork: The Anthropologist in the Field <www.truman.edu/academics/ss/faculty/tamakoshil/>. This site was created as a project of Truman State University by Professor Laura Tamakoshi. It is intended to deepen students' understanding of anthropological fieldwork. It draws heavily upon her own experiences in Papua New Guinea, but also provides helpful general advice on planning fieldwork, fieldwork notes, methodology and further references.

2.8.3 Area studies

HRAF Collection of Ethnography (New Haven, CA: HRAF Press) <www.yale.edu/hraf/collections.html>. The HRAF (Human Relations Area Files) Collection of Ethnography was founded in 1949 and aims to provide access to documentary materials relating to all cultures worldwide. It currently contains information files on more than 365 cultures past and present. Each file contains a variety of full-text documents including books, articles and manuscripts. They are indexed using a detailed culture and subject classification scheme which has been developed by HRAF. Prior to 1993, the collection was updated annually on microfiche. From 1993 onwards, the material has been available on CD-ROM or via the Internet. Subscription details and basic teaching guides can be found on the Website. The project also produces the *Native North Americans* (*see 2.3.3*).

2.8.4 Visual anthropology

Lacuna Project: Enhancing the Use of Video in Teaching and Learning in Anthropology <www.san.ed.ac.uk/lacuna/index.htm>. This project is funded by the National Network for Teaching and Learning Anthropology with the support of the Department of Social Anthropology at the University of Edinburgh. It aims to raise the awareness and use of films in anthropological teaching by acting as a centre for the dissemination of information. A database of available ethnographic films is being created on the site and it also aims to develop case studies and examples of how films can be used in teaching. For further information on the network *see 2.14.2.*

UR List – Web Resources for Visual Anthropology <www.usc.edu/dept/elab/urlist/index.html>. This list is available from the Website of the Center For Visual Anthropology at the University of Southern California. It indexes sites relevant to the study of visual anthropology and ethnographic film. Resources include: essays, bibliographies, audio-visual collections and photographs. Annotations are not provided, but the list is regularly updated and includes all the key sites for the discipline.

▶ 2.9 JOURNALS

2.9.1 General

See also 2.3.1 Anthropology Journals and Serials: an Annotated Guide for a bibliography of journals.

American Anthropologist <www.aaanet.org/aa/index.htm> (ISSN 0002–7294) (Washington, DC: American Anthropological Association, 1888–). Quarterly. The leading journal of the American Anthropological Association. Each issue contains five to 10 major articles, along with book and film reviews, obituaries and commentaries which offer replies and responses to previously published articles. Contents pages and abstracts from 1998 onwards are available on the journal's Website. *See also 2.14.1* for further information on the American Anthropological Association.

American Ethnologist <www.aaanet.org/aes> (ISSN 0094–0496) (Washington, DC: American Anthropological Association, 1974–). Quarterly. This refereed title is published by the American Ethnological Society Section of the American Anthropological Association and includes articles on all aspects of cultural anthropology including: the ecology, social organization, economics, politics and ethnicity of social groups worldwide. Book reviews are also included. Tables of contents and abstracts from 1998 onwards are offered on the Website.

Anthropological Quarterly (ISSN 0003–5491) (Washington, DC: Catholic University Press of America, 1953–). Quarterly. Continues *Primitive Man*, vols.1–25, 1928–52. This title publishes scholarly articles, book reviews and lists of books received in all areas of social and cultural anthropology. All articles are refereed.

Anthropology and Humanism <www.smcm.edu/sha/shapubs.htm> (ISSN 0192–5615) (Arlington, VA: American Anthropological Association,

1976–). Quarterly. This is the journal of the Society for Humanistic Anthropology, a subgroup of the American Anthropological Association, which seeks to explore the question of what it means to be human. It draws heavily upon the interrelationship between anthropological study and the humanities. The title is refereed and includes fiction, photographs and poetry as well as articles. The Website provides access to contents pages from 1998 onwards.

Anthropology News Online <www.aaanet.org/an/an.htm> (ISSN 0098–1605) (Arlington, VA: American Anthropological Association, 1947–). Monthly. This is the official newsletter of the American Anthropological Association. It is particularly noted for its information on current awareness, including calendars of forthcoming events, lists of recent publications, details of research funding and vacancies. It also has short articles and an obituary section. From 1996 onwards, parts of the newsletter were made available via the Internet. Principally, they include: death notices and lists of publications received.

Anthropology Today <www.aaanet.org/aa/index.htm> (ISSN 0268–540X) (London: Royal Anthropological Institute, 1985–). Three issues a year. Continues *RAIN: Royal Anthropological Institute News,* 1974–1984. This is the bimonthly newsletter of the Royal Anthropological Institute (RAI). It focuses specifically on current awareness and aims to promote debate in fields of applied anthropology including education and development studies. It includes calendars of forthcoming events, a vacancy supplement and film and exhibition reviews. Its Website provides electronic access to *Anthcal* – its events diary and VacancyLink its vacancy page. *See also 2.14* for further information on the RAI.

Anthropos <www.anthropos-journal.de/#Publications> (ISSN 0257–9774) (Sankt Augustin, Germany: Anthropos Institut, 1906–). Two issues a year. This title is devoted to the publication of articles relating to all aspects of cultural anthropology, including theoretical papers and ethnographic studies. It is renowned for its substantial international content, with each issue totalling, on average, over 700 pages of articles and reviews published in English, French or German. It also offers a large number of book reviews and a 'Review of Reviews Section' that provides a listing of the current contents of leading anthropology titles. Indexes from 1997 onwards are available from the Website.

Critique of Anthropology (ISSN 0308–275x) (London: Sage, 1974–). Quarterly. This journal is founded on the principle that anthropology must subject itself to continuous criticism if it is to continue to develop as a valid discipline. It frequently publishes articles that challenge established anthropological theory from a Marxist point of view and is also strong on analysing social and gender inequalities worldwide. Available electronically.

Cultural Anthropology <bernard.pitzer.edu/~cultanth/> (ISSN 0886–7356) (Arlington, VA: American Anthropological Association, 1986–).

Quarterly. This is the journal of the Society for Cultural Anthropology, the specialist subsection of the American Anthropological Association which focuses on cultural/social anthropology worldwide. It publishes articles, review essays, interviews and book reviews. Tables of contents for all issues since volume one and some supplementary audio and visual material are available from the Website. *See also 2.14.1.*

Current Anthropology (ISSN 0011–3204) (Chicago, IL: University of Chicago Press, 1960–). Five issues a year. This journal is refereed and international in scope. It covers the full range of anthropology, including: social/cultural anthropology, physical anthropology and linguistics. It offers particularly useful critical commentary and discussion on many of the longer research articles as well as shorter conference reports. Available electronically.

Dialectical Anthropology: an Independent International Journal in the Critical Tradition Committed to the Transformation of our Society and the Humane Union of Theory and Practice (ISSN 0304–4092) (Boston, MA Kluwer, 1975–). Quarterly. This refereed title publishes articles which are broadly Marxist in stance. They include theoretical and ethnographic studies. Book reviews are also provided. Available electronically.

Ethnology: an International Journal of Cultural and Social Anthropology (ISSN 0014–1828) (Pittsburgh, PA: Department of Anthropology, University of Pittsburgh, 1962–). Quarterly. This title was established in 1962 by George P. Murdock, the founder of the Human Relations Area Files. It is particularly strong in publishing articles, ethnographic studies and datasets relating to social and cultural anthropology. It has a diverse content of theoretical and topical articles of interest to both the academic scholar and general public.

Journal of Linguistic Anthropology (1055–1360) (Arlington, VA: American Anthropological society, 1990–). Two issues a year. This is the journal of the Society for Linguistic Anthropology, a section of the American Anthropological Association. It publishes refereed articles and book reviews relating to linguistic anthropology.

Journal of Peasant Studies <www.frankcass.com/jnls/jps.htm> (ISSN 0306–6150) (London: Frank Cass, 1974–). Quarterly. The primary focus of the journal is on the political economy of agrarian change. It frequently publishes articles and book reviews relating to the historical and current situation of peasants worldwide and is particularly good at highlighting issues relating to the social transformation of their societies. Some recent contents pages can be viewed on the Website.

Journal of the Royal Anthropological Institute <rai.anthropology.org.uk/pubs/jrai/jrai.html> (ISSN 1359–0987) (London: Royal Anthropological Institute, 1995–). Quarterly. Formally *Man* (0025–1496), this is the core publication of the Royal Anthropological Institute (RAI). It provides access to theoretical and research articles covering all aspects of social and physical anthropology. Also regularly included are book reviews, lists of books received and correspondence. Tables of contents from 1995 onwards are available from the Website. *See also 2.14.1* for further information on the RAI.

Theoretical Anthropology <www.univie.ac.at/voelkerkunde/theoretical-anthropology/welcome.html> (ISSN 1024–5804) (Vienna: Institut für Völkerkunde, 1994–). Irregular. *Theoretical Anthropology* is a free, full-text electronic journal produced at the Institut für Völkerkunde (Institute of Social Anthropology), University of Vienna. It is a co-project with the Commission on Theoretical Anthropology (COTA) of IUAES and the Society for Caribbean Research. The journal contains articles, training material, and information on symposia. Unfortunately, current issues are very irregular.

Transforming Anthropology <www.aaanet.org/aba/ta/index.htm> (ISSN 105–0559) (Arlington, VA: American Anthropological Association, 1993–). Semi-annual. A publication of the Association of Black Anthropologists section of the American Anthropological Association, it is primarily concerned with publishing theory and research which seeks to understand and explain racial, ethnic, class and gender inequalities in societies worldwide. It also aims to publish research which has involved members of the indigenous community and local scholars in its collection and dissemination. All articles are peer reviewed. *See also 2.14.1* for further information about the Association of Black Anthroplogists.

2.9.2 Applied anthropology

Anthropology in Action <lucy.ukc.ac.uk/Anthaction> (ISSN 0967–201X) (London: Anthropology in Action). Irregular. This title is the journal of Anthropology In Action (formerly known as the British Association for Social Anthropology in Policy and Practice) a professional grouping of practising anthropologists, academics and students concerned with applied anthropological issues such as the relationship of anthropology to health, social and community work and policy. Each issue contains several articles and reports of conferences and events. Recent topics covered include: anthropology and AIDS; kinship and new reproductive technologies; and ethnic violence. *See also 2.14.2* for further information about *Anthropology In Action.*

Culture and Agriculture <csbs3.utsa.edu/culture&agriculture/index.htm> (ISSN 1048–4876) (Arlington, VA: American Anthropological Association, 1978–). Three issues a year. This title is published by the Culture and Agriculture group of the American Anthropological Association. Its particular focus is upon applying anthropological theory and relevant methods to the study of agricultural practice and the management of the environment. It regularly includes analysis on class, cultural identity and gender relations in relation to the organization of agriculture and biodiversity issues. All articles are refereed and book reviews are also provided. *See also 2.14.2* for further information about the Culture and Agriculture group.

Human Organization <www.sfaa.net/ho/> (ISSN 0018–7259) (Arlington, VA: Society for Applied Anthropology, 1949–). Quarterly. Continues *Applied Anthropology,* vol.1–8, 1941–1948. This is the official journal of the Society for Applied Anthropology. Its main focus is on the application of anthropological study and principles to practical situations, such as development programmes. Each issue publishes articles, book reviews and case studies. In addition to some contents pages from recent issues, the Website offers additional online commentary on recent articles and the facility to sign up to receive contents pages via Email. *See also 2.14.2* for further information on the Society for Applied Anthropology.

2.9.3 Area studies

Eastern Anthropologist (ISSN 0012–8686) (Lucknow: Ethnographic and Folk Culture Society, 1947–). Quarterly. This is a leading title for anthropologists concerned with the study of the Asian subcontinent. It is the journal of the Ethnographic and Folk Culture Society of India and offers articles and book reviews on all aspects of social anthropology of the region. It includes material from indigenous writers.

Journal of Asian Studies <www.hum.utah.edu/jas/index.html> (ISSN 0021–9118) (Berkeley, CA: University of California Press, 1941–). Quarterly. Previously known as Far *Eastern Quarterly* 1941–1956. This is the journal of the Association for Asian Studies. Although not strictly anthropological in content, as it also focuses on contemporary politics and economics, cultural and ethnographic surveys of Asian societies are frequently published. Each issue contains four to five articles on the history, politics, culture and sociology of Asia, South Asia and Southeast Asia. There is also a substantial book review section.

Journal of Latin American Anthropology <www.northwestern.edu/jlaa/index.htm> (Arlington, VA: American Anthropological Association, 1995–). Semi annual. This peer-reviewed journal is sponsored by the Society of Latin American Anthropologists, a specialist subgroup of the American Anthropological Association. It provides access to articles and books reviews dealing with the anthropology of Latin America, the Caribbean and immigrant communities in the United States and elsewhere. It includes some publications from Latin American researchers.

Oceania (ISSN 0029–8077) (Sydney: Oceania Publications, 1930–). Quarterly. *Oceania* is of particular importance for the publication of social anthropological studies of the indigenous peoples of Australia, Melanesia and the South Pacific Islands. It includes refereed articles and book reviews.

2.9.4 Medical anthropology

Medical Anthropology: Cross–Cultural Studies in Health and Illness (ISSN: 0145–9740) (New York: Gordon and Breach, 1977–). Quarterly. This journal examines the relationship between human behaviour, social life and health from an anthropological perspective. It includes bio-cultural, historical and cross-cultural studies.

Medical Anthropology Quarterly: International Journal for the Analysis of Health <www.cudenver.edu//sma/medical_anthropology_quarterly.htm> (ISSN 0745–5194) (Arlington, VA: American Anthropological Association, 1987–). Quarterly. This is the journal of the Medical Anthropology Section of the American Anthropological Association. It publishes articles and book reviews relating to medical anthropology, exploring its relationship with health practice, medicine and anthropology as a whole. This covers a wide field including public health, concepts of illness and disease in a cross-cultural perspective, epidemiology, population, maternal and child health, the relationship between health and development, and health care services. Tables of contents from 1998 onwards are available from the Website.

2.9.5 Psychological anthropology

Anthropology of Consciousness <sunny.moorpark.cc.ca.us/~jbaker/sac/publications.htm> (ISSN 1053–4202) (Arlington, VA: American Anthropological Association, 1989–). Quarterly. This title is the main publication of the Society for the Anthropology of Consciousness, an interdisciplinary body within the American Anthropological Association which focuses upon cross-cultural and theoretical studies of consciousness. Key areas include: shamanic rituals, trances, the roles of psychic phenomena in traditional healing, and mysticism. Some abstracts of articles are available on the Website.

Ethos (ISSN 0091–2131) (Arlington, VA: American Anthropological Association, 1973–). Quarterly. A peer-reviewed publication of the Society for Psychological Anthropology, a specialist subsection of the American Anthropological Association which seeks to explore the interaction between psychological and socio/cultural processes, including such issues as socialization, motivation, self and identity and perceptions of culture. It includes articles, review essays and conference reports. *See also 2.14.5* for further information on the Society for Psychological Anthropology.

2.9.6 Urban anthropology

City and Society <www.aaanet.org/sunta/publications.htm> (ISSN 0893–0465) (Arlington, VA: American Anthropological Association, 1987–).

Annual. This is the annual review of the Society for Urban Anthropology, a section of the American Anthropological Association. It offers access to refereed articles, book reviews and case studies covering urban communities worldwide. Some articles give a historical approach to the subject field. *See also 2.14.6* for further information on the Society.

Urban Anthropology: Studies of Cultural Systems and World Encounters (ISSN 0363–2024) (New York: Institute for the Study of Man, 1972–). Quarterly. This refereed journal is concerned with urban anthropology and the study of the relationship between the Western industrialized nations and the developing countries in terms of development, imperialism and world systems theory.

2.9.7 Visual anthropology

Visual Anthropology Review <www.aaanet.org/pubs/svavar.htm> (ISSN 1058–7187) (Arlington, VA: American Anthropological Association, 1985–). Semi annual. This is the official publication of the Society for Visual Anthropology of the American Anthropological Association. It publishes refereed articles and review essays on both the visual aspects of human culture (such as art, museums and photography) and the use of ethnographic film in anthropological teaching. Ethnographic film essays can also be found in this publication. *See also 2.14.7* for further information on the Society for Visual Anthropology.

► 2.10 ABSTRACTS, INDEXES AND DATABASES

2.10.1 General

(a) Print

Abstracts in Anthropology <www.siftings.com/aa.html> (ISSN 0001–3455) (Amityville, NY: Baywood Publishing Company, 1970–). Eight issues a year. This title covers all fields of anthropology and is arranged into four main sections for archaeology, ethnology (social anthropology), linguistics and cultural anthropology. It currently indexes over 300 titles in the English language. Author and subject indexes are included in each quarterly issue with an annual accumulation. Users should, however, note that the subject index can be difficult to use as cross-referencing can be poor and many broad general headings are used.

Bulletin Signaletique: Ethnologie (ISSN 0765–1473) (Paris: Centre de Documentation Sciences Humaines, 1986–). Three issues a year. Previously known as the *Bulletin Signaletique 521: Sociologie-Ethnologie,* vols.24–39, 1970–1985. This is an important abstracting service for tracing European scholarship. Although the subject index is offered in French only, it is international in scope and includes many English language publications. From 1969 to 1986, cultural anthropology was classed with sociology. After that date, there is a separate anthropology section, classified by subject and subdivided by geographical region. Brief annotations of content are provided in French. The *Bulletin* forms part of the Ethnologie file on the *FRANCIS* database. *See (b) Electronic* below.

(b) Electronic

Anthropological Abstracts: Cultural/Social Anthropology from Austria, Germany, Switzerland <www.anthropology-online.de/Aga/Abstrcts.html> (Freiburg: German Anthropology Online, 1999–). Irregular. This title succeeds *Abstracts in German Anthropology* which was published 1980–1997. It aims to provide coverage of German language material, including journal articles, monographs and yearbooks. Abstracts are provided in English. The material is arranged geographically, but there are also author and subject keyword indexes. The main drawback at present is that lack of funding has made the publication very infrequent.

Anthropological Index Online <lucy.ukc.ac.uk/AIO.html> (London: Royal Anthropological Institute, 1963–). Quarterly. This is the online version of *The Anthropological Index to Current Periodicals in the Museum of Mankind Library*. From 1963 to 1976 it was known as the *Anthropological Index to Current Periodicals Received in the Library of the Royal Anthropological Institute*. One of the leading indexes in the field, it covers over 750 titles published worldwide and held in the Library of the Royal Anthropological Institute. They cover all subfields of anthropology and include many foreign language titles. The online database is currently undergoing development and at present little information is offered for the 1960s. Searches may be conducted by author, title or subject keyword. Abstracts are not provided.

Anthropological Literature (Cambridge, MA: Tozzer Library, Harvard University, 1984–). Quarterly. The online version of *Anthropological Literature: an Index to Periodical Articles and Essays* is available as an RLG Citation Resources CitaDel file. Further information can be obtained from the RLG Website at <www.rlg.org/cit-anl.html>. It is based on the holdings of the specialist Tozzer Anthropology Library at Harvard University and currently indexes more than 900 journals and monograph series held there. This covers all fields of physical and social anthropology and includes journal articles, reports and obituaries. Coverage dates back to the nineteenth century and includes all references to journal articles made in the original library catalogues of the Tozzer Library. The database may be searched by author, title and subject or geographical keyword. Updates are currently made monthly.

Anthropology Review Database (ARD) <wings.buffalo.edu/anthropology/ARD/>. ARD is maintained by the University of Buffalo and aims to provide a searchable database of anthropological books, films and videos, online resources and multimedia software. It may be searched by author, title, subject keyword, medium of publication or date. Typical reviews contain abstracts and full bibliographic details which conform to American Anthropological Association (AAA) standards.

FRANCIS <www.questel.orbit.com/EN/search.htm> (Paris: Questel. Orbit, 1972–). Monthly. *FRANCIS* is an online database for the humanities, social sciences and economics. As part of its content it contains the online version of the *Bulletin Signaletique Ethnologie* (*see (a) Print* above). It also includes other indexing services supplied by the Centre National de la Recherche Scientifique, Institut de l'Information Scientifique et Technique and Centre des Sciences Humaines et Socials. It provides abstracts of journal articles, monographs and conference proceedings from 1972 onwards. These include many items of importance for anthropologists. Searches may be conducted for author, title, subject, year of publication and geographic region. The primary language is French.

International Bibliography of the Social Sciences (*IBSS*) <www.lse.ac.uk/IBSS/> (London: IBSS, 1951–). *IBSS ONLINE* provides electronic access to the database of the *International Bibliography of the Social Sciences*. This is a specialist social science indexing service which has anthropology as one of its core subjects along with sociology, politics and economics.

Social Sciences Citation Index (SSCI) (Philadelphia, PA: Institute for Scientific Information, 1981–). SSCI is an index to journal articles in the social sciences which currently indexes over 2000 titles. These include substantial anthropological coverage, although foreign language materials are more readily traced via the *International Bibliography of the Social Sciences*. *See 1.10* for further information about both databases.

2.10.2 Applied anthropology

International Development Abstracts <www.elsevier.nl/inca/publications/store/4/0/5/8/8/8/> (ISSN 0262–0855) (Amsterdam: Elsevier, 1982–). Bimonthly the online version of this title is available as part of the GEOBASE file, currently available via DIALOG, ChemWeb and OCLC First Search. It is also published as a CD-ROM. Details of subscriptions can be obtained from the Website. It indexes over 500 journals, plus monographs, reports and conference proceedings relating to international development literature. While this includes human geography, politics and economics, it also regularly indexes cultural materials of relevance to anthropologists. In particular, literature relating to aid programmes and social policy in the fields of health, community development, education, housing and women's issues are well covered.

2.10.3 Area studies

(a) Print

Africa Bibliography (Edinburgh: Edinburgh University Press, 1984–). Annual. An index to over 5000 articles, books and essays, compiled in association with the International Africa Institute as an annual supplement to *Africa* journal. It is arranged by region/country and provides coverage of all aspects of African affairs. Relevant anthropological entries may be found in the social/cultural anthropology and sociology headings.

Index Islamicus: a Bibliography of Publications on Islam and the Muslim World (ISSN 1360–0982) (London: Bowker-Saur, 1958–). Quarterly. This title is renowned for its extensive coverage of publications relating to Islam and the Muslim world. In addition to materials on the arts and physical sciences, it also includes economic, political and cultural studies of relevance to anthropologists. Journal articles, monographs and collected essays are indexed. There is a subject index to specific peoples and topics. A cumulated edition of the index is available on CD-ROM, *see (b) Electronic* below.

(b) Electronic

Bibliography of Asian Studies <bas.umdl.umich.edu/b/bas/> (ISSN 0067–7159) (Ann Arbor, MI: Association for Asian Studies, 1971–). Quarterly. This index had its origins in an annual bibliography published in the *Far Eastern Quarterly* in 1936. The online version contains the contents of all printed editions from 1971 to the present day, with quarterly updates. It provides citations to western language journal articles, conference proceedings and some chapters in books covering the economic, political and social study of the region. Since 1992 monographs have been excluded. In the past, there have been considerable time lags between publication and indexing, extending in some instances to over four years, however, these are now in the process of being reduced. The database may be searched by region, or subject keyword.

Index Islamicus: a Bibliography of Publications on Islam and the Muslim World from 1906–1997 (London: Bowker-Saur). This CD-ROM contains all the information from the printed volumes of the Index (*see (a) Print* above) plus additional data covering materials from 1906 onwards. It may be searched by author, title or subject keyword.

▶ 2.11 OFFICIAL PUBLICATIONS

For the anthropologist, publications which originate from official bodies (such as governments and international organizations) are of most value in providing background information on the social, economic and political context of the particular culture in which fieldwork is to take place. They are also commonly used in applied anthropological work which is often involved in community development issues.

The *Food and Agricultural Organization of the United Nations (FAO)* <www.fao.org> publishes materials relating to agricultural production, poverty, nutrition, food aid and development programmes in its member nations. Its full catalogue of publications can be searched on the Internet at: <www.fao.org/catalog/giphome.htm>. Of particular note are its *Economic and Social Development Papers* series which discuss agricultural policy, structural adjustment and poverty alleviation programmes in specific nations. Also of importance are its many statistical publications, *see 2.12.1.*

The *IMF International Monetary Fund* <www.imf.org/> is an international organization of 182 member countries, established to promote international monetary cooperation, economic growth, exchange stability and orderly exchange. It is also one of the major organizations providing financial loans to developing countries. Its Website contains detailed information on its current activities. Of particular interest are the country report sections which provide listings of IMF publications about member countries, and an overview of individual financial relationships with the fund. A wealth of full-text periodical articles and working papers on financial arrangements, many of which are technical in nature, are also available for downloading from the site. These include *IMF Poverty Reduction Strategy Papers, Staff Country Reports* from 1997 to date and *IMF Working Papers* from 1997 onwards.

The *United Nations Development Program* (*UNDP*) <www.undp.org/> is a branch of the United Nations which seeks to encourage sustainable development by assisting countries to carry out development programmes in poverty eradication and employment regeneration. An important publication is the *Human Development Report* which has been issued annually since 1990. It provides snapshots of comparative human development worldwide compiled by independent advisers and UN officials, including rankings of nations by human development indicators, gender empowerment and poverty indices.

The *United Nations High Commissioner for Refugees.* (*UNHCR*) <www.unhcr.ch> publishes timely information on refugee crises and aid programmes worldwide. These include official statistics on refugee numbers as well as assessments of UN activity. Increasingly, information is being made available on its Website via *REFWORLD* <www.unhcr.ch/refworld/welcome.htm>. This is a database of official documents relating to refugeesand asylum seekers world wide which are compiled by the UNHCR's Centre for Documentation and Research. They include UN resolutions, legal documents, speeches of the High Commissioner for Refugees, US Department of State country reports, Amnesty International Country Reports and reports and statistics from individual aid programmes. Extensive links to other sites relating to refugees are also offered.

The Fourth World Documentation Project <www.cwis.org/un.html> is maintained by the Center for World Indigenous Studies, an independent US-based research institute which seeks to promote the rights of 'Fourth World' states. These are defined as states which are not internationally recognized, but whose indigenous peoples maintain a distinct political culture within the larger states which have absorbed or claimed their traditional territories. The database seeks to provide access via the Internet to the full-text of all official agreements relating to these peoples. They include United Nations documentation from the Working Group on Indigenous Peoples, multilateral treaties with native peoples and tribal resolutions. Coverage is international including native American Indians, tribes of Africa and peoples of Melanesia and Polynesia.

▶ 2.12 STATISTICS

As with official publications, the main value of statistics for the anthropologist is to provide background information on the particular society under study and to consider its position with regard to the world economic system. Many of the most useful sources are compiled by international and intergovernmental organizations. This section provides references to a selection of key organizations and titles.

United Nations (UN) Statistics Division <www.un.org/Depts/unsd/sd_databases.htm> Free access is provided to a series of the recent social indicators which provide basic data on population, health, literacy and economics worldwide. Other more detailed services are offered for subscription only. These include: the *Monthly Bulletin of Statistics* – a compilation of the most up-to-date social and economic data including demography, trade, national accounts and gender statistics. *Statistical Yearbook on CD-ROM* – a compilation of more than 400 series of economic and social statistics. Other key publications include: *Women's Indicators and Statistics Database (WISTAT)*. Currently, version four of this is available on CD-ROM and provides basic data on gender, population and development for 206 areas, covering the period 1970–1996. Information on subscription rates can be found on the Website which also offers a useful set of links to the homepages of the statistical departments of other international organizations such as the International Labour Organization and the Food and Agriculture Organization.

FAOSTAT <apps.fao.org> is a collection of online multilingual databases containing over one million time series of international statistics compiled by the Food and Agriculture Organization of the United Nations. It includes data on food production, land use, agricultural development and receipt of food aid shipments. The majority of statistics are available free of charge from the site, more comprehensive data is offered to subscribers only. Full details can be obtained from the Website. Some cumulative data is also available on CD-ROM. The *FAOSTAT 98 CD-ROM* covers 210 countries and territories with 3000 figures relating to agriculture, fisheries, forestry and nutrition, dating from 1961 to 1998. It includes subsections for Production, Trade, Food Balance Sheets, Food Aid Shipments, Fertilizers and Pesticides, Land Use and Irrigation, Fishery Products, Population and Agricultural Machinery.

Progress of Nations <www.unicef.org/pon99/mainmenu.htm> is an annual publication of UNICEF which provides a country by country report on child health and infant mortality. The most recent issue is available in full-text, free of charge from the Website. Topics covered include AIDS and the relationship between health and poverty.

WHO Statistical Information System <www.who.int/whosis>. This site provides access to health and health-related statistical information from the World Health Organization (WHO) Global Programme on Evidence for Health Policy. It includes the *World Health Report* data which provides a basic snapshot of health in individual WHO member countries worldwide. Also available are basic health indicators, mortality statistics, AIDS/HIV data and population estimates and projections. The latter is particularly detailed and contains data on ageing, the demographic impact of AIDS and projected population growth of individual nations to the year 2050. The site is fully searchable by subject keyword and nation. However, users should note that the online information tends to focus on current data. For historical materials users should refer to references given in the paper catalogues. The site also offers extensive links to other national health related Websites, which include Ministry of Health and Central Statistics Offices for the majority of WHO member nations.

► 2.13 RESEARCH IN PROGRESS

Anthro-l <www.anatomy.su.oz.au/danny/anthropology/anthro-l/archive/index.html>. This Website provides access to the mail archive of the general anthropology mailing list Anthro-l. It is an unmoderated list used as a forum for discussion on any anthropological topic and covers all fields including: social, cultural, physical and linguistic anthropology. Messages are stored from November 1993 onwards and may be searched by subject keyword to trace discussions on particular topics. Information on how to subscribe to the list is given on the site.

Anthro-teach-learn <www.jiscmail.ac.uk/lists/anthro-teach-learn.html>. This is a UK-based mailing list for higher education academic staff and students to discuss matters relating to teaching and learning anthropology. These include the use of information technology in the education of anthr pologists. Archived messages can be viewed on the site. Instructions on how to join are also available there.

Anthropology in the News <www.tamu.edu/anthropology/news.html>. This site offers links to news stories related to physical or social anthropology, compiled by Texas A&M University. They are taken from stories compiled from leading news sources including: *CNN*, *New York Times*, *USA Today*, *National Geographic* and university press releases. Some of the services require the user to register to retrieve the articles, but all are accessible free of charge. Information is available from October 1996 onwards. Check the section 'Breaking News' for the most recent stories and the subject related archives for older material.

UK Social Anthropology Theses <lucy.ukc.ac.uk/Theses/theses_intro.html>. This is a searchable database of abstracts of anthropology doctoral theses submitted since 1970 to UK and Irish universities. It is based on material taken from the annual volume of the ASLIB *Index to Theses* (*see 1.13*). Users should note that the site currently has a warning that the ASLIB classification of anthropology is rather narrow, consequently, some materials which originate from social anthropology departments have been indexed in other areas such as comparative religion or economics and are excluded from the database. Searches may be conducted by author, title or keyword.

▶ 2.14 ORGANIZATIONS

2.14.1 General

American Anthropological Association
4350 North Fairfax Drive, Suite 640, Arlington, VA 22203–1, USA
Tel: +1 703 528 1902
Fax: +1 703 528 3546
Web: <www.aaanet.org>

The American Anthropological Association was founded in 1902 and is the world's largest professional organization for anthropologists. It seeks to advance all subfields of anthropology, including physical, linguistic and social anthropology and currently has 30 specialist subgroups, covering such diverse areas as feminist anthropology, medical anthropology and urban anthropology. Its publications include the *American Anthropologist* and *Anthropology Newsletter* (*see* 2.9.1). Its Website is an up-to-date source of information on vacancies, funding, professional ethics and forthcoming events in the field. Membership is open to anyone with a professional or scholarly interest in the field.

Anthropology and Sociology Section (ANSS)
Association of College and Research Libraries, 50 East Huron Street, Chicago, Illinois 60611, USA
Email: jlogburn@u.washington.edu
Web: <www.lib.odu.edu/anss/anssWeb.html>

Formed in 1972, this is a special interest group of the Association of College and Research Libraries and aims to support the work of specialist librarians in the field. It regularly publishes useful bibliographies and annotated guides to reference sources.

Association for Feminist Anthropology
c/o American Anthropological Association, 4350 North Fairfax Drive, Suite 640, Arlington, VA 22203–1, USA
Tel: +1 703 528 1902
Fax: +1 703 528 3546
Web: <www.QAL.berkeley.edu/~afaWeb/>

This subgroup of the American Anthropological Association was founded in 1988 to encourage the development of feminist theory and research in all subfields of anthropology and to facilitate communication on gender related issues. Its main publication is *Voices: an Annual Review of Feminist Anthropological Research* (*see* 2.2.1). Membership of the society is open to all Anthropological Association Members.

Association for Political and Legal Anthropology
c/o American Anthropological Association, 4350 North Fairfax Drive, Suite 640, Arlington, VA 22203–1, USA
Tel: +1 703 528 1902
Fax: +1 703 528 3546
Web: <www.aaanet.org/apla/index.htm>

This body was established in 1976 as a special interest group of the American Anthropological Association, with the aim of fostering communication between scholars in the fields of political and legal anthropology. It covers such diverse issues as nationalism, refugees, state and civil society and political and legal processes. Activities include regular conferences, workshops and the publication of its journal *PoLAR: The Political and Legal Anthropology Review*.

Association of Black Anthropologists (ABA)
c/o American Anthropological Association, 4350 North Fairfax Drive, Suite 640, Arlington, VA 22203–1, USA
Tel: +1703 528 1902
Fax: +1 703 528 3546
Web: <www.aaanet.org/aba/index.htm>

The ABA is a special interest group of the American Anthropological Association which was founded in 1970 to provide a forum for the representation of African-American interests. It seeks to promote research on black peoples, to improve communication amongst black anthropologists and to involve local peoples in all stages of anthropological research and the dissemination of its results. It publishes the journal *Transforming Anthropology* (*see 2.9.1*).

Association of Social Anthropologists (ASA)
Enquiries c/o Audrey Dougall, Dept of Social Anthropology, University of Durham, 43 Old Elvet, Durham, DH1 3HN, UK
Email: Audrey.Dougall@durham.ac.uk
Web: <les1.man.ac.uk/asa/>

The ASA was founded in 1946 to promote the study and teaching of social anthropology. It regularly supports conferences and has an active publications programme which includes: monographs, the *Annals of the ASA*, a *Guide to University Departments in the UK and Commonwealth*, an annual report on each of the UK Anthropology Departments and a directory of members.

International Union of Anthropological and Ethnological Sciences (IUAES)
Office of the Secretary-General, IUAS, Faculty of Health Studies, University of Wales, Bangor, Gwynedd, LL57 2EF, UK
Tel.: +44 (0)1248 382000
Fax. +44 (0)1248 355830
Web: <lucy.ukc.ac.uk/IUAES/>

IUAES is a world organization of social and physical anthropologists which was originally established in 1948. It aims to facilitate research and communication among scholars worldwide and holds international congresses every five years to act as forums of discussion for the dissemination of research. The organization also regularly establishes commissions to work on areas of anthropological interest. Recent examples include: theoretical anthropology and the anthropology of women.

National Anthropological Archives / Human Studies Film Archive
National Museum of Natural History, Smithsonian Institution, 10th Street and Constitution Avenue, NW, Washington, DC 20560–0152, USA
Tel: +1 202 357 1976
Fax: +1 202 633 8049
Email: naa@nmnh.si.edu
Web: <www.nmnh.si.edu/naa/>

The National Anthropological Archives collects and preserves historical and contemporary anthropological materials that document the world's cultures and the history of the discipline. Its collections represent the four fields of anthropology: ethnology, linguistics, archaeology and physical anthropology. Manuscripts, fieldnotes, correspondence, photographs, maps, sound recordings, film and video created by Smithsonian anthropologists and other pre-eminent scholars are all represented within the collections.

The Royal Anthropological Institute (RAI)
50 Fitzroy Street, London W1P 5HS, UK
Tel: +44 (0)20 7387 0455
Fax: +44 (0)20 7383 4235
Email: rai@cix.compulink.co.uk
Web: <rai.anthropology.org.uk>

Originally established in 1843, the RAI promotes scholarship in all fields of social and physical anthropology. It publishes several leading journals (*Anthropology Today* and *Journal of the Royal Anthropological Institute, see 2.9.1*), has an extensive photographic collection and film lending library, organizes lectures and provides trust funds for research.

The Société d'Ethnologie Française
Musée National des Arts et Traditions Populaires, 6, Avenue du Mahatma Gandhi, 75116 Paris, France
Tel: +33 01 44 17 60 50
Fax: +33 01 44 17 60 60
Email: sef.atp@culture.fr
Web: <www.culture.fr/sef/s_e_f/ac_sef.htm>

Founded to further the social anthropological study of the French cultural domain, this body organizes conferences and training and publishes the journal *Ethnologie Française* which is a good source of information on ethnographies of francophone Africa and French language book reviews.

Society for the Anthropology of Work
c/o American Anthropological Association, 4350 North Fairfax Drive, Suite 640, Arlington, VA 22203–1, USA
Tel: +1 703 528 1902
Fax: +1 703 528 3546
Web: <www.aaanet.org/saw/index.htm>

A specialist subgroup of the American Anthropological Association which is concerned with the study of work from socio-cultural, biological, linguistic and applied anthropological perspectives. Members receive its quarterly publication *Anthropology of Work Review* which publishes articles, summaries of research and book reviews relating to the field.

Society for Cultural Anthropology
C/o American Anthropological Association, 4350 North Fairfax Drive, Suite 640, Arlington, VA 22203–1, USA
Tel: +1 703 528 1902
Fax: +1 703 528 3546
Web: <www.aaanet.org/sca/index.htm>

A section of the American Anthropological Association which is concerned with the analysis of cultural and social interaction. It sponsors the leading journal *Cultural Anthropology* (*see 2.9.1*) and organizes regular conferences and workshops.

The Wenner-Gren Foundation for Anthropological Research
220 Fifth Avenue, 16th Floor, New York, NY 10001–7708, USA
Tel: +1 212 683 5000
Fax: +1 212 683 9151
Web: <www.wennergren.org>

This is a private foundation which supports research in all fields of anthropology. It was created in 1941 as the Viking Fund by Axel Wenner-Gren. Its Website provides basic information on current trustees and how to apply for grants.

2.14.2 Applied Anthropology

Anthropology in Action
c/o Pam Groocock, 17 Marlborough Mansions, Cannon Hill, London, NW6 1JR, UK
Email: 106347.167@compuserve.com
Web: <lucy.ukc.ac.uk/Anthaction>

Previously known as the British Association for Social Anthropology in Policy and Practice, Anthropology in Action is a network of applied anthropologists concerned with social policy, health and community work. It publishes the journal *Anthropology in Action* (*see 2.9.2*) as well as organizing regular conferences and training events.

Centre for Learning and Teaching – Sociology, Anthropology and Politics (C–SAP)
The University of Birmingham, Edgbaston, Birmingham, B15 2TT, UK
Tel: + 44 (0)121 414 6063
Fax: +44 (0)121 414 6061
Email: s.a.wright@bham.ac.uk
Web: <www.c-sap.bham.ac.uk>

The Centre is one of 24 subject centres within the Learning and Teaching Support Network, funded by the UK Funding Councils for Higher Education. It aims to support the sharing of innovative practice in learning and teaching and, in particular, to encourage and support the use of communications and information technology.

Culture and Agriculture
c/o American Anthropological Association, 4350 North Fairfax Drive, Suite 640, Arlington, VA 22203–1, USA
Tel: +1 703 528 1902
Fax: +1 703 528 3546
Web: <csbs3.utsa.edu/culture&agriculture/index.htm>

Founded in 1976, membership of this group is open to all members of the American Anthropological Association who are interested in the study of agrarian systems, lifestyles and development. The group publishes the *Culture and Agriculture* journal, *see 2.9.3.*

Institute for Development Anthropology
99 Collier Street, Suite 302, PO Box 2207, Binghamton, NY 13902, USA
Tel: +1 607–772 6244
Fax: +1 607 773 8993
Email: devanth@binghamton.edu
Web: <www.devanth.org/>

This non-partisan body was founded in 1976 and specializes in international development issues. In particular, it promotes environmentally sustainable programmes and gender equality. Support is given to training applied anthropologists and it publishes the journal *Development Anthropologist* which regularly prints articles and reviews on specific development projects.

National Association for the Practice of Anthropology (NAPA)
c/o American Anthropological Association, 4350 North Fairfax Drive, Suite 640, Arlington, VA 22203–1, USA
Tel: +1 703 528 1902
Fax: +1 703 528 3546
Web: <www.aaanet.org/napa/index.htm>

NAPA is a specialist section of the American Anthropological Association and membership is restricted to AAA members. It was founded in 1983 to promote the interests of practising anthropologists who are usually defined as individuals employed in non-academic positions including local government, international organizations and community development programmes. It organizes regular training workshops and supports the publication of a *Directory of Professional Anthropologists*, *see 2.5.2*.

Society for Applied Anthropology (SfAA)
PO Box 24083, Oklahoma City, OK 73124, USA
Tel: +1 405 843 5113
Fax: +1 405 843 8553
Email: info@sfaa.net
Web: <www.sfaa.net>

SfAA was founded in 1941 and supports the work of applied anthropologists in a wide range of settings including: government, business and voluntary organizations. Its major publications include the journals: *Human Organization* and *Practising Anthropology*, *see 2.9.2*.

2.14.3 Area Studies

African Studies Association
Rutgers University, Douglass Campus, 132 George Street, New Brunswick, NJ 08901–1400, USA
Tel.: +1 732 932 8173
Fax: +1 732 932 3394
Email: callASA@rci.rutgers.edu
Web: <www.africanstudies.org/>

The African Studies Association was established in 1957 to facilitate communication amongst scholars concerned with all aspects of African affairs, including politics, sociology, economics and anthropology. Of particular interest are its publications which include: *African Studies Review*, a multi-disciplinary journal which appears three times annually and publishes research and book reviews which may be of interest to anthropologists.

Association for Africanist Anthropology
c/o American Anthropological Association, 4350 North Fairfax Drive, Suite 640, Arlington, VA 22203–1, USA
Tel: +1 703 528 1902
Fax: +1 703 528 3546
Web: <www.unc.edu/~mlambert/afaa>

A subgrouping of the American Anthropological Association which seeks to promote the anthropological study of Africa and to encourage collaboration with scholars in the region in order to develop a more 'African based perspective'.

Association for Asian Studies (AAS)
1021 East Huron Street, Ann Arbor, Michigan 48104, USA
Tel: +1 734 665 2490
Fax: +1 734 665 3801
Email: members@aasianst.org
Web: <www.aasianst.org/aboutaas.htm>

The AAS is a scholarly society, founded in 1941, which aims to promote the study and exchange of information on the political, social and economic aspects of East, South and South East Asia. Its main publication is the *Journal of Asian Studies* (*see 2.9.3*). It also regularly produces monographs and organizes conferences on issues of value to anthropologists.

Association of Latino and Latina Anthropologists
c/o American Anthropological Association, 4350 North Fairfax Drive, Suite 640, Arlington, VA 22203–1, USA
Tel: +1 703 528 1902
Fax: +1 703 528 3546
Web: <www.monterey.edu/academic/centers/sbsc/ALLA/index.html>

This is a special interest group of the American Anthropological Association which acts as a forum for support and the exchange of information between researchers who are interested in the anthropological study of Latino communities, or who are members of that community themselves.

International African Institute
School of Oriental and African Studies (SOAS), Thornhaugh Street, Russell Square, London, WC1H OXG, UK
Tel: +44 (0)20 7898 4420
Fax: +44 (0)20 7898 4419
Email: iai@soas.ac.uk
Web: <193.128.6.150/iai/mainpage.html>

Founded in 1926, this organization seeks to facilitate scholarly communication amongst Africanists. It is particularly notable for its publications programme which includes the monograph series, *Classics in African Anthropology*, a collection of famous ethnographic studies of the region. It also produces the quarterly journal *Africa* which publishes articles and book reviews on all aspects of African society and the *Africa Bibliography*, *see 2.10.3*.

Latin American Studies Association
946 William Pitt Union, University of Pittsburgh, Pittsburgh, PA 15260, USA
Tel: +44 412 648 7929
Fax: +44 412 624 7145
Email: lasa@pitt.edu
Web: <lasa.international.pitt.edu/>

This is the largest professional association for scholars interested in research into all aspects of Latin American study. It regularly organizes congresses and publishes the *Latin American Research Review* which contains articles relevant to the politics, economics, sociology and anthropology of Latin America, including many ethnographies which are of value to anthropologists. Other activities include the production of lists of relevant courses in North American universities.

Society for the Anthropology of Europe
c/o American Anthropological Association, 4350 North Fairfax Drive, Suite 640, Arlington, VA 22203–1, USA
Tel: +1 703 528 1902
Fax: +1 703 528 3546
Web: <www2.h-net.msu.edu/~sae/sae/>

A special interest group of the American Anthropological Association which was established in 1986 to foster communication amongst researchers engaged in the anthropological study of Europe. Its publications include regular newsletters and a membership directory. *See also* 2.5.3.

2.14.4 Medical anthropology

Society for Medical Anthropology
c/o American Anthropological Association, 4350 North Fairfax Drive, Suite 640, Arlington, VA 22203–1, USA
Tel: +1 703 528 1902
Fax: +1 703 528 3546
Web: <www.cudenver.edu/public/sma/>

The Society for Medical Anthropology is a subsection of the American Anthropological Association which was established in 1971 to promote research into the anthropological study of illness, health care and disease. It publishes the journal *Medical Anthropology Quarterly (see 2.9.4)* and has compiled directories of educational programmes related to the field.

2.14.5 Psychological anthropology

c/o American Anthropological Association, 4350 North Fairfax Drive, Suite 640, Arlington, VA 22203–1, USA
Tel: +1 703 528 1902
Fax: +1 703 528 3546
Web: <www.aaanet.org/spa/index.htm>

A leading organization in the study of the interaction between psychology, society and culture, this group is also a subsection of the American Anthropological Association. Its membership includes anthropologists and practising developmental psychologists and psychiatrists. Its main publication is the quarterly journal *Ethos*, *see 2.9.5*.

2.14.6 Urban anthropology

Society for Urban, National and Transnational/Global Anthropology (SUNTA)
c/o American Anthropological Association, 4350 North Fairfax Drive, Suite 640, Arlington, VA 22203–1, USA
Tel: +1 703 528 1902
Fax: +1 703 528 3546
Web: <www.aaanet.org/sunta>

SUNTA is a specialist section of the American Anthropological Association (AAA). It incorporates the former *Society for Urban Anthropology*. Its aim is to promote the anthropological study of all forms, processes and institutions of urban social life and to attempt to relate them to national and global systems. It is noted for its publications which include the journal *City and Society* (*see 2.9.6*). The Website also provides information on its electronic mailing list. Membership is open to all AAA members.

2.14.7 Visual anthropology

Royal Anthropological Institute, see 2.14.1.

National Anthropology Archives, see 2.14.1.

European Association of Social Anthropologists Visual Anthropology Network
Beate Engelbrecht, IWF, Nonnenstieg 72, D-37075 Göttingen, Germany
Tel. +49 551 5024 225
Fax: +49 551 5024 400
Email: <beate.engelbrecht@iwf.gwdg.de>

The Association aims to cover all aspects of visual anthropology, including photography, ethnographic film and multimedia. It was created in 1996 and serves as a forum for the communication of information between researchers. It also organizes conferences, training days and publishes resource guides.

Nordic Anthropological Film Association (NAFA)
NAFA Archive, c/o Ethnographic museum, Frederiks gate 2, N-0164 Oslo, Norway
Tel: +47 228 59300, +47 228 59964
Fax: +47 228 59960

An organization for cooperation among visual anthropologists from both within and outside the Nordic countries which has been active since the 1970s. It regularly organizes conferences and produces a quarterly newsletter called *NAFA-Network* which provides information on current research and events. It is creating an archive of anthropological films for use in teaching and research which is currently housed at the Ethnographic Museum in Oslo.

Society for Visual Anthropology
c/o American Anthropological Association, 4350 North Fairfax Drive, Suite 640, Arlington, VA 22203–1, USA
Tel: +1 703 528 1902
Fax: +1 703 528 3546
Web: <www.der.org/sva>

The Society for Visual Anthropology was established in 1984 as a subgroup of the American Anthropological Association in order to promote the use of visual and audio media in anthropological study. It regularly publishes handbooks and ethnographic film listings (*see* 2.3.7), in addition to its journal *Visual Anthropology Review* (*see* 2.9.7).

▶ REFERENCES

Keesing, Roger, M. (1988) *Cultural Anthropology: a Contemporary Perspective,* 3rd ed., London: Harcourt Brace College.

La Fontaine, J. S. (1985) *What is Social Anthropology?* London: Arnold.

Wolf, Eric (1980) 'They Divide and Subdivide and Call it Anthropology', in *New York Times,* 30 November, sec. 4: 9.

3 Sociology

Helen Fallon

▶ 3.1 NATURE AND SCOPE OF SOCIOLOGY

Sociology is concerned with the basic nature of human society and the ways in which people are organized into groups, classes, communities and institutions. The term has two stems – the Latin socius (companion) and the Greek logos (study of) (Abercrombie, Hill and Turner, 2000). It is the task of sociology to explore how institutionalized social forms are established and developed and how these influence people. These social forms include the family, peer group, religious institutions and economic, political and legal structures. In the context of these forms sociology has to explain social change and where the individual fits in society.

The term 'sociologie' was first used in 1824 by Auguste Comte (1798–1857). However, the study of society can be traced back to the writings of Plato and Aristotle in Greek philosophy, Ibn Khaldun in Islamic jurisprudence and the later European philosophers. They discussed much of the subject matter of sociology in philosophical, political and theological contexts. Indeed, sociology was not recognized as a discipline in its own right until the end of the nineteenth century.

The beginning of modern sociology lies in the philosophy and science of the eighteenth century period known as the 'Enlightenment'. The old order of agriculture and religion made way for the industrial revolution and an intellectual revolution which brought about a collapse of the feudal order and a new vision of society. The French revolution of 1789 was very much part of this.

Auguste Comte grew up in the aftermath of the French revolution, and was greatly influenced by it. He believed that the human world could be studied in exactly the same ways as the non-human world, and held that, just as observation and experiment had enabled men like Newton to discover the laws governing the physical world, so men like himself would be able to discover the laws governing the social world. This view came to be known as 'positivism' and was developed further by Emile Durkheim (1858–1917), one of sociology's founding fathers.

While the earliest sociologists were European, many developments took place in the United States particularly in the latter half of the nineteenth century. A society of high-speed change and capitalist expansion, America at the turn of the century was ripe for sociological inquiry. The first sociology course in the US was taught at Yale in 1875, while the first department of sociology was established by Albion Small in 1893 at the University of Chicago. With this came the beginning of the only major sociological journal of the time, the *American Journal of Sociology* and the establishment of the American Sociological Society (later the American Sociological Association) in 1905. Although the Chicago School, with its commitment to direct fieldwork and empirical study, dominated North American sociology during the first four decades of the twentieth century, in the 1940s the centre of sociological research in the United States shifted to Harvard and Columbia.

Sociological societies had been formed in England in 1903 and France in 1894. In 1907 the first British Chair in sociology was established at the London School of Economics. These developments aside, not a great deal happened in the world of sociology until after World War II, when there was a strong revival of interest in the subject throughout Europe. In the mid 1960s sociology was offered by the new British universities such as Lancaster, York, Essex and Kent. The discipline was coming of age.

The broadest of the social science disciplines, sociology overlaps with many other subjects including law, economics, education, psychology, anthropology and criminology. Increasing specialization in the second half of the twentieth century has led to more subfields including the sociology of medicine, the environment and gender. Throughout its history, sociology has been closely allied to social reform movements. Today it is increasingly being used to study a variety of social issues including drug abuse, genetic engineering and environmental degradation. Sociologists are employed across a wide range of work areas including government, industry, social services and various commercial and non-commercial support organizations.

Those interested in learning more about the development of sociology, and particularly American sociology, during the first half of the twentieth century should consult Lee Braude's essay, 'The Emergence of Sociology' (*Choice* October, 1994, 237–48). Lewis Coser's *Masters of Sociological Thought*, 2nd ed., (New York: Harcourt Brace Jovanovich, 1977) provides an introduction to the early theorists. A useful Website which draws on Coser's work is *the Dead Sociologist's Index* see *section 3.8*.

This chapter provides an evaluative guide to selected sociological resources, reflecting established and emergent subfields within the discipline.

▶ 3.2 ANNUALS

Reviews of research are particularly useful for synthesizing the literature of a discipline. Because of its cross-disciplinary nature, topical reviews of interest to sociologists can be found in a variety of annual publications including the *Annual Review of Psychology* (see 4.2) and the *Annual Review of Anthropology* (see 2.2).

3.2.1 General

(a) Print

The well-established *Annual Review of Sociology* (ISSN 0360 0572) (Palo Alto, CA: Annual Reviews, 1975–) gives original critical reviews of the significant literature and current developments in sociology. Each volume contains up to 20 articles organized under broad subject categories. Essays are written by sociologists and other social scientists, a fact which reflects the increasingly interdisciplinary nature of sociological research. Major topics are reconsidered for possible inclusion every five years. Recent essays have covered feminist theory and sociology, the family-responsive workplace, and the women's movements in the Third World. Authors summarize past and current literature on a topic, identifying aspects of the subject that merit further consideration by researchers. Each article is supplemented by an extensive bibliography. A subject index and cumulative indexes of authors and titles are included. Early volumes encountered some criticism for having an American bias, however the scope has broadened considerably. The work provides a useful addition to the literature of sociology, and is particularly useful for covering developments outside one's area of specialization.

Annual Editions: Sociology, 29th ed., edited by Kurt Finsterbusch is part of the McGraw-Hill Annual Editions series (Guilford, CT: Dushkin/McGraw-Hill, 2000). This volume brings together selected articles from magazines, newspapers and journals. Articles are topical, covering issues such as social inequality, gender, family, crime and cultural change. Finsterbusch is also editor of *Annual Editions: Social Problems*, 29th ed., (Guilford, CT: Dushkin/McGraw-Hill, 2001) which brings together articles from a variety of sources including: *American Educator, Nation, The Economist, Time* and *World Watch*. It also includes chapters from books which deal with social problems.

(b) Electronic

The full-text of the *Annual Review of Sociology* is now available on the World Wide Web from 1996 forward and tables of contents from 1984 to 1995. Subscribers can order and download articles. Abstracts and tables of contents are available free of charge. Further information is available at <soc.AnnualReviews.org>. The full text of volumes from 1975–1994 is also available on subscription via JSTOR (Journal STORage) <www.jstor.ac.uk>.

3.2.2 Ageing

Annual Review of Gerontology and Geriatrics (ISSN 0198–8794) (New York: Springer, 1980–). These volumes bring together the latest research on issues relating to ageing, death and dying. Articles are written by a variety of experts in the field. Volume 20 (2000) includes essays on medical decision-making toward the end of life; measuring the quality of medical care for dying persons and their families; friendship at the end of life; and clinical aspects of end-of-life care.

Annual Editions: Ageing, 13th ed., edited by Harold Cox (Guilford, CT: Dushkin/McGraw-Hill, 2000) is part of the McGraw-Hill Annual Editions series which aims to provide current, first-rate educational information in a range of subject areas. This series is appropriate for students, researchers and professionals in the field. Articles are drawn from a variety of magazine sources. The 13th edition of this title includes an article on confronting the boundaries of ageing from *American Scientist,* an article from *News & World Report* on how global ageing will challenge the world's economic wellbeing and an article on coping with ageing from *Psychology Today*. In all, 41 articles are included. There is an alphabetical subject index and two pages listing links to useful Websites.

3.2.3 Communication and media

Until relatively recently, there was no encyclopaedic treatment of communication. Therefore yearbooks, along with journals, have been very important for keeping people up to date with developments in the field. *Annual Editions: Mass Media*, 7th ed., edited by Joan Gorham (Guilford, CT: Dushkin/McGraw-Hill, 2000) is a compilation of carefully selected mass-media-related articles from magazines, newspapers and journals. See also the *Mass Communications Review Yearbook* (London: Sage in cooperation with the Center for Research in Public Communication, University of Maryland, 1980–1987). Although no longer published, this title may be of interest to those wishing to know about the most interesting and important work going on during the period in which it was produced. The yearbook contained some original articles in the field of mass communications and reprints of significant journal articles.

The *Communication Yearbook* (Newbury Park, CA: Sage, 1977–) is sponsored by the International Communication Association (ICA). Volumes 1 to 18 of this series offered a mix of essays, commentaries and research reports. With volume 19 the focus narrowed to that of a review series, presenting state-of-the-art literature reviews included as part of essays providing a comprehensive synthesis of a topic. The emphasis is on North American literature. Author and subject indexes are provided. This is a useful resource for students and researchers.

3.2.4 Politics and power

The *Annual Review of Political Science* edited by Nelson Polsby (Palo Alto, CA: Annual Reviews, 1998–) brings together essays on themes such as social capital and politics, identity politics and communication and opinion. The full-text is available electronically on subscription. Table of contents and abstracts are available free of charge from the Website: <polisci.annualreviews.org>.

▶ 3.3 BIBLIOGRAPHIES

Useful for both collection development purposes and as an excellent starting point for research on a topic, the range of bibliographies of potential interest to sociologists is enormous. This list concentrates on a few of the major bibliographies.

3.3.1 General

(a) Print

International Bibliography of Sociology. See section 3.10.1.
Bibliographies and Indexes in Sociology (Westport, CT: Greenwood Press, 1984–). Each volume in this really useful series provides a brief overview of the topic, an extensive annotated bibliography which covers books, dissertations and journal articles, and author and subject indexes. Recent titles in this series include: *Pro-Choice/Pro-Life Issues in the 1990s: An Annotated Selected Bibliography* by Richard P. Fitzsimmons and Joan Diana (Westport, CT: Greenwood Press, 1996); and *Homelessness in America, 1893–1992: An Annotated Bibliography* compiled by Rod Van Whitlock, Bernard Lubin and Jean R. Sailors (Westport, CT: Greenwood Press, 1994). Greenwood Press *Bibliographies and Indexes in Religious Studies* will also be of interest to those doing sociological research. Volumes in that series include: *Feminism and Christian Tradition: Annotated Bibliography and Critical Introduction to the Literature* by Mary Paula Walsh (Westport, CT: Greenwood Press, 1999); and *Jehovah's Witnesses: a Comprehensive and Selectively Annotated Bibliography* by Gerry Bergman (Westport, CT: Greenwood Press, 1999). A complete list of titles in the series can be accessed from the Greenwood Press homepage at <info.greenwood.com>.

Useful bibliographies for sociologists are also produced by Garland Press in their series *Garland Bibliographies of Modern Critics and Critical Schools, Garland Reference Library of the Social Sciences* including: *The Sociology of Mental Illness: an annotated Bibliography* by Richard R. Thomas (New York: Garland, 1989) which covers references from the

1970s and 1980s to books, book chapters and articles and provides an excellent overview of the topic. Another useful series is *Contemporary Social Issues* (Santa Cruz, CA: Reference and Research Service, 1986–). Bibliographies in this series bring together the popular and scholarly literature on a subject. Topics covered include: AIDS, homelessness, pornography and censorship, reproductive rights and domestic violence. Four bibliographies are issued per year. These are primarily geared towards undergraduate students. Another product of the same organization, *Social Theory: a Bibliographic Series* (Santa Cruz, CA: Reference and Research Service, 1986–), provides inexpensive access to the major works by and about important traditional and contemporary theorists including: Lukacs, Arendt, Derrida, Foucault, Lacan, Weber, De Beauvoir and Parsons. Bibliographies are generally between 50 and 70 pages in length and include approximately 500 references to books, articles, reviews and other articles by and about theorists. Organized into four sections, the first lists books written by the particular theorist, the second articles, while sections three and four list works about the theorist. A wide range of theoretical and ideological positions is covered.

Also of interest is *Sociology, Anthropology, and Development: an Annotated Bibliography of World Bank Publications 1975–1993* compiled by Michael M. Cernea, with April L. Adams (Washington, DC: World Bank, 1994). Annotations are grouped into several main sections with each publication listed once. An index of titles, authors, and geographic locations and populations is included.

(b) Electronic

The Bibliography of the United Nations Centre for Regional Development <www.virtualref.com/uncrd> provides extensive listings of journal articles, books, book chapters, working papers and conference papers. It is possible to search by author, subject or subject classification. Topics of interest to sociologists include poverty, homelessness, population, housing and other social areas.

3.3.2 Ageing

The Greenwood series *Bibliographies and Indexes in Gerontology* has a number of titles of interest to those involved in researching the sociology of ageing. These include: Thomas O. Blank's *Topics in Gerontology: Selected Annotated Bibliography* (Westport, CT: Greenwood Press, 1993) which presents essays and annotated bibliographies on topics such as the history of gerontology, death and dying, and health-care decision-making among the elderly. Books, book chapters, articles and conference proceedings are included. Substantial abstracts accompany entries and author and subject indexes are provided. In the same series Jean M. Coyle has compiled a bibliography *Families and Ageing: a Selected, Annotated Bibliography* (Westport, CT: Greenwood, 1991), which offers more than 700 citations covering books, articles, dissertations and other material from the period 1980 to 1990. Coyle also compiled *Women and Ageing: a Selected Annotated Bibliography* (Westport, CT: Greenwood, 1989) which offers over 600 annotated references, focusing on middle-aged and older women.

3.3.3 Communication and media

Greenwood Publishing Group's series *Bibliographies and Indexes in Mass Media and Communications* produce a number of titles relating to mass communications including: *Press Freedom and Development: a Research Guide and Selected Bibliography* by Clement E. Asante (Westport, CT: Greenwood Press, 1997); *Tabloid Journalism: an Annotated Bibliography of English Language Sources* by Gerard S. Greenberg (Westport, CT: Greenwood Press, 1996); and a *Bibliography of Cuban Mass Communication* by John A. Lent, (Westport, CT: Greenwood Press, 1992).

Mass Media: From Marconi to MTV compiled by Gerard V. Flannery (New York: University Press of America, 1989) brings together a select bibliography *of New York Times* Sunday magazine articles on communication covering the period 1900 to 1988. The bibliography is arranged by decades and there are author and subject indexes.

Eleanor Blum and Frances Coins Wilhoit compiled *Mass Media Bibliography: an Annotated Guide to Books and Journals for Research and Reference* (Urbana, IL: University of Illinois Press, 1990). The successor to the 1972 and 1980 editions of *Basic Books in the Mass Media*, this volume contains material up to and including 1987. Divided into eight sections, the first five of these are arranged by subject and cover general communications, broadcasting media, print media, film and advertising. This is followed by chapters detailing bibliographies, directories and handbooks, and journals and indexes in the area of mass media. Entries are annotated and there are author, title and subject indexes. This is a useful resource for students and researchers and those involved in collection development.

Media in Africa and Africa in the media: an Annotated Bibliography edited by Gretchen Walsh (Oxford: Hans Zell, 2000) is a bibliography of the literature on mass communication and the press in Africa and images of Africa in the media.

3.3.4 Cultural theory

The *Bibliography of Postmodernism and Critical Theory* <www.iath.virginia.edu/pmc/bibliography.html> is part of the Website of the electronic journal *Postmodern Culture*, published by Johns Hopkins University Press with support from the University of Virginia and Vassar College. It is possible to search the bibliography by author, title, keyword or contributor. Entries are annotated.

3.3.5 Family

Parenting: An Annotated Bibliography edited by Sandra Feinberg, Barbara Jordan and Michel Lauer-Bader (Lanham, MD: Scarecrow Press, 1995) provides annotated entries covering the various stages of parenting, from pregnancy and childbirth through the parenting of adult children. Entries cover topics such as: child development; health and safety; mental and physical disabilities; and books aimed at special groups such as teen parents and single parents. *Mothers and Mothering: an Annotated Feminist Bibliography* by Penelope Dixon (New York: Garland, 1991) gives references to over 300 books related to mothering. These are arranged in categories that correspond to strands of feminist thought, such as lesbian and black mothers and reproductive issues.

The Influence of the Family: a Review and Annotated Bibliography of Socialization, Ethnicity and Delinquency, 1975–1986 by Alan C. Acock and Jeffrey M. Clair (New York: Garland, 1986) is divided into three major sections: family influence, ethnicity and delinquency. Each section begins with an introductory chapter noting major research topics and trends. Publications within each section are arranged alphabetically by author. Coverage is from 1975 and source material is from the United States.

3.3.6 Gender

(a) Print

The Greenwood Publishing Series *Bibliographies and Indexes in Women's Studies* now has quite an extensive range of titles which will be of interest to sociologists. These include: *Women in Global Migration, 1945–2000: a Comprehensive Multidisciplinary Bibliography* (Westport, CT: Greenwood Press, 2000) by Eleanore O. Hofstett; and *Women and Mass Communications in the 90s: an International, Annotated Bibliography* (Westport, CT: Greenwood Press, 1999) by John A. Lent, which annotates books, periodicals, dissertations and conference papers. *Women in Japanese Society: an Annotated Bibliography of Selected English Language Materials* by Kristina Ruth Huber and Kathy Sparling (Westport, CT: Greenwood Press, 1992) contains more than 2300 annotated entries on the lives of women in Japan. *Sexual Harassment: a Selected, Annotated Bibliography* (Westport, CT: Greenwood Press, 1995) by Lynda Jones Hartel and Helena M. VonVille covers topics such as the sexual harassment of university students. Physical, psychological and economic consequences of sexual harassment and workplace strategies for dealing with sexual harassment are covered. Entries are briefly annotated.

Now in its second edition, *The New Men's Studies: a Selected and Annotated Interdisciplinary Bibliography* edited by Eugene R. August (Littleton, CO: Libraries Unlimited, 1994) gives some 1000 entries detailing books on subjects such as men's health, fathers, war and feminism. Entries describe book content and political stance. Author/title and subject indexes are included.

Volume nine in the *Research Guides in Military Studies Series* is *Women in the United States Military, 1901–1995: a Research Guide and Annotated Bibliography* compiled by Vicki L. Friedl (Westport, CT: Greenwood Press, 1996) which gives 850 references covering the period from 1901 until the Gulf War. Listed are interviews in journals, diaries, biographies, histories and other research work. Entries are annotated. Archival resources, women's military organizations, a chronology of women's services and military Webpages, are listed in appendices.

Women: a Selective Bibliography, 1988–1999 (Femmes, Bibliographie Sélective, 1988–1998) (Geneva: United Nations Library, 2000). This publication presents a selection of literature on women that is available in the United Nations libraries at Geneva and New York. The references, covering the period from 1988 up to and including December 1999, are arranged under the broad subject categories of women's rights, economic conditions, women at work, social conditions and women's health.

(b) Electronic

The Web provides a wide range of bibliographies on gender-related topics. The University of Maryland *Women's Studies Database* at <www.inform.umd.edu/WomensStudies> hosts approximately 50 bibliographies. Some of these, such as the *Women and Science Bibliography*, have an embedded search engine and are extremely comprehensive. The *Wisconsin Bibliographies in Women's Studies* at <www.library.wisc.edu/libraries/WomensStudies/bibliogs/biblmain.htm> offers a number of interesting bibliographies on gender-related topics. These include bibliographies on: information technology and women's lives; employment and health; and single parenthood. Most of the bibliographies have been prepared by librarians, women's studies faculty members, graduate students in library and information studies and staff members of the Women's Studies Librarian's Office at the University of Wisconsin.

3.3.7 Law

Now in its second edition, *The Sociology of Law: a Bibliography of Theoretical Literature* by A. Javier Trevino (New York: Edwin Mellen

Press, 1998) does not aim to be comprehensive. Rather, a relatively small number of the best and most enduring articles within the sociology of law are presented. The bibliography is organized around themes that place the theoretical literature of the sociology of law in both historical and comparative perspective. This is an extremely useful source for those involved in this branch of sociology.

3.3.8 Race and ethnicity

(a) Print

Race and Crime: an Annotated Bibliography compiled by Katheryn K. Russell, et al. (Westport, CT: Greenwood Press, 2000) is part of the *Garland Bibliographies and Indexes in Ethnic Studies* series. This volume covers the topic of race and crime in the United States from 1950–1999. It is divided into categories encompassing works on individual racial groups including American Indians, Asian Americans and Hispanics and multi-racial groups. There are author and subject indexes and a list of useful Web resources. Other bibliographies in the series can be identified from the Website at <info.greenwood.com/series/series.html>.

Discrimination and Prejudice: an Annotated Bibliography by Halford H. Fairchild et al (San Diego, CA: Westerfield Enterprises, 1992) offers over 4000 references to books, articles, dissertations and US government documents on the subject of prejudice and discrimination. Divided into five parts – African Americans; American Indians; Asian Americans; Hispanic Americans; and multi-ethnic groups – topics such as civil rights, education, health and public services are covered. References are briefly annotated. Broader in coverage is Meyer Weinberg's *World Racism and Related Inhumanities: a Country-by-Country Bibliography* (Wesport, CT: Greenwood Press, 1992) which cites over 12 000 books, articles and dissertations published worldwide on racism and related topics. Over 135 countries are included.

(b) Electronic

Annotated Bibliography of Psychology and Racism <www.apa.org/pi/oema/racebib/racebib.html>. Hosted by the American Psychological Association and compiled by Naijean Bernard et al, this bibliography focuses primarily on the published psychological literature and to a lesser extent on the published medical literature between 1974 and 1996. Divided into three sections: the first deals with the psychology of racism; the second gives details of articles on racism in psychology; and the third focuses on the psychology of anti-racism. Books, book chapters and journal articles are included. Entries are annotated. While there are no indexes, arrangement is alphabetical by author's name within each section and is straightforward to follow. This is a comprehensive and useful source for researchers.

3.3.9 Religion

Anthony J. Blasi and Michael W. Cuneo's *The Sociology of Religion: an Organizational Bibliography* (New York: Garland, 1990) is designed to complement their earlier bibliography, *Issues in the Sociology of Religion* (New York: Garland, 1986) which indexed the literature in the sociology of religion up to and including 1984. Instead of a topic arrangement this bibliography organizes entries by the names of specific religious traditions and organizations. Journal articles, books, theses, dissertations and anthologies in English or translated into English are included. Over 3000 entries are provided. Divided into five parts: the first covers the Asian traditions; the second gives sociological accounts of the Jewish, Hebrew and Islamic traditions; the third covers early Christianity; the fourth includes nine chapters on the post-Reformation Christian traditions; while the final part looks at newly evolving religions. Subject and author indexes are provided and some references are briefly annotated. Coverage is until 1990.

3.3.10 Social problems and social class

(a) Print

Homelessness: an Annotated Bibliography by James M. Henslin (New York: Garland, 1993) is part of the *Garland Reference Library of Social Sciences*. The work is in two volumes, the first of which is a straightforward annotated bibliography arranged by author. The second volume is arranged by subject. Entries in the first volume are annotated. These annotations are not repeated in the subject volume. This is a useful resource listing books, book chapters, newspaper articles, reports and US government publications. *Sociology of Poverty in the United States: an Annotated Bibliography* compiled by H. Paul Chalfant (Westport, CT: Greenwood Press, 1985) will be of use to those looking for historical material relating to the US.

(b) Electronic

The Public Policy Bibliography <spiu.gcal.ac.uk/policybib.html> produced by the Scottish Poverty Information Unit, gives a listing of some 20 books and journal articles on the topic of poverty. Most of these date from the late eighties and early nineties. Oslo University produces a useful series of

Web-based bibliographies on topics related to poverty at: <www.uio.no/~danbanik/povertybibliography.htm>. These include *Freedom and Liberty*, *Hunger and Ethics*, *Agriculture and Land Reforms* and *Poverty in India*. Working papers, journal articles and books are included. The entries are not annotated but it is a very comprehensive source and will prove a useful starting point for research. Albert Benschop at the Department of Sociology, University of Amsterdam, has compiled an extensive bibliography of both book and journal articles on the topic of social class at: <www.pscw.uva.nl/sociosite/CLASS/bibA.html>. Journal articles and books are included in this index arranged alphabetically by author's family name. Both Dutch and English citations are included.

3.3.11 Sociologists

(a) Print

Mary Jo Deegan is the editor of *Women in Sociology: a Bio-Bibliographical Sourcebook* (Westport, CT: Greenwood Press, 1991). Covering a total of 51 sociologists, all born before 1927, including Hannah Arendt, Harriet Martineau and Jane Addams, this work is arranged alphabetically. Entries are from seven to ten pages in length. They give summaries of achievements, short bibliographies, major themes in the subject's writings, sources for critiques and selective bibliographies of the most important primary and secondary materials. Name and subject indexes are provided.

(b) Electronic

The Durkheim Pages <www.lang.uiuc.edu/durkheim/index.html> offer a wide range of information about Emile Durkheim, including bibliographies of works by and about him. While a few references are to French language material, most are to articles in English.

Bibliography of Works About or Making Reference to the Work of Pierre Bourdieu <www.massey.ac.nz/~NZSRDA/bourdieu/home.htm>. Compiled by Henry Bernard at the University of Massey, New Zealand, the Pierre Bourdieu bibliography is a very comprehensive site, with French and English links to works about and by Bourdieu.

Norbert Elias and Process Sociology <www.usyd.edu.au/su/social/elias.html>. Hosted by the University of Sydney, this site provides links to Internet resources for social scientists working with the ideas of Norbert Elias and process sociology.

George's Page: the Mead Project Website <paradigm.soci.brocku.ca/~lward>. This is a Web-based repository for documents by, about and related to the work of George Herbert Mead, maintained by the

Department of Sociology, Brock University, St. Catherine's, Ontario, Canada.

3.3.12 Work

The Sociology of Work: a Critical Annotated Bibliography by Parvin Ghorayshi (New York: Garland, 1990) fills a bibliographic gap in the field of sociology. It offers a selective, annotated bibliography of books, articles and reports from sociology and related disciplines that relate to the sociology of work. Coverage is from the 1970s to 1989, a period which witnessed the change in focus from the micro problems of the workplace to the macro concerns of the global economy. Entries, many of which are cross-referenced, are consecutively numbered through the work's six chapters. Author and subject indexes are given. Ghorayshi is also the compiler of *Women and Work in Developing Countries: an Annotated Bibliography* (Westport, CT: Greenwood Press, 1994) which is organized geographically – Africa, Asia, Latin American and the Caribbean, and the Middle East – and within these divisions by various topics. A final chapter lists audiovisual resources. Entries are briefly annotated and cover books, articles, reports and dissertations. The book also contains an appendix of women's organizations and research centres and indexes by author, country/region and subject. This is a valuable work for those researching gender and development issues.

Work-Family Research: an Annotated Bibliography by Terri Ann Lilly, Marcie Pitt-Catsouphes and Bradley K. Goggins (Westport, CT: Greenwood Press, 1997) is divided into nine parts, each containing a number of essays on the following topics: women and work; work-family as structural and developmental concepts; work and family roles; work-family experiences among population groups; dependent care; work-family within human resources; time and place; public and private practices and policies; and linkages to corporate strategies and governance.

▶ 3.4 DICTIONARIES

3.4.1 General

Amongst the best short dictionaries of sociology, targeted at those who are new to the discipline is *The Collins Dictionary of Sociology*, 2nd ed., (Glasgow: Harper Collins, 1995) edited by David Jary and Julia Jary. This is an update of the *HarperCollins Dictionary of Sociology* (1991). The emphasis is on history and philosophy with less on recent development, methodology and applied fields. Brief definitions are given at the beginning of each entry. Sometimes these are followed by longer more encyclopaedic entries. Biographical sketches of key figures in sociology and social theory are also presented.

Another useful source for those who are new to the discipline is the *Dictionary of Sociology* edited by Gordon Marshall (Oxford: Oxford University Press, 1998). This is the second edition of the *The Concise Oxford Dictionary of Sociology* published in 1994. It adds more than 150 entries to the previous 2500 entries covering sociological terms, methods and concepts. Brief biographies of major sociologists are given. *The Penguin Dictionary of Sociology*, 4th ed., by N. Abercrombie, S. Hill and B. S. Turner (London: Penguin, 2000) is a good basic dictionary providing definitions of both traditional and contemporary sociological concepts and theories.

Also suitable for the undergraduate and those unfamiliar with the discipline is *The Encyclopedic Dictionary of Sociology* edited by Richard Lachmann (Guilford, CT: Dushkin, 1991) which offers short definitions of more than 1300 topics relating to sociology. *See* and *see also* references are given. Biographical sketches of prominent sociologists are provided and maps, diagrams, charts and tables supplement the text.

Appropriate for more advanced scholars is *A Critical Dictionary of Sociology* by Raymond Boudon and François Bourricaud (Chicago, Ill: University of Chicago Press, 1989). The first edition of this dictionary was published in France in 1982, a second abridged version appeared in 1986. This volume is translated and edited from the 1986 abridged edition. This is not a dictionary in the traditional sense, rather a collection of articles by the authors on a number of sociological concepts and themes. The entries are small essays, complete with bibliographical references, which taken together form a coherent critique of the sociological tradition that synthesizes American, British, French and German contributions. Essays on subjects such as bureaucracy, capitalism, family, suicide and utopia are presented. Discussion is well grounded in classical theory and is illustrated with many examples drawn from major sociological studies. Particularly informative are the sections on classical sociological theorists, such as Marx and Durkheim. Some 131 articles have been reproduced here, representing a cross-section of the best work on Durkheim which has appeared in scholarly journals published in English.

The Blackwell Dictionary of Twentieth-Century Social Thought edited by William Outhwaite and Tom Bottomore (Oxford: Blackwell, 1993) provides approximately 1000 entries that average 500–1000 words. These give an overview of main themes in social thought and their development from the beginning of the century (or sometimes earlier) to the present. Barbara Booth's *Thesaurus of Sociological Indexing Terms*, 4th ed., (San Diego, CA: Sociological Abstracts, 1996) lists the official subject terms used in *Sociological Abstracts*. It is an invaluable resource for thorough subject searching in *Sociological Abstracts* (*see 3.10*).

Allan G. Johnson is editor of the second edition of *The Blackwell Dictionary of Sociology: a User's Guide to Sociological Language* (Oxford: Blackwell, 2000), a book of immense value in the academic library. In an opening essay, Johnson explains the relationship of a discipline's vocabulary to the discipline. Primarily geared towards students, entries describe core sociological concepts. Dictionary entries are usually brief (three to four paragraphs) and include *see also* references. Suggested readings at the end of entries feature classic as well as more contemporary references. Methodological and statistical terminology is included. This new edition provides an additional 75 entries not included in the first edition, as well as an expanded biographical section, extensive revisions and updates, and more thorough cross-referencing. Unusually for an alphabetically arranged dictionary, there is an index to help further in cross-referencing and finding embedded topics and names. The volume concludes with a brief collection of over 150 biographical sketches.

3.4.2 Communication and media

The fourth edition of *A Dictionary of Communication and Media Studies* by James Watson and Anne Hill (London: Arnold, 1997) offers 1300 terms, which represents a 25 per cent expansion over the third edition. It includes many new terms from film studies, telecommunications, news reporting, and other topics related to the social and cultural aspects of communication. Individual subject entries, ranging from 20 to close to 1000 words, provide definitions, historical and theoretical contexts, and references to the professional literature and to other subject entries within the dictionary. Readers interested in short definitions of technical terms for journalism, mass media, or telecommunications would find Richard Weiner's *Webster's New World Dictionary of Media and Communication* (London: Macmillan, 1996) more useful.

3.4.3 Cultural theory

Peter Brooker's *A Concise Glossary of Cultural Theory* (London: Arnold, 1999) is an alphabetically arranged dictionary of key concepts in cultural theory. Entries of approximately one page present cultural theory as an active and continuing set of debates. Topics covered include: fundamentalism, nationalism, postmodernity, deconstruction and materialism. *See* and *See also* references are provided. A bibliography of books on the topic is also given. Clearly written, this glossary is a valuable guide to the changing meanings and issues in cultural studies. *Key Concepts in Cultural theory* edited by Andrew Edgar and Peter Sedgwick (London: Routledge, 1999) opens with an alphabetical list of key concepts. This is followed by a useful essay on the meaning of cultural theory. The main body of the work comprises of short pieces (usually about one page) covering the main concepts. References to further literature on a topic are given at the end of each entry. A bibliography of all texts referred to is included. This work will be particularly useful to those who are new to the discipline.

Though called an encyclopaedia, the *Encyclopaedia of Contemporary British Culture* edited by Peter Childs and Mike Storry (London: Routledge, 1999) is, in fact, a dictionary. Short entries (usually about four to a page) cover topics such as Asian fashions, marriage, performance art, pensioners, structuralism and street selling. More substantial entries are given to topics such as poetry in the 1990s, reggae, Indian communities and literary prizes. Brief biographies of people associated with film, fashion and other culture-related industries are given. There is a subject and person index. *See also* references are provided, together with references to further reading. This is a really useful, straightforward yet comprehensive, guide to contemporary British culture.

3.4.4 Feminism

From its development in the 1960s, women's studies has cut across a variety of academic disciplines including sociology and has begun to carve out for itself new interdisciplinary inquiries. Women's history and role in contemporary society is one of the many areas of interest to sociologists. Useful sources include *A Women's Thesaurus: an Index of Language Used to Describe and Locate Information by and About Women* edited by Mary Ellen S. Capek (New York: Harper & Row, 1997). Between the first (1989) and second edition of Maggie Humm's *Dictionary of Feminist Theory* (New York: Prentice Hall, 1995), feminist theory has grown exponentially. Humm gives general overviews of concepts and explains differences and distinctions within feminism. This is possibly the best scholarly source for defining French and American theory. A useful companion to this volume is *A Concise Glossary of Feminist Theory* by Sonya Andermahr, Terry Lovell and Carol Wolkowitz (London: Arnold, 1997). The authors seek to identify concepts within contemporary feminism (1969 forward) that have structured feminist theory over the past three decades. In addition to a traditional dictionary, Janet K. Boles and Diane Long Hoevel's *Historical Dictionary of Feminism* (Lanham, Md: Scarecrow, 1996) offers an extensive bibliography of books on topics related to the women's movement, including the labour movement and communications.

3.4.5 Gay liberation

Ronald J. Hunt is the compiler of the excellent *Historical Dictionary of the Gay Liberation Movement: Gay Men and the Quest for Social Justice*

(Lanham, Md: Scarecrow, 1999). The coverage is worldwide and chiefly twentieth century (although some earlier people and groups are covered). Besides the dictionary section, which has nearly 150 entries, there is a comprehensive introduction, a list of acronyms and a bibliography.

3.4.6 Medicine

Dictionary of Medical Sociology edited by William C. Cockerham and Ferris J. Ritchey (Westport, CT: Greenwood Press, 1997). Medical sociology has expanded so rapidly that it is now one of the largest specialized areas of sociology. This is the first dictionary on the terminology of the sociology of health and illness. An interesting introductory essay traces the history of medical sociology, from its beginnings in the years following World War II. Short alphabetically arranged entries were selected by reviewing the scholarly literature in medicine, sociology and medical sociology. Three types of term are included – generic terms created by medical sociologists; descriptive terms created by medical sociologists; and terms from related disciplines regularly used by medical sociologists. Extensive citations are given. This work would be valuable for students and researchers of medical sociology and for practitioners and researchers in related fields.

3.4.7 Quotations

Key Quotations in Sociology by Kenneth Thompson (London: Routledge, 1996) draws on key concepts and topics in sociology and aims to provide a core of quotations. Intended primarily as an aid to students writing papers for courses and examinations, entries vary in length from classic single-sentences to substantial passages from works.

3.4.8 Race and ethnicity

The fourth edition of the *Dictionary of Race and Ethnic Relations* by Ellis Cashmore (London: Routledge, 1996) covers topics such as: the media and racism; Darwinism; race relations; patriarchy and ethnicity; culture and colonial discourse; and affirmative action. Entries are signed and are primarily the work of academics in Britain and the United States, although there are also contributions from the University of Hong Kong, La Trobe University, Melbourne, the University of British Columbia and the University of Zimbabwe. Entries are short essays which give the history and development of a topic and references to further relevant readings. This work provides a useful background on a variety of topics relating to race in an informative, easy-to-read manner.

3.4.9 Research

Qualitative Enquiry: a Dictionary of Terms by Thomas A. Schwandt (Newbury Park, CA: Sage, 1997) offers in-depth explanations of terms used in the field of qualitative research. Definitions vary from one paragraph for relatively simple topics, to several paragraphs for more complex terms.

▶ 3.5 DIRECTORIES

3.5.1 General

There are a number of general publications (*see 1.5*) which list sociology and sociology-related organizations including: the *Encyclopedia of Associations: International Organizations*, 37th ed., (Farmington Hills, MI: Gale, 2001); and by the same publisher the *Research Centers Directory*, 28th ed., (Farmington Hills, MI: Gale, 2001). The latter gives details of university-related and other nonprofit, US research organizations carrying out research in areas including: medical sociology; government and public affairs; industrial sociology and the sociology of work; ageing; the family and education. The second edition of the *Directory of Social Research Organisations in the United Kingdom* edited by Wendy Sykes, Martin Bulmer and Marleen Schwerlzel (London: Mansell, 1999) and the *World Directory of Social Science Institutions* (Paris: UNESCO, 1990) would also be of use to sociologists. The American Sociological Association produces a number of print directories including a *Guide to Graduate Departments of Sociology* (Washington, DC: ASA, 1999) and a *Directory of Members, 1999–2000* (Washington, DC: ASA, 2000) which provides basic information on 13 000 ASA members, including mailing addresses, office phone numbers, Email addresses, and section memberships.

3.5.2 Ageing

Directory of Population Ageing Research in Europe (New York: United Nations, 1998). This directory describes approximately 300 projects sponsored by 150 institutions that are conducting research on a wide range of issues dealing with the ageing population in Europe. The directory is based on a survey of all European nations carried out in 1995 and 1996 by the Population Activities Unit of the United Nations Economic Commission for Europe in collaboration with the United States National Institute on Ageing. The work is arranged alphabetically by country, with an additional category entitled 'international'. Item and keyword indexes are included. Entries provide a general description of the research project and key contact details. This is a useful resource for those researching the topic of ageing and its regional effects.

3.5.3 Communication and media

The *International Media Guide* (New York: Directories International) is published in various versions – business/professional editions for Europe, Asia/Pacific, Middle East/Africa, the Americas – covering newspapers and consumer magazines worldwide. The business/professional editions are broken down into categories, within each of which publishers are listed with contact details, by region and country. The *World Media Handbook* (New York: United Nations) is a biennial publication which includes statistical information on literacy rates, together with telephone, newspaper and broadcasting data. A maximum of 16 major newspapers and 20 magazines, with standard directory information for each, are listed for each country.

Benn's Media Directory (Kent: Miller Freeman) is produced annually in three volumes covering the United Kingdom, Europe and the world. It provides information on the media including country-by-country listings of newspapers and journals. Media Websites are also included. *Willings Press Guide* ((Farmington Hills, MI: Gale) is produced annually in two volumes, one covering the United Kingdom, the other the international press. The work provides an extensive listing of international newspapers and periodicals.

3.5.4 Women

The National Women's Directory by LouLou Brown (London: Cassell, 1999) provides a comprehensive list of over 4800 women's organizations in England, Northern Ireland, and the Republic of Ireland, Scotland and Wales. Divided into two parts, the first lists over 800 national organizations set out in categories, while the second part lists 4000 local organizations by area within each country.

▶ 3.6 ENCYCLOPAEDIAS

Most academic disciplines have one or more specialized encyclopaedias. Articles written by experts in the field provide an overview of a topic and generally suggest additional reading. Because of the cross-disciplinary nature of sociology, researchers in the field may also need to consult encyclopaedias across the range of the social sciences.

3.6.1 General

(a) Print

The 17-volume *International Encyclopedia of the Social Sciences* (New York: Macmillan, 1968) with signed articles by experts and bibliographies covering all areas of the social sciences, will be of immense use to sociologists. Useful on a substantially smaller scale is the single volume second edition of the *Social Science Encyclopaedia* edited by Adam Kuper and Jessica Kuper (London: Routledge, 1996). *See also 1.6.*

As the first inclusive encyclopaedia of sociology, the *Encyclopedia of Sociology* edited by Edgar F. and Marie L. Borgatta (New York: Macmillan, 1992) represented a landmark in publishing. Aimed at an academic audience, this four-volume work edited by two scholars at the University of Washington, brings together the work of over 300 sociologists (mostly American). In 370 essay-like entries, arranged alphabetically, major sociological topics and theories are covered. Topics include: community health, the family, incest, prejudice, and race and world religions. Short bibliographies or reference lists follow each essay. This work, providing a good overview of topics, will be of use to students and practising sociologists.

International Encyclopaedia of Sociology edited by Frank N. Magill (London: Fitzroy Dearborn, 1995). Written for general readers, this encyclopaedia offers 338 alphabetically arranged essays on a variety of topics of interest to sociologists including theories, institutions and research techniques. Topics covered include: alcoholism; the cold war; industrial and post industrial economics; the sociology of education; and violence in the family. The text of each article is divided into three sections – the overview, the application and the context, which explains how the topic relates to sociology and its historical and cultural roots. There are no biographical articles, but contributions of prominent scholars to sociological theory can be traced through the index using their names. Bibliographies accompany each article and cross-references to other relevant essays are given. A select bibliography of sociology provided at the end of the volume lists key reference books and some core textbooks. This work provides really useful introductory essays.

Encyclopedia of Social Work, 19th ed., edited by Richard L. Edwards, et al (Washington, DC: National Association of Social Workers, 1995, supplement 1997). Of the topics addressed by the 290 articles, approximately 55 per cent are new to this edition. These include children's rights, family therapy, bisexuality and HIV/AIDS. Most of the 344 contributors are academics or practitioners. In addition to topical articles there is a biographical chapter which includes 142 entries. The eighteenth edition of the encyclopaedia will still be of use to the sociologist, as topics such as divorce and separation, parent training, infertility services, sex discrimination and inequality are not included in the nineteenth edition. This work will be extremely useful to practitioners, students preparing for practice and professionals in related fields. Published simultaneously with this edition of the encyclopaedia, the second edition of Leon Ginsburg's *Social Work Almanac* (Washington, DC: NASW Press, 1995) provides statistical tables, charts and graphs. *See also (b) Electronic* below.

(b) Electronic

The *Encyclopedia of Social Work*, 19th ed., edited by Richard L. Edwards, et al. (Washington, DC: National Association of Social Workers, 1995) is available on CD-ROM as the *Social Work Reference Library*. This incorporates the third edition of Robert L. Barker's *The Social Work Dictionary* (Washington, DC: NASW Press, 1995) and the second edition of the Leon Ginsberg's *Social Work Almanac* (Washington, DC: NASW Press, 1995).

3.6.2 Ageing

Encyclopaedia of Gerontology: Age, Ageing, and the Aged edited by James E. Birren (London: Academic Press, 1996). one hundred and ninety-six experts in the field have contributed scholarly essays to this two-volume work. Five major sections cover the biology, psychology, social science issues, health sciences issues and humanities issues of ageing. Each essay provides a brief outline, a short glossary, an introductory overview and a bibliography. This is a useful work for students and researchers. For general readers *The Encyclopedia of Ageing: a Comprehensive Resource in Gerontology and Geriatrics*, 2nd ed., by George L. Maddox, et al. (New York: Springer, 1995) provides over 600 clearly written articles. Roy F. Hampton and Charles Russell's *The Encyclopedia of Ageing and the Elderly* (New York: Facts on File, 1992) defines key concepts in the medical and sociological aspects of ageing. Acronyms and proper names for diseases, drugs and organizations are also given.

3.6.3 Communication and media

The *Encyclopedia of Television News* edited by Michael D. Murray (Phoenix, AZ: Oryx, 1999) offers over 300 signed entries which give biographical information about American journalists, alongside information about major issues and news themes in the later half of the twentieth century. The work includes black and white photographs and has an index. This is a useful resource for those involved in the study of journalism. A more academic work is the *Encyclopaedia of Television* edited by Horace Newcomb (London: Fitzroy Dearborn, 1997) which offers, in three volumes, over 1000 essays by academic writers on a large selection of famous English-language shows. It also covers: topics (e.g., high definition television and Vietnam on television); genres (e.g., science fiction, westerns); personalities (including actors, producers, journalists); and institutions associated with television. Essays on actors contain biographical and critical commentaries followed by filmographies and screen/stage appearances. Descriptions of television shows include programming history. Famous documentaries are also included. Most of the essays contain bibliographies and photographs. Although the emphasis is on the US, the encyclopaedia also provides overview essays on the history, institutional development, programming, and policies for television in Canada, Britain, and Australia. Less detailed, but useful nonetheless, is the third edition of *Les Brown's Encyclopedia of Television* edited by Les Brown (New York: Gale, 1992) an update of a 1977 work *The New York Times Encyclopedia of Television.* Television specialist, Brown and his 15 contributors, provide information on all aspects of the television industry in approximately 3000 brief entries.

Michael Shaw Findlay's *Language and Communication: a Cross-Cultural Encyclopaedia* (Oxford: ABC-Clio, 1998) aims to give worldwide coverage of language and communication patterns. Articles are brief, containing a definition with examples, *see also* references and brief bibliographies. Photographs are used occasionally to illustrate concepts. *From Talking Drums to the Internet: an Encyclopaedia of Communications Technology* by Robert Gardner and Dennis Shortelle (Oxford: ABC-Clio, 1997) focuses primarily on human communication. Each of the 210 alphabetical entries contains a lengthy description and end references. Some illustrations and photographs are included. The encyclopaedia covers forms of communication from prehistory to twentieth century innovations. The bulk of the entries deal with the twentieth century and the social implications of changing technologies. Because the encyclopaedia's scope is limited to technology, it deals only with a subset of the concepts covered in the *International Encyclopaedia of Communications* by Erik Barnouw (Oxford: Oxford University Press, 1989), where almost all of the same material is discussed in greater detail and with lengthier bibliographies. Whereas the latter is recommended for research libraries, Gardner and Shortelle is well suited to smaller, less specialized libraries.

3.6.4 Cultural theory

St. James Encyclopedia of Popular Culture edited by Tom Pendergast and Sara Pendergast (New York: Gale, 1999) offers in five illustrated volumes, over 2700 articles on all aspects of twentieth century popular culture.

Subjects covered include: social life, music, print culture, film, TV and radio, sports, and art and performance. Articles range in length from 75 to 3000 words. This is a particularly useful source for students of popular culture.

3.6.5 Demographics

Encyclopedia of Global Population and Demographics (Chicago, IL: Fitzroy Dearborn, 1999). Edited by Immanuel Ness and James Ciment this two-volume work begins with a selection of essays introducing the discipline of demography and cultural identity. Where available, figures are given for three years 1965, 1980 and 1995. Scope is global and statistics covered include those for: transport, health and health care, communication and education.

3.6.6 Education

International Encyclopaedia of the Sociology of Education edited by Lawrence J. Saha (London: Pergamon, 1997). In 1994, Pergamon published a second edition of the *International Encyclopaedia of Education.* Based on that the publishers began a series of one-volume specialized encyclopaedias under the title 'Resources in Education'. Some of Saha's material in the *International Encyclopaedia of Sociology of Education* is taken from the original work. There are also new articles in this 150-article volume. The articles are arranged into 10 broad subject areas. Contributors are drawn from several European countries, Australia and North America. This is an essential source for graduate collections in sociology and education.

3.6.7 Family

Encyclopedia of Marriage and the Family edited by David Levinson (New York: Simon and Schuster, 1995). This two-volume work presents 160 articles on a variety of topics relating to marriage and the family, including single parenthood, divorce, homelessness, poverty and gender roles. Entries range from two to seven pages and included biographies and references to related topics. This work will be very useful for those studying the family.

3.6.8 Race and ethnicity

Ethnic Relations: a Cross-Cultural Encyclopaedia edited by David Levinson (Oxford: ABC-Clio, 1998). Levinson, an anthropologist, examines definitions and cross-cultural information concerning a range of 53 race related concepts including anti-semitism, class hatred and ethnic cleansing. He also profiles 38 ethnic conflicts that he suggests, are representative of the world situation at the time of publication. An annotated directory of ethnic organizations throughout the world is provided, in addition to an extensive bibliography and a subject index. *The Encyclopaedia of Multiculturalism* edited by Susan Auerbach (New York: Marshall Cavendish, 1994) is a six-volume work which examines American history and society through the experience of racial, ethnic, national, religious and other marginalized groups. Entries vary from short paragraphs on basic terms to articles of up to 5000 words for major topics. Suggested readings follow articles together with references to related articles in other parts of the encyclopaedia.

3.6.9 Women

(a) Print

The *Encyclopedia of Feminist Theories* edited by Lorraine Code (New York: Routledge, 2000) offers a multidisciplinary insight into the field of feminist thought. Over 500 entries commissioned from an international team of contributors offer explanations of key themes and ideas. Each entry contains cross-references and a bibliographic guide to further reading. In addition, over 50 biographies are presented. The *Women's Studies Encyclopedia* edited by Helen Tierney (Westport, CT: Greenwood, 1999) is a three-volume revised and expanded edition of the 1989 edition. With close to 400 contributors, it offers new and expanded coverage of such areas as: violence against women; women in public life; and women in specific countries and regions. Many of the articles are new or completely rewritten. *See also (b) Electronic* below.

(b) Electronic

Women's Studies Encyclopedia (Westport, CT: Greenwood Press, 1999). Available as a CD-ROM from Greenwood Electronic Media and as a Web resource with hyperlinks between-cross references in the text. Over 700 entries bring together information about women from a variety of fields. The electronic versions support Boolean and natural language searching. Further details on the electronic product are available from <www.gem.greenwood.com>.

3.6.10 Work

The Blackwell Encyclopedic Dictionary of Organizational Behaviour edited by Nigel Nicholson (Oxford: Blackwell, 1998) contains over 400 entries from over 180 leading authorities in the field. Entries are short, from a half page to two to three pages and contain short bibliographies. The work contains an index of concepts and key people.

▶ 3.7 GUIDES AND HANDBOOKS

3.7.1 General

International Handbook of Contemporary Developments in Sociology edited by Raj Mohan and Arthur S. Wile (Westport, CT: Greenwood Press, 1994). Successor to the earlier edition (1975), this volume provides overviews of recent developments in sociology in various countries and regions. Arrangement is by six broad geographic categories: Western and Northern Europe; the Western Hemisphere; Eastern Europe; Southern Europe; Africa and the Middle East; and the East. The work aims to highlight the major theories, methods and substantive findings that have characterized sociological work since the mid-1970s in each of the nations listed. Both United States and European sociology receive substantial treatment. Coverage from other parts of the world is not as comprehensive. However, the essays are very informative regarding the international state of sociology. A selected bibliography is included at the end of each chapter. Name and subject indexes are also provided.

The *Handbook of Sociology* edited by Neil J. Smelser (Newbury Park, CA: Sage, 1988) is arranged in 22 lengthy chapters under four broad sections: theoretical and methodological issues; bases of inequality in society; major institutional and organizational settings; and social processes and change. Extensive bibliographies are provided with each article. Although the coverage has a strong US bias, this remains an extremely comprehensive work which will be of use to undergraduate students and researchers. The *Survey of Social Science: Sociology Series* edited by Frank N. Magill (Pasadena, CA: Salem Press, 1994) is a five-volume collection of over 300 articles covering specific topics related to the categories of social institutions, deviance and social control, ageing, sex and gender, demography, social change, race and ethnic relations.

The *Sage Studies in International Sociology* (SSIS) book series was established by the International Sociological Association (ISA) in 1974 in place of the *Transactions of the World Congress of Sociology* which had been published since 1949, the year of the Association's first congress. Titles in the series include: *Social Movements and Social Classes: the Future of Collective Action* (1995) edited by Louis Maheu; *Changing Classes: Stratification and Mobility in Post-Industrial Societies* edited by Gosta Esping-Andersen (1993); and *Gender, Work and Medicine Women and the Medical Division of Labour* edited by Elianne Riska and Katarina Wegar (1993). Each volume contains a number of essays by different specialists in the field. Volumes have a strong international flavour. From 2001, in addition to the book series, there will be two extra issues per year of the journal *Current Sociology* (*see 3.9*) devoted to SSIS monograph issues.

A number of detailed guides to the literature of sociology exist. Some are bibliographies, listing the core literature in the discipline. Stephen Aby's *Sociology: a Guide to Reference and Information Sources*, 2nd ed., (Englewood, CO: Libraries Unlimited, 1997) provides an extremely comprehensive guide to the literature. The earlier (1987) edition by the same author, covered the period 1970 to 1986 and was selected as an 'Outstanding Academic Book 1987-'88' by *Choice*. Aimed at researchers, students and librarians, it provides descriptions of sources published mainly between 1985 and 1996 in sociology, its subdisciplines, and related social sciences. The work is divided into four parts, the first of which deals with general social science reference sources. The various social science disciplines with details of relevant reference resources follow in the second part. Part three deals specifically with reference resources in sociology. The fourth and final part provides a breakdown of sociological fields with their reference sources. The book is extremely comprehensive with annotations, some of which have evaluative comments, from 60 to 250 words long. This is a core source for the sociology researcher and a valuable collection development tool for the librarian.

Not as current as Aby but useful nonetheless as a classic introduction to the field of sociology, is T. B. Bottomore's *Sociology: a Guide to Problems and Literature,* 3rd ed., (London: Allen & Unwin, 1987). *Finding the Source in Sociology and Anthropology: a Thesaurus-Index to the Reference Collection* (Westport, CT: Greenwood Press, 1987) is arranged by subject and serves as a general guide to a large range of sources. *Let's Go Sociology: Travels on the Internet* by Joan Ferrante and Angela Vaughan (Belmont, CA: Wadsworth, 1999) is now in its second edition and provides an extremely useful guide to Websites of interest to sociologists.

The *Student's Companion to Sociology,* edited by Jon Gubbay and Chris Middleton (Oxford: Blackwell, 1997) is a book to dip into rather than read from cover to cover. Arranged in six sections, it aims to guide students in their journeys through sociology. Essays are written in a lively interesting style, emphasizing the role of the sociologist in engaging with social problems and issues. Research methodology and information resources are covered, as are biographies of important sociologists.

3.7.2 Ageing

The *Handbook of Ageing and the Social Sciences*, 4th ed., edited by Robert H. Binstock and Linda K. George (San Diego, CA: Academic Press, 1996) is a comprehensive reference for students, researchers and practitioners. The volume is divided into four sections covering: theory and research methodology; ageing and social structure; social factors and social institutions associated with ageing; and social interventions. The *Handbook on Ethnicity, Ageing and Mental Health* (Westport, CT: Greenwood Press, 1995) edited by Deborah K. Padgett, focuses on the use of mental health services by elderly people of the following ethnic origins – African Americans, Hispanics, Asian Americans and Native Americans. A bibliography and subject indexes are included. Erdman B. Palmore is editor of *Developments and Research on Ageing: an International Handbook* (Westport, CT: Greenwood Press, 1993) which is a useful resource for students and planners in this area. It offers 25 chapters outlining programmes and research on ageing in a number of countries worldwide including Japan, Mexico, Israel, France, Germany and Italy. The essays give an overview of research, policy and services to the elderly in each country. An international directory of gerontological/geriatric associations, a selected bibliography and a name/title/subject index are also included.

3.7.3 Communication and media

Communication and the Mass Media: a Guide to the Reference Literature (Englewood, CO: Libraries Unlimited, 1991) by Eleanor S. Block and James K. Bracken covers bibliographies, dictionaries, encyclopaedias, handbooks, indexes and abstracts, biographical sources, library catalogues, directories and yearbooks, electronic sources, periodicals, research centres and associations. It is an excellent source giving annotated entries from the literature since 1970 and will be of cosiderable value to students and researchers. Useful also for undergraduates is *Communication Research: Strategies and Sources*, 5th ed., by Rebecca B. Rubin, Alan M. Rubin and Linda J. Piele (Belmont, CA: Wadsworth, 1999) which is designed as a textbook to guide communications students in their research and also lists the most important information sources in the subject area.

3.7.4 Economics

The Handbook of Economic Sociology (Princeton, NJ: Princeton University Press, 1994) edited by Neil J. Smelser and Richard Swedberg. The editors distinguish economic sociology from mainstream economics in its focus on the use of historical and comparative data to describe economic interaction. The 31 essays in this collection form the definitive compilation of recent research in the field of economic sociology. The volume provides a unique survey of this rapidly developing field of scholarship.

3.7.5 Education

The *Handbook of the Sociology of Education* edited by Maureen T. Hallinan (Dordrecht: Kluwer, 2000) provides a comprehensive overview of the field of education as viewed from a sociological perspective. Experts in the area present theoretical and empirical research on major educational issues and analyse the social processes that govern schooling, and the role of schools in and their impact on contemporary society. The work is divided into six major areas: Theoretical and Methodological Orientation; Developing and Expansion of Education; the Study of Access to Schooling; the Study of School Organization; the Study of School Outcomes; and Policy Implications of Research in the Sociology of Education. Hallinan's introduction presents an excellent overview of the sociology of education. The *Handbook of Theory and Research for the Sociology of Education* by John C. Richardson. (Westport, CT: Greenwood Press 1986) traces the development of the sociology of education, reviews the important classical European works in which the discipline is grounded and synthesizes major advances in the subject during the past decades. Each chapter is devoted to a major topic and provides an overview and a review of the literature.

3.7.6 Environment

International Handbook of Environmental Sociology edited by Michael Redclift and Graham Woodgate (Cheltenham: Edward Elgar, 1997). This work takes an interdisciplinary and international approach to a field that is very much in its early years. Divided into three main sections: concepts and theories; substantive issues (e.g., gender, science, technology, knowledge and lifestyles); and international perspectives (e.g., analyses of environmental crises and movements in Europe, Latin America, Japan and the Middle East). This is an excellent primary source making a major contribution to the field.

3.7.7 Family

Now in its second edition, the *Handbook of Marriage and the Family* edited by Marvin B. Sussman, Suzanne Steinmetz and G. W. Peterson (New York: Plenum, 1999) presents essays in four main sections: family diversity: past, present, and future; the family: theory and methods; changing family patterns and roles; and the family and other institutions. Within each category there are a number of essays written by a variety of experts in the field. There is an introductory essay which examines the family at the end of the second millennium. This is a thorough revision of the 1987 edition of the same title and will prove a valuable resource for those doing family research.

The *Handbook of Social Support and the Family* edited by Gregory R. Pierce, et al. (New York: Plenum, 1996) is divided into three sections: conceptual and methodological issues; the role social support plays in family relations; and real-world issues such as how social support, or the lack of it, affects family crises of various types and the early stages of family development. Fifty scholars have contributed to this work which will be of use to students and practitioners in sociological fields related to the family.

While the emphasis is on the US, *Domestic Violence: a Reference Handbook* by Margi Laird McCue (Oxford: ABC-Clio, 1995) has much that is relevant to the issue of domestic violence worldwide. It includes definitions of domestic violence; the types and causes of such abuse; short biographical sketches of people involved in the struggle for and against equal gender rights; a lengthy section of facts, statistics and legal issues involved in domestic violence; and a bibliography of books, articles, newsletters, professional publications and non-print resources.

3.7.8 Gender

Janet Saltzman Chafetz's *Handbook of the Sociology of Gender* (Dordrecht: Kluwer, 1999) offers in-depth discussions of the various aspects of the field. The work is divided into four sections, each with a number of chapters. Topics covered include feminist epistemology, gender theory, social movement and violence. Bibliographies are provided with each chapter. This handbook provides information about the current state of knowledge in gender sociology. Leonore Loeb Adler is editor of the *International Handbook on Gender Roles* (Westport, CT: Greenwood Press, 1994), a useful source for comparative data from 31 countries worldwide. An overview of the extent of inequality between males and females in each of the countries is provided, followed by a comparison of gender roles throughout the life cycle.

The *Handbook of Gender, Culture and Health* edited by Richard M. Eisler and Michel Hersen (Mahwah, NJ: L. Erlbaum, 2000) was developed to provide information for researchers, students and health care practitioners. The collection of articles emphasizes the importance of evaluating health risks and developing prevention and treatment programmes. The work is divided into four parts: stress in diverse populations; differences in health issues; specific health problems; and health problems of specific populations. In all there are 20 extensively referenced articles. Author and topic indexes are provided.

3.7.9 Medicine

Now in its fifth edition, the *Handbook of Medical Sociology* edited by Chloe Bird, Peter Conrad and Allen Fremont (Upper Saddle River, NJ: Prentice Hall, 2000) opens with a chapter on the history of medical sociology. The main body of the work is divided into six sections, written by leading specialists in the field, covering: the history of medical sociology; social contexts of health and illness; health and illness behaviour and experience; organization of health services; medical care and areas of collaboration; and future directions for medical sociology. This work is valuable for medical sociologists and other health and social scientists looking for a historical as well as contemporary perspective on the field. The *Blackwell Companion to Medical Sociology* edited by William C. Cockerham (Oxford: Blackwell, 2000) brings together 26 original essays by leading medical sociologists. The volume is divided into two parts. The first part covers the substantive areas of medical sociology, including essays on the sociology of the body, migration, health and stress, work stress, and health and social stratification. The second part of the volume applies those subjects to individual countries and societies in the Americas, Europe, the Middle East, Asia, and Africa.

3.7.10 Politics and power

The *Research in Political Sociology* series edited by Philo C. Wasburn of Purdue University (Greenwich, CT: JAI Press) was established in 1983 by the American Sociological Association section on Political Sociology. Its aim is 'to promote the scholarly research of those concerned with a sociological understanding of political phenomena' (Wasburn, 1998, p.ix). Each volume brings together a collection of essays which examine theoretical and methodological issues in political sociology.

3.7.11 Social problems

Homelessness: a Sourcebook by Rick Fantasia and Maurice Isserman. (New York: Facts on File, 1994) offers a really useful introductory essay on the history of homelessness as a social issue. This is followed by a dictionary of key terms and US organizations, persons and legislation relating to homelessness.

Poverty-a Global Review: Handbook on International Poverty Research edited by Else Oyen, S. M. Miller and Syed Abdus Samad (Cambridge, MA: Scandinavian University Press, 1996) provides a cross-disciplinary survey of poverty research within a global framework. Thirty-five contributors from several countries and a variety of disciplines discuss the theoretical foundation and the current state of poverty research. Essays explore the nature, shortcomings and goals of poverty research as well as the need to redefine concepts and methodologies. Four sections are devoted to the Asian, African, Western, and Latin American regions. Each chapter has an extensive bibliography. The volume serves as a literature review and will be of value to students and researchers.

Also useful to students of poverty is the *Statistical Handbook on Poverty in the Developing World* (Phoenix, AZ: Oryx, 1999) edited by Chandrika Kaul and Valerie Tomaselli-Moschovitis, which presents poverty statistics in the low and middle income countries of the world, as defined by the World Bank. The first section presents key global indicators. The rest of the volume deals with specific indicators (e.g., poverty measures, economic factors, demographics, health, AIDS, education, nutrition/food supply, women and poverty, children and poverty). Tables are organized by continent. Explanations of the indicators in each section are provided, and some useful Web addresses are included.

3.7.12 Women's studies

Eleanor B. Amico's *Reader's Guide to Women's Studies* (Chicago, Ill: Fitzroy Dearborn, 1998) provides a comprehensive guide to English language books covering more than 500 topics in the field of Women's Studies. Significant people in the field are also included. Entries are alphabetic and begin with a bibliography of books on the topic or person, followed by an essay. The scope is global and the volume is a useful guide to the secondary literature on the topic. The *International Handbook of Women's Studies* by Loulou Brown, Helen Collins, Pat Green and Maggie Humm (New York: Harvester Wheatsheaf, 1993) gives details of women's organizations, women's studies courses, research, centres, bookshops, libraries and publications worldwide.

3.7.13 Writing and research

(a) Print

The *Guide to Writing Sociology Papers,* 4th ed., edited by Rosanne Giarrusso, Judith Richlin Klonsky, William G. Roy and Ellen Strenski (Basingstoke: Palgrave, 1998) is divided into three parts, the first of which explains how to get started on writing a paper. This includes developing a proposal, time management, draft revisions, bibliographic citation formats and guidelines on submitting a paper. The second part of the work is concerned with locating information, taking notes, organizing data and writing up the paper. A sample student paper is provided. The final section contains a checklist for evaluating papers before they are submitted.

The Sociology Student Writer's Manual edited by William Archer Johnson (Upper Saddle River, NJ: Prentice Hall, 1999) is a reference manual for both beginning and advanced researchers. The work includes information on how to conduct various types of research; how to use libraries and the Internet; and how to write and format a variety of sociological papers. Another useful guide to using the library for the preparation of sociology papers is *The Student Sociologist's Handbook*, 4th ed., by Pauline Bart and Linda Frankel (New York: Random House, 1986). Chapters discuss journal literature, book reviews, handbooks, encyclopaedias, dictionaries, government publications and computers in sociology.

(b) Electronic

Formatting in Sociology <khorshid.ece.ut.ac.ir/misc/OWL/Files/60.html>. Produced by Purdue University, this Website explains how to cite according to the format recommended by the American Sociological Review. It gives examples of in-text citations, page references and footnotes. Interestingly, it does not include citing electronic resources.

▶ 3.8 WEBSITES

The range of Websites of potential interest to sociologists is daunting. Because of the nature of the discipline, information from the broadest possible range of Websites may be of interest to the sociologist. This list aims to bring together a few major gateways and large university Websites which will act as a springboard to other resources.

Allyn & Bacon's Sociology Links <www.abacon.com/sociology/soclinks/index.html>. This site provides links to a range of sociology-related sites in an easy-to-use alphabetical sequence. Topics covered include drugs, family, technology, social change and violence and abuse. The site is maintained by Cecil E. Greek for the publishers Allyn & Bacon.

BUBL LINK <link.bubl.ac.uk/sociology>. BUBL acts as a gateway to quality resources in a range of fields including sociology. Links are provided to sites that have been evaluated and deemed to be of high quality. Areas covered include social processes, interaction, change, population and race. BUBL provides a news page which carries details of job vacancies, forthcoming conferences, newspapers and news services. A current awareness facility exists whereby it is possible to receive the contents pages of journals via Email, while access to the contents pages of many journals is provided free of charge.

COOMBSWeb <coombs.anu.edu.au>. Established in 1994, and claiming to be the world's oldest Asian Studies networked research facility, COOMBSWeb provides a gateway to social science and Asian studies resources. It is hosted by the Australian National University and updated on a daily basis.

Dead Sociologists Index <www.runet.edu/~lridener/DSS/INDEX.HTML>. Compiled by Larry L. Ridener at Radford University, Virginia, the *Dead Sociologists Index* profiles major sociologists including Comte, Marx, Durkheim and Pareto. An overview of the person's ideas and some excerpts from key texts are given. Much of the information is based on Lewis Coser's book *Masters of Sociological Thought*, 2nd ed., (New York: Harcourt Brace Jovanovich, 1977). The Website also features a photo gallery giving thumbnail sketches that can be enlarged. This site provides a good introduction for newcomers to the works of these sociologists.

Julian Dierkes' Sociology Links at Princeton <www.princeton.edu/~sociolog/links.html>. An extremely comprehensive site that has been the recipient of a number of awards. The site provides links to an impressive range of sociology resources including associations, research institutes, mailing lists, e-journals, notable sociologists and directories of Web resources.

Sociology on Yahoo <dir.yahoo.com/Social_Science/Sociology>. This is a directory of Web resources providing links to Websites in a variety of categories including: criminal justice, social psychology, urban studies, together with access to electronic journals and organizations.

Sociology via the Social Science Information Gateway (SOSIG) <sosig.ac.uk/sociology>. Alphabetically arranged subject links to the main areas of sociology. Short informative descriptions of the Websites linked to are provided.

SocioSite <www.pscw.uva.nl/sociosite>. An excellent site, created and maintained by Albert Benschop of the faculty of Social Sciences at the University of Amsterdam. SocioSite gives access to European and International resources of interest to academic sociology. The main menu groups sociology resources into 24 categories, including subject areas, sociologists, libraries, departments, research centres, newsgroups and mailing lists. Sections are generally organized geographically with worldwide Websites (mainly US, Australian and Canadian) listed first, followed by European and then Dutch Websites. Over 140 subject areas are listed ranging from activism and ageing through family, leisure, rural studies and suicide. Brief descriptions of the Websites linked to are provided. Hypertext links to full or excerpted works of 55 noted sociologists are also provided. This Website has its own search engine. A valuable resource for sociology students and researchers.

Sociological Tour Through Cyberspace <www.trinity.edu/mkearl/index.html>. Provides links to a number of general sociology sites, followed by links to sociological theory, data resources, methods and statistics and links to sites which detail how to cite both print and electronic resources. The site has its own search engine.

SocioWeb <www.socioWeb.com/~markbl/socioWeb>. A useful guide providing access to a wide range of sociological information.

The World Wide Web Virtual Library – Sociology <www.mcmaster.ca/socscidocs/w3virtsoclib/index.htm>. Provides a gateway to an international range of resources. Listing is by continent then by country. The gateway provides connections to institutions (including departments of sociology), directories, discussion groups, electronic journals and organizations. The site is maintained by Dr. Carl Cuneo, Department of Sociology, McMaster University in Canada.

▶ 3.9 JOURNALS

This section includes descriptions of the major peer-reviewed journals within the field of sociology.

Administrative Science Quarterly (ISSN 0001–8392) (Ithaca, NY: Johnson Graduate School of Management, Cornell University, 1956–). Quarterly. This is a particularly important refereed title for those doing research on the sociology of organizations.

American Journal of Sociology (ISSN 0002–9602) (Chicago, Ill: University of Chicago Press, 1895–). Bimonthly. The first American scholarly journal for sociology, this is one of the major research sources in sociology. It publishes refereed articles and review essays on the history, theory, methods and practice of sociology. Available electronically.

American Sociological Review (ISSN 0003–1224) (Washington, DC: American Sociological Association, 1936–). Bimonthly. The official journal of the American Sociological Association, this journal encompasses the entire area of sociology. It publishes work on new theoretical developments, results of research, important methodological innovations and provides an extensive book reviews section. It is similar in scope to *Sociology* the official journal of the British Sociological Association. Available electronically.

American Sociologist (ISSN 0003–1232) (New Brunswick, NJ: Rutgers University, American Sociological Association, 1969–). Quarterly. Another title from the American Sociological Association, this journal publishes refereed research articles that examine the history, status and prospects of sociology as a profession and a discipline. The emphasis is on new trends in the profession.

British Journal of Sociology (ISSN 0007–1315) (London: Routledge, 1950–). Quarterly. Published by Routledge on behalf of the London School of Economics, this is one of the most prestigious and widely known sociology journals. While research tends to have a European focus subject coverage is broad. Available electronically.

Canadian Journal of Sociology/Cahiers Canadiens de Sociologie (ISSN 0318–6431) (Ontario: University of Toronto Press, 1974–). Quarterly. This refereed journal covers all aspects of sociology with particular emphasis on politics and history. Text is in English or French, abstracts in English and French. Available electronically.

Contemporary Sociology: a Journal of Reviews (ISSN 0094–3061) (Washington, DC: American Sociological Association, 1972–). Bimonthly. Another major publication from the American Sociological Association (ASA), this journal provides a collection of in-depth book reviews, critical surveys and discussions of new or recent important works in sociology. About 50 or 60 books are analysed per issue in signed reviews of varying length. This is a very useful selection tool for librarians. Available electronically.

Current Sociology/Sociologie Contemporaine (ISSN 0011–3921) (London: Sage, 1952–). Quarterly. Published by Sage for the International Sociological Association (ISA) in English and French, the focus is on the theory, research and methodology in contemporary international sociology. Each issue provides a substantial trend report on a particular sociological topic. Annotated bibliographies usually accompany these articles, making this a useful source for literature reviews. Avaiable electronically.

Electronic Journal of Sociology <www.sociology.org> (ISSN 1198–3655) (Alberta: University of Alberta, 1994–). Semi-annual. Available only electronically, this peer-reviewed journal began publication in September 1994, and publishes review essays, reviews of books, and reviews of software.

European Sociological Review (ISSN 0266–7215) (Oxford: Oxford University Press, 1985–). Quarterly. Published in association with the European Consortium for Sociological Research, this refereed journal publishes international research studies on all aspects of sociology. Available electronically.

International Journal of Sociology (ISSN 0020–7659) (New York: ME Sharpe, 1971–). Quarterly. Presents comparative research on macrosociological issues in non-English-speaking societies from around the world in English translation. Refereed journal.

International Journal of the Sociology of Language (ISSN 0165–2516) (New York: Walter de Gruyter, 1974–). Bimonthly. A journal dedicated to the development of the sociology of language as an international and interdisciplinary field in which various approaches complement each other.

International Sociology: Journal of the International Sociological Association (ISSN 0268–5809) (London: Sage, 1986–). Quarterly. The official publication of the International Sociological Association (ISA), this journal makes an important contribution to international sociological research. Available electronically.

Sociological Perspectives (ISSN 0731–1214) (Greenwich, CT: JAI Press, 1958–). Quarterly. The official journal of the Pacific Sociological Association, formerly (until 1982) known as the *Pacific Sociological Review*, this journal offers very broad subject coverage. A recent issue carried articles on employment chances in the academic job market in sociology and an examination of the effects of residential and church integration upon racial attitudes of whites. Special themed issues are also produced. The journal aims to advance research, theory, scholarship, and practice within sociology and related disciplines. It is the only sociology journal in the world to provide foreign abstracts in Spanish, Japanese and Chinese in every issue.

Sociological Research Online <www.socresonline.org.uk/> (ISSN 1360–7804) (University of Surrey, 1996–). Quarterly. Established under the Electronic Libraries Programme (eLib), this peer-reviewed journal has quickly established itself as a leading journal of sociology. Publishing articles in applied sociology, it focuses on theoretical, empirical and methodological discussions.

Sociological Review (ISSN 0038–0261) (Oxford: Blackwell, 1953–). Quarterly. Published on behalf of the University of Keele, this refereed journal discusses subjects relating to sociology, including essays on topics such as health and work, job training, equal opportunities and skills and family issues. Available electronically.

Sociology (ISSN 0038–0385) (Cambridge: Cambridge University Press, 1967–). Quarterly. The official journal of the British Sociological Association, it focuses on sociological research in the United Kingdom and Europe. A recent issue included articles on national identity, workplace identity and anti-traveller racism in Ireland. Extensive book reviews are given. Available electronically.

Sociology of Health & Illness (ISSN 0141–9889) (Oxford: Blackwell, 1979–). Bimonthly. This is an international, refereed journal with a European focus, which publishes sociological articles on all aspects of health, illness and medicine. It focuses particularly on empirical research, especially, though not exclusively, of a qualitative nature. Available electronically.

▶ 3.10 ABSTRACTS, INDEXES AND DATABASES

(a) Print

Combined Retrospective Index Set to Journals in Sociology, 1895–1974 (Washington, DC: Carrollton Press, 1978). These six volumes provide subject and author access to English language sociological articles in journals spanning an 89-year period. Over 100 journal titles are indexed. This is very useful for historical coverage of sociology.

Cumulative Index of Sociology Journals, 1971–1985. (Washington, DC: American Sociological Association, 1987). Compiled by Judith C. Lantz this index provides author and subject access to the contents of 19 major sociology journals, including: the *American Journal of Sociology*, the *American Sociological Review* and *Contemporary Sociology*.

International Bibliography of Sociology (London: British Library of Political and Economic Science, London School of Economics, 1951–). With its sister publications – *Anthropology*, *Economics* and *Political Sciences* – this volume makes up *The International Bibliography of Social Sciences*. Material from over 100 countries is included. Approximately 70 per cent of the records are in English, and articles in other languages are displayed with both the original language title and an English translation. Abstracts are available from 1997 onwards. It is possible to subscribe to the *International Bibliography of Sociology* without subscribing to the other sections of *The International Bibliography of Social Sciences* but only in the print format. Though the print volumes represent an edited version of the full bibliography, it is still a useful reference work. It contains approximately 6000 records while the electronic versions contain nearly two million. *See also (b) Electronic* below.

The Left Index: a Quarterly Index to Periodicals of the Left (ISSN 0733–2998) (Santa Cruz, CA: The Left Index, 1982–). This index cites articles from approximately 100 Marxist, radical and left periodicals. Sociological topics include social classes, social movements, social theory, race, work and sex roles.

Sociological Abstracts (ISSN 0038–0202) (San Diego, CA: Sociological Abstracts Inc., 1953–). Seven issues a year. This is one of the most important resources for accessing the research literature in sociology and its subdisciplines including: psychology, political science, philosophy, economics, education, community development, demography and medicine. Core journals in sociology are fully abstracted. Journals in related fields are selectively abstracted. Articles are screened by senior editors with backgrounds in the social sciences. Drawing information from an international selection of over 2600 journals and other serials publications, conference papers and dissertations, entries are arranged by author under a detailed classification scheme of 29 major subject headings that are further subdivided. Author, subject and reviewer indexes are included, as well as a source list giving names of all journals covered. *International Review of Publications in Sociology* (IRPS) is a supplement that lists reviews appearing in the same issue of *Sociological Abstracts*. An annual *Conference Abstracts Supplement* appears with the December issue. This supplement abstracts presentations made at various association meetings. Unfortunately these papers are seldom published; it is generally necessary to write to the author to obtain a copy. *See also (b) Electronic* below.

(b) Electronic

International Bibliography of Sociology is available as part of *The International Bibliography of Social Sciences*, as a Silverplatter CD-ROM (covering 1981 to date). The database from 1951 onward is available online via the Bath Information and Data Services (BIDS) at <www.bids.ac.uk>. The BIDS/ingenta service offers the option of downloading the full text of some of the articles.

JSTOR <www.jstor.ac.uk> provides a digital archive collection of the full-text of core scholarly journals, including 11 major sociology journals. Coverage of the *American Journal of Sociology* is from the beginning of the publication in 1895 to 1994. *American Sociological Review* is from 1936 to 1994. Titles in other fields such as statistics and education would also be of interest to sociologists.

Sociological Abstracts (1963–) <www.silverplatter.com>. This database covers publications from 1963 to date. Records added after 1974 contain in-depth and non-evaluative abstracts of journal articles. It also contains the *Social Planning/Policy & Development Abstracts, SOPODA*, database, which focuses on solutions to social problems. Coverage is from 1979 forward. *International Review of Publications in Sociology* is covered from 1980 forwards. *Sociological Abstracts* on WebSpirs uses a graphical interface. From the search screen, the user may select *Search Builder,* a pull-down menu, for step-by-step help in creating a search. Display options include citations with abstract, citation only, title only, complete record or selected fields. A number of search operators can be used. These are AND, NEAR, NOT, OR, ADJ and WITH. It is possible to execute complex searches using nesting within parentheses. An online thesaurus which lists broader, narrower and related terms is provided. This is an excellent database, which provides numerous indexes and searchable fields and extensive coverage of scholarly journals.

▶ 3.11 OFFICIAL PUBLICATIONS

Sociologists make use of a wide range of official publications. See *1.11* for a selection of general publications and the other subject chapters for more specialized resources which sociologists may have occasion to use.

▶ 3.12 STATISTICS

Useful sources for sociologists include: *The Labour Force Survey* (London: Office for National Statistics); *Social Trends* (ISSN 0306–7742) (London: Office for National Statistics); *Demographic Yearbook* (ISSN 0082–8041) (New York: Department for Economic and Social Information and Policy Analysis, United Nations, 1948–); *Compendium of Social Statistics and Indicators* by the Economic and Social Commission for Western Asia (ISSN 1012–7801) (New York: United Nations, 1991); and the *Statistical Abstract of the United States* (ISSN 0081–4741) (Washington, DC: GPO

1878–). Topics of interest to sociologists covered in the latter include population, immigration, vital statistics, education, and environment. A section of comparative international statistics is also available. *See also 1.12.*

▶ 3.13 RESEARCH IN PROGRESS

Electronic discussion lists make it possible for groups of people with similar research interests to carry out discussion related to that research interest. Sociology researchers may well need to look beyond the strict confines of the discipline and so a perusal of the mailing lists discussed in the other subject chapters is recommended. There are currently thousands of electronic discussion lists in existence and the number is increasing all the time. A few of the more well-established lists are indicated below.

APPSOC (to subscribe, send Email to majordomo@appliedsoc.org and in the body of the message type *subscribe appsoc-L*). This is the mailing list for the Society for Applied Sociology. Membership is open to those interested in the application of sociological knowledge.

Electronic-Sociology-L (to join the forum send Email to majordomo@coombs.anu.edu.au and in the body of the message type *subscribe Electronic-Sociology-L*). Provides a worldwide communications vehicle for the *Electronic Journal of Sociology* (EJS), a forum for discussing the issues of the EJS, and to initiate global connectivity within the discipline of sociology.

ESA-ALL <www.jiscmail.ac.uk/lists/esa-all.html>. Superlist for the discussion of lists of the European Sociological Association (ESA).

European-social-policy <www.jiscmail.ac.uk/lists/europeansocial.policy.html>. Deals with social policy and social welfare issues in Europe, including the EU. Of interest to academics in social policy, sociology, economics, political science, law, public administration and other fields, and also to others involved in policy debate.

European-sociologist <www.jiscmail.ac.uk/lists/european-sociologists.html>. Based on the newsletter of the European Sociological Association (ESA), this list acts as a forum for discussion, announcement and information for sociologists and other social scientists working in Europe or on European topics.

SOCED (to subscribe Send message to: majordomo@lists.stanford.edu). A list for those interested in the sociology of education.

Social-Theory <www.jiscmail.ac.uk/lists/social-theory.html>. A list devoted to the interdisiplinary discussion of social theory.

SOCREL <www.jiscmail.ac.uk/lists/socrel.html>. An open discussion and news list devoted to the sociology of religion. It is primarily for academics working in the field in (or about) the UK. The list grew out of discussions in the sociology of religion group of the British Sociological Association.

▶ 3.14 ORGANIZATIONS

American Sociological Association (ASA)
1307 New York Avenue, NW, Suite 700, Washington, DC 20005, USA
Tel: +1 202 383 9005
Fax: +1 202 638 0882
Email (general inquiries): executive.office@asanet.org
Web: <www.asanet.org>

Founded in 1902, this major American sociological association is dedicated to advancing sociology as a scientific discipline and profession serving the public good. It publishes a number of journals including the *American Sociological Review* (*see 3.9*), *Contemporary Sociology: A Journal of Reviews* (*see 3.9*), *Journal of Health and Social Behaviour* and *Teaching Sociology*. Its membership comprises sociologists, social scientists, and others with an interest in research, teaching and the application of sociology.

The Australian Sociological Association (TASA)
TASA Office, Dr Janeen Baxter – Associate Professor, Sociology, Anthropology & Archaeology, The University of Queensland, St. Lucia, 4072, Australia
Tel: +61 7 3365 2871
Fax: +61 7 3365 1544
Email: j.baxter@mailbox.uq.edu.au
Web: <www.newcastle.edu.au/department/so/tasa>

Established as the Sociological Association of Australia and New Zealand in 1963, this organization aims to promote the development of sociology in Australia. It publishes *The Australia and New Zealand Journal of Sociology* and holds an annual conference. TASA aims to further sociology in Australia, to provide a network for Australian sociologists and to address issues of relevance to Australian sociologists.

British Sociological Association
Unit 3F/G, Mountjoy Research Centre, Stockton Road, Durham, DH1 3UR, UK
Tel: +44 (0)191 383 0839
Fax: +44 (0)191 383 0782
Email: judith.mudd@britsoc.org.uk (executive officer)
Web: <www.britsoc.org.uk>

This is the professional association for sociologists in Britain. It acts as a communication and information network, hosts an annual conference at Easter, has a number of specialist study groups and publishes the journal *Sociology* (*see 3.9*).

Canadian Sociology & Anthropology Association (CSAA)
Concordia University, 1455 Boulevard de Maisoneuse E, Bureau LB-615, Montreal, PQ, Canada H3G IM8, Canada
Tel: +1 514 848 8780
Email: csaa@vax2.concordia.ca
Web: <www.arts.ubc.ca/csaa>

Founded in 1966, this organization seeks to further the study and teaching of sociology. It publishes the quarterly *Canadian Review of Sociology and Anthropology*.

Department of Sociology at the University of Chicago
1126 E 59th St. Chicago, IL 60637, USA
Tel: +1 773 702 8677
Fax: +1 773 702 4849
Email: sociology@uchicago.edu
Web: <social-sciences.uchicago.edu/sociology/>

The Department of Sociology at the University of Chicago is among the leading departments in the United States and a major centre for sociological research. Research and teaching in the department range over the principal areas of the discipline. A link to Library Resources offers information about where to find sociology materials in the library and also provides access to other Web-based sources. There is also a link to the Website of the Population Research Center (PRC), an interdisciplinary research organization designed to facilitate high-quality population research, an area in which the University of Chicago has traditionally excelled.

Department of Sociology at the University of Essex
Wivenhoe Park, Colchester, CO4 3SQ, UK
Tel: +44 (0)1206 873333
Fax: +44 (0)1206 873041
Web: <www.essex.ac.uk/sociology>

The Department, one of the largest in the UK, has an international reputation for scholarship and attracts students from across the world. Its Website is called *Essex Sociology Online* and not only provides a range of links to other sites but also gives access to online course materials, conferences and other useful information, including an innovative Resource Centre offering help and advice for sociology students.

European Sociological Association (ESA)
Plantage Muidergracht 4, 1018 TV Amsterdam, Netherlands
Tel. +31 20 5270 646
Fax: +31 20 622 9430
Email: esa@siswo.uva.nl
Web: <www.valt.helsinki.fi/esa>

Founded in 1992, the ESA is an academic association of sociologists and a non-profit Europe-wide association with over 700 members. It aims to facilitate European sociological research and to give sociology a central place in European affairs. Its official journal is *European Societies – The Official Journal of the European Sociological Association.*

International Sociological Association
Secretariat: Facultad CC Politicas y Sociologia, Universidad Complutense, 28223 Madrid, Spain
Tel: +34 913 527 650
Fax: +34 913 524 945
Email: isa@sis.ucm.es
Web: <www.ucm.es/ifno/isa>

Founded in 1949 under the auspices of UNESCO, this association aims to represent sociologists internationally.

Nihon Shakai Gakkai (Japan Sociological Society)
Secretariat of The Japan Sociological Society, The University of Tokyo, 7–3-1 Hongo, Bunkyo-ku, Tokyo 113–0033, Japan
Tel: +81 3 5841 8933
Fax: +81 3 5841 8932
Web: <wwwsoc.nacsis.ac.jp/jss/index-e.html>

Founded in 1924, this is an academic organization for sociologists in Japan which aims to encourage and promote sociological research. Current membership exceeds 3000 members. The organization's activities include holding general meetings and publishing the society's journal.

Society for Applied Sociology (SAS)
Baylor University, Center for Community Research and Development, PO Box 97131, Waco, Texas 76798–7131, USA
Tel: +1 254 710 3811
Fax: +1 254 710 3809
Email: info@appliedsoc.org
Web: <www.appliedsoc.org>

Founded in 1978, the society acts as an international organization for sociologists interested in applying sociological knowledge in a wide variety of settings.

▶ REFERENCES

Abercrombie, N., Hill, S. and Turner B. S. (2000) *The Penguin Dictionary of Sociology*. 4th ed., London: Penguin.

Wasburn, Philo C. (ed.) (1998) *Research in Political Sociology*, Vol. 8. Greenwich, CT: JAI Press.

4 Psychology

Eric L. Lang and Tamara Kuhn

► 4.1 NATURE AND SCOPE OF PSYCHOLOGY

Psychology is generally regarded as the science of mind and behaviour. Emerging as a unique discipline in the mid to late 1800s by distinguishing itself from philosophy and physiology, psychology initially had a relatively unified focus on the systematic exploration of the elements of conscious experience (for a detailed discussion of the early history of scientific psychology see Boring, 1957). Today, psychology is anything but unified. Many national psychology organizations support dozens of divergent subdisciplines that vary widely by focus and method, encompassing studies of animals, social groups, cognition, evolution, neurobiology, emotions, abnormalities and giftedness.

These disciplinary divisions, along with organizational pressures on psychologists to establish unique contributions, often promote professional and academic isolationism in which fine-grained specializations are valued more than interdisciplinary approaches. The consequence is missed opportunity for collaboration and insight, wasted resources and an inefficient cumulation of psychological science (Conner, 2001a, 2001b). This situation has been exacerbated by the recent explosion of social science information production and computerized access, resulting (as readers of this chapter may note) in a diverse collection of 'key' psychology references.

However, there are a few individuals who are beginning to argue for synthesis rather than division within psychology. One such agent for change (Kenrick, 2001) exhorts fellow psychologists in areas as diverse as cognitive science, evolutionary psychology and dynamical systems, to explore each other's methods and consider the productive commonalities across theories. We hope this chapter will help such efforts by offering a balanced guide to excellent information resources in the field of psychology at large and its major subdisciplines. In the same spirit, we exhort readers to explore other chapters in this book and to consider the wealth of stimulating information available across social science disciplines.

4.2 ANNUALS

4.2.1 General

(a) Print

The Annual Review of Psychology (Stanford, CA: Annual Reviews 1950–) consists of bibliographic essays published each year. This volume, which is international in scope, contains lengthy discussions on the best of the recent developments in psychology. The *Annual Review* includes both subject and author indexes and various disciplines within the field are updated at regular intervals. *See also (b) Electronic* below.

The *Mental Measurements Yearbook* (Lincoln, NE: University of Nebraska Press 1938–) provides critical evaluations and comprehensive coverage of commercially available standardized test materials. Readers are given descriptive information, references and reviews of English language tests for use in psychology and education. The *Mental Measurements Yearbook* is published biennially and updated by supplements published between issues of the yearbooks. *See also (b) Electronic* below. *Test Critique* edited by Daniel J. Keyser and Richard C. Sweetland, (Austin, TX: Pro-Ed, 1991–) is an excellent supplement to the *Mental Measurements Yearbook*. Each volume contains 100 critical essays.

(b) Electronic

The Annual Review of Psychology <psych.annualreviews.org/>. The online version offers the added value of full-text searching and the opportunity to view tables of contents of the volumes and abstracts of the papers without cost or the need to register. To view full-text articles an individual or institutional subscription is needed.

The *Mental Measurements Yearbook* is available as an Internet, CD-ROM and Hard Disk service from SilverPlatter Information <www.silverplatter.com>. The electronic service covers all *Yearbooks* from 1985 to date and is updated every six months. Its enhanced functionality over the print version includes author, publisher, subject and title searching.

4.2.2 Cognitive psychology

The annual publication, *Psychology of Learning and Motivation: Advances in Research and Theory* (San Diego, CA: Academic Press, Inc 1991–) summarizes the empirical and theoretical literature in cognitive and experimental psychology. Topics range from classical and instrumental conditioning to complex learning and problem solving. A subject index is included in each volume.

4.2.3 Developmental psychology

International literature in child development is summarized by the annual publication, *Advances in Child Development and Behavior* (San Diego, CA: Academic Press, 1963–). The serial provides scholarly technical articles with critical reviews, recent advances in research and fresh theoretical viewpoints. Cumulative contents of previous volumes and a current subject index are included in each volume.

▶ 4.3 BIBLIOGRAPHIES

The *Bibliographic Guide to Psychology* (Boston, MA: GK Hall, 1976–) is an annual bibliography with entries taken from the Library of Congress and the New York Public Library files of new books. It lists book literature, pamphlets, audiovisual material and other items catalogued by the New York Public Research Libraries in the field of psychology. *Psychology: an Introductory Bibliography* edited by Susan E. Beers (Lanham, MD: Scarecrow Press; Pasadena, CA: Salem Press, 1996) is designed to provide an introduction to the field of psychology. The bibliography of books, book chapters and articles encompass the 1970s through the 1990s, but significant historical works are also included.

Those who wish to explore the historical aspects of psychology in more depth might like to take a look at the *Century of Serial Publications in Psychology, 1850–1950: an International Bibliography* by Donald Osier and Robert Wozniak (Millwood, NY: Kraus International, 1984). It is an exhaustive two-volume set which provides international listings of all serial publications in psychology. This bibliography should be useful for locating serials for historical research. Of related interest is *The Psychological Index 1894–1935: an Annual Bibliography of the Literature of Psychology and Cognate Subjects* (Washington, DC: APA, 1894–1935) which comprises a 42 volume annual bibliography of the literature of psychology. The volumes contain a classified subject list with an author index. This resource precedes *Psychological Abstracts* (*see 4.10* (*a*)) and is useful for historical research.

Eminent Contributors to Psychology edited by Robert I. Watson, Sr. (New York: Springer, 1974–76) is a two-volume set. The first volume provides over 12 000 primary references, including useful biographical and philosophical information, for 500+ eminent contributors, living between 1600 and 1967. The second volume contains a selection of over 55 000 secondary references to the works of contributors included in volume one. *Women in Psychology: a Bio-Bibliographic Sourcebook* by Agnes N. O'Connell and Nancy Felipe Russo (New York: Greenwood, 1990) examines the lives and works of 36 women psychologists, both historical and current, who were selected using a comprehensive screening process. Those chosen for inclusion have sustained records of achievement and have made significant contributions to theories or methods. Each chapter is devoted to chronicling the personal and professional careers of each of these psychologists. Also included is a bibliographic chapter that identifies the most important sources of information in the field and references to biographical information on 185 women in psychology. This is an easy-to-read resource that will be useful to both professionals and students.

▶ 4.4 DICTIONARIES

4.4.1 General

The *Dictionary of Psychology* by Raymond J. Corsini (Philadelphia, PA: Brunner/Mazel, 1999) is probably the most comprehensive psychology dictionary available to date. Edited to serve professionals and students, this resource includes over 30 000 terms and 10 appendices. The *Dictionary of Concepts in General Psychology* by John Popplestone and Marion McPhersonis (Westport, CT: Greenwood, 1998) covers the major concepts in psychology. The entries include definitions of the current meaning of terms and often facts about their origins. Additional sources of information and/or a bibliography of references about each concept are given. J. E. Roeckelein's *Dictionary of Theories, Laws, and Concepts in Psychology* (Westport, CT: Greenwood Press, 1998) provides definitions and descriptions of significant generalized psychological concepts and theories. It also includes references for original sources and reviews in which the concepts are explained. British psychologist, Stuart Sutherland, has updated the second edition of the *International Dictionary of Psychology* (New York: Crossroad, 1996) by adding more than 1000 new terms. The dictionary provides concise explanations of terms found in psychological literature. It also includes terms from various neurological sciences, the social sciences and statistics.

The American Psychological Association's *Thesaurus of Psychological Index Terms*, 8th ed., (Washington, DC: APA, 1997) is the authoritative list of psychological terminology. Its relationship section presents terms in alphabetical order and lists synonyms and broader, narrower and related terms. The rotated alphabetical terms section lists each phrase alphabetically by each word contained in it. The thesaurus is also useful for determining subject headings used by *PsycInfo* and *Psychological Abstracts (see 4.10 (a))*. The *Dictionary of Behavioral Sciences* edited by Benjamin B. Wolman (San Diego, CA: Academic Press. 1989) covers all areas of psychology, including experimental and developmental psychology, applied psychology, educational psychology, learning and perception.

Also defined are terms related to the treatment of disorders within psychiatry, biochemistry, psychopharmacology and clinical practice.

The *Longman Dictionary of Psychology and Psychiatry* edited by Robert Goldenson (New York: Longman, 1984) is a single volume dictionary containing more than 21 000 entries relating to psychology and psychiatry. The volume also has significant coverage of neurological, physiological and medical terms, together with a large number of biographical entries. Of related interest is the *Biographical Dictionary of Psychology* edited by Noel Sheehy, Antony J. Chapman and Wendy Conroy (London; New York: Routledge, 1997). It is a valuable tool for researching biographical information on important contributors in psychology. It includes more than 500 well-written entries covering prominent figures from all branches of psychology from 1850 to the present.

4.4.2 Clinical psychology

Alan S. Bellack and Michel Hersen, editors of the *Dictionary of Behavioral Assessment Techniques* (New York: Pergamon Press, 1988) have provided a quick reference guide to assessment tools used to identify problems and disorders in children, adolescents, adults and the elderly. There are entries for more than 200 assessment techniques. The above authors have also edited the *Dictionary of Behavior Therapy Techniques* (New York: Pergamon Press, 1985), which includes more than 150 definitions from one to four pages in length, containing descriptions and evaluations of clinical applications, side-effects and expected outcomes of behavioural treatment techniques. Bibliographic references are also included. The *Psychiatric Dictionary*, 7th ed., by Robert Jean Campbell (New York: Oxford University Press, 1996) is a helpful guide to psychiatric terminology, incorporating the new terms of DSM-IV. It also covers the emerging language of neurobiology and neurophysiology.

In the *Dictionary of Counselling* (Albany, NY: SUNY, 1994) Donald A. Biggs and Gerald Porter provide a guide to the history, professional, ethical and legal aspects of counselling in the United States in the twentieth century. It includes 279 entries that encompass a broad range of terms, theories, concepts, strategies, people, major issues and organizations. Lists of important works for further research and reading accompany the entries. The authors have provided a helpful internal cross-reference structure between entries and a useful general index that makes this an easy-to-use resource.

4.4.3 Cognitive psychology

The *Blackwell Dictionary of Cognitive Psychology* (Oxford: Blackwell Reference, 1990) edited by Michael W. Eysenck, is an encyclopaedic dictionary dedicated to the field of cognitive psychology. It is a comprehensive and useful resource for those interested in this area. Definitions within the field of cognitive psychology, cognitive neuropsychology and artificial intelligence as they relate to human processes are included. A comprehensive index and bibliographies are provided. Of related interest is the *Dictionary of Cognitive Psychology* by Ian Stuart-Hamilton (London: Jessica Kingsley Publishers, 1995). It defines more than 2500 concepts and terms in cognition, including neurological and linguistic terms. Prominent theories and experiments are also explained. Undergraduates in psychology will find this publication particularly useful.

4.4.4 Developmental psychology

Students of psychology will find a useful reference in the *Dictionary of Developmental Psychology* by Ian Stuart-Hamilton (London: Jessica Kingsley Publishers, 1995). The dictionary provides more than 2500 definitions of key terms in the field, incorporating both American and British terminology and systems.

4.4.5 Neuropsychology

A Dictionary of Neuropsychology by Diana M. Goodwin (New York: Springer-Verlag, 1989) offers succinct definitions of terms used in neuropsychology. It includes definitions of syndromes and symptoms, as well as descriptions of methodologies and treatments. The *INS Dictionary of Neuropsychology* (New York: Oxford University Press, 1999) sponsored by the International Neuropsychological Society and edited by David W. Loring and Kimford J. Meador, is a useful resource for students, academics and clinicians. There are concise definitions for a wide range of topic areas including: clinical syndromes; neuropsychological tests; medical procedures; neurobehavioural abnormalities; and basic neuroscience. This book also provides other relevant and useful information including common abbreviations and acronyms, together with biographical information on figures important to the field. *The Blackwell Dictionary of Neuropsychology* edited by Graham Beaumont, Pamela Kenealy and Marcus Rogers (Malden, MA: Blackwell, 1999) is a sizeable single volume dictionary that covers the numerous technical terms employed within neuropsychology. There are more than 8000 extended entries that provide definition and discussion of the more important topics in the field. Additionally, there are a number of shorter entries (500 to 5000 words) and numerous cross-referenced glossary items.

▶ 4.5 DIRECTORIES

(a) Print

The American Psychological Association's *APA Membership Register* (Washington, DC: American Psychological Association) is an annual publication that provides up-to-date contact addresses, telephone and fax numbers, Email addresses, highest degree, membership status and divisional affiliation of its members. The current edition contains more than 83 000 entries of new and continuing members. The register also includes a separate section for newly elected members and cross-references for names that have been changed since the previous edition.

The *Directory of Unpublished Experimental Mental Measures* (New York: Human Sciences Press, 1974–) published on an irregular basis, is a supplement to the *Mental Measurements Yearbook (see 4.2.1 (a))*. It includes information on tests in a variety of fields that are not commercially available.

*Graduate Study in Psych*ology (Washington, DC: APA. Annual) provides useful information for nearly 600 graduate study programmes in psychology at universities in the United States and Canada. This is an important resource for those contemplating graduate study in the field.

(b) Electronic

The American Psychological Society provides a searchable online *Member Directory* on its Website: <www.psychologicalscience.org/membership/directory> for society members. Similarly, The British Psychological Society offers a directory of chartered psychologists in the UK at: <www.bps.org.uk/publications/register.cfm>.

▶ 4.6 ENCYCLOPAEDIAS

4.6.1 General

The *Encyclopedia of Psychology* edited by Alan E. Kazdin (Washington, DC: American Psychological Association; New York: Oxford University Press, 2000) is an eight-volume set, described as the 'reference work that defines the field' by the American Psychological Association. This set, which is the product of collaboration between Oxford University Press and the American Psychological Association, is international in scope, containing 1500 original entries written by more than 1000 distinguished experts. Organized alphabetically, the entries range in length from 500 to 7000 words, each with a bibliography. There are multi-article entries that examine key topics in depth, and there are more than 400 biographies. There is a comprehensive index that facilitates topic location and an extensive system of cross-referencing which makes researching a topic across articles easier. In addition to providing information about concepts, methods, theories, findings, major figures and schools of thought, the encyclopaedia covers contested fields, both in and outside psychology, such as repressed memory and the roles of nature and nurture. This is an encyclopaedia that will serve a wide range of users: students and educators in every area of psychology and related fields. Since it is one of the most comprehensive and current resources available, it should serve as a valuable reference source for many years to come.

The *Encyclopedia of Psychology*, edited by Raymond J. Corsini (New York: Wiley, 1994) is a four-volume set covering the entire field of psychology, with a focus more toward the social science aspects of psychology than to the scientific bases. Alphabetically arranged entries cover both subject and biographical information. A brief reference list is included with some entries and the bibliography, in volume four, houses complete citations. The set contains more than 2500 entries ranging from a single paragraph to several pages. Entries include concepts, terms, theories and several short biographies on important figures in the field. The subject index contains approximately 25 000 entries. This set is an excellent starting point for research on most topics, providing general and historical information, definitions and references for additional sources of information. There is also an appendix containing the APA's 'Ethical Principles of Psychologists and Code of Conduct'. This set is considered by some to be the best of its genre.

The *Companion Encyclopaedia of Psychology* (London: Routledge, 1994) edited by Andrew M. Colman, is a two-volume set covering all major branches of psychological research and professional practice. The contents are arranged thematically. Each topic is written by an acknowledged authority who is an active researcher or practitioner in the field. Topics covered include personality, emotion, motivation and the biological components of behaviour. Illustrations, references, a glossary, an index and suggestions for further reading are also provided.

The *Encyclopedia of Human Behavior* (San Diego, CA: Academic Press, 1994) is a four-volume encyclopaedia containing signed articles on topics including: psychology, psychiatry, neuroscience, cognitive science, medicine and philosophy. Entries are arranged alphabetically by subject. Bibliographies are provided, listing recent secondary sources focusing on more detailed and technical information. Each article contains an outline and is cross-referenced within the encyclopaedia. Volume four contains an index.

The *Encyclopedia of Psychoanalysis* edited by Ludwig Eidelberg (New York: Free Press, 1968) can be considered a classic work in the field of psychoanalysis. The encyclopaedia includes 642 entries for terms pertaining to the field of psychoanalysis. It provides a good starting point for most research, and is an excellent source for bibliographies on related sources. The *International Encyclopedia of Psychiatry, Psychology, Psychoanalysis and Neurology* (New York: Aesculapius, 1997) is unrivalled as a source of comprehensive and authoritative information on most areas of psychology and related fields. This 12-volume set, edited by Benjamin B. Wolman, provides entries containing lengthy discussions of broad issues. Most articles provide theory, historical development and professional opinion. The volumes contain name and subject indexes. Of related interest is the *Encyclopedia of Psychiatry, Psychology, and Psychoanalysis*, again edited by Benjamin B. Wolman (New York: Henry Holt and Company, 1996). More than 2500 entries are included, covering such topics as: cognitive theories in social psychology; genetic influences on personality development; sleep and dream research.

4.6.2 Cognitive psychology

The *MIT Encyclopedia of the Cognitive Sciences* edited by Robert A. Wilson and Frank C. Keil (Cambridge, MA: MIT Press, 1999) is a comprehensive resource containing 471 substantial entries covering diverse methodological and theoretical topics in this field. A number of biographical entries are also included. This book will prove to be an important resource for both researchers and students in a variety of fields. It is cross-indexed with a useful reference section.

4.6.3 Developmental psychology

The *Encyclopedia of Adult Development* edited by Robert Kastenbaum (Phoenix, AZ: Oryx Press, 1993). This single volume encyclopaedia shines as one of the few reference books on adult development. It contains 106 articles written by experts in the field and should be useful to both students and professionals. The *International Encyclopedia of Developmental and Instructional Psychology* (Elmsford, NY: Pergamon, 1996) edited by E. Decorte and Franz E. Weinert, is an incomparable resource for both students and more advanced scholars. The extent of its coverage of significant topics in human development and learning relevant to education is both comprehensive and exceptional. The volume covers: biological, cognitive, and social conceptions of development; theories and models of learning;

processes and outcomes of instruction; curriculum, educational settings, and technology; and individual differences in learning. The encyclopaedia includes 170 entries from a range of international contributors from 16 countries.

The *Encyclopedia of Ageing* (New York: Springer, 1995) edited by George L. Maddox, is an excellent one-volume multi-disciplinary encyclopaedia on ageing. The entries are written by expert contributors and cover a range of topics in ageing. It has a 130 page bibliography that is useful for additional research.

4.6.4 Mental health

The *Encyclopedia of Mental Health* edited by Howard S. Friedman (San Diego, CA: Academic Press, 1998) is a comprehensive work that encompasses all levels of analysis, from the biological, through the social and family, to the cultural. Although intended for students, practising clinicians and research professionals, the articles are also accessible and useful for lay users. The excellent survey essays cover such current topics as: Alzheimer's disease; Attention Deficit/Hyperactivity Disorder; HIV/AIDS and suicide. Articles are arranged alphabetically, with a topic outline, a glossary, cross-references and a bibliography.

4.6.5 Organizational behaviour

The Blackwell Encyclopedic Dictionary of Organizational Behavior (Cambridge, MA: Blackwell Publishers, 1995) edited by Nigel Nicholson, is a useful resource that covers the major topic areas of organizational behaviour. It provides more than 500 extended definitions and essays written by 180 experts in the areas of business administration, economics, organizational psychology and organization theory.

▶ 4.7 GUIDES AND HANDBOOKS

4.7.1 General

The International Handbook of Psychology edited by Kurt Pawlik and Mark R. Rosenzweig (Thousand Oaks, CA: Sage Publications, 2000) is a good resource examining the main areas of psychology. There are 31 chapters, written by experts from around the world, that cover topics such as: the foundations of psychology; methods; information processing and human behaviour; social processes; and applied psychology. The

Cambridge Handbook of Psychology, Health and Medicine edited by Andrew Baum, et al. (New York: Cambridge University Press, 1997) is an important work that integrates international and interdisciplinary expertise, to create a unique encyclopaedic handbook that will be of value to both medical practitioners and psychologists at all levels. There is extensive coverage in the areas of health, medicine and psychology and the interaction of those topics. The chapters are written with clarity, by respected experts in the field. This volume is intended to function primarily as a reference text, and readers will ordinarily seek out specific chapters. As a consequence, chapters have been arranged alphabetically and include cross-referencing.

The *Handbook of Psychological Assessment*, 3rd ed., by Gary Groth-Marnat (New York: Wiley, 1996) thoroughly covers the principles of psychological assessment, evaluation and referral, and reviews many frequently used assessment instruments.

Lawrence A. Pervin, the editor of the *Handbook of Personality: Theory and Research* (New York: Guilford Press, 1990) provides a nice overview of the field of personality. The handbook includes a brief history of modern personality theory and the intersection of personality with other fields such as: biology; social psychology; clinical psychology; cognitive psychology; and cultural psychology. Each chapter provides a bibliography and the volume is indexed.

The *Publication Manual of the American Psychological Association* (Washington, DC: American Psychological Association, 1994) is a comprehensive style guide for the writing and presentation of papers and reports in psychology.

4.7.2 Clinical psychology

The *Diagnostic and Statistical Manual of Mental Disorders* (DSM-IV) (Washington, DC: American Psychiatric Association, 1994) provides a reference for the classification of mental disorders. The text defines the psychiatric terminology of clinical diagnosis. A classification list contains disorders arranged under the specific headings and includes the ICD (International Classification of Diseases) number for each. The disorder entries list diagnostic features and criteria, associated disorders, course information and information on differential diagnosis. An annotated list of changes to the DSM-IV (since DSM III-R) is also included.

The *Clinical Handbook of Psychological Disorders* edited by David H. Barlow (New York: Guilford Press, 1993) is a concise, well-written treatment handbook. The contributions are prepared by leading clinicians who detail how to progress from abstract concepts to effective and practical treatment plans. *The Clinician's Handbook: Integrated Diagnostics, Assessment, and Intervention in Adult and Adolescent Psychopathology*,

4th ed., edited by Robert G. Meyer (Boston, MA: Allyn & Bacon, 1995) is considered a classic reference for clinicians. It integrates behavioural descriptors and diagnostic issues, test correlates and intervention options. Common symptoms, personality styles, test patterns and treatment recommendations are linked with the major psycho-diagnostic categories used by clinicians. DSM-IV information is integrated throughout the handbook.

The *Handbook of Clinical Child Psychology* edited by C. Eugene Walker (New York: Wiley, 2001) is one of the more complete resources for literature reviews in the field of child psychology. The topics covered are divided into three sections (infancy, childhood and adolescence) and include: abnormal and normal development; assessment and diagnosis; and strategies for intervention. Relevant research, a bibliography and guidelines for practice are included for each topic.

4.7.3 Cognitive psychology

The *Handbook of Applied Cognition* edited by Francis T. Durso (New York: John Wiley & Sons, 1999) analyses applied research in cognition. The work begins by examining the relationship between applied and basic research. It then provides an overview of applied research from various perspectives including: knowledge; memory; judgement and decision-making; human error; and social cognition. The book concludes with chapters that deal with specific applied settings: business and industry; computers and technology; information and instruction; and health and law. The chapter contributors include prestigious international researchers in the field. Edited by two key authors, Tim Dalgeish and Mick J. Power, the *Handbook of Cognition and Emotion* (New York: Wiley, 1999) gives an overview of the current state and recent developments of cognition and emotion research. The topics include memory, decision-making, anger, anxiety, sadness, jealousy and prominent theories. This handbook should be an important reference for both researchers and clinicians interested in cognition and emotion.

The *Handbook of Perception and Human Performance*, edited by Kenneth R. Boff , Lloyd Kaufman and James Thomas (New York: Wiley, 1986) is a two-volume set containing 45 articles, divided into seven topical sections. The first volume contains articles on theory and methods, basic sensory processes, and space and motion perception. Volume two contains articles on information processing, perceptual organization, cognition and human performance. For a useful resource which will prove valuable to researchers, practising psychologists and scholars interested in memory research see *The Oxford Handbook of Memory* edited by Endel Tulying and Fergus I. M. Craik (New York: Oxford University Press, 2000). It is a comprehensive 700-page handbook that covers the mammoth field of memory research. The book begins by introducing the terminology and issues, then presents essays written by experts in the field. The topics covered include: the development of memory; short-term memory; memory encoding; learning; meta-memory; memory at various life stages; and memory disorders.

4.7.4 Developmental psychology

The *Handbook of Developmental Psychology* by Benjamin B. Wolman (Englewood Cliffs, NJ: Prentice-Hall, 1982) provides thorough coverage of the areas of developmental psychology. It is divided into section areas that include infancy, childhood, adolescence, adulthood, ageing, theory and research methodology.

W. Damon and Rickard M. Lerner have edited a new edition of the *Handbook of Child Psychology* (New York: Wiley, 1998), the standard work on child development. This four-volume set includes: theoretical models of human development (volume 1); cognition, perception and language (volume 2); social, emotional and personality development (volume 3); and child psychology in practice (volume 4). The *Handbook of Child Psychopathology* edited by Thomas H. Ollendick and Michel Hersen (New York: Plenum Press, 1998) is a useful handbook comprising essays that detail a wide range of psychopathological issues that pertain to children.

The *Handbook of Infant Mental Health* (New York: The Guilford Press, 2000) edited by Charles H. Zeanah Jr., is a comprehensive, interdisciplinary handbook of the developmental, clinical and social aspects of infant mental health. The handbook covers models of development, risk conditions and protective factors, and social policy considerations, as well as assessment, evaluation and diagnosis for all children from birth to three years of age.

The *Handbook of Adolescent Psychology* edited by Vincent Van Hassel and Michel Hersen (New York: Pergamon Press, 1987) contains essays (with bibliographies) on adolescent psychology, psychopathology, psychiatry and other approaches to adolescent behaviour. Author and subject indexes are also included.

The *Handbook of the Psychology of Ageing* (Westport, CT: Greenwood, 1996) by James E. Birren and K. Warner Schaie is considered a classic in the field. It provides a comprehensive and authoritative overview to the numerous and expanding range of issues in the field of ageing. Of related interest is the *Handbook of Clinical Geropsychology* edited by Michel Hersen and Vincent B. Van Hasselt (New York: Plenum Press, 1998). This handbook contains a number of essays detailing a wide range of psychological issues that pertain to older adults. The *Handbook of Mental Health and Ageing*, 2nd ed., by James E. Birren, R. Bruce Sloane and Gene D. Cohen (San Diego, CA: Academic Press, 1992) is a comprehensive and useful handbook for advanced students, mental health professionals and researchers. The handbook has 33 chapters, covering a broad range of topics, including psychopathology and psychological assessment.

4.7.5 Educational psychology

The *Handbook of Educational Psychology,* edited by David C. Berliner and Robert C. Calfee (New York: MacMillan 1996) explores the intersection of psychology and education. This volume of more than 1000 pages summarizes the breadth and variety of theory, methods, practice and research in educational psychology. Educational psychology is placed in the context of the educational system and society at large. There are five major sections, each containing five to seven chapters written by experts, primarily from the United States, but also from Israel, England, Sweden, Norway, Belgium and Ireland. The sections review the current knowledge in areas such as cognition and motivation, child development, teaching, assessment methods and statistics. Bibliographies are included for each chapter.

The *Handbook of School Psychology*, 3rd ed., (New York: Wiley, 1999) edited by Cecil Reynolds, provides a comprehensive overview of the body of knowledge on which school psychology was founded, together with current research in the field. It includes sections on assessment, intervention with children and staff and legal and ethical issues. Also included are chapters on the history of school psychology and how other areas of psychology such as developmental, cognitive and behavioural have contributed to the topic area. There is an appendix containing the National Association of School Psychologists' Principles of Professional Ethics.

4.7.6 Experimental psychology

Steven's Handbook of Experimental Psychology, 2nd ed., edited by Richard C. Atkinson (New York: Wiley, 1988) is a two-volume set covering the major topic areas in experimental psychology. Subjects include: sensory perception, vision, emotion, learning and cognition, attention and memory. Articles, by a variety of authors, are grouped into four major sections. The first volume includes perception and motivation and the second volume covers learning and cognition. Bibliographies are provided for the chapters and a subject and author index are included for each volume.

4.7.7 History

(a) Print

The author of *A Chronology of Noteworthy Events in American Psychology* (Washington, DC: American Psychological Association, 1994) Warren R. Street, has compiled extensive, easy-to-access, factual notes on the history of psychology in chronological order. The entries include: dates of birth of notable figures; publication of books, journals and mental tests; passage of influential legislation; and events in the histories of psychological associations and institutions. The search for information can be cross-referenced with the Name Index, Subject Index, APA Division Index, or Calendar Index and quickly located by entry number. This resource provides an unusual view of the important moments in the field. *See also (b) Electronic* below. *A Source Book in the History of Psychology* edited by Richard J. Herrnstein and Edwin G. Boring (Cambridge, MA: Harvard University Press, 1966) is a collection of classic papers in psychology. The majority of the papers are pre-1900. The varied topics range from the nature of psychology to writings on learning and memory. The works include those by William James, Ebbinghaus, Aristotle, Locke, and Descartes. The *Guide to Manuscript Collections in the History of Psychology and Related Areas* compiled by Michael Sokal (Millwood, NY: Kraus, 1982) is a useful resource for historical study in the field. It includes collections of personal papers, manuscripts and correspondence.

(b) Electronic

An updated version of *A Chronology of Noteworthy Events in American Psychology* is available on the Web as *Today in the History of Psychology* at: <www.cwu.edu/~warren/today.html>. The online version has a unique 'pick a date' feature which allows the user to see the important events in psychology that transpired on any chosen day.

4.7.8 Neuropsychology

The *Handbook of Clinical and Experimental Neuropsychology* edited by Gianfranco Denes and Luigi Pizzamiglio (Hove, East Sussex: Psychology Press, 1999) is a comprehensive handbook comprising 38 chapters, each with extensive bibliographies. Each chapter provides in-depth overviews of specific experimental and applied neuropsychology topics. The topics include: dementia; movement disorders; language disorders; methodological problems; recognition disorders; special disorders; attention disorders; and recovery of functions. The authors give an integrated picture of cognitive functions, with a special emphasis on the clinical perspective. This resource is useful for both clinicians and researchers in neuropsychology. Of related interest is *The Neuropsychology Handbook* edited by Arthur MacNeill Horton, Jr, Danny Wedding and Jeffrey Webster (New York: Springer, 1997). Volume one presents essays on foundations and assessment. Volume two covers treatment issues and special populations. The *Handbook of Neuropsychology* edited by F. Boller and J. Grafman (Amsterdam: Elsevier, 1990) is a comprehensive work covering both the experimental and clinical aspects of neuropsychology.

4.7.9 Organizational behaviour

The *Handbook of Work and Organizational Psychology*, 2nd ed., edited by Pieter J. D. Drenth, Henk Thierry and Charles J. De Wolff (Hove, East Sussex: Psychology Press, 1998) is based on the findings of European organizational psychologists. The four-volume set presents a wide range of topics including: conflict resolution; employee selection and hiring; subjective perceptions of work; training and management; socialization to employment; participative management; and women and work.

The *Handbook of Industrial and Organizational Psychology* (Palo Alto, CA: Consulting Psychologists Press, 1990) edited Marvin D. Dunnette and Leaetta M. Hough, is an important work in the field of industrial and organizational psychology. The four-volume set covers a wide range of topics on: industrial psychology theory; individual and organization behaviour; organizational conflict; stress; and consumer behaviour. The authors provide useful reference lists, tables and statistics with each chapter. Technical terms are explained and the writing is easily accessible to a wide range of readers. Of related interest is The *Handbook of Organizational Behavior* edited by Jay W. Lorsch (Englewood Cliffs, NJ: Prentice Hall, 1987) which is a useful resource for beginning researchers and undergraduates. It includes almost 30 essays covering broad aspects of industrial psychology. Although the handbook provides an excellent overview, the lack of indexes makes finding information on specific topics difficult.

4.7.10 Research

Journals in Psychology: a Resource Listing for Authors (Washington, DC: American Psychological Association, 1997). This handbook lists over 300 professional and research journals for psychologists seeking publication for their manuscripts. It is also useful for students attempting to locate the appropriate scholarly journal for research.

Experimental and Quasi-Experimental Designs for Research by Donald Campbell and Julian Stanley (Chicago, Ill: Rand McNally, 1963) is the classic work on experimental and quasi-experimental research designs. This concise volume describes in detail experimental design and methods of controlling sources of 'invalidity' or error using various research models.

The *Handbook of Multivariate Experimental Psychology*, 2nd ed., edited by Raymond Cattell and John R. Nesselroade (New York: Plenum Press, 1988) provides a thorough review of multivariate experimental psychology. The articles are organized under major headings, including: multivariate method and theory construction; multivariate modelling and data analysis; and multivariate research and theory.

4.7.11 Social psychology

The *Handbook of Social Psychology*, 4th ed., edited by Daniel T. Gilbert, Susan T. Fiske and Garder Lindzey (Boston, MA: McGraw-Hill, 1998). This two-volume set is considered to be the standard handbook in social psychology. Each of the 38 chapters is authored by a leading figure in the field. The topics covered include both the traditional areas in social psychology and also newer topics such as stigma, emotion, evolutionary psychology and mental control. There are chapters on methodology and statistics and a number of historical essays. This is a well-organized and concise reference tool. *Social Psychology: Handbook of Basic Principles* edited by Tory Higgens and Arie W. Kruglanski (New York: Guilford Press, 1996) is a well-researched and technical reference book. It provides a comprehensive review of the major concepts in social psychology and reviews of research. The topics included are: the biological system; the cognitive system; the personal motivational system; the interpersonal system; and the group and cultural system. This is an excellent resource for advanced students and is often used as a textbook.

▶ 4.8 WEBSITES

Athabasca University Psychology Resources <server.bmod.athabascau.ca/html/aupr/psycres.htm>. This is a nicely organized list site with a focus on psychology links to departments and specific subtopics in psychology.

Center for Mental Health Services Knowledge Exchange Network <www.mentalhealth.org/>. This United States government-sponsored site is devoted to mental health and substance abuse. The site includes statistics and databases. Its mental health directory of 18 000+ organizations and annotated bibliography of state and local publications are particularly useful.

Classics in the History of Psychology <www.yorku.ca/dept/psych/classics/>. A valuable resource that makes the full text of a large number of historically significant public domain documents from the scholarly literature of psychology and related disciplines available on the World Wide Web. The initial documents were chosen by the editor of the project, Christopher D. Green of York University, in consultation with other historians of psychology. There are currently about 20 books and over 80 articles and chapters online, with 150 more links to relevant works posted elsewhere. Documents are text searchable and available sorted by topic and author. The site indicates that their target audience is researchers, teachers and students of the history of psychology. This is a particularly useful site that provides information not otherwise available online.

Cognitive and Psychological Sciences on the Internet <www-psych.stanford.edu/cogsci.html>. Compiled at Stanford University, this site is research oriented covering: departments, conferences, newsgroups, discussion lists and publishers. The journal list and lengthy miscellaneous section are both very good. Clinical and psychiatric fields are excluded.

Cognitive Sciences E-Print Archive <cogprints.soton.ac.uk/>. An archive for papers in any area of psychology, neuroscience and linguistics, and many areas of computer science, philosophy, anthropology, biology and medicine (including psychiatry and neurology) pertinent to the study of cognition. The site provides free access to scholarly and scientific research literature. The literature includes pre-refereed preprints and refereed, published reprints.

Internet Survival Guide of Industrial/Organizational Psychology <allserv.rug.ac.be/~flievens/guide.htm>. This is a well-maintained site with useful links to basic and applied information on human resource management and organizational psychology, as well as an excellent collection of research resources on statistics and methodology.

Mental Health Net <mentalhelp.net/>. A comprehensive, easy-to-use site, allowing users to search more than 8000 refereed resources in psychology, psychiatry and social work. Resources are organized into four sections: Disorders and Treatments; Professional Resources; a Reading Room; and Managed Care and Administration. The site rates and annotates the Websites of major mental health associations and organizations.

Psych Site <stange.simplenet.com/psycsite/>. A non-profit, public-service Internet site for psychologists and psychology students, focusing exclusively on research and science, excluding any self-help links. This site should be noted for the ease of navigation.

Psych Web <www.psychwww.com/>. This site is a useful resource oriented to the needs of students, teachers and laypersons, but it will be of limited use to researchers and academics. There are links to self-help pages, tips for undergraduate psychology majors, helpful tip sheets for using APA (American Psychological Association) writing style, guides for planning a graduate career and finding a job. This is one of the oldest and most student friendly Websites.

PsychCrawler <www.psychcrawler.com/>. This resource provides a search engine specifically designed for finding information on psychology-related sites. *PsychCrawler* is a product of the American Psychological Association created to provide fast and easy access to quality content in the field of psychology. This site is currently limited by the small number of indexed sites. In addition, most indexed sites are affiliated with the United States Government. However, the site claims that the product is under rapid development and that they will be adding many new sites. *PsychCrawler* indexes the Websites of the American Psychological Association, National Institute of Mental Health and the US Department of Health and Human Services, as well as a number of major substance abuse sites.

PsychNet-UK <www.psychnet-uk.com/>. Contains links to a variety of psychology pages, including sites not included on most other psychology Websites. There are gateways for mental health professionals, psychological training, corporate psychological services and those seeking help or counselling.

Psychological Online Documents (World Wide) <www.psychologie.uni-bonn.de/online-documents/lit_ww.htm>. This site, maintained at Bonn University, has an extensive list of online psychology-related papers from sources worldwide. Users should be cautioned that although new papers are added regularly, the site contains numerous broken links.

Psychology Resources <www.psychologyresources.net/>. This site was developed to serve academic psychologists engaged in research. For example, it contains a good description of various research-oriented Internet search methods.

Psychology Virtual Library <Web.clas.ufl.edu/users/gthursby/psi/>. The *Psychology Virtual Library* catalogues online psychology-related information as part of *The World Wide Web Virtual Library*. The *Virtual Library*, started by Tim Berners-Lee, is the oldest catalogue on the Web. Unlike commercial catalogues, it is run by volunteers, who compile links for particular areas in which they are expert. Although the *Virtual Library* is not one of the largest indexes, it is regarded as the one of the highest quality guides to particular sections of the Web. The *Virtual Library* only includes sites that have been inspected and evaluated by experts for their adequacy as information sources.

Resources for Psychology and Cognitive Sciences on the Internet <www.ke.shinshu-u.ac.jp/psych/index.html>. This is an excellent site produced by the Department of Kansei Engineering, Shinshu University (Japan). This comprehensive Website provides an extensive list of international links. It covers online journals, associations and conferences, but is particularly good for access to academic departments and research institutes. The site is searchable and fairly easily navigated.

Social Psychology Network <www.socialpsychology.org/>. The largest social psychology database on the Internet. This site contains more than 5000 links to psychology-related resources and electronic discussion forums for students and professionals. The strength of the *Social Psychology Network* is in creating a single list of organizations involved in current social psychological issues.

The *Social Science Information Gateway* (SOSIG) *Psychology Gateway* <sosig.esrc.bris.ac.uk/psychology/>. One of the most comprehensive and well-organized psychology resources. Each resource has been evaluated and categorised using the APA (American Psychological Association) PsycINFO coding scheme.

▶ 4.9 JOURNALS

4.9.1 General

American Psychologist (0003–066X) (Washington, DC: American Psychological Association, 1946–). Monthly. The official journal of the American Psychological Association. It publishes refereed articles on current issues in psychology, including empirical, theoretical and practical papers covering broad aspects of the discipline.

Australian Journal of Psychology (ISSN 0004–9530) (Victoria: Melbourne University Press, 1949–). Three issues a year. A refereed journal that includes articles and book reviews on any topic with a focus on psychology. Abstracts are available electronically at <www.psychsociety.com.au/member/ajpabstracts.html>.

British Journal of Psychology (ISSN 0007–1269) (Leicester: British Psychological Society). Quarterly. A peer-reviewed, general journal with a strong international reputation. Contributions cover a wide array of topic areas. Book reviews are also included. Available electronically.

Contemporary Psychology (ISSN 0010–7549) (Washington, DC: American Psychological Association, 1956–). Bimonthly. The journal publishes critical reviews of media relevant to psychology, including books, films and tapes. Peer-reviewed articles encompass a cross-section of topics within psychology and should appeal to a broad audience. Submissions are by invitation only.

European Psychologist (ISSN 1016–9040) (Kirkland, WA: Hogrefe & Huber, 1996–). Quarterly. A prominent, peer-reviewed journal that provides information about applied and research psychology throughout Europe. The journal contains articles written for a non-specialized general readership, and includes reviews, reports, commentaries and news.

The Indian Journal of Psychology (ISSN 0019–5553) (Calcutta: Indian Psychlogical Association, 1926–). Quarterly. The official publication of the Indian Psychological Association. The text of this journal is in English.

Japanese Journal of Psychology (ISSN 0021–5236) (Tokyo: Japanese Psychological Association, 1926–). Bimonthly. This peer-reviewed journal is an official publication of the Japanese Psychological Association. The text of the journal is in Japanese with the table of contents available in both Japanese and English. English translations of the abstracts are available on the major bibliographic databases, including *PsycINFO* (*see 4.10* (*b*)).

Journal of Comparative Psychology (ISSN 0735–7036) (Washington, DC: American Psychological Association, 1983–). Quarterly. This journal focuses on empirical and theoretical research from a comparative perspective. Topic areas include: social behaviour; behaviour genetics; behavioural rhythms; communication; comparative cognition; evolutionary psychology; methodology; sensory and perceptual processes; and social cognition.

Journal of Russian and East European Psychology. (ISSN 1061–0405) (Armonk, NY: ME Sharpe, 1992–). Bimonthly. A journal that focuses on developments in psychology in the Russian and East European region. The text is in English.

New Zealand Journal of Psychology (ISSN 0112–109X) (Christchurch: New Zealand Psychological Society, 1983–). Two issues a year. This publication of the New Zealand Psychological Society is the only journal from New Zealand dedicated to psychology. It includes contributions from both home and international authors.

Psychological Bulletin (ISSN 0033–2909) (Washington, DC: American Psychological Association, 1904–). Bimonthly. This is a peer-reviewed journal of evaluative and integrative reviews and interpretations of issues in scientific psychology.

Psychological Review (ISSN 0033–295X) (Washington, DC: American Psychological Association, 1925–). Quarterly. Publishes important, peer-reviewed theoretical contributions across all areas of scientific psychology.

Psychological Science (ISSN 0956–7976) (Washington, DC: American Psychological Society, 1990–). Bimonthly. This journal of the American Psychological Society explores research, theory and application in psychology and related sciences. Recently ranked eighth among 92 psychology journals for impact, *Psychological Science* publishes general articles, research articles, research reports, commentaries and letters.

Psycoloquy <www.princeton.edu/~harnad/psyc.html> is a refereed electronic journal sponsored by the American Psychological Association. The journal has a readership of more than 40 000. Journal coverage is international and interdisciplinary in scope. Authors submit brief research notes and book reviews.

Scandinavian Journal of Psychology (ISSN 0036–5564) (Stockholm: Almquist and Wiksell, 1960–). Quarterly. Published in association with the Nordic psychological associations, the journal contains high-quality articles from Scandinavia and elsewhere, covering a range of psychological topics with a special focus on experimental psychology. The journal's consistently high standards have helped it acquire readers worldwide. Available electronically.

South African Journal of Psychology (ISSN 0081–2463) (Pretoria: Bureau of Scientific Publications of the Foundation for Education, Science and Technology, 1970–). Quarterly. The journal, which focuses on developments in psychology in the area, is the largest publication in the social sciences in the Southern African region. Articles are in English and Afrikaans, with summaries in both languages.

4.9.2 Clinical psychology

British Journal of Clinical Psychology (ISSN 0144–6657) (Leicester: British Psychological Society, 1981–). Quarterly. A peer-reviewed publication that publishes original work contributing to scientific knowledge in clinical psychology. Paper topics include: descriptive comparisons and studies of the assessment; aetiology and treatment of people with a wide range of psychological problems in all age groups and settings. Available electronically.

Psychological Assessment (ISSN 1040–3590) (Washington, DC: American Psychological Association, 1989–). Quarterly. This peer-reviewed journal primarily publishes empirical articles with a focus on clinical assessment. These include: contributions on the development, validation, application and evaluation of psychological assessment instruments; clinical judgement and decision-making; methods of measurement of treatment process and outcome; and dimensions of individual differences as they relate to clinical assessment.

4.9.3 Cognitive psychology

European Journal of Cognitive Psychology (ISSN 0954–1446) (Hove, Hillsdale: Published for the European Society for Cognitive Psychology by L. Erlbaum Associates, 1989–). Quarterly. The official journal of the European Society for Cognitive Psychology. It focuses on the exchange and integration of ideas, research and training in European cognitive psychology. The journal includes reports of empirical work, theoretical discussions and literature reviews in all areas of cognitive psychology.

4.9.4 Developmental psychology

Developmental Psychology (ISSN 0012–1649) (Washington, DC: American Psychological Association, 1969–). Bimonthly. The peer-reviewed journal advances knowledge and theory about human development across the life-span. The focus is primarily on human development, although papers about other species are included if they have implications for human development.

4.9.5 Educational psychology

The British Journal of Educational Psychology (ISSN 0007–0998) (Leicester: British Psychological Society, 1931–). Quarterly. This refereed journal publishes articles that contribute to the understanding and practice of education and include: theoretical studies; case studies; action research; surveys; experimental studies; and psychometric and methodological research. Available electronically.

Journal of Educational Psychology (ISSN 0022–0663) (Baltimore, Md: Warwick & York, 1910–). Quarterly. A peer-reviewed journal that publishes original, primary psychological research pertaining to education at all educational levels. Topics include: cognition, instruction, emotion, social issues, motivation, development and special populations.

Journal Europeen de Psychologie de l'Education (European Journal of Psychology of Education) (ISSN 0256–2928) (Lisboa: ISPA/Instituto Superior de Psicologia Aplicada, 1986–). Quarterly. This journal covers the major topics in the psychology of education. Subjects include: special needs education; learning and communication; and educational achievement. Special themed issues are produced on an occasional basis. The journal is available in both English and French.

4.9.6 Experimental psychology

Canadian Journal of Experimental Psychology (ISSN 1196–1961) (Old Chelsea, Quebec: Canadian Psychological Association, 1993–). Quarterly. This peer-reviewed journal is a publication of the Canadian Psychological Association and continues the *Canadian Journal of Psychology*. It includes articles focused on topics in experimental psychology. The text is in both English and French.

Journal of Experimental Psychology: Applied (ISSN 1076–898X) (Washington, DC: American Psychological Association, 1995–). Quarterly. The journal publishes original, refereed, empirical investigations in experimental psychology that combine practically oriented problems with psychological theory. Topic areas include: applications of perception; attention; decision-making; reasoning; information processing; learning and performance.

4.9.7 Health psychology

British Journal of Health Psychology (ISSN 1359–107X) (Leicester: British Psychological Society, 1996–). Quarterly. This is a peer-reviewed journal that focuses on high quality research relating to health and illness. Common topics include: the management of acute and chronic illness; responses to ill-health; screening and medical procedures; and research on health behaviour and psychological aspects of prevention. Available electronically.

4.9.8 Research and methodology

Japanese Psychological Research (ISSN 0021–5368) (Oxford: Blackwell Publishers, 1954–). Quarterly. The journal publishes original articles from the members of the Japanese Psychological Association. This refereed journal has an international focus and attempts to raise awareness of psychological research in Japan.

Psychological Methods (ISSN 1082–989X) (Washington, DC: American Psychological Association, 1996–). Quarterly. This peer-reviewed journal publishes papers focused on methods for collecting, analysing, understanding and interpreting psychological data. The journal describes its purpose as the dissemination of innovations in research design, measurement, methodology, and quantitative and qualitative analysis to the psychological community.

4.9.9 Social psychology

British Journal of Social Psychology (ISSN 0144–6665) (Leicester: British Psychological Society, 1981–). Quarterly. The journal publishes peer-reviewed, original papers in all areas of social psychology. Topics include: attitudes; group processes; intergroup relations; self and identity; social cognition; social influence; and social psychological aspects of affect and emotion. Available electronically.

Current Research in Social Psychology: an Electronic Journal <www.uiowa.edu/~grpproc/crisp/crisp.html> (ISSN 1088–7423). A peer-reviewed, electronic journal covering all aspects of social psychology. The publication is sponsored by the Center for the Study of Group Processes at the University of Iowa which provides free access to its contents. The journal includes papers from both the psychological and sociological perspectives.

European Journal of Social Psychology (ISSN 0046–2772) (New York: Wiley 1971–). Quarterly. A refereed international journal with articles focusing on original research in all areas of social psychology. Most articles are based on empirical results, although a few theoretical or methodological articles may also be included. The text of this journal is in English with summaries in French, German and occasionally Russian. Available electronically.

Journal of Personality and Social Psychology (ISSN 0022–3514) (Washington, DC: American Psychological Association, 1965–). A peer-reviewed journal covering all areas of personality and social psychology. The journal includes three separately edited sections: attitudes and social cognition; interpersonal relations and group processes; and personality processes and individual differences.

► 4.10 ABSTRACTS, INDEXES AND DATABASES

(a) Print

The *Index of Psychoanalytic Writings* (New York: International Universities Press, 1956–1971) edited by Alexander Grinstein, is a comprehensive, international bibliography of psychoanalytic writings. This 14-volume set covers the period 1900–1969 and includes more than 200 000 references.

Psychological Abstracts (Washington, DC: American Psychological Association, 1927–) is the printed version of the *PsycINFO* database. This monthly publication contains summaries of English-language journals, technical reports, books and book chapters relevant to psychology. The summaries include abstracts and full bibliographic and indexing information. To facilitate browsing, *Psychological Abstracts* is organized by subject area based on the *PsycINFO* classification codes. Cumulative author and subject indexes, published annually, provide quick and easy access to each year's references. *See also PsycINFO* under *(b) Electronic* below.

L'annee Psychologique (Paris: Presses Universitaires de France. 1894–) is published twice a year and provides international coverage of all fields of psychology. It includes signed abstracts of journal articles and critical reviews of books. Both author and subject indexes are included.

(b) Electronic

ClinPSYC (Washington, DC: American Psychological Association) is a subset of *PsycINFO*. It is a rolling 10-year file with quarterly updates, covering only clinical topics in the journal literature. Topics covered include: mental disorders and treatments; the psychological aspects of physical disorders and treatments; psychopharmacology; and assessment methods. Given the specialized focus, this resource will be most helpful for individuals requiring clinical literature, including clinical psychologists, health psychologists, social workers, psychiatrists, physicians, nurses, and public health specialists. *ClinPSYC* is available from several suppliers including: SilverPlatter Information <www.silverplatter.com> (Hard Disk, CD-ROM and Internet) and Ovid <www.ovid.com> (CD-ROM and Internet).

The *ERIC/AE Test Locator* <ericae.net/testcol.htm> contains descriptions and reviews of over 10 000 tests and research instruments covering all fields. The database is searchable and indexed by keyword and *ERIC* descriptors. The database also includes Test Selection Tips: a Code of Fair Testing Practices; and the Test Review Locator and Test Publisher Locator.

ERIC (Educational Resources Information Center) <ericae.net/> (Rockville, MD: ERIC Processing and Reference Facility, 1966–). This data-base, sponsored by the US Department of Education, covers literature in the field of education and educational psychology. It includes articles on psychology as it relates to learning. The database indexes journal articles, books, theses, curricula, conference papers, standards and guidelines, and educational reports. *See 6.10* for further information about the database.

Linguistics and Language Behavior Abstracts (Bethesda, MD: Cambridge Scientific Abstracts) is a searchable database of over 285 000 bibliographic records, covering all aspects of the study of language including: phonetics, phonology, morphology, syntax and semantics. It focuses on three fundamental areas: research in linguistics; research in language; and research in speech, language and hearing pathology. The database is updated quarterly and includes abstracts from over 1300 journals from 50 countries. It is available from a number of suppliers including: SilverPlatter Information <www.silverplatter.com> (Hard Disk, CD-ROM and Internet) and Ovid <www.ovid.com> (CD-ROM and Internet).

Links to Psychological Journals <telehealth.net/armin/>. An index of more than 1600 online psychology and social science journals. The Website provides links to journal home pages and journal information on the Web. It indexes English, German, French, Dutch and Spanish language journals. The site is useful for gathering information on existing journals in the field, contacting publishers, browsing tables of contents and, in some cases abstracts, and locating available online articles.

MEDLINE (Bethesda, MD: National Library of Medicine). This database, developed by the National Library of Medicine, indexes the journal literature in the field of medicine, including psychiatry. It is available from a number of suppliers including: SilverPlatter Information <www.silverplatter.com> (CD-ROM, DVD and Internet) and Ovid <www.ovid. com> (CD-ROM and Internet).

PsycARTICLES (Washington, DC: American Psychological Association, 1988–) is an online database containing more than 25 000 searchable full-text articles from 42 journals published by the American Psychological Association and allied organizations. The database contains articles from 1988 to the present and covers general psychology and applied, clinical and theoretical research in psychology.

PsycINFO (Washington, DC: American Psychological Association, 1887–). The primary index in the field of psychology and a larger and more comprehensive online version of *PsycLit* on CD-ROM and *Psychological Abstracts* (See *(a) Print* above). *PsycINFO* includes citations and abstracts to journal articles, book chapters, technical reports, conference papers and dissertations. The database comprises more than 1.5 million references from 1887 to present. It includes literature relevant to psychology and related disciplines, including sociology, psychiatry, education, medicine and business. The database abstracts materials from over 1300 periodicals. Other useful features include the hypertext links to APA's *Thesaurus of Psychological Index Terms*. The database is available from a number of suppliers including: SilverPlatter Information <www.silverplatter.com> (Hard Disk, CD-ROM and Internet); and Ovid <www.ovid.com> (CD-ROM and Internet).

4.11 OFFICIAL PUBLICATIONS

Psychologists do not make particular use of a narrowly defined group of official publications. *See 1.11* for a general guide to official publications of interest to social scientists.

► 4.12 STATISTICS

4.12.1 Statistical reports

The *Center for Mental Health Services Locator* <iservices.cdmgroup.com/cmhsdata/cmhsdata.cfm> is a service of the Substance Abuse and Mental Health Services Administration, providing a searchable online database of mental health statistics, resources and services, by state. Information is limited to the United States.

The Numbers Count <www.nimh.nih.gov/publicat/numbers.cfm> produced by the US National Institute of Mental Health, provides current statistical summaries on national mental health conditions and issues in the USA.

4.12.2 Data archives useful for calculating statistics

The following data archives include many regional and population-based survey datasets. Although the datasets primarily contain demographic and sociological information, many also contain psychological information related to respondents' attitudes, opinions, motivations, expectations, beliefs, values and personality. These datasets can be used for secondary data analysis to calculate statistics on user-defined topics of interest.

The *Inter-University Consortium for Political and Social Research (ICPSR)* <www.icpsr.umich.edu> located within the Institute for Social Research at the University of Michigan (USA), is a membership-based, not-for-profit organization serving member colleges and universities in the United States and abroad. *ICPSR* provides access to the world's largest archive of computerized social science data. While some of these data is available only to those affiliated with member institutions, much of it is provided free of charge to the public through one or more of the topical data archives hosted by *ICPSR*: The Substance Abuse and Mental Health Data Archive; The International Archive of Education Data; The National Archive of Computerized Data on Ageing; and The National Archive of Criminal Justice Data.

The *UK Data Archive* <www.data-archive.ac.uk/> is a specialist national resource containing the largest collection of accessible computer readable data in the social sciences and humanities in the United Kingdom. Through their Web pages it is also possible to search the catalogues of other national archives for computer readable data and to use the services of the UK Data Archive to acquire these data on your behalf. See also 1.12.1 (b) Electronic.

▶ 4.13 RESEARCH IN PROGRESS

C-Psych (to subscribe contact listserv@MAELSTROM.STJOHNS.EDU) is a mailing list for researchers, practitioners, students and the lay public interested in cross-cultural psychology. This list was developed to discuss generic issues in cross-cultural psychology and connected areas, such as developmental, cognitive, personality and social psychology. A main focus of the list is the discussion of both quantitative and qualitative methodology, research, and generic issues in the study of cultures.

Clinical-Psychologist (to subscribe contact listserv@LISTSERV.NODAK.EDU putting 'subscribe clinical-psychologists' in the body of the message). This list is publicly available and provides an opportunity for the international community of clinical psychologists to share ideas, research and data encompassing the broad area of clinical psychology.

CRISP (Computer Retrieval of Information on Scientific Projects) <www-commons.cit.nih.gov/crisp/> is a searchable database of United States Government-funded biomedical research projects conducted at universities, hospitals and other research institutions. The *CRISP* database is maintained by the Office of Extramural Research at the National Institutes of Health (NIH). It includes projects funded by NIH, Substance Abuse and Mental Health Services Administration, Health Resources and Services Administration, Food and Drug Administration, Centers for Disease Control and Prevention, Agency for Healthcare Research and Quality and Office of Assistant Secretary of Health. *CRISP* is useful for searching for scientific concepts, emerging trends and techniques and identifying specific projects and investigators.

DIV12 (to subscribe Email listserv@LISTSERV.NODAK.EDU, putting 'subscribe div12' in the body of the message) is the official electronic forum for members of Division 12 (Clinical Psychology) of the American

Psychological Association. The main function of the list is to serve as a means of communication and rapid dissemination of knowledge on issues relating to the science and practice of clinical psychology.

The *Global School Psychology Network* <www.dac.neu.edu/cp/consult/> is described as an innovative Internet community for school psychologists. The network is committed to fostering professional development, peer support, problem-solving assistance and research. This site provides an interesting and creative graphical desktop. There are separate communities for practising school psychologists and graduate students.

National Center for the Workplace, Working Papers Series <violet.berkeley.edu/~iir/ncw/wpapers/index.html>. Produced by the Institute of Industrial Relations, University College, Berkeley, this site provides online access to the full text of working papers in the field of industrial relations. Common topics include job quality, training, performance and compensation.

Psych-methods <www.jiscmail.ac.uk/lists/psych-methods.html> is an electronic discussion list of qualitative and quantitative methods used in psychological research. The discussion topics can range from the appropriate methodology for a specific research project, to specific questions about the interpretations of a result.

SocPsy-L (to subscribe Email LISTSERV@UGA.CC.UGA.EDU, putting SUBSCRIBE SocPsy-L <name>). This list was created to encourage communication between researchers on topics relevant to social psychology. *SocPsy-L* provides an opportunity for individuals to discuss issues including current directions in theory and the application of social-psychological research.

▶ 4.14 ORGANIZATIONS

4.14.1 General

American Psychological Association
750 First St., NE Washington, DC 20002–4242, USA
Tel: +1 202 336 5500
Email: executiveoffice@apa.org
Web: <www.apa.org/>

The main scientific and professional organization representing psychology in the United States and the world's largest association of psychologists. Its membership includes more than 159 000 researchers, educators, clinicians, consultants and students. Through its divisions in 50 subfields of psychology and affiliations with 59 state, territorial and Canadian provincial associations, the association works to advance psychology as a science, as a profession and as a means of promoting human welfare.

American Psychological Society
1010 Vermont Avenue, NW, Suite 1100, Washington, DC 20005–4907, USA
Tel: +1 202 783 2077
Fax: +1 202 783 2083
Email: aps@aps.washington.dc.us
Web: <www.psychologicalscience.org/>

Founded in 1988, it is one of the leading psychological societies in the US, dedicated solely to scientific psychology. Its mission is to promote, protect and advance the interests of scientifically oriented psychology in research, application and the improvement of human welfare.

Australian Psychological Society
1 Grattan Street, Carlton, PO Box 126, Carlton South, Victoria 3053, Australia
Tel.: +61 3 8662 3300
Fax: +61 3 9663 6177
Email: natloff@psychsociety.com.au

Established in 1966 as the body that represents the interests of the science and profession of psychology nationwide. The mission of the society is 'to represent, promote and advance psychology and psychologists, within the context of improving community well being and scientific knowledge'. The organization has over 13 000 members.

Belgian Psychological Society
Vera Hoorens, Katholieke Universiteit Leuven, Departement Psychologie, Tiensestraat 102, B-3000 Leuven, Belgium
Email: fjvoverw@vub.ac.be
Web: <www.ulb.ac.be/bps/>

Founded in 1946, the aims of the society include: spreading information about the scientific development of psychology, organizing courses on career development and safeguarding the professional interests and stature of the psychologist.

The British Psychological Society
St. Andrews House, 48 Princess Road East, Leicester, LE1 7DR, UK
Tel: +44 (0)116 254 9568
Fax: +44 (0)116 247 0787
Email: enquiry@bps.org.uk
Web: <www.bps.org.uk/>

Founded in 1901, the society exists to promote the advancement of the study of psychology and its applications, and to maintain high standards of professional education and conduct. It currently has more than 32 000 members.

Canadian Psychological Association
151 Slater Street, Suite 205, Ottawa, Ontario K1P 5H3, Canada
Tel: +1 613 237 2144
Fax: +1 613 237 1674
Email: iparisien@cpa.ca
Web: <cpa.ca/>

Established in 1939 to ensure psychology's contribution to the war effort. Over the ensuing 60 years, the association has been active in promoting high standards in science, education and practice. It is a voluntary organization which represents the interests of all aspects of psychology in Canada, promoting unity, coherence and a sense of identity across the diverse scientific and professional interests.

European Federation of Professional Psychologists Association
EFPPA Head Office, Grasmarkt 105/18, B-1000 Brussels, Belgium
Tel: +32 2 503 49 53
Fax: +32 2 503 30 67
Email: efppa@skynet.be

The European Federation of Professional Psychologists' Association (EFPPA) is a federation of national psychology associations. It is the only European organization entitled to speak for European psychologists and it provides a forum for European cooperation in a wide range of fields of psychological practice and research. There are 30 member associations of *EFPPA* representing about 110 000 psychologists.

Finnish Psychological Society
Liisankatu 16 A, FIN-00170 Helsinki, Finland
Tel: +358 9 278 2122
Fax: +358 9 278 1300
Email: psykologia@genealogia.fi

The Finnish Psychological Society has about 1600 members. The aims of the society include supporting and developing psychological research and publishing in Finland, and acting as a link between representatives of basic psychological research and applied psychology in Finland. The society maintains links with similar organizations in other countries.

German Psychological Society
Sibylle Claßen, Hollandtstr. 61, 48161 Münster, Germany
Tel.: +49 251 862810
Fax: +49 251 869933
Email: dgps-gs@dgps.de
Web: <www.dgps.de/dgps_english.html>

Founded to promote scientific psychology in German speaking countries, the German Psychological Society has established 13 subject groups (divisions) to promote the development of the respective subdisciplines. The Website is primarily in German, but it does have a substantial number of pages in English.

National Institute of Mental Health (NIMH)
6001 Executive Boulevard, Rm. 8184, MSC 9663, Bethesda, MD 20892–9663, USA
Tel: +1 301 443 4513
Fax: +1 301 443 4279
Email: nimhinfo@nih.gov
Web: <www.nimh.nih.gov/>

Established in 1949, the NIMH is a mental health research institute funded by the US Government. Its mission is to diminish the burden of mental illness through research. The institute's mandate demands that it harness powerful scientific tools to achieve better understanding, treatment and, eventually, prevention of mental illness.

Norwegian Psychological Association
Storgt. 10A, Pb. 8733 Youngstorget, 0028 Oslo, Norway
Tel: +47 2310 3130
Fax: +47 2242 4292
Email: npfpost@psykol.no

The official psychological association in Norway. The 3500+ current members (94 per cent of all psychologists in Norway) have at least six and a half years of education and training in psychology. The association acts as a labour union negotiating wages and conditions for psychologists.

Spanish Psychological Association
Colegio Oficial de Psicologos, C/Conde de Peñalver, num. 45–5, E-28006 Madrid, Spain
Tel: +34 91 4449020
Fax: +34 91 3095615
Email: secop@correo.cop.es
Web: <www.cop.es/>

Founded in 1980 as the national organization representing the science and profession of psychology in Spain. The association currently has more than 24 000 members.

Swiss Psychological Association
SGP-SSP, Département de Psychologie, Rue Faucigny 2, 1700 Fribourg, Switzerland
Tel: +41 26 300 7640
Fax: +41 26 300 9712
Email: sgp-ssp@unifr.ch

Founded in 1943, this professional association has 430 members.

The Swedish Psychological Association
Sveriges Psykologförbund, Box 3287, 103 65 Stockholm, Sweden
Tel: +41 8567 06 400
Email: Webmaster@psykologforbundet.se

Founded in 1955 as both a trade union and a professional association. The association monitors the pay and employment conditions of its members. Its stated aims include: furthering the trade union and professional interests of its members; working for the appropriate training of psychologists; thorough monitoring of practical psychological activities in Sweden; promoting scientific development in psychology and its areas of application; promoting cooperation with Nordic and international associations; and working for the dissemination of knowledge about psychology.

4.14.2 Cross-cultural psychology

International Association for Cross Cultural Psychology
Klaus Boehnke, Secretary-General, Department of Sociology, Chemnitz University of Technology D-09107, Chemnitz, Germany
Tel: +49 371 5313925/2483

Founded in 1972, to facilitate communication between people interested in issues that involve the intersection of culture and psychology. The association has more than 800 members in over 65 countries.

4.14.3 Cognitive psychology

Cognitive Neuroscience Society
Dartmouth College, 6162 Moore Hall, Hanover, NH 03755, USA
Tel: +1 978 749 0021
Fax: +1 978 749 0025
Email: cns@dartmouth.edu

Founded in 1994, it currently has more than 1000 members worldwide. The society states that its members are committed to the development of mind and brain research aimed at the investigation of psychological, computational and neuroscientific bases of perception and cognition.

Cognitive Science Society
Cognitive Science Society Inc, PO Box 711012, Cincinnati, OH 45271–1012, USA
Tel: +1 512 471 2030
Fax: +1 512 471 3053
Email: cogsci@psy.utexas.edu

The Cognitive Science Society promotes scientific interchange among researchers in the various disciplines comprising the field of cognitive science. It aims to bring together researchers who focus on understanding the nature of the human mind.

4.14.4 Developmental psychology

Society for Research in Child Development
505 E. Huron, Suite 301, Ann Arbor, MI 48104–1567, USA
Tel: +1 734 998 6578
Fax: +1 734 998 6569
Email: srcd@umich.edu

An international, multidisciplinary, not-for-profit, professional association with more than 5000 members. The society promotes multidisciplinary research in the field of human development. It also stimulates information exchange among scientists and other professionals from various disciplines.

4.14.5 Neuropsychology

The British Neuropsychological Society
Dr Audrey Bowen, BNS Secretary, Human Communication and Deafness, Faculty of Education, University of Manchester, Oxford Road, Manchester, M13 9PL, UK
Tel: +44 (0)161 275 3401
Fax: +44 (0)161 275 3373
Email: Audrey.Bowen@man.ac.uk

Founded in 1989 to bring together persons interested in clinical and cognitive neuropsychology.

International Neuropsychological Society
700 Ackerman Road, Suite 550, Columbus, Ohio 43202, USA
Tel: +1 614 263 4200
Fax: +1 614 263 4366
Email: osu_ins@postbox.acs.ohio-state.edu

A multi-disciplinary non-profit organization dedicated to promoting research, service and education in neuropsychology, and to enhancing communication among the scientific disciplines that contribute to the understanding of brain-behaviour relationships. The society currently has more than 3700 members throughout the world.

National Academy of Neuropsychology
2121 South Oneida St. Suite 550, Denver, CO 80224–2594. USA
Tel: +1 303 691 3694
Fax: +1 303 691 5983
Email: office@NANonline.org

The membership of the National Academy of Neuropsychology includes clinicians, scientist-practitioners and researchers interested in neuropsychology. Its aims include: advancing the scientific study of brain-behaviour relationships using neuropsychological techniques; developing standards of practice for clinical neuropsychology; developing training standards and guidelines; developing standards of practice for clinical neuropsychology; and encouraging communication among neuropsychologists.

4.14.6 Political psychology

International Society of Political Psychology
ISPP Central Office, Pitzer College, 1050 N. Mills Ave., Claremont, CA 91711, USA
Tel: +1 909 621 8442
Fax: +1 909 621 8481
Email: ispp@pitzer.edui

A cross-disciplinary society that represents the many fields of inquiry focused on exploring the relationships between political and psychological processes. The society aims to advance the quality of scholarship in the field. Members come from all regions of the world including the Americas, Europe, Asia, the Middle East and Africa.

► REFERENCES

Boring, E. G. (1957) *History of Experimental Psychology,* 2nd ed., New York: Appelton-Century-Crofts.

Conner, A. (2001a) 'They all answer to 'psychologist'', in *APS Observer,* **14**(1), 1,8–9, 11.

Conner, A. (2001b) 'Territorial imperatives in psychological science', in *APS Observer,* **14**(2), 1,8–9, 11.

Kenrick, D. T. (2001) 'Evolutionary psychology, cognitive science, and dynamical systems: Building an integrative paradigm', in *Current Directions in Psychological Science,* **10**(1), 13–17.

5 Criminology

David Fisher

▶ 5.1 NATURE AND SCOPE OF CRIMINOLOGY

It is arguable that an interest in crime and criminals has its origins in the very earliest societies. Simultaneous with the creation of rules and laws of behaviour, is the opportunity to break them. Hot on the heels of the first miscreants are such age-old questions as: why do people break the rules? and what can be done to stop them? And thus one witnesses the first stirrings of a nascent criminology. However, the systematic development of criminology as a focus of intellectual curiosity only really took off in eighteenth century Europe. The reforming spirit of such writers as Montesquieu, Voltaire and Beccaria – the latter's *On Crimes and Punishments* (1764) stands out as a seminal early work – led to a critical analysis of the criminal justice system, which in turn paved the way for the upsurge in criminological interest in the nineteenth century. Two strands of activity are discernible: Belgian mathematician, Lambert Adolphe Jacques Quetelet, pioneered the application of statistical methods in the study of crime; whereas phrenologists such as Franz Joseph Gall and Johann K. Spurzheim were studying head shapes to predict types of criminal behaviour.

Italian physician, Cesare Lombroso, expanded theories linking physical features to personality and a criminal disposition. This led to an interest in genetics and hereditary factors as explanations for criminal behaviour. Enrico Ferri and Raffaele Garofalo developed Lombroso's work in important new directions. Whilst still interested in physical characteristics, they looked at how environmental and social forces external to the individual might influence criminal activity. Garofalo is credited with coining the term criminology in his book *Criminologia* published in 1885. Following the positivist school, these early figures believed in the scientific approach to the study of crime.

World War II was a turning point in scientific criminology, as Paul Friday (1983, p. 32) has noted, 'prior to this time most criminology focused on penal law or correctional issues, but after the war the orientation shifted to social science. Sociological and psychological research centred on crime, and the ISC (the International Society for Criminology, founded in 1938) became the primary organization for the dissemination of these new ideas.'

Academic criminology has witnessed many twists and turns in the half century since then, encompassing an interest in why some people and not others commit crimes, the creation of criminal and delinquent norms, the consequences of labelling individuals criminals and deviants, Marxist and radical criminologies, and renewed interest in crime control and prevention.

A current debate concerns the relationship between criminology and criminal justice. In the United States, the first university department established to study crime and justice was the School of Criminology at the University of California at Berkeley. However, it became a casualty of the political unrest in the 1960s and was subsequently closed. A new graduate programme at the State University of New York at Albany was named the School of Criminal Justice to disassociate it from Berkeley's unfortunate history. 1963 witnessed another key event in the separation of the International Association of Police Professors – to be called the Academy of Criminal Justice Sciences – from the American Society of Criminology. Criminal justice has become the preferred term in the USA, with criminology still finding favour in Europe and elsewhere.

So, is the criminology/criminal justice controversy merely a question of semantics, or are more fundamental issues at stake? This largely depends on who you speak to, but there seems to be a consensus developing which suggests both terms are reasonably interchangeable and share a common subject area – particularly in light of the apparently ever-widening boundaries of criminal justice. For further discussion see Benamati, et al. (1998). Cohn, Farrington and Wright (1998, pp. 121–2) have subjected the debate to citation analysis and note a 'fundamental complementarity' between the terms: 'Criminology and criminal justice now may be very much like Tweedledum and Tweedledee, who, as Alice discovered in *Through the Looking-Glass*, perpetually quarrelled, but still managed to finish each other's sentences.'

Criminology remains a multidisciplinary subject area and its key components – sociology, psychology, psychiatry, law and social policy – are reflected in the resources selected for this chapter. You will see that for clarity, rather than any ideological predilection, *Criminal Justice* is used as a separate heading, where appropriate.

▶ 5.2 ANNUALS

Michael Tonry is the general editor of a well-established series of publications, *Crime and Justice: a Review of Research* (Chicago, IL: University of Chicago Press) issued usually, but not invariably, on an annual basis. It is an excellent review series with each volume covering a different aspect of criminological research. *Advances in Criminological Theory* (ISSN 0894–2366) (Piscataway, NJ: Transaction Publishers, 1989–) is a journal produced on an annual basis by the School of Criminal Justice at Rutgers University, and acts as a forum for debate on all aspects of criminological theory.

McGraw-Hill are the publishers of a series called *Annual Editions;* they have a growing number of titles in their stable including: *Criminology*; *Criminal Justice*; *Juvenile Delinquency*; *Deviant Behavior*; and *Corrections*. The volumes collate articles from newspapers and key journals.

Sage Criminal Justice System Annuals is a useful series of edited volumes on a wide range of issues including: mental health, crime prevention, policing, capital punishment, victimology and prisons. The most recent volume is *Drug Treatment and Criminal Justice* edited by James A. Inciardi (Newbury Park, CA., London and New Delhi: Sage, 1993), whose 11 essays look at the various aspects of the drug abuse, offending and treatment equation. At the time of writing, the publishers have no plans for additional texts in the series.

A key series for those with a penchant for history is *Criminal Justice History: an International Annual* (London and Westport, CT: Greenwood Press, 1980–). An international platform for the discussion of the history of crime and criminal justice. The volumes typically include articles and book reviews. *See also 5.12* and *5.11* for annual statistical and official publications.

▶ 5.3 BIBLIOGRAPHIES

5.3.1 General

Criminology and the Administration of Criminal Justice: a Bibliography by Leon Radzinowicz and Roger Hood (London: Mansell, 1976) is a classic in the field. Although there are no entries beyond the mid-1970s, its scholarship is impeccable and has additional value as a record of the collaboration of two key criminologists. Its focus is sociological and ranges over a wide area of criminological research material (books, articles, reports) including: dimensions of crime and the problem of measurement; crime in its social setting; some categories of crime and criminals; the police; problems of sentencing; effectiveness of punishments and treatments; and international comparative references.

The US perspective is well-documented in *Criminology – a Bibliography: Research and Theory in the United States 1945–1972* (Philadelphia, PA: University of Pennsylvania Center for Studies in Criminology and

Criminal Law, 1974), which provides an extensive listing in two parts of over 3000 journal articles and more than 500 books published in the United States. For an exhaustive bibliographic essay on US criminology textbooks see Richard A. Wright's article, 'Criminology Textbooks, 1918 to 1993: a Comprehensive Bibliography' (*Journal of Criminal Justice Education* 5(2), 1994, 251–6). For a similar essay, but on Canadian literature see 'Canadian Books' by Andre Normandeau (*Canadian Journal of Criminology* 40(3), 1998, 329–41).

5.3.2 Comparative criminology

Comparative Criminology: an Annotated Bibliography by Piers Beirne and Joan Hill (London, New York and Westport, CT: Greenwood Press, 1991), abstracts 500 studies – books, chapters in books, journal articles, conference proceedings and unpublished papers – from the 1960s onwards. It is divided into three parts: Meaning and Measurement in Comparative Criminology; Cross-National Crime Rates; Social Control and Criminal Justice. Subject and author indexes are also provided. It is a key resource in this area of growing importance. For a critical review essay on the theoretical development of comparative criminology see T. D. Evans, R. L. LaGrange and C. L. Willis, 'Theoretical Development of Comparative Criminology: Rekindling an Interest' (*International Journal of Comparative and Applied Criminal Justice*, 20(1), 1996, 15–29).

5.3.3 Crime prevention

International Trends in Crime Prevention: an Annotated Bibliography by Irvin Waller and Brandon Welsh (Montreal: International Centre for the Prevention of Crime, 1995), covers 121 international publications written in English, French or Spanish. The focus of the bibliography is on the interaction between agencies and individuals and how this influences the causes of crime.

5.3.4 Criminal justice

Criminal Justice in America 1959–1984: an Annotated Bibliography by John D. Hewitt, Eric D. Poole and Robert M. Regoli (New York and London: Garland Publishing, 1985). The 813 entries are arranged into three main areas: law enforcement, courts and corrections, and each topic is further divided by the headings: history; organization; process and issues. Although 1984 is the cut-off point, the work does give an excellent introduction to the essential literature of the preceding 25 years. Name and subject indexes are included. A more historical perspective is adopted by *Canadian Criminal Justice History: an Annotated Bibliography* by Russell Smandych, Catherine Matthews and Sandra Cox (Toronto: University of Toronto Press, 1987). It covers around 1100 works written in English and French between 1867 and 1984.

Criminal Justice In Israel: an Annotated Bibliography of English language Publications, 1948–1993 compiled by Robert R. Friedmann (London and Westport, CT: Greenwood Press, 1995) is an excellent guide to materials – articles, books, book chapters and reports – published between 1948 and 1993. Topics include: corrections and treatment; addiction; crime by and among the aged; fear of crime; homicide, aggression and violence; juvenile delinquency and juvenile justice; organized crime; rape; terrorism; victimology; and white collar crime. A combined author, journal and subject index is included.

'Aids and the Criminal Justice System: an Annotated Bibliography' by John R. Austin and Rebecca S. Trammell (*Northern Illinois University Law Review* **11**(2/3), 1991, 481–527) is a useful review of the literature on the impact of HIV and AIDS on the criminal justice system.

Criminal Justice Ethics: Annotated Bibliography and Guide to Sources by Frank Schmalleger (London and Westport, CT: Greenwood Press, 1991) is a valuable resource from the Greenwood stable covering general criminal justice policy, police, courts, corrections and victim's rights. The book also lists additional sources (databases and organizations) for research on criminal justice ethics. For an international review of police and criminal justice accountability, take a look at *Accountability in the Administration of Criminal Justice: a Selective Annotated Bibliography* by Catherine J. Matthews (Toronto: Centre of Criminology, University of Toronto, 1993) which analyses material from the United States and Canada, Australia and New Zealand and the UK.

5.3.5 Criminologists

African-American Criminologists, 1970–1996: an Annotated Bibliography by Lee E. Ross (London and Westport, CT: Greenwood Press, 1998). This book showcases the work of around 45 African-American criminologists and provides abstracts of their key contributions to the literature. It also includes an essay by Lee E. Ross and Harvey L. McMurray on the challenges faced by African-American criminologists. For coverage of the period prior to the 1970s see H. T. Greene (ed.) *A Comprehensive Bibliography of Criminology and Criminal Justice Literature by Black Authors from 1895 to 1978* (Hyattsville, MD.: Ummah Publications, 1979). For directories of criminologists *see also 5.5.*

5.3.6 Deterrence

Deryck Beyleveld's *Bibliography on General Deterrence Research* (Farnborough: Saxon House, 1980) provides a critical review of the early literature on deterrence research covering the years 1946–1978. For an analysis of the characteristics of deterrence research publications 1950–1979 see A. DiChiara and J. F. Galliher, 'Thirty Years of Deterrence Research: Characteristics, Causes, and Consequences' (*Contemporary Crises*, 8(3), 1984, 243–63).

5.3.7 Domestic violence

Domestic Criminal Violence: a Selected Bibliography by Marvin E. Wolfgang, Neil A. Weiner and Donald Pointer (Washington, DC: US National Criminal Justice Reference Service, 1981) offers selected references from the National Criminal Justice Reference Service database for the years 1972–1980. Angela Patrignani and Renaud Ville have produced a useful review of works published between 1985 and 1992 in *Violence in the Family: an International Bibliography with Literature Review* (Rome: United Nations Interregional Crime and Justice Research Institute, 1995). The majority of studies are from the USA and Europe.

Eugene A. Engeldinger has put together an extensive collection of materials on partner violence in *Spouse Abuse: an Annotated Bibliography of Violence Between Mates* (Metuchen, NJ: Scarecrow Press, 1986). Violence against women is the subject of Nathan Aaron Rosen's *Battered Wives: a Comprehensive Annotated Bibliography of Articles, Books and Statutes in the United States of America* (New York: National Center for Women and Family Law, 1988). For the other side of the debate see 'References Examining Assaults by Women on Their Spouses/Partners' by Martin S. Fiebert (*Sexuality and Culture* **1**, 1997, 273–86), which reviews 85 works on violence in relationships.

5.3.8 Drugs

Drug Trafficking Research in the Americas: an Annotated Bibliography by B. M. Bagley (Coral Gables, FL: North-South Center Press, University of Miami, 1997). The bibliography details publications (journal articles, books, reports) covering the following geographical regions: US; Colombia; Ecuador; Peru: Brazil and the Southern Cone; Paraguay; Chile; Uruguay; Mexico, Central America and the Caribbean; and Bolivia. In several of the sections, chapters focus on specific issues – political, economic, judicial – relating to drug trafficking. Navigation would have been enhanced by the addition of an index, but nevertheless, this is a useful collection of resources for the researcher.

5.3.9 Economics of crime

Economics of Criminal Behavior <encyclo.findlaw.com/8100book.pdf> by Erling Eide, is a literature review and bibliography, published on the Web as part of the *Encyclopedia of Law and Economics* (*see 5.6.1* for the encyclopaedia's main entry).

5.3.10 Elderly

Crime and the Elderly: an Annotated Bibliography by Ron H. Day (London and Westport, CT: Greenwood Press, 1988) analyses the literature on the elderly as both offenders and victims of crime. For material on the abuse of the elderly see *Elder Neglect and Abuse: An Annotated Bibliography* edited by Tanya F. Johnson, James G. O'Brien and Margaret F. Hudson (London and Westport, CT: Greenwood Press, 1985).

5.3.11 FBI (Federal Bureau of Investigation)

The FBI: an Annotated Bibliography and Research Guide (New York: Garland, 1994) lists over a 1000 books and articles and also offers advice on searching for information on the FBI. *See also 5.7.6.*

5.3.12 Female offenders

In *Female Offenders: an Annotated Bibliography.* (London and Westport, CT: Greenwood Press, 1997), Kathleen O'Shea and Beverly Fletcher detail over 3000 English language materials (monographs, journal articles and dissertations) organized under the following headings: criminology; crimes; arrest, prosecution and sentencing; female juveniles; corrections; probation and parole; and political prisoners. The authors also include a bibliography of bibliographies on female offenders and related topics. Most entries date from the last three decades, but there is some coverage of older material, the earliest reference being an English Bill from 1820 to repeal the whipping of female offenders. Each citation is numbered which makes the subject index easy to use. In *A Bibliography of Resources Concerning Female Offenders* (Atlanta, GA: Planning, Evaluation and Statistics, Georgia Department of Corrections, 1994), Linda Lees and

Elaine DeCostanzo concentrate on the narrower topic of women's imprisonment. For a review of the earlier literature see Francyne Goyer-Michaud's article 'The Adult Female Offender: a Selected Bibliography', (*Criminal Justice and Behavior*, **1**(4), 340–56, 1974), which covers over 200 articles in English and French published between 1959 and 1974.

5.3.13 Gangs

(a) Print

Motorcycle Gangs: a Literature Search of Law Enforcement, Academic and Popular Sources with a Chronology of Canadian Print News Coverage by Tom Finlay and Catherine J. Matthews (Toronto: Centre of Criminology, University of Toronto, 1996). The 62-page booklet is organized according to the sections listed in the subtitle and covers materials (mostly books and journals) from the 1980s to about 1995. Although lacking annotations, this is nevertheless a useful collection of resources.

(b) Electronic

For an extensive, broad-based collection of around 1000 books, meeting/conference papers, journal articles and US Government documents see the *National Youth Gang Center Bibliography of Gang Literature* at <www.ncjrs.org/gangbi.htm>. The references range in date from the early part of the twentieth century to the mid 1990s.

5.3.14 Guns

Firearm Violence: an Annotated Bibliography by Krista Robinson, Jon Vernick and Stephen Teret (Baltimore, MD: Center for Gun Policy and Research, Johns Hopkins University, 1997) contains 195 entries on the US experience of guns.

5.3.15 History

Crime in Victorian Britain: an Annotated Bibliography from Nineteenth-Century British Magazines compiled by E. M. Palmegiano (London and Westport, CT: Greenwood Press, 1993), lists 1614 articles from 45 periodicals, with brief comments on each article. Palmegiano also provides an informative essay on nineteenth century crime based on his detailed knowledge of period magazines, covering such topics as: rates, types and causes of crime; law and enforcement; prosecution of criminals; sentencing; and classes of criminals.

Criminal Activity in the Deep South, 1700–1930: an Annotated Bibliography compiled by A. J. Wright (London and Westport, CT: Greenwood Press, 1989) is an excellent resource for scholars interested in tracking down hitherto elusive primary and secondary materials for this era. Through his annotations the author guides the reader around the available literature – fiction and non-fiction, published and unpublished – focusing on eight southern states: North Carolina, South Carolina, Georgia, Florida, Alabama, Mississippi, Louisiana, and Tennessee. Of related interest is Norton H. Moses' *Lynching and Vigilantism in the United States: an Annotated Bibliography* (London and Westport, CT: Greenwood Press, 1997). The book lists around 4200 items (books, journal articles, government documents, unpublished materials) covering a wide span of years from 1760 to 1996. Again, like Wright's work, the bibliography includes fiction as well as non-fiction sources.

5.3.16 Homicide

Homicide: a Bibliography, 2nd ed., by Bal K. Jerath and Rajinder Jerath (London and Ann Arbor, MI: CRC Press, 1993). The authors claim that '. . . no other single source . . . can provide the researcher with such a complete selection of homicide literature' (pp.vi–vii). It certainly represents an extensive trawl through most of the major abstracts and indexes, and covers both historical and contemporary (up until 1991, mainly journal-based) material. It is divided into 12 chapters: Introduction To Homicide; Statistics; The Murderer; The Victim; Murder Modes; Causes of Murder; Investigation; Case Reports; Homicide, Suicide and Accidents; Legal Aspects; Assassination; and Prevention and Control. Each of the chapters is further subdivided by topic. In summary, this is a useful collation of references, but the reader may find the lack of annotations (apart from keyword headings) a little disappointing.

5.3.17 Juvenile justice/Youth crime

For an investigation into the administration of juvenile justice systems see *Rationality in Juvenile Justice Decision Making: an Analytical Review of the Literature with Annotated Bibliography* by Michael Gottfredson and Carolyn Uihlein (Sacramento, CA: Justice Policy Research Group, 1992).

Gender Issues in Juvenile Justice: an Annotated Bibliography by Dr Loraine Gelshorpe (Lancaster: Information Systems, 1986), is an authoritative index of research on female crime and delinquency from the nineteenth century to the early 1980s. The author's stated aim is to be descriptive rather than critical, to 'encourage readers to examine the material for themselves and to form their own critical judgements' (p.x).

The US-based Youth Law Center has produced an annotated bibliography of 164 English language materials (journal articles, reports and monographs from the early 1970s to the mid-1990s), arranged alphabetically by author, on the *Disproportionate Representation of Minorities in the Juvenile Justice System* (San Francisco, CA; Washington, DC: Youth Law Center, 1996). *See also 5.3.22.*

Kim Openshaw, Roger Graves and Susan Ericksen cover two decades of research on sexual offences in 'Youthful Sexual Offenders: a Comprehensive Bibliography of Scholarly References' (*Family Relations* **42**, 1993, 222–6).

5.3.18 Mental health

Mental Health Services in Criminal Justice System Settings: a Selectively Annotated Bibliography, 1970–1997 compiled by Rodney Van Whitlock and Bernard Lubin (London and Westport, CT: Greenwood Press, 1999). 1264 entries – mainly journals, but some books and book chapters are covered – span 27 years of the literature. The references are arranged within 15 sections and include: mental disorders; institution and community-based programmes and services; prison suicide; sex offenders; female mentally ill offenders; ethical issues; and education and training. Separate subject and author indexes round off this useful compilation.

5.3.19 Organized crime

(a) Print

A Guide to the Literature on Organized Crime: an Annotated Bibliography Covering the Years 1967–81 by Eugene Doleschal, Anne Newton and William Hickey (Hackensack, NJ: National Council on Crime and Delinquency, 1981). This work presents of a useful summary of the earlier literature – monographs, journal articles, unpublished materials – on the topic. See also David Critchley's *International Perspectives on Organized Crime: a Bibliography* (Monticello, IL: Vance Bibliographies, 1984). *Organized Crime: a bibliography* by Joan Beavis and Greta Cumming (Ottawa: Law Enforcement Reference Centre, Canadian Police College, 1990) provides 500 entries divided into a variety of subject headings including: white-collar crime; the Mafia; gangs, prostitution; racketeering and extortion; and crime control and crime prevention.

(b) Electronic

Organized Crime and Illegal Markets <encyclo.findlaw.com/8400book.pdf> by Gianluc Fiorentini, is a literature review and bibliography, publishedas part of the *Encyclopedia of Law and Economics* (*see* 5.6.1 for the encyclopaedia's main entry). Of related interest is *Organized Crime in North America: a Bibliography* <www.yorku.ca/nathanson> compiled by Stephen Schneider of the Nathanson Centre for the Study of Organized Crime and Corruption in Canada. The bibliography covers a broad range of topics including: theories and conceptual models, types of activity, enforcement, and a section on special topics – narco-terrorism, transnational organized crime and women and organized crime.

5.3.20 Penology

Prisons

(a) Print

American Prisons: an Annotated Bibliography by Elizabeth Huffmaster Mcconnell and Laura J. Moriarty (London and Westport, CT: Greenwood Press, 1998), was written as a supplement to the *Encyclopedia of American Prisons* and contains annotations for selected references in the encyclopaedia, *see 5.6.5*. The references are presented alphabetically by topic from Accreditation to Youth in Prison.

Anger and Violence Management Programs in Correctional Services: an Annotated Bibliography by Ann Ward and Steve Baldwin (*The Prison Journal*, 77(4) December, 1997, 472–88), provides a useful analysis of the literature on anger and violence management programmes in American and British prisons between 1980 and 1995.

For a review of the privatization debate see *Privatization of Correctional Services: a Select Bibliography* by Catherine Matthews and Janet Chan (Kensington: University of New South Wales, 1992) which covers material from the USA, Australia and the UK.

(b) Electronic

The *Global Bibliography of Prison Systems* <www.uncjin.org/country/GBOPS/gbops.html> compiled by Philip L. Reichel contains 780 references from 117 countries; it is hosted by the *United Nations Crime and Justice Information Network* Website. *The Economics of Prisons* <encyclo.findlaw.com/8300book.pdf> by Kenneth L. Avio is a useful literature review and bibliography published on the Web as part of the *Encyclopedia of Law and Economics* (*see 5.6.1* for the encyclopaedia's main entry).

The *Deaths in Custody Bibliography* compiled by Vicki Dalton <www.aic.gov.au/services/biblio/index.html> results from the work of the Deaths in Custody Monitoring and Research Unit at the Australian Institute of Criminology. The Website suggests that the bibliography will be regularly updated. Whilst coverage has an emphasis on the Australian experience, some international research is included. Many different types of materials are listed: reports; books; book chapters; journal articles; unpublished papers; conference proceedings; and audiovisual aids. The database can be browsed by subject, and detailed abstracts are provided for each item. Deaths in prisons are covered as well as in other areas of the criminal justice system such as police custody.

Alternatives to imprisonment

(a) Print

The *International Bibliography on Alternatives to Imprisonment 1980–1989*, edited by Ugljesa Zvekic and Anna Alvazzi del Frate on behalf of the United Nations Interregional Crime and Justice Research Institute (Chicago, IL: Nelson-Hall, 1994), has 3599 entries arranged alphabetically by author on numerous penological topics including: probation; community service; electronic surveillance; and prison overcrowding. A subject index of broad key terms is included. The publication is volume two of *Alternatives to Imprisonment in Comparative Perspective*. *See section 5.7.13 Alternatives to Imprisonment* for details of the first volume of case study reports.

(b) Electronic

Alternative Sanctions <encyclo.findlaw.com/8200book.pdf>. A useful bibliography, published on the Web as part of the *Encyclopedia of Law and Economics* (*see 5.6.1* for the encyclopaedia's main entry). It also uses *Cruel Sanctions* as a supplementary title which is fitting as it does include materials on capital punishment – a rather severe alternative to imprisonment!

Restorative justice

Restorative Justice: an Annotated Bibliography by Paul McCold (Monsey, NY: Willow Tree Press, 1997) lists 552 entries – a mixture of books, journal articles and conference papers – about victim-offender mediations. The unhelpful alphabetical arrangement by author is ameliorated somewhat by a brief subject index. Despite these shortcomings, McCold has brought together a valuable collection of resources.

Capital punishment

The Capital Punishment Dilema 1950–1977: a Subject Bibliography by Charles Triche III (New York: Whitston, 1979) and *Capital Punishment in America: An Annotated Bibliography* by Michael Radelet and Margaret Vandiver (New York: Garland, 1988), provide informative reviews of the literature. *See also Alternative Sanctions* under *(b) Electronic* above.

5.3.21 Police

For a bibliography of books, dissertations and articles on American police history see *The Encyclopedia of Police Science* edited by William G. Bailey whose main entry is in 5.6.6. See also Bailey's *Police Science, 1964–1984: a Selected Annotated Bibliography* (New York: Garland, 1986). For the British perspective take a look at two books by Martin Stallion: *British Police Force Histories: a Bibliography* (Leigh-on-Sea: M.R. Stallion, 1997) and *A Life of Crime: a Bibliography of British Police Officers' Memoirs and Biographies* (Leigh-on-Sea: MR Stallion, 1998). Nehal Ashraf details the Indian experience in *Police and Policing in India: a Select Bibliography* (New Delhi: Commonwealth Publishers, 1992).

5.3.22 Race and ethnicity

Racism in the Criminal Justice System: a Bibliography by C. J. Matthews and L. Lewis (Toronto: Centre of Criminology, University of Toronto, 1995), provides 2132 entries on Canadian, British, North American and selected other jurisdictions covering English language materials published between 1980 and 1994. The compilers note that the emphasis is on American sources which include journal articles, monographs and reports. It is divided into seven sections: a general overview; police; courts; correctional system; women; youth; and native and aboriginal peoples. An author index is included, but the work would have benefited from annotated entries and, perhaps, a separate subject index. A related book focusing exclusively on the US is *Race, Crime and the Criminal Justice System: a Bibliography* by Joan Nordquist (Santa Cruz, CA: Reference and Research Services, 1997).

5.3.23 Rape and related crimes

Acquaintance and Date Rape: an Annotated Bibliography by Sally K. Ward, Jennifer Dziuba-Leatherman, Jane Gerard Stapleton, and Carrie L. Yodanis (London and Westport, CT: Greenwood Press, 1994), is a comprehensive collection of theoretical and research material covering such topics as campus, marital and gang rape, prevention programmes and the treatment of victims and perpetrators. See also Roberta Harmes' bibliography in: 'Marital Rape: A Selected Bibliography', (*Violence Against Women*, 5(9), 1999, 1082–1083).

5.3.24 Stalking

Mary Cooper has produced a useful guide to this relatively new area of interest in *Criminal Harassment and Potential for Treatment: Literature Review and Annotated Bibliography* (Vancouver, BC: BC Institute on Family Violence, 1994).

5.3.25 Terrorism

The key works in this field have been written by two authors Amos Lakos and Edward Mickolus who, between them, have the literature pretty well mapped. For early material see *Terrorism, 1970–1978, a Bibliography* by Amos Lakos (Waterloo, ON: University of Waterloo Library, 1979) and *The Literature of Terrorism: a Selectively Annotated Bibliography* by Edward F. Mickolus (London and Westport, CT: Greenwood Press, 1980). The following decade is covered by two works by Mickolus (with Peter A. Flemming) *Terrorism, 1980–1987: a Selectively Annotated Bibliography* (London and Westport, CT: Greenwood Press, 1988); *Terrorism, 1988–1991: a Chronology of Events and a Selectively Annotated Bibliography* (London and Westport, CT: Greenwood Press, 1993); together with Lakos' *International Terrorism: a Bibliography* (Boulder, CO: Westview and London: Mansell, 1986); and *Terrorism, 1980–1990: a Bibliography* (Boulder, CO and Oxford: Westview, 1991). For terrorism in the 1990s see *Terrorism, 1992–1995: a Chronology of Events and a Selectively Annotated Bibliography* by Edward F. Mickolus and Susan L. Simmons (London and Wesport, CT: Greenwood Press, 1997).

▶ 5.4 DICTIONARIES

5.4.1 General

At the time of writing criminology lacks an authoritative, up-to-date dictionary. The standard work is *A Dictionary of Criminology* edited by Dermot Walsh and Adrian Poole (London: Routledge and Kegan Paul, 1983) but this is now nearly two decades old. Individual entries are both detailed and of a high quality, but it cannot offer the reader any assistance with current trends in the discipline – there is no entry for victimology for instance. *See also 5.4.3.*

5.4.2 Crime

Crime Dictionary, rev. ed., by Ralph DeSola (New York: Facts on File, 1988). Although a number of years have passed since it was published, this is still a useful and comprehensive collection of some 10 000 crime-related definitions including legal and psychiatric terms, specific criminal and terrorist organizations, slang words, and references to fiction/non-fiction print sources. Of related interest is the *Dictionary of Crime* by Jay Robert Nash (London: Headline, 1993), which covers some of the same territory. In over 400 pages, it describes some 17 000 legal and crime-related terms, with an emphasis on the vernacular of the professional criminal. *See also 5.4.9.*

5.4.3 Criminal justice

Dictionary of American Criminal Justice: Key Terms and Major Supreme Court Cases by Dean J. Champion (London and New York: Fitzroy Dearborn, 1998). Its focus is intentionally interdisciplinary and it encompasses many topics of interest to criminologists. However, some of the entries are a little too sketchy: it has two lines on *penology* compared with Walsh and Poole's two pages. One particularly useful feature is the dictionary's inclusion of brief biographies of key figures in criminology and related fields. The emphasis is strongly American; you will seek in vain for any mention of Leon Radzinowicz for example, the Polish criminologist and leading figure in establishing academic criminology in the UK. Over half the volume is taken up with summaries of US Supreme Court Cases which will be of less value to those from other geographical areas and judicial systems.

Of related interest is George E. Rush's *Dictionary of Criminal Justice*, 5th ed., (Guilford, CT: Dushkin/McGraw-Hill, 2000) which contains over 3600 definitions of criminal justice topics and summaries of selected US Supreme Court cases. In addition, Rush also includes a small collection of relevant Websites, US doctoral programmes in criminal justice, forensic agencies and organizations, and key journals. Although *American* does not appear in the title, its perspective, like Champion's, is distinctly US-based. Unlike Champion's work, more of the text is devoted to the dictionary rather than the court cases, but again, many entries are quite brief. Colour is added by the inclusion of a sprinkling of famous figures in criminal justice/criminology and infamous criminals. Taken together, these two dictionaries go some way to compensating for the lack of an up-to-date dictionary of criminology.

5.4.4 Criminals

The *Dictionary of Culprits and Criminals*, 2nd ed., by George C. Kohn (Lanham, MD: Scarecrow, 1995) provides an entertaining collection of individuals – including murderers, terrorists, burglars, gangsters, and spies. Each entry gives details of the person's birth/death and criminal career. The miscreants are mostly American, with a few notorious Europeans added for good measure.

5.4.5 Drugs

Elsevier's Dictionary of Drug Traffic Terms: In English, Spanish, Portuguese, French and German by N. Illanes (Amsterdam: Elsevier, 1997 print, 1999 CD-ROM). This multilingual dictionary details terms in all key areas including: criminal justice, law enforcement, medical, psychological, social and economic. A substantial number of slang terms are also included.

5.4.6 Forensic psychology

A Dictionary of Forensic Psychology by L. R. C. Haward (Chichester: Medilaw/Barry Rose, 1990) covers all aspects of the field, from abduction to youth custody. Many entries offer additional references.

5.4.7 Penology

Dictionary of American Penology by Vergil L. Williams (London and Westport, CT: Greenwood Press 1996). This is a revised and expanded edition of the dictionary which first appeared in 1979. A thorough and well-researched work which covers all the main areas of penology, except, curiously, a definition of the term itself. The entries are detailed and include references, although the focus is exclusively American. A useful feature of the dictionary is that it not merely defines key terms, but also provides information on a vast range of US correctional systems. In addition, Williams provides the addresses of US prison systems and prison reform organizations, together with selected statistical tables from the United States Justice Department.

5.4.8 Police

(a) Print

The Police Dictionary and Encyclopedia by John J. Fay (Springfield, IL: Charles C. Thomas, 1988). Around 5000 terms are defined, including criminal slang. Useful, but the perspective is solidly American.

(b) Electronic

A work with a more European flavour is *Elsevier's Dictionary of Police and Criminal Law: English-French and French-English* by R. Ingleton (Amsterdam: Elsevier, 1992 print, 1999, CD-ROM). The entries cover all the topics you would expect to find, including: organization and functions of the police; drugs; terrorism; criminal law; and slang. In addition to the police and criminal justice systems in England and France, some reference is also made to other areas such as Scotland, USA, Belgium and Switzerland.

5.4.9 Slang

The classic work in this area is Eric Partridge's *Dictionary of the Underworld* (London: Routledge and Kegan Paul, 1950, 3rd ed. 1968), recently published as *The Wordsworth Dictionary of the Underworld* (Ware, Hertfordshire: Wordsworth Editions, 1995). This delightful book covers English, American, Canadian, Australian and South African terms. Its emphasis on the historical, makes it very good for etymological investigations. You will find definitions of a whole host of colourful terms from Abbott's teeth to ziff. For a more up-to-date publication you might try *Cop Speak: the Lingo of Law Enforcement and Crime* by Tom Philbin (New York: Wiley, 1996) which, in addition to defining the words, often delves into their origin. *See also 5.4.2.*

▶ 5.5 DIRECTORIES

(a) Print

The British of Directory of Criminology edited by A. Aizlewood and Roger Tarling (London: ISTD: the Centre for Crime and Justice Studies and The British Society of Criminology, 1999) lists UK institutions where criminology is taught and researched. It also gives detailed entries for individual criminologists covering their contact addresses, research areas, publications and activities. A particularly helpful final section matches researchers to an alphabetical listing of research topics.

The *NAPO Probation Directory* (London: Shaw and Sons for the National Association of Probation Officers) is produced annually, and lists all probation offices and officers, penal establishments, probation and bail hostels within the United Kingdom. It also includes details of other organizations and services such as NACRO (National Association for the Care and Resettlement of Offenders) and Mediation UK – an umbrella group for victim/offender, community and schools mediation services. A similar annual publication for the US is the *Probation and Parole Directory* (Lanham, MD: American Correctional Association, 1981–). See also the *Directory of Juvenile and Adult Correctional Departments, Institutions, Agencies, and Paroling Authorities, United States and Canada* (Lanham, MD: American Correctional Association, 1979–) and the *National Jail and Adult Detention Directory* (Lanhan, MD: American Correctional Association, 1979–).

Now in its ninth edition, the *Directory of Criminal Justice Information Sources* by Joyce Hutchinson (Washington, DC: Department of Justice, Office of Justice Programs, 1994) details US organizations which offer criminal justice information services. *A World Directory of Criminological Institutes,* 6th ed., edited by Carla M. Santoro (Rome: United Nations Interregional Crime and Justice Research Institute, 1995) is a useful publication (which first appeared in 1974) listing around 470 criminological institutions across 70 countries. See *(b) Electronic* below for its digital counterpart. The *Directory of Computerized Criminal Justice Information Systems* by Richard Scherpenzeel (The Hague: MITRA Foundation/Netherlands Ministry of Justice, 1995) details over 300 computerized criminal justice information systems used in Europe, Canada, Australia, Asia and Latin America.

(b) Electronic

World Directory of Criminological Resources <www.unicri.it/html/body_world_directory_of_criminologi.htm> is produced by the United Nations Interregional Crime and Justice Research Institute (UNICRI). This excellent resource has the same wide coverage (470 institutions in 70 countries) as its print counterpart, but benefits from being more up to date and searchable by name, country, and keyword. It provides contact and staff details for each organization as well as information about its activities, projects and library resources.

For directories of individual criminologists (in addition to *The British Directory of Criminology* discussed in *(a) Print* above), you might wish to consult the *American Society of Criminology – Directory of Members* <www.asc41.com/director/a.htm> which lists the names, institutional addresses, telephone numbers and Email addresses of members, and the

Australian Institute of Criminology – Directory of Researchers of Crime and Criminal Justice <www.aic.gov.au/services/directories/libraries/index.html> which provides contact details and information on current research. For criminology-related libraries in Australia see the *Australian Institute of Criminology – Directory of Criminal Justice Libraries: Australia and NewZealand* <www.aic.gov.au/services/directories/libraries/index.html>. This useful directory lists libraries by State/Territory and Agency/Organization. The individual entries provide full addresses and contact details of libraries and staff, together with information on the collections and services.

Restorative Justice Resources <ssw.che.umn.edu/rjp/Resources/Documents/cbar97a.pdf> is a regularly updated directory of organizations, bibliographies and training resources, by the Balanced and Restorative Justice Project, a joint project of the Community Justice Institute and the Center for Restorative Justice and Mediation. Of related interest is the *Directory of Victim Offender Mediation Programs in the US* <ssw.che.umn.edu/rjp/Resources/C%20Umb&Gre97b.pdf> produced by Mark S. Umbreit and Robert Schung of the Center for Restorative Justice and Peacemaking, University of Minnesota. First produced in 1997, the directory is under continual revision. Programmes are listed by state, city and name. Contact and activity details are provided for each programme entry. The *International Crime Victim Compensation Directory* <www.ojp.usdoj.gov/ovc/intdir/intdir.htm> produced by the Office for Victims of Crime of the US Department of Justice, lists victim compensation programmes in 29 countries, including full contact details of the organizations involved.

▶ 5.6 ENCYCLOPAEDIAS

5.6.1 General

(a) Print

The *Encyclopedia of Criminology* edited by Vernon C. Branham and Samuel B. Kutash (New York: The Philosophical Library, 1949) is a classic text in the field, boasting the likes of Marshall B. Clinard and Edwin H. Sutherland amongst its contributors. The text demonstrates the multidisciplinary nature of criminology at this early stage in its academic history. Much of the text is, of course, both dated and less than politically correct. Oddly, it fails to include an entry for the term *criminology*. However, it is of value as a slice of criminological history and for the entries by key figures, such as Sutherland's succinct overview of the white collar criminal.

Throughout the six volumes of the *Encyclopedia of World Crime: Criminal Justice, Criminology, and Law Enforcement* (Wilmett, IL:

CrimeBooks, 1989–1990) editor, Jay Robert Nash, discusses crime-related persons, places, events and cases from the earliest times to the late 1980s. Journalistic rather than academic in style the work is, nevertheless, the culmination of extensive research by Nash. Readers of all levels will find something of interest in it.

Encyclopedia of Law and Economics (Cheltenham and Northampton, MA: Edward Elgar, 2000). Published simultaneously in print and digital format. For main entry see *(b) Electronic* below.

The breadth of the three-volume *Encyclopedia of Violence, Peace and Conflict* edited by Lester Kurtz (London: Academic Press/Harcourt, 1999) goes far beyond the purely criminological, but it does offer both an overview of criminology and well-written articles on a host of other criminology-related topics such as: theories of criminal behaviour; death penalty; homicide; juvenile crime; television and violence; terrorism; and victimology.

(b) Electronic

Encyclopedia of Law and Economics (Cheltenham and Northampton, MA: Edward Elgar, 2000) <encyclo.findlaw.com/index.html>. The University of Ghent have made available the full text of the encyclopaedia on the Web. Obviously, its main focus is not criminology, but it does contain bibliographies of interest to criminologists including: Optimal Enforcement (sentencing); Corruption; Organized Crime and Illegal Markets; Economics of Criminal Behavior; Alternative Sanctions (Collateral Penalties, Cruel Sanctions, Capital Punishment); The Economics of Prisons; and Corporate Criminal Liability.

5.6.2 Criminal justice

Crime and the Justice System in America: an Encyclopedia edited by Frank Schmalleger (London and Westport, CT: Greenwood Press, 1997) is a key work in this area. In addition to defining major terms, the encyclopaedia discusses notable historical and contemporary figures, and precedent-setting cases. Many entries provide a selection of recommended reading. A bibliographical essay and index are also included. The *Encyclopedia of Crime and Justice*, Editor-in-Chief Sanford H. Kadish (New York: The Free Press, and London: Collier Macmillan, 1983) is a significantly earlier work, but with a somewhat broader focus. This substantial four-volume encyclopaedia offers a comprehensive, interdisciplinary overview of criminological topics, including: the nature and causes of crime; punishment and treatment of offenders; and the functioning of the institutions of criminal justice. The individual essays are well-referenced, and although there is a distinctly American flavour to the text (whose currency is limited to the state of knowledge in the early 1980s), individual countries can be traced via the detailed index.

5.6.3 Forensic science

A useful single volume work is Brian Lane's *Encyclopedia of Forensic Science* (London: Headline, 1993), which covers all the key aspects. A major new publication in this area is the three-volume *Encyclopedia of Forensic Sciences*, editor-in-chief Jay Siegel (New York and London: Academic Press, 2000). The publication consists of over 200 articles, covering all the major theories and methods. Also included is a glossary of key terms. The *Encyclopedia* is available in print and electronic formats.

5.6.4 Organized crime

World Encyclopedia of Organised Crime by Jay Robert Nash (London: Headline, 1993). Despite the appearance of '*world*' in the title, the United States dominates coverage within this volume. Journalistic rather than academic in style, it includes potted biographies and photographs of gangsters, as well as lively descriptions of crime gangs and (in)famous events from the nineteenth century onwards. *The Mafia Encyclopedia,* 2nd ed., by Carl Sifakis (New York: Facts on File, 1999) is an entertaining read as well as an authoritative who's who of the criminal underworld. The lives of over 400 Mafia members from Accardo to Zwillman are outlined within the pages of this attractively presented and illustrated work. Complementing the above two works by concentrating on the new ethnic criminal organizations of today is Robert J. Kelly's *Encyclopedia of Organized Crime in the United States: From Capone's Chicago to the New Urban Underworld* (London and Westport, CT: Greenwood Press, 2000).

5.6.5 Penology

Prisons

The *Encyclopedia of American Prisons* edited by Marilyn McShane and Frank P. Williams III (London and New York: Garland, 1996) provides the reader with around 160 quality essays on all aspects of the US prison system. Each essay has a bibliography of further reading and the inclusion of a combined author and subject index makes the collection easy to navigate. *See also 5.3.20 Prisons* for details of *American Prisons: an Annotated Bibliography* produced as a supplement to the *Encyclopedia.*

Capital punishment

Those interested in the ultimate sanction may wish to consult the *Encyclopedia of Capital Punishment* by Mark Grossman and Mike Dixon-Kennedy (Santa Barbara, CA: ABC-CLIO, 1998) which takes an historical approach to the subject, covering key figures – executioners, reformers, advocates, as well as those unfortunate enough to be executed – US court cases, methods of execution, statistics and concepts.

5.6.6 Police

World Encyclopedia of Police Forces and Penal Systems by George Thomas Kurian (New York and Oxford: Facts on File, 1989) is a comprehensive international survey organized A–Z by country. An attempt is made to provide information on police forces and penal systems in each country under four headings: history and background; structure and organization; recruitment, education and training; and penal system. In addition, there are appendices on: Interpol; a directory of police headquarters; and comparative statistics on police protection. Although now in need of updating – world geography has changed somewhat in the last few years – it is still a useful work, particularly in terms of its historical data.

A more current work, but focusing mainly on the US experience, is *The Encyclopedia of Police Science* edited by William G. Bailey (New York and London: Garland, 1995). The second edition adds another 70 entries to the 143 of the first to make a substantial and well-written contribution to the literature, covering everything from accidental death/murder of police officers to youth gangs. Its breadth means it will be of interest to criminologists generally and not just those specializing in police science.

5.6.7 Violence

The *Encyclopedia of Violence: Origins, Attitudes, and Consequences* by Margaret DiCanio (New York: Facts on File, 1993) is 'an album of snapshots of the places where violence enters everyday life in late twentieth century America as well as a taxonomy of some of the many varieties of violence' (p. ix). It's certainly an erudite and absorbing read, covering the theory and praxis of society's relationship with and response to violence. The appendices offer two additional essays on: 'Organized Crime: Roots of America's Drug Traffic'; and 'Limitations on Behavioral Science in Studying Violence'. An index, bibliography and directory of related organizations are also included.

▶ 5.7 GUIDES AND HANDBOOKS

5.7.1 General

The Oxford Handbook of Criminology edited by Mike Maguire, Rod Morgan and Robert Reiner (Oxford: Clarendon Press, 1997). Now in its second edition, this seminal work offers review essays by major scholars on all significant aspects of criminology. It is divided into four main areas: General Theories of Crime and Control; Social Dimensions of Crime and Justice; Forms of Crime and Criminality; and Criminal Justice Structures and Processes. The essays provide suggestions for further reading and detailed bibliographies.

A companion volume offering an American perspective, complementing the British focus of Maguire, et al, is *Criminology: a Contemporary Handbook* by Joseph F. Sheley (Belmont, CA: Wadsworth Publishing Company, 1999). Now in its third edition, it has been expanded to include the latest research and theories. Written by academic sociologists and criminologists, the handbook offers a coherent introduction to key criminological topics. Its forte has always been its clear exposition and this has been strengthened in the latest volume by including more chapter introductions and student discussion questions.

Criminology: a Reader's Guide edited by Jane Gladstone, Richard V. Ericson, and Clifford D. Shearing (Toronto: Centre of Criminology, University of Toronto, 1991) provides a platform for the Canadian experience. Divided into three parts:– Crime, Policing, and Punishment (including penology and historical aspects of crime and criminal justice in England and Canada); Law Reform and Policy (including politics, drugs and mental disorder); and Social Hierarchies, Crime and Justice (including feminism and juvenile justice/delinquency) – the guide offers brief essays linked to detailed reading lists of materials. Although the emphasis is on Canada, in many areas the focus is broadened to incorporate British and US perspectives. *Criminology Sourcebook* edited by Michael Doherty (London: Old Bailey Press, 1998) provides the reader with excerpts from key writers on most areas of criminology including: biological, psychological and social explanations of crime; crime prevention; the new criminology; feminist criminology; and juvenile crime and penology. Each extract is introduced by the editor, giving background information and guidance on the interpretation of the writings.

The Handbook of Crime and Punishment (New York and Oxford: Oxford University Press, 1998) was, says its editor, Michael Tonry, inspired by *The Oxford Handbook of Criminology* discussed above. Its 27 chapters are grouped within seven main subject areas: The Context (including an overview of crime and criminal justice with particular attention paid to ethnicity and gender); Topical Crime Problems (street gangs, white collar crime, organized crime, family violence, drug control); Causes of Crime (social, psychological and economic perspectives); Crime Reduction; Pre-conviction Processes and Institutions; Post-conviction Processes and Institutions; and Punishment. The focus is largely American, but contributions from criminologists in the UK, Australia and Canada are included. The high quality essays 'about the current state-of-the-art of knowledge ... from English-language sources' provide extensive references, and a combined author/organization/subject index assists the navigation of the volume's 776 pages.

The International Library of Criminology, Criminal Justice and Penology is, to quote the publishers Ashgate/Dartmouth, 'an important publishing initiative that brings together the most significant contemporary published journal essays in current criminology, criminal justice and penology'. Certainly the volumes, edited by well-known authorities, provide key collections of articles for students and researchers new to a particular area. Selected volumes are discussed within the specific subject areas below.

5.7.2 Comparative criminology

The *International Handbook of Contemporary Developments in Criminology* (London and Westport, CT: Greenwood Press, 1983) is a two-volume work edited by Elmer H. Johnson, and although somewhat dated, has an unequalled geographical breadth of coverage. Topics in volume one *General Issues and the Americas* include: international organizations for criminology; criminology in developing countries; an international perspective on women and criminology; and a section on radical criminology. The remainder of the volume looks at crime and criminology in the Americas: Argentina, Brazil, Canada, Chile, Costa Rica, Mexico and the United States. Volume two is subtitled: *Europe, Africa, the Middle East and Asia*. Its 33 chapters, one per country, are arranged alphabetically. Both volumes offer extensive bibliographies and combined subject/author indexes. Although a revised edition would be welcome, this well-researched work is still of value, particularly for its discussion of the historical development of crime and criminology within each region.

Issues in Comparative Criminology edited by Piers Beirne and David Nelken (Aldershot and Brookfield, NT: Ashgate/Dartmouth, 1997) provides 20 essays organized under three headings: the aims of comparison; measuring rates of crime and victimization; and varieties of comparative criminology. The geographical areas covered include: Edinburgh, Stockholm, Tanzania, Japan, Netherlands and the Third World. Issued as part of *The International Library of Criminology, Criminal Justice and Penology* series.

5.7.3 Computer crime

International Review of Criminal Policy – United Nations Manual on the Prevention and Control of Computer-Related Crime <www.uncjin.org/Documents/irpc4344.pdf> is a comprehensive international guide to all aspects of computer-related crime including: definition and prevalence of, criminal law and procedural issues; and crime prevention and international cooperation.

5.7.4 Criminal justice

(a) Print

Those new to the area should go straight to *Criminal Justice Information: How To Find It, How To Use It* by Dennis C. Benamati, Phyllis A. Schultze, Adam C. Bouloukos and Graeme R. Newman (Phoenix, AR: Oryx Press, 1998). Its nine chapters take the reader from the basics of using libraries to locating Websites. In between it covers all the main sources of information including: monographs, journals, abstracts and indexes, statistics, legal and official documentation. The emphasis is American but it does devote a chapter to international resources. Clearly presented and easy-to-use, this would make a rewarding purchase. Of related interest is *Criminal Justice Research Sources*, 4th ed., by Quint C. Thurman, Lee E. Parker and Robert L. O'Block (Cincinnati, OH: Anderson Publishing, 2000), which attempts to do a similar job but is not as comprehensive and detailed as Benamati, et al. above. *Criminal Justice: Concepts and Issues: an Anthology,* 3rd ed., by Chris W. Eskridge (Los Angeles, CA: Roxbury, 1999) covers all key areas of interest from capital punishment to victimization. Appendices include details of criminal justice organizations, information sources, and Supreme Court Cases.

Profiles of Criminal Justice Systems in Europe and North America edited by Kristiina Kangaspunta (HEUNI Publication No. 26. Helsinki: European Institute for Crime Prevention and Control, 1995), takes its data from responses to the Fourth United Nations Survey of Crime Trends and Operation of Criminal Justice Systems. Although geographically quite comprehensive, the detail given for individual countries is variable. For most countries the entries include background information and statistics. For some areas there is additional information on the organization and major principles of their respective criminal justice systems, resources allocated to such systems, selected key issues and suggestions for further reading. One of the volume's strengths is its inclusion of most of the independent states of the former USSR. There are also several collections of papers taking an international perspective on criminal justice systems which are worth consulting: *Comparative and International Criminal Justice Systems:*

Policing, Judiciary and Corrections edited by Obi N. Ignatius Ebbe (Boston, MA: Butterworth-Heinemann, 1996); and *Comparative Criminal Justice: Traditional and Non-traditional Systems of Law and Control* by Charles B. Fields and Richter H. Moore, Jr. (Prospect Heights, IL: Waveland, 1996).

(b) Electronic

The World Factbook of Criminal Justice Systems <www.ojp.usdoj.gov/bjs/abstract/wfcj.htm> hosted by the Bureau of Justice Statistics of the US Department of Justice, provides descriptions, penned by noted authorities, of criminal justice systems in 42 countries.

5.7.5 Drugs

Greenwood Press publish three comprehensive handbooks on the illegal drug trade and measures taken to control it: *Handbook of Research on the Illicit Drug Traffic: Socioeconomic and Political Consequences* by LaMond Tullis (London and Westport, CT: Greenwood Press, 1991); *International Handbook on Drug Control* edited by Scott B. MacDonald and Bruce Zagaris (London and Westport, CT: Greenwood Press, 1992); and *Handbook of Drug Control in the United States* edited by James A. Inciardi (London and Westport, CT: Greenwood Press, 1990).

5.7.6 FBI (Federal Bureau of Investigation)

The FBI: a Comprehensive Reference Guide edited by Athan G. Theoharis (Phoenix, AR: The Oryx Press, 1999) is a detailed and very readable guide to the Federal Bureau of Investigation. Its 10 chapters cover a wide range of topics including: a history of the FBI's role and powers; notable cases; traditions and culture; organization and activities; biographies of notable FBI personnel; and a chronology of key events. *See also 5.3.11.*

5.7.7 Forensic science

The three-volume *Forensic Science Handbook* edited by Richard Saferstein (Englewood Cliffs, NJ: Prentice-Hall, 1982, 1988, 1993) provides a good introduction to criminalistics.

5.7.8 Gangs

The Gang Intervention Handbook edited by Arnold P. Goldstein and Ronald C. Huff (Champaign, IL: Research Press, 1993) presents previously unpublished papers on various aspects of interventions with gangs including: historical, psychological and criminal justice perspectives.

5.7.9 Gender

Gender, Crime and Feminism edited by Ngaire Naffine (Aldershot and Brookfield, VT: Dartmouth, 1995). This volume contains 20 articles by key authors such as Maureen Cain, Pat Carlen and Loraine Gelsthorpe. The editor provides a useful overview of the relationship between feminism and modern criminology. The book is published in *The International Library of Criminology, Criminal Justice and Penology* series.

5.7.10 History

Criminal Ancestors: a Guide to Historical Criminal Records in England and Wales by David T. Hawkings (Stroud, Glos. and Wolfeboro Falls, NH: Alan Sutton Publishing Ltd., 1992). Hawkings is both an amiable and knowledgeable companion as he unravels the mysteries of tracing a wide variety of sources including: criminal and prison registers; court records; Home Office warrants and correspondence; prison hulk records; records of the Director of Public Prosecutions; and prison books and journals. Appendices offer full addresses of relevant collections, such as those held in police archives, prison service and county record offices. The book includes a bibliography, glossary of terms and indexes of personal/place names and prison hulks and ships. *The Origins and Growth of Criminology: Essays on Intellectual History, 1760–1945* edited by Piers Beirne (Aldershot and Brookfield, VT: Dartmouth, 1994) contains 15 articles published in the last 20 years charting the rise of criminology from Cesare Beccaria to Edwin Sutherland. Published in *The International Library of Criminology, Criminal Justice and Penology* series.

5.7.11 Juvenile justice/Youth crime

International Handbook on Juvenile Justice edited by Donald J. Shoemaker (London and Westport, CT: Greenwood Press, 1996). Written from both legal and social perspectives, the 19 chapters cover juvenile justice in: Australia; Brazil; Canada; China; Egypt; England; France; Germany; Greece; Hong Kong; India; Japan; Mexico; Nigeria; Philippines;

Poland; Russia; South Africa; and the United States. In addition to a short essay, most chapters also include references and details of key organizations. An index arranged by country facilitates searches for information on particular topics. The *Handbook of Juvenile Delinquency* edited by H. C. Quay (New York: John Wiley and Sons, 1987) presents 14 essays by respected academic psychologists, providing critical assessments of research and theory within the major psychological perspectives on juvenile delinquency including: epidemiology; social ecology; intelligence; personality; family interaction; and prediction and prevention models. Detailed chapter references are given and the book is easily navigated by means of subject and author indexes.

Elmer Johnson's *Handbook on Crime and Delinquency Prevention* (London and New York: Greenwood Press, 1987) provides the reader with 14 essays on juvenile crime prevention. Covering such topics as Crime Control; Deterrence and Target Hardening; The Community and Prevention; Schooling and Delinquency; and The Preventive Effects of the Family on Delinquency. The perspective is solidly American, but it does offer useful reviews of the literature and each chapter has its own bibliography. A supplementary selected bibliography and a directory of organizations are also included. *Street Crime* edited by Mike Maguire (Aldershot and Brookfield, VT: Dartmouth, 1996), contains 25 key articles on many aspects of street crime including: gangs, drugs, politics and policy. The editor offers a useful introduction entitled: 'From Chicago to Chicano: Shifting Perspectives in Street Crime'. Published in *The International Library of Criminology, Criminal Justice and Penology* series.

5.7.12 Organized crime

The *Handbook of Organized Crime in the United States*, edited by R. J. Kelly, K. L. Chin, and R. Schatzberg (London and Westport, CT: Greenwood Press, 1994) contains 21 essays by academics and criminal justice professionals, arranged under four headings: Background Issues; Perspectives on Organized Crime: Theory and Research; Organized Crime Groups and Operations; and Control and Containment: Law Enforcement Strategies. A bibliographic essay of further specialized readings is also provided, covering such topics as ethnicity and fiction.

Organized Crime: a Reference Handbook by Patrick J. Ryan (Santa Barbara, CA: ABC-CLIO, 1995) complements the above text in that it is targeted at the researcher who is new to the area, offering points of departure rather than the detailed analysis of Kelly, Chin and Schatzberg's volume. The two books are further connected in that Ryan (ex-New York City police officer and currently Associate Professor of Criminal Justice at Long Island University) contributed a chapter on the history of organized crime control to the *Handbook of Organized Crime*. Ryan's book is informative, well-presented and easy to read. In addition to a brief overview of the subject, there are chapters on organized crime groups and controlling organized crime, a chronology of events and a pot-pourri of facts, statistics and quotations. An interesting feature is the biographical sketches of criminals, crime-fighters, and academics. Usefully, Ryan also provides a directory of organizations and libraries and sections detailing print and electronic reference sources and services. Both handbooks focus mainly on the American experience.

5.7.13 Penology

The Handbook of Crime and Punishment edited by Michael Tonry (New York and Oxford: Oxford University Press, 1998) is a particularly useful work. *See 5.7.1* for its main entry. Of related interest is *The Sociology of Punishment: Soci-Structural Perspectives* edited by Dario Melossi (Aldershot and Brookfield, VT: Ashgate/Dartmouth, 1998), published in *The International Library of Criminology, Criminal Justice and Penology* series. This particular volume offers papers from such diverse authors as Durkheim, Mead, Sutherland, Ken Pease, David Garland, and Steven Box. It is divided into four parts: The Classics; Measuring and Comparing Punishment; Punishment: Self-regulation on the Economy?; and Culture, History and Changing Vocabularies of Punishment.

Prisons

(a) Print

The Prisons Handbook: 2000 edited by Mark Leech and Deborah Cheney (Winchester: Waterside Press, 1999) offers detailed information on every prison and young offenders institution in England and Wales. Topics covered include: the regime, visiting conditions, educational and medical facilities, disciplinary adjudication, workshops and prisoners' views. In addition, there are sections which provide advice to prisoners and information about relevant organizations, statutes and official reports. Selections from the book are available on the Web at: <www.tphbook.dircon.co.uk/>. The book first appeared in 1995 as the *Prisoners' Handbook* published by Oxford University Press, it was subsequently taken over by Pluto Press and since 1998 it has been published by Waterside Press who are committed to producing it annually, in December of each year.

The Oxford History of the Prison: the Practice of Punishment in Western Society edited by Norval Morris and David J. Rothman (New York and Oxford: Oxford University Press, 1995) offers an international perspective in part one on the development of prisons within England,

Europe,and the USA. In part two, particular themes are picked out including: the Australian colonies, women prisoners, the political prison and the depiction of prisons in fiction. Each of the 14 essays provides an annotated guide to further reading. A combined author/subject index is also included. *Prisons Around the World: Studies in International Penology* edited by Michael K. Carlie and Kevin I. Minor (Dubuque, IA: Wm. C. Brown Publishers, 1992) contains 24 key texts selected from 150 articles found during a two-year long search of the literature. It is divided into four sections: an overview of prisons around the world; offender rehabilitation and select prison problems; issues of policy and management; and prisoners' rights and protests. The book would have benefited from the inclusion of a subject index, but it does offer high quality contributions spanning diverse geographical areas.

(b) Electronic

Making Standards Work: an International Handbook on Good Prison Practice (The Hague: Penal Reform International, 1995) <www.rechten.unimaas.nl/straf&crim/PRI/manual.html>. Penal Reform International was founded in 1989 to provide an international focus for prison reform. The *Handbook*, which is freely available on the Internet, is the result of the collaboration of over a 100 governmental and non-governmental experts from more than 50 countries. To quote from the Preface: 'The Handbook attempts to present an overview of the UN rules on prison conditions and treatment of prisoners and explain concretely their value and meaning for prison policies and daily practice. The handbook is meant for use by all those working with prisoners or responsible for their care and treatment in any way.'

Alternatives to imprisonment

Alternatives to Imprisonment in Comparative Perspective edited by Ugljesa Zvekic on behalf of the United Nations Interregional Crime and Justice Research Institute (Chicago, IL: Nelson-Hall, 1994). This is an excellent collection of authoritative, comparative reports by experts in the field, which span the globe : Africa; Arab Countries; Asia and the Pacific Region; Australia; Europe; North America, Latin America and the Caribbean. Matti Joutsen and Ugljesa Zvekic introduce the collection with an extremely useful comparative overview. The case-study reports form volume one of the publication; volume two is an *International Bibliography on Alternatives to Imprisonment, 1980–1989*. For a discussion of the bibliography *see 5.3.20 Alternatives to Imprisonment (a) Print.*

Restorative justice

(a) Print

Restorative Justice: International Perspectives edited by Burt Galaway and Joe Hudson (Monsey, NY: Criminal Justice Press, and Amsterdam: Kugler Publications, 1996) is divided into four parts: Theory for Restorative Justice Practice; Restorative Justice Practice Among Indigenous Peoples; Restorative Justice Practice Issues; and Restorative Justice Program Applications. The geographical areas covered include: the United States, Japan, England and Wales, New Zealand, Canada, and The Netherlands. The chapters, authored by academic criminologists and practitioners, offer concise overviews and are fully referenced.

(b) Electronic

Guide for Implementing the Balanced and Restorative Justice Model <ssw.che.umn.edu/rjp/Resources/Implemen.htm> a report by Shay Bilchik, is intended to assist juvenile justice professionals in implementing balanced and restorative justice practices in their work. Paper copies are also available free from the Juvenile Justice Clearinghouse – further details are available on the Website.

Capital punishment

For a guide to the literature of a particularly controversial form of punishment see *The International Sourcebook on Capital Punishment* by William A. Schabas, Hugo Adam Bedau, and Peter Hodgkinson (Boston, MA: Northeastern University Press, 1997). It brings together an international selection of material – articles, book reviews, statistics – relating to the death penalty. *The Death Penalty: a World-Wide Perspective*, 2nd ed., by Roger Hood (Oxford and New York: Oxford University Press, 1996) is also an excellent contribution to the literature. Hood draws upon the work he did as consultant to the United Nations' Secretary-General's Report on the Fifth Quinquennial Survey on *Capital Punishment and Implementation of the Safeguards Guaranteeing the Protection of the Rights of those Facing the Death Penalty*, presented to the Economic and Social Council in June 1995. In particular, he discusses the abolitionist movement across the globe. An extensive bibliography of materials is also provided.

5.7.14 Police

Handbook of the World's Police by Harold K. Becker and Donna Lee Becker (Metuchen, NJ and London: Scarecrow Press, 1986). Although this text predates the break-up of the Soviet Union, it remains a useful summary of police systems in over a 170 countries. For each country brief data is given on demography, history, government and the organization of the police.

5.7.15 Politics

In *Politics, Crime Control and Culture* edited by Stuart A. Scheingold (Aldershot and Brookfield, VT: Ashgate/Dartmouth, 1997) 20 journal articles are organized within three main headings: politics, policy and punishment; public opinion and punishment; and the cultural construction of crime and punishment. The editor provides an introductory essay: 'Criminology and the Politicization of Crime and Punishment'. Issued as part of *The International Library of Criminology, Criminal Justice and Penology* series.

5.7.16 Probation

The *Handbook on Probation Services: Guidelines for Probation Practitioners and Managers* by J. F. Klaus (Rome: UNICRI, 1998) discusses the history and functions of probation and trends such as mediation, community service orders and restorative justice. The two main sections of the book look at the professional responsibilities of probation practitioners at pre- and post- sentence stages, and service management and administration.

5.7.17 Prostitution

Prostitution: an International Handbook on Trends, Problems, and Policies edited by Nanette J. Davis (London and Westport, CT: Greenwood Press, 1993). The word *international* is sometimes added to titles without any real justification, but this is one work which has more right than most to use it as it covers the following countries: Australia, Brazil, Canada, China, England, Germany, Italy, Japan, Netherlands, Norway, Portugal, Singapore, Taiwan, United States, Vietnam and Yugoslavia.

5.7.18 Psychology

The *Handbook of Psychology in Legal Contexts* edited by Ray Bull and David Carson (Chichester and New York: John Wiley and Sons, 1995) is a collection of high quality, often extensively referenced, essays by key international scholars on the use of psychology in a range of criminologically pertinent areas, including sections on: Investigations: Seeking, Obtaining, Interpreting and Assessing Information; Criminal Responsibility and Proceedings; and Trial and Decision-Making. A detailed subject index speeds the navigation of this well-presented volume. Another useful resource for academics and practitioners alike is the *Handbook of Psychological Approaches with Violent Offenders: Contemporary Strategies and Issues* edited by Vincent B. Van Hasselt and Michael Hersen (Dordrecht and New York: Kluwer Academic/Plenum Publishers, 1999). There are six main sections: Overview and Theoretical Perspectives; Violent Crime by Children and Adolescents; Homicide; Sexual Deviance and Assault; Family Violence; and Special Topics (including arson, neurology and psychiatry).

5.7.19 Race and ethnicity

Race, Crime and Justice edited by Barbara A. Hudson (Aldershot and Brookfield, VT: Dartmouth, 1996), tackles four areas: the courts; crime, policing and racial unrest; causes of black crime; and race and gender. The collection offers key papers published in North American and British Journals, forming part of the well-established *International Library of Criminology, Criminal Justice and Penology* series.

5.7.20 Rape and related crimes

Rape and Sexual Assault III: a Research Handbook edited by Ann Wolbert Burgess (New York: Garland, 1991) is the latest volume to date (the first appeared in 1985). The set provides a good introduction to the topic. *The Handbook of Forensic Sexology: Biomedical and Criminological Perspectives* edited by James J. Krivacska and John Money (Amherst, NY: Prometheus Books, 1994) collects together essays on a variety of deviant sexual activities including: paedophilia, rape, incest and exhibitionism.

5.7.21 Terrorism

Terrorism: a Reference Handbook by Stephen E. Atkins (Santa Barbara, CA: ABC-CLIO, 1992) adopts the same format as Patrick Ryan's

Organized Crime: a Reference Handbook (*see* 5.7.12), and provides a good launch pad for those new to the topic by offering a general overview of the subject, a chronology of events, a directory of organizations, statistics and a guide to print and electronic reference sources.

5.7.22 Victimology

Victimology edited by Paul Rock (Aldershot and Brookfield, VT: Dartmouth, 1994) presents 19 key articles divided into four main sections: the birth of victimology; crime surveys; patterns and representations of victimization; and remedies and conclusions. The book is published within *The International Library of Criminology, Criminal Justice and Penology* series. *The Victimology Handbook: Research Findings, Treatment, and Public Policy* edited by Emilio Viano (New York: Garland, 1990) makes available 26 papers presented at the World Congress of Criminology in three main sections: research findings; prevention and treatment; and public policy. The emphasis is on the US, but data from other countries are also included.

5.7.23 Violence

Statistical Handbook on Violence in America edited by Adam Dobrin and Brian Wiersema (Phoenix, AZ: Oryx Press, 1996). A useful sourcebook on US statistics, including such topics as: fatal violence; vulnerable groups and situations; and public opinion about violence. The appendix details the sources for all the statistics presented. *See also* 5.12.

5.7.24 World Wide Web

The Definitive Guide to Criminal Justice and Criminology on the World Wide Web produced by The Criminal Justice Distance Learning Consortium (Upper Saddle River, NJ: Prentice Hall, 1999). The book has a good pedigree, the preface having been written by Dr Frank Schmalleger, Director of The Justice Research Association and founder of The Criminal Justice Distance Learning Consortium. Although the guide is well presented and easy-to-use, it was perhaps a mistake to insert *definitive* into the title. Like most works of this type it allocates too much space to general topics – the history of the Internet, netiquette and search engines – and only devotes one chapter to criminology and criminal justice Websites. That said, it does provide details of a wide variety of Websites (predominantly American, but with a smattering of international resources) and is a good starting point for those new to the area. The contents page and a sample chapter of the book can be found at: <www.cjcentral.com/cjdlc/TOC.htm>. A particularly useful feature of the publication is the option to be able to trace updates of the listed Websites at <talkjustice.com/files/guide.htm>.

▶ 5.8 WEBSITES

A selection of quality gateways to criminological and criminal justice information. For the Websites of key organizations *see section 5.14*.

Criminal Justice Links <www.criminology.fsu.edu/cj.html>. An award-winning collection of resources maintained by Cecil Greek of the School of Criminology and Criminal Justice at Florida State University, USA. Topics include: juvenile delinquency, drugs, police, law, forensics, and criminal justice in the media.

Criminal Justice Web Links <www.leeds.ac.uk/law/ccjs/ukWeb.htm>. Numerous links to criminal justice in the UK, as well as selected collections of sites for Continental Europe, North America and the rest of the world. The pages are maintained by Professor Clive Walker, Director of the Centre for Criminal Justice Studies, University of Leeds, UK.

Criminology <www.cf.ac.uk/infos/information/subject/criminology/subject.html>. Extensive resources from the Arts and Social Studies Resource Centre at the University of Cardiff, UK. Subjects covered include: crime prevention, domestic violence, drugs, penology, race and white collar crime.

Criminology at BUBL <link.bubl.ac.uk/crime/>. Selected resources from the respected UK service based at the Andersonian Library, Strathclyde University, UK.

Criminology at YAHOO! <dir.yahoo.com/Social_Science/Sociology/Criminology/>. European and international resources from one of the Internet's major directories.

Criminology Links <www.law.cam.ac.uk/crim/crimlink.htm>. Worldwide sources of information on most criminological topics including: crime prevention, forensics, drugs, ethnicity, gender and sexuality, the police, restorative justice/mediation, and victimology. The site is hosted by the Institute of Criminology, University of Cambridge, UK.

The Criminology Mega-Site <faculty.ncwc.edu/toconnor/criminology.htm>. An entertaining and informative site by Dr Tom O'Connor of the Justice Studies Department, North Carolina Wesleyan College, USA – particularly good for criminological theory.

Criminology Resources <www.ntu.ac.uk/lis/crim.htm>. A useful gateway to criminological Websites based at The Nottingham Trent University, UK. Subjects covered encompass: police, criminal justice, law, prisons, media and victimology.

Dr Frank Schmalleger's Talk Justice <talkjustice.com/>. The site is directed by the noted US academic and offers bulletin boards for the discussion of topics such as the police, courts and victims of crime, as well as links via the *Cybrary* to other Webpages on a variety of subjects including: computer crime, death penalty, forensics, gangs, prisons, sentencing, statistics and violence against women.

International Victimology Website <www.victimology.nl>. Launched in June 1999 as 'a resource for all those interested in improving justice for victims of crime and the abuse of power'. The site is hosted by the Research and Documentation Centre of the Dutch Ministry of Justice and sponsored by the World Society of Victimology and the United Nations Centre for International Crime Prevention. It is an excellent resource giving access to full-text United Nations publications, related international links, and two databases: Victimology Research (providing details of ongoing research worldwide) and Victim Services and Victimization Prevention (giving information about victim support schemes and victimization prevention programmes).

National Criminal Justice Reference Service <www.ncjrs.org>. It describes itself as a 'federally sponsored information clearinghouse for people . . . involved with research, policy, and practice related to criminal and juvenile justice and drug control'. The site provides links to a vast array of documentation and Websites covering many criminological topics: corrections, courts, drugs, juvenile justice, law enforcement and victims of crime.

Organized Crime Web Links <www.yorku.ca/nathanson/Links/links.htm>. Extensive international resources on organized crime, presented under the following main headings: comprehensive and reference sites; academic and research centres; media sources on organized crime; discussion groups; organized crime genres; organized crime activities; transnational organized crime; and organized crime enforcement. The site is maintained by the Nathanson Centre for the Study of Organized Crime and Corruption, Ontario, Canada.

The Redwood Highway: Crime, Law and Related Links on the Web <www.sonoma.edu/cja/info/infos.html>. Quality, annotated links to a wide range of sites, maintained by Pat Jackson of the Department of Criminal Justice Administration, Sonoma State University, USA.

Subject Index to Internet Resources in Criminology <www.library.utoronto.ca/libraries_crim/centre/links.htm>. The site covers a broad range of topics: computer crime, drugs, death penalty, family violence, female offenders and women inmates, forensics, gangs, homicide, juvenile justice, prostitution, restorative justice and victims of crime. The pages are maintained by the Centre of Criminology, University of Toronto, Canada.

United Nations Crime and Justice Information Network <www.uncjin.org>. Access to international information and documentation on crime and crime prevention from this key network.

World Justice Information Network <www.justinfo.net/>. Supported by the National Institute of Justice of the United States Department of Justice, the site is subtitled: 'An Experiment on Building a Global Network of Knowledge About Crime and Justice'. A useful networking tool.

▶ 5.9 JOURNALS

An international selection of major journal titles is discussed in this section. As many titles are available in both print and digital versions, I have not included a separate section of electronic journals, but simply indicated if available electronically within the entry. Where a title is freely available via the Internet the Web address is included. Whilst all selections are inherently subjective, a degree of objectivity has been imposed upon the collection by selecting key journals from the chapter 'Who Lands the Luminaries? Rating the Prestige of Criminology and Criminal Justice Journals Through an Analysis of Where Scholars' publish in: *Evaluating Criminology and Criminal Justice* by Cohn, Farrington and Wright (1998) which statistically ranks titles by the number of articles penned by renowned scholars.

Australian and New Zealand Journal of Criminology (ISSN 0004–8658) (New South Wales, Australia: Butterworths, 1968–). Three issues a year. A key refereed journal for these countries, covering all aspects of criminology, aimed at both academics and professionals.

The British Journal of Criminology (ISSN 0007–0955) (Oxford: Oxford University Press for ISTD: the Centre for Crime and Justice Studies, 1950–). Quarterly. A noted UK-based publication with international coverage of all criminological issues. Available electronically.

The British Criminology Conferences: Selected Proceedings <www.lboro.ac.uk/departments/ss/bsc/bccsp/INDEX.HTM> (Loughborough: British Society of Criminology, 1998–). Irregular. An electronic journal published on an occasional basis to disseminate papers given at the biennial British Criminology Conference.

Canadian Journal of Criminology/Revue Canadienne De Criminologie (ISSN 0704–9722) (Ottawa: Canadian Criminal Justice Association. 1958–). Quarterly. This journal publishes both theoretical and more pragmatic, policy oriented articles. The perspective is international, but with a natural emphasis on the Canadian experience. Available electronically.

Crime and Delinquency (ISSN 0011–1287) (Thousand Oaks, CA: Sage Publications, 1955–). Quarterly. A peer-reviewed journal publishing policy-oriented qualitative and quantitative articles. Available electronically.

Crime, Law and Social Change (ISSN 0093–8548) (Dordrecht, Netherlands: Kluwer Academic Press, 1977–). Eight issues a year. A refereed journal focusing on organized crime, financial crime, political corruption, environmental crime and human rights.

Criminal Behaviour and Mental Health (ISSN 0957–9664) (London: Whurr Publishers, 1991–). Quarterly. This refereed journal focuses on mental health issues and their relationship with criminal activity. Available electronically.

Criminal Justice Ethics (ISSN 0731–129X) (New York: John Jay College of Criminal Justice, City University of New York, 1982–). Semiannual. A refereed publication of The Institute for Criminal Justice Ethics at John Jay College (*see 5.14* for information about the College), aimed at both criminal justice practitioners and academics. Available electronically.

Criminology (ISSN 0011–1384) (Columbus, OH: American Society of Criminology, 1963–). Quarterly. A key journal with an interdisciplinary focus, publishing original empirical research as well as literature reviews and theoretical debates.

Critical Criminology (ISSN 1205–8629) (Richmond, BC: Collective Press for American Society of Criminology, Division of Critical Criminology, 1989–). Semiannual. Formerly called *Journal of Human Justice*, this refereed journal focuses on social justice from an interdisciplinary perspective.

Deviant Behavior (ISSN 0163–9625) (Rankine, Hants. and Bristol, PA: Taylor and Francis, 1979–). Quarterly. A refereed journal covering all aspects of deviancy from an international perspective. Available electronically.

European Journal of Crime, Criminal Law and Criminal Justice (ISSN 0928–9569) (The Hague: Kluwer Law International, 1993–). Quarterly. Available electronically. Refereed. *European Journal on Criminal Policy and Research* (ISSN 0928–1371) (Dordrecht, Netherlands: Kluwer Academic Publishers, 1993–). Quarterly. Available electronically. Both of these titles are of interest for their discussion of European policies on crime and criminal justice.

Federal Probation (ISSN 0014–9128) (Washington, DC: Administrative Office of the United States Courts, 1937–). Semiannual. A long-established US Government publication featuring articles by academics and practitioners on corrections and alternatives to imprisonment. *See also* the *Probation Journal* below.

The Howard Journal of Criminal Justice (ISSN 0265–5527) (Oxford: Blackwell Publishers for The Howard League, 1941–). Quarterly. A renowned title which publishes articles on key aspects of criminal justice.

International Journal of Comparative and Applied Criminal Justice (ISSN 0192–4036) (Wichita, KS: Department of Criminal Justice, Wichita State University 1977–). Semi-annual. Emphasis is on the presentation of original empirical research from around the world.

International Journal of Offender Therapy and Comparative Criminology (ISSN 0306–624X) (Thousand Oaks, CA: Sage Publications, 1957–). Quarterly. This long-established, refereed journal prides itself on its international coverage of the treatment of offenders. *See also* the *Journal of Offender Rehabilitation* below.

International Journal of the Sociology of Law (ISSN 0194–6595) (London: Academic Press, 1972–). Quarterly. Ranges widely, both geographically and conceptually, over criminological and criminal justice issues. Until volume seven, 1979 it was called the *International Journal of Criminology and Penology*. Available electronically.

International Review of Victimology (ISSN 0269–7580) (Bicester, Oxon: A B Academic Publishers, 1990–). Quarterly. Published in association with the World Society of Victimology, this refereed journal covers all aspects of victimological research.

Journal of Contemporary Criminal Justice (ISSN 1043–9862) (Thousand Oaks, CA: Sage, 1978–). Quarterly. Each issue is devoted to a particular theme, which allows in-depth, international coverage of topics. Available electronically.

Journal of Criminal Justice (ISSN 0047–2352) (Kidlington, Oxford: Elsevier Science, 1973–). Bimonthly. A refereed, multidisciplinary and international journal encompassing all aspects of criminal justice.

Journal of Criminal Justice and Popular Culture <www.albany.edu/scj/jcjpc/index.html> (ISSN 1070–8286) (New York: University at Albany, State University of New York, 1993–). Irregular. A peer-reviewed electronic journal concerned with the intersection of crime, criminal justice and popular culture.

Journal of Criminal Law and Criminology (ISSN 0091–4169) (Chicago: Northwestern University School of Law, 1910–). Quarterly. A long-established title with an emphasis on policy and legal issues.

Journal of Interpersonal Violence (ISSN 0886–2605) (Thousand Oaks, CA: Sage, 1986). Monthly. Focuses on both the victims and perpetrators of violence. It has an interdisciplinary perspective with a bias towards quantitative research. Available electronically.

Journal of Offender Rehabilitation (ISSN 1050–9674) (New York: Haworth Press, 1976–). Quarterly. This refereed journal is a forum for interdisciplinary research on the rehabilitation of offenders. *See also* the *International Journal of Offender Therapy and Comparative Criminology* above.

Journal of Quantitative Criminology (ISSN 0748–4518) (New York: Kluwer Academic/Plenum, 1984–). Quarterly. A refereed journal focusing, as its title suggests, on the publication of quantitative research. Available electronically.

Journal of Research in Crime and Delinquency (ISSN 0022–4278) (Thousand Oaks, CA: Sage, 1964–). Quarterly. Published in association with the US National Council on Crime and Delinquency, presenting both qualitative and quantitative empirical research, as well as theoretical discussions. Available electronically.

Justice Quarterly (ISSN 0741–8825) (Highland Heights, KY: Northern Kentucky University, 1984–). Quarterly. The official journal of The Academy of Criminal Justice Sciences, it promotes a multidisciplinary approach to all aspects of criminal justice.

Legal and Criminological Psychology (ISSN 1355–3259) (Leicester: The British Psychological Society, 1996–). Semiannual. An international, refereed journal which publishes papers (both theoretical and empirical) on a broad range of topics including: victimology, mental health, penology and crime prevention. Available electronically.

The Police Journal (ISSN 0032–258X) (Ashford, Kent: Vathek Publishing, 1928–). Quarterly. Its subtitle bills it as 'a quarterly review for the police of the world' and while it publishes a preponderance of material about the UK, it does also reflect the international scene.

Policing (ISSN 1363–951X) (Bradford: MCB University Press, 1978–). Quarterly. Formerly known as *Police Studies*, and incorporating the *American Journal of Police*. A good source of international and comparative academic studies on all aspects of policing. Available electronically.

Policing and Society (ISSN 1043–9463) (Chur, Switzerland: Gordon and Breach/Harwood Academic, 1991–). Quarterly. A refereed journal concerned with key aspects – social, political, legal and policy – of policing from an international perspective.

The Prison Journal (ISSN 0032–8855) (Thousand Oaks, CA: Sage, 1845–). Quarterly. This refereed publication is the official journal of the Pennsylvania Prison Society which was founded in 1787. A respected title covering all aspects of prison and corrections systems. Available electronically.

Probation Journal (ISSN 0264–5505) (London: National Association of Probation Officers, 1929–). Quarterly. A refereed journal which was established to act as a forum for sharing good practice and developing debate about the theory and practice of work with offenders. *See also Federal Probation* above.

Scientific Testimony: an Online Journal <www.scientific.org/> (Irvine, CA: Department of Criminology, University of California). This electronic journal publishes articles, news reports and commentary about the use of scientific evidence in legal proceedings.

Theoretical Criminology (ISSN 1362–4806) (London: Sage, 1997–). Quarterly. A relatively new refereed title concerned, as its name suggests, with the theories, concepts, narratives and myths of crime. Available electronically.

The Victimologist <www.world-society-victimology.de> (World Society of Victimology, 1997–). Irregular. As the official journal of the World Society of Victimology *(see section 5.13)* it publishes short articles by members, interviews with victimologists, and news about conferences, services and publications.

Western Criminology Review <wcr.sonoma.edu> (ISSN 1096–4886) (Carmichael, CA: Western Society of Criminology, 1998–). Irregular. A peer-reviewed electronic journal focusing on the discussion of theory, research, policy and practice within criminology and criminal justice.

▶ 5.10 ABSTRACTS, INDEXES AND DATABASES

Key abstracting and indexing services in criminology are covered in this section. Services that are available in both print and electronic formats are cross-referenced with more detail provided about the electronic version. Due to the multidisciplinary nature of their subject area, criminologists may need to consult a wide range of databases in related areas such as sociology (Chapter 3) and psychology (Chapter 4). The reader is thus also directed to the relevant sections within those chapters (*3.10* and *4.10*) and to the more general resources of Chapter 1 (*1.10*).

(a) Print

Criminal Justice Abstracts (Monsey, New York: Willow Tree Press, 1968–). Updated quarterly. Previously known as *Abstracts on Crime and Juvenile Delinquency*; *Crime and Delinquency Literature*. Formed by the merger of: *Information Review on Crime and Delinquency*; *Selected Highlights of Crime and Delinquency*. For further details see entry under *(b) Electronic.*

Criminal Justice Periodical Index (Ann Arbor, MI: UMI, 1975–) Published three times a year. It is also available online from The Dialog Corporation and as an Internet database from ProQuest Information and Learning. For further details see entry under *(b) Electronic.*

Criminology, Penology and Police Science Abstracts (Amsterdam: Kugler Publications, 1961–1997). Published bimonthly, ceased publication in December 1997. This well-respected abstracting service is international in scope, covering a broad range of criminological topics in both monograph and journal literature including: offences, deviant behaviour, victim studies, juvenile justice and delinquency, criminal law, police, and criminal justice system. The arrangement of material is by main subject headings, which are supplemented by subject and author indexes. The last issue of each year contains cumulative indexes.

W. H. Nagel, Professor of Criminology, University of Leyden, founded this service in 1961 as *Excerpta Criminologica*, becoming *Abstracts on Criminology and Penology* in 1969, and *Criminology and Penology Abstracts* in 1982. In 1992 *Criminology and Penology Abstracts* joined with *Police Science Abstracts* to become *Criminology, Penology and Police Science Abstracts*. The Criminologica Foundation has been associated with the service since its inception and for many years it was jointly produced in conjunction with the Research and Documentation Centre and Crime Prevention Unit of the Netherlands Ministry of Justice; the Police Study Centre, Warnveld; and the Detective Training School, Zutphen. The demise of this service will be much missed by scholars and leaves a gap in the indexing of criminological literature.

Organized Crime Digest (Fairfax, VA: Washington Crime News Services). Patrick Ryan in *Organized Crime: a Reference Handbook* (for main entry *see 5.7.12*) says of the service that it is the 'only reference source dedicated to collecting newspaper articles dealing with organized crime ... Articles are reprinted verbatim in a series of newspaper-style "bulletins" that provide a lot of information but suffer from lack of detail and references to sources cited' (p.248). *See also* the *Organized Crime and Corruption Bibliographic Database* below under *(b) Electronic* below.

Violence and Abuse Abstracts: Current Literature in Interpersonal Violence (ISSN 1077–2197) (London and Thousand Oaks, CA: Sage Publications, 1995–). Quarterly. This journal is an abstracting service of academic literature on interpersonal violence – journal articles, books, reports and unpublished conference papers. Key areas covered include: child abuse, gender, family violence, perpetrator profile and assessment, victim profiles, criminology of violence and abuse, criminal law, and penology. Entries are arranged by topic, but separate author and subject indexes are also included. It is now also available electronically but does not in itself offer any additional features in this format. Of course, certain journal subscription agents do offer limited search facilities for electronic journals.

(b) Electronic

Criminal Justice Abstracts (Monsey, NY: Willow Tree Press, 1968–). Available as an Internet, CD-ROM or Hard Disk database from SilverPlatter <www.silverplatter.com>, updated quarterly or annually. The database, produced in association with the Criminal Justice Collection of Rutgers University Library, is international in scope and abstracts journals, books, reports, dissertations and unpublished papers. Topics covered include: crime trends, crime prevention, juvenile delinquency, police, courts, punishment and sentencing. In its digital SilverPlatter format, the database is quite straightforward to use, sharing the same interface as related databases, *Sociological Abstracts* (*see 3.10*) and *Psyclit* (*see 4.10*). It allows searching of all fields of the record and uses standard Boolean operators *AND, OR* and *NOT.* * is used to truncate terms. Whilst international in coverage, it does have an emphasis on US data. Nevertheless, it is a key abstracting service for criminology, particularly in light of the discontinuation of *Criminology, Penology and Police Science Abstracts.*

Criminal Justice Periodical Index (Ann Arbor, MI: ProQuest Information and Learning, 1975–). The Internet version of this database is easy to navigate as it uses Proquest's Web-based delivery platform (*see*: <www.umi.com)>. Like *Criminal Justice Abstracts*, it has an American slant, but it does cover many of the key criminology journals. It employs standard Boolean logic and truncation symbols. The main advantage of the database over its rivals is that it offers the full text of selected journals, including: *The British Journal of Criminology*, *Canadian Journal of Criminology*, *Journal of Research in Crime and Delinquency*, and *Criminology*.

Forensic Science Society: Journal Bibliography Search <www.forensic-science-society.org.uk/biblisea.html>. A useful specialized database, produced by the UK-based Forensic Science Society, searchable by keywords, covering references to the journals *Science & Justice* and *Journal of the Forensic Science Society*, and additional monograph material. Not a large database, but it is regularly updated and free!

LMS Bibliographic Collection <www.unicri.it/html/body_databases.htm>. Produced by the United Nations Interregional Crime and Justice Research Institute (UNICRI), this is an extensive database of over 6000 authors, 300 series and 600 publishers. It lists and abstracts material on crime prevention, deviance and related areas such as drug abuse, held in the UNICRI Documentation Centre. The database is searchable by title, author, publisher, series, publication year and keyword.

National Criminal Justice Reference Service (NCJRS) Abstracts Database <www.ncjrs.org./ncjdb.htm>. This Website gives access to abstracts of more than 145 000 criminal justice publications published by the US Department of Justice, other local, State, and Federal government agencies, international organizations and the private sector. It is available online from <www.ncjrs.org/search.html> and also in CD-ROM format and as a Dialog file. The online version links to full-text publications where available.

Organized Crime and Corruption Bibliographic Database <www.yorku.ca/nathanson/search.htm>. Maintained by the respected Nathanson Centre for the Study of Organized Crime and Corruption (*see 5.14* for more information about the Centre) in Canada. The extensive international database currently holds details of around 6000 references and is continually updated. Searchable by name, title, or keyword.

▶ 5.11 OFFICIAL PUBLICATIONS

5.11.1 United Kingdom

(a) Print

As a starting point when looking for UK official publications, readers may wish to consult: *A Researcher's Guide to Sources of Official and Unofficial Information: the Police, Crime and the Criminal Justice System* by M. J. Gafour (Reading, Berkshire: Osborne, 1997), which is a useful tool for researchers interested in UK sources. It covers general resources – government information, legislation, courts, libraries – details of UK police forces and their public enquiry and research facilities, together with a directory of organizations. Its clear, A4 format makes it easy to use, and navigation is further assisted by a subject index. Of related interest is *Law and Order: a Select Guide to the Official Publications* by Frank Gregory (Cambridge: Chadwyck-Healey, 1994), an annotated bibliography of official publications on: the crime and criminal justice system; the court system; the police service; and the prison system in the UK, from 1979 to the early 1990s.

The *Report of Her Majesty's Chief Inspector of Constabulary* (London: The Stationery Office) is an annual review of police forces in England and Wales. Similarly, the *Report of Her Majesty's Chief Inspector of Prisons* (London: The Stationery Office) provides a yearly review of the prison service. Both of these reports and many other official publications are available in digital format, see *Home Office: A–Z Index* under *(b) Electronic* below.

(b) Electronic

CJS online <www.criminal-justice-system.gov.uk/>. This Webpage provides access to some useful full-text documents on the Criminal Justice System in England and Wales, including the service's strategic plan.

Home Office: A–Z Index <www.homeoffice.gov.uk/atoz/index.htm>. Via the alphabetical subject headings, this Website provides access to all full-text UK official documents produced by the Home Office which are available on the Web.

5.11.2 United States

(a) Print

See section 1.11.3 of Chapter one for general guides to US official publications. Of a more specific nature is *Criminal Justice Issues in the States* (Washington, DC: Justice Research and Statistics Association, 1984–) which lists the research publications and activities of State-level criminal justice agencies. *Uniform Crime Reports for the United States* (Washington, DC: Federal Bureau of Investigation, 1930–) is a key source of nationwide information. *See 5.12.2* for its main entry.

(b) Electronic

For access to the publications of the *US Department of Justice* go to: <www.ojp.usdoj.gov/reportsinfo.htm>.

The National Criminal Justice Reference Service (NCJRS) <www.ncjrs.org/> acts as a clearinghouse for many thousands of US official publications – see their *Abstracts Database* in section *5.10(b), see also 5.12.2.*

5.11.3 International

The *United Nations Interregional Crime and Justice Research Institute (UNICRI)* publishes extensively on international crime issues. For a list of both their printed and digital materials take a look at the following Website: <www.unicri.it/html/body_publications.htm>.

For materials relating to the establishment of an *International Criminal Court* (first proposed in United Nations resolution 260 of 9th December 1948) see <www.un.org/law/icc/index.html>. The *United Nations Crime and Justice Information Network* <www.uncjin.org> provides links to an excellent range of international documentation. The *National Criminal Justice Reference Service* also gives access to an international range of publications at: <virlib.ncjrs.org/International.asp>.

▶ 5.12 STATISTICS

5.12.1 United Kingdom

(a) Print

Criminal Statistics England and Wales, produced annually by the Home Office (London: The Stationery Office). The main feature of the publication is the provision of data on notifiable offences recorded by the police, court proceedings and sentencing within England and Wales, but a summary chapter on recorded crime also provides comparative international statistics. The Home Office also produces more specific series of statistical data on crime, see for instance, *Drug Seizure and Offender Statistics, United Kingdom* (London: Home Office). For information about the *Home Office Statistical Bulletin* and *Research Findings* (London: Home Office, Research Development and Statistics Directorate) see under *(b) Electronic* below.

Prison Statistics England and Wales (London: The Stationery Office) is an annual publication of the Home Office, presenting a statistical analysis of the prison population. *Probation Statistics England and Wales* (London: Home Office, annual) provides statistical data on the probation service and personnel. See also CIPFA's (Chartered Institute of Public Finance and Accountancy) *Probation Service Statistics* (London: The Chartered Institute of Public Finance and Accountancy), for financial expenditure on the service. In addition, CIPFA produces several other annual statistical publications including: *Administration of Justice: Estimates and Actuals* and *Police Statistics*.

The Lord Chancellor's Department produces an annual report, *Judicial Statistics* (London: The Stationery Office), detailing information about the traffic through the court system from Appellate to Crown Courts, as well as sections on family matters, the judiciary and legal aid. See also the Lord Chancellor's Department's *Statistics on Magistrates' Courts Information Bulletin*.

(b) Electronic

Home Office Research Development and Statistics Directorate <www.homeoffice.gov.uk/rds/index.htm>. This Web address provides access to the publications discussed below.

Home Office Statistical Bulletin issued on a regular basis, the bulletins (average length 30 pages) present statistics on a range of criminal justice topics. Mainly, but not exclusively about the UK, a recent bulletin, for instance, provided an international comparison of criminal justice statistics. *Research Findings* (average length four pages) provide statistical summaries on a similar range of criminal justice issues. For a statistical review of criminal justice in the UK see *Information on the Criminal Justice System*, again available from the above Home Office Research Development and Statistics Directorate Website.

5.12.2 United States

(a) Print

Sourcebook of Criminal Justice Statistics (Washington, DC: Bureau of Justice Statistics) is produced annually and available in print, CD-ROM and Web formats; *Uniform Crime Reports for the United States* (Washington, DC: Federal Bureau of Investigation, 1930–) provides an overview of crime in the US; *Bureau of Justice Statistics Reports* (Washington, DC: US Department of Justice) are produced on a variety of topics including expenditure on the criminal justice system, victimization and capital punishment. For information about the digital versions of all the above resources see under *(b) Electronic* below.

For comparative crime statistics on US cities see the annual publication *City Crime Rankings: Crime in Metropolitan America* (Lawrence, KS: Morgan Quitno Corporation). Of related interest is *Crime State Rankings* (Lawrence, KS: Morgan Quitno Corporation) which is also published annually.

Statistics on prison populations and the correctional system are produced on an annual basis by several bodies and include the following publications: *Juvenile and Adult Correctional Departments, Institutions, Agencies, and Paroling Authorities, United States and Canada* (Lanham, MD: American Correctional Association, 1979–); *Correctional Populations in the United States* (Washington, DC: US Department of Justice, Bureau of Statistics, 1985–); and *Statistical Report* (Washington, DC: US Federal Bureau of Prisons, 1930/31–).

The Bureau of Justice Statistics publishes a wide range of specialized statistical reports on crime and the criminal justice system, see the Websites listed under *(b) Electronic* below which give access to many of them.

(b) Electronic

Bureau of Justice Statistics <www.ojp.usdoj.gov/bjs> is part of the US Department of Justice and the main official source of American criminal statistics. For a complete A–Z listing of all the *US Department of Justice Bureau of Statistics Publications* see: <www.ojp.usdoj.gov/bjs/pubalp2.htm> many of which are available electronically in full-text format. The Bureau produces *Crime & Justice Electronic Data Abstracts* <www.ojp.usdoj.gov/bjs/dtdata.htm>. The data is provided in spreadsheet format by jurisdiction (Federal, State, County, City) and topic: crime and arrest; criminal justice; corrections; and demographic information.

Of related interest is the *Sourcebook of Criminal Justice Statistics Online* <www.albany.edu/sourcebook>. Produced again by the Bureau of Justice Statistics, this annual publication collates data on all aspects of criminal justice in the United States. It is divided into six main areas: characteristics of the criminal justice systems; public attitudes toward crime; nature and distribution of known offences; characteristics and distribution of persons arrested; judicial processing of defendants; and persons under correctional supervision. The database can be browsed or searched by keyword. A comprehensive source of statistical information on crime in the USA. Cumulations of data from the last five years are available on CD-ROM.

Uniform Crime Reports <www.fbi.gov/ucr/ucr.htm> produced by the Federal Bureau of Investigation (FBI), provide 'a nationwide view of crime based on the submission of statistics by law enforcement agencies throughout the country.' The reports cover the following categories of crimes: murder and nonnegligent manslaughter; forcible rape; robbery; aggravated assault; burglary; larceny-theft; motor vehicle theft; and arson.

The *National Archive of Criminal Justice Data* <www.icpsr.umich.edu/NACJD/index.html> is a branch of the Inter-university Consortium for Political and Social Research at the University of Michigan. The site provides access to hundreds of criminal justice data collections covering 11 areas: attitude surveys; community studies; corrections; court case processing; courts; criminal justice system; crime and delinquency; official statistics; police; victimization; and drugs, alcohol, and crime. The data are mainly US-based, but some international statistics are included.

The National Criminal Justice Reference Service (NCJRS) of the National Institute of Justice – the research and development agency of the US Department of Justice – provides an extensive collection of *Criminal Justice Statistics* at <virlib.ncjrs.org/Statistics.asp>.

5.12.3 International

The United Nations Crime and Justice Information Network has created a very useful Webpage, *Statistics and Research Sources* <www.uncjin.org/Statistics/statistics.html> which links to an extensive range of international statistics. The National Criminal Justice Reference Service (NCJRS) provides access to international and country-specific statistics from a Website called, *Statistics: Additional Resources* at <www.ncjrs.org/statwww.html>. You will need to scroll down past the US sites until you reach the International Statistics section. *See also* the *National Criminal Justice Reference Service* in *section 5.11.3* and the *National Archive of Criminal Justice Data* in *section 5.12.2(b).*

▶ 5.13 RESEARCH IN PROGRESS

Electronic discussion groups and mailing lists are a good way of keeping up to date with current research and the topical concerns of practitioners and academics. Below is a selection of lists with Web addresses and/or details of how to subscribe. *See also 5.14* for details of relevant research organizations, and *5.5* for directories of researchers and institutes.

BLKCRIM (to subscribe send Email to <Listserv@umdd.umd.edu> stating 'subscribe BLKCRIM First Name Last Name). A discussion group for black criminologists hosted by the University of Maryland.

C-J-S-Forum <www.jiscmail.ac.uk/lists/c-j-s-forum.html>. A discussion list 'designed to encourage open discussion of all aspects of the UK Criminal Justice System'.

CJTREAT (to subscribe send Email to <Majordomo@lists.downcity.net> stating 'subscribe CJTREAT'). A mailing list concerned with treatment and rehabilitation issues within prison and probation services.

CJUST-L (to subscribe send Email to LISTSERV@LISTSERV.CUNY.EDU stating 'subscribe CJUST-L First Name Last Name'). Hosted by the City University of New York's John Jay College of Criminal Justice (*see 5.14)*, this is a large, international mailing list devoted to the discussion of criminal justice issues.

Crimebooks <groups.yahoo.com/group/crimebooks/join>. A useful way to keep abreast of new books, but discussion also ranges over broader topics of criminological interest.

Criminology <www.jiscmail.ac.uk/lists/criminology.html>. A list for those working in UK higher education and interested in criminology, criminal justice and socio-legal studies.

Criminology (to subscribe send Email to LISTSERV@LISTSERV.GMD.DE stating 'subscribe criminology First Name Last Name'). A German academic list, but discussion is usually in English.

CrimNet <www.law.usyd.edu.au/mailman/listinfo.cgi/crimnet>. A mailing list for criminal justice professionals throughout Australia and across the world. Hosted by the Institute of Criminology, Faculty of Law, University of Sydney.

CRIT-L (to subscribe send Email to listproc@sun.soci.niu.edu stating 'subscribe CRIT-L First Name Last Name). The discussion list of the Critical Criminology Division of the American Society of Criminology.

European-Group-Criminology <www.jiscmail.ac.uk/lists/european-group-criminology.html>. This list is for 'academic criminologists in Britain, principally those who are associated with the European Group for the Study of Deviance and Social Control.' A forum for finding news about research initiatives and making requests for collaborators and information.

Fear-Of-Crime-Research <www.jiscmail.ac.uk/lists/fear-of-crime-research.html>. Although UK-based, this list is intended to attract an international membership to discuss all issues around the fear of crime.

JUSTICE (to subscribe send Email to majordomo@scn.org stating 'subscribe justice'). An international list for the discussion of justice and penological issues.

JUSTINFO (to subscribe send Email to listproc@ncjrs.org stating 'subscribe JUSTINFO First Name Last Name). A service of the US Department of Justice, providing up-to-date criminal justice news.

Leanalyst <www.inteltec.com/leanalyst/>. A discussion group for law enforcement professionals.

Leofficer <groups.yahoo.com/group/Leofficer/join>. A discussion forum for professional law enforcement, corrections and probation personnel.

LMS ALERT SERVICE <www.unicri.it/html/body_alert_service.htm>. A useful current awareness service which alerts subscribers to additions to the United Nations Interregional Crime and Justice Research Institute (UNICRI) library. The service can be customized to individual research interests.

Organized Crime Discussion Groups <www.yorku.ca/nathanson/Links/links.htm#Discussion>. A collection of discussion groups/mailing lists selected by the renowned Nathanson Centre for the Study of Organized Crime and Corruption *(see 5.14)*, York University, Canada.

POLICE-L (to subscribe send Email to LISTSERV@CUNYVM.CUNY.EDU stating 'subscribe POLICE-L First Name Last Name). Like *Leanalyst* above, membership of this list is restricted to current or former law enforcement officers.

PRISON-L (to subscribe send Email to listproc@lists.yale.edu stating 'subscribe PRISON-L First Name Last Name). Hosted by Yale University, this list debates all prison-related topics.

Probation-Practice <www.jiscmail.ac.uk/lists/probation-practice .html>. The list says it is intended to 'act as a network for those in educational institutions and in the field to discuss and debate any issues pertaining to probation practice'.

Talkjustice <talkjustice.com/cgi-bin/dcforum/dcboard.cgi>. Part of *Dr Frank Schmalleger's Talk Justice* site (*see 5.8*), offering access to a number of discussion forums. Specialist topic areas include: police, courts, prisons, death penalty, crime prevention, criminal law, guns, victims of crime, terrorism, forensics, juvenile justice and delinquency, and international criminal justice.

UNCJIN-L (to subscribe send Email to listserv@lserv.un.or.at stating 'subscribe UNCJIN-L First Name Last Name'). This list is a vehicle for the dissemination of information about the activities of the United Nations Crime and Justice Information Network, and more generally for the discussion of crime prevention and criminal justice issues.

▶ 5.14 ORGANIZATIONS

The intention of this section is to feature a selection of international organizations within the field, giving contact details and brief descriptions of their primary functions. *See also 5.5* for details of comprehensive listings of criminological associations, institutes, libraries and other organizations.

American Society of Criminology
1314 Kinnear Road, Columbus, OH 43212–1156, USA
Tel: +1 614 292 9207
Fax: +1 614 292 6767
Email: asc41@infinet.com
Web: <www.asc41.com>

Its aims are to foster scholarship, encourage cooperation amongst criminologists and disseminate criminological knowledge. Its excellent Website provides in-depth information about the ASC and related criminological topics.

Australian Institute of Criminology
GPO Box 2944, Canberra, ACT 2601, Australia
Tel: +61 2 6260 9200
Fax: +61 2 6260 9201
Email: Front.Desk@aic.gov.au
Web: <www.aic.gov.au/institute/contacts.html>

Founded in 1973, the Institute is 'the national focus for the study of crime and criminal justice in Australia and for the dissemination of criminal justice information.'

British Society of Criminology
Loughborough University, Department of Social Sciences, Loughborough, Leicestershire, LE11 3TU, UK
Tel: +44 (0)1509 228365
Fax: +44 (0)1509 228365
Email: BritSocCrim@lboro.ac.uk
Web:<www.lboro.ac.uk/departments/ss/BSC/homepage/HOMEPAGE.htm>.

The UK's main criminology society boasts a membership of 800, including some international members. It is involved in publishing and in organizing the biennial British Criminology Conference.

Centre for Comparative Criminology and Criminal Justice
School of Sociology and Social Policy, University of Wales, Bangor, Gwynedd, LL57 2DG, UK
Tel: +44 (0)1248 382215
Fax: +44 (0)1248 382085
Email: sasp@bangor.ac.uk
Web: <www.bangor.ac.uk/so/4cj/4cjhome.htm>

Directed by Professor Roy King, the Centre, which was established in 1991, carries out research into a variety of areas including: prisons (from both institutional and comparative perspectives, focusing particularly on Russia and Eastern Euorpe); rural-urban comparative research; and socio-criminological research.

Centre for Crime and Justice Studies (ISTD)
King's College London, 8th Floor, 75–79, York Road, London, SE1 7AW, UK
Tel: +44 (0)20 7401 2425
Email: istd.enq@kcl.ac.uk
Web: <www.kcl.ac.uk/ccjs>

The centre was founded in 1931 as The Institute for the Scientific Study of Delinquency. The centre's aims are to advance the education of the public and criminal justice practitioners, in the causes and prevention of crime and delinquency and the treatment of offenders, acting as a forum for debate and research. It publishes numerous reports and papers, and owns the *British Journal of Criminology* (*see* 5.9).

The European Institute for Crime Prevention and Control (HEUNI)
Heuni, POB 161, 00131 Helsinki, Finland
Tel: +358 9 1825 7880
Fax: +358 9 1825 7890
Email: heuni@om.vn.fi
Web: <www.vn.fi/om/heuni>

The Institute was created in 1981, as the European link in the network of institutes operating within the United Nations Crime Prevention and Criminal Justice Programme, to 'promote the exchange of information on crime prevention and criminal justice among European countries.'

Federal Bureau of Investigation (FBI)
J. Edgar Hoover Building, 935 Pennsylvania Avenue, NW, Washington, DC 20535–0001, USA
Tel: +1 324 3000
Web: <www.fbi.gov>

Founded in 1908, the organization assumed its present name in 1935. The FBI is the main investigative arm of the United States Department of Justice. It produces the country's *Uniform Crime Reports* (*see 5.12.2*), accessible via the above Website – a key statistical resource on US crime.

Home Office
50 Queen Anne's Gate, London, SW1H 9AT, UK
Tel: +44 (0)20 7273 4000
Fax: +44 (0)20 7273 2065
Email: public.enquiries@homeoffice.gsi.gov.uk
Web: <www.homeoffice.gov.uk>

The government department responsible for internal affairs in England and Wales. It undertakes research and develops policy in a number of areas including criminal justice, crime reduction and crime prevention.

Howard League for Penal Reform
1 Ardleigh Road, London, N1 4HS, UK
Tel: +44 (0)20 7249 7373
Fax: +44 (0)20 7249 7788
Email: howard.league@ukonline.co.uk
Web: <Web.ukonline.co.uk/howard.league>

Established in 1886 and named after John Howard, the founder of the penal reform movement. An independent charity working for 'humane, effective, and efficient reform of the penal system'. As a publisher, the League produces many reports and papers including the journals: *Howard Journal of Criminal Justice* (*see 5.9*) and *Howard League Magazine*.

Institute of Criminology
University of Cambridge, 7 West Road, Cambridge, CB3 9DT, UK
Tel: +44 (0)1223 335360
Fax: +44 (0)1223 335356
Email: crim-enquiries@lists.cam.ac.uk
Web: <www.law.cam.ac.uk/crim/iochpg.htm>

Founded in 1959, this is a major centre for criminological research and teaching. A multidisciplinary approach is taken covering the fields of sociology, social policy, psychology, psychiatry and law. The Institute's Radzinowicz Library of Criminology houses one of the world's largest collections of criminological publications.

Institutes of the United Nations Crime Prevention and Criminal Justice Programme Network

For examples of member institutes in this section see: *The European Institute for Crime Prevention and Control; International Institute of Higher Studies in Criminal Sciences; National Institute of Justice; United Nations Interregional Crime and Justice Research Institute; United Nations Asia and Far East Institute for the Prevention of Crime and the Treatment of Offenders* in this section. For a complete list of affiliated institutes see <www.uncjin.org/Institutes/institutes.html>.

International Center for Comparative Criminology/Centre Internationale de Criminologie Comparée
University of Montreal, 3150 rue Jean Brillant, Case postale 6128, Succursale Centre-ville Montreal, H3C 3J7 Quebec, Canada
Tel: +1 514 343 7065
Fax: +1 514 343 2269
Web: <www.cicc.umontreal.ca/frameset_english.html>

Founded in 1969 by Professor Denis Szabo, its research interests focus on three interrelated areas: criminal phenomenon; people; and penal system. It is one of three centres (the others are in Genoa, Italy and San Sebastian, Spain) affiliated with the Société Internationale de Criminologie.

International Institute of Higher Studies in Criminal Sciences (ISISC)
Via Agaati, 12, 96100 Siracusa, Italy
Tel: +39 931 35511 or 35611
Fax: +39 931 442605

Founded in September 1972, it is an educational and scientific institution and an affiliate of the United Nations Crime Prevention and Criminal Justice Programme Network. Between 1973 and 1993 it organized 152 conferences and meetings of experts with the participation of 9875 people from 107 countries.

International Society for Criminology/Société Internationale de Criminologie Comparée
4–14 rue Ferrus, 75014 Paris, France
Tel: +33 (01) 45 88 00 27
Fax: +33 (01) 45 88 96 40
Email: crim.sic@wanadoo.fr
Web: <perso.wanadoo.fr/societe.internationale.de.criminologie>

Founded in 1938, the society is a non-governmental organization with nearly 1000 members. Its objective is to 'promote activities and research designed to further a better understanding of the crime phenomenon on an international scale.'

International Society of Crime Prevention Practitioners
266 Sandy Point Road, Emlenton, PA 16373, USA
Tel: +1 724 867 1000
Fax: +1 724 867 1200
Web: <ourworld.compuserve.com/homepages/iscpp/>

The society was founded in 1977, by graduates of the National Crime Prevention Institute. Their mission is: 'to establish and support a permanent network of crime prevention practitioners who can provide leadership, foster cooperation, encourage information exchanges, and extend and improve crime prevention education and programs internationally.'

John Jay College of Criminal Justice
The City University of New York, 899 Tenth Avenue, New York, NY 10019, USA
Tel: +1 212 237 8000
Web: <www.jjay.cuny.edu>

Founded in 1964, the College 'serves as a major center for research in criminal justice, law enforcement, forensic sciences, and as a ... training facility for local, state, federal, international law enforcement agencies, and private security personnel.' The Library is noted for its special collections of historical material – including diaries and personal correspondence of key figures, as well as published reports – relating to the history of criminal justice in the UK and the USA.

Nathanson Centre for the Study of Organized Crime and Corruption
Osgoode Hall Law School, York University, 4700 Keele Street, Toronto, Ontario, M3J 1P3, Canada
Tel: +1 416 736 5907
Fax: +1 416 650 4321
Email: orgcrime@yorku.ca
Web: <www.yorku.ca/nathanson/default.htm>

A key centre for multidisciplinary research into organized crime. See reference to their bibliographies and databases respectively in the following sections: *5.3.19 (b) Electronic* and *5.10 (b) Electronic.*

National Institute of Justice
810 7th Street, Suite 700 Washington, DC 20531, USA
Tel: +1 202 307 2942
Fax: +1 202 307 6394
Web: <www.ojp.usdoj.gov/nij>

Created in 1968, it is the research agency of the US Department of Justice. Over recent years it has been developing a more international focus through membership of the United Nations Crime Prevention and Criminal Justice Network.

Scarman Centre for the Study of Public Order
University of Leicester, The Friars, 154 Upper New Walk, Leicester, LE1 7QA, UK
Tel: +44 (0)116 252 2458/5703
Fax: +44 (0)116 252 3944/5766
Email: scarman.centre@le.ac.uk
Web: <www.le.ac.uk/scarman>

Established in 1987, to 'undertake research, teaching and professional training in the study of public disorder, crime and punishment, policing, crime prevention and security management'. The centre has developed international links, in particular with the John Jay College of Criminal Justice in New York and the Gong An University in Beijing.

United Nations Asia and Far East Institute for the Prevention of Crime and the Treatment of Offenders (UNAFEI)
1–26, Harumi-cho, Fuchu-shi, Tokyo, Japan
Tel: +81 423 33 7021
Fax: +81 423 33 7024
Email: staff@unafei.or.jp
Web: <www.unafei.or.jp>

Founded in 1962, the Institute organizes international seminars and training courses. It is an affiliated organization of the United Nations Crime Prevention and Criminal Justice Programme Network.

United Nations Interregional Crime and Justice Research Institute (UNICRI)
Via Giulia 52, 00186 Rome, Italy.
Tel: +39 6 6877437
Fax: +39 6 6892638
Email: unicri@unicri.it
Web: <www.unicri.it>

Established in 1968, the objective of UNICRI is 'to contribute, through research, training, field activities and the collection, exchange and dissemination of information, to the formulation and implementation of improved policies in the field of crime prevention and control.' It operates at local, national and international levels. A member of the United Nations Crime Prevention and Criminal Justice Programme Network.

United Nations Office for Drug Control and Crime Prevention
Vienna International Centre, PO Box 500, A-1400 Vienna, Austria
Tel: +43 1 26060 0
Fax: +43 1 26060 5866
Email: odccp@odccp.org
Web: <www.odccp.org>

The Office consists of two main elements: the United Nations International Drug Control Programme and the United Nations Centre for International Crime Prevention. Its aim is to help the United Nations 'to focus and enhance its capacity to address the interrelated issues of drug control, crime prevention and international terrorism'. The *United Nations Crime and Justice Information Network* www.uncjin.org acts as an electronic clearinghouse for information produced by the above organizations.

▶ REFERENCES

Benamati, D. C. *et al* (1998) *Criminal Justice Information: How To Find It, How To Use It.* Phoenix, AR: Oryx Press.

Cohn, G., Farrington, David P. and Wright Richard A. (1998) *Evaluating Criminology and Criminal Justice.* London and Westport, CT: Greenwood Press.

Friday, P. (1983) 'International Organizations: An Introduction', in *International Handbook of Contemporary Developments in Criminology*, E. H. Johnson (ed.) pp.32–6. London and Westport, CT: Greenwood Press.

6 Education

Roy Kirk

► 6.1 NATURE AND SCOPE OF EDUCATION

Unlike academic subjects with a longer pedigree, the study of education as a subject is of comparatively recent origin. Originally, 'education' was linked solely to the training of teachers. In the UK, for instance, the formal training of teachers came into being in 1846 when the Committee of Council on Education established a system of Queen's Scholarships, which provided financial support for pupil teachers studying at training colleges. Certificate examinations were also introduced for teachers who had undertaken a form of professional preparation. The 1872 syllabus for the certificate examination shows the essentially practical nature of the training.

The introduction of the application of psychology to courses of education did not take place until the last decade of the nineteenth century. For those who stayed on their training course for a third year the syllabus was headed 'The Art, Theory and History of Teaching'. The course texts indicate the introduction of the study of educational psychology and the history of education into training courses. Educational psychology was the core subject of teacher training courses from the turn of the century to World War II. In the 1950s, the sociology of education became an equally important strand of teacher training courses, stimulated by sociology becoming a subject area in its own right for study and research. This expansion of teacher training from a practical exercise to a partial academic subject led to the growth in texts and explanations, histories and treatises. In effect, the beginning of the literature of education.

At the same time, the establishment of national educational research associations began to see the rise of research and the close study of education in all its facets. The American Educational Research Association, the Australian Association for Research in Education and the New Zealand Education Research Association were all founded before 1940 and the British Educational Research Association followed after. All have promoted research into education with the subsequent growth in the number of publications being made available.

Today, education is conceived of as an important element of economic prosperity. A well-educated and trained population is the key to the wealth of nations. Since the 1960s, the UK Government has taken an interest in the development of education at all levels, leading to the publication of reports and memoranda, circulars and Education Department papers. From 1975 onwards the government's focus on education has become intense and the attempt to improve the curriculum, improve the quality of teacher training and to ensure that every citizen leaves school – or better still, higher and further education – with qualifications to prove their worth has resulted in a vast mountain of literature; literature that takes a myriad of forms from reports, books, legal documentation through to articles in periodicals and papers at conferences. At the same time the study of education as a discipline has developed and now, in addition to the professional degree of BEd and postgraduate certificates, there are MEds, MBAs, PhDs and EdDs, which produce their own wealth of literature in the form of theses and dissertations.

This brief guide to the literature is intended to point the way for those who are researching the comparatively new area of education, for those needing to keep up to date as administrators and for parents who play a significant role in the education process.

► 6.2 ANNUALS

6.2.1 General

The *World Yearbook of Education* (London: Kogan Page, 1931–) is the best known of the British education yearbooks and it is international in scope. Each issue deals with a specific theme or topic in a series of chapters which cover developments in different parts of the world, with very useful bibliographies. Originally known only as the *Yearbook of Education*, it was not published between 1975 and 1978 and then reappeared under a new publisher. Topics covered over the years include examinations (1969), universities facing the future (1972–73), recurrent education and life-long learning (1979), computers and education (1982–83), and assessment and evaluation (1990).

International Yearbook of Education (Strasbourg: UNESCO, 1948–). First published in Britain in 1948 it contained descriptions of national education systems with statistical appendices. In 1980, after a period of non-publication, the content became based on the biennial International Conference on Education held in Geneva. The 1986 yearbook entitled *Primary Education on the Threshold of the Twenty-first Century* began a series of thematic yearbooks, still based on the biennial International Conference on Education. Information for the yearbooks is drawn largely from the national reports and replies to questionnaires presented by the member states of the United Nations Educational, Scientific, and Cultural Organization (UNESCO).

International Yearbook of Educational and Training Technology (London: Kogan Page). Until 1988 it was known as the *International Yearbook of Educational and International Technology*. It is both a yearbook and a directory, providing an overview of educational technology worldwide, reviewing trends and developments in the field. Of related interest is *Aspects of Educational and Training Technology* (London: Kogan Page). Formally known as *Aspects of Educational Technology*, it is the record of the proceedings of the Annual Conference of the Association for Educational and Training Technology (AETT). Each volume deals with different aspects of educational technology with some very useful bibliographies. See also the *Educational Media and Technology Yearbook* (New York: Littleton Libraries Unlimited). There are two sections, one on particular aspects of educational technology and the second is a list of media-related organizations throughout the world. There is also a 'mediagraphy'.

6.2.2 Europe

Paedagogica Europea: a Review of Education in Europe. (New York: Westermann, 1965–1978). This yearbook covered new developments in European education and again each volume was concerned with a particular theme. The earlier volumes were more general in scope, but the research aspect was always prominent. After 1978 the yearbook became the *European Journal of Education: Research, Development and Policies*. Each quarterly issue of the periodical still deals with a particular theme (*See 6.9*). Also of interest is the *Eudised European Educational Research Yearbook* (Munich: KG Saur, 1996–). This annual publication continues the *EUDISED R&D Bulletin* and is a very useful tool for researchers.

European Schools and the European Baccalaureate: Guidance for Universities and Colleges (London: DFE Publications, 1994). Produced by the Department for Education in the UK, this publication has a wider applicability beyond its utility for university and college administrations. *A Guide to Higher Education Systems and Qualifications in the EU and EEA Countries*, 2nd ed., (Luxembourg: Office for Official Publications of the European Union, 1998) is a most helpful document. It is relatively up-to-date and one of the many official education documents coming from the European Union.

6.2.3 United States

Yearbook of Special Education (New York: Marquis Academic Media). The emphasis of this publication is on special education in the US. The *Yearbook of American Universities and Colleges* (New York: Garland, 1986–) gives a review of developments in US higher education. It aims to preserve the most meaningful data and events and it is organized under subject headings. From its inception, each volume has contained a bibliographic guide. The *Yearbook of the National Society for the Study of Education.* (Chicago, IL: University Press) is published in two volumes. Each edition tends to be devoted to a separate topic. Some of the subjects covered are very general, e.g. policy making in education (1982), others are far more specific, e.g. microcomputers and education (1986).

6.2.4 Australia

Melbourne Studies in Education (Melbourne: University Press) is an Australian yearbook which has been appearing regularly since 1957. As you would expect, emphasis is mainly on the Australian educational scene, but there are articles of wider interest.

▶ 6.3 BIBLIOGRAPHIES

6.3.1 General

(a) Print

Finding Out in Education: a Guide to Sources of Information, 2nd ed., (London: Longman, 1993). Compiled by Peter Clarke, this is a marvellous repository of sources in the field of education. Divided into sections, it has a good subject index and title index. It is an indispensable tool, but beginning to become dated. Of related interest is *Researching Education: Reference Tools and Networks* (Hull: Librarians of Institutes and Schools of Education, 1999). Compiled by Bob Smeaton this is the second edition of a very popular earlier work. Slimmer than the Clarke volume, it is more-up-to date and includes tips on searching. It is less international in scope, but very much a working tool for the PhD, EdD or Masters students.

(b) Electronic

TES Bookfind (London: BookData, monthly). A joint service with the *Times Educational Supplement*, the CD-ROM is designed for schools and colleges. Descriptive information about books is included, together with reviews and publication details of non-book materials.

6.3.2 Adult education

A Select Bibliography of Adult Continuing Education, 5th ed., (Leicester: National Institute of Adult Continuing Education, NIACE, 1988). Edited by J. H. Davies and J. E. Thomas, this is a very useful bibliography, but becoming a little dated.

6.3.3 Bilingualism

Bilingualism and Education: a Bibliography on European Regional or Minority Languages (Ljouwert: Fryske Akademy/Mercator-Education, 1996). Edited by R. S. Tjeerdsma and M. B. Stuijt, this is a helpful bibliography of materials in a specialized field.

6.3.4 Comparative education

The 'Comparative and International Education Bibliography' written by I. Epstein (*Comparative Education Review*, 37(3), 1992, pp. 341–62) is a very useful starting point for anyone studying the area. Of related interest is the *International Bibliography of Comparative Education* (New York: Praeger, 1981), which is an excellent complementary work detailing earlier materials by P. G. Altbach, a well-known author in this field.

Education in South East Asia: Select Bibliography of English Language Materials (London: Gower, 1985). Written by C. Inglis and others, this is a valuable starting point for researchers in this area. See also *Education in South Asia: a Selected Annotated Bibliography* (New York: Garland, 1987), another title written by P. G. Altbach, in the *Garland Reference Books on International Education* series. Others in this series include: *Education in Japan: a Source Book* by E. R. Beauchamp and R. Rubinger (New York: Garland, 1988); *Education in Russia from the Middle Ages to the Present* by W. W. Brickman (New York: Garland, 1986); and *Education in the People's Republic of China, Past and Present: an Annotated Bibliography* by F. Parker and B. J. Parker (New York: Garland, 1986).

6.3.5 Geography

A Bibliography of Geographical Education 1970–1997 by N. Foskett and B. Marsden (Sheffield: Geographical Association, 1998). An official publication of the Geographical Association, charting the development of the field during the last 30 years.

6.3.6 History of education

Sources for the History of Education (London: Library Association, 1968). Compiled by Winifred Higson, this is a finding list as well as an authoritative bibliography of books on education published from the sixteenth century to 1918. It also contains information about children's literature and lists the member libraries of the Librarians of Institutes and Schools of Education (LISE) who hold copies of all titles listed. A supplement was published in 1976. *Histories of Girls' Schools and Related Bibliographical Material: a Union List of Books in the Stock of Education Libraries in British Universities* compiled by Barbara Barr (Leicester: LISE, 1984) is divided into five parts: schools; general works; schools by name; biographies; and biographies and autobiographies. There is only a short introduction and no annotations.

6.3.7 Learning

Co-operative Learning: a Guide to Research (London: Garland, 1992). Written by S. Totten and others, this is a useful guide.

6.3.8 Teachers

Compiled by P. E. Lester, *Teacher Job Satisfaction: an Annotated Bibliography and Guide to Research* (London: Garland, 1986) is a good starting point for those interested in this area.

► 6.4 DICTIONARIES

6.4.1 General

Dictionary of Education, 2nd ed., (London: Hodder & Stoughton, 1996). Written by Denis Lawton and Peter Gordon, this dictionary is divided into four sections. Section one provides brief discussions of key ideas in education. Section two gives short definitions and section three contains some background historical information. Section four provides an up-to-date list of acronyms and abbreviations. Of related interest is the *Dictionary of Educational Terms* by David Blake and Vincent Hanley (Aldershot: Arena, 1995), which is another example of a useful dictionary of educational terms.

A Guide to English Education Terms by Peter Gordon and Denis Lawton (London: Batsford, 1984) is an essential reference source for anyone wishing to find out the meaning of educational terminology. It has the added advantage of giving excellent summaries of the numerous official reports that have been published in the UK during the last 200 years. The object of *A Critical Dictionary of Educational Concepts*, 2nd ed., by Robin Barrow and G. Milburn (Brighton: Harvester and Wheatsheaf, 1990) is to offer in-depth analysis of important educational concepts. It has a very personal view on many of the themes covered. Both authors are Canadian professors.

In *A Dictionary of Education* (London: Harper & Row, 1981) the author, Derek Rowntree has tried to produce references to as many educational terms as possible. Some have a paragraph devoted to them, some only a few lines. Summaries of major reports and potted biographies of key figures are also included. Like the *International Dictionary of Education* by G. Terry Page and J. B. Thomas, with A. R. Manhold (London: Kogan Page, 1977) it remains a work worth consulting, but both tomes are now becoming somewhat dated.

6.4.2 Management

Educational Management Today: a Concise Dictionary and Guide by David Oldroyd, Danuta Elsner and Cyrila Poster (London: Paul Chapman, 1996). This book is in three main parts. Firstly, there is a section giving concise terms likely to be encountered by students, particularly from overseas, interested in the management of education in Britain. Secondly, there is a series of short essays which give a concise overview of concepts. Finally, the third section lists abbreviations and acronyms.

6.4.3 Higher education

Academic Keywords: a Devil's Dictionary for Higher Education (New York and London: Routledge, 1999). Written by Gary Nelson and Stephen Watt, this useful volume includes 10 pages of bibliographical references and an index.

6.4.4 Adult education

International Dictionary of Adult Education by Peter Jarvis (London: Kogan Page, 1999). This revised edition (previously published as *An International Dictionary of Adult and Continuing Education* in 1990) is an essential tool for practitioners and researchers interested in lifelong learning and continuing education. It is international in scope and contains over 2500 references.

6.4.5 Special education

A Glossary of Special Education by P. A. Williams (Milton Keynes: Open UP, 1987). Aimed at teachers, administrators and parents, it includes definitions, the more important psychological and educational tests and a list of organizations. As its title suggests, the *Resource Guide to Special Education: Terms, Laws, Assessment, Procedures, Organizations*, 2nd ed., by W. E. Davis (New York: Allyn & Bacon, 1986) is much more than just a dictionary. It lists terms, abbreviations and acronyms, tests, legislation and organizations. It is written from a US perspective.

6.4.6 Instructional technology

Dictionary of Instructional Technology (London: Kogan Page, 1986). H. Ellington and D. Harris have written a very helpful dictionary covering not only mainline instructional technology but also the fields impinging on it including TV production, photography and computing. It includes UK and US terminology.

6.4.7 United States

Historical Dictionary of Women's Education in the United States (Westport, CT: Greenwood Press, 1999). Edited by Linda Eisenmann, this volume is a collection of signed articles. Each article has bibliographical references. The *Dictionary of Education* (Washington, DC: Facts on File, 1989), written by R. Koeppe and J. Shafritz, contains about 5000 terms, concepts and processes used in the study of education. Most of the entries are specific to North America.

6.4.8 Acronyms and abbreviations

Acronyms and Initialisms in Education: a Handlist by John Hutchins (Swansea: LISE, 1995), is the sixth edition of what has proved to be a very useful handlist. Based on the findings of British education librarians, the volume reflects the working needs of the profession where acronyms continue to grow. For the American perspective see the *Dictionary of Educational Acronyms, Abbreviations and Initialisms*, 2nd ed., by J. C. Palmer and A. Y. Colby (Phoenix, AZ: Oryx Press, 1985). The book contains an alphabetical list of over 4000 acronyms. In addition, the acronyms are also listed separately in their unabbreviated form. The lists are derived from the *ERIC* Clearing House. *See 6.10.*

6.4.9 Thesauri

The *British Education Thesaurus*, 2nd ed., edited by Joan Marder (Leeds: University Press, 1991), contains over 8000 terms, with particular attention paid to British terminology. There is an Alphabetical Descriptor Display of terms used in the *British Education Index* (*see 6.10*) and a Rotated Descriptor Display which provides an alphabetical index to all the words found in the descriptors. It is based on the *Thesaurus of ERIC Descriptors* (see below). The *Thesaurus* is also available on the CD-ROM version of *International ERIC, see 6.10.*

Thesaurus of ERIC Descriptors (Phoenix, AZ: Oryx Press, 1996). A new edition is published every few years and an up-to-date version is available on the *ERIC* database (*see 6.10*). This thesaurus will be of most value to those involved in serious educational research.

Thesaurus of Vocational Training, 2nd ed., (London: HMSO, 1988). Produced by the Centre for the Development of European Vocational Training (CEDEFOP) this is a specialized thesaurus for those involved in training and human resource development.

▶ 6.5 DIRECTORIES

6.5.1 General

(a) Print

Education Yearbook (London: Pearson). Although called a yearbook this valuable volume is, in fact, a directory. Divided into 27 sections covering addresses of local authorities, schools, colleges, universities and information on educational publishing and organizations, it is difficult to do justice to this bible for education. In addition to the above information there are sections on education statistics, a guide to abbreviations, a guide to reports and a guide to legislation, amongst others.

Education Authorities Directory and Annual (Redhill: School Government Publishing Co.). A similar publication to the *Education Yearbook*, it contains very much the same information. Divided into sections again, it has information on government departments, local education authorities, schools, colleges and universities. It also has sections on organizations, equipment suppliers and consultants. However, there is no statistical or report information in this publication.

(b) Electronic

Directory of Organizations in Educational Management <eric.uoregon.edu/directory/index.html>. The purpose of this directory is to link users with a wide range of information on topics related to educational policy, management, leadership and organization of K-12 schools. The directory lists service and research organizations in the field.

6.5.2 Adult education

Yearbook of Adult and Continuing Education: a Directory of Opportunities (Leicester: National Institute of Adult Continuing Education). Annual. This directory provides details of Local Education Authorities (LEAs) in England and Wales, adult education providers at all levels and relevant organizations. A list of key journals is also included. The *Open Learning Directory* (Oxford: Pergamon Open Learning, 1995) is a definitive source of information on open learning opportunities. It is aimed at employers, trainers, advisers and those who wish to study. It is an eminently useable directory which began in 1985 and has maintained an up-to-date image ever since.

ECCTIS Handbook: a Guide to Credit Transfer Opportunities Offered by Advanced Further and Higher Education Institutions in the UK (London: Educational Counselling and Credit Transfer Information Service). Annual. The information in this directory would be of great value to mature students. The term ‘credit transfer’ is defined in a helpful way.

6.5.3 Curriculum

The American Curriculum: a Documentary History (Westport, CT: Greenwood Publishing, 1993) is a useful primary resource collection edited by George Willis and William H. Schubert. A volume in the *Greenwood Documentary Reference Collection series*. Of related interest is *Transforming American Education: a Directory of Practice to Help the Nation Achieve the Six National Education Goals* (Washington, DC: United States Department of Education Office of Policy and Planning, 1992). A practical directory for teachers and educators in the United States.

6.5.4 Further education

Directory of Vocational and Further Education (London: Financial Times and Pitman Publishing). Annual. Similar to the *Education Yearbook* (*see 6.5.1*), this very useful directory has 13 sections listing, amongst others, further education colleges, sixth form colleges, GNVQ and NVQ lead bodies and educational/allied organizations. There is a very good general index and an equally good subject index. A very important directory publication.

6.5.5 Grant-providing bodies

Directory of Grant Making Trusts (Tonbridge: Charities Aid Foundation). Bi-annual. A particularly important directory in these days of fund-seeking. It claims to make applying for grants an efficient process, as it demonstrates quite clearly the policies and guidelines being followed by each grant-making trust. There is a good index and education is prominent with a breakdown by level. The *Education Funding Guide* edited by Susan Forrester, Anne Mountfield and Alka Patel (London: Directory of Social Change, 1995) is introduced by a series of essays on various levels of education and which are followed by sections on charitable trusts, the National Lottery and funding by major companies. A valuable source of information and help for everyone concerned with education from every aspect and every level.

Charity Choice (London: Waterlow Information Services). Annual. This is described as the encyclopaedia of charities and like all those mentioned in this section is a useful source of information. The book is divided into 22 categories and within each category is an index page which indicates the range of organizations listed. Twenty pages are devoted specifically to education, but many of the other sections could also be of use. The *Grants Register* (Basingstoke: Macmillan) Annual. This is an international guide for students from the US, Canada, UK, Ireland, Australia, New Zealand and South Africa. It has a detailed subject index and then pages of award-granting bodies. To use the directory properly you are advised to read the 'How to use the grants register' chapter first.

6.5.6 Higher education

The *World of Learning* (London: Europa Publications). Annual. This global directory (available in print and CD-ROM formats) gives addresses of universities, learned institutions, societies and museums, together with lists of senior professionals in the institutions listed. Of related interest is the *World List of Universities: Other Institutions of Higher Education and University Organizations* (London: Macmillan). Triennial. This directory is published in two editions, British and American. It is divided into two sections: part one is arranged alphabetically by country; and part two comprises a guide to organizations, regional and international, connected with higher education.

The *Commonwealth Universities Yearbook*: *a Directory to Universities of the Commonwealth and the Handbook of Associations* in two volumes (London: Association of Commonwealth Universities). Annual. This is a key guide for higher education institutions throughout the Commonwealth. It provides information on all the universities listed, together with staff lists. It is particularly useful for information on UK universities when it is not possible to have a sight of individual calendars and handbooks.

American Universities and Colleges (Washington, DC: American Council on Education). Every four years. This is the standard guide to institutions of higher education in the United States. All institutions are dealt with in detail, but there are also essays on higher education policies in the United States. A number of very useful indexes are included. *American Universities and Colleges*, 15th ed., (New York: Walter de Gruyter, 1997) produced in collaboration with the American Council on Education, is also a key directory on post secondary education in the United States. In addition to details of over 1900 institutions, the volume also provides information on the evolution and future of higher education.

The following publications are examples of directories which will be of particular use to those engaged in comparative research on higher education systems: the *Guide to Higher Education in Africa* (London: Macmillan Reference, 1999), is produced by the Association of African Universities and the International Association of Universities and is an extremely good, up-to-date directory; and *Asian Higher Education: an International Handbook and Reference Guide* edited by Gerard A. Postiglione and C. L. Grace (Westport, CT: Greenwood Press, 1997), is a wide-ranging publication containing useful bibliographical references and an index.

6.5.7 Qualifications

British Vocational Qualifications: a Directory of Vocational Qualifications Available From All Awarding Bodies in Britain, 3rd ed., (London: Kogan

Page, 1998). It is very difficult keeping up with qualifications, awarding bodies and the continual flow of new developments. This guide is probably one of the best in the field and will be of value to anyone seeking information that is as up to date as possible. Also worth consulting is *British Qualifications: a Complete Guide to Educational, Technical, Professional and Academic Qualifications in Britain* (London: Kogan Page). Annual. Yet another very important publication for those who want to keep abreast of the vast world of qualifications.

6.5.8 Schools

Primary Education Directory (London: School Government Publishing). Annual. The *Education Yearbook* (see *6.5.1)* does not cover primary education but this publication does. It is arranged geographically and includes names of headteachers and pupil numbers. The *Independent Schools Yearbook: Boys' Schools, Girls' schools, Co-educational Schools & Preparatory Schools* (London: A & C Black). Annual. This is the official book of reference of all the independent school associations and is arranged in order of each body.

Choose the Right Primary School: a Guide to Primary Schools in England, Scotland and Wales (London: Stationery Office, 1998); *Choose the Right Secondary School: a Guide to Secondary Schools in England, Scotland and Wales* (London: Stationery Office, 1998). Both books are written by Bob Findlay and represent a vast quantity of work. Each book is divided into five sections: background information; the examinations system; advice to parents; Scottish education; and Standard Assessment Tests (SATs) and performance statistics.

The International Schools Directory (Petersfield: European Council of International Schools). Annual. This is aimed at expatriate parents seeking an appropriate education for their children and gives full details of the schools listed. It is also intended for companies, governments and organizations to consult. It is a valuable tool for the educational researcher.

6.5.9 Scotland

The *Scottish Companion* (Glasgow: Carrick). Biennial. This covers all aspects of public life in Scotland. In 1989 it began to list all Scottish secondary schools and has replaced the *Scottish Education Directory* which was a valuable source of Scottish educational information.

6.5.10 Special education

The *Special Education Directory* (Redhill: School Government Publishing). Annual. This lists schools and support services, local education authorities, psychological services and organizations offering further help. There are detailed indexes under specific aspects of special education. Of related interest is *Special Schools in Britain: Including Further Education Colleges* (London: Network Publishing Ltd., 1994), which covers all aspects of special needs. Now becoming dated, but still basically a useful and valued directory.

6.5.11 Teacher training

Handbook of Initial Teacher Training in England and Wales (London: NATFHE). Annual. Compiled, edited and published by the National Association for Teachers in Further and Higher Education, this is a useful guide to initial teacher training courses on offer in England and Wales. It covers both undergraduate and Postgraduate Certificate in Education courses. Arranged in alphabetical order of institution, there is detailed information about courses provided and an indication of professional development courses offered. An index of courses is also included. For a more global perspective see the *World Directory of Teacher-Training Institutions* (Arlington: International Council on Education for Teaching and France: UNESCO). Annual. This is a unique resource guide providing access to national government agencies, professional associations and college and university level institutions devoted to the training and development of teachers. Over 170 countries and 5000 institutions are covered.

▶ 6.6 ENCYCLOPAEDIAS

The *International Encyclopaedia of Education*, 2nd ed., by T. Husen and T. N. Postlethwaite (London: Pergamon, 1994) is a 12-volume work consisting of seminal articles written by experts from across the world, with particularly good bibliographies appended. Educational systems of different countries are well covered and there is a good, detailed index volume. The *International Encyclopaedia of Teaching and Teacher Education* edited by Michael Dunkin (Oxford: Pergamon, 1987), is designed to enable readers to learn about key concepts from scholarly and authoritative sources. The work is divided into six sections, each section is subdivided into relevant chapters. Topics covered include: concepts and models, methods and paradigms for research, teaching methods and techniques, classroom processes, contextual factors and teacher education.

Those interested in the topic of language and education might like to look at the *Encyclopedia of Language and Education* edited by D. Corson (Dordrecht, The Netherlands: Kluwer, 1997). The eight-volume work tackles a number of different issues: literacy; oral discourse and education; second language education; language testing and assessment; research methods in language and education; and bilingual education. For those who wish to pursue the latter topic in more depth see the *Encyclopedia of Bilingualism and Bilingual Education* (Clevedon: Multilingual matters, 1998). Compiled by Colin Baker and Sylvia Prys Jones the work has a two-fold aim of promoting the subject of bilingualism and of being an academically sound review of the topic. Aimed at an international audience, it is divided into three main sections: individual bilingualism; bilingualism in society; and bilingual education. An extensive bibliography on bilingualism is included.

Evaluation is a key topic of educational discourse and *The International Encyclopaedia of Educational Evaluation* edited by Hernert J. Walberg and Geneva D. Haertel (Oxford: Pergamon, 1990), provides a useful introduction to the issues. Published as part of a series entitled Advances in Education, the aim of the encyclopaedia is to bring together studies that had previously been scattered throughout the literature. The *Encyclopedia of Higher Education* (Oxford: Pergamon, 1992) is a four-volume work edited by Burton R. Clark and Guy R. Neave. Volume one covers national systems of higher education, volumes two and three give analytical perspectives and volume four deals with academic disciplines and indexes. Covering over 135 national systems of higher education, this is a valuable resource for those undertaking comparative studies.

▶ 6.7 GUIDES AND HANDBOOKS

6.7.1 General

Handbook of Educational Ideas and Practices (London: Routledge, 1990). The general editor for this work is Noel Entwistle, aided by eight associate editors. The book is composed of 100 specially commissioned articles. Each article presents a critique of the key questions in present day education. It is a valuable sourcebook. *The Blackwell Handbook of Education* by Michael Farrell, Trevor Kerry and Carolle Kerry (Oxford: Blackwell, 1995), is a practical handbook covering a wide range of topics including: curriculum and assessment, pedagogy, and roles and people. There are separate sections on acronyms, legislation and organizations. The *Routledge International Companion to Education* edited by Bob Moon, Miriam Ben-Peretz and Sally Brown (London: Routledge, 2000), uses authoritative authors to cover the major contemporary education debates. A valuable overview for all those involved in educational research.

6.7.2 Curriculum

Handbook of Research on Curriculum (New York: Macmillan Publishing, 1992). A project of the American Educational Research Association, this impressive volume was edited by Philip W. Jackson. Described as 'groundbreaking work' the handbook provides a comprehensive overview of what is currently known about a wide range of curricula issues.

National Curriculum for England, Handbook for Primary Teachers in England: Keystages One and Two (London: Stationery Office for Department for Education and Employment and Qualification and Curriculum Authority, 1999). Sets out the legal requirements of the National Curriculum in England for pupils aged five to 11 and provides information to help teachers implement the National Curriculum in schools. Separate subject booklets for the 12 National Curriculum subjects are also available. *The National Curriculum in England, Handbook for Secondary Teachers in England: Keystages Three and Four* (London: Stationery Office for Department for Education and Employment and Qualification and Curriculum Authority, 1999), is the companion volume to key stages one and two, and is written specifically for secondary teachers to help them understand the National Curriculum and to apply it correctly in their schools. Again, separate booklets for the National Curriculum subjects are also available.

Many handbooks and guides are available for those engaged in comparative European curricula studies, the following is a selection of key titles. *Basic Education and Competence in the Member States of the European Community* (Brussels: EURYDICE European Unit, 1988), is an analysis of core curriculum requirements in member states of the European Union at the end of the 1980s. *Core Curricula for Basic Education in Western Europe: Perspectives and Implementation* (Emchede: Consortium of Institutions for Development and Research in Europe, 1991). Edited by Gert van den Brink and Hans Hoogoff this is a revised edition of a useful source document. *Levels and Pluriformity of Higher Education: on Comparing Curricula* (The Hague: Institute of Education, Groningen University and NUFFIC, 1992), is a volume that compares higher education curricula across Europe at the beginning of the 1990s.

Primary Education in Europe: Evaluation of New Curricula in Ten European Countries (Frascati: Centro European Dell 'Educazione and NATO, 1990). Written by Lucio Pusci, this is a good starting point when looking at the curricula across the continent. See also the *Handbook of Primary Education in Europe* (London: Fulton, 1989), edited by Maurice Galton and Alan Blyth, and published in association with the Council of

Europe. It gives a full overview, from the viewpoint of experts in the field, of primary education in the major European countries. An authoritative volume that still has weight in this field; a full bibliography is included. *Secondary Education Across Europe: Curricula and School Examinations Systems* (London: Centre for Educational Research, London School of Economics and Political Science, 1999). Written by Anne West, Ann Edge and Eleanor Stokes this publication updates some of the earlier documents already mentioned in this section. Finally, *ATEE – Guide to Institutions of Teacher Education in Europe (AGITE)* (Brussels: Association for Teacher Education in Europe, 1992), edited by Friederich Buchberger, is a comprehensive guide to teacher training institutions across the countries of Europe.

6.7.3 Mathematics

International Handbook of Mathematics Education edited by a team led by Alan J. Bishop (Dordrecht: Kluwer, 1996). This two-volume work aims to bring together the vast amount of research carried out in the area of mathematics education over the last 20 years. Of related interest is the *Handbook of Research on Mathematics Teaching and Learning* (New York: Macmillan, 1992). Edited by Douglas A. Grouws, this volume represents a project promoted by the National Council of Teachers of Mathematics. Again, its purpose is to highlight the research carried out in the area of mathematics education over the last two decades.

6.7.4 Multicultural education

Handbook of Research on Multicultural Education edited by James A. Bank (New York: Macmillan, 1995). This volume draws together 30 years of research and scholarship in 47 chapters, each written by an expert in the field.

6.7.5 Science education

Handbook of Research on Science Teaching and Learning edited by Dorothy L. Gabel (New York: Macmillan, 1994). Sponsored by the National Science Teachers Association the work not only summarizes recent research in science education, but examines current debates and evaluates new developments. See also the *International Handbook of Science Education* edited by Barry J. Fraser and Kenneth G. Tobin (Dordrecht: Kluwer, 1998), which similarly aims to bring together past research and current thinking in the field of science education.

6.7.6 Teacher education

Handbook of Research on Teaching, 3rd ed., edited by Merlin C. Wittrock for the American Educational Research Association (New York: Macmillan, 1986). The 35 articles reflect the many changes that have occurred in educational research during 1970s and 1980s. A new edition would now be welcome. The *Handbook of Teacher Training in Europe: Issues and Trends* edited by Maurice Galton and Bob Mann (London: Fulton, 1994), produced in association with the Council of Europe, is the essential, authoritative text for teacher training practices in Europe.

▶ 6.8 WEBSITES

6.8.1 General

BBC Education Schools Online <www.bbc.co.uk/education/schools/>. Educational resources (including revision materials) for children of all age groups. Also includes many useful links to other Websites.

British Library Education Website <www.education.bl.uk/>. At the heart of the Website is a projects area. Interactive topics draw on the British Library's diversity of historical, social and literacy source material in a series of activities and guided investigations across a range of curriculum issues.

BUBL News WWW Subject Tree for Education <link.bubl.ac.uk/education/>. BUBL has always retained a strong library element, but now provides a subject-based service to the wider academic community. The *Subject Tree for Education* is the UK's main gateway to more than 500 educational resources. It is worth noting that the resources are not solely UK-based, but international in scope.

Deliberations <www.lgu.ac.uk/deliberations/>. Deliberations is based in the Educational Development unit at London Guildhall University. It is a resource for educational developers, librarians, academic staff and managers in education. It is also a forum for readers to discuss and develop ideas and to identify resources that will aid their work.

EARLI (European Association for Research on Learning and Instruction) <www.earli.eu.org/>. Over 1000 researchers in 40 countries use this network to discuss important issues. An excellent tool for the researcher in education.

Ednow.com <www.ednow.com/>. An American Website that supports the work of teachers, librarians and administrators. It has a wide variety of search facilities and its strength lies in up-to-date news and information. The site will Email Ednow.com announcements directly to customers if they so desire.

Educational Research Forum (ERF) <telematics3.ex.ac.uk/ERF>. An international resource for those undertaking research into new technologies in education. It offers opportunities for collaboration in research.

Education Guardian <education.guardian.co.uk/>. This is a Website for teachers, parents and lecturers in further and higher education. It combines all the *Guardian* and *Observer's* educational content with special reports, exclusive online features and hundreds of recommended sites.

Education-line <brs.leeds.ac.uk/~beiwww/beid.html>. This Website gives access to educational documents online. Searches can be done in three main ways: browsing through the *British Education Thesaurus*, searching the list of indexed words in the author, title or subject fields, or by carrying out a direct search in fields of your own choosing.

Education Network Australia (EdNA) <www.edna.edu.au/EdNA>. EdNA Online is a Website pointing to thousands of resources identified and contributed by Australian educators. It networks the bodies responsible for Australian education. Discussions and notice boards are offered on the site, making it a meta-network of Australian education practitioners.

Education 2000 <education2000.co.uk/>. A Website for managers and administrators in schools, colleges and universities. The site-map covers such subjects as appointments, associations, news and information, subject listings, equipment, apparatus, furniture, staff development and a whole host of other topic areas.

Education Virtual Library <www.csu.edu.au/education/library.html>. This virtual library of education organizes resources by education level, resources provided, type of site and country.

EduWeb <www.eduWeb.co.uk/>. EduWeb is an Internet service for use by teachers and pupils, and is packed full of educational resources and links. Special care has been taken to make the Website suitable for both teachers and pupils; an age filter to ensure the appropriateness of the site found is provided.

Europa-Campus <www.europa.eu.int>. A Website giving a single point of entry for European Union policies, programmes and sources of information of relevance to the educational sector.

Eurydice <www.eurydice.org>. An information network on education in Europe and a database of European Education systems.

National Grid for Learning <www.ngfl.gov.uk>. Launched in 1998, this Website has grown considerably in only that short time. There are around 60 000 pages of information and it is still growing. It links to other Websites and education services to support teaching, learning and administration in schools, libraries, universities, colleges, the workplace and home.

NISS Education <www.niss.ac.uk>. NISS is a UK organization providing access to electronic information for the academic community. There is a useful education section offering access to UK government departments and agencies, academic institutions, schools and current projects and initiatives.

Overview of Education Review <www.ed.asu.ed/edrev/overview.html>. *Education Review* publishes review articles of recently published books in education. It contains 16 sections covering the whole range of educational scholarship and is intended to promote wider understanding of the latest and best research in this field.

Schoolsnet <www.schoolsnet.com>. An excellent Website for teachers. It offers a variety of facilities including information on other Websites, up-to-date news and interactive lessons.

Social Science Information Gateway (SOSIG) <www.sosig.ac.uk/>. Emanating from the University of Bristol's Institute for Learning and Research Technology, this is one of a family of gateways giving access to data that has been given peer approval. One major danger of electronic information lies in its normally unassessed quality; SOSIG removes all of these fears. SOSIG organizes social science resources, but much of it is very useful for educational research. Research reports are a significant feature of this database.

Thematic Network of Teacher Education in Europe <tntee.umu.se/>. The main objective of this network is to establish a flexible, multilingual trans-national forum for the development of teacher education in Europe.

Times Higher Internet Service <www.thesis.co.uk/>. The service provided by the *Times Higher Education Supplement* (*THES*) presents news, reviews and features in the current *THES* including announcements of chairs, honorary degrees, appointments, grants and events. There is even a section of job advertisements from around the world.

Virtual Teachers Centre (National Grid for Learning) <www.vtc.ngfl.gov.uk/vtc/meeting.current.html>. This is a discussion group for the dissemination of good practice in teaching. There are four discussion groups currently, including one for senior managers.

World Wide Web Virtual Library for Education <www.csu.edu.au/education/library.htm>. This site provides links to education resources by site, level and country. It offers links to newsgroups relevant to education in addition to a variety of education-based Websites.

Yahoo Education <dir.yahoo.com/education/index.html>. This search engine provides links to a vast range of resources including electronic journals, online teaching and learning databases, television and news. A portfolio of useful and interesting Websites.

6.8.2 Adult education

Lifelong Learning Network <www.life-learning.net/>. This Website gives details of events, publications and news items related to lifelong learning. It also includes links to other relevant sites, contact details of people and organizations and online discussion groups.

University for Industry (UFI) <www.ufiltd.co.uk/>. UFI works with businesses and education and training providers. It uses modern technologies to make learning available at a time and place to suit the learner.

6.8.3 Further education

National Learning Network (NLN) <www.nln.ac.uk>. The NLN is a national initiative supported by the UK Government to help transform the further education learning environment. It is designed to raise standards, widen access, promote and support employability and improve competition for UK business.

FE Resources for Learning: FERL <ferl.becta.org.uk/>. FERL is an Internet-based information service for lecturers and other practitioners in further education. The service is funded by the Further Education Funding Council (FEFC) and managed by the British Educational Communications and Technology Agency (*see 6.13*). FERL aims to help colleges get the most out of information and learning technologies.

6.8.4 Higher education

Braintrack <www.braintrack.com>. Braintrack is a worldwide University Index on the Internet. It contains Internet addresses of universities, polytechnics, colleges and other higher education institutes all over the world. It is based in Zurich in Switzerland.

ORTELIUS <ortelius.unifi.it/>.A database of information on Higher Education in Europe. It was set up under the auspices of the European Commission to provide accurate and up-to-date information on higher education in Europe.

6.8.5 Language teaching

ESL on the net <www.nceltr.mq.edu.au/eslnet.html>. Contains gateways to English as a second language resources, places to visit, lists, newspapers, Muds and Moos, journals, software and useful references.

Lingu@NET <www.lingunet.org.uk/>. A virtual Language Centre on the World Wide Web, providing quality-assured information and resources for language teachers, learners and researchers. Developed by the Centre for Information on Language Teaching and Research (CILT) and the British Educational Communications and Technology Agency (BECTA).

TESL/TEFL/TESOL/ESL/EFL/ESOL links <www.aitech.ac.ip/~iteslj/>. Provides links of interest to students and teachers of English as a second language.

▶ 6.9 JOURNALS

American Educational Research Journal (ISSN 0002–8312) (Washington, DC: American Educational Research Association, 1963–). Quarterly. A refereed publication of the American Educational Research Association, it publishes original research, both empirical and theoretical. It also includes brief synopses of research.

Australian and New Zealand Journal of Vocational Education Research (ISSN 1039–4001) (Leabrook: National Centre for Vocational Education Research Ltd., 1992–). Two issues a year. Provides articles based on vocational education and training and research and development activities in Australia and New Zealand.

Australian Educational Researcher (ISSN 0311–6999) (New South Wales: University of New England, 1973–). Three issues a year. This was formerly the *AARE Newsletter* and is published by the Australian Association for Research in Education.

Australian Journal of Education (ISSN 0004–9441) (Hawthorn: Australian Council for Educational Research Inc., 1956–). Three issues a year. A publication of the Australian Council for Educational Research, it contains papers on the theory and practice of education.

Australian Journal of Teacher Education (ISSN 0313–5373) (Katoomba: Social Science Press, 1975–). Two issues a year. The main Australian publication for articles on teacher training in all its aspects.

British Educational Research Journal (ISSN 0141–1926) (Basingstoke: Carfax Publishing, 1975–). Five issues a year. A major vehicle (called *Research Intelligence* until 1978) for the publication of research articles. The approach is interdisciplinary and includes reports, discussions and accounts of research in progress. The flagship refereed publication of the British Educational Research Association. Available electronically.

British Journal of Educational Psychology (ISSN 0007–0998) (Letchworth: British Psychological Society, 1931–). Quarterly. Refereed publication featuring major articles contributing to the understanding and practice of education. Case-study, action research and psychometric/statistical methods are encouraged. Available electronically.

British Journal of Educational Studies (ISSN 0007–1005) (Oxford: Blackwell Publishers, 1952–). Quarterly. This refereed title covers recent developments in education policy in the United Kingdom and elsewhere. Available electronically.

Cambridge Journal of Education (ISSN 0305–764X) (Basingstoke: Carfax Publishing, 1971–). Three issues a year. Emphasis is placed on articles that span the divide between academic researchers and teachers. Available electronically.

Comparative Education (ISSN 0305–764X) (Basingstoke: Carfax Publishing, 1964–). Three issues a year. This refereed journal concentrates on the implications of comparative studies for the formation and implementation of policies. Available electronically.

CORE (Collected Original Resources in Education) (ISSN 0308–6909) (Basingstoke: Carfax Publishing, 1976–). Three issues a year. A research oriented journal with an international scope. Published in microfiche format.

Curriculum Journal (ISSN 0958–5176) (London: Routledge, 1990–). Three issues a year. UK-oriented, it concentrates on theoretical research on curriculum issues. Includes an update on National Curriculum documents. Available electronically.

Education and the Law (ISSN 0953–9964) (Basingstoke: Carfax Publishing, 1989–). Quarterly. An up-to-date source of information on all aspects of the law relating to primary, secondary, tertiary and higher education. Available electronically.

Educational Management & Administration (0263–211X) (London: Sage, 1972–). Quarterly. A refereed journal publishing articles on educational administration and management in the widest sense. Research reports, accounts of new methods and controversial issues are all covered. Available electronically.

Educational Leadership (ISSN 0013–1784) (Vancouver: Association for Supervision and Curriculum Development, 1942–). Eight issues a year. Each issue is devoted to an important contemporary theme in learning and teaching at all levels. Views are shared on social, psychological and pedagogical topics.

Educational Psychology (ISSN 0144–3410) (Basingstoke: Carfax Publishing, 1980–). Quarterly. A refereed journal providing an international forum for the discussion and rapid dissemination of research findings in psychology relevant to education. Available electronically.

Educational Research (ISSN 0013–1881) (London: Routledge, 1958–). Three issues a year. The academic journal of the National Foundation for Educational Research. Articles of new informed thinking and empirical research are included. Available electronically.

Educational Researcher (ISSN 0013–189X) (Washington, DC: American Educational Research Association, 1972–). Nine issues a year. A refereed publication of the American Educational Research Association, containing news and features of general significance in educational research.

Educational Review (ISSN 0013–1911) (Basingstoke: Carfax Publishing, 1948–). Three issues a year. Publishes articles and accounts of research of interest to teachers, lecturers, researchers in education and psychology and to students of education. Available electronically.

Education Review <www.ed.asu.edu/edrev/>. This electronic journal publishes review articles of recently published books in education. All articles are published online and disseminated via an Email distribution list.

Educational Studies (ISSN 0305–5698) (Basingstoke: Carfax Publishing, 1975–). Three issues a year. This refereed journal publishes papers which cover applied and theoretical approaches to the study of education and its closely related disciplines. Available electronically.

Education Guardian <education:guardian.co.uk/>. The online version of the useful *Guardian* Tuesday education supplement.

E-Journal of Instructural Science and Technology (e-JIST) <www.us.usq.edu.au/electpub/e-jist/>. *e-JIST* is an international peer-reviewed electronic journal. Based at the Distance Education Centre of the University of Southern Queensland, it provides articles covering a wide range of areas including, amongst other topics, instructional science practice in education and training.

Electronic Journal of Science Education <unr.edu/homepage/jcannon/ejse.html>. A peer-reviewed online journal, developed and designed to offer the science education community a vehicle with which to share ideas, information and research. It is published by the University of Nevada, Reno.

European Journal of Education (ISSN 0141–8211) (Basingstoke: Carfax Publishing, 1964–). Quarterly. This refereed journal devotes its attention to educational reforms and general developments in Western and Eastern Europe and, in particular, to policy implications. Available electronically.

European Journal of Teacher Education (ISSN 0261–9768) (Basingstoke: Carfax Publishing 1997–). Three issues a year. The official journal of the Association for Teacher Education in Europe (ATEE), it examines policies, theories and practices related to teacher education. Available electronically.

Harvard Educational Review (ISSN 0017–8055) (Cambridge, MA: Harvard University, 1930–). Quarterly. A scholarly journal of opinion and research in education. Since 1930 it has been one of the most prestigious journals in education. Available electronically.

Higher Education in Europe (ISSN 0379–7724) (Basingstoke: Carfax Publishing, 1975–). Quarterly. A review published on behalf of the European Centre for Higher Education. A scholarly journal dealing with major problems and trends in contemporary higher education. Mainly European in coverage, it does publish articles on other areas of the world. Available electronically.

History of Education (ISSN 0046–760X) (Basingstoke: Carfax Publishing, 1972–). Quarterly. The official refereed journal of the History of Education Society. Contains original papers on the history of education. Available electronically.

International Journal of Educational Management (ISSN 0951–354X) (Bradford: MCB University Press, 1986–). Bimonthly. This journal aims to bridge the gap between the academic approach to educational management and basic practice. Available electronically.

International Journal of Lifelong Education (ISSN 0260–1370) (Basingstoke: Carfax Publishing, 1982–). Bimonthly. A refereed journal launched at the beginning of 1982, to provide an international forum for the debate of principles and practices of lifelong education. Available electronically.

International Journal of Science Education (ISSN 0950–0693) (Basingstoke: Carfax Publishing, 1979–). Monthly. This refereed publication reports major advances in the theory and practice of research into science education. Emphasis is placed on research that has a practical application. Available electronically.

International Review of Education (ISSN 0020–8566) (Dordrecht, The Netherlands: Kluwer Academic. 1955–). Bimonthly. A refereed journal sponsored by the UNESCO Institute for Education. Its aim is to disseminate scholarly information on major educational issues. Available electronically.

The Internet TESL Journal: for teachers of English as a second language <www.aitech.ac.ip/~iteslj/>. This monthly online journal contains articles, lesson plans, classroom handouts, teaching ideas and links to other sites.

Journal for Research in Mathematics Education (ISSN 0021–8251) (Vancouver: National Council of Teachers of Mathematics Inc.. 1969–). Five issues a year. The official refereed journal of the National Council of Teachers of Mathematics, includes research reports and reviews on the teaching and learning of mathematics at all levels. Available electronically.

Journal of Curriculum Studies (ISSN 0022–0272) (Basingstoke: Carfax Publishing, 1968–). Bimonthly. Publishes original, refereed contributions to theory and practice and policy-making, with emphasis on curriculum issues and the assessment of teaching. Available electronically.

Journal of Education Policy (ISSN 0268–0939) (Basingstoke: Carfax Publishing, 1985–). Bimonthly. A refereed publication which ranges broadly over issues of management, curriculum and the social and cultural context of education policy. The journal maintains an international perspective. Available electronically.

Journal of Education for Teaching (ISSN 0260–7476) (Basingstoke: Carfax Publishing, 1975–). Three issues a year. Publishes original, refereed contributions on the subject of teacher education in its widest sense. Available electronically.

Journal of Educational Psychology (ISSN 0022–0663) (Washington, DC: American Psychological Association, 1910–). Quarterly. A refereed publication of the American Psychological Association, this journal provides a forum for the discussion of learning and cognition, psychological development, relationships and social adjustment of the individual. All levels of education and all age groups are covered. Available electronically.

Journal of Further and Higher Education (ISSN 0309–877X) (Basingstoke: Carfax Publishing, 1943–). Three issues a year. A professional rather than a scholarly journal, most of its articles offer informed investigation, analysis and argument without the support of the full process of research. Published by the National Association of Teachers in Further and Higher Education (NATFAR) it offers a discussion forum for all staff across the adult, further and higher education spectrum. Available electronically.

Journal of Higher Education Policy and Management (ISSN 1360–080X) (Basingstoke: Carfax Publishing, 1979–). Two issues a year. An international peer-reviewed publication which seeks to cater for the information needs of managers and administrators in higher education. Available electronically.

Journal of Research in Science Teaching (ISSN 0022–4308) (New York: John Wiley, 1963–). Ten issues a year. Publishes research articles related to teaching strategies, curriculum development and other topics relevant to the teaching of science. Articles written from historical and philosophical perspectives are also included. Available electronically.

Journal of Computing in Teacher Education (ISSN 1040–2454) (Eugene, Or: International Society for Technology in Education, 1967–). Quarterly. Formerly *Journal of Research on Computing in Teacher Education* and *Journal of Research on Computing in Education,* this journal provides a forum for researchers at teacher training institutions who are confronting issues of providing computer and technology education for teachers in training at all levels. Available electronically.

Oxford Review of Education (ISSN 0305–4985) (Basingstoke: Carfax Publishing, 1975–). Quarterly. The main object of this refereed journal is to advance the study of education. Available electronically.

Reading (ISSN 0074–0472) (Oxford: Blackwell Publishing, 1967–). Three issues a year. A journal for those interested in the study of literacy and language. The official refereed journal of the United Kingdom Reading Association. Available electronically.

Reading Research Quarterly (ISSN 0034–0553) (Detroit, IL: International Reading Association Inc., 1965–). Quarterly. Provides peer-reviewed, technical studies for those interested in research into reading. Available electronically.

Research in Education (ISSN 0034–5237) (Manchester: Manchester University Press, 1969–). Two issues a year. Aims to present empirical and experimental findings from research into educational problems. Available electronically.

Research in Science & Technological Education (ISSN 0263–5143) (Basingstoke: Carfax Publishing, 1983–). Two issues a year. Publishes refereed articles on original research from throughout the world, focusing on the dual topics of science education and technological education. Available electronically.

Research in the Teaching of English (ISSN 0034–527X) (Champaign, IL: National Council of Teachers of English, 1966–). Quarterly. Deals with all aspects of English from teaching to linguistics and psycholinguistics. Articles are research-based. Available electronically.

Research Papers in Education (ISSN 0267–1522) (London: Routledge, 1986–). Quarterly. Publishes research articles related to policy and practice in education. Available electronically.

Review of Educational Research (ISSN 0034–6543) (Washington, DC: American Educational Research Association, 1931–). Quarterly. A refereed publication of the American Educational Research Association. Available electronically.

School Effectiveness and School Improvement (ISSN 0924–3453) (Lisse: Swets & Zeitlinger B.V., 1990–). Quarterly. A refereed journal published by the International Congress for School Effectiveness and Improvement. Articles from both practitioner and research perspectives are included. Available electronically.

School Leadership & Management (ISSN 1363–2434) (Basingstoke: Carfax Publishing, 1997–). Quarterly. Continues *School Organisation* which was first published in 1980. A refereed journal concerned primarily with the improvement of practice. Available electronically.

Teachers and Teaching: Theory and Practice (ISSN 1354–0602) (Basingstoke: Carfax Publishing, 1995–). Three issues a year. Publishes qualitative and quantitative research on teaching from around the world. Focus is on the social, political and historical contexts of teaching. Available electronically.

Teaching & Teacher Education (ISSN 0742–051X) (Oxford: Elsevier Science, 1985–). Eight issues a year. This refereed journal aims to enhance theory, research and practice in teaching and teacher education. Available electronically.

Teachers College Record (ISSN 0161–4681) (New York: Columbia University, 1900–). Bimonthly. A refereed journal of research, analysis and commentary in the field of education. Available electronically.

Times Educational Supplement (TES) <www.tes.org.uk/>. The online version of the weekly educational newspaper. Archived back to 1995, it is an excellent way of researching educational issues.

▶ 6.10 ABSTRACTS, INDEXES AND DATABASES

(a) Print

British Education Index (Leeds: University Press, 1954–). Published five times a year, including the cumulative volume. This is one of the most important sources of periodical literature for British education . For further details *see also International ERIC* and the *British Education Index* under *(b) Electronic* below.

Education Index (New York: HW Wilson, 1983–). Published monthly, except July and August, with an annual cumulation. It indexes 582 English-language journals and yearbooks published in the United

States and elsewhere. It offers detailed coverage of all educational topics including adult education, higher education, multicultural/ethnic education, teacher education and vocational education. A useful database, but with an emphasis on the educational scene in the United States. *See also Education Index* under *(b) Electronic* below.

Educational Technology Abstracts (Basingstoke: Carfax, 1985–). Covering approximately 600 international journals, the subject areas included range across all aspects of educational technology, learning theory, issues of assessment and evaluation and many more. There are six issues a year. *See also Educational Technology Abstracts* under *(b) Electronic* below.

Multicultural Education Abstracts (Basingstoke: Carfax, 1985). A current awareness service which draws on a wide range of international sources in order to serve the information needs of those throughout the world who are concerned with multicultural education. Abstracts books as well as journals. *See also Educational Research Abstracts* under *(b) Electronic* below.

Research into Higher Education Abstracts (Basingstoke: Carfax, 1968–). Published on behalf of the Society for Research into Higher Education, the service provides a regular survey of international periodicals relevant to the theory and practice of higher education, and also offers selective coverage of books and monographs. *See also Educational Research Abstracts* under *(b) Electronic* below.

Educational Management Abstracts (Basingstoke: Carfax, 1982–). Published four times a year, this is an international current awareness service focusing on the organization and management of the school as a complex organization. *See also Educational Research Abstracts* under *(b) Electronic* below.

Sociology of Education Abstracts (Basingstoke: Carfax, 1965–). This abstracting service provides a complete guide to essential resources in the research and teaching of the sociology of education. *See also Educational Research Abstracts* under *(b) Electronic* below.

Special Educational Needs Abstracts (Basingstoke: Carfax, 1989–). A quarterly information service for professionals concerned with the education of children and adults who have special needs (physical, intellectual and social). *See also Educational Research Abstracts* under *(b) Electronic* below.

Technical Education & Training Abstracts (Basingstoke: Carfax, 1961–). The information needs of those teaching mathematics, science and design and technology at all levels are covered in this publication,. In addition, it also specializes in vocational, further and continuing education, with an emphasis on human resource development. *See also Educational Research Abstracts* under *(b) Electronic* below.

Contents Pages in Education (Basingstoke: Carfax, 1986–). Covering over 600 journals, this publication lists the contents pages of the journals concerned. Supported by subject and author indexes, this is a useful way of scanning a wide selection of international literature.

Current Index to Journals in Education (Phoenix, AZ: Oryx Press, 1966–). Published monthly, this is the paper version of *ERIC* and gives access to international literature in periodical form. It is sponsored by the US Department of Education. *See also ERIC* under *(b) Electronic* below.

Resources in Education (Phoenix, AZ: Oryx Press, 1966–) Like the *Current Index to Journals in Education*, this is updated monthly and covers a vast quantity of report literature, much of it unpublished, or semi-published. *See also ERIC* under *(b) Electronic* below.

Psychological Abstracts (Arlington, VA: American Psychological Association, 1972–). An important abstracting journal for its coverage of the psychological aspects of education. *See also PsycINFO* under *(b) Electronic* below.

(b) Electronic

Educational Research Abstracts (ERA) <www.tandf.co.uk/era>. Providing material from 1995 onwards, *ERA* is aimed at the academic community, but is also of use to practitioners. Its breadth of coverage is wide and includes electronic bibliographic access to the following print titles: *Educational Management Abstracts*, *Educational Technology Abstracts*, *Multicultural Education Abstracts*, *Research into Higher Education Abstracts*, *Sociology of Education Abstracts*, *Special Educational Needs Abstracts*, and *Technical Education & Training Abstracts*. Usefully, the service links to full-text articles where available.

British Education Index <www.education.bids.ac.uk/>. This electronic version of the *British Education Index* (*see (a) Print* above) is available as part of BIDS (Bath Information Data Services) via an OVID interface. It covers over 360 British education journals from 1986 onwards. The coverage of report and conference literature is increasing.

International ERIC (Mountain View, CA: Knight-Ridder Information Inc.) This is a CD-ROM version of the *British Education Index* (*see (a) Print* above) and includes the *Australian Education Index*, the *Canadian Education Index*, the *Bibliography of Education Theses in Australia* and the *British Education Thesis Index*. Searches can be made across all databases using the same keywords. Abstracts are not normally available, but more report literature is being covered in succeeding yearly parts. Updated quarterly. Some selected European English language titles are being included, too. It is very straightforward to use, working on a simple topic or author approach. The database is also available through Bath Information and Data Services (BIDS) <www.bids.ac.uk> and OCLC FirstSearch at: <firstsearch.oclc.org>.

ERIC (Educational Resources Information Center, 1966–) <ericfac.piccard.csc.com>. Available from Dialog and the BIDS Education

Data Services via an OVID interface. Containing over 700 000 citations and currently the largest education database in the world, this online version of the *Current Index to Journals in Education* and *Resources in Education* (*see (a) Print* above), provides a powerful way of searching international literature in education. Simple and complex searches are possible (including the facility to search by journal or report titles) together with a variety of print-capture features. While education is its principal focus, its reach extends into a large number of related fields. The inclusion of abstracts makes this database very valuable indeed.

Education Index, *Education Abstracts* and *Education Full Text* (New York: HW Wilson, 1983–). A trio of electronic databases which complement the printed index discussed in *(a) Print* above. The abstracting service commenced in 1994 and greatly added to the value of the service. *Educational Abstracts* retains the broad coverage of the *Index* and includes 50–150 word summaries for each indexed item. *Education Full Text* offers yet more added value by providing access to the full-text of more than 133 journals in the database. The services are available with monthly updates on CD-ROM and via the Internet. For more information see: <www.hwwilson.com/>. ProQuest Information and Learning also offers a Web version of the database with full-text links called *Education PlusText*. For more information see: <www.umi.com>.

ICT in Education News (Coventry: BECTa, 1998–) <www.becta.org.uk/information/ictnews.html>. This monthly online service provides abstracts of articles which have appeared in national newspapers and the educational press. It focuses on information technology in education under four main sections: general issues, innovative uses, hardware and software news and telecommunications and broadcasting.

Web of Science <wos.mimas.ac.uk/>. A general electronic database with access to *Science, Social Science* and *Arts & Humanities*, Citation Indexes. It provides broad coverage of education topics. *See 1.10* for a detailed discussion of the database.

Periodical Contents Index (London: Chadwyck Healey) <www.edina.ac.uk>. A very useful general index that is good for historical research and therefore for the history of education. Available via the EDINA Website with an ATHENS username and password.

British Newspaper Index (London: Primary Source Media, 1992–). Covers *The Times* group of newspapers and others. It is possible to restrict searches to the *Times Educational Supplement*.

PsycINFO (Washington, DC: American Psychological Association). Produces very good references to educational psychology articles and related subjects like dyslexia, behaviour modification and counselling. *See 4.10* for a full discussion of this and other psychological databases.

▶ 6.11 OFFICIAL PUBLICATIONS

6.11.1 United Kingdom

(a) Print

Education and Employment Publications (London: DFEE, monthly). Specifically listing the publications produced by the Department for Education and Employment, this unassuming publication is essential for anyone tracking down DFEE publications. Arranged by subject, it is fairly easy to search by scanning the pages. A wide variety of documents are included, amongst them OFSTED reports, circulars and Social Fund documents. *See also (b) Electronic* below for information about the publications of the recently established Department for Education and Skills, which has replaced the Department for Education and Employment.

The Law of Education (London: Butterworths, loose-leaf format). This publication is an important legal guide to the law of education. It is updated quarterly with new pages and instructions on how to add pages and to withdraw out-of-date material. There is a very good index and in addition to statutes, it includes circulars, administrative memoranda and statutory instruments.

The following publications will be of use to those conducting historical investigations into official publications in the field of education. *British Government Publications in Education During the Nineteenth Century* (Leicester: History of Education Society, 1971). This volume was written by Michael Argles and he then followed this with *British Government Publications Concerning Education During the Twentieth Century* 4th ed. (Leicester: History of Education Society, 1982) which he co-authored with John E. Vaughan. Both publications give a wonderful overview of official education documentation in the nineteenth and twentieth centuries (up to 1982). Invaluable material for education historians.

Of related interest is *Educational Documents: England and Wales, 1816 to the Present Day*, 5th ed., (London: Methuen, 1986). Edited by J. S. Maclure, the volume follows, through public and official documentation, the progressive development from elementary, primary, secondary to technical and higher education and from private to public. A good index is included. *Scottish Public Educational Documents 1560–1960* by H. Hutchinson (Edinburgh: SCRE, 1973), was the first volume to include Scottish official documentation. The monograph provides extracts from 220 documents covering a period of 400 years. There is a comprehensive index to the work. *A Guide to the Study of British Further Education: Published Sources on the Contemporary System* edited by A. J. Peters (Windsor: NFER, 1967), is a unique document for the history of further education. Appendix two is a list of reports mentioned which are commonly known by the Chairman's name.

(b) Electronic

Department for Education and Skills, (DfES) <www.dfes.gov.uk>. The Website gives access to publications by topic and publication type (e.g., circulars and research reports). The DfES Publications database can also be searched by keyword(s).

UK Online Open Government Information Service <www.open.gov.uk/>. This is the key Website for non-parliamentary official material. Use the topic index to select Education. This brings together a select list of the official bodies associated with education. Included are the Department for Education and Skills, the Higher Education Statistics Agency, The Teacher Training Agency and the funding Councils. There is also an A–Z directory of higher education universities and colleges.

NISS (National Information on Software and Services) <www.niss.ac.uk/>. This is a vital Website for any researcher, or student of education following the development of education. Particularly valuable for further and higher education, the full text of all major reports is available. Higginson, Dearing, papers from the Committee of Vice Chancellors and Principals (CVCP) and publications of such bodies as the Quality Assurance Agency for Higher Education are all there in full text.

6.11.2 Europe

EURYDICE – The Information Network on Education in Europe <www.eurydice.org>. Part of Socrates, the European Commission's Community Programme on Education. This site provides details (often including summaries) of its extensive range of publications.

6.11.3 United States

For details (including some full-text access) of the official publications of the *US Department of Education* go to the following Website: <www.ed.gov>.

6.12 STATISTICS

6.12.1 United Kingdom

(a) Print

Education Statistics for the United Kingdom (London: Stationery Office). This annual volume covers a wide range of educational topics. Of particular value is the introductory section. The following examples from the *Statistics of Education* series of titles provide information on a wide variety of topics. *Statistics of Education: Schools* (London: Stationery Office). Annual. Contains detailed information on pupils and teachers in schools in each Local Education Authority (LEA). *Statistics of Education: Public Examinations GCSE/GNVQ and GCE in England* (London: Stationery Office). Annual. This provides statistics on public examinations in England in schools and further education. Subject group and gender tables are included. *Statistics of Education: Teachers* (London: Stationery Office). Annual. Offers information on, amongst other topics, teacher numbers, age, qualifications and salaries. Further and higher education (post 1992 universities) is included. *Statistics of Education: Student Support, England and Wales* (London: Stationery Office). Annual. Includes statistics on mandatory and discretionary awards to students in further and higher education.

For a concise summary of educational statistics see *Education in the UK: Facts and Figures*, 3rd ed., by Donald Mackinnon and June Statham (London: Hodder and Stoughton, 1999). The previous edition was entitled *Education Fact File*. The authors emphasize that the book is not one of original research, almost all of the information is derived from other published sources. However, as it collates material from disparate sources it is a useful one-stop-shop for general facts and figures.

Higher Education Statistics for the United Kingdom (London: Higher Education Statistical Agency). Annual. This is the official statistical overview of higher education in the UK. The most recent editions also include information about the further education sector. *See also (b) Electronic* below.

(b) Electronic

DfES Statistics <www.dfes.gov.uk/statistics/>. The Department for Education and Skills produce statistics covering education, training and life-long learning.

Higher Education Statistics Agency (HESA) <Hesa.ac.uk/>. Set up in 1992 by UK universities and higher education colleges to collect, analyse and report on HE statistics to form the basis of a comprehensive management system for publicly funded higher education in the UK. Coverage includes data on students, staff and finance.

6.12.2 Europe

Key data on Education in the European Union (Brussels: The Commission). Published annually since 1994, this publication covers a variety of data on all levels of education. Presented in an attractive and understandable way with highlighted comments on specific issues. Concise volumes like *Education in Western Europe: Facts and Figures* (London: Hodder & Stoughton in association with the Open University, 1997) are extremely useful for a broad statistical sweep across a number of countries. Written by a team led by Donald McKinnon, this work was put together to support an Open University course.

6.12.3 United States

(a) Print

The section on education in the annual *Statistical Abstract of the United States* (Washington, DC: US Bureau of the Census) presents data at various levels and for public and private schools. The emphasis is on national data, but there are tables on regions and individual states. The *Digest of Education Statistics* (Washington, DC: National Center for Education Statistics 1962–) is an annual publication which provides a good overview for anyone seeking general statistics of education in the United States.

(b) Electronic

FedStats: Education Statistics <www.fedstats.gov/programs/educ.html>. Provides access to statistics from both the National Center for Education Statistics in the US Department of Education, and the National Science Foundation which publishes statistics on the science and engineering higher educational system in the United States.

6.12.4 International

(a) Print

See *Education at a Glance: OECD Indicators* (Paris: Organization for Economic Cooperation and Development 1992–) for indicators of education systems, educational output, educational costs and performance indicators in OECD countries. *See also (b) Electronic* below. Of related interest is *OECD Education Statistics 1985–1992* (Paris: Organization for Economic Cooperation and Development, 1995). Prepared by Wendy Simpson, these represent a very important set of statistics for anyone looking for worldwide figures. They cover Europe, United States, Canada, Australia, New Zealand and Japan.

(b) Electronic

For a digital version of *Education at Glance: OECD Indicators* see the Website: <www.oecd.org/publications/e-book/960004le.pdf>.

6.12 Research in progress

A useful publication for keeping track of current research is *Focus on Educational Research in the United Kingdom* (Windsor: National Foundation for Educational Research (NFER). Biannual. This is the renamed two-volume work which has replaced the *Register of Educational Research*, from the same source. The *Register* was published every two years and was an important source of information, specifically on research being carried out in the subject area of education. The changed title will not make the work any less valuable. It is intended to mount the database on the NFER Website in due course. Meanwhile, the database is continually updated and searches can be made for data added between publications.

See below for details of key discussion lists which researchers can use as a valuable networking tool and as a means of keeping up to date with current debates.

english-ltsn <www.jiscmail.ac.uk/lists/english-ltsn.html>. This list provides a supportive network of communication and activities to advance the practice of teaching English across the range of higher education awards in the UK. This list service provides a forum to discuss the evolving pedagogy of professional English studies.

lis-access <www.jiscmail.ac.uk/lists/lis-access.html>. This list aims to look at library support for 'non-traditional' students. It is concerned with the issues relating to library access and how best to support those students disadvantaged in this respect (part-time, distance students and similar categories).

lis-educ <www.jiscmail.ac.uk/lists/lis-educ.html>. A list produced under the auspices of the Education Librarians Group (ELG) (*see 6.14*). Its prime function is as a list for the discussion of the provision of information to those involved in educational research, teacher training and the study of education.

lis-lise <www.jiscmail.ac.uk/lists/lis-lise.html>. This is a closed list for Librarians of Institutes and Schools of Education (LISE) (*see 6.14*). Its aim is to cover the activities and communications of LISE.

lis-research support <www.jiscmail.ac.uk/lists/lis-researchsupport.html>. A list intended for librarians in universities, colleges of higher education and research institutions to facilitate discussion about library support for researchers. It aims to encourage the sharing of ideas and good practice and to help create a network of research support librarians.

sl-net (to subscribe to the list a message needs to be sent to listserve@jimmy.qmuc.ac.uk. More information is available by Email: jherring@qmuc.ac.uk). A list produced to enhance communication between school libraries. The originator was James Herring of Queen Margaret University College, Edinburgh.

▶ 6.14 ORGANIZATIONS

In this selection of key organizations from around the world, I have focused on those bodies which make a significant contribution to research, pedagogy and training within the educational field.

Advisory Centre for Education (ACE)
1b Aberdeen Studios, Highbury Grove, London, N5 2DQ, UK
Tel: +44 (0)20 7354 8318
Fax: +44 (0)20 7354 9069
Email: ace.ed@easynet.co.uk
Web: <www.ace.ed.org.uk>

An independent non-profit making body offering confidential advice to parents and others on the maintained school system through its free advice lines.

American Educational Research Association(AERA)
1230 17th Street, NW, Washington DC, 20036–3708, USA
Tel: +1 202 223 9485
Fax: +1 202 775 1824
Email: aera@gmu.edu
Web: <www.tikkun.ed.asu.edu/aera/home.htm/>

AERA encourages scholarly inquiry related to education and then disseminates the results of that research. It has a membership of over 22 000 members who represent a broad range of disciplines including education, psychology, statistics, economics and political science.

Association for Science Education (ASE)
College Lane, Hatfield, Hertfordshire, AL10 9AA, UK
Tel: +44 (0)1707 283000
Fax: +44 (0)1707 266532
Web: <www.ase.org.uk/>

ASE is for all concerned with science in education. It supports and develops science education from primary through to tertiary levels. It is a registered charity funded by members' contributions.

Association of Commonwealth Universities (ACU)
36 Gordon Square, London, WC1H 0PF, UK
Tel: +44 (0)207 380 6700
Fax: +44 (0)207 387 2655
Email: info@acu.ac.uk
Web: <www.acu.ac.uk/>

The ACU serves nearly 500 member institutions from commonwealth countries around the world. Its major function is to advance cooperation and understanding in higher education.

Australian Council for Educational Research Ltd.(ACER)
Private Bag 55, Camberwell, Victoria 3124, Australia
Tel: +61 3 9277 5555
Fax: +61 3 9277 5500
Email: mceetya@curriculum.ed.au
Web: <www.acer.edu.au>

ACER was established in 1930 and its work falls into three areas: research and development projects, services provided on a user-pay basis, including testing services, conferences and sales of publications. Since 1987, ACER's research programme has been organized thematically on a triennial basis.

British Council
10 Spring Gardens, London, SW1A 2BN, UK
Tel: +44 (0)20 7930 8466
Web: <www.britcoun.org/>

The British Council is the UK's international organization for educational and cultural relations. The Website gives in-depth information for those coming to Britain to study. Facilities include libraries and information collections in over 108 countries around the world.

British Educational Communications and Technology Agency (BECTa)
Millburn Hill Road, Science Park, Coventry, CV4 7JJ, UK
Tel: +44 (0)1203 416994
Email: becta@becta.org.uk
Web: <www.becta.org.uk>

BECTa supports government and national agencies in the use and development of information and communications technology with the aim of raising standards in education. The National Grid for Learning is being nurtured through BECTa.

British Educational Research Association (BERA)
15 St John Street, Edinburgh, EH8 8JR, UK
Tel: +44 (0)131 557 2944
Fax: +44 (0)131 556 9454
Email: bera@scre.ac.uk
Web: <www.scre.ac.uk/bera>

The aim of BERA is to encourage the pursuit of educational research and its applications both for the improvement of education and the general benefit of the community. It holds an annual conference and publishes research through the *British Education Research Journal* (*see* 6.9). Membership is open to anyone interested in educational research.

Department for Education and Skills
Sanctuary Buildings, Great Smith Street, London, SW1P 3BT, UK
Tel: +44 (0) 870 000 2288
Fax: +44 (0) 1928 79 4248
Email: info@dfes.gsi.gov.uk
Web: <www.dfes.gov.uk>

A new Government department formed in 2001, after the restructuring of the Department of Education and Employment and the Department of Social Security. It has responsibility for education, training and lifelong learning.

Educational Management Information Exchange (EMIE)
NFER, The Mere, Upton Park, Slough, SL1 2DQ, UK
Tel: +44 (0)1753 574123
Fax: +44 (0)1753 531458
Email: emie@nfer.ac.uk
Web: <www.nfer.ac.uk/emie>

EMIE is an information service designed primarily for education officers and advisers/inspectors in Local Education Authorities. The LEAs contribute the information and make use of their combined input. There is an enquiry desk, and a wide selection of papers and reports are published. An online database is available on the Website.

Education Librarians Group (ELG)
Ward Freeman School, Bowling Green Lane, Buntingford, SG9 9BT, UK
Tel: +44 (0)1763 271 818
Email: dcrolf@aol.com
Web: <www.la-hq.org.uk/groups/elg/elg.html>

The Education Librarians Group is one of the subject based support groups belonging to the UK Library Association. Its major objective is to provide continuing professional development support for librarians involved with education as a subject. This is done mainly by regional meetings and through the channel of *ELG News*, the group's newsletter. In addition, the group provides expert advice to the Library Association when responses to relevant government and other bodies' discussion papers are needed. Unlike *Librarians of Institutes and School of Education* (LISE), ELG is a group for librarians to join as individuals.

European Centre for the Development of Vocational Training (CEDEFOP)
P O Box 22427, GR55102, Thessaloniki, Greece
Tel: +30 31 490111
Fax: +30 31 490102
Email: info@cedefop.eu.int
Web: www.cedefop.eu.int
Interactive Web: <www.trainingvillage.gr>

CEDEFOP is the European agency that helps policy-makers and practitioners across Europe make informed choices about vocational education. It makes available the latest information on the present state and future trends in vocational education and training. Publications are a major part of its programme and a catalogue is available for most European countries.

European Educational Research Association (EERA)
Professional Development Unit, Faculty of Education, University of Strathclyde, 76 Southbrae Drive, Glasgow, G13 1PP, UK
Tel: +44 (0)141 950 3772
Fax: +44 (0)141 950 3210
Email: eera@strath.ac.uk
Web: <www.eera.ac.uk/?>

EERA aims to foster the exchange of ideas amongst European researchers, promote collaborative research, improve research quality and to offer independent advice on educational research. The Association is for the use of both administrators and practitioners. There is a programme of publications and conferences to support the dissemination of research.

Further Education Development Agency(FEDA)
Citadel Place, Tinworth Street, London, SE11 5EH, UK
Tel: +44 (0)20 7840 5400
Fax: +44 (0)20 7840 5401

FEDA was established in 1995 to provide a service to further education, to maintain and improve standards and conduct research. Training and conference facilities are provided and collaboration with both the further education and other sectors takes place.

Higher Education Statistics Agency (HESA)
18 Royal Crescent, Cheltenham, Gloucester, GL50 4RH, UK
Tel: +44 (0)1242 255577
Fax: +44 (0)1242 211122
Email: customer.services@hesa.ac.uk
Web: <www.hesa.ac.uk>

Set up in 1992 by United Kingdom universities and higher education colleges, HRSA collects, analyses and reports on higher education statistics. Three streams of data are kept – student data, staff data and finance data.

The Institute for Learning and Teaching (ILT)
Genesis 3, Innovation Way, York Science Park, Heslington, York, YO10 5DQ, UK
Tel: +44 (0)1904 434222
Fax: +44 (0)1904 434241
Email: enquiries@ilt.ac.uk
Web: <www.ilt.ac.uk>

The Institute for Learning and Teaching is a professional body for all who teach and support learning in higher education in the UK. ILT fosters research and innovation as well as providing accreditation for those teaching in higher education.

Librarians of Institutes and School of Education (LISE)
The Library, Anglia Polytechnic University, Sawyers Hall Lane, Brentwood, Essex, CM15 9BT, UK
Tel: +44 (0)1277 264 504
Fax: +44 (0)1277 211 363
Email: Lbryab@vaxe.anglia.ac.uk
Web: <www.educ.cam.ac.uk/lise/index.html>

Formed in 1954, LISE is a group comprising librarians from all UK higher education institutions that provide initial teacher training, continuing professional development for teachers or which carry out educational research. The major role of the group is to provide bibliographical support for librarians in the subject area of education. The *British Education Index* (*see* 6.19) began its life as a LISE publication and there have been a variety of publications over the years covering the areas of children's books, history of education and more general areas. The group is now responsible for *Education Libraries Journal* which it took over from the London University Institute of Education Library in 1994. LISE members represent their institutions and this has enabled a considerable amount of cooperative activity to take place during the life of the group.

National Association for Primary Education (NAPE)
School of Education, University of Leicester, Barrack Road, Northampton, NN2 6AF, UK
Tel: +44 (0)1604 636326
Fax: +44 (0)1604 636328
Email: nationaloffice@nape.org.uk
Web: <nape.org.uk/>

NAPE has a membership of some 200 000 people including parents, teachers, school governors, inspectors, education officers and entire schools. Members are surveyed regularly about issues concerning primary education and about the work of NAPE itself.

National Association for Special Educational Needs (NASEN)
NASEN House, 4–5 Amber Business Village, Amber Close, Armington, Tamworth, Staffordshire, B77 4RP, UK
Tel: +44 (0)1827 311500
Email: welcome@nasen.org.uk
Web: <nasen.org.uk>

An organization that has been set up specially to look at resources and other topics of concern. It also offers information and advice to teachers and parents.

National Children's Bureau (NCB)
8 Wakley Street, London, EC1V 7QE, UK
Tel: +44 (0)20 7843 6000
Fax: +44 (0)20 7278 9512
Web: <www.ncb.org.uk/>

The National Children's Bureau is a registered charity which promotes the interests and wellbeing of children and young people. It undertakes high quality research and promotes cross-agency partnerships.

National Foundation for Educational Research (NFER)
The Mere, Upton Park, Slough, SL1 2DQ, UK
Tel: +44 (0)1753 574123
Fax: +44 (0)1753 691632
Web: <www.nfer.ac.uk>

NFER is an independent organization which carries out research in education and educational psychology, constructs tests and provides information and advice on research developments. The *Register of Educational Research in the UK* (*see 6.13*), *Research Papers in Education* and the journal *Educational Research* (see *6.9*) are all products of this important research body.

National Institute of Adult Continuing Education (NIACE)
21 De Montfort Street, Leicester, LE1 7GE, UK
Tel: +44 (0)116 204 4200
Fax: +44 (0)116 285 4514
Web: <www.niace.org.uk/>

The national centre for research in all forms of adult education, NIACE also provides advice and information in this sector. It has a governing Council with wide representation from Local Education Authorities (LEAs), universities, the Home Office and numerous voluntary bodies. NIACE publishes journals, monographs and a yearbook. It has an information centre, supported by a library and organizes a variety of conferences.

National Society for Education in Art & Design (NSEAD)
The Gatehouse, Corsham Court, Corsham, Wiltshire, SN13 0BZ, UK
Tel: +44 (0)1249 714825
Fax: +44 (0)1249 716138
Web: <www.nsead.org/>

The National Society for Education in Art & Design is the leading national authority concerned with art, craft and design across all phases of education in the United Kingdom.

New Zealand Council for Educational Research (NZCER)
PO Box 3237, Wellington, New Zealand
Tel: +64 4384 7939
Fax: +64 4384 7933
Web: <www.nzcer.org.nz/>

NZCER was set up in 1934 and the NZCER Act of 1972 states that the function of the Council shall be to foster the study of research into education and to prepare and publish reports on any findings, and to furnish information and advice to persons and organizations concerned with education. NZCER has a strong standing in the international community.

Open College
St Pauls, 78 Wilmslow Road, Didsbury, Manchester, M20 2RW, UK
Tel: +44 (0)161 345 3300
Fax: +44 (0)161 245 3301

The Open College produces open learning training materials for business and education. In addition, support programmes, often specially tailored for the recipient, are provided and a consultancy service offered.

Quality Assurance Agency (QAA)
Southgate House, Southgate Street, Gloucester, GL1 1UB, UK
Tel: +44 (0)1452 557000
Fax: +44 (0)1452 557070
Email: comms@qaa.ac.uk
Web: <www.qaa.ac.uk/>

The Quality Assurance Agency was established to safeguard and enhance quality of provision and standards of awards in higher education. Institutions are audited and the results are published in traditional form and on their Website.

The Research and Information on State Education Trust (RISE)
54 Broadwalk, London, E18 2DW, UK
Tel: +44 (0)20 8989 43356
Email: barbara.collins@risetrust.org.uk
Web: <www.risetrust.org.uk>

RISE promotes research on state education in a form 'accessible to parents and other bodies responsible for the education of young children, young persons or adults in the publicly maintained sector of education'. The research carried out, sometimes funded by the Department for Education and Skills, is published on a regular basis. Statistical surveys are being made more widely available on the RISE Website.

Scottish Council for Research in Education (SCRE)
15 St. John Street, Edinburgh, EH8 8JR, UK
Tel: +44 (0)131 557 2944
Fax: +44 (0)131 556 9454
Email: scre@scre.ac.uk
Web: <www.scre.ac.uk/>

The director of this prestigious research Council is Professor Wyonne Harlen, the eminent researcher into science teaching. SCRE aims to conduct, sponsor and coordinate educational research in Scotland, to publish that research, maintain registers of research and to give grants for research to be carried out. The SCRE was re-appraised and restructured in 1986 and, as a result of this, a Forum on Educational Research in Scotland was established. Membership includes teachers, researchers and administrators.

Society for Research into Higher Education (SRHE)
3 Devonshire Street, London, W1N 2BA, UK
Tel: +44 (0)20 7637 2766
Fax: +44 (0)20 7637 2781
Email: srhe@mailbox.u/cc.ac.uk
Web: <www.srhe.ac.uk/srhe.htm>

SRHE was established in 1965 to stimulate and coordinate research into all aspects of higher education. It is a specialist publisher of research under the imprint SRHE & Open University and there are currently about 100 titles in print. The society publishes *Studies in Higher Education*, *Higher Education Quarterly* and *Research into Higher Education Abstracts* (*see* 6.9). Regular seminars and an annual conference are held for the members.

Teacher Training Agency (TTA)
Portland House, Stag Place, London, SW1 5TT, UK
Tel: +44 (0)1245 454454
Email: publications@ttalit.co.uk
Web: <www.teach.tta.gov.uk/index.htm>

The Teacher Training Agency was established in 1994 with the purpose of raising standards in schools by attracting able people into teaching.

Workers Educational Association(WEA)
Temple House, 17 Victoria Park Square, London, E2 9PB, UK
Tel: +44 (0)20 8983 1515
Fax: +44 (0)20 8983 4840
Email: info@wea.org.uk
Web: <www.wea.org.uk>

The WEA is the largest voluntary provider of adult education in the UK, with over 10 000 courses and 140 000 students. It was formed in 1903 and is very much involved in international work. Currently the organization is at the forefront of exploring the educational possibilities of the new communication technologies. It is a registered charity.

▶ REFERENCES

Christie, T. and Papasolomontos C. (1998) 'Using national surveys: a review of secondary analysis with special reference to education', in *Educational Research,* **40**(3), 295–310.

Daly, P. (2000) 'Recent critiques of school effectiveness research', in *School Effectiveness and School Improvement* **11**(1), 131–43.

Gorard, S. (1999) '"Well. That about wraps it up for school choice research": a state of the art review', in *School Leadership and Management,* **19**(1), 25–47.

Gregory, S., Thoutenhoofd, E. D. and Powers S. (1999) 'The educational achievements of deaf children: a literature review: executive summary', in *Deafness and Education International,* **1**(1), 1–9.

Hammersley, M. and Foster P. (1998) 'A review of reviews: structure and function in reviews of educational research', in *British Educational Research Journal,* **24**(5), 609–28.

Harris, A. (1998) 'Effective teaching: a review of the literature', in *School Leadership and Management,* **18**(2), 169–83.

Johnstone, R. (2000) 'Research on language teaching and learning: 1999', in *Language Teaching* **33**(3), 141–62.

Laws, P. (1996) 'Undergraduate science education: a review of research', in *Studies in Science Education,* **28**, 1–85.

MacDonald, D. (1999) 'Teacher attrition: a review of literature', in *Teaching and Teacher Education,* **15**(8), 835–48.

Mastropieri, M. A., Boon, R. and Scruggs T. E. (1998) 'Science education for students with disabilities: a review of recent research', in *Studies in Science Education,* **32**, 21–44.

Muijs, R. D. and Reynolds D. (1999) 'The effective teaching of mathematics: a review of research', in *School Leadership and Management*, **19**(3), 273–88.

Podmore, V. N. (1998) 'Class size in the first years at school: a New Zealand perspective on the international literature', in *International Journal of Educational Research*, **29**(8), 711–21.

Rees, G., Gorard, S. and Salisbury J. (1999) 'Accounting for the differential attainment of boys and girls at school', in *School Leadership and Management*, **19**(4), 403–26.

Richardson, J. T. E. (1994) 'Mature students in higher education: I, a literature survey on approaches to studying', in *Studies in Higher Education* **19**(3), 309–25.

Segers, M., Sluijsmans, D. and Dochy F. (1999) 'The use of self-, peer- and co-assessment in higher education: a review', in *Studies in Higher Education*, **24**(3), 331–50.

Southworth, G. and Hall V. (1997) 'Headship', in *School Leadership and Management*, **17**(2), 1551–70.

Tight, M. (1995) 'Education, work and adult life: a literature review', in *Research Papers in Education* **10**(3), 383–400.

7 Political science

Craig Conkie

▶ 7.1 NATURE AND SCOPE OF POLITICAL SCIENCE

The formal development of political science has its roots in the nineteenth century, although Aristotle may be considered as the first political scientist. It has been heavily influenced by many other disciplines, although these influences are difficult to quantify. In Europe, different approaches to the subject reflect its national origins. Political science emerged from constitutional law in France and Italy, which influenced its development right up until the 1950s. By comparison, in Germany and central Europe, political science reflected its philosophical antecedents.

The development of political science in the United States, in the latter part of the nineteenth century, was heavily influenced by the teaching approach used in German universities that considered political science as 'Stattswissenschaft', or the science of the state. Many American scholars carried out graduate work at German universities and they brought back to the United States the rational and analytical approach to the subject. The behaviourist approach to political science became established in the United States before World War II, but it was only in the post-1945 period that it became the dominant approach in the US and it gradually spread to Europe. It stresses the importance of using political concepts and models that are subject to empirical validation and that may be employed in solving practical political problems. A consequence of the behaviourist approach has been to spawn a diverse range of political concepts and methods. Professor Heinz Eulau wrote that 'Political Science carries the burden of both past and future. It is, of necessity, a historical discipline, and, of equal necessity, a predictive science' (Eulau, 1964, p.358).

Clifton Brock, in his 1969 publication *The Literature of Political Science*, wrote 'The logical starting point for a search, whether for a specific book or for 'subject' information, is the library card catalogue'

(Brock, 1969, p.8). The quotation illustrates how far information retrieval has evolved in the 30 years since the publication was written. Political science, as with most other areas of academic study and research, has been profoundly affected by the growth of electronic sources and, principally, the Internet. It has opened a whole new vista of possibilities for publishing political science research.

This chapter is divided into a number of broad subject groupings in order to examine a selection of the key publications within the literature.

▶ 7.2 ANNUALS

(a) Print

Two standard reference works, which are produced annually, are *The Europa World Year Book* (London: Europa Publications) and *The Statesman's Yearbook (*London: Macmillan). The latter contains information on current affairs, comparative statistics and facts for 192 countries of the world. *The Europa World Year Book* is published in two volumes and contains a detailed analysis of the 250 countries of the world together with information on major international organizations. *See also 1.2.*

Whereas the *Europa World Year Book* focuses on current affairs, the emphasis of the *Political Handbook of the World* (New York: McGraw-Hill. Published for the Center for Comparative Political Research of SUNY Binghamton and for the Council on Foreign Relations) is inherently political. The publication has information on political parties, constitutions and legislatures in each country. It also analyses key issues in public policy. Two more research-focused annuals are *British Political Science* (Oxford: Blackwell) and the *Annual Review of Political Science (*Palo Alto, CA: Annual Reviews, Inc.). The publishers of the United Kingdom's leading political science journal, *Political Studies* (*see 7.9.1*) produce an additional volume (*British Political Science*) under the aegis of a guest editor and on a special theme. The 2000 edition of *British Political Science* was a special edition to celebrate the 50th anniversary of the journal. Edited by Patrick Dunleavy, P. J. Kelly and Michael Moran, it contains 19 essays on various aspects of British political life.

The *Annual Review of Political Science* is one of 29 subjects in a series produced by Annual Review Inc., a non-profit making publisher dedicated to the intelligent dissemination of research. The Website search facility allows the user to search the contents of the last three political science reviews <polisci.annualreviews.org/>. Once selected, users may view the abstracts, but access to the full-text of articles requires payment.

A more general resource is *Keesing's Record of World Events* (Bethesda, MD; and Cambridge: Keesing's Worldwide, 1931–) which has objectively reported every significant world event since 1931. *Keesing's Record of World Events Online Archive* consists of 40 years and 30 000 pages of contemporary world history with original international news reports.

The period since the end of World War II has seen some progress in protecting individual rights around the world through steps such as the adoption of the Universal Declaration of Human Rights and the European Convention of Human Rights. *Freedom in the World: the Annual Survey of Political Rights and Civil Liberties* (New York: Freedom House) charts the status of the individual in the world's political systems, recording improvements or declines in civil liberties in 192 countries and approximately 50 disputed territories.

(b) Electronic

The CIA World Factbook <www.cia.gov/cia/publications/factbook/index.html> is the Internet at its best: high quality information, freely available, from the Central Intelligence Agency Website. It has information on all countries of the world, including government and geographical data. The publication is also available in print and on CD-ROM.

The Political Reference Almanac 1999–2000 <www.polisci.com/almanac/almanac.htm> is a useful free resource on the World Wide Web. The content of the online edition largely mirrors the print edition, *The Political Reference Almanac 1999–2000* (Arlington, VA: PoliSci Books, 1999).

Human Rights Watch produces an annual report, *Human Rights Watch World Report* <www.hrw.org/wr2k/> that details the rights of individuals worldwide. *The Human Rights Watch Report* is supplemented by special reports on recent troublespots or particular problems. There is no keyword search facility, but countries are grouped by continent and can be easily identified.

► 7.3 BIBLIOGRAPHIES

7.3.1 General

Bibliographic publications for political science fall into two groups: those focusing exclusively on political science and others featuring political science as part of the broader social sciences. One publication, which falls into both groupings, is the *International Bibliography of the Social Sciences* (IBSS) (Andover, Hants: Taylor and Francis/Routledge). The IBSS provides comprehensive bibliographic services for the main social science disciplines of political science, anthropology, economics and sociology. *See also section 1.3.*

Bibliographic publications published in the period before 1990 lack the currency of more recent works. However, they do provide important reviews of the political science literature from the period. From a United States standpoint, Frederick Holler's work *Information Sources of Political Science* (Santa Barbara, CA: ABC-Clio, 1986) provides broad coverage of key political science resources: the role of bibliographies, journals, newspapers and government documents. A *Guide to Resources and Services of the Inter-University Consortium for Political and Social Research, 1976–1977* (Ann Arbor, MI: Inter-University Consortium for Political and Social Research, 1976) is another useful bibliography.

A truly international political science bibliography is to be found in *International Bibliography of Political Science/Bibliographie Internationale de Science Politique* (Paris: UNESCO 1953–1970). The publication is now dated, but it provides a classified list of books, periodicals and pamphlets for the 1953 to 1970 period. The *Bibliography* was produced by the International Committee of the Social Sciences.

7.3.2 Constitution and legal system

(a) Print

Few bibliographical publications have been compiled in the last decade on legal systems or constitutional law. Where such works exist, they reflect the traditional strength of North American scholarly work in this area. Two such publications are: *The American Constitution: an Annotated Bibliography* by Robert Janosik (Pasadena, Ca: Salem Press, 1991); and at state level *The Constitutions of the States: a State by State Guide and Bibliography of Current Scholarly Research* by Bernard Reams and Stuart Yoak (Dobbs Ferry, NY: Oceana Publications, 1988).

The 1980s in Canada witnessed intensive efforts to find a permanent resolution to the demands of the French majority in Quebec province and the counter demands of the English-speaking majority within the Canadian Confederation. This situation was reflected in the large quantity of bibliographical literature from the period. Two of the key bibliographies for the Canadian Constitution are Robert J. Jackson's *Canadian Government and Politics* (Ottawa: Department of the Secretary of State of Canada, 1988) and Eric Swanick and Doreen Whalen's *The Lake Meech Accord: a Bibliography* (Monticello, IL: Vance Bibliographies, 1988).

(b) Electronic

Encyclopedia of Law & Economics Bibliographical Database <allserv.rug.ac.be/~gdegeest/bibsearch.html>. This encyclopaedia attempts to survey the key literature on law and economics. Each entry contains a review of the literature, written by an authoritative figure in the field, and a bibliography.

7.3.3 Electoral systems

A detailed bibliography on electoral systems is available in Richard Katz's *International Bibliography on Electoral Systems* (Ottawa: International Political Science Association, 1989).

7.3.4 International relations

The United Nations Educational, Scientific and Cultural Organization (UNESCO) produces approximately 60 databases covering bibliographic, referral and factual databases within its areas of competence. UNESBIB <unesdoc.unesco.org/ulis/unesbib.html> is the bibliographical records database for UNESCO documents, publications and library collections.

7.3.5 Political behaviour

(a) Print

Polling and Survey Research Methods, 1935–1979: an Annotated Bibliography (London and Westport, CT: Greenwood Press, 1996) by Graham Walden, covers research studies on public opinion surveys in the United States, from the first opinion surveys in the 1930s.

(b) Electronic

National Election Studies (NES) Bibliography <www.umich.edu/~nes/resources/biblio/bib_q.htm> has approximately 3000 citations from the political science fields of electoral politics, public opinion and political participation, reflecting the emphasis of the organization. The bibliography is not, however, comprehensive because it only contains research which has incorporated NES datasets.

A Survey Research Bibliography <www.ukans.edu/cwis/units/coms2/po/srvbib.html> was prepared by Shelly Carden, of the University of Kansas, and it provides some valuable leads on survey research. It has, however, not been updated since 1996.

7.3.6 Political institutions

(a) Print

Two bibliographical compilations on Canadian political institutions are: Beatrice Corbett's *Canada: the Political Panorama* (London: Academic Relations Unit, Canadian High Commission, 1999); and Gregory Mahler's *Contemporary Canadian Politics, 1988–1994: an Annotated Bibliography* (Westport, CT: Greenwood Press, 1995).

The political scientist, Robert Goehlert, has been one of the most prolific compilers of bibliographies on political science topics. He has written extensively on parliamentary institutions. In 1990, his reference work, *The Parliament of Canada: a Select Bibliography* (Monticello, Il: Vance Bibliographies, 1990) was published. He has also written two sister publications, *The European Parliament: a* Bibliography (Monticello, IL: Vance Bibliographies, 1982) and *The Parliament of Great Britain: a Bibliography* (Lexington, MS: Lexington Books, 1982).

Within the United States, Robert Goehlert and Fenton S. Martin have compiled bibliographies on the three foundations of the American political system: The Presidency, Congress and The Supreme Court. They are: *The American Presidency: a Bibliography* (Washington, DC: Congressional Quarterly, 1987); *The US Supreme Court: a Bibliography* (Washington, DC: Congressional Quarterly, 1990); and *The United States Congress: an Annotated Bibliography, 1980–1993* (Washington, DC: Congressional Quarterly, 1995).

The British Council's *Bibliography on UK Governance* (London: British Council, 1997) lists sources of information on UK government developments, covering official publications, papers and articles. Robert Bunyan's *Researching the European State: a Critical Guide* (London: Statewatch, 1996) provides a comprehensive bibliography for the European Union and its politics since 1945.

(b) Electronic

Parlit Database <www.ipu.org/parlit-e/parlitsearch.asp> enables bibliographic references on parliamentary law and practice to be searched. *See also 7.8.*

7.3.7 Political theory

(a) Print

Gregory Brunk's publication, *Theories of Political Processes: a Bibliographic Guide to the Journal Literature, 1965–1995* (London and Westport, CT: Greenwood Press, 1997), is based on the premise that the large increase in the number of social science journals since the 1960s has reinforced the compartmentalisation of individual disciplines within the social sciences. In it he provides a general guide to important journal articles about politics from the mid-1960s to the 1990s.

Western Political Thought: a Bibliographical Guide to Post-war Research (Manchester and New York: Manchester University Press, 1995) by Michael Kenny and Robert Eccleshall, is a comprehensive guide to the published literature on political thought since 1945. Annotations are provided for most entries and, where appropriate, the author has indicated the significance of the entries.

(b) Electronic

Women in Politics: Bibliographic Database <www.ipu.org/bdf-e/BDfsearch.asp> currently holds 650 titles of recent works concerned with women in politics, drawn from books, reports and journal articles. The search facility allows users to specify type of document, geographic region, publishing organization, subject matter, author, title of periodical, and year of publication. There is also a subject keyword search facility.

7.3.8 Public policy and administration

(a) Print

The *Garland Annotated Bibliography Series* includes: *Public Policy Analysis: an Annotated Bibliography* edited by John S. Robey (New York: Garland Publishing, 1984); and *American Public Administration: a Bibliographical Guide to the Literature* by Gerald E. Caiden (New York: Garland Publishing, 1983). Howard E. McCurdy has produced another important bibliography covering public administration: *Public Administration: a Bibliographic Guide to the Literature* (New York: Dekker, 1986).

Although the *Encyclopedia of Public Affairs Information Sources*, edited by Paul Wasserman, James Kelly and Desider Vikor (Detroit, MI: Gale, 1988) is described as an encyclopaedia, it fits more appropriately into the bibliography section. The work contains more than 8000 citations for publications, organizations and other information sources for subjects related to public affairs.

(b) Electronic

SCAD Database <europa.eu.int/scad/index.htm> is a bibliographical database containing more than 300 000 records of European Community legislation, European Union (EU) official publications, articles from periodicals and opinions. The database can be searched by free text searching on the abstract or title, author, language, publication year, source and keywords. However, following a reorganization of Commission services, the *SCAD* database has no longer been updated from 1 March 2001. The database will nonetheless remain available. *See also section 7.11.*

BOPCRIS: British Official Publications Collaborative Reader Information Service <www.bopcris.ac.uk/> is a project to add all British official publications over the period 1688–1995 to a Web-based bibliographic database. The resource will be a valuable time-saver for researchers. The scale of the project is mammoth as there are estimated to be more than 250 000 parliamentary papers and an unknown number of non-Parliamentary publications.

▶ 7.4 DICTIONARIES

7.4.1 General

(a) Print

Frank Bealey and A. G. Johnson have compiled the excellent publication *The Blackwell Dictionary of Political Science* (Oxford: Blackwell Publishers, 1999). It guides readers through the terminology used in political science taking as its starting point a minimal level of subject knowledge. The dictionary is an invaluable reference tool, with more than 1000 political terms covered in the work and many terms are cross-referenced. Three other political dictionaries worthy of note are: *Cassell Dictionary of Modern Politics* compiled by CIRCA Research and Reference Information (London: Cassell, 1995); *The Concise Oxford Dictionary of Politics* edited by Ian McLean (Oxford: Oxford University Press, 1996); and David Robertson's *A Dictionary of Modern Politics* (London: Europa Publications, 1993).

On a lighter note, the quirky approach adopted by *Brewer's Politics: a Phrase and Fable Dictionary* (London: Cassell, 1995) to political terms that have become part of everyday language makes for colourful reading. The dictionary contains around 5000 entries.

(b) Electronic

This Nation political glossary <www.thisnation.com/glossary.html>. The terms are primarily of interest to a US audience.

7.4.2 Constitution and legal system

The Illustrated Dictionary of Constitutional Concepts (Washington, DC: Congressional Quarterly, 1996) by Robert L. Maddex, covers 400 common terms and ideas shared by constitutions worldwide. Many terms are cross-referenced and there is an abundant use of illustrations.

7.4.3 International relations

(a) Print

J. Denis Derbyshire and Ian Derbyshire's publication *Political Systems of the World* (Oxford: Helicon, 1999) is now in its third edition. They scrutinize different political systems in 165 nation states and 55 semi-sovereign states around the world. The tome has three sections: a comparative assessment of political systems; a description of the political system in each nation state and each semi-sovereign state; and coverage of regional and global organizations. A useful reference work for terms linked to twentieth century international politics is *The Dictionary of Twentieth Century World Politics* by J. M. Shafritz, P. Williams and R. S. Calinger (New York: H. Holt, 1993). It defines 4000 terms on topics ranging from people, doctrines, crises and events.

(b) Electronic

Dictionary of Politics, International Relations, Human Rights <home.t-online.de/home/Georg.Finsterwald/eortpage.htm> was compiled by George Finsterwald, and contains several thousand terms in German and English. It was, however, last updated in 1997.

7.4.4 Political theory

Roger Scruton's *A Dictionary of Political Thought* (London: Macmillan, 1996) is an authoritative dictionary on political philosophy. It has 1700 entries which summarize the thoughts of major political philosophers.

France has contributed some of the most important figures and concepts to political philosophy since the Enlightenment. *Dictionnaire de Philosophie Politique* by Philippe Raynaud and Stéphane Rials (Paris: Presses Universitaires de France, 1998) is not simply an alphabetical listing of political concepts, authors and their publications. Given the special importance of political philosophy to philosophy as a discipline and French culture, the publication aims to illuminate the traditional debates over, for example, sovereignty and power.

James Russell's *Marx-Engels Dictionary* (Westport, CT: Greenwood Press, 1980) is a useful guide to Marxian terminology. It contains only terms appearing in the writings of Marx and Engels and includes economic and philosophical terms.

7.4.5 Political institutions

(a) Print

The American political system is unique in the world because of its power structure and separation of powers. Much of the terminology used to describe the US political process comes from the Founding Fathers and the US Constitution. *The Dorsey Dictionary of American Government and Politics* (Chicago, IL: Dorsey Press, 1988) by J. Sharitz, is a useful aide to the terminology and processes. It also has a series of appendices containing the US Constitution and a guide to statistical sources of American Government information.

(b) Electronic

The Fast Times Political Dictionary <www.fast-times.com/political/political.html> seeks to empower citizens by increasing understanding of the political process and political terminology. Its target audience is everyone from high-school students to political editors. The dictionary is a useful and handy guide to terms, but it does have a distinct American slant. There is no overall search facility, merely 14 categories into which terms are arranged alphabetically.

7.4.6 Public policy and administration

(a) Print

William Fox and Ivan H. Meyer's *Public Administration Dictionary* (Hanekom, South Africa: Juta & Co., 1995) is a comprehensive guide to terminology in public administration. It defines terms, concepts, institutions, theories and law relative to the field.

(b) Electronic

A Glossary of Political Economy Terms <www.duc.auburn.edu/~johnspm/glossind.html> is produced by Paul Johnson of Auburn University, Alabama and is a useful guide to the language of political economy.

► 7.5 DIRECTORIES

7.5.1 General

(a) Print

The *Handbook of West European Political Science* (Colchester, Essex: European Consortium for Political Research, 1995) and its sister volume the *Handbook of Central and East European: Political Science* (Colchester, Essex: European Consortium for Political Research, 1994) were produced by Kenneth Newton and Claire Dekker. They provide information on political scientists based at higher education establishments in Europe, including their research interests. *See also 7.14.*

The American Political Science Association's *Biographical Directory* (Washington, DC: American Political Science Association, 1988) is the foremost directory of information on American political scientists available. It includes contact information, a representative list of publications and professional awards, together with employment histories for political scientists who are members of the Association. The Association's *Centennial Biographical Directory* is currently being compiled. It represents the first major update in more than 10 years and it will feature essays on political science's history and practice.

(b) Electronic

For information on European-based political scientists, the European Centre for Political Research (ECPR) is the obvious starting point. The *ECPR Directory of Members 2000* <www2.essex.ac.uk/ecpr-scripts/search.asp> is a fully searchable database of 6000 political scientists in ECPR member institutions. Previously, the information was only available in paper form. *See also 7.9* and *7.14.*

Address Directory: Politicians of the World <www.sneadsferry.com/community/politicians_of_the_world.htm> covers 196 countries and provides addresses for Monarchs, Presidents, Prime Ministers and Regional Governors.

NIRA's (National Institute for Research Advancement) World Directory of Think Tanks 1999 <gate.nira.go.jp/ice/tt-info/nwdtt99/id-nor.html#304> is freely available on the World Wide Web. It provides detailed information on all types of organizations and it is worldwide in its coverage.

7.5.2 Constitution and legal systems

Richard Kimber's *Constitutions, Treaties and Declarations* <www.psr.keele.ac.uk/const.htm> is a full listing of constitutional links in many countries. He also includes links to the conventions on human rights treaties on trade and commerce.

7.5.3 Electoral systems

In *Governments on the WWW: Institutions in the Area 'Elections'* <www.gksoft.com/govt/en/elections.html> each country entry has details of the relevant electoral organization or commission that oversees national elections. Another useful directory is *Elections and Electoral Systems around the World* <www.psr.keele.ac.uk/election.htm>. Richard Kimber's list of hyperlinks is organized into non-specific election resources and then by country.

7.5.4 International relations

Directory of International Organisations/Organisations Internationales et Européennes. (Washington, DC: Georgetown University Press, 1996) was produced by H. A. Schraeper. This directory provides information on international organizations that focus on the political, cultural and economic areas of world affairs. Entries include statements of purpose, membership and contact details for branch offices and headquarters.

7.5.5 Political institutions

The *Washington Information Directory* (Washington, DC: Congressional Quarterly). Annual. This directory provides address and fax details for government agencies, congressional committees and non-profit groups operating in the US capital. Two other directories which guide the user through the jungle of American government are the *Official Congressional Directory, 1999–2000* (Washington, DC: Congressional Quarterly, 1999) and the ninth edition of *Federal Regulatory Directory* (Washington, DC: Congressional Quarterly, 1999). The latter contains directory information about 113 federal regulatory agencies.

7.5.6 Political parties

Governments on the WWW: Political Parties <www.gksoft.com/govt/en/parties.html> is a comprehensive directory of political parties throughout the world arranged by country. Each political party name is displayed in its native language and the appropriate translation is given in square brackets after the original. This Website, which is maintained by Gunnar Anzinger, has won the Free Speech Blue Ribbon Online campaign award. Richard Kimber's *List of Political Parties* <www.psr.keele.ac.uk/parties.htm> is another excellent list of hyperlinks for political party Websites around the world.

▶ 7.6 ENCYCLOPAEDIAS

7.6.1 General

Two invaluable sources for gleaning background knowledge on aspects of political science are: the *Encyclopaedia of Government and Politics* by Maurice Kogan and Mary Hawkesworth (London: Routledge, 1992); and the *Survey of Social Science: Government and Politics Series (*Pasadena, CA: Salem Press, 1995*)* by Frank Magill and Joseph Bessette. The *Government and Politics Series*, by Salem Press, is the fourth in the series covering social science subjects. The large number of articles are divided into 13 general areas of study, including comparative government and political philosophy.

7.6.2 Constitution and legal systems

Encyclopedia of Law & Economics <encyclo.findlaw.com/index.html> is a site by Boudewijn Bouckaert (University of Ghent) and Gerrit De Geest (University of Ghent and University of Utrecht) which, they claim, surveys the whole of the literature for economics and law. The site has a number of sections: a bibliographical database, literature reviews and Web resources. *See also 7.3.*

7.6.3 Political institutions

World Encyclopedia of Parliaments and Legislatures (Washington, DC: Congressional Quarterly, 1997) is a two-volume set that covers the legislatures of all democracies in constitutional terms, as well as in practice. It is made up of more than 200 articles encapsulating country entries and essays on particular topics. Key characteristics of each legislature are scrutinised in detail: parliamentary procedures; relations with the executive branch and judiciary; and elections. This publication is the most authoritative available on democratic legislatures. Another useful publication, but slightly more dated is *The Blackwell Encyclopedia of Political Institutions* (Oxford: Blackwell Publishing, 1991) edited by Vernon Bogdanor. A companion volume to the similarly named *Blackwell Encyclopedia of Political Thought,* the same format of short, signed essays is used to describe the political institutions of the Western democracies, which are the focus of this publication. There are bibliographies for major political figures, concepts and institutions.

7.6.4 Political theory

(a) Print

The *Blackwell Encyclopaedia of Political Thought* (Oxford: Blackwell Publishing, 1987) is arguably the most comprehensive guide to political thought to have been collated. It covers the whole spectrum of the history and theory of politics, from Socrates to Rawls. The entries vary from shorter definitions to lengthy articles. The key concepts are defined and considered in their current and historical context.

In 1995, the renowned political scientist, Seymour Lipset, was editor-in-chief of the major, four-volume, scholarly work *The Encyclopedia of Democracy* (Washington, DC: Congressional Quarterly, 1995). This 1900-page tome considers democracy from its beginnings to the recent arrival of democracy in Eastern Europe. A concise version of the publication is available titled: *The Concise Encyclopedia of Democracy (*Washington, DC: Congressional Quarterly, 2000). It contains a large bibliographical section and it is aimed specifically at introductory college courses.

Kathlyn and Martin Gaye have produced the *Encyclopedia of Political Anarchy* (Santa Barbara, CA: ABC-Clio 1999) which charts individuals, political organizations and theories of anarchy that have existed during the last 300 years. Biographical entries range from Baader-Meinhoff to Emiliano Zapata.

(b) Electronic

The Internet Encyclopedia of Philosophy <www.utm.edu/research/iep/x> is a useful resource for a range of political ideas and the philosophers behind the ideas.

7.6.5 Public policy and administration

International Encyclopaedia of Public Policy and Administration (Oxford: Blackwell Publishing, 1998), edited by Jay Schafritz, is an exhaustive resource covering public policy and administration literature. It contains contributions from more than 400 authors over 850 articles. For each topic there is a description, explanation, history and bibliography. Part of Dekkers's *Public Administration and Public Policy Series* is the second edition of the *Encyclopedia of Policy Studies* (New York: Dekker, 1994). Edited by Stuart Nagel, it covers all aspects of policy studies – including concepts, utilization, formation and implementation – across all levels of government. This publication is an invaluable reference text.

▶ 7.7 GUIDES AND HANDBOOKS

7.7.1 General

A New Handbook of Political Science edited by Robert Goodin and Hans-Dieter Klingemann (Oxford: Oxford University Press, 1996) reviews developments in political science over the last two decades and places the changes in a historical context. It includes sections on; the discipline of political science; political institutions; political behaviour; comparative politics; international relations; political theory; public policy and administration; political economy; and political methodology. Forty-two academics have contributed commentaries to this expansive work. A more dated guide to the discipline of political science is available in the publication *Information Sources in Politics and Political Science Worldwide: a Survey Worldwide* (London: Butterworths, 1984), edited by Dermot Englefield and Gavin Drewry. The publication provides a British perspective on political science through a series of bibliographical essays.

An American perspective is available in *Political Science: a Guide to Reference and Information Sources* (Englewood, CO: Libraries Unlimited, 1990). Henry E. York's guide covers general social and political science resources, including reference books, databases and associations. Other European languages do not have the same breadth of coverage for political science. An important German publication, though now dated, is *Die Politische Dokumentation in der Bundesrepublik Deutschland* (Munchen-Pullach: Verlag okumentation, 1971) by W. Krumholz.

7.7.2 Electoral systems

Involvement by citizens in the election of representatives is the bedrock of most participatory styles of political system. *Campaign and Election Reform: a Reference Handbook* edited by G. Utter and R. Strickland (Santa Barbara, CA: ABC-Clio, 1997) reviews a number of contemporary election issues, such as electoral reform and the cost of elections. Whilst the US is its main focus, it does make some attempt to consider the broader, international perspective.

Details of the United Kingdom Labour Party's win in the 1997 General Election are included in the sixth edition of Robert Waller and Byron Criddle's publication, *The Almanac of British Politics* (London: Routledge, 1999). *The Almanac* is the definitive guide to Westminster constituencies and the political identity of the United Kingdom's regions. It profiles the social, economic and political characteristics of each Member of Parliament's constituency and also includes regional surveys.

Within the United States, *The Almanac of American Politics 2000: the Senate, the Representatives and the Governors: Their Records and Election Results, their States and Districts* (Washington, DC: National Journal Group Inc., 1999) edited by M. Barone and G. Ujifusais, is a comprehensive guide to all of the Congressional and Governorship incumbents in the 50 US states. Every congressional and gubernatorial seat is analysed for social and economic makeup.

The International Almanac of Electoral History by Tom Mackie (London: Macmillan, 1991) covers the election results for all Western industrialized nations, from the first election in individual countries.

7.7.3 International relations

Much political science research focuses on Europe and North America, a factor which skews the depiction of research undertaken elsewhere. Greenwood Press published a series of publications focusing on political science research within distinct geographical areas in the 1990s. David Dent edited the *Handbook of Political Science Research on Latin America: Trends from the 1960s to the 1990s* (Westport, CT: Greenwood Press, 1990) which examines 30 years of political science research in Latin America and the Caribbean region. The first section focuses on countries and regions in a comparative context, the second examines patterns of international relations, and the third contains a select bibliography of reference works on Latin American politics and details of major political research centres in the region.

Three other Greenwood Press publications which take a similar geographical approach are: the *Handbook of Political Science Research on the USSR and Eastern Europe: Trends from the 1950s to the 1990s* edited by Raymond Taras (Westport, CT: Greenwood Press, 1992); the *Handbook of Political Science Research on SubSaharan Africa: Trends from the 1960s to the 1990s* edited by Mark DeLancey (Westport, CT: Greenwood Press, 1992); and the *Handbook of Political Science Research on the Middle East and North Africa* edited by Bernard Reich (Westport, CT: Greenwood Press, 1998). The latter features a series of bibliographic essays by a variety of authors and covers research undertaken in the post-World War II period on the politics of Israel and the Arab States, and the seemingly intractable problem of a Palestinian state.

Ann Kelleher and Laura Klein use case studies to illustrate four global issues: international peace and conflict; the environment; cultural diversity; and global economic development, in *Global Perspectives: a Handbook for Understanding International Issues* (Upper Saddle River, NJ: Prentice Hall, 1998).

7.7.4 Political institutions

International Handbook of Local and Regional Government: a Comparative Analysis of Advanced Democracies (Brookfield, VT: Edward Elgar, 1993) by Alan Norton, provides detailed information on local and regional systems of government in advanced democracies. He focuses particularly on France, Germany, Sweden, Denmark, Italy, Britain, the United States and Japan.

7.7.5 Political methodology

D. Schmidt's *Expository Writing in Political Science: a Practical Guide* (New York: HarperCollins College Publishers, 1993) provides guidance on writing about politics and subjects related to political science. It is aimed at undergraduate and postgraduate students. Three other publications which are worth mentioning are: *Methods for Political Inquiry: the Discipline, Philosophy, and Analysis of Politics* edited by Stella Z. Theodoulou and Rory O'Brien (Upper Saddle River, NJ: Prentice Hall, 1999); *Case Study Research: Design and Methods* by Robert Yin (Thousand Oaks, CA: Sage Publications, 1994); and *Methods and Models: a Guide to the Empirical Analysis of Formal Models in Political Science* (Cambridge and New York: Cambridge University Press, 1999) by Rebecca Morton.

7.7.6 Political parties

The three-volume *World Encyclopedia of Political Systems and Parties* (New York: Facts On File Inc., 1999) is an authoritative source on political parties and political structures. Its 1600 pages provide a global perspective and depth of information that cannot be matched elsewhere.

The complexity of Europe's national and regional political parties is covered extremely well by F. Jacobs' *Western European Political Parties – a Comprehensive Guide* (Harlow, Essex: Longman Group, 1989). The book divides political parties into three categories: political parties in the context of European Union member countries; other West European democracies; and Western European political groupings, such as the Council of Europe. The parties themselves provided all the background information. The history and main features of each country's political system are analysed in the book. The greatest drawback to the publication is the amount of time that has passed since it was published. There has been a great deal of change over the intervening period and the topical policy issues in the book are somewhat dated. *Political Parties of the Americas and the Caribbean: a Reference Guide* (Harlow, Essex: Longman Group, 1992) by John Coggins and D. S. Lewis, is a useful reference work for political parties in the region.

7.7.7 Political theory

A Companion to Contemporary Political Philosophy (Oxford: Blackwell, 1993) edited by Robert E. Goode and Philip Pettit, comprises two sections. The first section examines the contribution other social science disciplines make to discussions on political philosophy and the second section is an examination of political ideologies themselves. There is also coverage of topics of current concern, such as environmentalism.

▶ 7.8 WEBSITES

7.8.1 General

National Political Index <www.politicalindex.com>. It aspires to be 'a one-stop-shop for substantive political information', providing links to 3500 Websites and adding a further 50 each month. It aims to empower individuals and counteract the influence of television advertising within the US political system. Although links are provided to non-US oriented Websites, the focus of NPI is primarily the United States. Thirty-two categories are used to subdivide the Web links on the site, which range from 'Federal Elected Officials' and 'State and Local Officials' to 'Online Political Magazines'.

ThisNation: the American Government and Politics Portal <www.thisnation.com/index.html>. This site describes itself as 'the most comprehensive guide to American government and politics on the net'. It was created and is maintained by Dr Jonathan Mott, formerly a political science professor at the University of Oklahoma and Brigham Young University. It features an extensive library of important documents in American political history; daily political briefings with hypertext links to major media outlets; a search engine covering 5000 political Websites;

and a 'Capital Watch'. The Website provides an online textbook on American government and politics and other learning tools for teachers and students.

Political Resources on the Net <www.politicalresources.net>. This resource has links to political parties, organizations, government and media sites available on the World Wide Web, categorized by country. In terms of its coverage – more than 20 000 hyperlinks to politically oriented Websites at the last count – there is no other Website, which can surpass it. The global nature of the coverage is also breathtaking. A good additional feature is the Political Site of the Week.

British Politics Pages <www.ukpol.co.uk/>. A wealth of information on British politics: biographies and contact details for Members of Parliament, links to UK local authorities and Non-Governmental Organizations and an interesting diary feature.

Polis: the Starting Point to European Union politics <www.polis.net/>. This site combines up-to-date news of events within the European Union with hyperlinks categorized within specific subject areas. These include governments, parliaments and elections.

Some of the best gateways are available through United States university Websites. Four key sites are:

Political Science Resources <sun3.lib.uci.edu/~dtsang/pol.htm>. This comprehensive listing of political Websites was drawn-up by the social science bibliographer, Daniel S. Tsang, from the University of California, Irvine. A table of contents is used to subdivide the links into searchable groups. Some of the categories in the table of contents reflect the California base of the author. There is also a large number of links in the 'General Resource', 'Journals and Newsletters' and 'Political and Related Data Sources'.

Poly-Cy - Internet Resources for Political Science <www.polsci.wvu.edu/polycy/>. This Website has a good list of links covering most areas of political science and is updated regularly. The Poly-Cy site was only one of four political science resources to receive the seal of approval from the Argus Clearing House.

Political Science Research Resources <www.vanderbilt.edu/~rtucker/polisci/miscpol.html>. A very well indexed list of links.

Ultimate Political Science Links Page <ednet.rvc.cc.il.us/~PeterR/PSLinks.htm>. This gateway is very clearly laid out and links to a valuable range of resources. It includes a list of Websites for political science text publishers.

From a British perspective, two of the best political science gateways are *Richard Kimber's Political Science Resources* <www.psr.keele.ac.uk/psr.htm> and *Political Science Association Gateway to WWW* <www.psa.ac.uk/www/>. The Political Science Association Website has more than 3000 links. There is the usual indexing of links by constitution, media and archives, but the site has the added benefit of having an internal search engine, which allows for focused searching.

Globally, the hyperlinks listed at the *International Political Science Association Guide to General Politics Resources* <www.ucd.ie/~ipsa/genpols.html> is difficult to match. The list of hyperlinks is broken down into general links, political subfields, basic information, official servers, periodicals and news resources and miscellaneous. The only unfortunate aspect is that the links page does not appear to be regularly updated.

The WWW Virtual Library: International Affairs Resources <www.etown.edu/vl/>. There are more than 2000 links available from this Website on international relations topics.

7.8.2 Political theory

Four excellent Webpages listing political philosophy links are:

Richard Kimber's Directory of Political Thought Hyperlinks <www.psr.keele.ac.uk/thought.htm>. It is a very comprehensive list and it ranges from links for Aristotle's discourses to the Federalist Papers.

Political Philosophy/Political Theory <www.library.ubc.ca/poli/theory.html>. An excellent list of links on political philosophy, prepared by Iza Laponce.

Yahoo Political Theory <dir.yahoo.com/Social_Science/Political_Science/Political_Theory/>. A useful site from this well-known Internet directory.

Thinking Politica's Political Theory Section <home.freeuk.net/ethos/theory.htm> has links to electronic versions of political philosophy texts. These include *The Social Contract* by J. J. Rousseau and Immanuel Kant's *Perpetual Peace*. There are also a number of essays and papers on key philosophical questions.

Although Marxism has lost some of its political relevancy with the fall of the Soviet Union and the Eastern Bloc, its influence on the social sciences is still manifest.

Marxism <www.theglobalsite.ac.uk/marxism.htm> is an extremely useful directory of Marxist texts. The Website has a keyword search facility. *The Civil Society & Democracy* <www.theglobalsite.ac.uk/civilsociety.htm> section of the Website is also worth scanning. The *Global Site* is maintained by the University of Sussex and its remit is world politics, society and culture.

7.8.3 Constitution and legal system

French Studies Web: Politics and Government – Constitutions and Civil Codes <www.lib.byu.edu/~rdh/wess/fren/constitu.html> provides English translations of the French, Belgian, Swiss and Luxembourg constitutions.

7.8.4 Electoral systems

As its title suggests *Elections from Around the World* <www.agora.it/elections/election.htm> is excellent for information on elections. The site also has an electoral calendar for forthcoming elections, information on political parties, political institutions and political databases.

7.8.5 Political institutions

Assessing Egovernment (Brown Policy Report) <www.insidepolitics.org>. The Internet opens up a completely new perspective for how citizens communicate with government or their elected representatives. Potentially, the Internet could spell an improvement in government operations in terms of response times and efficiency. A team of researchers, led by Professor Darrell West, from the Taubman Centre for Public Policy, Brown University, examined the content of 1813 US Federal and State Government Websites. The researchers analysed the sites for 27 different features and rated them out of a 100.

The Inter-Parliamentary Union's *Parline Database* – a derivative of *Parliaments Online* – at <www.ipu.org/parline-e/parlinesearch.asp> provides comprehensive and up-to-date information on parliaments around the globe. There is a simple search facility that lists all countries alphabetically and a more advanced search capability for experienced users. For each country where a national legislature exists, the database provides general information on the Parliament's chambers, a description of the electoral system used, the result of the most recent election, details of the Presidency of the Chamber and information on the mandate and status of parliamentary members.

Governments on the WWW: Parliaments <www.gksoft.com/govt/en/parliaments.html>. A comprehensive list of hyperlinks to national parliamentary Websites.

7.8.6 Public policy and administration

ARENA (Advanced Research on the Europeanisation of the Nation State) is a research programme on the changes taking place in Europe, focusing on the role of the nation state within this framework. The programme is under the auspices of the Research Council of Norway and there is a coordinating unit, *ARENA*, based at the University of Oslo. Information is provided in Norwegian and English. There are two Websites: <olymp.wu-wien.ac.at/erpa/arena.htm> and <www.sv.uio.no/arena/>.

A related archive that is aimed at providing a common access point for working papers in the field of European integration research is available at the *European Research Paper Archive (ERPA)* <olymp.wu-wien.ac.at/erpa/>. There are currently 387 papers on the ERPA database.

7.8.7 Political methodology

There are few Websites that are devoted to political methodology. One such site is Richard Tucker's *Statistics and Computing* <www.vanderbilt.edu/~rtucker/methods/econometrics> list. It has links for Game Theory, Dynamic Models, Data Archives and Artificial Intelligence.

▶ 7.9 JOURNALS

The selection criteria for journals included in this section is their appearance in the *Journal Citation Reports: Social Sciences Edition* (Philadelphia, PA: Institute for Scientific Information) and their reputation as core journals in the political science field.

7.9.1 General

American Journal of Political Science (ISSN 0092–5853) (Madison, WI: University of Wisconsin Press,1950–). Quarterly. This refereed journal covers the major areas of political science including American policy, public policy, international relations, comparative politics, political methodology and political theory. It also has a workshop section covering new developments in research methodology. Available electronically.

American Political Science Review (ISSN 0003–0554) (Washington, DC: American Political Science Association. 1906–). Quarterly. This refereed title was first published in 1906. It covers all aspects of political science and it includes a large book review section in each issue. Available electronically.

Annals of The American Academy of Political And Social Science (ISSN 0002–7162) (Thousand Oaks, CA: Sage Publications, 1891–). Bimonthly. Few refereed journals in an age of specialization can match the breadth of coverage offered by the *Annals*. Each bi-monthly edition focuses on a significant topic of interest.

AntePodium (AtP) <www.vuw.ac.nz/atp> (Wellington, New Zealand: Victoria University of Wellington; School of Political Science and International Relations, 1995–). Irregular. *AntePodium* is an electronic, peer-reviewed journal that aims to transcend the traditional boundaries of political science. It draws on other disciplines for published articles in the areas of politico-strategic, politico-economic and politico-cultural aspects of international relations.

Australian Journal of Political Science (ISSN 1036–1146) (Basingstoke: Carfax Publishing, 1966–). Three issues a year. This refereed journal is a key title within Australian political science. Available electronically.

Australian Journal of Politics And History (ISSN 0004–9522) (Oxford: Blackwell Publishing Ltd., 1955–). Quarterly. A peer-reviewed journal focusing on international relations, political studies and history, with particular reference to Australia and modern Europe. Available electronically.

British Journal of Political Science (ISSN 0007–1234) (Cambridge and New York: Cambridge University Press, 1971–). Three issues a year. This broad-based, refereed journal draws scholarly articles from all areas of political science and across a wide range of countries. Available electronically.

Canadian Journal of Political Science/Revue Canadienne De Science Politique (ISSN 0008–4239) (Waterloo, Canada: Wilfrid Laurier University Press, 1968–). Quarterly. A refereed publication of the Canadian Political Science Association.

Comparative Political Studies (ISSN 0010–4140) (Thousand Oaks, CA: Sage Publications, 1968–). Ten issues a year. An excellent forum for the disussion of comparative politics. Available electronically.

East European Politics And Societies (ISSN 0888–3254) (Berkeley, CA: University of California Press, 1967–). Three issues a year. A quality, refereed publication, focusing on a fascinating area for political study.

European Journal of Political Research (ISSN 0304–4130) (Dordrecht, The Netherlands: Kluwer Academic, 1973–). Eight issues a year. The journal is composed of refereed articles, research notes and book reviews. Available electronically.

Government Information Quarterly (ISSN 0740–624X) (New York: Elsevier Science, 1984–). Quarterly. The refereed journal is cross-disciplinary in approach and analyses current government information policy, its philosophical background and new trends. Available electronically.

Harvard International Journal of Press-Politics (ISSN 1081–180X) (Cambridge, MA: M I T Press, 1996–). Quarterly. A refereed journal dedicated to analysing the interaction of the press, politics, and public policymaking. It seeks to address the gap between political science research and the broader world of the media.

International Political Science Review (ISSN 0192–5121) (London: Sage Publications, 1980–). Quarterly. The official, refereed journal of the International Political Science Association. It is dedicated to creating and disseminating rigorous political enquiry. Available electronically.

Journal of Conflict Resolution (ISSN 0022–0027) (Thousand Oaks, CA: Sage Publications, 1956–). Bimonthly. This refereed title focuses on war and peace, between and within nations. Available electronically.

Journal of Government Information (ISSN 1352–0237) (Oxford: Pergamon-Elsevier Science, 1974–). Bimonthly. A refereed journal which publishes articles on all types of government information, including bibliographical control. Available electronically.

Journal of Political Economy (ISSN 0022–3808) (Chicago, Ill: University of Chicago Press, 1892–). Bimonthly. This refereed journal publishes analytical, interpretative, and empirical studies in traditional political economy areas, such as fiscal theory and macro-economic policy, but also in interdisciplinary fields such as the history of economic thought.

The Journal of Politics (ISSN 0022–3816) (New York: Blackwell Publishers, 1939–). Quarterly. The journal of the Southern Political Science Association, is the oldest regional journal in the United States. It publishes refereed articles on political theory, American politics, comparative politics and international politics. Available electronically.

Mediterranean Politics (ISSN 1362–9395) (London: Frank Cass, 1996–). Three issues a year. The refereed journal's focus is the problems of the whole Mediterranean basin, including the challenges imposed by Islamic fundamentalism, environmental degradation and increasing migration. Available electronically.

New Republic (ISSN 0028–6583) (Washington, DC: New Republic Inc., 1914–). Weekly. A 'journal of opinion' that provides commentary on current political, economic, social and cultural issues.

Osterreichische Zeitschrift Fur Politikwissenschaft (ISSN 0378–5149) (Vienna, Austria: Verlag Gesellschaftskritik, 1972–). Quarterly. Text is in German and English. The journal publishes political science articles with a special emphasis on Austria. Available electronically.

Political Geography (ISSN 0962–6298) (Oxford: Elsevier Science). Eight issues a year. An interdisciplinary, refereed journal which brings together three strands in political geography research: quantitative studies (such as electoral geography), political economy approaches, and traditional topics (such as the spatial structure of the state). Available electronically.

Political Science Manuscripts (PSM) <www.tenj.edu/~psm> (Ewing, NJ: Department of Political Science, College of New Jersey) was created by Dr. William J Ball in a project to distribute political science research and scholarship online. All the abstracts and manuscripts on *PSM* are searchable.

The Political Quarterly (ISSN 0032–3179) (Oxford: Blackwell Publishing, 1930–). Bi-monthly. A long-established, refereed title providing an international forum for debate. Available electronically.

Political Science Quarterly (ISSN 0032–3195) (New York: Academy of Political Science, 1886–). Quarterly. It is the oldest continuously produced journal in the discipline, covering public and international affairs. Selected full-text, refereed articles are available online. The journal also has an extensive book review section.

Political Studies (ISSN 0032–3217) (Guildford: Butterworth Scientific, 1953–). Five issues a year. The leading United Kingdom political science journal, publishing peer-reviewed, scholarly work from across the whole range of the discipline. Available electronically.

Politics and Society (ISSN 0032–3292) (Thousand Oaks, CA: Sage Publications, 1970–). Quarterly. A key refereed title, which takes a multi-disciplinary approach to the role of politics in society. Available electronically.

Politics And The Life Sciences (ISSN 0730–9384) (Guildford: Beech Tree Publishing, 1982–). Semiannual. This refereed journal provides a forum for academics interested in researching the area where politics and the life sciences meet.

PS: Political Science and Politics (ISSN 1049–0965) (Washington, DC: American Political Science Association, 1969–). Quarterly. The aim of this journal is to act as a record for the political science profession in the United States. It is the best source of career opportunities in the political science field in the US.

Revue Francais de Science Politique (ISSN 0035–2950) (Paris: Presses de la Fondation Nationale des Sciences Politiques, 1951–). Bimonthly. The journal is the most prestigious French language journal in political science. It covers the area of French politics, international relations, sociological and institutional analysis, political history and philosophy. It aims to present the best material in observation, thinking and methodological criticism.

Scandinavian Political Studies (ISSN 0080–6757) (Oxford: Blackwell Publishing, 1966–). Quarterly. Refereed journal. Political studies in Scandinavia are presented to a international forum of political scientists and sociologists. Text in English. Available electronically.

Schweizerische Zeitschrift für politische Wissenschaft/Revue Suisse de Politique/ Swiss Political Science Review (ISSN 1420–3529) (Zurich: Seismo Press for the Swiss Political Science Association, 1995–). Quarterly. Articles are published in English, French and German. Available electronically.

West European Politics (ISSN 0140–2382) (London: Frank Cass, 1978–). Quarterly. This refereed journal covers political and social issues in Western Europe, including coverage of all national elections. Available electronically.

Women & Politics (ISSN 0195–7732)(New York: Haworth Press, 1980–). Quarterly. A peer-reviewed journal of research and policy studies.

7.9.2 Constitution and legal system

Harvard Journal On Legislation (ISSN 0017–808X) (Cambridge, MA: Harvard Law School, 1964–). Semiannual. This refereed journal examines the current state of law and the theorectical background to legisation. The publishers also print a biannual Congress Issue, which includes essays written by members of Congress.

7.9.3 Electoral systems

Electoral Studies (ISSN 0261–3794) (Amsterdam: Elsevier Science, 1982–). Quarterly. A refereed journal covering all aspects of voting, publishing papers on such topics as the relationship between votes and seats. Available electronically.

7.9.4 International relations

Foreign Affairs (ISSN: 0015–7120)(New York: Council of Foreign Relations, 1922–). Bimonthly. A scholarly journal dedicated to the discussion of international politics and economic thought.

International Affairs (ISSN 0020–5850) (Oxford: Blackwell Publishing, 1922–). Quarterly. Britain's leading journal of international relations, which has been particularly influential in European policy debates. Available electronically.

International Studies Quarterly (ISSN 0020–8833) (Malden, MA: Blackwell Publishers, 1957–). Quarterly. The refereed journal provides an Asian perspective on international affairs and regional studies. Available electronically.

Peace and Conflict Studies <www.trenton.edu/~psm/pcs> (Fairfax, VA: Lentz Peace Research Association on behalf of The Network of Peace and Conflict Studies, 1994–). Irregular. The online publication is sponsored by Political Science Manuscripts. The journal aims to highlight various issues in peace research and conflict analysis.

Review of International Studies (ISSN 0260–2105) (Cambridge and New York: Cambridge University Press, 1974–). Quarterly. The journal reviews law, politics and history in the international arena. Available electronically

Review of International Political Economy (ISSN 0969–2290) (London: Routledge, 1994–). Quarterly. The journal is interdisciplinary in its approach and is committed to publishing innovative research. Available electronically.

World Policy Journal (ISSN 0740–2775) (New York: World Policy Institute, 1983–). Quarterly. The journal was cited by the *New York Times* as one of the leading journals in international relations in 1998.

7.9.5 Political behaviour

American Politics Research (ISSN 0044–7803) (Thousand Oaks, CA: Sage Publications, 1973–). Quarterly. This journal was formerly entitled *American Politics Quarterly*. The journal promotes research into all areas of US political behaviour, as well as social problems requiring political solutions. Available electronically.

Politique et Societé (ISSN 1203–9438) (Montreal, Canada: Societé Quebecoise de Science Politique, Université de Quebec à Montreal, 1982–). Three issues a year. The journal text is primarily in French, but summaries are in English and French.

Political Behavior (ISSN 0190–9320) (New York: Kluwer Academic/ Plenum Publishing, 1979–). Quarterly. An interdisciplinary, refereed journal examining the interaction of individuals and groups with the policy process. Available electronically.

Political Psychology (ISSN 0162–895X) (Malden, MA: Blackwell Publishers, 1979–). Quarterly. An interdisciplinary journal covering the application of psychology within political studies. Available electronically.

7.9.6 Political institutions

Journal of Democracy (ISSN 1045–5736) (Baltimore, MA: Johns Hopkins University Press, 1990–). Quarterly. A scholarly journal dedicated to the study of democracy and democratic institutions. Available electronically.

Parliamentary Affairs (ISSN 0031–2290) (Oxford: Oxford University Press, 1947–). Quarterly. The journal covers all aspects of Parliamentary democracy in the United Kingdom and elsewhere.

7.9.7 Political methodology

Journal of Policy Modeling (ISSN 0161–8938) (New York: Elsevier Science, 1979–). Bimonthly. The refereed periodical examines the interdependence of economic, social and political forces in the relationship between national and regional systems. Available electronically.

Political Analysis (ISSN 1047–1987) (Boulder, CO: Westview Press, 1989–). The journal was previously published on an annual basis. From 1999 it has been issued quarterly. *Political Analysis* is the official journal of the Society for Political Methodology and the Political Methodology Section of the American Political Science Association. It is concerned with the entire range of interests and topics that fall within the gamut of political research, though the emphasis is on how such research should be conducted. Available electronically.

Public Choice (ISSN 0048–5829) (Dordrecht, The Netherlands: Kluwer Academic Publishers, 1966–). Sixteen issues a year. The journal considers the application of economic methods to political problems. Available electronically.

7.9.8 Political parties

Party Politics (ISSN 1354–0688) (Thousand Oaks, CA: Sage Publications, 1995–). Quarterly. A forum for examining the character and organization of political parties within their respective national systems. Available electronically.

7.9.9 Political theory

Journal of Theoretical Politics (ISSN 0951–6298) (Thousand Oaks, CA: Sage Publications, 1989–). Quarterly. This refereed journal seeks to encourage the development of theory in the study of the political process. Available electronically.

Political Theory (ISSN 0090–5917) (Thousand Oaks, Ca: Sage Publications , 1973–). Bimonthly. A key journal within this area. Available electronically.

7.9.10 Public policy and administration

Administration & Society (ISSN 0095–3997) (Thousand Oaks, CA: Sage Publications, 1974–). Bimonthly. This highly regarded, refereed journal aims to advance understanding of human and public service organizations, their administrative processes and the consequent effect upon society. Available electronically.

American Review of Public Administration (ISSN 0275–0740) (Thousand Oaks, CA: Sage Publications, 1967–). Quarterly. A key refereed journal. Available electronically.

Journal of European Public Policy (ISSN 1350–1763) (London: Routledge, 1994–). Quarterly. This refereed journal publishes analytical articles on public policy in Europe.

Policy and Politics (ISSN 0305–5736) (Bristol: Policy Press, University of Bristol, 1972–). Quarterly. Refereed journal. The text is in English, with abstracts available in French and Spanish. The journal covers the origin, implementation and impact of public policy.

Policy Studies Journal (ISSN 0190–292X) (Urbana, IL: Policy Studies Organization, University of Illinois, 1972–). Quarterly. The focus of this refereed journal is on the application of political and social science to public policy problems.

Public Administration (ISSN 0033–3298) (Oxford: Blackwell Publishing, 1923–). Quarterly. A key title covering all aspects of public administration. Available electronically.

Public Administration Review (ISSN 0033–3352) (Washington, DC: American Society for Public Administration, 1940–). Bimonthly.

An important, refereed title from the American Society for Public Administration.

► 7.10 ABSTRACTS, INDEXES AND DATABASES

(a) Print

International Political Science Abstracts (Paris: Fondation Nationale des Sciences Politique, 1950–) is published by The International Political Science Association from the Fondation Nationale des Sciences Politique. It is updated six times a year and has a comprehensive index. The key abstract sources for IPSA are international scholarly journals and yearbooks. A special emphasis is placed on countries or areas where information is scarce. The main areas covered are: methodology and theory; political ideas; institutions and process; international relations; and national and regional studies. *See also (b) Electronic* below.

PAIS International in Print (New York: OCLC Public Affairs Information Service, 1972–). *PAIS* is published monthly and an annual subscription includes monthly issues, author and subject indexes. *PAIS* subject headings, containing 8000 indexing terms are available in the print version for users, for more effective searching of the indexed material. The subject areas covered are current events, economics, foreign affairs, government regulations, political science, public administration and social issues. The primary objective of *PAIS* is to provide better access to public affairs literature at all levels. *See also (b) Electronic* below.

ABC Pol Sci – A Bibliography of Contents (Santa Barbara, CA: ABC-Clio 1969–). *ABC Pol Sci* lists and indexes the tables of contents for 300 international journals in their original languages. Approximately 10 000 new records are added to the bibliographical database each year. Its primary focus is political science and government, and on a secondary level, sociology, law and economics. The main section of *ABC Pol Sci* is arranged alphabetically by journal title, and in each edition there are also separate subject and author indexes. *ABC Pol Sci* is currently available on CD-ROM and it will soon become available on the Internet.

(b) Electronic

The Brown Electronic Article Review Service (Bears) in Moral and Political Philosophy <www.brown.edu/Departments/Philosophy/bears/homepage.html> is the type of information resource which, in terms of quality, puts the Internet on a level with dedicated databases. *Bears* provides comprehensive coverage of the political philosophy literature and its entries include: essays, primary texts, reviews and published books.

International Political Science Abstracts (Paris: Fondation Nationale des Sciences Politique, 1950–). CD-ROM and Internet versions are available from SilverPlatter Information <www.silverplatter.com>. IPSA follows a policy of completely indexing approximately 45 core journals, though this may vary year on year. In addition, articles in another 900 journals are indexed on a selective basis. There are currently more than 64 000 abstracts available on the database covering the period 1989 to present. Around 7400 new abstracts are added annually. The vast majority of abstracts are in English and the remainder in French. IPSA's indexing allows records to be accessed by searching on a variety of fields including descriptors, title, journal name index and abstract.

PAIS International <www.pais.org/products/index.stm> (New York: OCLC Public Affairs Information Service, 1972–). The *PAIS* online database (now merged with OCLC to form the *OCLC Public Affairs Information Service*) contains 440 000 indexed records and another 14 000 records are added annually. The sources used are published in 60 countries and in six languages. They include: government publications, statistical yearbooks, conference proceedings, books and reports as well as journals. All abstracts and subject headings used in indexed records are in English. One of the great strengths of *PAIS* is its indexing of grey literature. In 1999, *PAIS* indexed 951 journals, 1036 Internet documents and 5600 books, reports and pamphlets. *PAIS* is also available on CD-ROM and can be accessed through online database hosts and fee-based services on the Internet. *See also 1.10.*

Spicers' Centre for Europe is a commercial database that provides citations and abstracts of articles appearing in a wide range of European Union publications. The database holds 70 000 abstracts dating from 1987 onwards and a further 10 000 are added each year. In 1998, *Spicers Centre for Europe* was purchased by Lawtel and the database is now only available through *EU Interactive* <www.euinteractive.com>.

▶ 7.11 OFFICIAL PUBLICATIONS

Government publications have been affected by the same revolution that has changed academic publishing so fundamentally over the last 10 years. Electronic versions of government publications are replacing the printed version for search, retrieval and storage purposes as the preferred option for librarians and researchers. This section is subdivided by country or region.

7.11.1 United Kingdom

The Daily List (London: The Stationery Office) provides details of government publications. It includes Parliamentary Publications, Statutory

Instruments, Official and Agency Publications, and publications from the devolved Assemblies. *The Daily List* is also available from the Stationery Office bookshop Website at: <www.clicktso.com>.

Two key Websites for parliamentary information are the homepages of the *House of Commons* <www.parliament.the-stationery-office.co.uk/pa/cm/home.htm> and the *House of Lords* <www.parliament.the-stationery-office.co.uk/pa/ld/ldhome.htm>. The House of Commons site includes access to: *Hansard* (the Official Report of Debates in the House of Commons); the *Weekly Information Bulletin* – which provides details of the recent and forthcoming business of the House of Commons; *House of Commons Order Papers* – published each day when the House of Commons is in session, providing details of questions, motions and other business to be considered on that day; *House of Commons Select Committee Reports*; and *House of Commons Factsheets* – brief, informative descriptions of various facets of the work of and background to; the House of Commons. The House of Lords pages include access to *Hansard* (the Official Report of Debates in the House of Lords); *House of Lords Select Committee Reports*; and the *Weekly Information Bulletin* – which includes details of much of the recent and forthcoming business of the House of Lords.

BOPCAS – British Official Publications Current Awareness Service <www.soton.ac.uk/~bopcas/>. BOPCAS aims to increase the productivity of UK policy related research work by reducing the amount of time spent searching for relevant government publications. The BOPCAS database is available on the Internet and United Kingdom Parliamentary or Departmental publications are indexed by date, publication type and policy area. The *UK Online Open Government Information Service* Website <www.open.gov.uk/search/search.htm> provides access to all UK Government departments and agencies, as well as public sector organizations. Some official publications are available in full-text through this Website by selecting the government department required. *See also 1.11.1.*

7.11.2 France

Le Journal Officiel 'Lois et Décrets' (Paris: Direction des Journaux Officiel) is the official record of the French Government. The JO is published daily and it contains the text of French laws and regulations. Publication in the JO marks the point at which the legislation is enacted. The text can also be searched on the Website at: <www.journal-officiel.gouv.fr>/.

Details of French legislation, Parliamentary proceedings and jurisprudence can be searched from 1990 onwards at the *Jurifrance* Website <www.jurifrance.com/>. In addition, the entire contents of *Le Journal officiel 'Lois et Décrets'* for the last decade can be searched.

7.11.3 European Union

The Official Journal of the European Communities (OJ) is the daily record of the European Union. It is made up of a number of separate publications including: 'C' series – Information and Notices and 'L' Series – Law. 'C' and 'L' versions of the OJ are available on the *EUR-LEX Portal to European Union Law* at: <europa.eu.int/eur-lex/en/oj/index.html>. In addition, the OJ is also available from *CELEX* <europa.eu.int/celex/htm/celec_en.htm> a key resource for European Union law. *See also 1.11.2.*

7.11.4 United States, Canada and Australia

The *United States Government Printing Office* (GPO) <www.access.gpo.gov/su_docs/index.html>. Users can search the GPO Website for current US Government publications which are indexed by categories such as legislative, judicial and administrative decisions. The *Federal Register* (Washington, DC: Office of Federal Register) is the official daily publication for Rules, Proposed Rules, and Notices of Federal agencies and organizations, as well as Executive Orders and other Presidential Documents. The GPO Access Webpage allows users to search the *Federal Register* from 1995 onwards. The *Congressional Record* (Washington, DC: Joint Committee on Printing, Congress of the United States), the official daily record of Congressional proceedings, can be searched via the same Website.

A new government portal *FirstGov* <www.firstgov.gov/> provides a one-stop Website for more than 20 000 US Federal Government resources. The site aims to 'expand the reach of democracy and make government more responsive to citizens.' *See also 1.11.3.*

Australian publications of the Australian Commonwealth Government can be searched on the Australian Government Index of Publications (AGIP) database by clicking on the AGIP logo at the following Website: <Webpac.ausinfo.gov.au/>. Simple and advanced search options can be used to scrutinize bibliographical entries of Commonwealth publications.

Canadian Government Publications <canada.gc.ca/publications/publication_e.html>. This Website lists publications that have been published by the Parliament of Canada, Federal Departments and Statistics Canada. Users can browse the publications which are indexed by subject.

▶ 7.12 STATISTICS

7.12.1 General

The Inter-university Consortium for Political and Social Research (ICPSR) <www.icpsr.umich.edu>. ICSPR is a not-for-profit organization, located at the University of Michigan's Institute for Social Research, which allows access to the world's largest archive of computerised social science data. Archive users can view study datasets and abstracts. The studies are broadly split into a United States category and nations other than the United States.

Governments on the WWW: Institutions in the Area 'Statistics' <www.gksoft.com/govt/en/statistics.html>. This Website has an excellent list of links to national and regional statistical offices.

Statistical Resources on the Web <www.lib.umich.edu/libhome/Documents.center/stats.html>. A useful general listing, not exclusively concerned with political science.

The Society for Political Methodology and the Political Methodology Section of the American Political Science Association <polmeth.calpoly.edu/>. The Website's main function is to serve as a gateway to the society's Electronic Paper Archive and to its *Political Analysis Journal* and *Political Methodologist Newsletter*. Political methodology focuses on the examination of empirical data and, consequently, there are a number of links to published and unpublished data sets on the Research and Teaching Webpage.

Poly-Cy <www.polsci.wvu.edu/polycy/psstat.html>. The Website has an excellent list of links to research methodology, statistics and data sources.

Data on the Net <odwin.ucsd.edu/idata/>. This Website has available 851 indexed sites of social science statistical data and data catalogues.

Online Survey Research/Public Opinion Centers: a Worldwide Listing <www.ukans.edu/cwis/units/coms2/po/index.html>. An excellent page of hyperlinks maintained by the Department of Communication Studies at the University of Kansas. The listing has links to university-based research centres in the United States and around the world, professional associations, public opinion survey firms and other relevant areas.

7.12.2 United States

National Election Studies <www.umich.edu/~nes> National Election Studies (NES) has been conducting surveys of US political behaviour since 1948. NES conducts time series surveys in Presidential election and mid-term election years, based on a representative sample of the American electorate. The great benefit of the NES time series is that the length of time over which surveys have been conducted allows long-term trends and the political impact of historical events to be identified. Each study addresses a number of themes: the election outcome; attention to campaign coverage, perception of candidates and their parties, trust in government, economic well being; and views on a number of economic and social issues. The years between elections in the American political cycle are used for developing and refining instrumentation and study design for the Time Series Studies.

The Pew Research Center <www.people-press.org/>. An independent opinion research group that examines public attitudes towards the press, politics and public policy issues. Survey results on a variety of issues are available on the Website.

7.12.3 Canada

Canadian Public Opinion Archives <jeff-lab.queensu.ca/opinion/>. Data from more than 350 opinion surveys conducted between the 1970s and the present are available within the archive. However, for contractual reasons, access to the data is limited to Queen's University Staff and Students, or external researchers receiving authorization from Queen's.

▶ 7.13 RESEARCH IN PROGRESS

See *7.14* for a number of research organizations which organize conferences, workshops and other events, which facilitate networking within the research community.

Working and conference papers provide useful means of disseminating research findings without the need to face the time-consuming rigour of the peer review process for publication. *Political Research Online (PROceedings)* <pro.harvard.edu/> is a joint project between Harvard University Library and the American Political Science Association (APSA) offering online papers that were presented at the 2000 Annual Meeting of APSA.

Email lists are one of the best facilitators of topical discussion on issues. In the United Kingdom, JISCmail provides electronic discussion lists for UK academic and support staff. Currently, there are more than 3000 lists, but they vary in terms of activity. Among the most useful lists are those provided by the *British Official Publications Current Awareness Service* (BOPCAS) *See also 1.11.1* and *7.11.1*. Each of the 28 lists offers weekly updates of the latest Government publications related to a list's particular interest. For example, *bopcas-wales* <www.jiscmail.ac.uk/lists/bopcas-wales.html> is concerned with government publications related to Wales and provides a forum to discuss matters arising from them.

Gary Klass and his associates at the Department of Political Science, Illinois State University, have put together a wonderfully comprehensive list of Email groups. *The Political Science List of Lists* <coyote.its.ilstu.edu/tango/gmklass/listsrch.qry> covers topics related to politics and political science. The groups are all to be found on the Listserv, Listproc, Majordomo and JISCmail servers. However, there is no system for verifying how active the groups are or whether access is restricted.

▶ 7.14 ORGANIZATIONS

American Political Science Association (APSA)
1527 New Hampshire Ave., NW Washington, DC 20036–1206, USA
Tel: +1 202 483 2512
Fax: +1 202 483 2657
Email: apsa@apsanet.org
Web: <www.apsanet.org/>

For political scientists within the United States, the American Political Science Association is the most significant professional organization. It is based in Washington, DC and stages an annual meeting at which political scientists from around the world present their research and engage in scholarly debate. APSA maintains and publicizes a schedule of professional conferences held throughout the year. The two notable journals, which APSA produces, are the *American Political Science Review* and *PS: Politics and Political Science* (*see 7.9.1*). In 2000, APSA produced a biographical directory for the first time since 1988. It incorporated APSA members contact details, a representative list of publications and employment history. The directory also features essays on the discipline's history and practice.

The Brookings Institution
1775 Massachusetts Ave. NW, Washington, DC 20036, USA
Tel: +1 202 7976000
Fax: +1 202 797 6004
Email: brookinfo@brook.edu
Web: <www.brook.edu/about/aboutbi.htm>

The Brookings Institution can trace its origins back to 1916. It publishes research findings on public policy issues. Its aim is to function as a bridge between scholarship and public policy.

Canadian Political Science Association
260 Dalhousie Street, suite 204, Ottawa, Ontario, K1N 7E4, Canada
Tel: +1 613 562 1202
Fax: +1 613 241 0019
Email: cpsa@csse.ca.
Web: <www.uottawa.ca/associations/cpsa-acsp/>

The Association aims to encourage and develop political science and its relationship with other disciplines. It publishes the *Canadian Journal of Political Science – see 7.9.1.*

Carnegie Endowment for International Peace (CEIP)
1779 Massachusetts Avenue, NW Washington, DC 20036, USA
Tel: +1 202 483 7600
Fax: +1 202 483 1840
Email: carnegie@ceip.org
Web: <www.ceip.org>

The Carnegie Endowment was founded in 1910. It remains dedicated to analysing and influencing debate on the central issues affecting US foreign relations, security and defence.

The Cato Institute
1000 Massachusetts Avenue, NW Washington, DC 20001–5403, USA
Tel: +1 202 842 0200
Fax: +1 202 842 3490
Email: librarian@cato.org
Web: <www.cato.org>

The Cato Institute seeks to broaden the parameters of public policy debate to allow consideration of more options that are consistent with the traditional American principles of limited government, individual liberty, and peace.

Center for Responsive Politics
1101 Fourteenth Street NW, Suite 1030, Washington , DC 20005, USA
Tel: +1 202 857 0044
Fax: +1 202 857 7809
Email: info@crp.org
Web: <www.opensecrets.org/home/index.asp>

The CRP is a non-partisan, non-profit making research group that analyses the financing of political campaigns. The centre aims to create 'a more educated voter, involved citizenry, and a more involved government.' The amount of money raised by political candidates and who is contributing financially to the campaign can be identified. The site even breaks down contributions by geography and names top contributors. It also provides a search engine for its database of information.

C.enter for the Study of Democracy
School of Social Sciences, University of California, Irvine CA, 92697, USA.
Fax: +1 949 824 8762
Email: rdalton@uci.edu
Web: <hypatia.ss.uci.edu/democ/center.htm>

The Center for the Study of Democracy is an Organized Research Unit (ORU) at the University of California, Irvine. The Center fosters academic research and education that aims to provide a better understanding of the democratic process, and the steps that may be taken to strengthen democracy at home and abroad.

Demos
9 Bridewell Place, London, EC4V 6AP, UK
Tel: +44 (0)20 7353 4479
Fax: +44 (0)20 7353 4481
Email: mail@demos.co.uk
Web: <www.demos.co.uk>

The organization was launched to help reinvigorate British public policy and the political system, which were seen as increasingly falling prey to short-term policy formulation. Demos is dedicated to the renewal of British politics and its reconnection with popular concerns. Among its areas of study are work on democratic innovation and family and gender.

The European Consortium for Political Research Central Services (ECPR)
University of Essex, Wivenhoe Park, Colchester, Essex, C04 3SQ, UK
Tel: +44 (0)1206 872501
Fax: +44 (0)1206 872500
Email: ecpr@essex.ac.uk
Web: <www.essex.ac.uk/ECPR/index.htm>

The ECPR is a private, scholarly association representing European political scientists. It is the administrative centre for more than 5000 political scientists in Europe and it aims to foster collaboration among them. It is a registered charity under British law and has its headquarters at the University of Essex, UK. Among its activities are organizing workshops and conferences.

The Heritage Foundation
214 Massachusetts Ave., NE, Washington, DC 20002, USA
Tel: +1 202 546 4400
Fax: +1 202 546 8328
Email: info@heritage.org
Web: <www.heritage.org>

The Heritage Foundation represents a conservative or classical liberal perspective towards public policy. Its primary objective is to influence policymakers, particularly the US Congress, by the provision of factual and timely information on topical issues.

The Institute for Public Policy Research
30–32 Southampton Street, London, WC2E 7RA, UK
Tel: +44 (0)20 7470 6100
Email: postmaster@ippr.org.uk.
Web: <www.ippr.org.uk/>

The Institute for Public Policy Research is Britain's leading centre-left think tank. Among the projects in which it is involved is the Public Involvement Programme for developing new ways of involving the public in decision-making.

Institute of Governance Studies
Department of Political Science, Simon Fraser University, Burnaby, BC, V5A 1S6, Canada
Tel: +1 604 291 4293
Fax: +1 604 291 4786
Email: igs@sfu.ca
Web: <www.sfu.ca/igs>

The Institute pursues multidisciplinary research into problems on contemporary governance with a special focus on British Columbia.

International Political Science Association (IPSA)
Department of Politics, University College Dublin, Belfield, Dublin 4, Ireland
Tel: +353 1 706 8182
Fax: +353 1 706 1171
Email: ipsa@ucd.ie
Web: <www.ipsa-aisp.org/>

IPSA is one of the most notable organizations, if not the most influential, within the political science field. It holds international congresses and it has a network of 49 Research committees made up of international scholars. The committees are each committed to the study of major themes in political science, ranging from 'Biology in Politics' to 'Military Rule and 'Democratization in the Third World'. IPSA's major publications include the *International Political Science Review* (*see 7.9.1*) and *International Political Science Abstracts* (*see 7.10*).

The Inter-university Consortium for Political and Social Research (ICPSR)
The University of Michigan, Institute for Social Research, PO Box 1248, Ann Arbor, MI 48106–1248, USA
Tel: +1 734 998 9900
Fax: +1 734 998 9889
Email: netmail@icpsr.umich.edu
Web: <www.icpsr.umich.edu>

ICPSR is located at the Institute of Social Research within the University of Michigan. It provides access to the world's largest archive of social science data. *See also 7.12.1.*

Observatoire Interregionel du Politique
71 boulevard Raspail, 75006, Paris
Tel: +33 (0) 1 45 49 72 64
Fax: +33 (0) 1 45 49 72 65
Email: info@oip.sciences-po.fr
Web: <www-bdsp.upmf-grenoble.fr/oip/oipf_gen.htm>

The Observatoire Interregional du Politique was set up in 1985 to provide opinion data on regional politics, the policy of regionalization and decentralization. The Website is currently only available in French, but an English version is under construction.

The Political Studies Association of the UK (PSA)
Department of Politics, University of Newcastle, Newcastle-upon-Tyne, NE1 7RU, UK
Tel: +44 (0)191 222 8021
Fax: +44 (0)191 222 5069
Email: psa@ncl.ac.uk
Web: <www.psa.ac.uk/>

PSA, which celebrated its 50th anniversary in 2000, aims to develop and promote the study of political science. It publishes the leading UK journal *Political Studies* (*see 7.9.1*) and it recently launched the new journal *The British Journal of Politics and International Relations*. The PSA's Politics Forum is an important arena for academic debate and analysis. A resource listing for political science is also available through the PSA Website.

The Policy Studies Institute (PSI)
100 Park Village East, London, NW1 3SR, UK
Tel: +44 (0)20 7468 0468
Fax: +44 (0)20 7388 0914
Email: postmaster@psi.org.uk
Web: <www.psi.org.uk>

The Institute focuses on two key policy areas, namely, employment and social policy. It is an independent subsidiary of the University of Westminster.

Social Market Foundation (SMF)
11 Tufton Street, London, SW1P 3QB, UK
Tel: +44 (0)20 7222 7060
Fax: +44 (0)20 7222 0310
Email: info@smf.co.uk
Web: <www.smf.co.uk>

The SMF is an independent institute, which develops ideas that are 'pro-market'. Unlike other think tanks of the orthodox right, SMF believes in promoting 'sustainable welfare systems'. Its three main areas of research are education, public sector performance and health care.

Southern Political Science Association
Department of Political Science, University of Mississippi, University, MS 38677, USA
Tel: +1 622 915 5673
Fax: +1 622 915 5672
Email: ERC@olem.iss.edu
Web: <www.olemiss.edu/orgs/spsa/>

The Southern Political Science Association produces The *Journal of Politics* (*see 7.9.1*), the oldest regional journal in the United States.

▶ REFERENCES

Brock, C. (1969) *The Literature of Political Science: a Guide for Students, Librarians and Teachers*. London: RR Bowker.

Eulau, H. (1964) 'Political Science' in: C. M. White, (ed.), *Sources of Information in the Social Sciences: a Guide to the Literature*. Totowa, NJ: Bedminster Press.

8 Economics

Alison Sharman

▶ 8.1 NATURE AND SCOPE OF ECONOMICS

Ask a lay person to define economics and you will probably receive an answer that states the contents covered by the subject rather than an actual definition. They would probably include the topics of exchange rates, inflation, unemployment and international trade. However, adequately defining the discipline of economics becomes increasingly difficult the more involved you are with the subject. This is because there are a variety of different schools of thought, all with differing opinions of what economics is and how it should be studied. The preferred definition of economics will thus vary depending upon your point of view. However, there are a few well-known definitions of economics in existence including the two quoted below:

> 'Economics is a study of mankind in the everyday business of life' Marshall (1890, p.1).
>
> 'Economics is the science which studies human behaviour as a relationship between ends and scarce means which have alternative uses' Lord Robbins (1932) 'Essay on the nature and significance of economic science', in Partington (1992, p.541).

Economics, as a separate discipline, is usually taken to have started with the work of Adam Smith and his book *An Enquiry into the Nature and Causes of the Wealth of Nations* (1776). However, many earlier writers may well have concerned themselves with economics. The Greek philosophers certainly did so and in the Middle Ages St. Thomas Aquinas discussed price formation in theological terms and talked of a 'just' price. It was only after Smith, however, that the subject of political economy became a discipline in its own right, rather than a branch of moral philosophy. This was later shortened to economics with the advent of the Neoclassical School of Thought which stemmed from the marginalist revolution of the 1870s.

There are a number of schools of thought in economics. These comprise the Austrian School, the Neoclassical School, the Chicago School, the Post-Keynesian School, the Institutionalist (Evolutionary) School and the Marxist School.

The focus of economics has moved on from being concerned with ideas and hypothesis, to mathematical formulas and empirical research. The *Economics Journal* in the 1930s, for example, had a predominance of articles discussing the ideas and theories comprising economics. Today, however, it tends to be full of articles containing detailed mathematical equations. Neoclassical economics, the dominant school of thought, probably takes us in this direction.

An excellent book which presents a detailed investigation of the seven schools of economic thought is *A Modern Guide to Economic Thought* edited by Douglas Mair and Anne G. Miller (Aldershot: Edward Elgar, 1991). Each chapter is written by a leading specialist in that particular school of thought. In a similar vein is *Why Economists Disagree* edited by David L. Prychitko (Albany, NY: State University of New York Press, 1998). Finally, a highly recommended book which debates the whole subject of economics, what it means and how it should be studied, is *Foundations of Research in Economics: How do Economists do Economics?* by Steve G. Medma, and Warren J. Samuels (Cheltenham: Edward Elgar, 1996). The book is a collection of essays, with each contributing author writing on the subject of how they believe 'economics should be done'.

Economics encompasses a broad range of subject areas and it has not been possible to include all of the reference material within this one chapter. However, it does aim to cover the main sources of economic information including gateways to important Websites and reference material.

▶ 8.2 ANNUALS

8.2.1 General

The Statesman's Yearbook: the Politics, Cultures and Economies of the World edited by Barry Turner (London: Macmillan Reference Limited, 1864–). A succinct country-by-country guide to the world, including economic factors such as energy and natural resources, industry, international trade and the economy.

8.2.2 Business

Euromonitor produce a number of excellent publications which are usually published on an annual basis and provide an informative overview of a country or region. A good example is *Consumer Europe* (London: Euromonitor, 1976–), a compendium of data on a variety of products, identifying the significant consumer trends of Western Europe. It is also a useful source for locating socio-economic factors pertaining to each country. It is also available in electronic format on CD-ROM. Other titles are: *Consumer Asia* (London: Euromonitor, 1993–); *Consumer International* (London: Euromonitor, 1994–); and *Consumer China* (London: Euromonitor, 1994–).

Macmillan's Unquoted Companies (London: Waterlow) is a profile of the top 20 000 UK unquoted companies. It is published in two volumes: the first volume includes companies with a turnover exceeding 13 million pounds sterling; and the second volume covers companies with a turnover below 13 million pounds. Each entry includes contact details, personnel, and financial data. Organized alphabetically by company, it also includes industrial league tables.

The Times 1000 (London: Times Books) has been published since 1966. It includes a ranking of the top 50 international industrial companies, the top 100 European companies and the top 100 UK companies, all with a commentary. Other lists include the leading 1000 UK and European Companies, and the foremost 100 companies from Japan, North America, Australia, New Zealand and Southeast Asia. An overview of the global economy is also provided.

World Business Rankings Annual by Robert Lazich (Detroit, MI: Gale) comprises classified lists on business-related subjects, with the source acknowledged at the end of each list. It ranges from the brand value of fashion accessories listed in millions of US dollars, to the number of aircraft accidents listed in a given phase of flight over a period of time. The work is organized by subject, but there are also indexes categorized by company, geographical region and Standard Industrial Classification (SIC).

The Macmillan Stock Exchange Yearbook edited by Martin C. Timbrell and Diana L. Tweedie (London: Waterlow Specialist Information Publishing) is an easy-to-use reference book that provides information for over 4000 'companies, corporations and securities listed on the London and Dublin Stock Exchanges, and all those traded on the Alternative Investment Market'. The publication comprises a brief history of the company, a list of directors, registered address and financial data such as the consolidated balance-sheet, assets and liabilities, capital and recent dividends.

8.2.3 Environmental

The International Yearbook of Environmental and Resource Economics edited by Tom Tietenberg and Henry Folmer (Cheltenham: Edward Elgar) examines the issues at the forefront of environmental and resource economics, covering such topics as water use, solid waste management, and the environment in developing countries. It also provides a survey of current research.

► 8.3 BIBLIOGRAPHIES

Although this section is dedicated to bibliographies, other sections also contain reference to bibliographies, most notably the dictionaries listed in *8.4*, e.g. for bibliographies on individual economists, *see* the biographical dictionaries in *8.4.2*, and the encyclopaedias in *8.6*.

8.3.1 General

(a) Print

The *Bibliographical Guide to Business and Economics* (Boston, MS: G K Hall) is an annual publication that started its life in 1975. It contains bibliographical citations of all business and economic sources catalogued in the current year by the Library of Congress and the Research Libraries of New York. However, the entries are not annotated and there is no cumulative volume, which makes retrospective searching a little more difficult.

International Bibliography of Economics (London and New York: Routledge, 1952–). An annual annotated bibliography with references to books, journals and documents, organized by topic and divided into 15 sections which include a history of economic thought, international economics and prices and markets.

(b) Electronic

NetEc <netec.mcc.ac.uk/>. A useful resource, created with the aim of improving the dissemination of economic resources available through the Internet. It comprises: *BibEc*: details of printed working papers; *WoPEc*: details of electronic working papers; *WebEc*: economic resources available via the Internet; and *JokEc*: jokes about the economic profession. A search combining these sources can be conducted. The site is accessed in the UK through MIMAS (Manchester Information and Associated services)and it is mirrored in America and Japan.

There are details of bibliographical databases and information on Bill Goffe's excellent *Resources for Economists on the Internet* found at <rfe.wustl.edu/ScholComm/Bib/index.html>. It provides links to and a brief description of eight bibliographical tools that can be found on the Internet.

One of the sources included is *IDEAS* which claims to the largest economic bibliographical database to be found on the Web. It can be accessed at <ideas.uqam.ca/>. It appears to be a very comprehensive database, providing information on working papers, journals, software, many of which have a *Journal of Economic Literature* (see 8.9.1) classification.

8.3.2 Biographies

A series on bio-bibliographies has been published by Greenwood Press. The publications are divided into three chapters comprising a biography of the life of the chosen economist, an annotated bibliography of their publications and an annotated bibliography of salient works written about the particular person. Examples include: *William J. Fellner: a Bio-Bibliography* by James N. Marshall (Westport, CT: Greenwood Press, 1992); *Joan Robinson: a Bio-Bibliography* by James Cicarelli and Julianne Cicarelli (Westport, CT: Greenwood Press, 1996); and *Joseph Alois Schumpter: a Bibliography, 1905–1984* by Michael I. Stevenson (Westport, CT: Greenwood Press, 1985).

8.3.3 Methodology

Economic Methodology: a Bibliography with References to Works in the Philosophy of Science, 1860– compiled by Deborah A. Redman (Westport, CT: Greenwood Press, 1989). This bibliography of economic methodology includes 2244 entries originating from 1860 onwards. The work is divided into two parts: the first is dedicated to 25 categories of economic methodology including work from the great exponents of the subject such as Friedman and Samuelson as well as addressing the theory and ideas; the second part deals with the philosophy of science.

8.3.4 Political

Marxists.org Internet Archive Online Library <csf.colorado.edu/mirrors/marxists.org/>. Set up by volunteers from all over the world, this extensive resource comprises original documents, photographs and biographies of Marxist writers and those defined by the contributors as non-Marxist writers such as Adam Smith, Hegel and most controversially Joseph Stalin. It also contains an encyclopaedia of Marxism, as detailed in *8.6.5(b) Electronic*.

Articles Discussing Friedrich Hayek and His Work <www.hayek-center.org/friedrichhayek/articles.htm>. This bibliography of Hayek's writings is categorized by: abstracts and outlines; book reviews; and books and interviews by Hayek. There are no descriptions of any of the sources, just links to the material.

▶ 8.4. DICTIONARIES

8.4.1 General

(a) Print

The New Palgrave Dictionary of Economics (London: Palgrave, 1998) was previously published in three volumes under the name *Dictionary of Political Economy: the New Palgrave Dictionary of Economics and the Law* edited by Peter Newman (London: Palgrave Reference, 1998). *See 8.6.1* and *8.6.2* for further information about both of these publications.

Collins Dictionary of Economics by Christopher Pass, Bryan Lowes and Leslie Davies, 3rd ed., (London: Harper-Collins, 2000) explains over 2500 key economics phrases and terms in an A–Z format. It also covers important economic concepts and principles. The *Dictionary of Economics* by Graham Bannock, R. E. Baxter and Evan Davis (London: Profile Books, 1998) discusses the meaning of economic terminology in a concise manner, including those terms pertaining to statistics and econometrics. Economic history is also included, as are biographies of eminent economists. There is a plethora of cross-referencing of terms, aiding the understanding of the terminology. The *Routledge Dictionary of Economics* by Donald Rutherford (London: Routledge, 1995) is an outstanding dictionary with over 4200 A–Z entries explaining the key concepts, terms, and issues concerning modern day economics. It also gives a biographical account of the key figures to feature in the history of economics. Where applicable, annotated bibliographies are included after the entries.

Roberts' Dictionary of Industrial Relations, 4th ed., by Harold Selig Roberts (Washington, DC: Bureau of National Affairs, 1994) contains an explanation of the language used in industrial relations. It also includes details of international trade unions, government bodies, important court cases and significant legislation. Bibliographical references are usefully provided.

(b) Electronic

Economics Glossary <www.bized.ac.uk/stafsup/options/aec/glos.htm> is a searchable glossary of basic economic terms, some with featured diagrams where appropriate. *See also 8.8.1.*

A Journalist's Guide to Economic Terms <www.facsnet.org/tools/ref_tutor/econo_term/glossary.html>. Created to help reporters and journalists understand a variety of economic terms, this Website comprises 213 economic phrases with an explanation arranged in alphabetical order.

8.4.2 Biographical

Biographical Dictionary of Dissenting Economists, 2nd ed., by Philip Arestis (Cheltenham: Edward Elgar, 2000) is a biographical dictionary covers over 1000 prominent economists, giving a broad overview of their lives plus bibliographical information. *Who's who in Economics,* 3rd ed., edited by Mark Blaug (Cheltenham: Edward Elgar, 1999) presents entries on key economists. As well as giving biographical information, the dictionary also provides a critical commentary and a detailed bibliography of their works.

A Biographical Dictionary of Women Economists edited by Robert W. Dimand, Mary Ann Diamand and Evelyn L. Forget, (Cheltenham: Edward Elgar, 2000). The dictionary presents specially commissioned articles on the lives and research of over 100 women economists from around the world who have made a significant contribution to the field of economics. Bibliographical references are included. The *Dictionary of Twentieth Century British Business Leaders* by Dr David Jeremy and Dr Geoffrey Twiddle (London: Bowker Saur, 1994) gives biographical details of major British business leaders presented in an A–Z format. As well as detailing the major achievements and education of the subject, bibliographical citations on significant works by the person are also included. There is a useful company index at the back of the volume.

8.4.3 Monetary

The New Palgrave Dictionary of Money and Finance edited by Peter Newman, Murray Milgate and John Eatwell (London: Macmillan Press, 1992). *See 8.6.3* for further information.

Reuters Glossary of International Financial and Economic Terms, 3rd ed., (Harlow: Longman, 1994). Compiled by the staff at Reuters, this publication contains around 3000 entries in an A–Z format explaining the terms used in banking, business management, trading and exporting.

Brian Butler has edited the *Dictionary of Finance and Banking,* 2nd ed., (Oxford: Oxford University Press, 1997) with the help of experts from Lloyds Bank. This reference tool is a compilation of over 4000 entries covering the language of the finance world. As well as explaining concepts and terms, it provides an historical background to the various international financial centres and also highlights some of the main financial publications.

The *Dictionary of Free-market Economics* by Fred E. Foldvary and John F. Kennedy (Aldershot: Edward Elgar, 1994), explains terms connected to the free market economy, arranged in alphabetical order with cross-referencing where appropriate. Theories are defined, empirical studies identified and biographies of free-market economists included. Bibliographies of relevant published works are also presented.

The *International Dictionary of Finance*, 3rd ed., by Graham Bannock and William Manser (London: Penguin, 1999) provides an explanation of the concepts and terms used in banking, commodity markets, insurance and security markets. Cross-references are included. There are explanations of the foreign language terms and also acronyms and abbreviations. There is a useful foreword that explains how the dictionary operates.

8.4.4 Econometrics

A Dictionary of Econometrics by Adrian C. Darnell (Aldershot: Edward Elgar, 1994) contains short entries in an A–Z format on the theories and ideas comprising econometrics with references to further reading. The further reading also provides a guide to additional material available to supplement reading in the field.

▶ 8.5 DIRECTORIES

8.5.1 General

(a) Print

The *Directory of Economic Institutions* by Forrest Capie (London: Macmillan and New York: Stockton Press, 1988) provides details of institutions engaged in economic research, making or influencing economic policy and working to further economic understanding and knowledge. Data are arranged by country and includes research interests, publications and activities. The *Directory of International Economic Organizations* by Hans-Albrecht Schraepler (Washington, DC: Georgetown University Press, 1999) is a valuable source for research as it contains information on a wide range of international economic organizations.

(b) Electronic

Economists on the World Wide Web <eclab.ch.pdx.edu/ecwww/>. A searchable collection of the home pages of many economists from around the world.

8.5.2 Business

(a) Print

The *Business and Economics Research Directory* (London: Europa, 1996) provides information for over 1500 business and economics research centres and institutions from more than 150 countries. It also contains a list of around 1000 business and economics journals. *Business Information from Government, 1998* edited by Liz Lampard (East Grinstead: Bowker Saur, 1998) is a valuable guide to the range of sources held by Government departments and official organizations.

D and B Europa (High Wycombe, Bucks: Dun and Bradstreet, 1999). First published in 1989, this work of four volumes details 65 000 leading companies from the member states of the European Union and the European Free Trade Association. The chosen companies are from all areas of business, and statistical information is provided for each. The fourth volume is particularly useful with pages devoted to lists of companies ranked by sales, employees and main business activity.

The Hambro Company Guide (London: Hemmington-Scott, 1978–) is a quarterly publication providing financial details of all UK listed companies, compiled from individual company reports and accounts. The information comprises each company's main business activities, address of head office, shareholders, bankers and financial advisors, as well as financial information such as turnover, pre-tax profit and fixed assets. *Hoovers Handbook of World Business* by Patrick J. Spain and James R. Talbot (Austin, TX: Hoover, 2001) focuses on 750 major US companies.

The *International Directory of Company Histories* (Detroit, MI: St James Press, 1998) details the history of a range of international companies including their mission, goals, ideals, principal subsidiaries and articles for further reading. Companies are included on the premise of having a minimum annual sales of 100 million US dollars.

Key British Enterprises (High Wycombe, Bucks: Dun and Bradstreet, 2001). This directory spans six volumes and comprises a series of lists providing details on 50 000 corporations, categorized by a variety of criteria and cross-referenced where appropriate. Details provided include an alphabetical compilation of companies with criteria such as name, address, description of business activity and brief financial information. These are categorized by industry by Standard Industrial Classification (SIC) codes and geographical regions. There are also listings of brand names, organizations doing business in specific export markets and directors' names. Finally, there is a ranked list of the top 5000 employing companies organized by sales, county, industrial groupings and number of employees.

A very similar publication to *Key British Enterprises* is *UK Kompass Register* (East Grinstead: Reed Business Information, 1962–). This key reference work is an excellent source of company information and provides details of around 41 000 products and services offered by British companies. It also contains company information according to geographical area as well as financial data, parent companies, subsidiaries and international trade names. There are also versions for most European countries and many other countries including Australia, New Zealand, China, South Africa and Mexico. *Kompass* is also available electronically.

Graham and Whiteside, an imprint of the Gale Group, produce an impressive set of annual publications on major companies of certain regions of the world. Included in this are: *Major Companies of Latin America and the Caribbean 2001* (London: Graham and Whiteside, 2001); *Major Companies of South West Asia 2001* (London: Graham and Whiteside, 2001); and *Major Companies of Central and Eastern Europe and the Commonwealth of Independent States 2001* (London: Graham and Whiteside, 2001).

Sources of European Economic and Business Information, 6th ed., edited by the British Library Business Information Service (Aldershot: Gower, 1995), provides a comprehensive list of relevant international economic and business statistical sources for 32 European countries. Topics covered include public finance, industry, business, commerce and socio-economic conditions. There is a separate section for each country. *Wards Business Directory of US Private and Public Companies 2001* (Detroit, MI: Gale Group, 2001) is published in eight volumes and covers approximately 100 000 US companies. Information is provided on small and medium sized enterprises, details of which can often prove hard to find.

Who Owns Whom (High Wycombe, Bucks: Dun and Bradstreet, 1958–) is an excellent series to consult when requiring the identification of the parent, subsidiary or associate company of an organization. All corporate groups are included. The corporation simply has to be owned by another corporation. The series includes the UK and Ireland, continental Europe, North and South America, Australasia, Asia, the Middle East and Africa.

The World Directory of Business Information Websites, 4th ed., (London: Euromonitor, 2001) details significant business information Websites that are available free of charge and includes an index of Websites by sector and type. A good starting point to use in any information search. *The World Directory of Trade and Business Associations*, 3rd ed., (London: Euromonitor, 2000) is an indexed list of international organizations with contact details and Web addresses. Background information on each organization is provided, along with information on their aims and objectives. A useful feature is that publications from each of the profiled associations are listed.

The *Environment Business Directory* (London: Information for Industry, 1994–) is a collection of environmental addresses and contacts, including company profiles, an A–Z phone book, a regional list of companies, enforcers and regulators (including those from the European Union as well as national and regional) and consultancy companies. This work is published on an annual basis.

(b) Electronic

Hemscott Net <www.hemscott.co.uk/>. A good source of UK company information can be found at the *Hemscott* Website from which information concerning UK companies can be accessed free of charge. Information includes the five-year summary plus balance-sheet, daily share price and share price graph.

Hoover's UK at <www.hoovers.co.uk/uk/>. *Hoovers UK* is the European site of *Hoovers Online*, an American online company directory offering company, industry, people and product information. There is a subscription to use the service. However, free information is provided including the company's full legal name, contact details, list of competitors, subsidiaries with Web links, brief company history, information about the operations of the company and details about the industry. Key financial information is also supplied including the share prices and the annual and financial report. Links are provided to other online business directories. The American version can be found at <www.hoover.com/>.

▶ 8.6 ENCYCLOPAEDIAS

8.6.1 General

The key economic encyclopaedic dictionary is *The New Palgrave Dictionary of Economics* (London: Palgrave, 1998). It contains over 2000 entries spanning four volumes and was written by more than 900 contributors. At least 700 of the entries are biographical, encompassing the world's most important economists and their literature. Essays are provided on numerous contemporary economic topics such as the division of labour, economic markets and political economy, presenting a diversity of views and opinions with appropriate cross-referencing. The *Gale Encylopedia of US Economic History* (Farmington Hills, MI: Gale Group, 1999) presents information on the people, businesses, industries, events, movements and trends that comprise the economic history of the US from 1691 to 1998.

8.6.2 Economics and law

(a) Print

The New Palgrave Dictionary of Economics and the Law edited by Peter Newman (London: Palgrave Reference, 1998). This book comprises 399 essays arranged alphabetically by title, the majority of which involve some aspects of either law or economics or both. At the end of each title, there are cross-references to other related articles. The essays are also categorized into broader subject areas by a numbered subject classification including the headings of society, economy, polity, law in general, common law systems, regulation and biography. Each essay includes a useful bibliography listing full details of the references alluded to in the article and a list of further reading.

Encyclopedia of Law and Economics, Volumes 1–5, edited by Boudewijn Bouckaert (Cheltenham: Edward Elgar 2000). A five-volume encyclopaedia reviewing the literature of law and economics, covering such subjects as the history and methodology of law and economics, civil law and economics, the regulation of contracts, and the economics of public and tax law. Subject Bibliographies also are included. *See also (b) Electronic* below.

(b) Electronic

Encyclopedia of Law and Economics at <encyclo.findlaw.com/>. Produced by Edward Elgar in collaboration with the University of Ghent, this is a one-stop-shop to the literature on law and economics. The aim is to make literature of this inter-disciplinary subject matter accessible to the non-law specialist. The entries in this online encyclopaedia are around 10 000 words and usually contain a review of the literature and a bibliography. There are also some excellent links to other relevant Websites. *See also (a) Print* above.

8.6.3 Monetary

(a) Print

The New Palgrave Dictionary of Money and Finance edited by Peter Newman, Murray Milgate and John Eatwell (London: Macmillan Press, 1992). This reference work includes at least 1000 essays from over 800 contributors. It covers national and international areas of money, banking and finance. Each article is cross-referenced and there is also an extensive bibliography which lists the full details of publications highlighted in the articles, and also references to further reading. A subject index is included.

(b) Electronic

Wired: Encyclopedia of the New Economy <hotwired.lycos.com/special/ene/>. Sponsored by Andersen Consulting, this is an online encyclopaedia of the terms used in international economics and E-commerce. Includes new economic terms as well as older, more traditional ones.

8.6.4 Business

The *Encyclopedia of Emerging Industries* edited by Jennifer L. Carman and Holly M. Selden (London: Gale, 1999) presents information about over 108 new and developing US industries including electronic commerce, Internet service providers and multimedia computers, arranged alphabetically by industry. There are two indexes: one organized by the Standard Industrial Classification (SIC) code; and a broader index detailing company names, people, locations and legislation. Comprehensive cross-referencing is included. Information includes the background to and overview of the industry, the structure of the organization, industrial leaders and how the industry is thriving in the rest of the world.

Encyclopedia of Business, 2nd ed., (London: Gale Group, 1999). This two-volume encyclopaedia contains around 700 signed articles on the major concepts and theories pertaining to the world of business. The *Encyclopaedia of Global Industries*, 2nd ed., (London: Gale Group, 1998) covers 115 world industries. Entries are arranged by industry, but a table of contents listed alphabetically is also provided.

International Encyclopedia of Business and Management edited by Malcolm Warner (London and New York, Routledge 1996). A six volume encyclopaedia that contains 517 terms organized in alphabetical order. Extensive cross-referencing is used and volume six provides a very useful index to the concepts, countries and names covered in the other five volumes.

8.6.5 Political economy

(a) Print

An Encyclopedia of Keynesian Economics edited by Thomas Cate, Geoff Harcourt and David C. Colander (Cheltenham: Edward Elgar, 1997). An excellent guide to the theoretical concepts presented by Keynesian economics and the literature of John Maynard Keynes. It includes articles not only by authors supporting the ideas and concepts expounded by Keynes, but by those opposed to the theories.

The *Encyclopedia of Political Economy* edited by Phillip Anthony O'Hara (London: Routledge, 1999) is a refereed encyclopaedia that demands little economic understanding prior to reading. It has been compiled with the help of 300 international authors, editors, referees and advisors. There are around 450 entries arranged alphabetically. Cross-references are provided to related subjects with references for further reading. A subject classification comprises 20 A–Z lists which include the labour market, financial markets, global capitalist economy and history of political economy.

(b) Electronic

The Encyclopedia of Marxism <csf.colorado.edu/mirrors/marxists.org/admin/intro/index.htm>. Established in September 1999, this is an ongoing project of the Marxist Internet Archive with the aim of being 'the most complete reference guide to Marxism'. The encyclopaedia is divided into six glossaries comprising people, events, places, organizations, terms and periodicals. It can be navigated by a search engine, subject indexes or by browsing manually. The main attributed sources for the encyclopaedia are non-copyright footnotes from the Institute of Marxism-Leninism. *See also 8.3.4.*

8.6.6 Environmental

The Environment Encyclopedia and Directory, 3rd ed., (London: Europa, 2001). A detailed guide to international environmental issues in an A–Z format. It also includes a directory of national and international organizations arranged alphabetically by country with contact details. There is also a useful bibliography of appropriate environmental journals.

► 8.7 GUIDES AND HANDBOOKS

8.7.1 General

(a) Print

A Guide to Modern Economics by David Greenaway (London and New York: Routledge, 1996). Previously published as *Companion to Contemporary Econ-omic Thought* in 1991, this publication provides a review of the development and implications of economic theory between 1985 and 1995. *Information Sources in Economics*, 2nd ed., edited by J. Fletcher (London: Butterworths, 1984) was originally published as *The Use of Economics Literature* (London: Butterworths, 1971). This second edition is an excellent guide to economic information sources covering aspects such as reference and bibliographical tools, journals, British official publications, statistical sources and dictionaries.

The Handbook of Economic Methodology edited by John B David, D. Wade Hands and Uskali Maki (Cheltenham: Edward Elgar, 1998) comprises over 100 essays on the subject of economic methodology by specialists from around the globe. The themes covered are those that have been topical in the field of economic methodology for the past couple of decades as well as the issues that are at the forefront of current research. Each article includes a useful bibliography. Biographical entries of the main exponents are also included. This book would also appeal to those interested in the philosophical debates concerning economics and the history of economic thought.

The *Companion to Contemporary Economic Thought* by David Greenaway, Michael Bleaney and Ian Steward (London: Routledge, 1999) presents 41 essays written predominantly by UK, US and Australian authors. Each section commences with a commentary by one of the editors. References and a bibliography are provided after each essay.

The *Elgar Companion Series* is a useful series to consult about a variety of economic perspectives. *The Elgar Companion to Austrian Economics* edited by Peter J. Boettke (Aldershot: Edward Elgar, 1994) comprises 80 articles written on all elements of Austrian economics with a list of suggested references for further reading. *The Elgar Companion to Institutional and Evolutionary Economics* by Geoffrey M Hodgson (Aldershot: Edward Elgar, 1994) provides a guide to institutional and evolutionary economics, focusing on the Veblenian and Schumpeterian schools of thought along with other theories and concepts. *The Elgar Companion to Classical Economics* edited by Heinz D Kruz and Neri Salvadori (Cheltenham: Edward Elgar, 1998) comprises two volumes of approximately 200 short entries on the significant perspectives from the classical tradition of economics. *The Elgar Companion to Law and Economics* by Jürgen G. Backhaus (Cheltenham: Edward Elgar, 1999) provides an overview of the main theories and concepts relating to law and economics. It includes 22 biographies in which the work of the major exponents of the field is discussed. *The Elgar Companion to Radical Political Economy* edited by Philip Arestis and Malcolm Sawyer (Aldershot: Edward Elgar, 1994) includes over 100 entries written by specialists in the field of political economy. International in scope, it encompasses a broad range of theories, concepts and ideas including the Post Keynesian, Marxist, and Sraffian schools of thought.

The Economist Guide to Economic Indicators: Making Sense of Economics by Richard Stutely (London: Profile Books, 1997) explains the concept of economic indicators (such as balance of payments, exchange rates, fiscal indicators, investment and savings), describing precisely why they are such an essential tool in the field of economics. It also gives tips on how to interpret the data.

The *Guide to the European Union*, 7th ed., by Dick Leonard (London: Profile Books, 2000) discusses, in 39 concise chapters, the development and workings of the European Union. Topics covered include trade, competition policy, economic and financial policy, energy, transport, aid and development.

The *Handbook on the Globalization of the World Economy* edited by Amnon Levy-Livermore. (Cheltenham: Edward Elgar, 1998) is concerned with the increasing breakdown of economic boundaries between countries and groups of countries and investigates the consequences of greater economic interdependence.

Regional Surveys of the World (London: Europa) is an excellent series constituting a comprehensive guide to seven world regions. Seven titles are available: *Western Europe 2000*; *Eastern Europe and the Commonwealth of Independent States 1999*; *South America, Central America and the Caribbean 2000*; *Africa South of the Sahara 2000*; *The Middle East and North Africa 2000*; *The Far East and Australasia 2000*; and *The USA and Canada 1998*. Each book includes an extensive synopsis of each country, demographic and key economic statistics, a bibliography and names and contact details for prominent organizations.

World Economic Factbook 2000/2001 (London: Euromonitor, 2000) provides a compilation of political and economic information for 205 countries of the world. It has written analyses of each country, with a complete data set (1997–1999) for all key indicators. Another useful Euromonitor publication is the *World Economic Prospects 2000,* 2nd ed., (London: Euromonitor, 2000). This title surveys the variables that play a part in shaping economic growth across 52 countries.

(b) Electronic

Winecon <www.Webecon.bris.ac.uk/winecon> is an interactive tutorial, introducing students to the concept of economics by means of online teaching, quizzes, etc. A joint venture between a group of UK universities and five publishers, *Winecon* is available via CD-ROM. There is an introductory version and further details are available from the *Winecon* Website.

8.7.2 Monetary

(a) Print

The *Guide to Financial Markets*, 2nd ed., by Marc Levinson (London: Profile Books, 2000) provides an explanation of the different types of existing financial markets, how they operate and their main traders. It also explains the influencing factors that change prices and rates. The topics covered include foreign exchange, bonds, equities and commodities.

The *Handbook of United States Economic and Financial Indicators* by Frederick O'Hara and Robert Sicignano (Westport, CT: Greenwood, 2000) presents a broad overview of 284 economic indicators including details on how they are calculated, how they are applied and in which publications they can be found. The book is in alphabetical order with cross-referencing and a useful index.

(b) Electronic

Economic Growth Resources <www.nuff.ox.ac.uk/Economics/Growth/>. This Website is maintained by Jonathan Temple, at Oxford University. It provides resources on economic growth including critical evaluation of existing literature, links to relevant journals, links to working papers, data sets and links to other Websites.

8.7.3 Business

(a) Print

Business Information Sources by Lorna M. Daniells (Oxford and Berkeley, CA: University of California Press, 1993). A good, comprehensive guide to literature in the business world, although it does have a US bias. Information provided includes foreign statistics and economic trends, basic US statistical sources, information on companies, organizations and individual business personnel. There is a subject index and an author/title index. *Business Information Basics: a Guide to Key Information Sources 2000* edited by Pam Foster (East Grinstead: Bowker Saur, 1999) is highly recommended for international business information in both electronic and printed formats. There is a very useful section on global economics and statistics, as well as government forecasts, ranking lists and financial data. The guide includes company, regional and name indexes as well as an alphabetical listing of business related Webpages.

The Business and Economy Internet Resource Handbook edited by Phil Bradley (London: Library Association Publishing, 2000). A useful reference tool for tracing business and economic Websites, written by a number of contributing authors. The book includes subjects such as international economy, government information, E-commerce, and small and medium-sized enterprises. It also offers advice on how to keep up to date on what is being published in the business and economics field on the Web. The book details predominantly UK sites, but does mention a few international Web pages.

Business Research Sources: a Reference Navigator by F. Patrick Butler (Boston and London: McGraw-Hill, 1999) is a comprehensive guide to international business reference guides. Types of information covered include encyclopaedias, directories, almanacs, international sources, international and regional journals, and statistical sources. As well as a description of each publication, tables of contents and sample pages are also provided.

IEBM Handbook of International Business edited by Rosalie L Tung (London: International Thompson Business Press, 1999). A useful handbook containing short essays written mainly by leading international academics in the field of business globalization. The *Handbook of*

Latin American Trade in Manufactures edited by Montague J. Lord (Cheltenham: Edward Elgar, 1998) is a comprehensive guide to the globalization and expansion of the South American manufacturing trade.

(b) Electronic

Corporate Watch <www.corporatewatch.org.uk/publications/diy_research.html> is an excellent site for company information. This site provides: a brief overview of locating company profiles; industrial sites from the World Wide Web; listings of trade journals; business directories; and directions to other physical sources of information such as Companies House.

8.7.4 Labour

International Handbook of Labour Market Policy and Evaluation edited by Günther Schmid, Jacqueline O'Reilly and Klaus Schöman (Aldershot: Edward Elgar, 1996). This work provides an in-depth analysis of the existing international labour markets as well as examining policies employed to control unemployment.

8.7.5 Environmental

Environment and Trade: a Handbook by the International Institute of Sustainable Development and the UN Environment Programme (Winnipeg, Canada: International Institute of Sustainable Development, 2000). This handbook examines the relationship between trade and the environment, describing how one can have an effect on the other and ultimately have an effect on the development on a particular country. The book is available online at <www.iisd.org/trade/handbook/default.htm>.

The *Handbook of Environmental and Resource Economics* edited by Jeroen C. J. M van den Bergh (Aldershot: Edward Elgar 1996) is an extensive compilation of articles written by international authors addressing a wide range of global issues pertaining to the environmental and resource economics field.

▶ 8.8 WEBSITES

8.8.1 General

About.Com <economics.about.com>. A well-organized site that is useful for both newcomers to the discipline and the experienced economist. It contains a glossary, news and analysis, forecasts, a free newsletter, links to other economic resources on the Internet, and feature articles written by John S. Irons, an economics professor working at Amherst College in the US.

Biz/ed <www.bized.ac.uk>. Developed by the Institute for Learning and Research Technology at the University of Bristol, this Website is an essential Internet directory, providing links to many reputable sources of business and economic information. *See also 8.4.1 (b) Electronic.*

Centre for the Study of African Economies <users.ox.ac.uk/~csae info>. This Website contains the working papers series published by the Centre for the Study of African Economics, part of Oxford University's Institute of Economics and Statistics. Many of the papers are available in full-text pdf format. The contents pages of the *Journal of African Economies*, also produced by the centre, can be browsed via this Website.

Dismal Scientist <www.dismal.com/>. This site provides analysis of major economic global events by economists from the Economy.com network.

Economics Centre of the Learning and Teaching Support Network <www.economics.ltsn.ac.uk/>. Based at Bristol University, this Website has been developed by the LTSN whose remit is to enhance the teaching, learning and assessment of subjects within higher education establishments. They have developed an impressive online economic tutorial named *Internet Economist*. It includes a tour of some of the key economics Internet sites.

Economicsearch.com <www.economicsearch.com/research>. Includes a section dedicated to research with information on specific subjects grouped together in an easy-to-read format. Topics include: statistics; economic international forecasts and analysis; policy analysis and commentaries; links to organizations; conferences; and journals.

Financial Times <www.financialtimes.com/>. As well as including a variety of facts and figures, this site contains a very useful search facility enabling the researcher to search over three years to retrieve articles and news reports. It is also available on CD-ROM.

Freepint <www.freepint.com>. Published electronically twice per month, this is an excellent free resource for keeping up to date with Internet sites. It also offers helpful tips on searching facilities as well as reviews of a variety of Websites. The edition published in February 2001 (issue 82) contains a review of economic Webpages by Paul Pedley and can be found at <www.freepint.com/issues/150201.htm#tips>.

Inomics <www.inomics.scom>. Includes Econsearch, a search engine for economic information, plus a directory of economics Internet resources. It also has details of jobs plus details of the latest conferences and summer schools.

NISS Gateway <www.niss.ac.uk/cgi-bin/GetUdc.pl?33>. Provides a useful list of economic-related Websites from journals, newspapers, Internet directories and mailing lists.

Resources for Economists <www.rfe.org/>. Edited by Bill Goffe and sponsored by the American Economic Association, this Website provides details of 1194 resources of interest to academic staff and students of economics. The site is well organized and the table of contents includes the following sections: data; economists; departments and universities; forecasting and consulting; mailing lists; meetings and conferences; news media; Internet guides; scholarly communication; and software. The sources appear to be biased in favour of US sites, but there are sections on non-US resources. *See also 8.3.1 (b).*

Scout Report for Business and Economics <www.scout.cs.wisc.edu/report/busecon/current/index.html>. A weekly Email service from the Internet Scout Project based at the Department of Computer Sciences, University of Wisconsin. It details international economics and business research Websites, useful learning resources, general interest sites, working papers and journal articles. The quality of each recommended site is assessed. There is a UK mirror version at <www.ilrt.bris.ac.uk/mirrors/scout/report/busecon/current/index.html>.

SOSIG <www.sosig.ac.uk/economics>. This social science gateway is a recommended starting point for finding links to quality economic Internet resources. There are several searchable subcategories within the field of economics, and each one lists various Websites under resource type. A comprehensive description of each site by a subject specialist is included.

Sloman Economics Companion Website <cw.booksites.net/bookbind/pubbooks/sloman_ema/index.html>. A Website designed to accompany three economic textbooks written by Sloman. As well as including resources for students and teaching staff, there are many hotlinks to relevant economic sites, as well as recent news items with suggested references to encourage further reading.

Virtual Library on International Development <w3.acdi-cida.gc.ca/virtual.nsf>. Developed in Canada, this Website provides some useful links to global resources on development.

Yahoo! <dir.yahoo.com/Business_and_Economy/Directories/>. A comprehensive set of links to international business and economics pages. For Websites specific to the UK, see <uk.dir.yahoo.com/Business_and_Economy/Directories/>.

8.8.2 Business

The Business Accountant Magazine at <www.businessed.net/>. Published weekly by BusinessEd.net. Contains information on 40 international companies, detailing mergers, economic news, strategic direction, etc. In each issue one particular company is examined in depth. The free Email distribution list, available to academic staff and librarians, is well worth subscribing to for up-to-date company information.

Business Information and the Internet <www.business.dis.strath.ac.uk/>. A very comprehensive Website acting as a gateway for business economic sources and an excellent starting point for any search. However, this is no longer updated so some of the Web addressess may not be valid.

BusinessWeb <pinstripe.opentext.com/>. An impressive resource of business information, encompassing news and resources of 11 major industries. Each industry has a page providing current news, links to other relevant Websites, a directory, the facility to search for information about companies within the sector and links to appropriate news groups.

E-business Forum at <www.ebusinessforum.com>. Compiled by the Economist Intelligent Unit, this is a one-stop-shop for all you need to know on E-business. It contains global news and analysis, the latest developments in the industry, featured articles and the E-business strategies of major international competitors. It also has an excellent section on E-business research including research reports and links to Internet pages charting international E-business trends. The information is categorized into five main sections: market trends; business strategies; executive surveys; benchmarks; and resources making the information quick and easy to browse. It is possible to register on the free Email alerting service.

Europages: the European Business Directory <www.europages.com/business-info-en.html>. Provides an effective overview of the main market trends in Europe and each report can be downloaded free of charge. Topics discussed are the European Monetary Union (EMU), transport, education, etc. There is a link to the yellow pages of European countries. European data on 21 sectors are presented, divulging the main trend of each one by a series of tables, maps and graphs.

European Industrial Relations Observatory online (EIROnline) <www.eiro.eurofound.ie/>. Contains details on industrial relations in the EU member states plus Norway. The most recent additions to the Webpage are documented in chronological order on the front page of the Website. More detailed information can also be accessed by country, including feature length articles and news briefs.

Ide-Jetro: Institute of Developing Economies <www.ide.go.jp/English/index4.html>. Developed by the Institute of Developing Economics, this site provides a link to the latest press releases on East Asian issues. It also comprises links to publications such as summaries from the recent editions of Developing Economies (quarterly), an academic forum for the discussion of issues in developing countries and spot surveys on Asian economies.

The Labour Economics Gateway <labour.ceps.lu/>. Created by Jacques Brosius, an economics PhD students studying in Luxembourg. This gateway provides access to resources on labour economics, including: links to online journals; online books; working papers and articles; links to research institutes; statistics and datasets; discussion forum; and forthcoming conferences.

Market-Eye <www.marketeye.com/>. A Website that is useful for keeping up to date with company share prices, and the European and North American stock markets. It is part of Thompson Financial. It includes the Investor Service which is available free of charge but registration is required in order to access data. This service includes current prices, market news and has the option to allow the user to track certain stocks. A subscription is necessary for the Premium Service which includes Email updates and a sophisticated charting facility.

North Hall Library Business and Economics <www.mnsfld.edu/depts/lib/business.html>. An extensive resource of business and economic Websites compiled at Mansfield University, including the top five sites, general business resources, business reference resources, numeric data, and US and international economics.

8.8.3 Political economy

IPEnet <csf.colorado.edu/ipe>. A comprehensive gateway on global political economy resources. There are links to electronic mailing lists, electronic journals, PhD dissertations and electronic archives.

8.8.4 Environmental

AAEA Online: Links for Agricultural Economists <www.aaea.org/resources.html>. The official site of the American Agricultural Economics Association. The site includes useful links to academic departments, agribusiness, agricultural and economics associations, links to journals, details of meetings and conferences, and other significant links.

▶ 8.9 JOURNALS

This is not an exhaustive list of journal titles pertaining to economics. However, the ones featured below have been carefully chosen and are considered to have high academic reputations and are key journals in their area.

8.9.1 General

American Economic Review (ISSN 0002–8282) (Nashville, TN: American Economic Association, 1911–). Five issues a year, with an extra issue being published every fourth year. Academically, it is one of the most highly regarded economics journals, covering economic theory and applied economics. Economic policy, both in the US and abroad, is extensively covered. Available electronically.

Cambridge Journal of Economics (ISSN 0309–166X) (Oxford: Oxford University Press. 1977–). Bimonthly. This multi disciplinary journal is produced by the Cambridge Political Economy Society. It includes, with empirical evidence, contemporary issues such as social production, globalization, and unemployment.

Economic Affairs (ISSN 0265–0665) (Oxford: Blackwell Publishers 1980–). Quarterly. Formerly named *Journal of Economic Affairs*, this Institute of Economic Affairs journal tackles issues of an economic and social nature with each issue focusing on a different topic. Previous issues have included articles around the future of the Common Agricultural Policy, the National Dock Labour Scheme and the Economics of Sport. Articles from regular columnists specializing in IT, welfare, education, environmental issues and city news are also featured. Available electronically.

The Economic History Review (ISSN 0013–0117) (Oxford: Blackwell Publishers, 1927–). Quarterly. Covers a broad spectrum of topics including business, finance, political and gender issues. It reviews the literature published on economic history during a specified year. Available electronically.

The Economic Journal: the Journal of the Royal Economic Society (ISSN 0013–0133) (Oxford: Blackwell Publishers, 1891–). Eight issues a year. Refereed articles of an empirical, theoretical and applied nature are published by authors of international distinction. It has a high mathematical content and is currently regarded as one of the most prestigious British economics journals. Available electronically.

The Economic Review <www.soton.ac.uk/~peters/er/ecrew.html> (ISSN 0265–0290) (Oxford: Philip Allan 1982–). Five issues a year. The *Economic Review* won the Anbar Golden Page Award winner in 2000 for its readability. It is edited by staff at the University of Southampton and applies economic theory to real-life economic issues. It explains economic concepts and gives advice to students on answering examination questions. Available electronically.

Economica (ISSN 0013–0427) (Oxford: Blackwell Publishers, 1921–). Quarterly. Produced by the London School of Economics and Political Science, this key international journal concentrates on research that is currently being conducted in all fields of economics and includes theoretical as well as empirical articles, often with a statistical emphasis. Each issue contains a comprehensive review section examining recent economic material. Available electronically.

The Economist <www.economist.com> (ISSN 0013–0613) (London: The Economist Newspaper, 1843–). Weekly. Contains news summaries, letters, leaders special reports on issues of global significance, reviews of what is occurring around the world, finance and economics, science and technology. Available electronically. Some full-text articles can be downloaded free of charge.

Journal of Economic History (ISSN 0022–0507) (Cambridge: Cambridge University Press, 1940–). Quarterly. This journal is published on behalf of the Economic History Association and examines economic history from a wide range of perspectives, with the aim of promoting scholarly discussion. The subject coverage is very broad with topics such as capitalism, income tax policy, agricultural policy, wages and banking. The geographical coverage is predominately American and British but other countries and regions are covered. Available electronically.

Journal of Economic Literature (ISSN 0022–0515) (Nashville, TN: American Economic Association, 1963–). Quarterly. A key economic journal title that serves as a guide to economic research and publications. *See also 8.10.*

Journal of Economic Perspectives <www.e-jep.org/> (ISSN 0895–3309) (Nashville, TN: American Economic Association, 1987–). Quarterly. This refereed journal examines current issues relating to the field of economics, such as the future direction of economic research, economics as a discipline, and the education and future of the economist. The journal describes itself as filling a gap between academic economic journals and more generalist periodicals. Available electronically.

Journal of Post Keynesian Economics <www.mesharpe.com/pke_main.htm> (ISSN 0160–3477) (New York: M.E. Sharpe, 1978–). Quarterly. This international journal with a US bias addresses issues such as globalization and balance of payments. Available electronically.

The Manchester School (ISSN 0205–2034) (Oxford: Blackwell Publishers, 1930–). Bimonthly. This refereed journal covers a broad range of economic research, although there is a concentration on microeconomics, macroeconomics, econometrics and labour. Available electronically.

National Institute Economic Review <www.niesr.ac.uk/niesr/pdfframe.htm> (ISSN 0027–9501) (London: National Institute of Economic and Social Research, 1959–). Quarterly. The journal of the independent National Institute for Economic and Social Research contains a commentary on the current international economic climate. It also includes an analysis on the condition of the UK economy, forecasting future trends. Available electronically.

Oxford Economic Papers (ISSN 0030–7653) (Oxford: Oxford University Press, 1938–). Quarterly. Produced by economic researchers at Oxford University, this journal contains articles of a theoretical and applied economic nature and often devotes whole issues to an area of topical concern, such as the labour market.

Oxford Review of Economic Policy (ISSN 0266–903X) (Oxford: Oxford University Press, 1985–). Quarterly. A refereed journal. Each issue examines a topical subject pertaining to economic policy. Topics covered include the labour market, the Japanese economy, the Internet,

European network infrastructures, finance and growth. Available electronically.

Quarterly Journal of Economics (ISSN 0033–5533) (Cambridge, MA: MIT Press., 1886–). Quarterly. Edited by the Department of Economics at Harvard University, this highly regarded academic journal covers an extensive range of economics subjects and is one of the oldest published economics journals. Traditionally concentrating on theory, it now includes articles of an empirical as well as theoretical nature. Available electronically.

Review of Economic Studies (ISSN 0034–6527) (Oxford: Blackwell Publishers, 1933–). Quarterly. Established by British and American economists, this journal is one of the leading publications in its field. It has become very mathematically orientated, although it began life as a general economics journal.

Review of Economics and Statistics (ISSN 0034–6535) (Cambridge, MA: MIT Press, 1919–). Quarterly. This journal of high academic standing has an emphasis on empirical economics. It covers an extensive range of subjects including agricultural economics, monetary economics, labour force, international trade and business economics, etc. It is aimed at academic researchers. Available electronically.

Scottish Journal of Political Economy (ISSN 0036–9292) (Oxford: Blackwell Publishers, 1954–). Five issues a year. A high quality journal that publishes on a range of subjects including regional economics and the history of economic thought.

8.9.2 Development

Development and Change (ISSN 0012–155X) (Oxford: Blackwell Publishers, 1969–). Quarterly. Produced by the Institute of Social Studies in the Netherlands, this is a key interdisciplinary journal devoted to the critical analysis and discussion of current issues of development.

Economic Development and Cultural Change (ISSN 0013–0079) (Chicago, IL: The University of Chicago Press 1952–). Quarterly. This journal reviews the economic and social forces that affect development and the impact of development on culture. A key title in the economic development field.

Journal of Development Economics (ISSN 0304–3878) (Amsterdam: Elsevier, 1974–). Bimonthly. This journal covers a variety of issues concerning economic development.

Journal of Development Studies (ISSN 0022–0388) (Ilford, Essex: Frank Cass, 1964–). Bimonthly. A reputable interdisciplinary journal, examining the social, political and economic concepts of development. It is based at the Institute of Development Studies.

World Development (ISSN 0305–750X) (Oxford: Pergamon Press, 1973–). Monthly. This journal also concentrates upon the social, political and economic concepts of development, examining the issues and efforts taken to reduce and eliminate poverty, disease and illiteracy.

8.9.3 Methodology

Journal of Economic Methodology (ISSN 1350–178X) (London: Routledge, 1989–). Biannual. Examines the methodological concepts of historical and contemporary economics.

Journal of Economic Theory (ISSN 0022–0531) (San Diego, CA: Academic Press, 1969–). Monthly. It is a leading journal in the area of economic theory containing original research and emphasizing the 'theoretical analysis of economic models, including the study of related mathematics techniques'. Available electronically.

8.9.4 European

Economic Policy: a European Forum (ISSN 0266–4658) (Oxford: Blackwell Publishers, 1985–). Biannual. It covers international economics, concentrating on European issues, ranging from the labour force to European football, an analysis of the economics of the lotteries to the minimum wage. Available electronically.

European Journal of the History of Economic Thought (ISSN 0967-2567) (London: Routledge, 1993–). Quarterly. A refereed journal that comprises articles and discussions concerning economic history. Book reviews are also included. Available electronically.

Journal of Common Market Studies (ISSN 0221–9886) (Oxford: Blackwell Publishers, 1962–). Five issues a year. It has a reputation for producing quality articles on current and emerging EU issues. It tackles a broad range of economic topics including international relations, public policy, and monetary and fiscal economics. Once a year there is a report included on the events that have occurred within the European Union during the previous year.

Journal of European Public Policy (ISSN 1350–1763) (London: Routledge, 1994–). Five issues a year. This highly distinguished journal is written with the aim of amalgamating theoretical arguments with empirical evidence concerning European integration and public policy. Special issues are occasionally published in which a certain topic is highlighted.

8.9.5 Monetary

Journal of Finance (ISSN 0022–1082) (Oxford: Blackwell Publishers Press, 1946–). Bimonthly. An official Publication of the American Finance Association, this journal publishes research in the field of financial economics.

Journal of Monetary Economics (ISSN 0304–3932) (Amsterdam: Elsevier Science, 1975–). Three issues a year. Publishes research carried out on monetary analysis, financial institutions, changes in the structure of banking, and the workings of credit markets. Available electronically.

Journal of Money Credit and Banking (ISSN 0022–2879) (Columbus, OH: Ohio State University Press, 1969–). Quarterly. A journal devoted to the study of monetary and fiscal policy, money and banking, credit markets and financial institutions. Available electronically.

Wall Street Journal <interactive.wsj.com/home.html> (New York: Dow Jones Publishing Company, 1889–). Dedicated to business and finance matters. Available electronically.

First Monday: Articles on Internet Economics <www.firstmonday.dk/subjects/economics.html>. First started in 1996, this monthly peer reviewed e-journal, contains articles written on the economics of the Internet and its usage in the world of business.

8.9.6 Econometrics

Econometrica (ISSN 0012–9682) (Oxford: Blackwell Publishers, 1933–). Bimonthly. A high quality, refereed journal for post-graduate students produced by the Econometric Society and published in the US. It has an international team of editors and covers a wide range of theoretical and empirical subject matter, concentrating upon econometric issues. Available electronically.

The Econometrics Journal (ISSN 1368–4221) (Oxford: The Royal Economic Society and Blackwell Publishers, 1998–). Biannual. Covers all areas of econometrics: applied; methodological; computational; practical; and theoretical. It invites key figures to comment on pertinent issues and is first published on the Web to avoid a delay in publication. Available electronically.

Journal of Applied Econometrics (ISSN 0883–7252) (Chichester: John Wiley, 1986–). Bimonthly. This international journal focuses on applying existing, as well as new, econometric theory to a variety of economic situations.

Journal of Econometrics (ISSN 0304–4076) (Amsterdam: Elsevier Science, 1973–). Monthly. This journal focuses on theoretical and applied econometrics. It includes a supplement titled: *Annals of Applied Econometrics.*

8.9.7 Political

Journal of Political Economy <www.journals.uchicago.edu/JPE/journal/index.html> (ISSN 0022–3808) (Chicago, IL: The University of Chicago Press, 1892–). Bimonthly. This journal has one of the widest subject coverages of all the economics journals and is a key title in the area of political economy. Produced by the Chicago School, it includes articles embracing not only the history of economic thought, but also the labour market, monetary economics, micro and macroeconomic theory and international trade. Available electronically.

New Political Economy (ISSN 1356–3467) (Abingdon: Carfax Publishing, 1996–). Three issues a year. A relatively new journal first published in March 1996 with a focus on issues relating to the international political economy, and which marry together theoretical and empirical approaches. Topics covered include the environmental political economy, social welfare and globalization. Available electronically.

Review of International Political Economy (ISSN 0969–2290) (London: Routledge, 1993–). Quarterly. This interdisciplinary journal deals with issues such as international trade, finance and consumption in the context of the global environment. Available electronically.

8.9.8 Environment and regions

Agricultural Economics (ISSN 0169–5150) (Amsterdam: Elsevier Science, 1986–). Bimonthly. Discusses the theoretical aspects of agricultural economics. It also explores issues such as farm management, technology, energy, the environment and practical solutions to common problems. Available electronically.

Ecological Economics (ISSN 0921–8009) (Amsterdam: Elsevier Science, 1989–). Monthly. An interdisciplinary journal, distinguished by the fact that it recognizes that the economic and environmental systems are interdependent, and studies the joint economy-environment system. It has more of an ecological influence than the afore-mentioned journals.

Environment and Planning (ISSN 0308–518X) (London: Pion Publishing, 1969–). Monthly. This journal concentrates on international regional and urban issues.

The following journals are concerned with the application of economic theory and methods to environmental resource issues that require sectoral environmental policy impact analysis, environmental quality indicators, modelling and simulation, resource pricing and valuation of environmental goods:

American Journal of Agricultural Economics (ISSN 0021–857X) (Ashford, Kent: Agricultural Economics Society, 1968–). Five issues a year; *Environmental and Resource Economics* (ISSN 0924–6460)

(Dordrecht: Kluwer Academic, 1991–). Eight issues a year; *Journal of Agricultural Economics* (ISSN 0021–857X) (Ashford, Kent: Wye College (University of London), 1928–). Quarterly; *Journal of Environmental Economics and Management* (ISSN 0095–0696) (San Diego, CA: Academic Press, 1975–). Nine issues a year; and *Land Economics* (ISSN 0023–7639) (Madison, WI: University of Wisconsin Press, 1925–). Quarterly.

European Urban and Regional Studies (ISSN 0969–7764). (London: Sage Publications, 1994–). Quarterly. A forum for discussion between the varying European components of the urban and regional tradition.

Journal of Environmental Management (ISSN 0301–4797) (London: Academic Press, 1973–). Monthly. This journal focuses predominantly on management issues related to the environment. It is less mathematical than the other environmental journals previously listed but addresses similar issues.

Regional Studies (ISSN 0034–3404) (Abingdon: Carfax Publications, 1966–). Eight issues a year. This journal deals with regional issues such as housing, migration, labour markets and transport. It is a journal that focuses almost entirely on economic geography.

Urban Studies (ISSN 1360–063X) (Abingdon: Carfax Publishing, 1964–). Monthly. This journal has an emphasis on urban studies covering issues such as transport and housing.

8.9.9 Transport

Journal of Transport Economics and Policy (ISSN 0022–5258) (Bath: The University of Bath, 1967–). Three issues a year. This refereed journal has an international editorial board and contains abstracts from articles in each issue written in English, German and French.

▶ 8.10 ABSTRACTS, INDEXES AND DATABASES

The following section details some of the main economic services. *See also 1.10* for relevant broader-based services.

(a) Print

Journal of Economic Literature (JEL) (ISSN 0022–0515) (Nashville, TN: American Economic Association, 1963–). Quarterly. As well as publishing articles, this journal is a bibliographical index to material published in all fields of economics. It contains the contents pages of each journal covered by JEL, journal articles categorized by author and subject using its own classification system, and an index to dissertations each December. *See also (b) Electronic.*

Research Index <www.researchindex.co.uk/> (Lincoln: Business Surveys Ltd, 1965–). Published fortnightly since 1965, this publication indexes major international company and industrial news as reported by the UK press and a variety of key business journals. It is updated twice weekly. Available electronically.

World Banking Abstracts: the International Journal of the Financial Services Industry (ISSN 0265–9484) (London: World Banking Intelligence, 1984–) (Oxford: Blackwell Publishers, 1991–). Bimonthly. Provides concise 75 word abstracts from articles published in over 400 international banking and finance publications, organized by subject. It has a comprehensive index and full-text articles can be accessed through a service provided by the Institute of European Finance and the Chartered Institute of Bankers. Available electronically.

(b) Electronic

One of the most authoritative abstracting and indexing services of economic research is *EconLit*, <www.econlit.org/econlit/ellistjn.html> (Norwood, MA: Silverplatter). *Econlit* is an electronic database containing over 600 international journals from 1969 to the present including the titles indexed in the *Journal of Economic Literature.* As well as journals, other material documented include books of over 60 pages in length, book reviews, abstracts of working papers from Cambridge University Press, and economic doctoral dissertations. *EconLit* is also available on a CD-ROM that is updated on a monthly basis.

e-JEL <www.e-jel.org/> (Nashville, TN: American Economic Association). This is the electronic version of the *Journal of Economic Literature,* free to all AEA members using the Internet. It has a much more extensive range of journals than those provided by its print counterpart. It lists each record in hypertext format linking to abstracts and complete *EconLit* records. Author and subject indexes to dissertations published by North American Universities for that current year are also included. An indexed archive provides articles published since December 1994 in pdf-format. *JEL-CD* (Pittsburgh, PA: American Economic Association) indexes the contents of selected journals, as well as providing an index to author and subject. It also contains articles and critical reviews of new and forthcoming books. Similarly to *e-JEL,* the December issue includes an index to dissertations published by American Universities during the year. The CD-ROM is cumulative and the most current disc includes entries from the *Journal of Economic Literature* going back to 1994.

ABI/INFORM <www.umi.com/pqdauto> (Cambridge: Chadwyck Healey, part of Bell and Howell Information and Learning). The Internet version of this database is available through ProQuest and contains bibliographic details and abstracts from 1971 and full-text articles from 1992, although not all journals are available in full-text format. The global edition contains over 1300 high-quality international journals containing business, finance, and economic information, with over half available in full text. There is also a research edition (covering 800 journal titles) and a select edition (with over 350 titles). The database is also available on CD-ROM.

Business Source Premier (Ipswich, MA: EBSCO Publishing). Available from EBSCO Publishing, it has full-text access to a very impressive range of 1830 journals including economics and business titles. Full-text backfiles are in the process of being created going back to 1965.

EIU CountryData <eiu.com> (London: Economist Intelligence Unit). An extensive source of economic indicators and forecasts for 117 countries enabling retrospective searching back to 1980 and forecasting to 2005. Over 270 economic series are presented and the data is updated on a monthly basis. Other databases produced by the EIU include *EIU Country Forecasts,* that presents forecasts of economic trends of 60 countries from the Asia-Pacific, Western Europe, Eastern Europe, America and the Middle East. The figures are updated monthly. *EIU Country Reports* provides extensive data and analysis on the political, economic and business trends on six international regions including SubSaharan Africa as well as the ones cited for *EIU Country Forecasts.*

FAME (Financial Analysis Made Easy) (New York: Bureau Van Dijk). A recommended database for company information available via the Internet, on CD-ROM and DVD-ROM. It contains the financial accounts of over 550 000 public and private companies in the UK and Ireland, from information received from Companies House. Key historical information, such as balance sheets, profit and loss accounts, ratios and trends, and number of employees are provided for each company. Searches can also be performed using other criteria such as company name, geographical region, SIC codes, number of employees, and financial criteria such as turnover. Other databases detailing company information from Bureau Van Dijk include: *Amadeus* (four million companies from 32 European countries); *REACH* (varying degrees of information for 1.2 million Dutch companies); *ICARUS* (over 250 000 US companies); and included as part of the BvD suite, *JADE* (over 100 000 Japanese companies).

Goldsmiths' Kress Library of Economic Literature Index (Farmington Hills, MI: Primary Source Microfilm, Gale). An excellent resource of early economic literature dating back to the latter half of the fifteenth century and continuing through to the first half of the twentieth century, including rare editions, texts in foreign languages and anonymous works. The index was produced from the combined collections of the University of London's Goldsmith's Library of Economic Literature and the Kress Library of Business and Economics at the Harvard University Graduate School of Business Administration. The printed and microfilm versions are searchable by author or title, whereas the CD-ROM has the added advantage of an online search facility to search over 60 000 titles.

Hydra (Luton: Synergy Software). *Hydra*, formerly known as *Sequencer* is a relatively easy-to-use and valuable tool for tracing share price and market data for the past 10 years, financial ratios and balance sheets going back five years, and profit and loss data. Details can be found at <www.synsoft.co.uk/sequencer/index.htm>.

Reuters Business Briefing, www.briefing.reuters.com (London: Factiva) provides access to over 600 publications from around the world, including major newspapers, newswires and a wide selection of journals. Full-text access is available for the majority of articles written in English, while foreign language articles are usually supplied as translated abstracts.

8.11 OFFICIAL PUBLICATIONS

8.11.1 United Kingdom

A number of official UK economic publications are referred to in the statistics section at *8.12. See also section 1.11.*

Department of Trade and Industry <www.dti.gov.uk>. Provides access to a range of trade and industry statistics, press releases, recent speeches by Government ministers, plus information on DTI policy and objectives including the strategic framework 2000–2001, and expenditure plans.

HM Treasury <www.hm-treasury.gov.uk/>. This Website includes *Forecasts for the UK Economy* downloadable in pdf format. There is also a selection of published material by several forecasting organizations, latest Economic indicators, budgetary information since 1994, speeches by ministers, and latest news items.

8.11.2 Europe

(a) Print

Bulletin of the European Union (ISSN 1016–8702) (European Commission Luxembourg: Office for Official Publications, 1968–). Eleven issues a year. Published in the official languages of the European Union, this publication concentrates on the issues concerning the European Commission and its institutions. It is available in two sections: recent activities; and documentation. A subject index is included at the back of each volume with a cumulative annual index in the January edition covering the previous year. It is published with a supplement which contains official Commission material such as Commission Documents (COM DOCs).

European Economy (Brussels: Commission of the European Communities, 1978–). Monthly. A publication which reports on the economic developments and trends of the European Union. It is accompanied by three supplements: *Supplement A*: *Economic Trends* (1984–) published every month except August and concentrates on a particular economic theme with accompanying graphs and tables; *Supplement B* (1985–) *Business and Consumer Survey Results* which appears monthly apart from August and comprises tables of confidence indicators and surveys from the manufacturing, retail and construction industries and tables of consumer opinion of the economic and financial situations; and *Supplement C* (1986–) *Economic Reform Monitor*, which checks out the economic situation in the Eastern and Central European Countries.

(b) Electronic

Rapid: *the Press and Communication Service of the European Commission* <europa.eu.int/rapid/start/welcome.htm> service provides full-text access to the press releases issued by the Institutions of the European Commission. Press releases from the European Commission, Council of Ministers, Court of Justice, Court of Auditors, Economic and Social Committee, and the Committee of the Regions are made available as soon as they are released from the Institution.

Week in Europe <www.cec.org.uk/pubs/we/index.htm>. An excellent concise weekly overview of events and occurrences within the EU, issued electronically and in paper format on a Thursday from the London European Commission Press Office. This is a recommended publication for keeping abreast of EU developments with relevant Internet and postal addresses and links to reports and other documentation.

8.11.3 United States

FirstGov <www.FirstGov.gov>. An official government portal launched in September 2000 which provides free electronic access to official US Government documents.

▶ 8.12 STATISTICS

8.12.1 United Kingdom

General

There are several good places to start searching for UK economic statistics. *See 1.12* for some of the more general resources.

(a) Print

Bank of England Quarterly Bulletin (London: Bank of England, 1960–). Quarterly. This publication provides analysis of recent economic and financial developments both within the UK and worldwide. It also includes a commentary on domestic financial policy, research and analysis conducted by the bank, and articles on a wide range of pertinent global monetary issues. A useful summary page detailing the information presented in the articles has been in operation since 1994. The Bank of England Website provides a summary of each edition of the Bulletin from November 1998 along with the contents pages. The Website is: <www.bankofengland.co.uk/qb/index.htm> *See also 8.14.1.*

The *Consumer Price Indices (Business Monitor)* (London: The Stationery Office, 1962–). Monthly. Includes a summary of the latest retail price index including figures for the current month and the significant changes that took place during the previous month. Historical data going back over the last 20 years are contained, plus the European Union Harmonised Indices of consumer prices. Data are available free of charge on the Office for National Statistics Website. *See also (b) Electronic (ONS).*

Economic Trends produced by the Office for National Statistics (London: The Stationery Office, 1953–). Monthly. Contains macro economic statistics on subjects such as UK economic accounts, prices, gross domestic product (GDP), national account aggregates, the labour market and recent trends in the UK economy. It also includes analytical articles including an 'Economic Update' in which a topical issue illustrated by recently released statistics is analysed. *Economic Trends Annual Supplement* produced by the ONS (London: The Stationery Office, 1977–) is an accompanying volume to *Economic Trends* with similar content, although it has historical data dating back to up to 50 years ago making it a significant publication in its own right.

The UK Economic Accounts (London: The Stationery Office). Quarterly. This publication is also a supplement to *Economic Trends*. It provides key data on UK national and financial accounts of central and local government as well as companies and financial institutions, industrial and commercial companies, and the balance of payments. It supersedes the articles on national accounts and balance of payments published in *Economic Trends*. As well as statistical tables, each issue contains two topical articles written on the current developments of that particular quarter and estimates of UK economic accounts, focusing particularly on the balance of payments, but also including figures on GDP, household expenditure and imports and exports.

Family Expenditure Survey (London: The Stationery Office). Annual. This is a survey conducted by the Office for National Statistics and the Northern Ireland Statistics and Research Agency on 7000 households in the UK. It conveys information about household expenditure on a whole variety of goods and services. It also contains details of household income, producing information on UK patterns of spending for the Retail Price Index and provides figures for calculating consumers' expenditure in the National Accounts.

Financial Statistics (London: The Stationery Office). Monthly. Contains data on a wide range of topics within the broader subjects of: Part 1 General Financial Statistics (updated as soon as data becomes available); and Part 2 Financial and Sector Accounts (updated quarterly). Themes available include public sector finance, acquisitions and mergers, insolvencies, exchange, interest and inflation rates, financial accounts by sectors, and key economic indicators.

A Guide to Everyday Economic Statistics, 4th ed., by Gary E. Clayton and Martin Gerhard Giesbrecht (London: McGraw-Hill, 1990) is an easy-to-understand guide to economic statistics. Its coverage includes production and growth, employment, prices and financial markets.

Inflation Report (London: Bank of England, 1993–). Quarterly. The Report is available as part of the subscription to the *Bank of England Quarterly Bulletin* or as a separate publication. It is a significant resource, giving not only an in-depth commentary of the UK's economic trends (including the labour market, prices, interest and exchange rates and supply and demand) but also providing projections about forthcoming inflation rates. The Bank of England Website includes a full-text version of the current and previous edition of the report, <www.bankofengland.co.uk/inflationreport/index.htm>. *See also 8.14.1.*

Input-Output Supply and Use Tables (London: The Stationery Office). Annual. Provides data on the inputs and outputs of the UK Economy and essential criteria to consider when examining Gross Domestic Product.

Monthly Review of External Trade Statistics (Business Monitor MM24) (London: The Stationery Office). Monthly. A statistical source concentrating on trade in goods, particularly on balance of payments and overseas trade statistics. Organized according to the Standard International Trade Classification (SITC). The data are categorized according to commodity or country and is seasonally adjusted. The publication also comprises price indices and seasonally adjusted volume indices for commodity groups. Data correspond with that provided by the *IMF Balance of Payments Manual*, 5th ed., (Washington, DC: IMF, 1993). Figures can be downloaded free of charge from the Office for National Statistics Website. *See also (b) Electronic.*

The UK Balance of Payments (the Pink Book) (London: The Stationery office, 1948–). Annual. Includes estimates of the UK Balance of Payments, with each edition providing figures for the previous 10 years. From September 1998, the Pink Book data correspond with the fifth edition of the *IMF Balance of Payments Manual* (Washington, DC: IMF, 1993).

The UK National Accounts (Blue Book) (London: The Stationery Office, 1984–). Annual. Comprises estimates of the domestic and national income, product and expenditure of the United Kingdom, sector financial accounts and central government. Data are provided in all tables going back at least nine years with summary tables going back another 10 years. Chapter one of the publication has a useful analysis of national accounts with information on how the statistics are calculated.

(b) Electronic

Biz/ed <www.bized.ac.uk>. Contains statistics from 500 companies from the Extel database. Statistical information is provided by the UK Office for National Statistics. Monthly, quarterly and/or annual datasets are provided from 1960 onwards up to 1992 on topics such as gross domestic product (GDP), gross national product (GNP), and population for a variety of countries. *See also 8.8.1* and *8.4.1 (b) Electronic.*

England PLC <www.englandplc.com>. This Website is a summary of the annual publication *England PLC.* It covers areas such as regeneration, transport, local government, the economy, etc. There are also listings, rankings, maps, commentary and contacts.

MIMAS <www.mimas.ac.uk>. Provides access to key macroeconomics statistical data including the OECD Main Economic Indicators, the UNIDO Databases which includes industrial statistics and the commodity balance statistics, IMF databanks and National Statistics data. *See also 1.12.1.(b) Electronic.*

The *National Statistics: the Official UK Statistics site* <www.statistics.gov.uk/>. Includes a databank section that provides access to historical data published over a specified time period, national statistical sources such as the *Balance of Payments* (Pink Book) and *National Accounts* (Blue Book). There is a charge for using this service. *See 1.12.1(b) Electronic.*

SOSIG <www.sosig.ac.uk/roads/subject-listing/World-cat/stats.html> includes a bibliography of international statistical Websites. *See also 8.8.1* and *1.8.*

Business

(a) Print

Key Business Ratios (High Wycombe: Dun and Bradstreet, 1996). Provides a variety of financial ratios and statistics for over 370 industrial sectors based on the audited accounts of the UK companies within the industry. Data on Great Britain Ltd are provided first, this is an accumulation of all the financial figures and gives an overall picture of the whole economy, followed by data and graphics analysing each one of the major industrial sectors. The main section comprises statistical data for each individual industry, showing the norms, balance sheets, profit and loss accounts, and financial ratios.

Labour Market Trends (London: The Stationery Office, 1893–). Monthly. Presents various tables and graphs detailing the latest trends and figures, topical employment news items and analytical articles featuring data from the *Labour Force Survey*, details of current research, and labour market data covering the topics employment/unemployment statistics, labour market activity, labour disputes and earnings.

The Office for National Statistics have produced a series of guides to understanding labour market statistics, including *Guide to Regional and Local Labour Market Statistics* (London: The Stationery Office, 1999) and *Guide to Labour Market Statistics Releases* (London: The Stationery Office, 2000).

Producer Price Indices (London: The Stationery Office). Monthly. Contains data series that measure the changes in the price of goods bought and sold by manufacturers. Producer price indices of materials and fuels purchased are also included, as well as commodities produced in the UK, imports into the UK and quantities produced by the manufacturing industry categorized by sector.

(b) Electronic

<*Nomis* www.nomisWeb.co.uk>. Since 1978, Nomis has been developed and operated by staff at Durham University, run on behalf of the Office for National Statistics. It is an online database through which up-to-date official government statistical information on the UK labour market can be accessed. It includes statistics on employment/unemployment, job centre vacancies, labour force survey and census of populations. It also provides historic (going back to the 1980s) and specified regional data, even for electoral ward and postcode areas. There is a charge for using this database either through a subscription or a pay per use basis.

8.12.2 International

General

(a) Print

Economic Indicators Handbook, 5th ed., edited by Arsen J. Darnay (Farmington Hills, MI: Gale Group, 2000). A useful source of aggregate national statistics for the US economy. Includes the consumer price index, gross national product, rate of inflation and nearly 175 other US economic facts.

International Financial Statistics (Washington, DC: International Monetary Fund, 1948–). Monthly. Provides data on exchange rates, prices, production, international banking, interest rates, national accounts in tables presented by each individual country, and also accumulated into tables according to area. A separate yearbook is published and is entitled *International Financial Statistics Yearbook* (Washington, DC: International Monetary Fund, 1976–).

International Yearbook of Labour Statistics (Geneva: International Labour Office). Annual. Contains statistics from over 180 countries on subjects such as population, employment, unemployment, average hours worked and labour costs.

Main Economic Indicators (Paris: OECD, 1965–). Monthly. Provides statistics for the 29 OECD countries plus 10 non-member countries, highlighting recent economic changes. It is also available on CD-ROM.

OECD Economic Outlook (Paris: OECD, 1967–) Semiannual. This publication reviews the trends of the past year of the OECD countries. It contains future projections of economic activity on aspects such as output, prices and employment for the forthcoming two years also are presented. It also recommends economic policies to be applied in order to maintain economic growth.

OECD Economic Surveys (Paris: OECD, 1953–). Annual reports detailing recent trends and macroeconomic policy for each member country and also selected non-member countries. Key statistical information is provided on employment, balance of payments, production, wages etc. It is now available via the Internet (See <electrade.gfi.fr/cgi-bin/OECDBookShop.storefront/> for details) as well as in printed format.

Russian Economic Trends <www.hhs.se/site/ret/ret.htm> (Oxford: Blackwell Publishers, 1992–). Quarterly. This publication provides a statistical analysis of the current macroeconomic trends and policies in Russia. Each month an update is published which provides up-to-date key economic indicators.

Statistics Europe, 6th ed., edited by Joan Harvey (Beckenham: CBD Research, 1997). Provides over 1200 different sources of statistical information for economic, social and market research across Europe. The titles are classified by country.

World Economic Outlook (Washington, DC: International Monetary Fund, 1980–). Semi-annual. Contains data gathered by the IMF in collaboration with member countries. It was first published on an annual basis in 1980. In 1984 it started being published semi-annually. As well as providing charts and tables on key economic indicators, detailed analysis is also included, gathered from individual countries and groups of countries from advanced, developing and transition economies. Tables of detailed statistics are usefully provided at the end of the publication with figures going back at least 10 years. An up-to-date copy of the publication in pdf format is provided free of charge at <www.imf.org>.

The UN Statistical Yearbook (New York: United Nations, 1948–). Annual. The yearbook is organized into four main sections: world and region summary; comprising key world and regional data; population and social topics; economic activity which includes tables on production organized by International Standard Industrial Classification (ISIC); and inter-national economic relations, including exports and imports, balance of payments and international tourism. The data are gathered from the United Nations statistical division with the figures going back nine years. *See also 1.12.2.(a) Print.*

The *World Economic Survey and Social Survey* (New York: United Nations, 1948–). Monthly. This publication deals with major trends and events relating to the international economy, concentrating on international trade, production and the balance of payments.

(b) Electronic

Asian Demographics <www.asiandemographics.com>. Socio-Economic Asian statistics compiled by Asian Demographics Ltd on 14 Asian countries from 1970 until 1996. There is a fee for using the service, but statistics from 1995 are available free of charge for each of the countries, with figures projected until 2006. Key data for 1980 and 1990 are available. Statistics include demographic information, GDP and household expenditure.

Econdata.net econdata.net. An impressive Website featuring links to US regional economic data. Includes a link to the 10 best sites from the information gathered from their data user survey. It also incorporates links from 10 different subject areas.

Economagic <www.economagic.com/>. Provides access to over 100 000 economic time series data, predominantly from the US, although there is detailed coverage of statistics from other countries, including Australia, Canada, and Japan.

Economics and Development Resource Centre: Statistics and Datasystems Division <internotes.asiandevbank.org/notes/edr0006p/>. Produced by the Asian Development Bank (ADB), this Website contains a database of statistics from ADB's developing member countries from the Far East. It covers national accounts, trade, financial data and other statistics such as labour force, between the years 1998–1998. There is also a regional database which encompasses statistics including population, health indicators and poverty. Links to other statistical sites are provided.

EIA <www.eia.doe.gov/>. A Website produced by the statistical agency in the US Department of Energy. It provides data and information on a variety of fuels in the US. International statistics from countries around the world are also included, as well as projections and forecasts of world-wide energy consumption by fuel types and carbon emissions.

Handbook of International Economic Statistics <www.cia.gov/cia/di/products/hies/index.html>. A compendium of key international economic statistics collated by the Central Intelligence Agency. Areas covered include energy, agriculture, external trade, as well as economic profiles of individual countries.

History of European Integration Site: International Sources for European Statistical Data <www.let.leidenuniv.nl/history/rtg/res1/CBS.htm>. The History of European Integration Department located at Leiden University, The Netherlands, has produced a bibliography of sources of European statistical information with a description of each source.

Offstat: Official Statistics on the Web <www.auckland.ac.nz/lbr/stats/offstats/OFFSTATSmain.htm>. A comprehensive collection of Websites that offer free social and economic data gathered from official sources. The Websites have been grouped according to country and topic with figures obtained from mainly official sources. A large majority of the data can be downloaded into Excel spreadsheets.

Oxford Economic Forecasting <www.oef.com>. A useful site for obtaining a monthly economic forecast for countries worldwide. This is available free of charge. Detailed country reports are available via a subscription.

Resources for Economists on the Internet <rfe.org/Data/index.html>. Provides data on the US economy, international data from around the world, finance and financial markets plus links to academic online journals.

SIGMA (The Bulletin of European Statistics) <europa.eu.int/en/comm/eurostat/serven/part7/7a.htm>. A quarterly bulletin reporting on the methods of European data collection. A full-text version published in English, French and German is available via the Internet in pdf format. Each issue is often dedicated to a specific theme such as the quality of European data collection and statistics and the Internet.

Statistical Agencies <www.unece.org/stats/links.htm>. A bibliography of international statistical agencies compiled by the UN's Economic Commission for Europe.

Statistics – a Guide to Library Resources: <library.Adelaide.edu.au/gen/Stats.html>. An excellent guide to both printed and electronic world-wide statistical sources.

Uncle Sam's Reference Shelf <www.census.gov/statab/www/>. Provides selected data from various publications that deal with economic and social statistics of the US. It provides a useful link to 'frequently requested tables' which contains data on stock prices and yields, industrial production indexes by industry, retail sales and consumer price index. It also has a link to *USA Statistics in Brief* which covers subjects from energy to business, income to employment, and finance to business. The data go back to 1990 and are collected annually. It also provides a profile of each state, gathering data on the 1992 Economic Census, income and poverty, and Government finances as well as a guide to State statistical abstracts. *See also 1.12.2 (b) Electronic.*

United Nations <www.un.org/depts/unsd>. This Website contains National Data sources and links to various official statistical sources belonging to each country. There are also links to the Webpages of the various projects of the UN Statistical division. As well as being a useful update on the news and publications of the various organizations, annual statistics are provided on a variety of subjects including statistics from the International Monetary Fund (IMF) and the International Labour Organisation (ILO).

Business

Manufacturing Worldwide Industry Analysis Statistics, 3rd ed., by Arsen Darnay (Detroit, MI and London: Gale, 1999). Data are provided on 500 manufactured products and commodities. It examines over 4000 companies from a total of 119 countries, arranged by 37 key industry sectors and by around 500 products.

Panorama of EU industry: (Luxembourg: Office for Official Publications, 1994–). Annual. This publication, formerly called *Panorama of EC industry,* is a source of statistical data on the manufacturing and service industries of the European Union. The statistics are mainly obtained from Eurostat, Data for European Business Analysis (DEBA) and professional trade associations. At the front of the publication are special feature articles examining topical global issues. The remainder of the book is divided into an analysis of industrial sectors with reviews and forecasts written for each one, classified by the NACE coding system. Statistics are presented in a time series going back over the last 10 years.

Virtual International Business and Economic Sources (VIBES) <libWeb.uncc.edu/ref-bus/vibehome.htm>. VIBES contains over 1600 links to international economic Websites. The site is divided up into: 'comprehensive' which includes all areas of the world; 'regional' limiting the information to continents or regions; and 'national' reducing the information to a specific country. Topics include banking, business and marketing, general country information, stock markets, law, trade issues and statistics. It includes many links, pointing out what it deems are excellent sites.

World Market Share Reporter, 3rd ed., (Detroit, MI: Gale, 1998). Presents data on shares from around the world. It also contains rankings on companies, services and products. There are around 1670 entries.

▶ 8.13 RESEARCH IN PROGRESS

8.13.1 United Kingdom

The Economic and Social Research Council (ESRC) <www.esrc.ac.uk/home.html> is a good starting point for investigating current research being carried out in Britain. It describes the ESRC funding schemes available. An annual report is provided listing the work of the various research centres. There are useful links to the Websites of other research organizations. *See also 1.13. and 1.14.*

BUBL <www.bubl.ac.uk/link/e/economicsresearch.htm>. Provides a quick reference A–Z guide of current international economics research. It includes links to institutions specialising in economic research, results of statistical surveys, working papers and links to journals.

8.13.2 International

The primary source of European funding for research is the European Commission. It distributes the majority of its resources to highly publicized programmes. One of the major European research initiatives is the *Community Research and Development Information Service* (Cordis) <www.cordis.lu/>. The service is dedicated to EU research and innovation, it helps individuals and organizations partake in EU research initiatives. The Website contains recent press releases, information about the research priorities established by the member state holding the EU Council presidency, as well as the Cordis database which is free to use and is available in five European languages: English, French German, Spanish and Italian. Another good source of Website links is the *Labour Economics Gateway* found at <labour.ceps.lu/LEGcentres.html>. It contains links to European and International research centres, institutions and associations.

Research Papers in Economics (RePEc) <ideas.uqam.ca/>. This is the work of a group of over 100 individuals from around 25 countries whose main aim is to improve knowledge about the range of economic research that has been conducted and create a central point where details can be accessed. With this aim, they have created a database named *IDEAS*, an impressive resource that can be searched for working papers, journal articles, information concerning authors, institutions, etc. Details of working papers can also be Emailed to individuals. This project is sponsored by NetEc. *See also 8.3.1 (b) Electronic.*

The National Bureau of Economic Research <www.nber.org> is an independent, non-profit body devoted to promoting a greater understanding about the workings of the economy. Research is conducted by over 500 university professors around the US.

The Stanford Institute for Economic Policy Research (SIEPR) www-cepr.stanford.edu/ was created in 1982. It has two centres: the Center for Research on Economic Developments and Policy Reform (CREDPR); and the Center for Research on Employment and Economic Growth (CREEG). Areas of research include the Japanese Economy Program, tax and budget policy program, technology and economic growth program.

8.13.3 Mailing and discussion lists

A comprehensive list of economics mailing lists can be found on the *JISC National Academic Mailing List Service* <www.jiscmail.ac.uk/>. The mail groups have been set up for the UK academic and research community. Another useful Website for mailing lists is the *Resources for Economists Internet* site <rfe.wustl.edu/sc.html>, previously mentioned in *8.3.1 (b) Electronic* and *8.8.1*.

econ-bused-research (econ.bused-research@jiscmail.ac.uk) is aimed at researchers in economics and business education.

econ-business-educators econ-business-educators@jiscmail.ac.uk is aimed at teachers and lectures of economics so that issues affecting the curriculum can be discussed.

*economic-geography (*economic-geography@jiscmail.ac.uk) is an electronic discussion group available for members of the Economic Geography Research.

economicdynamics (economicdynamics@jiscmail.ac.uk) is for those researching economic dynamics, especially DGE modelling.

econ-cea-uk <www.jiscmail.ac.uk/lists/econ-cea-uk> is a mailing list pertaining to the Chinese Economic Association (UK) and is aimed at researchers interested in issues relating to the Chinese economy.

Econ-ltsn is a list is for discussions and information relating to the Economics section of the Learning And Teaching Support Network. *See also 8.8.1*. Instructions on how to join can be found at <www.jiscmail.ac.uk/lists/econ-ltsn.html>.

econ-soc-devt is a list for those interested in the area of economic and social development, particularly in relation to Third World countries. Further information available at <www.jiscmail.ac.uk/lists/econ-soc-devt.html>.

econ-value <www.greenwich.ac.uk/~fa03/iwgvt> is a discussion group for the announcements about the activities of the International Working Group on Value Theory (IWGVT).

▶ 8.14 ORGANIZATIONS

8.14.1 United Kingdom

Bank of England
Threadneedle Street, London, EC2R 8AH, UK
Tel: +44 (0)20 7601 4444
Email: enquiries@bankofengland.co.uk
Web: <www.bankofengland.co.uk>.

The Bank of England is the United Kingdom's central bank and was established in 1694. It was nationalised in 1946 but it became an independent organisation in 1997. It ensures the financial stability and monetary efficiency of the UK's economy. The bank has a useful Website containing up-to-date monetary information including retrospective monthly press releases and annual reports. Contains pages created by the Monetary and Finance Statistics Division including the *Bank of England Statistical Abstract: parts 1 and 2*, available free of charge. It also includes Base Rate information, financial statistics, and interest and exchange rates.

Centre for Economic Performance
Houghton Street, London , WC2A 2AE, UK
Tel: +44 (0)20 7955 7284
Fax: +44 (0)20 7955 7595
Email: info@cep.lse.ac.uk
Web: <cep.lse.ac.uk/>

Located at the London School of Economics and Political Science, the CEP was founded in 1990 by the Economic and Social Research Council (ESRC). It concentrates around three main areas that comprise labour markets, technology and growth, and global markets.

Centre for Economic Policy Research (CEPR)
90–98 Goswell Road, London , EC1V 7RR, UK
Tel: +44 (0)20 7878 2900
Fax: +44 (0)20 7878 2999
Email: cepr@cepr.org
Web: <www.cepr.org/home_ns.asp>

The Centre implements and obtains funding for research projects, provides workshops and conferences, and publishes research findings.

Centre for the Study of African Economies
Department of Economics, University of Oxford, Manor Road, Oxford , OX1 3UL, UK
Tel: +44 (0)1865 271084
Fax: +44 (0)1865 281447
Email: home.ulh.ac.uk/LearningSystem/Start.asp
Web: <www.csae.ox.ac.uk/>

One of the designated research centres of the Economic and Social Research Council. Conducts micro- and macroeconomic research on relating to the African economy.

Economist Intelligence Unit
15 Regent Street, London, SW1Y 4LR, UK
Tel: +44 (0)20 7830 1007
Fax: +44 (0)20 7830 1023
Email: London@eiu.com
Web: <www.eiu.com/>

Established in London in 1950, the Economist Intelligent Unit now has offices worldwide. It provides forecasts and analysis on political, economic and business trends in around 180 countries.

Employment Research Unit (ERU)
Aberconway Building, Colum Drive, Cardiff, CF1 3EU, UK
Tel: +44 (0)29 2087 4270
Fax: +44 (0)29 2087 4419
Email: PooleM@Cardiff.ac.uk
Web: <www.vista.ac.za/vista/units/eru/home.html>

Established in 1986, the ERU is a forum for research on work and employment.

Institute of Economic Affairs (IEA)
2 Lord North Street, Westminster, London, SW1P 3LB, UK
Tel: +44 (0)20 7799 8900
Fax: +44 (0)20 7799 2137
Email: iea@iea.org.uk
Web: <www.iea.org.uk/>

A completely independent organization educating the public in the role market economies play in providing a solution to economic and social problems.

Institute for Fiscal Studies
Third floor of 7 Ridgmount Street, London, WC1E 7AE, UK
Tel: +44 (0)20 7291 4800
Fax: +44 (0)20 7323 4780
Email: mailbox@ifs.org.uk
Web: <www.ifs.org.uk/>

An independent research institute dedicated to providing detailed economic analysis, focusing in particular on the UK tax system and examining the effects of fiscal policy on the public. The Institute has a well-designed Website split up into 15 subsections of activity. It details current research with either full-text access or provides publishing details. Recent working papers can be downloaded free of charge.

Institute for Social and Economic Research (ISER)
Wivenhoe Park, Colchester, CO4 3SQ, UK
Tel: +44 (0)1206 872957
Fax: +44 (0)1206 873151
Email: iser@essex.ac.uk
Web: <ideas.uqam.ca/EDIRC/data/isessuk.html>

The Institute is based at the University of Essex and receives funding from the Economic and Social Research Council (ESRC). It combines the ESRC Research Centre of Micro-social Change, ESRC UK Longitudinal Studies Centre and the European Centre for Analysis in the Social Sciences.

National Institute of Economic and Social Research
2 Dean Trench Street, Smith Square, London, SW1P 3HE, UK
Tel: +44 (0)20 7222 7665
Fax: +44 (0)20 7654 1900
Web: <www.niesr.ac.uk/>

Formed in 1938, this organization is independent of any university or political body. It carries out research into issues which will have implications on UK economic performance.

Royal Economic Society
Dept of Economics, London Business School, Sussex Place, Regent's Park, London NW1 4SA, UK
Tel: +44 (0)171 262 5050 Ext 3383
Fax: +44 (0)171 724 1598
Web: <www.res.org.uk/indexhtml>

Founded in 1890, this organization proclaims to be one of the oldest economic associations in the world. It provides training to 3300 individual members, provides a forum for the exchange of professional ideas, communication of economic information and knowledge, and liaison with international economic associations.

Scottish Economic Society (SES)
Department of Economics, University of Glasgow, Adam Smith Building, Glasgow, G12 8RT., UK
Tel: +44 (0)141 330 5534
Fax: +44 (0)141 330 4940
Email: F. G. Hay@socsci.gla.ac.uk
Web: <www.scoteconsoc.org>

Set up to promote the study and teaching of economics in line with the Adam Smith Scottish tradition of Political Economy, and to offer a platform of discussion for economic and social problems pertaining to Scotland. The society publishes the journal *Scottish Journal of Political Economy. See also 8.9.1.*

Society of Business Economists
11 Bay Tree Walk, Watford, WD1 3RX, UK
Tel: +44 (0)1923 237287
Email: 106376.3274@compuserve.com
Web: <www sbe.co.uk>

The Business Economists Group was formed in 1953, changing to its current name in 1969. This society supports and gives advice to those individuals and organizations who need to have an awareness of economic issues and developments as part of their work.

STICERD (Suntory and Toyota International Centres for Economics and Related Disciplines)
London School of Economics and Political Science, Houghton Street, London,WC2A 2AE, UK
Tel: +44(0)20 7955 6699
Fax: +44(0)20 7955 6951
Email: sticerd@lse.ac.uk
Web: <sticerd.lse.ac.uk>

Founded in 1978 with money donated by Suntory Limited and Toyota, STICERD conducts research based around four programmes: the Japanese Studies Programme (JS); Programme for the Study of Economic Organization and Public Policy (EOPP); Distributional Analysis Research Programme (DARP); and Economics of Industry (EI). It is also home to the Economic and Social Research Council (ESRC) Research Centre for the Analysis of Social Exclusion (CASE).

8.14.2 International

African Economic Community(AEC)
c/o OAU, PO Box 3243, Addis Ababa, Ethiopia, Africa
Tel: +2511 517700
Fax: +2511 512622
Web: <fp.chasque.net:8081/ngonet/trade/procesos/aec.htm>

Founded in Abuja, Nigeria in 1991, following the adoption of the Abuja Treaty. The AEC is part of the Organization of African Unity (OAU), it aims to foster African Economic integration as well as encouraging economic, social and cultural development.

African Economic Research Consortium (AERC)
International House, 8th Floor, PO Box 62882, Nairobi, Kenya, Africa
Tel: +2542 225234
Fax: +2542 219308
Email: aerc@elci.gn.apc.org
Web: <www.aercafrica.org/>

Promotes independent investigation into the economic problems of the sub-Saharan region of Africa. Established in August 1988.

AISEC: International Association of Students in Economics and Management
AIESEC International, Teilingerstraat 126, 3032-AW, Rotterdam, The Netherlands
Tel: +31 10 443 4383
Fax: +31 10 265 1386
Email: info@ai.aisec.org
Web: <www.aiesec.org/>

Founded in Stockholm in 1949. Proclaimed to be the largest international student organization with a membership of around 50 000, its specific aim is to mobilize students into the global community by encouraging them to participate in international exchange projects.

American Economic Association
2014 Broadway, Suite 305, Nashville, TN 37203, USA
Tel: +1 615 322 2595
Fax: +1 615 343 7590
Email: aeainfo@ctrvax.vanderbilt.edu
Web: <www.vanderbilt.edu/AEA/>

Founded in 1885 at Saratoga, New York, this organization is devoted to the production of historical and statistical research.

Canadian Economics Association (CEA)
President: James MacKinnon, Department of Economics, Queen's University, Kingston, ON K7L 3N6.
Tel: +1 613 533 2293
Email: jgm@qed.econ.queensu.ca
Web: <economics.ca/>

Scholarly organization for Canadian academic economists.

Center for Economic Policy Analysis (CEPA)
80 Fifth Avenue, Fifth Floor, New York, NY 10011 8002, USA
Tel: +1 212 229 5901
Fax: +1 212 229 5903
Email: cepa@newschool.edu
Web: <www.newschool.edu/cepa>

Created in 1995, devoted to economic policy research, concentrating on macroeconomic policy, inequality and poverty, and globalization.

The Chinese Economists Society (CES)
733 15th St, NW, Suite 910, Washington, DC 20005, USA
Tel: +1 202 347 8588
Fax: +1 202 347 8510
Email: vmcorp@aol.com
Web: <china-ces.org/>

An academic organization dedicated to encouraging a Chinese economy based on market forces, furthering international communication by Chinese academics and research into the Chinese economy.

Economic Policy Institute
1660 L Street NW, Suite 1200, Washington, DC, 20036, USA
Tel: +1 202 775 8810
Fax: +1 202 775 0819
Email: epi@epinet.org
Web: <epinet.org/>

Founded in 1986 by a group of Economic policy experts, EPI is committed to conducting research on economic issues, recommending policy as a result of the findings, and sharing its activities with relevant audiences.

The Econometrics Society
Executive Director Secretary, Department of Economics, Northwestern University, Evanston, 60208 2600, Illinois, USA
Tel: +1 847 491 3615
Email: es@<www.econometricsociety.org
Web: <gemini.econ.yale.edu/es/>

Founded in 1930 by international economists, mathematicians and statisticians, this organization concentrates on analysing economic theory in relation to statistics and mathematics, as well as promoting research which combines a theoretical and empirical approach to economic problems.

European Central Bank
European Monetary Institute, PO Box 10 20 31, D-60020, Frankfurt-Main, Germany
Tel: +49 69 24 00 06 91
Fax: +49 69 24 00 06 99
Web: <www.ecb.int/>

Created in June 1998 after an idea that was initiated in the 1992 Maastricht Treaty. It forms the European System of Central Banks (ESCB) along with the Central Banks from another 11 EU member states. It formulates the monetary policy of the Euro area and ensures its implementation either by its own actions or through the instruction of the national central banks.

European Economic Association (EEA)
34, voie du Roman Pays, B-1348 Louvain-la-Neuve, Belgium
Tel: +32 10 472 012
Fax: +32 10 474 021
Email: eea@core.ucl.ac.be
Web: <www.core.ucl.ac.be/eea>/

Established in 1985 with the aim of developing economics as a science in Europe, enhancing the communication and exchange of ideas between students, lecturers and researchers, and improving liaison between European academic institutions and research organizations.

Institute for International Economics
11 Dupont Circle, NW Washington, DC 20038, USA
Tel: +1 202 328 9000
Fax: +1 202 328 5432
Web: <www.iie.com/>

An independent think-tank on international economic policy that was established in 1981.

International Development Information Centre
Canadian International Development Agency, Place du centre, 200 Promenade du Portage, Hull, Québec, K1A 0G4, Canada
Tel: +1 819 953 1035
Fax: +1 819 953 8132
Email: _cidi-idic@acdi-cida.gc.ca
Web: <w3.acdi-cida.gc.ca/INDEX-E.HTM>

Supports sustainable development activities with the aim of reducing global poverty.

International Monetary Fund (IMF)
700 19th Street, N W, Washington, DC 20431, USA
Tel +1 202 623 7000
Fax: +1 202 623 4661
Email: publicaffairs@imf.org
Web: <www.imf.org/>

The IMF was founded to encourage economic growth, foster the stability of the exchange rate, promote high employment levels and provide financial assistance to aid countries alleviate the balance of payment adjustment. The IMF has a membership of 183 countries.

Latin American and Caribbean Economic Association (LACEA)
Center for International Economics, 4118 Tydings Hall, University of Maryland College Park, MD 20742, USA
Tel: +1 301 405 4536
Fax: +1 301 405 7835
Email: stanton@econ.umd.edu
Web: <www.lacea.org/>

Since its formation in 1992, this organization has sought to be a forum for international economists to discuss issues pertaining to the economies of Latin America and the Caribbean.

Middle Eastern Economics Association
Jeffrey B Nugent, Executive Secretary c/o Dept of Economics, University of Southern California,, University Park, Los Angeles, CA 90089 0253, USA
Fax: +1 213 740 8543
Email: nugent@rcf.USC.edu
Web: <www.gsb.luc.edu/depts/economics/meea.htm>

An academic organization promoting scholarly discussion and research on Middle Eastern economics.

National Bureau of Economic Research (NBER)
1050 Massachusetts Ave, Cambridge, MA 02138, USA
Tel: +1 617 868 3900
Web: <www.nber.org/>

Since its foundation in 1920, this independent organization has conducted research on the aggregate economy including Milton Friedman's study on money and consumer spending. It now proclaims to have over 500 eminent US university professors researching and analysing trends in the US economy.

Organization for Economic Co-operation and Development (OECD)
2, rue André Pascal, F-75775 Paris Cedex 16, France
Tel: +33 1 45 24 82 00
Email: news.contact@oecd.org
Web: <www.oecd.org/>

An organization in which 29 member countries can discuss and exchange information, seek solutions to common problems and make economic and social policy decisions.

UNU World Institute for Development Economics Research
UNU/WIDER, Katajanokanlaituri 6 B, FIN-00160 Helsinki, Finland
Tel: +358 9 61 59911
Email: wider@wider.unu.edu
Web: <www.wider.unu.edu/>

A research and training centre that aims to carry out studies with the single purpose of improving quality of life for both individuals and for the community.

World Bank
1818 H Street, N W, Washington, DC 20433, USA
Tel: +1 202 477 1234
Fax: +1 202 477 6391
Web: <www.worldbank.org/>

Provides financial backing and support to over 100 developing countries, helping them to eradicate poverty and ensure a degree of economic stability.

World Trade Organization
Centre William Rapard, Rue de Lausanne 154, CH-1211 Geneva 21, Switzerland
Tel: +41 22 739 51 11
Fax: +41 22 731 42 06
Email: enquiries@wto.org
Web: <www.wto.org/wto/index.htm>

Founded in 1995, the World Trade Organization is the successor to GATT. Its remit is 'to consider the legal and institutional foundation of the multi-lateral trading system and how governments frame and implement trade legislation and regulation.' The World Trade Organization Website is available in English, French and Spanish. It contains full-text information that can be downloaded free of charge, for example the annual report, news archives and press releases.

▶ REFERENCES

Marshall, A. (1890) *Principles of Economics.* London: Macmillan.

Robbins, Lord. (1932) 'Essay on the nature and significance of economic science', in A. Partington, (1992) (ed.) *The Oxford Dictionary of Quotations.* Oxford: Oxford University Press, p.541.

Sutherland, S. and Blake A. (2000) 'Nomis via the Web', in *Labour Market Trends,* **108**(7), 349–52.

▶ ACKNOWLEDGEMENTS

Special acknowledgements for their help and encouragement with this chapter go to Peter Clarke, David Gray, Julian Beckton and Richard High.

9 Human services

Mark Watson and Angela Upton

▶ 9.1 NATURE AND SCOPE OF HUMAN SERVICES

Human Services is a term used in a number of countries to cover those services which work alongside health services to support individuals, families and groups of people, and as such covers areas referred to variously as welfare services, personal social services, social work and variations thereof. The exact nature of those services varies between countries, in legal, administrative, practical and cultural aspects. The Department of Health and Human Services in the US administers services delivered on a federal and local level, typically by departments of social services. In the UK, the Department of Health is responsible for 'social care'. The term originally relating to a subset of social work, but one which now has transformed into a broader definition which encompasses social work. In Northern Ireland, there is a Department of Health and Social Services and Public Services, and in Scotland the Scottish Executive has transferred responsibility for some social services from the Social Work Department to other parts of the Executive. Departments and ministries of social welfare are common in some European countries, whilst others have radically different structures.

Even the term 'social worker' hides a multitude of variations. The average US social worker takes a college route through bachelor and masters degrees, and will often practise as a clinical social worker with an emphasis on counselling and therapeutic interventions, often in private practice. Many European countries and Australia, follow a similar academic route, whilst the UK social worker typically qualifies professionally in their early 30s, having had several years experience within the field – although a three-year undergraduate degree level social work qualification is now an option. In other European countries, roles such as 'assistant social', 'social educateur' and 'social pedagogue' cover tasks which will typically be carried out by social workers, community workers and youth workers. This tends to make the transferability of information across borders in the wide area denoted by human services more problematic than is the case in other disciplines, and many information sources in the human services will not travel well – for example, the *Encyclopedia of Social Work* produced in, and a key resource for, the US will not be directly helpful to a social worker in the UK (*see 9.6.1 (a)*).

This chapter will look, wherever possible, at broad information resources covering the human services. Due to the issue of terminology raised above, not all will feature the term 'human services' in their names, and many will use related terms such as social services, social welfare or social work. In addition to these broad scope resources, a selection of exemplars from more specific subject areas covered by human services will be identified. For the sake of geographical comprehensiveness, the chapter will attempt to draw resources from as many countries as is possible, even to the extent of identifying some which are not written in English.

► 9.2 ANNUALS

Annual publications in the human services include annual reviews of social services and social policy, annual reports from government organizations, journals, statistics and handbooks. Statistics and handbooks are listed in the relevant sections (*9.12* and *9.7* respectively), and annual reports from government are in Official Publications (*9.11*). This section presents some representative examples from other categories of annual publications.

One major annual in the social services field in the UK is the *Guide to the Social Services* (London: Waterlow Professional Publishing), which is produced by the Family Welfare Association. The guide first appeared in 1882, when it formed the introduction to the first edition of the *Charities Register and Digest*, published by the Charity Organization Society. It was then published separately and called *How to Help Cases of Distress: a Handy Reference Book for Almoners*. The book was intended to meet the need for information on law, regulations and available services. Even more relevant to United Kingdom practice today, with people in the caring professions having to cope with ever increasing change, the *Guide* provides clear, up-to-date, basic information about the services available and the legal framework underpinning them. The *Guide* defines 'social services' as 'services . . . provided by the community to meet certain individual needs' (p.vii) and is organized by type of service provided. It contains sections, clearly laid out with paragraph headings, on: organization and administration of public social services; services for children and families; community care; health services; welfare benefits and pensions; taxation;

housing; education; employment; the law and legal services; nationality, immigration and race equality; and information, advice, help and useful addresses. It also contains appendices on: training for the personal social services; social services departments and the Social Services Inspectorate; social services in Scotland; and a bibliography. It concludes with a directory of addresses and an index.

In the United States, the National Association of Social Workers produces *Social Work Speaks: NASW Policy Statements* (Washington, DC: NASW Press) on a regular basis. NASW (*see 9.14.3*) is the professional body for social workers in the United States and the policy statements present NASW's position on the full range of contemporary social issues and the role of social work and the human services. The statements are presented in alphabetical order (from Abortion to Youth Suicide) and recent policy statements include Correctional Social Work, Environmental Policy, Technology and Social Work and Transgender and Gender Identity Issues. The NASW Code of Ethics is also included in this comprehensive volume.

The Social Policy Association's *Social Policy Review* (London: Social Policy Association) started in 1972 as *The Year Book of Social Policy*, changing its title with the 1989–90 edition. The *Social Policy Review* focuses on the policies and policy formulation processes influencing social care and takes the form of an annual collection of 16 or more essays. The focus is mainly on United Kingdom policy, but each edition includes four or five chapters on significant social policy changes or events in other countries. For example, the 1997 edition focuses on the shifting boundaries of social policy, with papers on social policy and the arts, and the impact on British women of raising their pension age to 65. Internationally, there were papers on, for example, Australian social policy towards 2000 and changing social policy in South Africa.

Many Eastern European countries are gearing up to provide social services along a more Western model and have begun to produce annual reviews of social services which often include abstracts of articles in English. An example is *Ljetopis Studijskog Centra Socialnog Rada* (ISSN 1330–6456) (Zagreb: Pravni fakultet Sveucilista u Zagrebu. Studijski Centar Socijalnog Rada, 1994).

An annual journal with an international focus is the *New Global Development Journal of International and Comparative Social Welfare* (ISSN 1080–9716) (Baton Rouge, LA: Dialogues, 1985). The journal 'seeks to reflect the post Cold War zeitgeist of international and comparative social welfare'. A typical issue included articles on: the politics of human need; changing social welfare systems in Nordic countries; and Sartre's existentialism and social work. This annual is about to be launched on the Web as <www.newglobaldevelopment.com>.

In the UK, *The Mental Health Research Review* (ISSN 1353–2650) (Canterbury: University of Kent. Personal Social Services Research Unit,

1994) appears annually. It is, essentially, an annual introduction to some of the mental health research work, either in progress or complete, produced by the Personal Social Services Research Unit (*see 9.14.1*) and the Institute of Psychiatry's Centre for the Economics of Mental Health. The review is split into a series of short articles highlighting the salient policy issues and background to each project, along with key results and conclusions.

► 9.3 BIBLIOGRAPHIES

9.3.1 General

Printed bibliographies were a mainstay of human services information provision in the UK in the 1970s and 1980s. Examples of these include the Library Association's *Personal Social Services Bibliography* edited by Gill Stewart (London: Library Association: 1st ed., 1978; and 2nd ed., 1980). The third edition was actually a supplement: *The Social Services Bibliography 1980–1985* edited by Gill Stewart and John Stewart (Lancaster: University of Lancaster, Department of Social Administration, 1985). These were the first attempts to draw together the literature on the new personal social services structures implemented at the beginning of the 1970s and a reflection on the lower volume of literature being published in those days.

The sheer volume of literature being published in the personal social services alone would nowadays preclude any attempt at a comprehensive listing as done by Stewart – the National Institute for Social Work's monthly abstracting service *Caredata Abstracts* (*see 9.10.1* (*b*)) lists over 4000 articles and books each year.

The Department of Health Library was one of the main providers of bibliographies during the 1970s and 1980s with a series of ready-made listings on all aspects of the personal social services which numbered several hundred. The establishment of their monthly *Social Services Abstracts* (*see 9.10.1* (*a*)) and subsequently the online *DHSS-DATA* (*see 9.10.1* (*b*)) will doubtless have been a factor in the discontinuation of this service. More focused bibliographies are therefore the rule, and a selection of these is provided below.

9.3.2 Social work

Hong-Chan Li's *Social Work Education: a Bibliography* (Methuen, NJ: Scarecrow Press, 1978) featuring literature after 1960 (but with some earlier items), and its supplement *Social Work Education II: a Bibliography 1977–1987* (Metchuen, NJ: Scarecrow Press, 1989) are detailed bibliographies with a US focus. Both volumes conclude with a section on international social work education.

A Bibliography of European Studies in Social Work (Lyme Regis: Russell House, 2000) by Steven Shardlow and Stacey Cooper, is part of a three-year multinational project sponsored by the Socrates Programme of the European Union and is unique in that no other similar bibliography exists. It contains details of documents published in English after 1980 and each entry provides a concise outline of the content of the item. The bibliography includes: comparative studies of social work that feature at least two European states; comparative studies of social work that include at least one European state and one non-European state; general theoretical material on comparative studies in social work; and single country studies. This is an essential resource for identifying comparative literature, and for finding out about social work in other countries.

Spiritual Diversity and Social Work: a Comprehensive Bibliography with Annotations compiled by Edward R. Canda, Mitsuko Nakashima, Virginia Burgess and Robin Russel (Alexandria, VA: Council on Social Work Education, 1999) aims to be a comprehensive listing of more than 550 writings on spirituality and social work in the English language. Spirituality is defined as a universal aspect of human experience concerned with the search for a sense of meaning and purpose. While the main focus of the bibliography is on North American literature, many of the items listed are relevant to cross-cultural social work in any setting or country. Divided into five sections: religious and non religious spiritual perspectives; cultural perspectives and issues pertaining to spirituality; spirituality in various fields of social work; general concepts, concerns and approaches to spirituality and religion; and ethics, values and moral issues.

9.3.3 Homelessness

The National Homeless Alliance's *Bibliography: a First List of Publications Relevant to Homelessness* (London: National Homeless Alliance, 1999) has been produced primarily for day centre staff, but is also of use to a wider audience. The unannotated listing covers a range of publications dealing with management matters and the services provided to homeless people who are day centre users, as well as providing background reading on both general and particular aspects of homelessness. The bibliography is arranged under subject headings and has a comprehensive list of relevant organizations at the end. However, the lack of any abstracts or annotations to the entries makes this listing less useful than it might have been.

9.3.4 Mental health

The mental health of people from minority ethnic groups is a controversial issue of current concern in psychiatry, mental health services and social services. Introduced by an executive summary, Dinesh Bhugra's timely bibliography and literature review *Mental Health of Ethnic Minorities: an Annotated Bibliography* (London: Gaskell, 1999) contains the most important research published in this area during the 1980s and 1990s. Each entry consists of a detailed but concise and accessible summary. Aimed at clinicians, researchers, mental health professionals and all those involved in providing cross-cultural mental health services, it is an important source of information.

9.3.5 Older people

Long Term Care: an Annotated Bibliography compiled by Theodore H. Koff and Kristine M. Bursac (Westport, CT: Greenwood Press, 1995), focuses on long-term care in the United States, and as such many of the items listed are not directly relevant to practice in other countries. However, an ageing population is common to many countries and many of the issues discussed in the documents in this bibliography are useful on a comparative basis. The listing covers literature published between 1980 and 1995 and is arranged into 12 subject chapters, covering such topics as the past and future of long-term care, community services, non-institutional care and ethics. Each entry has a short abstract. *Gold Standards: a Guide to Professional Targets for the Care of Elderly People; a Selected Bibliography* (London: Age Concern, Royal College of Physicians, 1994) is designed to provide a list of guidelines and standards on all aspects of good quality care for older people. Produced by a range of organizations, including government and professional bodies, the bibliography is organized under subject headings and covers both social and health care. Entries include annotations and date from 1985 to 1994. This is an extremely useful resource for all those interested in services for older people, though other sources need to be consulted for post-1994 data.

Part of a series of detailed bibliographies designed to heighten awareness of existing practice, to serve the process of search and discovery, and to help Local Authorities learn from each other, *Inlogov Informs on the Third Age,* compiled and edited by Lesley Grayson and Margaret Hobson (Birmingham: University of Birmingham. Institute of Local Government Studies, 1994/95), contains sections on a wide range of topics relating to older people and an ageing society. A detailed introduction precedes the 11 separate sections, each with introductory articles looking at issues and policies, followed by the entries, each with an abstract. Documents published from the late 1980s to 1995 are included. Topics covered comprise: trends and issues in ageing; the attitudes and values of older people and society to older people; income and pensions; working life and retirement; housing; health and wellbeing; lifestyles; older women; carers; black elders; and elder abuse.

9.3.6 HIV/AIDS

Research in AIDS Care: an Annotated Bibliography of Social Research in HIV and AIDS Care in the United Kingdom, 1982–1995 compiled by Rayah Feldman, Ruth Garside and Philip Gatter (London: NAM Publications and South Bank University, 1996), brings together published research materials relating specifically to AIDS care in the UK. The focus is on social rather than medical aspects of AIDS and includes entries on HIV testing and counselling. Service provision is considered at a number of levels, from national through to organizational level policy, management, and service delivery. The bibliography is divided into four sections: client groups; professionals and volunteers; service provision; and research methods. Each entry includes a detailed abstract. One of the aims of the bibliography is to improve the links between research and practice. This is a clearly laid out, easy-to-use document of interest to both practitioners and users of HIV/AIDS services.

9.3.7 Children and young people

(a) Print

For service providers, particularly managers, wanting to evaluate the quality and effectiveness of their work with children, *Help with Evaluation: an Annotated Bibliography for Managers and Practitioners* compiled by Sophie Laws (London: Save the Children, 1995) is a good, basic bibliography with entries dating from 1986 to 1995. Each item contains a short abstract and a critical evaluation. Variations on the bibliography include the National Children's Bureau's *Highlights Series*, which typically covers one topic on two sides of A4, discussing the key literature and then listing the sources. Recent issues have included *Evidence-based Child Care Practice* (London: National Children's Bureau, 1999) and *Bullying in Schools* (London: National Children's Bureau, 2000).

(b) Electronic

The Nordic Youth Research Information Bibliography (Stockholm: EPM Data AB) is the result of Nordic (Denmark, Finland, Iceland, Norway, and Sweden) cooperation on the documentation of youth research. Particularly strong on grey literature, the bibliography has a primarily academic focus. From 1988 to 1996, the bibliography was produced annually in print form. In 1998, it merged with the *European Youth Research Bibliography* (Strasbourg-Wacken, France: Council of Europe, Youth Directorate, European Youth Centre). Now only available in electronic form, it can be accessed on the World Wide Web at <eyrb.epm.se/>.

The Australian National Child Protection Clearing House produces a comprehensive range of *Bibliographies* (Melbourne: National Child Protection Clearing House) which represent a selection of regularly updated references from the *Australian Family & Society Abstracts* database. All documents listed are held in the Australian Institute of Family Studies library. The bibliographies are available free on the World Wide Web at: <www.aifs.org.au/nch/bibmenu.html>.

9.3.8 Drug and alcohol misuse

The Library at the Canadian Addiction Research Foundation, based at the University of Toronto, produces a wide range of bibliographies, freely downloadable from the World Wide Web, on drug and alcohol misuse. The *Bibliographies* (Toronto: University of Toronto. The Addiction Research Foundation), updated to 1998, are at <www. arf.org/isd/bib/list.html>. For later material the site directs you to <www.camh.net/>.

Exploring the Links between Substance Use and Mental Health: an Annotated Bibliography and a Detailed Analysis (Ottawa: Health Canada, 1996) is designed to investigate the links and relationships between substance use and mental health. A wide selection of articles is covered and the bibliography has the added value of an analysis of the literature in each section. The document is freely available on the World Wide Web at: <www.hc-sc.gc.ca/hppb/alcohol-otherdrugs/pdf/bib_e.pdf>.

▶ 9.4 DICTIONARIES

9.4.1 General

(a) Print

The major social work dictionary emanates from the United States – The National Association of Social Workers, *Social Work Dictionary*, 4th ed., edited by Robert L. Barker (Washington, DC: National Association of Social Workers, 1999). This volume contains nearly 8000 terms covering concepts, organizations, historical figures and values that define the profession in the United States of America (*see also (b) Electronic* below).

Whilst many of the values underpinning social work practice are constant throughout most of the world, the history, structures, practices and legislation are markedly different. As such, this dictionary would not be as useful for those in the UK as the following title.

The *Social Welfare Word Book* by Alan Dearling, (Harlow: Longman, 1993) begins with a particularly handy 17 pages of acronyms and abbreviations. Entries in the main A–Z (A–Y in actual fact) sequence of words and phrases have a paragraph or two describing them. Entries also contain useful see also references – for example, 'Milieu Therapy' describes this form of therapy which usually takes place in residential care settings with socially or mentally disordered people, and refers the reader to Residential Care, Therapy and Token Economy. In addition to practice issues, management is also covered – for example, Quality Assurance, which refers the reader to entries for Audit, British Standard BS5750, Quality Circles, Standards, Total Quality Management and Value Analysis. This latter example highlights the way in which some areas of human services change more than others – the management techniques described would now be seen as 'very mid-1990s'. This useful volume, now somewhat dated, rather undersells itself in its title, and could more accurately be described as an encyclopaedia. At a similar time, the *Dictionary of Social Work*, edited by Martin Thomas and John Pierson (London: Collins Educational, 1994) was published, which is also worth consulting.

Prior to the above volumes, the key UK dictionary was the *Dictionary of Social Welfare* edited by Noel Timms and Rita Timms (London: Routledge and Kegan Paul, 1982). This offers an interesting historical perspective, although one has a sneaking suspicion that copies may still be lurking on some library shelves as a current resource!

(b) Electronic

The National Association of Social Workers, *Social Work Dictionary* (*see (a) Print* above), *The Encyclopedia of Social Work* (*see 9.6.1*(*a*)) and the *Social Work Almanac* (*see 9.12.2*(*a*)) have been brought together in electronic format on CD-ROM as the *Social Work Reference Library* (Washington, DC: NASW, 1998–).

9.4.2 Multilingual

As already stated, the culturally specific nature of human services poses a problem in providing information which can be relevant in different systems. Language also poses a problem. An interesting example of a multi-lingual dictionary is the *Glossary of Social Care Terms: English, French, German, Spanish* edited by Marian Dickinson, Adrian Greenwood and John Mitchell (Canterbury: European Institute of Social Services,

University of Kent, 1995). At 27 pages it is a slim volume, alphabetically arranged by English terms only, as opposed to having a separate sequence for each language. A more traditionally arranged multi-lingual dictionary is the *Glossary of Child, Social Care and Social Work Terms* (Zurich: International Federation of Educative Communities, 1991), which is worth consulting.

9.4.3 Learning disability

The degree to which dictionaries can date is variable. In addition to content, the titles themselves can suffer – take, for example, *The Dictionary of Mental Handicap* edited by Mary P. Lindsey (London: Routledge, 1989). While 'mental handicap' is still (although decreasingly so) used in health, the phrases 'learning disabilities' and 'learning difficulties' have taken the place of mental handicap in social care – although not in the US, where the phrase 'mental retardation' still persists. Although fast approaching its 'sell by' date, the encyclopaedic coverage of this dictionary makes it still worth consulting.

9.4.4. Race

The *Dictionary of Race and Ethnic Relations*, 4th ed., edited by Ellis Cashmore, et al. (London: Routledge 1996) contains detailed entries which typically cover a couple of pages and provides useful further reading suggestions as well as *see also* references. An idea of the scope can be seen by the consecutive entries: Scarman Report, Segregation, Self-Fulfilling Prophecy, Skinheads, Slavery and Social Darwinism – a good international mix of coverage, general theoretical concepts and historical detail. In addition to being a reference tool, this volume could quite easily, and perhaps more appropriately, be suggested as a standard introductory read for anyone studying in the human services field.

9.4.5 Family therapy

The Dictionary of Family Psychology and Family Therapy, 2nd ed., by S. Richard Sauber, Luciano L'Abate and Gerald R. Weeks (London: Sage, 1993) briefly defines over 1500 terms. Each entry provides information relating to the origin of the term, an example and a source. It updates Sauber's previous work *Family Therapy: Basic Concepts and Terms* published in 1985.

9.4.6 Biographical

The Biographical Dictionary of Social Welfare in America by Walter I. Trattner (Westport, CT: Greenwood Press, 1986) provides biographical sketches of some 300 prominent Americans who were active in social work or other related fields. Entries usefully include a list of sources for further information and critical comments about their lives.

► 9.5 DIRECTORIES

9.5.1 Social care

(a) Print

For European Union addresses *The Europe Directory: a Research and Resource Guide* (London: Stationery Office, 1992–) edited by Antony Inglis and Charles Leonard is worth looking at. It includes information on: the single European market; EU legislation; institutions and decision-making processes; a bibliography; and a comprehensive list of addresses.

The IHSM Health and Social Services Year Book (London: Institute of Health Services Management, 1888–), edited by Guy Howland and produced annually, contains detailed entries for relevant organizations, but is more health than social care focused. It has a section on central government and other health related organizations, followed by sections on health purchasers and health providers. A shorter listing on social services organizations for England, Wales and Scotland follows. The directory also includes a full listing of *Health Circulars*.

The Social Services Yearbook (London: Pearson Education, 1972–) is produced annually and is an essential reference tool for any organization involved in social services and social welfare in the United Kingdom. It aims to be a comprehensive guide and to reflect the changing functions of the organizations involved in providing social and health care in the statutory, private and voluntary sectors. The directory is arranged in two parts. Part one provides details on relevant central and local government organizations, and education and health services throughout the UK. It also includes information on legal issues. Part two provides data on voluntary, private and non-statutory services. It also contains sections on: education and training in health, welfare and social work; research and development organizations; and on social services media. *See also (b) Electronic* below.

The Public Human Services Directory (Washington, DC: American Public Human Services Association, 1940–) is the main directory for the public human services in the United States, with over 30 000 personnel listed in 70 programme areas. It includes contacts for such programmes as child welfare, welfare-to-work, education, housing, Medicaid, public health, information systems, and employment and training. The Council on Social Work Education produces the *Directory of Colleges and Universities with Accredited Social Work Programs* (Alexandria, Va: Council on Social Work Education, 1952–). This annual publication is an excellent source of information on social work education and the organizations that run courses on the human services in the United States.

The Voluntary Agencies Directory (London: National Council for Voluntary Organizations, 1973–) appears semi-annually and is an important UK reference source, covering a wide range of voluntary organizations. The directory is arranged in alphabetical order by organization name and each entry includes a short description of what the organization does. There is also a useful classified index at the end.

(b) Electronic

For finding addresses and other information on European social welfare organizations, and on how social welfare is organized in individual European countries, perhaps the best starting point is the *European Social Welfare Information Network* (ESWIN) Website at <www.eswin.net/>. ESWIN includes links to social welfare organizations in Austria, Belgium (the Flemish region), Israel, the Netherlands, Luxembourg, Spain and the United Kingdom. A comprehensive searchable database of organizations, with browseable category listings (similar to *Yahoo*), is included as part of the Website.

The *Social Services Yearbook* (*see (a)Print* above) is also available on CD-ROM, and although this is an expensive option, among other advantages it offers a freely downloadable addresses and address labels facility. In the United States, the *Department of Health and Human Services* has an easily navigable Website which includes a ‘gateway’ page <www.hhs.gov/gateway/> containing links to relevant state and federal organizations and is probably the best starting point for contact addresses for US Governmental organizations dealing with the human services.

9.5.2 Black and minority ethnic people

The *Directory 2000 of Black Voluntary Organizations Working with Black Children and Families* (London: Race Equality Unit, 2000–) is much more than a list of addresses. In addition to contact details, each entry contains information on services provided, geographical areas served, and community languages used by staff. *The Diversity Directory: Your Guide to Equality and Diversity Consultancies* (Turvey: Diversity UK, 1983–) is produced annually. Each entry contains detailed background information on the consultancies listed. The directory also contains: feature articles; areas of work index; equal opportunities issues index; and an index to the consultancies listed. For European addresses, *Ethnic Minority and Migrant Organizations: European Directory* (London: Joint Council for the Welfare of Immigrants, 1991–) compiled and edited by Ciaran O'Maolain is a good starting point.

9.5.3 Disabled people

The UK *Directory for Disabled People: a Handbook of Information for Everyone Involved in Disability* compiled by Ann Darborough and Derek Kinrade (Hemel Hempstead: Prentice Hall/Harvester Wheatsheaf, 1988–) is produced annually and provides a guide to the whole range of services, facilities and opportunities available to disabled people and to those who care for them. Each section contains a description of statutory services available, details of legislation, what is available from the voluntary sector, details of relevant organizations and much more. It begins with a section on general statutory services and goes on to provide information on: money (including social security benefits); aids and equipment; housing and home; education; further and higher education and training; employment; mobility and motoring; holidays; leisure activities; sex and personal relationships; legislation; and access.

9.5.4 Older people

The European Directory of Older Age: Information and Organizations Concerned with Older People in the 12 EC Member States (London: Centre for Policy on Ageing, 1993–) compiled by Gillian Crosby, Anna King, Nat Lievesley and Frances Perry, presents a general overview of older people across the EC, including statistics, and goes on to provide country-by-country information on the full range of services available to older people.

9.5.5 Probation

NAPO Probation Directory (Crayford, Kent: Shaw and Sons for the National Association of Probation Officers, 1977–) compiled by Owen Wells appears annually and is an essential reference book for all those working with offenders. It contains addresses and details of contact names and aims to list: every probation officer and probation office in the UK; penal establishments, probation and bail hostels; details of Home Office probation, mental health and prison departments; prisons ombudsman; relevant

Scottish organizations; National Association for the Care and Resettlement of Offenders (NACRO) offices and projects; specialist accommodation for offenders; services for drug misusers, problem drinkers and gamblers; victim/offender mediation services; and many other useful addresses.

▶ 9.6 ENCYCLOPAEDIAS

9.6.1 General

(a) Print

The pre-eminent human services encyclopaedia is produced by the National Association of Social Workers (NASW) in Washington DC, with the qualification that its main focus is on human services in the United States. *The Encyclopedia of Social Work,* 19th ed., (Washington, DC: NASW, 1995) is a hefty resource which will be a mainstay of many a North American social work library, and fully justifies its claims to be 'the field's most comprehensive reference work for the general knowledge base of the profession'. Three volumes provide nearly 3000 pages of information on virtually every aspect of social work; all of the edition's 290 entries have been newly written, and several areas of interest are covered in greater depth than before. Expanded content areas include: new technologies; research; global changes; policy developments in the US; evolving roles for social workers, and knowledge development.

Each volume contains a complete table of contents, a full index, *Reader's Guides* that list all the entries that relate to a topic and *see also* references to ensure that readers find all the information related to a topic. Keywords for each entry provide another search tool to help readers find the content they require. The focus of the text is naturally that of social work delivery in the US, and as the nature of social work practice and delivery is radically different between countries, these volumes will be of substantially less use to those outside of the United States.

A notable gap in this type of resource for the UK has been filled with the publication of *The Blackwell Encyclopaedia of Social Work* (Oxford: Blackwell, 2000) edited by Martin Davies, building on the author's *Companion to Social Work* from the same publisher in 1977. More accessibly sized, and priced, than the NASW encyclopaedia, in a single volume of 412 pages, the encyclopaedia has 400 topics, which are categorized as either 100-word short items which aim to provide a definition, 200-word glossary items giving a brief explanation and suggesting further reading, or 1000-word major items. The traditional two-column layout is used for the first two of these categories, but major items cover the whole page width and are presented in a box, which does not work particularly well when the entry spans more than one page. A lexicon is provided at the front, which usefully categorizes the headings under broad topics – abuse and domestic violence, addiction and problem drug use, black perspectives, carers and so forth. There will inevitably be issues over interpretation and coverage in a volume such as this. One example is the brief coverage of 'community social work', which is given the smallest possible coverage, on a par with the likes of the somewhat less high profile European social action model of intervention 'animation'.

Both the above titles give coverage well beyond a narrow 'social work' definition. The UK will also benefit from a forthcoming companion volume from Blackwell's, covering social policy – *The Blackwell Encyclopaedia of Social Policy* (Oxford: Blackwell, 2001), edited by Maggie May. In addition to the broad coverage of the resources discussed above, there are a large number of more subject-specific encyclopaedias. Exemplars of the range of subject encyclopaedias which those in the human services may wish to consider when building up a library collection are provided in the numbered sections below.

(b) Electronic

The *Encyclopedia of Social Work* (*see (a) Print* above) and the National Association of Social Workers' *Social Work Dictionary* (*see 9.4.1 (a)*) and the *Social Work Almanac,* (*see 9.12.2 (a)*) have been brought together in electronic format on CD-ROM as the *Social Work Reference Library* (Washington, DC: NASW, 1998–).

9.6.2 Children

The *Gale Encyclopedia of Childhood and Adolescence* edited by Jerome Kagan (Detroit, IL: Gale Group, 1996) has over 700 pages and over 900 signed articles covering aspects of child development from birth to young adulthood, with topics ranging from anorexia nervosa to thumb-sucking. *The Encyclopedia of Child Abuse*, 2nd ed., compiled by Robin E. Clark, Judith Freeman Clark and Christine Adamec (New York: Facts on File, 2000) contains 500 entries over 368 pages. It has a US focus, and is part of the *Facts on File Library of Health and Living Series*, other volumes cover adoption, blindness and vision impairment, deafness and hearing disorders, mental health, alcohol and drugs. These titles appear to be aimed more at the general reader, rather than specialists in the various fields. A major issue in looking at information sources is, of course, the extent to which they remain relevant. A title such as *The Encyclopaedia of Social Services and Child Care Law* edited by Richard M. Jones (London: Sweet & Maxwell, 1993) is very much at risk from major legislative and practice change, and a reliance on subscribers interfiling updates.

9.6.3 Mental health

The Encyclopedia of Mental Health edited by Howard S. Friedman, et al. (San Diego, CA: Academic Press, 1998) contains 1700 pages over three volumes, covering genetic, neurological, social and psychological factors that affect mental health. As this is an expensive publication, its potential utility may need to be carefully evaluated before purchasing, as a number of journal titles and monographs could be acquired for the same money.

9.6.4 AIDS/HIV

The Encyclopaedia of AIDS: a Social, Political, Cultural and Scientific Record of the HIV Epidemic (London: Penguin, 2001) is more of a discursive than encyclopaedic overview, but its 832 pages certainly offer value for money.

9.6.5 Older people

The Encyclopaedia of Ageing, 2nd ed., edited by George L. Maddox (Edinburgh: Churchill Livingstone 1996) contains over 1200 pages and provides a much needed revision of the first edition which was published nine years previously.

▶ 9.7 GUIDES AND HANDBOOKS

There are many handbooks and guides currently available for the human services. Some are specifically aimed at practitioners, while others are targeted at a more general readership, including students and researchers. Below are some representative examples including handbooks on the United Kingdom, comparative studies of social work in other countries and handbooks for work in specific areas.

9.7.1 General

Henry Neil Mendleshon's *Guide to Information Sources for Social Work and the Human Services* (Phoenix, AZ: Oryx Press, 1987) is one of the few broad-based guides and a useful introduction to the literature. Reference books, newspaper and journal articles, social work journals, online sources and statistical sources are included. However, it is now becoming somewhat dated.

An Introduction to Social Services in England and Wales by John Mitchell (Canterbury: University of Kent, European Institute of Social Services, 1998) is a short, practical, jargon-free description of the principal legislation, policies and types of social services provided in England and Wales. It covers services for all user groups, as well as social work training. It also provides concise summaries of other major services that impact on social services, such as education, health, employment and training, housing, social security, and work with offenders. Tony Byrne and Colin F. Padfield's *Social Services*, 4th ed., (Oxford: Made Simple Books, 1990) is part of the *Made Simple* series of books. Although there has been no new edition since 1990, the book is still useful in that it gives a clear and concise historical introduction to social services in the United Kingdom, an outline of the UK Government and puts social services into the context of the welfare state.

Understanding Health and Social Care: an Introductory Reader (London: Sage in Association with the Open University, 1998) edited by Margaret Allott and Martin Robb, provides a wide-ranging collection of key texts in the field of health and social care, cutting across the traditional boundaries between the two services. Classic articles and selected chapters are featured alongside papers that reflect current policy and practice. Service users are also given a voice, and insights from academic debate and research are included. The idea is to pull together essential reading for students of social work, nursing, health and social policy, as well as for those already qualified or undertaking research.

The *International Handbook on Social Work Theory and Practice* (Westport, CT: Greenwood Press, 1997) edited by Nazneen S. Mayadas, Thomas D. Watts and Doreen Elliott, with a foreword by Phyllida Parsloe, presents brief overviews of social work and the theories and values underpinning it in a range of countries. It is designed to give a starting point for understanding social work and social policy throughout the world. The countries covered are: United States, Canada, Mexico, Argentina, Brazil, Germany, Sweden, United Kingdom, Poland, Egypt, Israel, India, Japan, China, Ghana, South Africa and Australia. There is a concluding section on international social work. This is an important reference source for anyone interested in social work in other countries. *The Old and the New: Changes in Social Care in Central and Eastern Europe* edited by Brian Munday and George Lane (Canterbury: University of Kent, European Institute of Social Services, 1998) is the first major study of emerging systems of social care in the former communist countries of Central and Eastern Europe. Ten countries are covered: Albania, Bulgaria, Czech Republic, East Germany, Estonia, Hungary, Macedonia, Poland, Romania and Russia. Writers from these countries compare the previous ideology and practice of social care with what is now replacing it. Each chapter is organized according to the same framework. It is aimed at all those interested in comparative social work, or working with or in

Central and Eastern Europe, as well as practitioners in the countries featured.

The *Handbook of Care Planning* by Kate Atherton, Althea Brandon and David Brandon (London: Positive Publications, 1996) is a short, clearly presented text on user centred care planning, with an emphasis on the rights of the individual. It is designed to be both theoretical and practical.

The Field of Adult Services: Social Work Practice and Administration edited by Gary M. Nelson, Ann C. Eller, Dennis W. Streets and Margaret L. Morse (Washington, DC: NASW Press, 1997) is one of a range of practical texts produced by the National Association of Social Workers in the United States. The text aims to create a definition of adult services and to build clinical skills as well as skills in strategic planning and management and programme and staff development. Case-studies are used to help identify and overcome barriers to good practice. The book is aimed at students and lecturers, but is also designed as a handbook and reference tool for qualified social workers, supervisors, managers and administrators working in the human services in the US.

9.7.2 Disabled people

Compiled by Michael Mandelstem, *How to Get Equipment for Disability*, 3rd ed., (London: Jessica Kingsley for The Disabled Living Foundation, 1993) describes how equipment is provided for people with disabilities in the United Kingdom. It explains the statutory framework and how the system works in practice. Intended to be a practical handbook, the book can also be used as a directory. It aims to give a simple account of an often complicated procedure that involves going through a number of channels. Aimed at service providers and people, and agencies providing advice and information to disabled people, it contains sections on: daily living equipment; home adaptations; home nursing equipment; medical equipment; wheelchairs; cars; walking aids; footwear; orthotic appliances; prostheses; communications equipment; equipment for people with hearing impairment; equipment for visually impaired people; environmental controls; and equipment for the management of incontinence. No new edition of this well laid out and useful handbook has been produced since 1993.

9.7.3 Older people

CareFully: a Handbook for Home Care Assistants, 2nd ed., by Lesley Bell (London: Age Concern England, 1999) is an example of a practical handbook aimed at social care staff. It contains guidance and detailed information on good practice and recent developments in home care provision. It is used as a textbook for vocational qualifications in social care and includes chapters on: the importance of core values; the health of older people; taking care of yourself; basic skills for home care assistants; and the user's perspective on receiving home care.

Social Work Practice with the Elderly, 2nd ed., (Washington, DC: NASW Press, 1996) edited by Michael J. Holosko and Marvin D. Feit is a detailed text focusing on the knowledge and skills needed for work with older people. The book includes information on areas such as counselling, psychosocial assessments, and health and social services for older people. A comprehensive text, it is aimed at all those in the United States and Canada working with older people, and is a useful handbook as it covers all areas of human services.

9.7.4 Social security benefits

The Child Poverty Action Group publishes two handbooks annually, aimed at: welfare rights advisers; social workers; solicitors; community care and financial assessors; claimants; service users; and carers. These are: *Paying for Care Handbook: a Guide to Services, Charges and Welfare Benefits for Adults in Need of Care in the Community or in Residential or Nursing Care Homes* (London: Child Poverty Action Group); and *Welfare Benefits Handbook, Volumes 1 and 2* (London: Child Poverty Action Group). Designed as practical reference tools, the guides are clearly laid out, jargon-free and include indexes.

9.7.5 Drug and alcohol misuse

Management of Drug Users in the Community: a Practical Handbook edited by Roy Robertson (London: Arnold, 1998) is a practical and comprehensive guide to working in the community with people who misuse drugs. The book stresses the importance of understanding the causes of drug dependency and how this impacts on the lives of drug abusers. The treatment for related problems such as AIDS and hepatitis is also dealt with. Issues around public health and political and international policies are looked at, as well as the practical aspects of day-to-day management of services for drug misusers. Currently available treatments are detailed and the increasing role of the non-specialist worker is examined. This book is an essential tool for new and experienced social and health care workers, and for students undertaking courses related to community care.

▶ 9.8 WEBSITES

As in many fields, the Internet and the World Wide Web have had – and continue to have – a major impact in making information available to those in the human services field. Whilst academics in the human services will have had access to a range of information resources in their university library, practitioners in public service, voluntary and private sector organizations will traditionally have been less well served. The explosion of Websites may be starting to redress the balance somewhat. Discussing the ever-increasing number of human services Websites, in a small section in one chapter of a book such as this, requires self-discipline and clarity. The focus in this section is on Web gateways to human services Websites and the development of 'dot.com' activity in the field.

9.8.1 Web gateways

A list of links is evidently deemed a prerequisite for any Website, and it would be possible to fill several pages by merely listing those human services Websites which have major lists of links to other Websites. Rather than do this, a few properly structured and major sites are discussed, with some poorer examples used for contrast.

One of the longest established gateway Websites is the *World Wide Web Resources for Social Workers* <www.nyu.edu/socialwork/wwwrsw/> maintained by Gary Holden and colleagues at the New York University's Ehrenkranz School of Social Work, and the Division of Social Work and Behavioural Science, Mount Sinai School of Medicine. It boasts some 51 000+links and is regularly updated. A top-level hierarchical structure drills down to government, higher education, journals and newsletters, professional associations, reference and search engines, and social work. This latter category is further subdivided into 11 (including research and practice). Following the 'Research link' produces a page with specific links to research centres in the USA and elsewhere in the world. The long list of links elsewhere is in simple alphabetical order with no geographical subdivision, and each link stands (or falls) on the basis of its title – there is no additional information given other than the link. The resource as a whole is searchable; a search on the journal title *Research Policy and Planning* for instance, quickly brings up the one link to that journal.

The *Social Policy and Social Work Learning and Teaching Support Network* site <www.swap.ac.uk> offers a comprehensive selection of quality gateways and more narrowly focused social policy links.

The *Centre for Human Service Technology* Website <www.chst.ac.uk> is also worth consulting as it provides an impressive social work gateway. Topics covered include addictions, community care, disability, ethnicity, gerontology and ageing, homelessness and welfare rights.

One of the key UK resources is the *Social Science Information* Gateway (SOSIG) <www.sosig.ac.uk> a major initiative in the academic sector which covers the whole of the social sciences. SOSIG is developed collaboratively with 'section editors' in other organizations, and at this stage we should declare that one of the authors of this chapter is a section editor for the *Social Welfare* section. The *Social Welfare* section is further subdivided into 20 subsections and has links to other sections within SOSIG (criminal justice, psychology, social policy and so forth). Records on the gateway are given, at times, a lengthy summary. Simple and advanced search options, including a thesaurus, and an option for a weekly Email update alert add to the functionality of this service.

The *European Social Welfare Information Network* at <www.eswin.net> provides structured gateways into a variety of European countries.

9.8.2 Human services dot.coms

The human services have not been immune to dot.com frenzy, and it will be equally as interesting to see which survive to provide a service in the long term. Those wishing to make sense of what is on the Web in the area of human services, as in any field, should take a close look beyond the dot.com name and design.

Take for example *Child Welfare* <www.childwelfare.com>, which was set up in 1997 through the School of Public Policy and Social Research. The home page shows a quite recent 'last updated' date, but the pages therein are an eclectic collection of off-site links, many of which are broken and what purports to be an electronic journal is a similarly dated collection of links and materials. Assessed against even the most generous of criteria this Website would be graded as poor. A matter of a letter or two difference in the Web address is the *Child Welfare Resource Centre* <www.childwelfare.ca> which offers as its mission 'building links in the world of child welfare', and provides a focused range of materials for those in the child welfare field in Canada and the USA. It is up to date and well designed.

Social Work Search.com <www.socialworksearch.com> starts with 17 categories and has a look and feel similar to the likes of *Yahoo*. Following the 'Research and Statistics link' (as per the example with Holden in *9.8.1* above) provides a somewhat disappointing five links. Searching for 'research policy and planning' does not meet with success. In addition to online forums and chatrooms, there is a research section which aims 'to provide the largest online database of information for social workers by social workers'. Several months after launch, less than two dozen pieces are available and some of those are of dubious quality. A list of the 'Top 20' sites reveals a large number of personal homepage Websites.

A recent addition in the UK is *CareandHealth.com* <www.careandhealth.com>. This is a well-resourced development that provides a range of resources for those in health and social care. In addition to the ubiquitous links database, interviews, articles and databases of training courses provide a range of material of interest to those in the human services. However, this site is in competition with the likes of <www.community-care.co.uk> – the 30-years-old weekly care journal, *Community Care* which offers a similar range of content, and also the substantial <www.society-guardian.co.uk> which provides content from *The Guardian* newspaper. These offer useful content, in contrast to sites such as the *British Social Work Site* <www.social-work.co.uk>, which, at first glance, might strike the casual surfer as potentially a top Website, but it is not – it is a site with very limited content, thus, emphasizing the need to look beyond the name and carefully assess the quality of resources being provided, including their currency and who is providing them.

The *Child Abuse Prevention Network* <www.child-abuse.com> provides access to a range of material on the Website, including reference to a number of specific listserves. One of the key players in this field is Cornell University, which was also instrumental in setting up the *Children's House* at <www.child-abuse.com/childhouse>. This international initiative has a lot of information held in the various rooms of the house, although identifying how recently the pages have been updated, and the extent of those updates, is not always easy. The *Centre for Europe's Children* <Eurochild.gla> in the Documentation and Information Centre for the Council of Europe Programme for Children, hosts a range of full-text documents, databases and other useful resources.

▶ 9.9 JOURNALS

There are journal titles covering the whole of the human services from a wide range of countries and a selection of these appear in 9.9.1. The reamaining subsections cover specific user groups in social care. These titles are often produced by voluntary organizations and only a selection of what is available is listed. They have been chosen for their academic content, while still being useful for practitioners, policy makers and all those interested in social care for different user groups.

9.9.1 General

Asia Pacific Journal of Social Work (ISSN 0218–5385) (Singapore: Times Academic Press of Singapore, 1991–). Quarterly. Published by Times Academic Press for the National University of Singapore Department of Social Work and Psychology, this journal is an international (but with specific focus on the Asia Pacific area), peer-reviewed, academic publication. It aims to enhance the understanding of human behaviour and the social environment in all its diversity, focusing on the implications for human services of: cross-cultural dynamics; human needs; gender and racial issues; and the analysis of social welfare history and trends andsocial policy.

Australian Social Work (ISSN 0312 407X) (Barton, ACT: Australian Association of Social Workers, 1978–). Quarterly. This is the professional journal of the Australian Association of Social Workers. The publication seeks to promote the interests of the profession in Australia in the context of the whole range of human services and publishes peer-reviewed original research, practice and theoretical articles. A typical issue offered an excellent range of topics with both an academic and practical slant, including: the accommodation and support needs of people with mental health problems; understanding the complexity of decision-making around residential placement in aged care; working with parents with serious mental health problems; social work with centenarians; social workers and mediators; family preservation; supervision of counsellors; and video conferencing applications in the human services. Available electronically.

The British Journal of Social Work (ISSN 0045–3102) (Oxford: Oxford University Press for British Association of Social Workers, 1971–). Bimonthly. An essential academic title for all those interested in social work in the United Kingdom, this journal publishes a wide range of articles on all aspects of social work, including theory, practice, research and education. The editorial aim is to provide articles that are both scholarly and readable. While the focus is mainly on the UK, articles from other countries are also included. The journal has an international, as well as a UK, readership. Available electronically.

Canadian Social Work Review (ISSN 0820–909X) (Ottawa: Canadian Association of Schools of Social Work, 1984–). Biannual. With articles in both French and English, this peer-reviewed journal aims to advance social work scholarship, practice and education in Canada. Scholarly and theoretical in content, a typical issue contained articles on: linking research paradigms to practice; supervision of student social workers; a critical reflection on feminist intervention; and human rights.

Community Care (ISSN 0307–5508) (Haywards Heath, West Sussex: Reed Business Publishing, 1974–). Weekly. This journal is essential reading for people working in the human services in the UK. A weekly journal in magazine format, it features news, articles on current issues, editorial and other comment, reviews, a practice advice shop, and job and other adverts. Aimed at practitioners, students, managers, academics and anyone interested in keeping up to date with what is happening in social work. Available electronically.

Critical Social Policy (ISSN 0261–0183) (London: Sage, 1981–). Quarterly. A number of journals focusing on the social policy underpinning social welfare exist. This quarterly journal aims to provide a forum for developing an understanding of social welfare from a socialist, feminist, anti-racist and radical perspective, in a UK and international context. Aimed at practitioners, academics, researchers, consumer groups and all those interested in social policy, the journal contains clear and accessible articles and usually provides a balance of articles looking at both ideas and practice in each issue. Available electronically.

European Journal of Social Work (ISSN 1369–1457) (Oxford: Oxford University Press, 1998–). Three issues a year. This journal aims to provide a forum for the social professions in all parts of Europe and beyond. It analyses and promotes European and international developments in social policy, social services organizations and strategies for social change by publishing refereed papers on contemporary key issues. This journal is an essential read for anyone looking at the human services in a global context. A typical issue contained articles on: recognising diversity and developing skills in transcultural communication; young people leaving care in England, Northern Ireland and Ireland; attitudes to reform of children's services in Romania; a Finnish perspective on the personal qualities needed by social workers; a comparative look at social work education in Europe; and social policy and social work in New Zealand. The articles include theoretical debate, empirical studies, good practice examples, topical essays, and commentary. Available electronically.

International Journal of Social Welfare (ISSN 1369–6866) (Oxford/ Boston, MA: Blackwell, 1990–). Quarterly. Produced as a joint venture between: the Department of Social Work, Stockholm University, Sweden and the School of Social Welfare, University of California, Berkeley. This journal publishes articles in English on social work and social welfare, with the aim of encouraging debate about the global implications of contemporary social welfare issues. Contributors span the globe and the journal contains empirical studies, conceptual analysis of trends and issues, comparative studies, case-studies, evaluative studies, and articles on theory, practice and methodology, all from an international perspective. Available electronically.

International Social Work (ISSN 0020–8728) (London: Sage, 1959–). Quarterly. This is the journal of the International Association of Schools of Social Work, the International Council on Social Welfare and the International Federation of Social Workers and is scholarly in focus. The emphasis of the journal is on cross-national research and comparative analysis, as well as on trends and issues in social welfare and social policy in a global context. It is an ideal publication for those interested in comparative studies on an international level. Available electronically.

Journal of European Social Policy (ISSN 0958–9287) (London: Sage, 1991–). Quarterly. As the title suggests, the focus of this journal is on policy and is aimed at policy makers at European Union, national and local levels. It includes refereed articles offering analysis of key developments. The journal covers a broad range of subject areas, including equal opportunities, social exclusion, housing and health. It can be used as an excellent source of data on the policies behind human services in Europe. Available electronically.

Maatskaplike Werk/Social Work (ISSN 0037–8054) (Stellenbosch, Republic of South Africa: University of Stellenbosch, Department of Social Work, 1964–). Quarterly. With articles in English and Afrikaans, this peer-reviewed journal contains a range of articles with a South African context and is an important resource for all those interested in tracking the development of social work, social welfare and human services in the new South Africa.

Practice (ISSN 0950–3153) (Birmingham: Venture Press, 1987–). Quarterly. Aimed mainly at practitioners, the British Association of Social Worker's journal *Practice* aims to stimulate practice development in an accessible way by presenting articles on topical issues. The articles are quite short but wide-ranging and scholarly. The journal is useful for managers, lecturers, students and policy makers.

Research Policy and Planning (ISSN 0264–519X) (Bradford: Social Services Research Group, 1983–). Three issues a year. This journal is devoted to publishing research by practitioners working in UK local and central government, voluntary organizations and other relevant contributors.

Social Work (ISSN 0037–8046) (Washington, DC: National Association of Social Workers, 1959–). Quarterly. A long-established, scholarly journal from the professional association for social workers in the United States, the publication aims to improve practice and advance knowledge in social work and social welfare. It has a wide-ranging remit, with a call for articles focusing particularly on: research on social problems; evaluation of social work practice; advancement of developmental and practice theory; culture and ethnicity; and social policy, advocacy, and administration. It is essential reading for those interested in the human services in a United States context.

Social Work in Europe. (ISSN 1353 1670) (Lyme Regis: Russell House, 1994–). Three issues a year. This journal does not state its aims as such, but a glance at the contents page shows a truly Europe wide coverage of a broad range of topics. A typical issue contained articles on: cross-national research; social workers in England and Romania; socially excluded Romani in Central and Eastern Europe; the Mediation Commission; and social and psychiatric services for children in Greece. The articles are academic in content, while being clearly laid out and accessible.

9.9.2 Children

Adoption and Fostering (ISSN 0308–5759) (London: British Agencies for Adoption and Fostering, 1976–). Quarterly. This long-established UK journal provides an inter-disciplinary, all round perspective on new developments in policy, practice, law and research in the UK concerning adoption, fostering and children's services in general. It is a useful publication for all those interested in the subject, including researchers, academics, practitioners and students.

Adoption Quarterly (ISSN 1092–8755) (Binghampton, NY: Haworth Press, 1997–). Quarterly. One of the Haworth Press stable of academic journals from the United States, *Adoption Quarterly* aims to bring research to bear on the theory, policy and practice of adoption. Multidisciplinary in focus it is useful for all those in the human services involved in adoption issues.

Child Abuse Review (ISSN 0952–9136) (Chichester, West Sussex: Wiley for the British Association for the Study and Prevention of Child Abuse and Neglect, 1987–). Bimonthly. Each issue of this journal contains a mix of refereed research and practice papers, training updates, and case studies with a practice-oriented focus. The aim is to promote, for all those interested in evidence-based practice, relevant research and to facilitate the use of research findings to improve practice and influence policy. Available electronically.

Children and Society (ISSN 0951–0605) (London: National Children's Bureau, 1987–). Quarterly. This journal seeks to promote multidisciplinary and multi professional approaches to children's services and to inform practice by making available the latest research.

Journal of Child Sexual Abuse (ISSN 1053–8712) (Binghampton, NY: Haworth Press, 1992–). Quarterly. A multidisciplinary journal focusing on contemporary research, intervention techniques, services, legal issues and reviews on all aspects of child sexual abuse in the United States with the aim of promoting dialogue between researchers, practitioners and others interested in the field. However, the articles are manifestly academic in style.

9.9.3 Disabled people

Disability and Society (ISSN 0968–7599) (Abingdon, Oxfordshire: Carfax/Taylor & Francis, 1993–). Bimonthly. This journal is aimed at an international audience but publishes articles in English mainly from the United Kingdom and the United States. The aims and scope of the journal are not stated but a typical issue contained articles on: a comparison of disability with race, sex and sexual orientation statuses in the United States; inequalities, the social model and families with disabled children in the United Kingdom; the role of human services in supporting

Asian deaf young people and their families in the United Kingdom; and creating disability in the home and the role of environmental barriers in the United States. Available electronically.

9.9.4 Mental health

Journal of Mental Health (ISSN 0963–8237) (Basingstoke, Hants.: Carfax/ Taylor & Francis, 1996–). Bimonthly. This journal has a primarily UK focus, with the aim of providing a forum for all mental health professionals and managers to keep up to date with the latest research and evidence. Available electronically.

9.9.5 Older people

Ageing and Society (ISSN 0144–686X) (Cambridge: Cambridge University Press, 1981–). Bimonthly. This is the journal of the Centre for Policy on Ageing and the British Society of Gerontology and is aimed at an international and multidisciplinary readership. A typical issue shows a truly international focus, with articles (in English) on Turkey, Canada, Sweden, Australia and the United Kingdom. For all those interested in older people, society and the human services worldwide. Available electronically.

Journal of Gerontological Social Work (ISSN 0163–4372) (Binghampton, NY: Haworth Press, 1980–). Quarterly. This journal is devoted to the study of social work theory and practice in the field of ageing. While academic in content, it is aimed primarily at practitioners in a wide range of human services.

9.9.6 People with learning difficulties

British Journal of Learning Disabilities (ISSN 1354–4187) (Oxford: Blackwell Science, 1983–). Quarterly. The official journal of the British Institute of Learning Disabilities, this is an interdisciplinary publication with refereed papers and a focus on informing practice with research. It is an important title for all those in the human services working with people with learning difficulties. Available electronically.

Tizard Learning Disability Review (ISSN 1359–5474) (Brighton, East Sussex: Pavilion, 1996–). Quarterly. It is the journal of the Tizard Centre, University of Kent at Canterbury, and supports service development and innovation in the field of learning difficulties. It has a UK focus, but also includes international articles. The journal attempts to bridge the experience of managers, practitioners, academics, users and carers, and to establish a dialogue between these varying interest groups.

▶ 9.10 ABSTRACTS, INDEXES AND DATABASES

9.10.1 General

(a) Print

A dearth of abstracting and indexing services in the area of social welfare was bemoaned in the UK in the 1970s in *Information Sources in Social Welfare* by Jane Hustwit and Maureen Webley (London: National Institute for Social Work, 1977). *Social Work Abstracts*, (Washington, DC: NASW, 1965–) published by the National Association of Social Workers in the USA was the only major abstracting service in the Human Services at this time. The title continues to this day, having for a number of years been merged with a sister title to become *Social Work Research and Abstracts*, before being once again separated. The quarterly publication lists about 600 abstracts per issue in subject categories, with an annual subject and author index. *See also (b) Electronic* below.

In 1977, the (then) Department of Health and Social Security in the UK launched *Social Services Abstracts* (*see also (b) Electronic* below) which was published monthly until 1996. A triumph of consistency – the very last issue was almost identical in format to the very first issue! Subsequently, a number of social welfare organizations in the UK began to publish monthly abstracting services based on their library collections, which are detailed below.

Caredata ABSTRACTS (London: National Institute for Social Work, 1987–2000), was launched in 1987 as *Social Care Updated*, renamed in 1994 with the launch of the *Caredata* database (*see (b) Electronic* below). Publication of the printed version ceased at the end of 2000, migrating to a Web-only version. Coverage is broad, including services to all client groups, management, policy and research, arranged by broad subject.

(b) Electronic

The National Association of Social Worker's *Social Work Abstracts Plus* (Boston, MA: SilverPlatter), the electronic complement to the printed service of the same name (*see (a) Print* above) went online initially with host BRS, subsequently moving to SilverPlatter. It is the major human services database, with 65 000+records. However, subject retrieval is not always as easy as it could be, due to the individual abstracts having been keyworded by three different sets of standards over the years the database has been built. The content is primarily North American.

DHSS-DATA (London: Department of Health) was launched by the then Department of Health and Social Security, the online version of its *Social Services Abstracts* (*see (a) Print* above). Health content predominates and the social work element reduced to a minor element in the mid-1990s when *Social Services Abstracts* ceased production.

The Department of Health is now a partner with the King's Fund and Nuffield Institute in producing *HMIC – Health Management Information Consortium* (Boston, MA: SilverPlatter) which is strong in the administration and management of health care. The boundary between health services and social services in the UK is rapidly being removed and there will increasingly be useful material for those in social services in the UK on this database. Content is from the Department of Health Library & Information Services, the King's Fund Library & Information Service and the Nuffield Institute for Health.

Caredata (London: National Institute for Social Work) was launched in 1994 as the CD-ROM version of the monthly *Caredata ABSTRACTS* (*see (a) Print* above). Initially containing 25 000 abstracts, this figure has now doubled, with the addition of a range of full-text briefings from the Joseph Rowntree Foundation, Scottish Executive, and articles from journals including *Social Work in Europe*, *Practice*, *Research Policy and Planning*, and *Adoption and Fostering*. A Web version is also available – originally updated on a monthly basis, it is planned that it will become a continually updated service during 2001.

Social Services Abstracts (Bethesda, MD: Cambridge Scientific Abstracts) has been relaunched by CSA, having been available as the somewhat less catchy *Social Planning and Development Abstracts* for some years, a subset of the major *Sociological Abstracts* database (*see 3.10*).

9.10.2 Older people

(a) Print

New Literature on Old Age (London: Centre for Policy on Ageing) is a bimonthly publication, covering areas as diverse as abuse, and arts and music. This service is now online in the form of *AgeInfo* (*see (b) Electronic* below).

(b) Electronic

AgeInfo (London: Centre for Policy on Ageing) is the library database of the CPA. A searchable, online version of the database is available through the CPA Website <www.cpa.org.uk>.

AgeLine (Boston, MA: SilverPlatter) is a similar database in terms of size and scope, with the focus on North American literature. The 59 000+records cover books, journals, research reports, consumer guides and book chapters.

9.10.3 Children

(a) Print

ChildData Abstracts (London: National Children's Bureau) was launched in 1996 following the establishment of the electronic *ChildData* database (*see (b) Electronic* below). It has an alphabetical categorization, but no listing of those categories at the beginning of the issue, which makes retrieval somewhat more difficult than should be the case.

(b) Electronic

ChildData (Caterham: Oxmill Publishing) is the National Children's Bureau's library database, containing abstracts and full-text of the NCB journal *Children in Society*. The database is published in CD-ROM format and on the Web.

The Australian Institute of Family Studies have their library database available on their Website <www.aifs.org.au> and their *Australian Family and Society Abstracts* database is available online through Informit and the National Information Services Corporation (NISC) <www.nisc.com> as part of its *Child Abuse & Neglect* database. NISC provides free access to this database through the Website. The predominantly USA coverage of this database and the key-wording system do make finding material appropriate to other countries an interesting challenge! The *Family Process* CD-ROM <www.familyprocess.org> provides the full-text version of almost 40 years of articles from the family therapy journal title of the same name. The UK National Youth Agency have made their library database available over the Web at <www.nya.org.uk>.

9.10.4 Learning disabilities

The *BILD Current Awareness Service* (Kidderminster: BILD), previously the *BIMH Current Awareness Bulletin*, provides comprehensive coverage of learning disabilities literature (mental handicap/mental retardation/intellectual impairment as it is referred to in other countries) – books and journals, in addition to events and audio-visual materials.

9.10.5 Alcohol misuse

Social care in the UK has been an interesting example of how small, specialist libraries can make available their library database to others. CD-ROM was the big leap forward in the early 1990s, and now the Web offers further possibilities. The Alcohol Concern charity now have their library database available on their Website <www.alcoholconcern.org.uk>.

▶ 9.11 OFFICIAL PUBLICATIONS

The World Wide Web has freed up access to official publications in a way that was unimaginable 10 years ago. Many countries, as well as international organizations, provide the freely downloadable full-text of most, and in many cases all, of their official documents. This section covers only those official publications that are narrowly relevant to the human services. More general publications are covered in *1.11*. Statistical publications from government departments are listed in *9.12*.

9.11.1 United Kingdom

The most important government department for human services in England is the Department of Health. For direct access, the Web address is <www.doh.gov.uk>. The social care group is particularly relevant. The Department produces a range of documents, including social services inspection and social care reports, guidance, regulations, standards, consultation papers and research studies. The Department of Health now provides much easier access to publications in hard copy. For people who are unable to download PDF documents from the Internet, or who prefer bound copies, these may be obtained from: Department of Health, PO Box 777, London, SE1 6XH, Fax 01623 724 524, Email doh@prologistics.co.uk. The Department also produces the *Communications Summary*, a printed listing of documents published each month.

For Scottish documents the Scottish Executive site at <www.scotland.gov.uk> is an excellent starting point, and for Wales the site of the National Assembly for Wales at <www.wales.gov.uk/>. For Northern Ireland, the site of the Department of Health, Social Services and Public Safety at <www.nics.gov.uk/hss.htm> is the most important.

Other government departments relevant to UK human services are the Department for Work and Pensions formerly the Department of Social Security at <www.dss.gov.uk/> (UK wide); the Home Office at <www.homeoffice.gov.uk/> (responsible for home affairs for England and Wales); the Cabinet Office at <www.cabinet-office.gov.uk/>; and the Department for Social Development at <www.dsdni.gov.uk/> (the Northern Ireland Department with responsibility for urban regeneration, community and voluntary sector development, housing, social security benefits, pensions and child support).

The UK Department of Health Social Services Inspectorate, which is responsible for maintaining standards and ensuring quality in Social Services Departments, produces a *Chief Inspector's Report* each year (London: DH Publications) which draws on the inspection and performance review activities of the Inspectorate, with the aim of providing an assessment of the current position of social services. Full-text versions of the reports are available in PDF format at <www.doh.gov.uk/scg/socialc.htm>.

The Audit Commission, established in the UK in 1983 to appoint and regulate the external auditors of local authorities in England and Wales, and from 1990 to also audit the National Health Service, operates independently of local and central government. It produces the annual *Local Authority Performance Indicators* (London: Audit Commission). The indicators relevant to the human services are: the provision of housing; housing the homeless; the local environment; social services; education; and spending and income generally. The Audit Commission and the Social Services Inspectorate embarked on a series of joint reviews of social services in 1996 with the aim of providing independent assessments of how well social services departments are performing. Summaries of the findings and conclusions of the joint reviews are produced annually. The full-text copies of these, as well as the individual reviews, are available on the World Wide Web at: <www.joint-reviews.gov.uk/>.

A useful print source for UK official publications is the *TSO Weekly List* (London: The Stationery Office), a weekly rundown of all Government papers, including those relevant to the human services, published by the official publisher of the UK Government. Parliamentary, statutory and departmental publications are covered, as well as some relevant EU, UN and other international items. Another good source is the *Social Services Parliamentary Monitor* (London: Cadmus Newsletters) published fortnightly while Parliament sits. This is an expensive publication, however, though the subscription does include access to the electronic version on the Cadmus Website at <www.cadmus.co.uk/>.

9.11.2 Europe

The *European Social Welfare Information Network* (*ESWIN*) <www.eswin.net/> includes contact details and Web and Email addresses for a range of organizations, including central government, for the United Kingdom, Belgium, Spain, Israel, Austria, Hungary, Luxembourg, and the Netherlands.

9.11.3 United States

An easy to navigate and well laid out Website, *State and Local Government on the Net* at: <www.piperinfo.com/state/index.cfm> provides a way in to State information, with comprehensive listings of each government department within each State, including those relevant to the human services. The Department of Health and Human Services <www.hhs.gov/> and the Social Security Administration <www.ssa.gov/> are the main Federal government departments with responsibility for social welfare. Both sites are very easy to navigate and contain some documents for download. Full contact details for obtaining information that is not on the Web are also available.

▶ 9.12 STATISTICS

9.12.1 United Kingdom

A range of official statistics relevant to the human services is produced by central government in the United Kingdom. These vary in their coverage – some are UK wide, others cover only England, Wales, Scotland or Northern Ireland.

(a) Print

The publications listed below contain statistics on social services in England, Wales, Scotland and Northern Ireland. Where electronic versions of the statistics are available, they are listed in the *(b) Electronic* section. Also included is a selection of publications giving a statistical overview of various population groups in the UK that would need to be taken into account when planning human services.

A New Social Atlas of Britain (Chichester: Wiley, 1995) by Daniel Dorling from the University of Newcastle, is based on the 1991 census and other social data. It is included in this section because it presents data in map rather than table form, giving an overview of a range of data on how people work and live from a geographical perspective. This makes it a key source of statistical information for health authorities, social services departments and all those interested in area based data for England, Wales and Scotland. Particularly useful sections include: population; demography; housing; health; and society. Many of these sections also include information on black and ethnic minority people.

The *Social Focus* series (London: The Stationery Office) is produced by the Office for National Statistics and is designed to paint a picture of different groups of people in contemporary society in the whole of the UK. Examples of the population groups studied to date are ethnic minorities, young people, older people, children and families. Aimed at a wide range of professionals, the booklets contain the following statistics of interest to those in human services: population; families; victims and offenders, employment and unemployment; and health and health services.

Social Trends (London: The Stationery Office) is another Office for National Statistics publication, produced annually. Covering the whole of the UK in some tables, and Great Britain only in others, it draws together statistics from a range of government departments and other organizations to present a broad picture of British society. Easy on the eye, attract-ively laid out, and including succinct commentary, it presents data both as tables and as graphs and diagrams. Relevant to human services are sections on: population; education and training; labour market; income and wealth; expenditure; health; social protection (including data on sick and disabled people, older people and families); crime and justice; hous-ing; and lifestyles and social participation. (*see 1.12.1 (a)*)

Personal Social Services Statistics (London: Chartered Institute of Public Finance and Accountancy) is produced annually, first as 'estimates' and then when figures are finalized, as 'actuals'. Covering England, Wales and Scotland, it contains details of expenditure and income on the personal social services, together with non-financial data. The series is unique in its collation of financial statistics.

The Department of Health produces a number of annual statistical publications on social services in England that are essential tools for the human services. These include: *Health and Personal Social Services Statistics for England* (London: Stationery Office); and *Community Care Statistics: Residential Personal Social Services for Adults; Detailed Statistics on Residential and Nursing Care Homes and Local Authority Supported Residents* (London: Stationery Office). *Social Services Performance: the Personal Social Services Performance Assessment Framework Indicators* (London: Department of Health Social Care Group and Office for National Statistics) appears annually and provides comparative statistics on how well social services are performing. The Department of Health has also started producing *Statistical Bulletins* (*see also (b) Electronic* below) providing information on social care across services and user groups.

(b) Electronic

An annual statistical publication from the Department of Health, produced on CD-ROM, is *Key Indicators Graphical System* (*KIGS*) (London: Department of Health). This contains data back to 1990 on social services budgets, expenditure, unit costs, home care, staffing, day centres, meals services, places in residential homes, supported residents, secure accommodation, children looked after, child protection, nursery schools and census based indicators. The data can be accessed by seven different types of tables and charts.

The Department also publishes *Statistics on the Web* at <www.doh.gov.uk/public/stats3.htm>, allowing easy, free access to a wide range of social welfare data, including the *Statistical Bulletins*. The Website includes statistics on: community care; the social services workforce; local authority personal social services finance; and children on child protection registers.

The Northern Ireland Department of Health, Social Services and Public Safety (formerly the Department of Health and Social Services) produces an annual statistical publication *Community Statistics* (Belfast: Northern Ireland, Department of Health and Social Services. Regional Information Branch) covering: programmes of care; family and child care; older people;

mental health; learning disabilities; physical and sensory disabilities; health promotion; and primary health care. The statistics are also freely available from <www.dhssni.gov.uk/hpss/statistics> and are an important resource for information on social services and social welfare in Northern Ireland.

The Scottish Office produces regular, clearly laid out, statistical bulletins on an annual basis on all aspects of social care in Scotland. Examples are: *Staff of Scottish Social Work Departments; Children in Care or Under Supervision; Community Care; and Child ProtectionManagement Information* (all published by and available from: Edinburgh: Stationery Office). The statistical bulletins are also freely available on the WWW from <www.scotland.gov.uk> but some trawling through the site is needed before they can be found. The Welsh Office offers a range of annual statistical publications. These include: *Social Services Statistics for Wales* (London: Stationery Office); and *Child Protection Register: Statistics for Wales* (London: The Stationery Office). The National Assembly for Wales publishes freely downloadable statistics at: <www.wales.gov.uk/keypubforstatistic swales/index.htm>.

9.12.2 United States

(a) Print

The *Social Work Almanac*, 2nd ed., compiled by Leon Ginsberg (Washington, DC: NASW Press, 1997) is designed to make it easier for human services professionals in the United States to find their way through the maze of social welfare statistics available. It is a succinct but comprehensive source of statistics and contains data on: basic demographic data for the United States; children; crime; health and mortality statistics; education; mental health; older people; social welfare; social security benefits; housing; homelessness; and professional social work issues. *See also (b) Electronic* below.

Statistics on Social Work Education in the United States (Alexandria, Va: Council on Social Work Education) is produced annually by the Council on Social Work Education. This is based on an annual survey of all baccalaureate and master's degree programmes in social work accredited by the Council, and provides data not only on course and student numbers and qualifications, but also on recent trends in social work education in the United States.

(b) Electronic

The Social Work Almanac (*see (a) Print* above,) *The National Association of Social Workers' Dictionary* (*see* 9.4.1) and *The Encyclopedia of Social Work* (*see* 9.6.1) have been brought together in electronic format on

CD-ROM as the *Social Work Reference Library* (Washington, DC: NASW, 1998–).

The United States Department of Health and Human Services Website contains a wealth of statistical data on the human services. This, however, can be difficult to find, as it is not obvious where the statistics are. In fact, they are usually contained under the headings for services or service users. The site is plain and functional in design and after a certain amount of searching a great deal of useful, free data can be teased out. The best starting point is via the Department's home page at <www.hhs.gov/>.

9.12.3 International

Internationally, human services statistics are provided by local, regional and national governments, and by supranational governments or organizations such as the European Union, the United Nations, the World Health Organization and the World Bank. All these organizations produce statistics in printed versions, as well as holding freely available data on their Websites. Some of the sites are easier to access than others. The World Bank site is at <www.worldbank.com/> and contains easily accessible data, with a link from the home page to a wide range of clearly organized statistics of interest to those in the Human Services, particularly with an international, comparative focus.

The United Nations site contains *Social Indicators* at <www.un.org/Depts/unsd/social/>. These cover a wide range of data and are compiled by the Statistics Division, Department of Economic and Social Affairs of the United Nations Secretariat, from a wide range of national and international sources. The site contains statistics on: population; youth and older people; populations; housing; health; birth rates and childbearing; education; income and economic activity; and unemployment. The statistics are freely available, and are extremely useful for those interested in the human services from a comparative point of view.

The European Union site is a different matter, and it is probably easier to use printed material rather than struggle with navigating the EU site or with using their search facility. The best way in is to go straight to the EU publications pages at <eur-op.eu.int/general/en/index.htm>. One print publication that includes social statistics is *Europe in Figures*, 4th ed., (Brussels: Euro-Op. Office for Publications, 2001), which offers a clear and concise presentation of figures of the most important aspects of the EU.

An example of online statistics from an individual country is the Australian Institute of Health and Welfare's data at <www.aihw.gov.au/publications/welfare.html>. The AIHW is the nation's authoritative source of information on welfare services expenditure, children's and family services, child protection, housing assistance, crisis accommodation and support services, services for older people and disability services. The statistical reports are free to download or print out.

▶ 9.13 RESEARCH IN PROGRESS

9.13.1 Research registers

(a) Print

Social work in the United Kingdom was well served for many years by the journal *Clearing House for Local Authority Research* (Birmingham: University of Birmingham Department of Social Administration, 1972–1983). Whilst three issues per year published research articles, the quarterly journal dedicated one issue per year to a listing of current research projects. It was a good exemplar of such a directory: comprehensive, as relatively current as could be the case prior to the widespread use of IT, and containing useful information. The journal changed its name to *Social Services Research* (Birmingham: University of Birmingham Department of Social Administration, 1984–1998), and sadly the annual issue containing details of current research dwindled from a peak in which the number of records numbered in the hundreds, to having only a couple of dozen in the final register. This title ceased publication in 1998, and with it a valuable tool for finding out about research in local authority and academic settings in the human services.

(b) Electronic

In addition to electronic resources mentioned in the introductory chapter (*see 1.13*), such as the *REGARD* database of ESRC (Economic and Social Research Council) funded research, which has a substantial amount of content of relevance to the human services, there are some more specific Websites of note.

The National Research Register <doh.gov.uk/research/nrr.htm> from the Department of Health, provides details of DOH-funded completed and ongoing research projects. More recently established is the *ReFer – Research Findings Register* <www.doh.gov.uk/research/rd3/information/findings.htm#refer> which requires those carrying out DH-funded research to submit abstracts of work in progress.

The Joseph Rowntree Foundation is another major funder of research in the United Kingdom, and has had for several years a comprehensive Website <www.jrf.org.uk> which makes available briefings from those commissioned research projects, in addition to other resources. Their Work in Progress section provides details of current research, searchable by keyword, researcher name or organization, project title or research theme. The returned results are displayed with title and researcher name initially supplied, and a click link to a page with an abstract, status of publications, and other information. In addition to specific research databases such as these, the ease with which it is possible to set up Web bulletin boards has led to a plethora of online discussion forums, and anyone setting up a Website will see a Java-chat room as an easy-to-implement additional resource to their site.

9.13.2 Mailing lists and discussion groups

The extent to which Email discussion groups provide a useful route into ongoing research will vary on a number of factors, not least the culture within a specific field in a particular country. A drive to publish research can come from the need to achieve personal tenure, as is the case in the US and other countries. In the UK, it could be said that the quinquennial Research Assessment Exercise, which grades universities on research and influences subsequent funding, fosters competition rather than collaboration.

The facility with which individuals in a particular field engage with Information Technology will impact on the use of list-serves to exchange information. Social workers are 'people people', as the National Association of Social Worker's button badge proudly proclaims, and perhaps less inclined to network electronically than other professions?

A number of Websites have attempted to keep track of mailing lists and discussion groups in the field. The following variously cover the human services field, although none are comprehensive.

Listsoft's list of lists <www.lsoft.com/scripts/wl.exe?qL=social+work&F=L&F=T> provides a list of lists in social work (the Human Services category is virtually empty). Similarly, *<lizst.com>* identifies over 20 lists. The advantage of these Websites is that they regularly trawl listserves to check that they are still operational. *Colorado State's List of Social Work Lists,* <www.colostate.edu/Depts.SocWork/lists>is also a good starting point. The Website of the *Centre for Human Service Technology* <www.chst.soton.ac.uk> is worth consulting as they provide access to five social work/human services discussion lists which they host.

The UK has been particularly well served by the *Mailbase* initiative, enabling academics to set up listserves with ease. Now transferred to the rather less than elegantly named JISCmail service <www.jiscmail.ac.uk> the wide range of lists provided, and Web archives, will give those looking to contact experts and researchers in a particular field plenty to go on. E-groups Websites such as <www.yahoogroups.com> enable many groups to network electronically. *The Social Services Research Group* <www.ssrg.demon.co.uk> in the UK uses a mailing list to facilitate discussion amongst members.

Prior to current developments, there was substantial electronic networking in the human services through the *Computer Users in Social Services Network* (CUSSnet), which used dial-in bulletin boards on the Fidonet network to exchange messages. In the early to mid-1990s, a number of human services listserves developed, including the original *Socwork* list maintained by Harris Chaiklin at the University of Maryland at Baltimore. This particular list soon became a victim of its own success, in terms of the huge numbers of messages posted each week. Research by Berman (1996) identified a variety of uses the list was put to: information transfer (people providing information pro-actively e.g., details of forthcoming conferences and books), information requests and discussion. Berman concluded:

> 'In spite of its interactive setting the discussion group has not devolved into a forum through which the social work practitioner can use it as a medium for knowledge transfer. Social worker practitioners have not increased their access to practice wisdom even though the technology to make it accessible exists' (p.32).

The extent to which any electronic discussion group meets each of these needs will be a key element of their usefulness for those seeking information on current research. There has been an explosion in the number of listserves, and Web-based bulletin boards and forums are now commonplace. Below is a selection of a few key resources.

Socwork (to join, send a message to majordomo@uwrf.edu with the first line of your Email stating subscribe socwork) moderated by Ogden Rogers, at the University of Wisconsin-River Falls, describes itself as '... an open, unmoderated, general discussion listserver, whose purpose is to enable broad discussion of information and issues of concern to the social work community. You will find that there are other, more directed lists elsewhere for more defined social work discussion; SOCWORK tends to be "wide-open". We like to think of it of as sort of a crowded lunchroom: a place with a lot of people talkin' about social work, and a lot of social workers talkin'.'

Uksocwork (to join, send a message to jiscmail@jiscmail.ac.uk with the first line of your message reading join uksocwork) was established in 1995 and is maintained by the Centre for Human Service Technology <www.chst.soton.ac.uk>. A list for all those interested in social work and social care issues.

Intsocwork (to join, send a message to jiscmail@jiscmail.ac.uk with the first line of your message reading join intsocwork) focuses on international/comparative social work, and is similarly maintained by the Centre for Human Service Technology.

Social-Work-LTSN (to join, send a message to jiscmail@jismail.ac.uk with the first line of your message reading join Social-Work-LTSN) is managed by the Social Policy and Social Work Learning and Teaching Support Network <www.swap.ac.uk> and promotes innovation in learning and teaching within social work.

Social-Policy-LTSN (to join, send a message to jiscmail@jismail.ac.uk with the first line of your message reading join Social-Policy-LTSN) is similarly managed by the Social Policy and Social Work Learning and Teaching Support Network and promotes innovation in learning and teaching within social policy.

In addition to the more general resources discussed above, there are numerous specialized mailing lists which concentrate on particular areas of research in the human services. A brief selection is provided below.

Child-maltreatment-research (to join, send a message to listproc@cornell.edu with the first line of your Email stating subscribe child-maltreatment-research Your Name), a long-established list maintained by Cornell University and one of the key players in developing electronic access to resources in child abuse.

Downs-research (to join, send a message to jiscmail@jiscmail.ac.uk with the first line of your Email stating join downs-research Your Name) is one of several research focused lists on the UK academic Jiscmail service is, which discusses social and cognitive functioning in those with Down's Syndrome.

Disability-research (to join, send a message to jiscmail@jiscmail.ac.uk with the first line of your Email stating join disability-research Your Name), managed by the Centre for Disability Research at the University of Leeds, is a useful forum for the discussion of research in this field.

▶ 9.14 ORGANIZATIONS

As social welfare systems, structures and practices vary widely between countries emphasis has been given to UK organizations and key international bodies.

9.14.1 United Kingdom

In the United Kingdom, there are a large number and wide range of voluntary organizations in the social welfare field. One consequence of this is that, as opposed to other countries, central government has had less of a role to play in the provision of information. Voluntary organizations typically provide information through a variety of means: monographs; journals; newsletters; briefing papers; library services; and increasingly the Web. Listed below is a cross section of the main UK organizations dealing with the human services.

Education and training

Central Council for Education and Training in Social Work (CCETSW)
Derbyshire House, St. Chad's Street, London, WC1H 8AD, UK
Tel: +44 (0)20 7278 2455
Web: <www.ccetsw.org.uk>

CETTSW is responsible for promoting and approving education and training for social work and social care staff throughout the UK.

Training Organization for the Personal Social Services (TOPSS)
TOPSS England, 26 Park Row, Leeds, LS1 5QB, UK
Tel: +44 (0)113 245 1716
Fax: +44 (0)113 243 6417
Email: info@topssengland.org.uk
Web: <www.topss.org.uk>

TOPSS aims to work closely with and on behalf of employers from all sectors of care to enhance the quality of staff and services in social care. The organization also has offices in Wales, Scotland and Northern Ireland.

Government

Department of Health
Wellington House, 135–155 Waterloo Road, London, SE1 8UE, UK
Tel: +44 (0)20 7972 2000
Email: dhmail@doh.gsi.gov.uk
Web: <www.doh.gov.uk>

The aim of the Department of Health is to improve the health and wellbeing of people in England. The Social Care Group is related to social services in England and consists of three business areas: Social Care Policy Branches, Social Care Regions, and the Social Care Inspection Division. A wide range of information, including freely downloadable full-text documents, is available on the Department's Website.

Department for Work and Pensions
Richmond House, 79 Whitehall, London, SW1A 2NS, UK
Tel: +44 (0)20 7238 0800
Fax: +44 (0)20 7238 0831
Email peo@ms41.dss.gov.uk
Web: <www.dss.gov.uk/>

The UK-wide Department: helps with the costs of raising children and with arranging child support maintenance; supports people who are looking for work or cannot work; and promotes financial security in retirement. A wide range of information, including freely downloadable full-text documents, is available on the Department's Website.

Scottish Executive Social Work Services Inspectorate (SWSI)
James Craig Walk, Edinburgh EH1 3BA, UK
Tel: +44 (0)131 556 8400
Fax: +44 (0)131 244 8240
Email: ceu@scotland.gov.uk
Web: <www.scotland.gov.uk/>

The SWSI works with others to continually improve social work services in Scotland, so that they genuinely meet people's needs. The provision of advice about social work services to the First Minister and the Scottish Executive, and the management of workforce regulation, and education and training programmes for social work staff are also part of the SWSI remit.

Northern Ireland Executive Department of Health, Social Services and Public Safety
Castle Buildings, Stormont, Belfast, BT4 3SJ, UK
Tel: +44 (0)28 9052 0500
Email: Webmaster@dhsspsni.gov.uk
Web: <www.northernireland.gov.uk/hss.htm>

The Department administers the business of health and personal social services, public health and public safety and its overall aim is to improve the health and social wellbeing of the people of Northern Ireland.

National Assembly for Wales
The Public Information and Education Service, The National Assembly for Wales,
Cardiff Bay, Cardiff, CF99 1NA, UK
Tel: +44 (0)29 20 898200
Email: Assembly.Info@wales.gsi.gov.uk
Web: <www.wales.gov.uk/>

Following the transfer of the devolved powers and responsibilities of the Secretary of State for Wales to the National Assembly on 1 July 1999, the National Assembly will decide on its priorities and allocate the funds made available to Wales from the Treasury in England.

Professional bodies

British Association for Counselling (BAC)
1 Regent Place, Rugby, Warwickshire, CV21 2PJ, UK
Tel: +44 (0)1788 550899
Fax: +44 (0)1788 562189
Email: bac@bac.co.uk
Web: <www.counselling.co.uk>

The BAC was established in 1977 and currently has a membership of over 16 000. The association has a number of associated groups and it is affiliated to the National Council for Voluntary Organizations. It supports both counsellors and those who use counselling skills within their work by providing an information service, research, publications, training and numerous events.

British Association of Social Workers (BASW)
16 Kent Street, Birmingham, B5 6RD, UK
Tel: +44 (0)121 622 3911
Fax: +44 (0)121 4860
Email: info@basw.co.uk
Web: <www.basw.org.uk>

BASW is the association representing social work and social workers in the UK. *See 9.9.1 Journals* for information on the BASW journals: *British Journal of Social Work* and *Practice.*

Research

Other organizations in *9.14.1* carry out research, but as part of a range of other organizational objectives. The following, however, are primarily concerned with research, and all, except the Joseph Rowntree Foundation, are university based.

Joseph Rowntree Foundation
Homestead, 40 Water End, York, Y030 6WP, UK
Tel: +44 (0)1904 629241
Fax: +44 (0)1904 620072
Web: <www.jrf.org.uk>

The JRF carries out research and development across the whole of human services in the United Kingdom, publishing briefing papers, and research studies.

Personal Social Services Research Unit (PSSRU)
Cornwallis Building, George Allen Wing, University of Kent at Canterbury, Canterbury, Kent, CT2 7NF, UK
Tel: +44 (0)1227 827672
Fax: +44 (0)1227 827038
Web: <www.ukc.ac.uk/PSSRU/>

Established in 1974, its mission is 'to conduct research and policy analysis aimed at the improvement of equity and efficiency in community and long-term care'.

Social Policy Research Unit (SPRU)
University of York, Heslington, York, YO10 5DD, UK
Tel: +44 (0)1904 433608
Fax: +44 (0)1904 433618
Email SPRUINFO@york.ac.uk
Web <www.york.ac.uk/inst/spru/>

An independent unit within the Department of Social Policy and Social Work at York University, it has an international reputation for research in health, social care, social security and employment.

Voluntary organizations

Age Concern England
Astral House, 1268 London Road, London, SW16 4ER, UK
Tel: +44 (0)20 8765 7200
Fax: +44 (0)20 8765 7211
Email: ace@ace.org.uk
Web: <www.ace.org.uk>

As the National Council on Ageing they coordinate a network of local Age Concern organizations and national organizations, making them the 'leading charitable movement in the UK concerned with ageing and older people'.

Barnardos
Tanners Lane, Barkingside, Ilford, Essex, IG8 1QG, UK
Tel: +44 (0)20 8550 8822
Fax: +44 (0)20 6870
Web: <www.barnardos.org.uk/>

Barnardos is a long-established charity that used to run children's homes and residential schools. The organization retains very few homes, and instead focuses on UK wide community based projects for children and young people and their families.

British Agencies for Adoption and Fostering (BAAF)
Skyline House, 200 Union Street, London, SE1 OLX, UK
Tel: +44 (0)20 7593 2000
Fax: +44 (0)20 7593 2001
Web: <www.baaf.org.uk/>

BAAF provides advice, information and training for social workers, lawyers and doctors, to adoptive parents, foster carers and members of the public with an interest in adoption and fostering. See *9.9.2* for information about the BAAF journal *Adoption and Fostering.*

British Institute of Learning Disabilities (BILD)
Wolverhampton Road, Kidderminster, Worcestershire, DY10 3PP, UK
Tel: +44 (0)1562 850251
Fax: +44 (0)1562 851970
Email: bild@bild.demon.co.uk
Web: <www.bild.org.uk>

BILD provides services that promote good practice in the provision of health and social care services for people with learning difficulties. *See 9.9.6* for information on the BILD journal *British Journal of Learning Disabilities.*

MENCAP (Royal Society for Mentally Handicapped Children and Adults)
123 Golden Lane, London, EC1Y ORT, UK
Tel: +44 (0)20 7454 0454
Fax: +44 (0)20 7608 3254
Email: Information@mencap.org.uk
Web: <www. mencap.org.uk/>

MENCAP provides advice and support to people with learning difficulties and their families and carers through divisional offices, district offices and a network of local societies. The organization also runs residential, employment, training and leisure services.

MIND, the Mental Health Charity
15–19 Broadway, London, E15 4BQ, UK
Tel: +44 (0)20 8519 2122
Fax: +44 (0)20 8522 1725
Email: contact@mind.org.uk
Web: <www.mind.org.uk/>

MIND offers a national information line, a legal network, publications, the bi-monthly journal *Open Mind*, conferences, training and the MindLink network for service users. The organization campaigns for rights for people with mental health problems, and offers community services via a network of regional offices and local associations.

National Children's Bureau (NCB)
8 Wakley Street, London, EC1V 7QE, UK
Tel: +44 (0)20 7843 6000
Fax: +44 (0)20 7287 5912
Web: <www.ncb.org.uk/>

The National Children's Bureau undertakes research, policy and practice development and provides an information service, seminars and training for all those interested in children's services and childcare. *See* 9.9.2 for information on the NCB quarterly journal *Children and Society.*

National Society for the Prevention of Cruelty to Children (NSPCC)
42 Curtain Road, London, EC2A 3NH, UK
Tel: +44 (0)20 7825 2500
Fax: +44 (0)20 7825 2525
Web: <www.nspcc.org.uk/>

The NSPCC runs more than 120 child protection teams/projects in England, Wales and Northern Ireland, responding to the local needs of children and families. The organization provides training, and operates the free 24-hour *National Child Protection Helpline.*

RADAR (Royal Association for Disability and Rehabilitation)
12 City Forum, 250 City Road, London, EC1V 8AF, UK
Tel: +44 (0)20 7250 3222
Fax: +44 (0)20 7250 0212
Web: <www.radar.org.uk/>

RADAR operates as a coordinating body for over 500 member associations, acting as a pressure group on central and local government. The organization's particular focus is on access, education, employment, holidays, housing, mobility and social services for all people with disabilities.

RNIB (Royal National Institute for the Blind)
224 Great Portland Street, London, W1N 6AA, UK
Tel: +44 (0)20 7388 1266
Fax: +44 (0)20 7388 2034
Web: <rnib.org.uk/>

The RNIB aims to challenge blindness and to achieve a world in which blind and partially sighted people enjoy the same rights, freedoms, responsibilities and quality of life that sighted people have. The organization offers a wide range of services and information products.

RNID (Royal National Institute for Deaf People)
19–23 Feathersonte Street, London, EC1Y 8SL, UK
Tel: +44 (0)20 7296 8000
Fax: +44 (0)20 7296 8199
Web: <www.rnid.org.uk>

The RNID works towards enabling deaf people to exercise their rights to full citizenship and to enjoy equal opportunities by providing a wide range of services, including assistive technology, support services and information.

Social Care Association
Thornton House, Hook Road, Surbiton, Surrey, KT6 5AU, UK
Tel: +44 (0)20 8397 1411
Fax: +44 (0)20 8397 1436
Email: sca@scaed.demon.co.uk
Web: <www.socialcareassoc.com>

The association, founded in 1949, exists to promote high standards in social care.

9.14.2 Europe

European Centre for Social Welfare Policy and Research
Berggasse 17, A-1090 Wien, Austria
Tel: +43 1 319 4505 0
Fax: +43 1 319 450519
Email: ec@euro.centre.org
Web: <www.euro.centre.org>

The European Centre is an international centre for social research, policy, information and training. It is an intergovernmental organization focused on social welfare, particularly in Europe, and affiliated to the United Nations.

Nederlands Instituut voor Zorg en Welzijn (Netherlands Institute of Care and Welfare) (NIZW)
Postbus 19152, 3501 DD Utrecht, Netherlands
Tel: +31 30 230 6373
Fax: +31 30 231 9641
Email: H.Braakenburg@nizw.nl
Web: <www.knoware.nl/nizw/>

NIZW is an independent institute for innovation and improvement which provides services to organizations in the care and welfare sector in the Netherlands. NIZW works in close cooperation with these organizations to develop practice, service quality and interagency cooperation. It organizes conferences and training programmes, publishes books, reports and newsletters, and databases. It also runs a telephone helpline and information service.

STAKES
PO Box 220, FIN-00531 Helsinki, Finland
Tel: +358 9 39 671
Fax: +358 761 307
Web: <www.stakes.fi/english/>

STAKES, the Finish National Research and Development Centre for Welfare and Health, promotes the wellbeing and health of people in Finland, and aims to help in the securing of equal access for all to high-quality and effective social care and health services. The organization produces information and knowledge in the field of human services and uses this to influence policy makers. It is a centre of expertise overseen by the Ministry of Social Affairs and Health in Finland.

9.14.3 United States

Council on Social Work Education (CSWE)
1600 Duke Street, Suite 300, Alexandria, Virginia 22314–3421, USA
Tel: +1 703 683 8080
Fax: +1 703 683 8099

The Council on Social Work Education (CSWE) is responsible for social work education in the United States. The organization works to ensure the preparation of competent social work professionals by providing national leadership and a forum for collective action. In addition, the CSWE aims to stimulate knowledge and curriculum development, to advance social justice, and to strengthen community and individual wellbeing.

Department of Health and Human Services
200 Independence Avenue, SW, Washington, DC 20201, USA
Tel: +1 202 619 0257
Email: hhsmail@os.dhhs.gov
Web: <www.hhs.gov/>

The Department of Health and Human Services is the United States Government's principal agency for protecting the health of all Americans and providing essential Human Services, especially for those who are least able to help themselves. The best way in to finding out how this government department works is to visit the Website, which is plainly designed and easy to navigate.

National Association of Social Workers (NASW)
50 First Street NE, Suite 700, Washington, DC 20002–4241, USA
Tel: +1 202 408 8600
Email: info@naswdc.org
Web: <www.naswdc.org/>

The National Association of Social Workers (NASW) is the professional organization for social workers in the United States, with more than 155 000 members. NASW works to enhance the professional growth and development of its members, to create and maintain professional standards, and to advance sound social policies. The organization produces publications, aims to influence policy in the human services in the United States and publishes the journal's *Social Work* (*see 9.9 1*) and *Health and Social Work*, as well as providing a comprehensive range of services to its membership.

9.14.4 International

Asian and Pacific Association For Social Work Education (APASWE)
Dr Romeo Quieta, College of Social Work & Community Development, University of the Philippines, Diliman, Quezon City 1126, Philippines
Tel: +632 020 0491
Fax: +632 929 8438
Email: quiet@info.com.ph
Web: <social1.socialnet.uq.edu.au/apaswepost/>

The Asian and Pacific Association for Social Work Education publishes the twice yearly *APASWE Post*, runs conferences and organizes events to facilitate the exchange of information, ideas and issues of interest to social work educators in the Asia Pacific region.

International Association of Schools of Social Work (IASSW)
Applied Community Studies, Manchester Metropolitan University, 799 Wilmslow Road, Didsbury, Manchester, M20 2RR, UK
Email: iassw@socsci.soton.ac.uk
Web: <www.iassw.soton.ac.uk/map.htm>

The International Association of Schools of Social Work (IASSW) is an international association of institutions of social work education, organizations supporting social work education and social work educators. Its mission is to develop and promote excellence in social work education, research and scholarship globally in order to: enhance human wellbeing; to create and maintain a dynamic community of social work educators and their programmes; support and facilitate participation in mutual exchanges of information and expertise; and represent social work education at the international level.

International Council on Social Welfare (ICSW)
5 Tavistock Place, London, WC1H 9SN, UK
Tel: +44 (0)20 7383 5381
Fax: +44 (0)20 7 388 5363
Email: icsw@icsw.org
Web: <www.icsw.org/>

The International Council on Social Welfare is a non-governmental organization representing national and local organizations in more than 80 countries throughout the world. The membership also includes a number of major international organizations. Member organizations collectively represent tens of thousands of community organizations that work directly at the grassroots with people in poverty, hardship or distress. Worldwide, within people's own communities, the network of organizations provides help for a wide range of people who are poor, ill, disabled, unemployed, frail or oppressed. These include young people, older people, families, indigenous peoples, migrants, refugees and others who are experiencing special hardship or vulnerability.

International Federation of Social Workers
Postfach 6875, Schwarztorstrasse 20, CH-3001 Berne, Switzerland
Tel: +41 31 382 6015
Fax: +41 31 381 1222
Email: secr.gen@ifsw.org
Web: <www.ifsw.org/>

The organization aims to promote social work as a profession through cooperation and action on an international basis, especially as regards professional values, standards, ethics, human rights, recognition, training and working conditions, and to promote the establishment of national associations of social workers where they do not yet exist. 59 national associations belong to the Federation. It publishes *The Ethics of Social Work*, a manual on human rights and a newsletter. Lists of publications and activities are also included.

▶ REFERENCES

Berman, Y. (1996) 'Discussion groups on the Internet as sources of information: the case of social work', in *Aslib Proceedings,* **48**(2) February, 31–36.

Hustwit, J. and Webley, M. (1977) *Information in Social Welfare: a Survey of Resources.* London: National Institute for Social Work.

Streatfield, D. (1982) *Social Work: an Information Sourcebook.* London: Capital Planning Information Ltd.

10 Human geography

Caedmon Staddon, Alan Terry, Krystyna Brown, Richard Spalding, Rosemary Burton

▶ 10.1 NATURE AND SCOPE OF HUMAN GEOGRAPHY

Human geography is a diverse and constantly changing discipline. Though its fundamental concern is with understanding spatial variation in human processes, such variation may appertain to economic, social, cultural, historical, political or other phenomena. Human geographers, for example, have specialized in topics as diverse as industrial plant location dynamics, ethnic relations at the urban scale, electoral geography and representations of space and place in art. Thus it may sometimes seem that geographers are always practitioners of at least two disciplines: geography and political studies, geography and economics, etc. Such a duality in professional identity has long led some geographers to suggest that geography may be a common (if unsung) core to all social sciences (Cloke, Philo and Sadler, 1992; Fenneman, 1919).

This diversity and heterogeneity does not however imply that human geography is somehow secondary to other disciplines. On the contrary, one can fairly wonder why most other social sciences have been slow to realize the very real difference that space makes to human affairs. In sociology, for example, this realization is of only recent provenance but it has played a vital role in the reconsideration of the discipline over the past 20 years (Giddens, 1984; Urry, 1988). Other disciplines, including economics, political science and cultural studies have recently argued that the 'geographical imagination' ought to be quite central to their areas of research and teaching.

It is, therefore, possible to conclude that human geography maintains a strong coherent identity forged around the study of what Doreen Massey (1984) has called 'the difference that space makes' in all types of human process and phenomena. It is this 'geographical imagination' – only partly defined in terms of careful regional description – that unites all human geographers regardless of their actual area of specialization, providingcommon ground for economic, social, cultural, historical and other geographers (cf. Hart, 1984).

Like many other social sciences, geography (we are now speaking more generally about a 'geography' which includes physical as well as human geographical studies) only became institutionalized as an academic discipline in the nineteenth century. Its roots, however, go back much further. Some histories of human geography trace the beginnings of the discipline to the work of Eratosthenes, Posidonius and other philosophers that began to appear in the late Greek and early Roman periods. Best known of these is the first century BC *Geography* of Strabo which attempted to provide an integrated account of the physical and human characteristics of the inhabited world. Its attempt at 'integration' however, is more akin to a Gazetteer or Baedecker than a modern textbook, as it was explicitly intended to provide useful information to statesmen who must know about countries, coastlines, natural resources and political systems. Today, Strabo's *Geography* is primarily remembered for its essentially descriptive and often fragmentary character, as well as its occasional forays into more mythological geographies. Another prominent early geographical work is Ptolemy's second century AD *Geography*, though this is in fact primarily a work of astronomy, geodesy and mathematics.

During Western Europe's 'Dark Ages' geographical thinking and research was preserved and carried forward by several Moslem scholars including: Abu Abeyd Ab Allah Al-Bakri, an eleventh century government minister and author of two books of descriptive geography; Ash Sharif Al-Idrisi, whose twelfth century *Pleasurable Excursions* was written for Roger II of Sicily; and Ibn Battutah, the fourteenth century 'traveller of Islam'. During the Renaissance, Western Europeans began again to take up geographic research, as is shown in the work of Jean Bodin (sixteenth century) and William Purchas (sixteenth century) though neither of these authors thought of himself specifically as a *geographer*. Modern geography really begins with the short-lived seventeenth century Dutch geographer and mathematician, Bernhardus Varenius, whose *Geographia Generalis* (1649) once again sought to unify the mathematical description of the globe (general geography) with the description of its inhabitants, nations, economies, etc. (special geography).

In the twentieth century human geography has emerged as a strong independent discipline, whose focus on what Massey (1984) calls 'the difference that space makes' renders it distinct and viable notwithstanding its frequent conceptual borrowings from other social sciences. Former president of the American Association of Geographers, John Fraser Hart, called regional description the essence of the geographer's art (Hart, 1984). Together with anthropology this may be what most distinguishes geographers for the general public – descriptions of far off places and exotic peoples (though in the geographers' case, with maps). While such 'capes and bays' geography is no longer considered the acme of disciplinary practice, it remains true that many geographers are very good regionalists. Such regionalisms are, however, married together with topical specialisms in economic, political, cultural and other processes to create the vibrant and progressive modern discipline.

The aim of this chapter is to highlight important sources of information. In each subsection which follows, the reader will find references which are obviously (according to their titles) 'geographical' together with other less obviously geographical material, these latter include materials that the geographers who prepared this chapter have found very useful in their own teaching and research. Decisions about the inclusion of a particular reference have been made solely with regard to whether or not geographers are currently making significant use of that reference.

▶ 10.2 ANNUALS

There are relatively few annuals of specifically geographical information. Even so, human geographers do make use of a wide variety of annual publications produced by national and international organizations and by other cognate disciplines, usually for the purposes of furthering economic development or the understanding of important social issues, such as population growth, environmental awareness or cultural exchange. These are described below under subheadings for specific subspecialties within human geography. In addition, a number of broad-based annual publications (such as the *Europa World Year Book*) which are discussed in section *1.2*, are worth consulting for brief overviews of individual countries.

10.2.1 Regional geography/area studies

Several organizations, including the World Bank <www.wds.worldbank.org> the Organization for Economic Cooperation and Development (OECD) <www.oecd.org> and the Economist Intelligence Unit (EIU) publish an annual or biannual round of country reports. The latter also provides, through its Website <www.eiu.com> a comprehensive range of macroeconomic and social development data for more than 100 countries around the world. In addition to country and regional reports, the World Bank also publishes global level annual data sources such as *World Development Indicators* (Washington, DC: World Bank, 1997–) and a wide range of more thematically focused studies on countries and regions. The *World Development Report 2000–2001* (New York: Oxford University Press) is subtitled *Attacking Poverty* and is part of the World Bank's ongoing efforts to portray itself in a less technocratic and more caring light.

The *African Development Report* (Oxford: Oxford University Press) has been produced annually by the African Development Bank since 1964. It covers issues related to all countries on the African continent including: Africa in the world economy; fostering private sector development in Africa; and economic and social statistics on Africa. Like the World Bank and OECD reports discussed above, each *African Development Report* adopts a specific theme for further focused investigation. Thus, the 1999 theme was 'Infrastructure Development in Africa', the 1998 theme was 'Human Capital Development in Africa' and the 1997 theme was Fostering Private Sector Development in Africa'. Some years of this report and related reports are available as portable pdf files on the African Development Bank Website <www.afdb.org>.

The Inter-American Development Bank (IADB) publishes annual reports for Central and South America covering economic and social development issues. Like those of the African Development Bank, the IADB annuals are organized around specific themes that change from year to year. The 2001 report, the 51st annual edition, is entitled *Development Beyond Economics: Economic and Social Progress in Latin America 2000* (Washington, DC: Inter-American Development Bank). The *Asian Development Outlook 2000* (New York: Asian Development Bank) is the Asian Development Bank's annual survey of economic developments in its developing member countries in the Asian and Pacific region. The United Nations' *Economic and Social Survey of Asia and the Pacific 1999* (Geneva: United Nations Press) surveys and analyses recent economic and social developments in the region with particular emphasis on economic and social policy issues and broad development strategies. An essential resource for every multinational corporation intending to expand their business into Asia or to invest in the region.

Southeast Asian Affairs (Los Angeles, CA: Institute for Southeast Asian Studies) of which there are now 26 in the series (published each May), is an annual review of significant developments and trends in the region, with particular emphasis on ASEAN countries. The publication aims primarily at giving the enquiring reader a broad grasp of current regional affairs. Readable and easily understood analyses are made of major political, economic, social, and strategic developments within South East Asia.

What are the challenges facing the new leadership in Indonesia? How is the Anwar Ibrahim case affecting the politics of Malaysia? How sustainable are the economic recoveries in regional countries? *Regional Outlook: Southeast Asia* (Los Angeles, CA: Institute for Southeast Asian Studies) attempts to answer these and many other questions with succinct yet substantive analyses of current political and economic trends in the region and the likely developments over the next year or two. It is written by a team of international and local experts for the busy non-specialist reader who does not have the time for lengthy academic analyses.

10.2.2 Development geography

Perhaps no subdiscipline makes greater use of annual publications than development geography, where the need for good quality, up-to-date social and economic data is incessant and voracious. In addition to the country or regional reports listed above, frequent use is made of the many annual publications produced by the United Nations, World Bank and Organization for Economic Cooperation and Development (OECD). The most general, and perhaps most widely used of these, is the annual *Human Development Report* (New York: Oxford University Press, 1990–) produced by the United Nations Development Programme. This publication endeavours to include basic social and economic statistics for every country in the world within the context of careful analysis. For example, *Human Development Report 2000* looks at human rights as an intrinsic part of development and at development as a means to realizing human rights. It shows how human rights bring principles of accountability and social justice to the process of human development. The quality of the data is good and, for most indicators, there is now an excellent run of data to facilitate longitudinal studies. Also included is a reference section on key terms, technical notes on computing human development indices, country fact sheets listing key data and tables reflecting the status of United Nations treaties.

Various UN agencies also produce annual reports on their activities which can be very useful for researching issues of development. See, for example, The *UNEP Annual Report 1999* (Nairobi, Kenya: UNEP, 1999) which presents the challenges and work accomplished by the United Nations Environment Programme (UNEP). This report is structured on the foundation of five priority areas: environmental information, assessment and research; enhanced coordination of environmental conventions and development of policy instruments; fresh water; technology transfer and industry; and support to Africa.

Other UN agency annuals include The United Nations High Commission for Refugees' (UNHCR) flagship publication, *The State of the World's Refugees* (Oxford: Oxford University Press) which is, perhaps, the best available annual review and dataset on world refugee populations, their movements and their living conditions. *The World's Women 2000: Trends and Statistics* (New York: United Nations, 2000) is a unique compilation of the latest data and analysis documenting progress for women worldwide in six areas such as health, human rights and political decision-making, and families. On related issues see also the *Country Reports on Human Rights Practices for 1999* (Washington, DC: US Department of State, 1999). Also useful is the United Nations Children's Education Fund's (UNICEF) annual, *The State of the World's Children,* (New York: UNICEF) which publishes high quality analysis and data on children's welfare issues, especially in developing countries. The areas covered are population; education and training; economic activity; health and child-bearing; and households and marital status. It is written for the non-specialist.

Published by the World Health Organization (WHO), *The World Health Report 2000* (Geneva: WHO, 2000) is an expert analysis of the increasingly important influence of health systems in the daily lives of people worldwide. To an unprecedented degree, it takes account of the role of people as providers and consumers of health services, as financial contributors to health systems, as workers within them, and as citizens engaged in their responsible management or stewardship. *The Yearbook of Labour Statistics* (Geneva: ILO, 1942–) is produced by the International Labour Organization, the United Nations specialized agency which seeks the promotion of social justice and internationally recognized human and labour rights.

10.2.3 Environmental geography

Key annual sources of information and analysis for environmental topics include the *State of the World* (Washington, DC: Worldwatch Institute) reports produced by Lester Brown and his colleagues at the Worldwatch Institute in Washington DC. In addition to providing useful, and consistently high quality global data on environmental conditions, the *State of the World* reports also include a range of analytical chapters on topical issues of the year. The 1990 *State of the World* report, for example, included chapters on environmental conditions in the former Soviet Bloc, then just emerging from decades of communist central planning. Because the specific content of the chapters changes annually it is always worth browsing the table of contents to see what specific issues will be covered in that issue.

Another provider of environmental data at global and national levels is the World Resources Institute. Its *World Resources* publications (Oxford: Oxford University Press) coproduced with UNEP, is also a basic resource for geographers and social scientists researching global environmental issues. *World Resources 2000–2001: People and Ecosystems, the Fraying Web of Life* (Oxford: Oxford University Press, 2000), for example, adopts an ecosystem approach in an attempt to provide a comprehensive evaluation of the state of the earth at the beginning of the twenty-first century together with indicators from 150 different countries.

Detailed environmental data at the national or subnational level can be harder to come by, unless specific national governments publish 'State of the Environment' reports. Many, such as Canada, do but publication can be erratic and more than a year can easily pass between editions. Increasingly, these reports are now being published first or even exclusively on the Internet as, for example, on the Canadian Government's 'Green Lane' Website at <www.ec.gc.ca>. One source that attempts to periodically round up high quality environmental data at the European level is the publication *Europe's Environment* (Luxembourg: Office for Official Publications of the European Communities, 1995) the update for which is in production at the time of writing.

The United Nations Food and Agriculture Organisation also produces a wide variety of annual information (data and analysis), treating issues related to global food production and the management of living natural resources, including fisheries and forestry, much of it now available on their extensive Website at <www.fao.org>.

10.2.4 Tourism geography

The most comprehensive source of tourism information on each country of the world is contained in the Columbus Press annual publication, *The World Travel Guide*. It provides up-to-date information on climate, attractions, political history, travel, health and passport requirements (but not any statistics on tourism). It also includes addresses and contact details of tourist offices for every country. Available electronically at <www.wtgonline.com>.

▶ 10.3 BIBLIOGRAPHIES

10.3.1 General

Due to the diversity and wide-ranging nature of the discipline there are currently no comprehensive and up-to-date bibliographies covering the entire subject. Moreover, there are relatively few up-to-date bibliographies of even subdisciplines such as economic geography or political geography. One partial exception is the *World Bibliography of Geographical Bibliographies* (Tsukuba, Japan: Institute of Geoscience, University of Tsukuba, 1992–5) produced by T. Okuno at the Institute of Geoscience at University of Tsukuba. This is essentially a list of bibliographies of books and pamphlets in European languages published before the mid-1980s. Arrangement is both topical and regional. Unfortunately, an index is not provided.

The American Geographical Society (AGS) publishes several useful general bibliographies and catalogues including its *Current Geographical Publications: Additions to the Research Catalogue of the American Geographical Society, 1938–1984*. An online version covering years after 1984 is included on the AGS Website <leardo.iib.uwm.edu/cgp>. Both versions incorporate indexes of international literature: books, articles, atlases and maps, under both topical and regional subjects. It uses the American Geographical Society's classification system. Where appropriate, titles are listed in both the systematic and regional sections. Recent books are also featured in a separate list.

10.3.2 Sub-areas of human geography

C. L. Brown and J. O. Wheeler's *Bibliography of Geographic Thought* (New York: Greenwood Press, 1989) provides a useful entry point into the English language literature on the history and philosophy of the discipline. B. L. Sukhwal's *Political Geography: a Comprehensive, Systematic Bibliography* (New York: AMS Press, 1996) is a useful and up-to-date bibliography of English language publications in political geography. It is nicely augmented by G. J. Walters' *Human Rights in Theory and Practice: a Selected and Annotated Bibliography* (Metuchen, NJ: Scarecrow Press, 1995).

The Canadian Council on Urban and Regional Research has published *Urban and Regional References* annually since 1945 and it is a fine source for regional, as well as urban, scale studies of economic and social development issues, especially for those with a North American research interest. An excellent sourcebook for references on the technical aspects of environmental protection is Eagle and Deschamps' *Information Sources in Environmental Protection* (London: Bowker Saur, 1998). On more general environmental issues see J. A. Miller and S. M. Freidman's *The Island Press Bibliography of Environmental Literature* (Washington, DC: Island Press, 1993), and on the related topical issue of sea and ocean governance see also *Law of the Sea: a Select Bibliography* (New York: United Nations, 1999) which is divided into 23 subject categories based mainly on the major topics of the United Nations Convention on the Law of the Sea. The books and articles within each category are listed alphabetically by author and a complete author index is also included.

Professor Thomas Rumney of the University of New York at Plattsburgh, has virtually made a career out of publishing area studies bibliographies, including: *A Scholar's Guide and Bibliography on the Geographical Study of Southeast Asia* (New York: AMS Press, forthcoming); *The Geography of Canada Bibliography Series* in seven volumes (Plattsburgh: Centre for the Study of Canada, 2000); and *The Geography of Eastern Europe: a Selected Bibliography* (Monticello, IL: Vance Bibliographies, 1989). Rumney has also published several topical bibliographies including 'The Geography of Sport: a Compendium of Published Works, Theses, and Dissertations' (*Sports Place*, **9**(1), 1995, 4–30) and *The Study of Agricultural Geography: a Scholar's Guide and Bibliography* (Lanham, MD: Scarecrow Press, 2000).

Other useful area studies bibliographies include C. D. Harris' *Bibliography of Geography: Regional: the United States of America* (Chicago, Ill: University of Chicago Press, 1984) and James Sanchez'

Bibliography for Soviet Geography: With Special Reference to Cultural, Historical, and Economic Geography (Chicago, Ill: CPL Bibliographies, 1985). See also the *World Bibliographical Series* which publishes bibliographies on many countries of the world – for example, Ruby A. Bell-Gam and David Uru Iyam's *Nigeria* (Oxford: ABC Clio, 2000).

► 10.4 DICTIONARIES

By their very nature social science dictionaries tend to be relatively non-specific and human geography, covering such a broad range of topics, does not easily lend itself to concise dictionary-style treatment. Having said that, there are a number of recent dictionaries for human geography which contain annotated entries of excellent quality. These make a fine starting point for studies in a wide variety of subbranches of the discipline. Perhaps the most important is *The Dictionary of Human Geography* (Oxford: Blackwell, 2000) edited by R. J. Johnston, et al. Now in its fourth edition, the dictionary has become a basic reference work for all subbranches of human geography and is now quite comprehensive in its coverage. Other dictionaries currently in use include Susan Mayhew's *Dictionary of Geography*, 2nd ed., (Oxford and New York: OUP, 1997) and R. P. Larkin and G. L. Peters' *Dictionary of Concepts in Human Geography* (Westport, CT: Greenwood Press, 1983).

Steve Pile and Nigel Thrift's *City A–Z* (New York: Routledge, 2000) is a rather unusual 'dictionary' of urban geography, preferring the discursive and Socratic approach to key concepts and terms rather than the more usual synoptic one. It is nevertheless quite stimulating and, like William's *Keywords* (discussed below) is likely to become something of a classic.

Other, slightly more specialized, dictionaries include: Tom Bottomore's *A Dictionary of Marxist Thought*, 2nd ed., (Oxford: Blackwell, 1991); K. B. Hadjor's *Dictionary of Third World Terms* (London: Penguin, 1993); Wolfgang Sachs' *The Development Dictionary: a Guide to Knowledge as Power* (London: Zed Books, 1992); and Andy Crump's *The A–Z of World Development* (Oxford: New Internationalist, 1998). Although these works might be more directly linked to political studies, economics and sociology, they are all widely consulted by human geographers with relevant theoretical or topical interests and are therefore included here.

A different approach is taken by the many biographical guides to contemporary and past geographers starting with T. F. Barton and P. P. Karan's *Leaders in American Geography* (Mesilla, NM: New Mexico Geographical Society, 1992). Other similar publications include: P. H. Armstrong and G. J. Martin's *Geographers: Biobibliographical Studies*

(London: Continuum, 2000); and R. P. Larkin's *Biographical Dictionary of Geography* (Westport, CT: Greenwood, 1993). The latter contains sketches of 77 figures, from Aristotle to David Harvey, who have made a significant contribution to the development of the discipline. In a similar vein is E. Ehlers' *Orbis Geographicus/World Directory of Geography* (Stuttgart: Franz Steiner, 1992).

For environmental issues, Paul D. Kemp's *Environment Dictionary* (London: Routledge, 1998) and Julian and Katherine Dunster's *Dictionary of Natural Resource Management* (Wallingford: CAB International, 1996) are well worth consulting for their up-to-date and (mostly) annotated entries. S. Medlik's *Dictionary of Travel, Tourism and Hospitality*, 2nd ed., (Oxford: Butterworth-Heinemann, 1996) includes more than 3000 terms, and lists key data for over 200 countries. Of the current textbooks, David Weaver and Martin Oppermann's *Tourism Management* (Chichester: Wiley, 2000) has excellent summaries of key terms at the end of each chapter, a useful glossary, plus a few good Websites. It is a student friendly and accessible text. Designed for the Australian market, it has plenty of up-to-date Australian case-studies and examples, but also offers good global coverage

Raymond Williams' *Keywords: a Vocabulary of Culture and Society* (Oxford and New York: Oxford University Press, 1983) is a somewhat more eclectic, though still useful compendium of terminology. More than merely a collection of synoptic definitions, *Keywords* tends towards the genealogical, offering its readers fascinating glimpses into the history of key terms.

▶ 10.5 DIRECTORIES

General directories consulted by geographers include the *Guide to Programs in Geography in the United States and Canada 2000–2001/AAG Handbook and Directory of Geographers* (Washington, DC: Association of American Geographers:, 2000) and the *Handbook of Canadian Geography Departments* (Windsor, Ontario: Canadian Association of Geographers). Both claim to provide comprehensive coverage of undergraduate and postgraduate geographical education in the US and Canada with information about all degree-granting geography programmes, including programme structures, information about lecturing staff, numbers of students and student societies. Similar information for UK geography programmes is published by a number of organizations including *Which? Magazine* and the Universities and Colleges Admissions Service (UCAS). Worldwide coverage is provided, via the Internet, by the University of Innsbruck in Austria at <geowww.uibk.ac.at/geolinks/ index.html>.

G. Shirley's *The Third World Directory,* (London: Directory of Social Change, 1990) is a useful, though rapidly dating guide to organizations working for Third World development. Other directories, more orientated towards environmental issues include: L. S. Katz, S. Orrick and R. Honig's *Environmental Profiles: a Global Guide to Projects and People* (New York: Garland, 1993); Monica Frisch's *Directory for the Environment: Organisations, Initiatives and Campaigns in the British Isles*, 4th ed., (London: Green Print, 1994); and the *World Who is Who and Does What in Environment and Conservation* compiled by Lynn M. Curme and edited by Nichola Polunin (London: Earthscan Press, 1997). Despite its title, *Who's Who in the Environment: England*, 3rd ed., edited by Kate Aldous, Rachel Adatia and Kim Milton (London: Environment Council, 1995) is actually a directory of organizations rather than people. Entries, arranged A–Z by name, give a fair amount of detail. A useful subject index is also included. Of course, no directory can stay accurate for very long, but between them, these directories should help interested researchers make contact with environmental organizations operating around the world.

▶ 10.6 ENCYCLOPAEDIAS

10.6.1 General

Good general introductions to key concepts and terms can be sought in the large multi-volume encyclopaedias discussed in *1.6*. Professor Peter Haggett has recently updated and revised his *Encyclopaedia of World Geography* (New York: Marshall Cavendish, 2001) as a source for students from middle school onwards with current data on physical geography, economy, government and the people of more than 190 countries. Two aspects which make the work particularly interesting are the more than 2500 photographs and the emphasis placed on regional information.

The *Companion Encyclopedia of Geography* edited by Ian Douglas, Richard Huggett and Mike Robinson (London: Routledge, 1996) is divided into six parts: a differentiated world; a world transformed; the growth of a global economy; the global scale of habitat modification; a world of questions; and changing worlds, changing geographies. Chapters of particular interest for human geographers are: human welfare and social justice; environmental hazards; the nature of Third World cities; changes in global demography; and unity and division in global political geography. The five-volume *Worldmark Encyclopedia of the Nations*, 9th ed., (Farmington Hills, MI: The Gale Group, 1998) is also worth consulting. It provides data on 200 countries and dependencies across the world.

10.6.2 Development geography

The Encyclopedia of the Third World, 4th ed., edited by George Kurian (New York: Facts on File, 1992) details the political, economic and social systems of 126 developing countries. Topics include: demography, health, government, labour, climate and education. It remains a useful review, but a new edition would enhance its utility. *Women in the Third World: an Encyclopedia of Contemporary Issues* edited by Nelly P. Stromquist (Westport, CT: Garland, 1998) is an excellent introduction to the lives of women in the developing world. Subjects covered include: health issues – including AIDS; domestic and sexual violence; nutrition; gender consequences of ecological devastation; and the creation of women-friendly cities.

10.6.3 Environmental geography

As there are a number of encyclopaedias on environmental issues, we will highlight a selection of the most recent and comprehensive works. The third edition of *The Environment Encyclopedia and Directory 2001* by Celia Jaes Falicov (London: Europa, 2001), is a welcome revision of this standard text which first appeared in 1994 (2nd ed., 1998). Its perspective is global and contains detailed and clear explanations of terms and concepts. Maps, a bibliography and a who's who section are included. Of related interest is the *Encyclopedia of Environmental Science* edited by David E. Alexander (Dordrecht: Kluwer Academic, 1999) which collates the work of 228 authors from 25 countries. The authors are drawn from a wide spectrum of disparate fields including: geography, ecology, climatology, political science and biology. Its multidisciplinary perspective is particularly suited to the information needs of human geographers. Also worth consulting is the *Environmental Encyclopedia*, 2nd ed., (Farmington Hills, MI: Gale Group, 1998) which provides 1300 cross-referenced articles on a wide range of environmental issues from acid rain to water pollution. An index and around 250 maps are included. A forthcoming publication, the *International Encyclopedia of Environmental Politics* edited by John Barry and Gene E. Frankland (London: Taylor & Francis, 2001) will be worth watching out for.

10.6.4 Tourism geography

VNR's Encyclopedia of Hospitality and Tourism edited by M. A. Khan, M. D. Olsen, and T. Var (New York: Van Norstrand Reinhold, 1993) has a good range of short articles on issues, theories and types of tourism. C. K. Brown's *Encyclopaedia of Travel Literature* (Santa Barbara, CA:

ABC-Clio, 2000) is a valuable and up-to-date source of information. David Weaver's forthcoming *Encyclopedia of Ecotourism*, (CABI Press) is likely to become a key reference resource for students and researchers interested in ecotourism issues.

▶ 10.7 GUIDES, HANDBOOKS, ATLASES AND GAZETTEERS

10.7.1 General

Guides to human geography, written along discursive lines include: the National Research Council's *Rediscovering Geography: New Relevance for Science and Society* (Washington, DC: National Academy Press, 1997); *The Student's Companion to Geography* edited by A. Rogers, H. Viles and A. Goudie (Oxford: Blackwell, 1992); and A. Holt-Jensen's *Geography: History and Concepts: a Student's Guide*, 3rd ed., (London: Sage, 1996). These are all predominantly guides to essential geographical concepts/paradigms and to the contemporary discipline, covering such areas as what geographers do, sources of information, careers and graduate work. Discussion of geography's subject matter, tools and perspectives is directed toward people outside the field to show them what geography can offer to their concerns. On the topic of information resources, Stephen Goddard edited the *Guide to Information Sources in the Geographical Sciences* (London: Croom Helm, 1983), though this is now rather dated.

A somewhat more unusual guide to human geography is *New Models in Geography: the Political-Economy Perspective*, 2 vols, edited by R. Peet and N. Thrift (London: Unwin Hyman, 1989). It is, however, a very valuable volume as it brings together review articles on most of the major streams of human geographical thinking in the late 1980s allied to the political economy tradition. Michael Redclift's chapter on environmental issues, for example, is still well worth reading.

Those interested in teaching methods in university-level geography can turn to John R. Gold, et al *Teaching Geography in Higher Education: a Manual of Good Practice* (Oxford: Blackwell, 1991), which is considered one of the key volumes in the field of geographic pedagogy. Also on the theme of geography teaching is Jones', 'A Guide to English-Language Journals for Geography Education' (*Journal of Geography (Indiana)*, **100**(1), 2001, 14–23). Those with a penchant for historical geography should consult M. P. Conzen, T. A. Rumney and G. Wynn's *A Scholar's Guide to Geographical Writing on the American and Canadian Past* (Chicago, Ill: University of Chicago Press, 1993), for easy reference to over 10 000 books, dissertations and journal articles published from 1850 to 1990. Three introductory essays summarize the subfields of scholarship treated.

Numerous guides and handbooks have also been produced for various regions and countries around the world, for example: Korean Overseas Information Service, *A Handbook of Korea*, 9th ed., (Seoul: Korean Overseas Information Service, 1993); T. Bainbridge's *The Penguin Companion to European Union*, 2nd ed., (London: Penguin, 1998); and G. Arnold's *The Third World Handbook*, 2nd ed., (London: Cassell, 1994). The *Handbook of Latin American Studies* (Austin, TX: University of Texas Press, 1935–) is an annual bibliography of humanities and social science publications. It covers publications in such disciplines as: geography, public administration, anthropology, economics, politics, international relations, history, women's studies, art, literature, music and philosophy. There are, of course, very many more such volumes, often produced in series by major publishers, but the above selection should give the interested reader an idea of what is available.

There are now a number of guides to new technological resources including, C. Harder's *Serving Maps on the Internet: Geographic Information on the World Wide Web* (Redlands, CA: Environmental Systems Research Institute, 1998), which discusses how public and private sector institutions use Web-based geographic information systems to improve their businesses. A recent attempt to summarize geography Web resources is P. Vileno's 'Geography Resources on the Internet' (*College & Research Libraries News*, 58(7), 1997, 471–4). This annotated sampling of World Wide Web sites by a Canadian librarian provides descriptions and addresses for sites covering many different geographical subjects.

The *Guide to Environment and Development Sources of Information on CD-ROM and the Internet* (New York: UNEP, 1998) will assist users in locating worldwide information sources on the environment and sustainable development that are available in electronic format. The information is presented in two sections – subject and country. Three indexes are provided – subject headings, a narrower subject index and a title index. Entries appear only once in the book. Each entry gives the name of the source of information; mailing and Email addresses; telephone and fax numbers; and the type of information available. The CD-ROM information and/or Internet location are given. Guidelines on how to use the Internet are also provided. In *Internet Resources for Leisure and Tourism* (Oxford: Butterworth-Heinemann, 1999), W. F. Theobald and H. E. Dunsmore have produced a fine guide to free resources on the Internet that will be especially useful for travel and tourism students.

10.7.2 Research, fieldwork and statistical methods

There is a large amount of literature in the areas of geographical research and techniques. Some of this literature seeks to introduce readers to the basic elements of good research practice, such as M. H. Matthews and I. D. L. Foster's *Fieldwork Exercises in Human and Physical Geography* (London: Edward Arnold, 1986) and *Research in Human Geography: Introductions and Investigations* edited by John Eyles (Oxford: Blackwell, 1988). Eyles' book, however, takes a much more philosophical perspective on the subject of research methods.

More intended as handbooks for university-level students are Tony Parsons and Peter Knight's *How To Do Your Dissertation in Geography and Related Disciplines* (London: Chapman & Hall, 1995) and *Methods in Human Geography: a Guide for Students Doing a Research Project* edited by R. Flowerdew and D. Martin (London, Longman, 1997). Both of these volumes are well-known and have been well-received as standard treatments of research project and undergraduate dissertation issues.

The use of statistics in geographical research has also occasioned a great many handbooks, textbooks and guides. G. Shaw and D. Wheeler's *Statistical Techniques in Geographical Analysis*, 2nd ed.' (London: David Fulton, 1994): D. Ebdon's *Statistics in Geography*, 2nd ed., (Oxford: Blackwell, 1985): and More's *Elementary Statistics for Geographers* (Harlow: Longman, 1999) are three of the best known handbooks for geographical statistics and are widely available. *Methods of Presenting Fieldwork Data*, rev. ed., (Sheffield: Geographical Association, 1997) and *Methods of Statistical Analysis of Fieldwork Data*, rev. ed., (Sheffield: Geographical Association, 1996), both by Peter St. John and Dave Richardson, are two useful treatments of geographical research and statistical analysis, produced under the auspices of the Geographical Association (UK).

10.7.3 Geographical information systems (GIS) and remote sensing

GIS and Remote Sensing has developed its own distinct set of handbooks and guides. For concepts and methods I. Heywood, S. Cornelius and S. Carver's *Introduction to Geographical Information Systems* (Harlow: Longman, 1998) and K. C. Clarke's *Getting Started with Geographic Information Systems*, 3rd ed., (Upper Saddle River, NJ: Prentice Hall 2001) are both useful. Heywood is particularly good for detailed and clear explanations of GIS terms as well as techniques. Clarke's book adopts a more historical approach but both books include key terms and definitions, which are invaluable to the novice reader. P. A. Burrough and R. A. McDonnell's *Principles of Geographical Information Systems* (Oxford: Oxford University Press, 1998) is another well-established handbook for GIS.

As introductory guides to remote sensing, T. M. Lilles and R. W. Kiefer's *Remote Sensing and Image Interpretation*, 4th ed., (New York: Wiley, 2000) and J. B. Campbell's *Introduction to Remote Sensing*, 2nd ed., (London: Taylor and Francis, 1996) offer comprehensive accounts of the principles involved in aerial photography and satellite data. They also include useful lists of organizations which provide such data. Robert Arnold's book, *Interpretation of Airphotos and Remotely Sensed Imagery* (London: Prentice Hall, 1997) is a reliable guide dealing with fundamental concepts as well as exercises on working with maps and aerial images. Methods of analysing remotely sensed data by digital image processing is the focus of P. M. Mather's *Computer Processing of Remotely-Sensed Images*, 2nd ed., (Chichester: Wiley, 1999). It is a detailed but somewhat daunting book for the novice.

GIS techniques for ecological research and the software involved are the focus of *GIS for Ecology: An Introduction* by R. Wadsworth and J. Treweek (Harlow: Longman, 1999). Many socioeconomic applications of GIS are discussed in Paul Martin's *Geographic Information System: Socioeconomic Applications*, 2nd ed., (London: Routledge, 1996). *Ground Truth: The Social Implications of Geographic Information Systems* edited by John Pickles (Guildford Press, New York, 1995), consists of a diverse range of opinions that address these issues.

10.7.4 Atlases

Information sources possibly unique to geography, are the many atlases which collect and collate complex social, environmental and other data within a specifically geographical frame. They are legion in number and only a few examples are included here to give the reader a flavour of what is available. Good basic world atlases such as *The Times Atlas of the World: Concise Edition*, rev. 7th ed., (London: Times Books, 1997) are invaluable sources for determining the location of places large and small. Of course, a good atlas will also be well indexed and use official spellings for potentially troublesome place names such as Dushanbe and Nizhny Novgorod. Other excellent atlases are produced by Rand McNally and the New York Times in the USA and Oxford University Press in the UK.

Thematic atlases can be very useful for getting a sense of the basic geography of things or processes prior to researching them more deeply and there is quite an art to clearly encoding complex data into various sorts of maps (choropleth, area cartograms, etc.). Andrew Boyd's *An Atlas of World Affairs*, 10th ed., (London: Routledge, 1998) and E. W. Anderson's *An Atlas of World Political Flashpoints: a Sourcebook of Geopolitical Crisis* (London: Pinter, 1993) both portray contemporary social, economic and political events in a geographical context. More analytical is the *Atlas of Mineral Resources of the ESCAP Region: Geology and Mineral Resources of Kyrgyzstan* (Geneva: UNEP, 1999) which shows the distribution of mineral deposits and occurrences in Kyrgyzstan. Other volumes provide information about other countries of the Asia and Pacific region irrespective of their economic significance and provide information on their contained commodities, reserves, geographic locations, their relation to the geological environment and other characteristics. There are all manner of environmental atlases including: G. Lean and D. Hinrichsen's *Atlas of the Environment*, 2nd ed., (London: Harper-Collins, 1992); J. Seagar's *The State of Women in the World Atlas*, 2nd ed., (London: Penguin, 1997); and A. S. Goudie and D. Brunsden's *The Environment of the British Isles: an Atlas* (Oxford: Clarendon, 1994).

Atlases are becoming much more interactive. For example, the *National Atlas of Canada* has recently launched an initiative involving schools and communities in what is called the Canadian Communities Atlas Project. By participating and creating a Community Atlas Website, schools will be able to be part of the *National Atlas of Canada*. An Internet version of the *National Atlas of Canada* is currently underway and will provide the very best geographical and geospatial information and data to Canadians.

10.7.5 Place name gazetteers

Place name gazetteers attempt to bring together the most up-to-date information on the correct spelling, pronunciation and precise location of all places within a nation, major world region or even the globe itself. When in doubt about the correct spelling of 'Beijing', or the exact location of 'Dushanbe', the correct Gazetteer can be invaluable. *The Columbia Gazetteer of the World*, rev. ed., edited by Saul B. Cohen (New York: Columbia University Press, 1998) contains 165 000 entries, covering both the political and physical spheres, including national parks and monuments. The *GEOnet Names Server* <164.214.2.59/gns/html/index.html> is an online gazetteer which features place names outside the US on the National Imagery and Mapping Agency database, providing location data, name and type of feature. Country names are current to the date after each name, as approved by the US Board on Geographic Names. *Place Names of the World – Europe* by John Everett-Heath (London: Palgrave, 2000) provides information on the origins of place names within the 38 countries of Europe.

The *Gazetteer of Great Britain*, 4th ed., produced by the Ordnance Survey (London: Macmillan, 1999) contains all the names that appear on Ordnance Survey 1:50 000 scale Landranger maps of Great Britain. The *US Gazetteer* <www.census.gov/cgi-bin/gazetteer> identifies populated places, providing type of place, location, 1990 population, and a link to a map in the Bureau of the Census Tiger map server (TIGER is the system used by the US Bureau of the Census to organize spatial boundary information and census statistical data within the US). The Canadian government provides a *Canadian Gazetteer* through the Department Natural Resources Canada <geonames.nrcan.gc.ca>. It includes over 500 000 geographical names in Canada, from the Canadian Permanent Committee on Geographical Names. Location information and map links are provided.

▶ 10.8 WEBSITES

10.8.1 General

There has been a tremendous proliferation of Web-based materials in human geography over the past decade. Part of this proliferation has involved the transfer of traditional paper-based materials, such as government statistics and journals, onto the Web, and part of this has involved the development of more innovative uses of the Web for the publication of geographical information. Recently, several lead institutions have developed what are called 'Virtual Geography Departments', bringing course information, lecturers, research and jobs together with the more traditional bibliographies and abstracting services. The University of Colorado operates one such Virtual Geography Department at <www.colorado.edu/geography/virtdept/contents.html>, endorsed by the Association of American Geographers and the (US) National Council for Geographic Education, which is a good starting place for interested non-experts attempting to find geographical research or sources on thematic or regional issues.

Below is a selection of key gateways to quality geography and human geography Websites:

BUBL: Geography Links <bubl.ac.uk/link/g/geographylinks.htm>. Resources selected by the well-known Bulletin Board for Libraries (BUBL). It offers easy access to a number of gateway sites.

CTI: Human Geography <www.geog.le.ac.uk/cti/hum.html>. This site is produced as part of the Computers in Teaching (CTI) initiative, established in 1984 to support the use of Communication and Information technologies in higher education. Topics covered include: cultural and social geography, development geography, economic geography, geography of gender, historical geography, political/electoral geography and urban geography. Maintained by the Geography, Geology and Meteorology Department at the University of Leicester, UK.

Directory of Networked Resources: Geography <www.niss.ac.uk/cgi-bin/GetUdc.pl?91>. Links to an excellent range of international resources of use to human geographers, provided by NISS (National Information Services and Systems), which has been maintaining online information services for the UK education sector since 1988.

GEOSOURCE <www.library.uu.nl/geosource>. Web resources for human geography, physical geography, planning, geoscience and environmental science, maintained by Jeron Bosman of the Library Centre Uithof (BCU), Utrecht University, The Netherlands.

SOSIG: Social Geography <www.sosig.ac.uk/roads/subject-listing/World/socgeog.html>. A vast array of social geography resources from around the world, offered as part of the respected *Social Science Information Gateway* (see *1.8*).

The World Wide Web Virtual Library: Geography <geography.pinetree.org>. An easy-to-navigate site providing links to numerous Webpages of value to those seeking information in human geography. Maintained by Gordon Dewis for the World Wide Web Virtual Library.

Basic country information can be obtained on the CIA Website at: <www.odci.gov/cia/publications/factbook/index.html>. On this site one can find a range of editions of the *CIA World Fact Book* which provides a brief overview (including: population, government and economy) and access to downloadable maps for each country of the world.

The World Bank Group <www.worldbank.org> has developed a truly enormous Website containing everything from economic development statistics for all WB member countries, sectoral policy documents, databases of WB loans to specific countries and even some press releases and official correspondence with national governments.

The European Commission <europa.eu.int/comm/index.htm> Website is also quite large, and it is probably best thought of as a collection of Websites, one for each of the dozen or so directorates that coordinate EC/EU policy on everything from transport to environment. Though daunting and often slow, the Website can yield a great deal of high quality data.

10.8.2 Regional geography/area studies

At the national scale every government in Europe now operates at least a modest Website. Prospective EU member countries like the Czech Republic and Bulgaria tend to have comparatively complete and easy-to-use sites. Others, like the UK, can be hard to access because there is simply so much material available from government departments, as widely disparate as the Department for International Development <www.dfid.gov.uk>, the Environment Agency<www.environmentagency.gov.uk> and the 'UK Drinking Water Inspectorate' <www.dwi.gov.uk>.

The University of Texas at Austin *Centre for Middle Eastern Studies* link.lanic.utexas.edu/menicc is an excellent gateway to information about Middle Eastern countries, including cultural, political, economic and other information. Its complement, for the former communist states of Eastern Europe and Eurasia is *REESWEB*, the *Russian and Eastern European Studies Web* located at <www.ucis.pitt.edu/reesWeb/Hist/histind.html>.

The Latin American Network Information Centre <lanic.utexas.edu> provides similar service for the countries of that region.

10.8.3 Development geography

The Institute for Development Studies (IDS), based at Sussex University in the UK, maintains a Website called *Eldis: the Gateway to Development Information* <www.ids.ac.uk/eldis>. It provides links to development information organized under the following headings: Social, Agriculture, Environment, Economics, Disasters, Management and Reference. *Eldis* is an excellent first port of call for those needing to locate high quality materials on a range of development orientated subjects.

Several Western governments maintain large Websites showcasing their own development projects around the world. These include: the British Government's *Department for International Development* <www.dfid.org.uk>; the Canadian Government's *Canadian International Development Agency* <www.cida.ca>; and the *American Agency for International Development* <www.usaid.org>.

The critical social development subject of HIV is very well covered by what is perhaps the largest HIV-dedicated Website in the world at <www.aegis.org>.

The *International Labour Organization* is the UN agency which seeks the promotion of social justice and internationally recognized human and labour rights. It was founded in 1919 and is the only surviving major creation of the Treaty of Versailles which brought the League of Nations into being and it became the first specialized agency of the UN in 1946. It maintains a large and very informative Website at <www.ilo.org>.

10.8.4 Environmental geography

There are numerous environmental information gateways on the Internet. See *The Guide to Environment and Development Sources of Information on CD-ROM and the Internet* in *section 10.7.1* above for assistance in selecting the best resources. The *Urban Environmental Management* site at <www.gdrc.org/uem> is an excellent starting point. It is the homepage of the Urban Environmental Management Research Initiative (UEMRI) and was created to assist communication and information exchange between researchers of urban environments around the world. The site hosts a wealth of information related to urban environments and their management.

The United Nations' *Food and Agriculture Organisation* (FAO) maintains a large and useful Website for data and analysis within its purview at <www.fao.org>. Its information about forestry is especially good as are its links to other related sites including the global *Forest Conservation Portal* <www.forests.org>.

For environmental information about Central and Eastern Europe see: *Environmental Information in Central and Eastern Europe and the Newly Independent States* <www.grida.no/enrin> provided by the Environment and Natural Resources Information Network (ERIN), part of the United Nations Environment Programme, and the *Regional Environmental Center for Central and Eastern Europe* <www.rec.org>.

Environmental organizations often have excellent Websites which provide both information and access to links. See, for example, the sites maintained by the *Friends of the Earth* <www.foe.org.uk> and the *Soil Association* <www.soilassociation.org>.

10.8.5 Political geography

Elections Around the World <www.stm.it/elections/election/main.htm> is a useful gateway to international information about elections from across the globe.

10.8.6 Rural geography

The University of Newcastle Upon Tyne's *Centre for Rural Economy* maintains an excellent Website at <www.ncl.ac.uk/cre> for those interested in rural geography and development. The *UK Countryside Agency* produces a good Website with many useful links at <www.countryside.gov.uk>. The *Countryside and Community Research Unit*, Cheltenham and Gloucester College of Higher Education at <www.chelt.ac.uk/el/ccru> provides a useful gateway for rural geography issues.

10.8.7 Geographical information systems (GIS) and remote sensing

A good starting point for information is *GI News* <www.ginews.co.uk> which is an online magazine and Website providing news and feature articles about the industry, as well as software and book reviews, a product directory and links to other sites.

GIS and remote sensing organizations have their own Websites and often provide examples of applications and free data. Unfortunately many of these sites are ephemeral; hence, it is with some trepidation that we put forward a short list of those that we use.

United Kingdom Ordnance Survey <www.ordsvy.gov.uk> is the mapping agency of the United Kingdom. This site contains a great deal of information relating to their maps.

NOAA CLIMVIS <www.usgs.gov>. Data downloaded from this site are immensely useful. The National Oceanic and Atmospheric Administration (NOAA) offers a vast range of variables including continuous daily climatic variables with weather stations located all over the world. Latitude and longitude for each station is supplied as well as the elevation.

Microsoft Terraserver <terraserver.microsoft.com>. For a synoptic view of an area, a satellite image is extremely useful. This site holds a huge range of locations around the world.

Websites exclusively about a particular satellite give examples of the images and related information. Here is a selection:

Landsat <geo.arc.nasa.gov/esd/esdstaff/landsat/landsat.html>.

SPOT <www.spotimage.fr>.

Meteosat <www.nottingham.ac.uk/meteosat>.

IKONOS satellite <www.gisrs.com/Gallery1.html>. This Website it the first to offer images of the new high spatial resolution data available from the IKONOS satellite. The spatial resolution (4km and 1km) is the best available commercially.

NASA Remote Sensing Tutorial by Nicholas Short <rst.gsfc.nasa.gov/TofC/Coverpage.html>. A comprehensive introduction to the concepts and techniques of remote sensing.

Xerox PARC Viewer <pubWeb.parc.xerox.com/mapdocs/mapviewer.html>. Some interesting ways of viewing geographic data.

A real world interactive GIS is found on the *Friends of the Earth* Website at <www.foe.org.uk>. Under its Factory Watch banner there is an interactive GIS which provides information on pollutants released by factories in the United Kingdom. The essence of this program is that by putting in a postcode (a surrogate for a geographical location), the GIS will return either a map giving location, or simply a list of the factories in the vicinity of that postcode. Attribute data from the associated databases describe the chemical products released to air, water and land. The query option allows the user to select on type of materials released, or factories operated by a particular company, or search on the chemicals which are associated with health hazards. All of this information is in the public domain but it is the manipulation and query capacity of this GIS that make the information accessible. It is a model of GIS functionality.

10.8.8 Tourism geography

For travel and tourism issues there are various umbrella sites that will give links to other organizations and the Websites of individual countries. See, in particular, the *Tourism Industry Professionals Site* at <www.tourismtrade.org.uk>.

▶ 10.9 JOURNALS

10.9.1 General

Annals of the Association of American Geographers (ISSN 0004–5608) (Malden, MA: Blackwell, 1911–). Quarterly. One of the flagship publications of the discipline, *Annals* publishes a wide range of high quality refereed articles. Available electronically.

Antipode (ISSN 0066–4812) (Malden, MA: Blackwell, 1969–). Quarterly. The journal attracts the best and most provocative of radical geographical theory and research, particularly that which contributes to politics and practice. Available electronically.

Area (ISSN 0004–0894) (London: Royal Geographical Society/Institute of British Geographers, 1973–). Quarterly. It publishes shorter more review-style articles, compared to its sibling publication the *Transactions of the Institute of British Geographers* (see below).

Canadian Geographer (ISSN 0008–3658) (Toronto: Canadian Association of Geographers, 1957–). Quarterly. Publishes a broad range of articles on topics from economic change to historical geography and cultural theory, though mostly tries to maintain a Canadian focus.

Ecumene (ISSN 0967–4608) (London: Edward Arnold, 1996–). Quarterly. *Ecumene* has established a reputation for stylish, scholarly and informed research writing on the cultural appropriation, both material and imaginative, of nature, landscape and the environment. It is a forum for the growing number of scholars and practitioners in the arts, humanities and environmental sciences who are interested in the ways that people imagine, interpret and transform their physical and social worlds. Available electronically.

Environment and Planning A (ISSN 0308–518X) (London: Pion, 1969–). Monthly. An interdisciplinary, refereed journal of urban and regional research. It is the only journal in the field which, because of its size and frequency, can provide the breadth of coverage which allows it to maintain its core interests while simultaneously developing new fields of research as they emerge. The journal is primarily concerned with the fate of cities and regions. Available electronically.

Environment and Planning B: Planning and Design (ISSN 0265–8135) (London: Pion, 1974–). Bimonthly. The journal has as its goal the publication of high quality, refereed articles which report leading edge research in the application of formal methods, methods models and theories to spatial problems, which involve the built environment and the spatial structure of cities and regions. Available electronically.

Environment and Planning C: Government and Policy (ISSN 0263–744X) (London: Pion, 1983–). Quarterly. A refereed journal committed to interdisciplinary research on issues of government and policy with an international perspective. The journal is interested in theoretical papers and empirical assessment and is committed to a broad range of policy questions, not just those related to government and public policy. Available electronically.

Environment and Planning D: Society and Space (ISSN 0263–7758) (London: Pion, 1983–). Bimonthly. An interdisciplinary, refereed journal that leads internationally in discussions about the relations between society and space. Space is broadly conceived: from landscapes of the body to global geographies; from cyberspace to old growth forests; as metaphorical and material; as theoretical construct and empirical fact. Interpretations move across theoretical spectrums, from psychoanalysis to political economy. Available electronically.

European Urban and Regional Studies (ISSN 0969–7764) (London: Sage, 1994–). Quarterly. This major journal provides a means of dialogue between different European traditions of intellectual enquiry on urban and regional development issues. In addition to exploring the ways in which space makes a difference to the future economic, social and political map of Europe, *European Urban and Regional Studies* highlights the connections between theoretical analysis and policy development. The journal also places changes in Europe in a broader global context. Available electronically.

Gender, Place and Culture (ISSN 0966–369X) (London: Carfax, 1984–). Quarterly. Aims to provide a forum for debate in human geography and related disciplines on theoretically-informed research concerned with gender issues. It also seeks to highlight the significance of such research for feminism and women's studies. Available electronically.

Geoforum (ISSN 0016–7185) (Kidlington, Oxon: Elsevier Science, 1970–). Quarterly. An international, interdisciplinary, refereed journal, global in outlook and integrative in approach. The broad focus of *Geoforum* is the organization of economic, political, social and environmental systems through space and over time. The journal also includes a Critical Review section which features critical assessments of research in all the above areas.

Geografisker Annaler B: Human Geography (ISSN 0435–3684) (Oxford: Blackwell, 1923–). Quarterly. A prestigious and international journal, publishing articles covering all theoretical and empirical aspects of human and economic geography. The journal has no specific regional profile but some attention is paid to research from the Nordic countries, as well as from countries around the Baltic Sea.

Geographical Journal, The (ISSN 0016–7398) (London: Royal Geographical Society/ Institute of British Geographers, 1831–). Quarterly. The journal is the Society's key publication of report. It has the highest circulation of any British academic journal in its field and publishes original research papers and review articles, which range across the entire subject of geography. The academic articles are complemented by book reviews and a Society news section.

Local Environment (ISSN 1354–9839) (Basingstoke: Carfax,1996–). Quarterly. An international, refereed journal which focuses on local environmental and sustainability policy, politics and action. It is a forum for the examination, evaluation and discussion of the environmental, social and economic policies and strategies which will be needed in the move towards sustainable development at local, national and global levels. Associated with the *International Council for Local Environmental Initiatives (ICLEI)*.

Professional Geographer (ISSN 0033–0124) (Oxford: Blackwell, 1911–). Quarterly. As one of the core journals in the discipline, *The Professional Geographer* is read primarily by geographers and its papers are often cited in other geography publications.

Progress in Human Geography: an International Review of Geographical Work in the Social Sciences and Humanities (ISSN 0309–1325) (London: Arnold, 1977–). Quarterly. Contains bibliographical essays and progress reports on recent research. A useful source for reviewing the direction of research in human geography. Available electronically.

Regional Studies (ISSN 0034–3404) (Basingstoke: Carfax, 1976–). Nine issues a year. It has developed an international reputation for the publication of original research and reviews on urban and regional development. The journal is of special interest to economists, geographers, sociologists, planners and policy-makers for its cross-disciplinary approach to topics such as industrial, retail and office location, labour markets, housing, migration, recreation, transport, communications and the evaluation of public policy.

Tijdschrift voor Economische en Sociale Geografie/Journal of Economic and Social Geography (ISSN 0040–747X) (Oxford: Blackwell, 1910–). Quarterly. A leading international journal on contemporary issues in human geography, committed to promoting rigorous academic work on the field. Through its scholarly articles and special 'dossiers' on topics of interest, it publishes the latest research findings from Europe and around the world in authoritative scientific contributions. The journal bridges the gap between continental European practices of geography and the Anglo-American traditions by including articles from both regions. Available electronically.

Transactions of the Institute of British Geographers (ISSN 0020–2754) (London: Royal Geographical Society/Institute of British Geographers, 1977–). Quarterly. One of the world's leading English language journals of geographical research. It publishes substantial, internationally refereed articles of the highest scholarly standard. Available electronically.

10.9.2 Regional geography/area studies

Asia Pacific Viewpoint (ISSN 1360–7456) (Oxford: Blackwell,1960–). Three issues a year. Publishes the research of geographers and other disciplines on the economic and social development of countries in the Asia Pacific region. Particular attention is paid to the interplay between development and the environment and to the growing inter-connections between countries in the region. Available electronically.

Australian Geographer (ISSN 0004–9182) (Basingstoke: Carfax, 1928–). Three issues a year. Concentrates primarily on two areas of research: Australia and its region, including development issues and policies in Australia, the western pacific, the Indian Ocean, Asia and Antarctica; and environmental studies. Available electronically.

Australian Geographical Studies (ISSN 0004–9190) (Oxford: Blackwell, 1963–). Three issues a year. Primarily concerned with the geography of Australia and its Pacific, Asian and Antarctic neighbourhoods. Available electronically.

The *Review of African Political Economy* (ISSN 0305–6244) (Basingstoke: Carfax, 1974–). Quarterly. It has provided radical analysis and commentary on trends and issues in Africa since 1974. It pays particular attention to class and gender analysis, and to Marxist interpretations of change in Africa.

Singapore Journal of Tropical Geography (ISSN 0129–7619) (Oxford: Blackwell, 1980–). Semi-annual. It provides a forum for the discussion of problems and issues in the tropical world. It publishes theoretical and empirical refereed articles that deal with the physical and human environments and development issues from geographical and interrelated disciplinary viewpoints. Available electronically.

Third World Quarterly (ISSN 0143–6597) (Basingstoke: Carfax, 1980–). Bimonthly. A leading journal of scholarship and policy in the field of international studies. Available electronically.

10.9.3 Development geography

European Journal of Development Research (ISSN 0957–8811) (London: Frank Cass, 1990–). Two issues a year. It aims to achieve the highest standards of debate and analysis on matters of policy, theory and practice, in all aspects of development studies. It exists, in particular, to publish research carried out in Europe, or in cooperation with European institutions. Most issues are special issues with a common theme.

Gender and Development (ISSN 1355–2074) (Basingstoke: Carfax, 1993–). Three issues a year. The journal has become essential reading for development practitioners, policy makers and academics. It offers articles drawing on Oxfam's strength as a leading organization working in the gender field. It is grounded in the experience of gender-sensitive development. Available electronically.

Journal of Development Studies, The (ISSN 0022–0388) (London: Frank Cass, 1964–). Bimonthly. It was the first and is one of the best known international journals in the area of development studies. Since its foundation in 1964, it has published many seminal articles on development and opened up new areas of debate.

10.9.4 Environmental geography

International Journal of Water Resources Development (ISSN 0790–0627) (Basingstoke: Carfax, 1985–). Quarterly. The journal covers all aspects of water development and management in both industrialized and Third World countries. Contents focus on the practical implementation of policies for water resources development, monitoring and evaluation of technical projects, and, to a lesser extent, water resources research. Available electronically.

Journal of Environment and Development (ISSN 1070–4965) (London: Sage, 1982–). Quarterly. The only international forum that combines discussion of environmental and developmental issues. The journal publishes research and debate from the regional to international level, and includes scholarship from disciplines as diverse as political science, economics, law and public policy. Available electronically.

Journal of Environmental Management, The (ISSN 0301–4797) (San Diego, CA: Academic Press, 1973–). Monthly. Publishes papers on all aspects of the management and use of the environment, both natural and man-made. It is aimed not only at the environmental manager, but at everyone concerned with the wise use of environmental resources. The journal endeavours to publish examples of the use of modern mathematical and computer techniques and encourages contributions from the developing countries. Available electronically.

Natural Resources Forum (ISSN 0165–0203) (Kidlington, Oxon: Elsevier, 1976–). Quarterly. It has evolved over the years from a refereed journal concerned mainly with technical issues of extraction, development and efficient exploitation of resources, to one which seeks to meet the need for an international, multidisciplinary journal focused on the sustainable development and management of natural resources in developing countries. In recent years, following the growing importance of social policy and programmes at the United Nations, the journal's editorial policy has also shifted to socio-economic aspects of the sustainable development of water, energy and mineral resources. Available electronically.

Society and Natural Resources (ISSN 0894–1920) (London: Taylor and Francis, 1988–). Ten issues a year. It provides a forum for scientific, refereed research from multidisciplinary and interdisciplinary social science perspectives. Available electronically.

10.9.5 Political geography

Political Geography (ISSN: 0962–6298) (Kidlington, Oxon: Elsevier, 1981–). Eight issues a year. An interdisciplinary journal for all students of political studies with an interest in geographical and spatial aspects. Available electronically.

10.9.6 Economic geography

Economic Geography (ISSN 0013–0095) (Worcester, MA: Clark University, 1925–). Quarterly. Until recently, it was the only journal published in English specializing in economic geography. The journal has worldwide distribution. Available electronically.

Journal of Economic Geography (ISSN 1468–2710) (Oxford: Oxford University Press, 2001–). Biannual. The journal aims to redefine and reinvigorate the intersection between economics and geography and to provide a world class journal in the field for the new millennium. Available electronically.

10.9.7 Urban geography

Cities (ISSN 0264–2751) (Kidlington, Oxon: Elsevier, 1984–). Bimonthly. It offers a comprehensive range of articles on all aspects of urban policy. The primary aims of the journal are to analyse and assess past and present urban development and management as a reflection of effective, ineffective and non-existent planning policies; and the promotion of the implementation of appropriate urban policies in both the developed and the developing world. Available electronically.

International Journal of Urban and Regional Research (ISSN 0309–1317) (Oxford: Blackwell, 1977–). Quarterly. The leading international journal for urban studies. Since its inception in 1977 as a groundbreaking forum for intellectual debate, it has remained at the forefront of its field. Available electronically.

Urban Geography (ISSN 0272–3638) (Columbia, MD: Bellwether Publishing, 1980–). Eight issues a year. The journal offers original papers on problem-oriented current research by geographers and other social scientists on: urban policy; race, poverty and ethnicity in the city; international differences in urban form and function; historical preservation; the urban housing market; and provision of services and urban economic activity.

Urban Studies (ISSN 0042–0980) (Basingstoke: Carfax, 1964–). Thirteen issues a year. A very good journal providing an international forum for the discussion of issues in the fields of urban and regional analysis and planning. It publishes leading articles from urban scholars working from within a variety of disciplines, including geography, economics, sociology, political science, as well as planning and public administration. Available electronically.

10.9.8 Tourism geography

Tourism Geographies (ISSN 1461–6688) (London: Routledge, 1999–). Quarterly. It publishes good, research-based articles by renowned geographers.

Annals of Tourism Research (ISSN 0160–7383) (Kidlington, Oxon: Elsevier 1973–). Quarterly. The major social science research journal on tourism. While striving for a balance of theory and application, *Annals* is ultimately dedicated to developing theoretical constructs.

Journal of Sustainable Tourism (ISSN 0966–9582) (Clevedon: Channel View, 1993–). Bimonthly. Good for theoretical and research based papers on many aspects of sustainable tourism, including ecotourism.

Journal of Ecotourism (ISSN 14724049) (Clevedon: Channel View, 2001–). The launch of the journal illustrates the dramatic rise in interest in ecotourism issues. The publishers state it 'will seek to advance the field by examining the social, economic and ecological aspects of ecotourism at a number of scales, and including regions from around the world'. During its first year the journal will be circulated free of charge to subscribers of the *Journal of Sustainable Tourism* and *Current Issues in Tourism*.

Journal of Travel Research (ISSN 0047–2875) (London: Sage, 1961–). Quarterly. It serves as a medium through which the latest ideas and developments in travel research and marketing are disseminated. It includes new techniques and information, creative views and general articles on travel research and marketing, from both industry practitioners and academics.

Journal of Tourism Studies (ISSN 1035–4662) (Townsville, Australia: James Cook University of North Queensland, 1990–). Semiannual. It publishes refereed articles on tourism from scholars and practitioners in a range of disciplines including economics, commerce, biological and physical sciences, social sciences and humanities. It aims to be international in scope and inclusive in its coverage.

Current Issues in Tourism (ISSN 1368–3500) (Clevedon: Channel View Publications, 1998–). Publishes major review articles. Available electronically.

Tourism Management (ISSN 0261–5177) (Kidlington, Oxon: Elsevier, 1980–). Bimonthly. *Tourism Economics* (ISSN 1354–8166)

(London: IP Publishing, 1995–). Quarterly. Refereed journal. Available electronically.

Both of the above titles deal with more specialized aspects of tourism from a multi-disciplinary perspective, but contain much material of use to human geographers.

10.9.9 GIS and remote sensing

International Journal of Remote Sensing (ISSN 0143–1161) (London: Taylor and Francis, 1980–). Eighteen issues a year. It continues to be a reliable source of academic papers on new data and applications of remotely sensed data. Available electronically.

International Journal of Geographical Information Science (ISSN 1365–8816) (London: Taylor and Francis, 1987–). Eight issues a year. Available electronically.

Remote Sensing of Environment (ISSN 0034–4207) (Kidlington, Oxon: Elsevier, 1969–). Monthly. ISPRS Journal of Photogrammetry and Remote Sensing (ISSN 0924–2716) (Exeter: Elsevier, 1965–). Bimonthly. Available electronically.

The above journals are not easy reading, but they offer the best of the new research.

10.9.10 Rural geography

Journal of Rural Studies (ISSN 0743–0167) (Kidlington, Oxon: Elsevier, 1985–). Quarterly. Publishes research articles relating to such rural issues as society, demography, housing, employment, transport, services, land-use, recreation, agriculture and conservation. Available electronically.

Sociologia Ruralis (ISSN 0038–0199) (Oxford: Blackwell, 1951–). Quarterly. Over the past 40 years the journal has been an international forum for social scientists engaged in a wide variety of disciplines focusing on social, political and cultural aspects of rural development. *Sociologia Ruralis* covers a wide range of subjects, from farming, natural resources and food systems, to rural communities, rural identities and the restructuring of rurality. Available electronically.

▶ 10.10 ABSTRACTS, INDEXES AND DATABASES

(a) Print

Geographical Abstracts (ISSN 0953–9611) (Kidlington, Oxon: Elsevier Science). Preceded by *Geomorphological Abstracts*, 1960–1965. Began in four parts in 1966, expanded to seven parts in the 1970s as *Geoabstracts*. It has been published in two parts from 1989 to the present as: *Human Geography* and *Physical Geography*. It is the major indexing tool in geography covering periodical articles, plus books, conference proceedings, reports and theses. Each subseries is issued monthly. Citations, most with detailed abstracts are arranged in a classified sequence. There is an Index in each issue, cumulated annually. Be sure to use the latter for rapid retrieval and when undertaking an extensive subject search. The publication is arranged by fields of human and physical geography. The *Human Geography* subseries contains 11 000 abstracts from 1100 core journals. Topics covered include: environment, cultural and political geography, rural and urban studies, transport and communications, recreational geography and GIS applications. The series is included in *GEOBASE* from 1980, *see (b) Electronic* below.

Current Geographical Publications (New York: The American Geographical Society) which commenced in 1938, is issued 10 times a year and provides bibliographical references to books, periodical articles, government documents, maps and atlases in the American Geographical Society collection held at the University of Wisconsin-Milwaukee. *See also* the *Online Geographical Bibliography* in *(b) Electronic* below.

Ecological Abstracts (ISSN 0305–196X) (Kidlington, Oxon: Elsevier, 1974–) is a companion publication to *Geographical Abstracts* (above) and published on a monthly basis with an annual cumulated index. It gives wide coverage of environmental issues including sections on nature conservation and economic ecology. It provides 14 000 abstracts from over 3000 journals in the fields of ecology, environmental science and biology. Books, conference proceedings and reports are also covered. It is included in *GEOBASE*, *see (b) Electronic* below.

International Development Abstracts (ISSN 0262–0855) (Amsterdam: Elsevier, 1982–). Bimonthly. The online version of this title is available as part of the GEOBASE file (*see (b) Electronic* below). It indexes over 500 journals, plus monographs, reports and conference proceedings relating to the international development literature. Much of the information indexed is relevant to human geography, politics and economics.

Sage Urban Studies Abstracts (ISSN 0090–5747) (London: Sage, 1962–). Quarterly. It covers all aspects of urban studies and is very useful. Look up your city in the subject index and be surprised at how much published research exists on even modest towns and cities, especially in North America. *See also (b) Electronic* below.

Leisure, Recreation and Tourism Abstracts (ISSN 0261–1392) (London: CABI, 1976–) is the best abstracting service in this field available in English and reviews a very wide range of books, journals, reports and conferences. It also has English abstracts of some foreign language articles. Topics covered include: leisure and tourism policies; tourism and leisure industries; travel and transport; facility management and planning;

recreation, entertainment and sport; and natural resources and the environment. *See also TOURCD* in *(b) Electronic* below.

(b) Electronic

EDINA <Digimap edina.ac.uk/digimap/> is a service that delivers Ordnance Survey Map Data to UK Higher Education. Data are available either to download to use with appropriate application software such as GIS or CAD, or as maps generated by Digimap online. As with some of the other electronic and print sources listed above, universities usually have blanket subscriptions to these services providing staff and students with the passwords necessary to access these databases from home as well as via university-based terminals.

EIU DataServices <countrydata.bvdep.com> (London: Economist Intelligence Unit). A suite of databases comprising: *EIU CountryData* – economic indicators and forecasts, covering 270 statistical variables for 115 countries from 1980 onwards; *EIU CountryIndicators* – economic, demographic, consumption and industry data for 60 countries worldwide from 1990 onwards; and *EIU CityData* – a global database of over 300 price and salary levels, providing information on the cost of living in 123 cities from across the world from 1990 onwards.

GEOBASE (available as a CD-ROM from Silver Platter and online via DIALOG, ChemWeb and OCLC First Search). It is a vast database which contains over 500 000 citations from many thousands of journals. *GEOBASE* incorporates both *Geographical Abstracts*, *Ecological Abstracts* and *International Development Abstracts* (*see (a) Print* above). It indexes journal articles, books, conference proceedings, reports, irregular publications, maps, dissertations and working papers. Coverage includes physical geography, as well as economic, political, and social geography. As such, it is a particularly good source for literature on geology, climate, environmental issues, regionalism, economic development, local politics, local government, public policy and planning. Some foreign language literature is included.

Online Geographical Bibliography – American Geographical Society Collection <geobib.lib.uwm.edu>. This is the electronic version of *Current Geographical Publications* (*see (a) Print* above) and provides access to the collections of the American Geographical Society at the University of Wisconsin-Milwaukee. The online database covers 1985 to date and can be freely accessed from the above Website. The database can be searched by title keyword, author and subject.

Sage Urban Studies Abstracts <www.sagepub.co.uk/journals/> (ISSN 0090–5747) (London: Sage, 1962–). Quarterly. The abstracting service is available as a full-text electronic journal as part of an institutional subscription to the print version (*see (a) Print* above). Additional search facilities may be available if using one of a number of intermediaries such as NESLI or SwetsnetNavigator. All aspects of urban studies are covered including: policy, transportation, spatial analysis, planning, environment and comparative urban analysis.

TOURCD: Leisure, Recreation and Tourism Abstracts on CD-ROM. It is the electronic version of *Leisure, Recreation and Tourism Abstracts* discussed in *(a) Print* above. The CD-ROM contains citations to more than 32 000 documents published since 1976. It is updated on a yearly basis, those requiring more regular updates would need to subscribe to the quarterly print publication.

Urbadisc <www.london-research.gov.uk/rl/rlurba.htm> (London: London Research Centre/Greater London Authority, 1970–). Issued twice a year on CD-ROM, *Urbadisc* is a cooperative production from Britain, France, Germany, Italy and Spain. It collates over 600 000 bibliographic references from major European urban affairs databases. Its broad coverage of urban issues includes: social policy, architecture, transportation, leisure and tourism, economic development and the environment.

Worldwide Hospitality & Tourism Trends <www.whatt.net> (London: HCIMA, 1985–). Produced by the Hotel and Catering International Management Association, this database gives subscribers global perspectives on hospitality and tourism from the academic and professional journal literature. Full-text articles are made seamlessly available to users via ingenta.

▶ 10.11 OFFICIAL PUBLICATIONS

Official publications are discussed within various sections of this chapter. Due to the broad focus of human geography, recourse may need to be to made to a bewilderingly wide variety of sources which it is impractical to attempt to list here. Rather, the reader is directed to the official publications sections of the other chapters in this volume and, in particular, to *1.11* which should act as a good starting point for general resources of this kind.

▶ 10.12 STATISTICS

(a) Print

Trends in Europe and North America: Statistical Yearbook of the Economic Commission for Europe (New York: United Nations, 1999) provides basic data on the 55 countries of the United Nations Economic Commission for Europe, which includes all countries of the former Soviet

Union; Central, Eastern and Western Europe; Israel; the United States of America and Canada. The first part of the book presents economic and social profiles in statistics and the second part, with 13 chapters, paints a broad picture of recent social and economic life in the respective countries.

The *African Statistical Yearbook* (New York: United Nations) presents data arranged on a country basis for 53 African countries and covers statistics on population and employment, national accounts, finance, agriculture, forestry and fishing, industry, transport and communications, foreign trade, prices and social statistics.

Issued four times a year, *Statistical Indicators for Asia and the Pacific* (New York: United Nations) provides data for assessing demographic and economic trends in countries and areas of the Asia and the Pacific region. Data are presented for multiple years on a month-by-month basis, facilitates comparative analysis.

Migration in the CIS (Geneva: International Organization for Migration, 1999) provides a comprehensive description of the migration situation and migration flows in each of the CIS (Commonwealth of Independent States) countries. This issue updates to early 1998, the 1996 *CIS Migration Report* and includes all relevant developments of the countries' official policies concerning migrations.

Statistical Charts and Indicators on the Situation of Youth (New York: United Nations, 1980–) is a statistical and analytical sourcebook that uses charts and graphs to highlight the main aspects and trends in the aforementioned area from 1980 to 1995 in 177 countries. The topics covered are: population; education and training; economic activity; health and child-bearing; and households and marital status. It is written for the non-specialist.

The *International Trade Statistics Yearbook* (New York: United Nations) is useful for analysing trade by country and by commodity; performing trend analysis and projections; understanding economic development planning; and developing marketing strategies. This publication provides statistical information for 174 countries or reporting customs areas.

The *Handbook of World Mineral Trade Statistics* (Geneva: UNCTAD, 1998) offers comprehensive, up-to-date statistics at world, regional and country levels for the international trade of major non-fuel minerals and metals, from primary to semi-processed forms for the years 1993–1998.

The *Energy Statistics Yearbook* (New York: United Nations) is comprehensive and reliable, provides a global framework of comparable data on long-term trends in the supply of mainly commercial, primary and secondary forms of energy. Valuable and precise data for each type of fuel and aggregate data for the total mix of commercial fuels for individual countries and areas are summarized into regional and world totals.

Forest Resources of Europe, CIS, North America, Australia, Japan and New Zealand (Industrialized Temperate/Boreal Countries) UN-ECE/FAO Contribution in the Global Forest Resources Assessment 2000: Main Report (New York: United Nations, 2000) presents the national replies to a detailed enquiry on forest resources. The volume includes statistical and descriptive information together with analyses undertaken by high level experts in the following specific thematic areas: forest and other wooded land (OWL); ownership and management status; wood supply and carbon sequestration; biological diversity and environmental protection; forest condition and damage; and protective and socio-economic functions. More than 80 main tables with the validated national statistics on the different parameters of forest resources are included in the publication.

(b) Electronic

The Organization for Economic Cooperation and Development *(OECD)* maintains a large Website located at <www.oecd.org> where it is possible to find detailed macroeconomic statistics for all OECD countries (*see also 1.12* and *8.12*).

The *Labour Force Statistics Database* (LFSD) (New York: United Nations, 1999) provides statistics in three major areas for the member countries and areas of Western Asia: economically active population distributed by marital status, educational attainment, employment status, occupational groups and industrial divisions; the unemployed population distributed by educational attainment and employment status; and the population in general distributed by age group and sex, by educational attainment, and by activity status and age group. Available on five floppy disks covering the period 1950–1994, the system allows the production and printing of reports. A user's manual is also included.

The Population Reference Bureau <www.prb.org> provides copious amounts of demographic data for virtually all countries in the world. Some analysis and policy documents are also included.

The World Tourism Organization (WTO) publishes the *Annual Compendium of Tourism Statistics*, which summarizes the current year and four previous years' data for all countries in the world. The more detailed *Yearbook of Tourism Statistics* provides regional summaries and statistics on inbound tourism on a country by country basis. See the WTO Website at <www.world-tourism.org>.

Star UK <www.staruk.org.uk> is the official site of the UK Research Liaison Group. It provides UK tourism facts, information on national research projects, relevant publications and links to other Websites. For UK information on expenditure on leisure and tourism in family spending see the report of the annual *Family Expenditure Survey* (London: The Stationery Office). Leisure participation is reported every three years in the report of the *General Household Survey* (London: The Stationery Office). Both are available electronically from the Office for National Statistics at <www.statistics.gov.uk>.

▶ 10.13 RESEARCH IN PROGRESS

Major funders of geographical research are also good sources of information about current research. In the UK, the Economic and Social Research Council (*see Regard* database in *1.13* and information about the organization in *1.14*) is the major funder of academic geographic research and is a reliable source of information about cutting edge research that has won public funding through a very rigorous proposal review process. Public funding bodies in other countries are also potentially good sources of information, including the USA's National Science Foundation and the Canadian Social Science and Humanities Research Council.

A more efficient way of learning about where research is going in certain areas is to consult the Websites or contact the officers for any of the Royal Geographical Society/Institute of British Geographers speciality groups. There are very many of these (*see* <www.rgs.org>), two are specifically listed below for illustrative purposes:

Economic Geography Research Group <www.econgeog.org.uk>. The Economic Geography Research Group aims to foster research and its dissemination in economic geography by organizing meetings, developing contact and cooperation among geographers and other social scientists, and promoting the publication of research.

Post-Socialist Geography Research Group <www.geog.plym.ac.uk/postsocialist>. The group's main objectives are to bring together a scattered research community from within geography and neighbouring disciplines, linked by their common interest in post-socialism and to encourage discussions about the relationship between post-socialist and other concepts of transformation or transition, such as Third World development. They organize and host conferences and workshops dedicated to post-socialist questions.

There is a plethora of Email discussion lists where information about ongoing research often appears. The *Critical Geography Forum* <www.jiscmail.ac.uk/lists/crit-geog-forum.html> is a UK-based group, devoted to the discussion of critical and radical perspectives in geography. For an annotated list of key forums from around the world consult *Geography Discussion/Mailing Lists* <www.geog.le.ac.uk/cti/other/geog_lists.html> provided by the excellent CTI (Computers in Teaching Initiative) Centre for Geography, Geology and Meteorology at the University of Leicester, UK. *See 10.8.1* for more information about their human geography Website.

▸ 10.14 ORGANIZATIONS

In the English-speaking world the most prominent professional societies are: the Institute of British Geographers (with the Royal Geographical Society), the Association of American Geographers, the National Geographic Society and the Canadian Association of Geographers, all of which are discussed in more detail below, together with other key organizations.

Association of American Geographers
1710 Sixteenth Street NW, Washington, DC 20009–3198, USA
Tel: +1 202 234 1450
Fax: +1 202 234 2744
Web: <www.aag.org>

The Association of American Geographers (AAG) is a scientific and educational society founded in 1904. Its 6500 members share interests in the theory, methods, and practice of geography, which they cultivate through the AAG's Annual Meeting, two scholarly journals (the *Annals of the Association of American Geographers* (*see 10.9.1*) and *The Professional Geographer*), the monthly *AAG Newsletter*, and the activities of its two affinity groups, nine regional divisions and 53 specialty groups. The AAG conducts educational and research projects that further its interests and programs.

Canadian Association of Geographers
McGill University, Burnside Hall, 805 Sherbrooke St. West, Room 425
Montreal, Quebec, H3A 2K6, Canada
Tel: +1 514 398 4946
Fax: +1 514 398 7437
Web: <www.uwindsor.ca/cag/>

The Canadian Association of Geographers (CAG) is the professional organization for academic geographers working in Canada. Though the organization welcomes geographers with all regional and thematic interests, there is a strong tendency for its members and its conferences to reflect a preoccupation with Canadian issues.

Department for Transport, Local Government and the Regions (DTLR)
Eland House, Bressenden Place, London, SW1E 5DU, UK
Tel: +44 (0)20 7944 3000
Web: <www.dtlr.gov.uk>

The DTLR is an important source of official information on key topics of interest to human geographers. The Department's Website provides full-text access to its annual reports from 1996 onwards, as well as information and documentation on specific areas including: construction, environmental protection, housing, supporting people, sustainable development and urban issues.

GeoData Institute
University of Southampton, Highfield, Southampton, SO17 1BJ, UK
Tel: +44 (0)23 8059 2719
Fax: +44 (0)23 8059 2849
Email: geodata@soton.ac.uk
Web: <www.geodata.soton.ac.uk>

From 1984 the Institute has 'coordinated interdisciplinary research projects and consultancy services focused on the acquisition, processing and communication of data and information'. Its remit covers the whole field of environmental issues, as well as social and economic evaluation and development. It utilizes a number of technologies including Geographic Information Systems (GIS).

International Geographical Union
Web: <www.igu-net.org>

A truly virtual organization unencumbered by a physical location, the International Geographical Union (IGC) aims to: promote the study of geographical problems; initiate and coordinate international geographical research; facilitate the collection and diffusion of geographical data and documentation in and between all member countries; and promote international standardization or compatibility of methods, nomenclature, and symbols employed in geography. The IGC seeks to achieve its goals through the ongoing work of its speciality commission and its International Geographical Congresses, held in various cities of the world every two years.

Institut Geographique National
136 bis, rue de Grenelle, Paris, France
Web: <www.ign.fr>

France's national mapping agency, the French equivalent of the UK's Ordnance Survey.

The National Council for Geographic Education
Indiana University of Pennsylvania, 16A Leonard Hall, Indiana, PA 15705–1087, USA
Tel: +1 724 357 6290
Fax: +1 724 357 7708
Web: <www.ncge.org>

The National Council for Geographical Education (NCGE) works to enhance the status and quality of geography teaching in the US. It is both a political lobby group which lobbies state and federal authorities to improve geography provision in higher education and a professional association which organizes conferences, workshops, publications and training schemes for its members.

Ordnance Survey
Romsey Road, Southampton, SO16 4GU, UK
Tel: +44 (0)23 8079 2913
Fax: +44 (0)23 8079 2535
Web: <www.ordsvy.gov.uk>

Great Britain's national mapping agency. Two centuries after its creation its military title remains, but it has been a civilian organization since 1983. Although its focus is on Great Britain, it has carried out work in 60 countries across the world.

Royal Geographical Society/Institute of British Geographers
1 Kensington Gore, London SW7 2AR, UK
Tel: +44 (0)20 7591 3000
Fax: +44 (0)20 7591 3001
Email: info@rgs.org
Web: <www.rgs.org>

The Royal Geographical Society (with The Institute of British Geographers) is the Learned Society representing Geography and Geographers. It was founded in 1830 for the advancement of geographical science and has been amongst the most active of the learned societies ever since. The largest geographical society in Europe, and one of the largest in the world, the RGS-IBG operates at regional, national and international scales. The Society supports research, education and training, and the wider public understanding and enjoyment of geography.

University of California at Berkeley
Department of Geography, 507 McCone Hall, 4740 Berkeley, CA 94720–4740, USA
Tel: +1 510 642 3903
Fax: +1 510 642 3370
Web: <geography.berkeley.edu/>

The Berkeley Department is one of the strongest and best-known in North America. Its programmes are divided into three major areas: Development and Environment; Local and Global Relations; and Global Environmental Change. Within these domains a wide range of topics are represented: political ecology, economic geography, cultural geography, modernity studies, urban studies, and the geography of race and gender.

University of Edinburgh
Department of Geography, Drummond Street, Edinburgh, EH8 9XP, UK
Tel: +44 (0)131 650 2565
Fax: +44 (0)131 650 2524
Email: office@geo.ed.ac.uk
Web: <www.geo.ed.ac.uk>

The Department's research themes, spanning the whole of geography, include social and cultural geography, geographical information systems (GIS), and area studies with an emphasis on Scotland.

University of Oxford

School of Geography and the Environment, Mansfield Road, Oxford, OX1 3TB, UK

Tel: +44 (0)1865 271919

Fax: +44 (0)1865 271929

Web: <www.geog.ox.ac.uk>

This is one of the UK's oldest and strongest Geography Departments, with particular expertise in economic geography, environmental management and politics, and social and cultural geography, as well as physical geography. Strong research and teaching linkages are maintained with the Environmental Change Institute, the Transport Studies Institute and with a wide range of interdisciplinary research centres throughout the university system. One particularly exciting recent development is the establishment, with significant funding from the Economic and Social Research Council, of the 'Transnational Communities' research programme, led by Dr. Alistair Rogers.

University of Toronto

Department of Geography, St. George Campus, Sidney Smith Hall, 100 St George St, Room 5047 Toronto Ontario, M5S 3G3, Canada

Tel: +1 416 978 3375

Fax: +1 416 946 3886

Web: <www.geog.utoronto.ca/>

The University of Toronto's Department of Geography is one of the oldest and largest geography departments in North America. Founded in 1935, the department offers both undergraduate and postgraduate programmes.

▶ REFERENCES

Bowen, M. (1980) *Empiricism and Geographical Thought: from Francis Bacon to Alexander von Humboldt*. Cambridge: Cambridge University Press.

Cloke, P., Philo C. and Sadler, D. (1992) *Approaching Human Geography: an Introduction to Contemporary Theoretical Ddebates*. New York: Guilford Press.

Fenneman, N. (1919) 'The Circumference of Geography', in *Annals of the Association of American Geographers*, **9**, 3–11.

Giddens, A. (1984) *The Constitution of Society: Volume One of a Contemporary Critique of Historical Materialism*. Berkeley, CA: University of California Press.

Hart, J. F. (1984) 'The Highest Form of the Geographer's Art', in *Annals of the Association of American Geographers*, **72**, 1–29.

Massey, D. and Allen, J. (eds) (1984) *Geography Matters! a Reader*. Cambridge: Cambridge University Press.

Rediscovering Geography Committee, National Research Council, (1997). *Rediscovering Geography: New Relevance for Science and Society.* Washington, DC: National Academy Press.

Urry, J. (1988) 'Some Notes on Realism and the Analysis of Space', in *International Journal of Urban and Regional Research*, **7**(1), 122–7.

Index